SYNOPSIS

ACCESS TO SOCIAL EUROPE

Guide to ... ammes

Edited by European Study Service

ISBN 2-930119-36-5

Avenue Paola, 43 - B-1330 Rixensart
Tel: (+32 2) 6521184 - Fax: (+32 2) 6530180
RCN: 51 147 - TVA BE 659 309 394

TABLE OF CONTENTS

ANNEXES

Chapter 1

INTRODUCTION TO EUROPEAN INTEGRATION

This book is based on the 13th edition of the general book of the same author known in its English edition as ***Access to European Union: Law, Economics, Policies***. Hence, the present analysis of one of the many common policies of the European Community/Union (EC/EU) is based on the global work and refers to it on many aspects of other common policies, which are intertwined with the common social policy. Indeed, a good understanding of one common policy, such as social, requires a comprehensive view of the complex organisation that is the EC/EU and some knowledge of its development over time.

Access to European Union aspires to being a textbook for any student of European integration, whether academic student of the economic integration of Europe, lawyer interested in Community law, which is ceaselessly growing and modified, economist wishing to acquire the latest information on European economic policies, historian wanting to understand the recent history of the continent or businessman seeking to understand the mechanisms of the large market in which he operates. In fact, European integration cannot be properly approached with the particular methods and tools of political science, international relations, economics or law. *Access to EU* follows, therefore, an interdisciplinary, pragmatic approach, which is somewhat distinct from the precise lines of the established disciplines.

Access to European Union presents an empirical approach to European policies as they are in a particular year: what they try to achieve; what they have achieved so far; which are their main shortcomings; and, finally, which are their short-term prospects. Indeed, a theory on multinational integration is advanced in that book, based on the setting up and development of common policies by the participating states. This approach is neither dogmatic nor purely theoretical. European policies, as all public policies, have both positive and negative aspects and can therefore be approached either in a positive or a negative way according to the viewpoint of the writer. Moreover, European policies are in a state of perpetual evolution. At a certain point of time, one can reasonably extol their achievements or deplore their failures. The empirical or pragmatic approach endeavours to study European policies as they are, with a minimum of value judgments as to their performance. The same empirical approach is followed in ***Access to Social Europe***.

To help the reader easily find the details of this policy and the measures he or she is interested in and/or deduce in an unprejudiced way whether a certain measure is good or bad or whether it has achieved the objectives assigned to it, facts and references are presented in a precise, almost scholastic, manner. All statements about past, present and future developments of the policy as well as all references to the relevant European law are based on the official texts of Community acts, published in the **Official Journal of the European Union (OJ)** or in Commission publications, such as the monthly **Bulletin of the European Union** and the annual **General**

Report on the Activities of the European Union. In addition to their documentary purpose, the references to the OJ are also meant to help interested persons find the official texts of their particular interest, as published in the collections of the OJ or in the electronic database EUR-Lex in the Europa server of the Commission.

1.1. Introduction to the European Treaties

The first European Treaty, the one establishing the **European Coal and Steel Community (ECSC)**, was signed in Paris on 18 April 1951 and entered into force on 23 July 1952. Its main objective was to eliminate the various barriers to trade and to create a common market in which coal and steel products from the Member States could move freely in order to meet the needs of all Community inhabitants, without discrimination on grounds of nationality. Capital and workers in both sectors should also circulate freely. In order that all this could be achieved, the Treaty laid down certain rules on investment and financial aid, on production and prices, on agreements and concentrations of businesses and on transport and Community institutions, including a High Authority and a special Council (of Ministers), the decisions of which would be binding on all Member States. Ambitious despite its restricted scope, the ECSC Treaty introduced a European Assembly and a European Court of Justice. The avowed intentions of the founders of the ECSC were, indeed, that it should be an experiment, which could gradually be extended to other economic spheres, culminating in a "European Federation". For this reason, the duration of the ECSC Treaty was limited to fifty years. On 23 July 2002, when it expired, the specific rules concerning the coal and steel sectors were integrated in the Community law and their particular resources, programmes and international obligations were taken over by the European Community[1].

The **Treaty establishing the European Atomic Energy Community (EAEC**, but more commonly known as **Euratom)** was signed in Rome on 25 March 1957 and came into force on 1 January 1958. Its aim was to create a common market for nuclear materials and equipment, establish common nuclear legislation, introduce a common system for supplies of fissile materials, introduce a system for supervising the peaceful use of nuclear energy and common standards for nuclear safety and for health and safety protection of the population and workers against ionising radiation. The key elements in this Treaty were, however, the coordination of the research programmes of the Member States and a joint research programme, implemented in a Joint Research Centre, which was to develop technology and stimulate nuclear production in Europe. Although it was very much in the spotlight at the time of its establishment, Euratom has experienced many ups and downs as a result both of disillusionment as regards the economic prospects for nuclear energy and of the ambition of some Member States to develop their own nuclear industry, and not purely for civil purposes. Nevertheless, the EAEC Treaty is still in force.

Signed at the same time as the Euratom Treaty on the Capitol Hill in Rome on 25 March 1957, the Treaty establishing the **European Economic Community (EEC)** was likewise brought into force on 1 January 1958. Although the EEC and EAEC treaties are sometimes referred to as the "Treaties of Rome", the "Treaty of Rome" is obviously the EEC Treaty. The essential task, which the Treaty of Rome assigned to the Community institutions, was the creation of a common market between the Member States. That involved: (a) the achievement of a customs union entailing, on the one hand, the abolition of customs duties, import quotas and other barriers to trade between Member States and, on the other hand, the introduction of a Common Customs Tariff (CCT) vis-à-vis third countries; and (b) the implementation, *inter alia* through common policies,

[1] Decision 2002/234, OJ L 79, 22.03.2002, Decisions 2002/595 and 2002/596, OJ L 194, 23.07.2002 and Decisions 2003/76 and 2003/77, OJ L 29, 05.02.2003.

of **four fundamental freedoms**: freedom of movement of goods, of course, but also freedom of movement of salaried workers, freedom of establishment and freedom to provide services by independent persons and companies and, finally, freedom of capital movements.

An important amendment to the Treaties establishing the European Communities took place on 1 July 1987 with the coming into force of the **Single European Act**. Supplementing in particular the EEC Treaty, the Single Act committed the Community to adopt measures with the aim of progressively establishing the internal market over a period expiring on 31 December 1992. At the same time it consecrated the European Council, European cooperation on foreign policy and social and economic cohesion between Member States. Lastly, it served as a legal base for numerous common policies, notably, social, environmental, research and technology.

The **Treaty on European Union (TEU), signed in Maastricht** on 7 February 1992, marked a new stage in the process of creating an ever closer union among the peoples of Europe. The Union was founded on the European Communities and supplemented by new policies and forms of cooperation. In fact, the Treaty of Maastricht was made up of two separate but interlinked Treaties: the Treaty on the European Union (TEU); and the Treaty establishing the European Community (TEC). These two Treaties separated the European construction into three pillars or edifices, distinguished mainly on the basis of the decision-making process: the main pillar or edifice, which is the European Community and where the common work of the participants is regulated by the TEC and where the Community method prevails; the pillar or edifice of justice and home affairs; and the pillar or edifice of the common foreign and security policy (CFSP) [see annex 1.1.]. The method of construction of the two new pillars or edifices was based on intergovernmental cooperation, since the TEU required unanimity for decision-making and, hence, any Member States could veto a common action.

Within the main edifice - the European Community - the Maastricht Treaty brought about profound changes, since it strengthened certain common policies and instituted several others, such as economic and monetary union, education and youth, culture, public health and consumer protection. It is clear that even before completing the single market, the Member States felt the need to complement it with a single currency and to enrich it with new or strengthened common policies, thus confirming the evolutionary nature of the multinational integration process.

On 17 June 1997, at Amsterdam, the Heads of State and Government of the fifteen countries of the EU revised the Treaty on European Union. The **Treaty of Amsterdam** deepened European integration by placing justice and home affairs under the Community orbit, by reinforcing the common foreign and security policy and by initiating new common policies, notably concerning employment and social protection. The Treaty of Amsterdam, which as its predecessor was composed of two Treaties, on the EU and on the EC, marked some progress in the European integration process:

- it placed employment and citizens' rights at the heart of the Union. While confirming that the Member States bear primary responsibility for employment, the revised Treaty on the European Community engaged them to act together to find solutions to unemployment;

- it secured freedom of movement of persons, while strengthening security, by consolidating and "communitarising" the cooperation of the Member States in the fields of justice and home affairs;

- it gave Europe a stronger voice in world affairs by making the European Council (heads of State or government) responsible for defining common strategies to be implemented by the

Union and the Member States and by designating a High Representative for the CFSP (the Secretary General of the Council) and a Policy Planning and Early Warning Unit under his responsibility;

- it made the Union's institutional structure more efficient by extending the co-decision procedure (Parliament/Council) and qualified majority voting in the Council.

In view of the new enlargement of the Union, the European Council of Nice (7-9 December 2000), meeting at Intergovernmental Conference, adopted the **Treaty of Nice**, which came into force o 1 February 2003. Under the heading of the city in which it was signed, the Treaty of Nice, as the repealed Treaties of Maastricht and Amsterdam, includes in fact two Treaties[1] [see annex 1.2.]. The first sets the goals and the arrangements concerning the European Union, namely the common foreign and security policy. The second, which concerns the European Community, determines the objectives and means for achieving the three first stages of European integration: the customs union, the common and economic and monetary union. This book follows the numbering of the articles of the TEU and the TEC adopted in Nice [see annex 2.1.], except when referring to past legislation based on the original versions of the Treaties.

The Treaty of Nice brought changes mainly to four institutional matters: the size and composition of the Commission, the weighting of votes in the Council, replacement of unanimity by qualified majority in decision-making procedures, and enhanced cooperation.

- As regards the composition of the Commission, the decision is that, after the enlargement of the Union, each Member State will continue to have one Commissioner until such time as the 27th Member State joins the European Union, but thereafter the number of Commissioners will be smaller than the number of Member States. Furthermore, the powers of the Commission President are to be enhanced and he will henceforth be appointed by the European Council on a qualified majority basis.

- The decision-making process will be altered, with effect from 1 January 2005, as follows: a qualified majority will be obtained if the decision receives a specified number of votes and is approved by a majority of Member States. The qualified majority will replace unanimity in the case of some thirty provisions, notably concerning judicial cooperation in civil matters, the common commercial policy and industrial policy.

- The enhanced cooperation of some Member States will be reinforced and facilitated.

The entry into force of the Nice Treaty, on the 1st February 2003, does not end the process of constant reform of the EC/EU. Indeed, in view of the enlargement of the Union to ten more States, the Nice European Council called for a new Intergovernmental Conference to make appropriate institutional changes founded on a new Treaty. In order to prepare for the Intergovernmental Conference as broadly and transparently as possible, the Laeken European Council (14-15 December 2001) decided to convene a **Convention on the Future of Europe**, with the former President of the French Republic, Mr Giscard d'Estaing, as Chairman. The Conference brought together representatives of: the governments and national parliaments of the Member States; the European Parliament and the Commission; the accession candidate countries; the Economic and Social Committee; the social partners; the Committee of the Regions; and the European Ombudsman[2]. In order to widen the debate further and to involve all citizens, a Forum was made

---

[1] OJ C 325, 24.12.2002.

[2] Decision 2002/176, OJ L 60, 01.03.2002 and interinstitutional agreement, OJ C 54, 01.03.2002.

available to organisations representing civil society (the social partners, the business world, NGOs, academia, etc.).

The European Council meeting in Thessaloniki (19-20 June 2003) welcomed the **draft constitutional treaty** presented by the Chairman of the Convention. It decided that the text of the draft constitutional treaty was a good basis for starting in the intergovernmental conference (IGC), which should be convened in October 2003, with the participation of the acceding Member States, and agree the constitutional treaty as soon as possible and in time for it to become known to European citizens before the June 2004 elections for the European Parliament. Although there are several misgivings, concerning particularly the role and the structure of the European Commission in relation to the proposed creation of a permanent president of the Council, the draft constitutional treaty breaks new ground on several fronts regarding the tasks of the Union and the institutional architecture, mainly as regards:

- incorporating the Charter of Fundamental Rights into the body of the Treaty;
- conferring on the Union a single legal personality;
- economic governance and external representation of the euro;
- generalising the codecision legislative procedure;
- extending the use of qualified majority voting within the Council;
- clarifying the competencies of the Union and the Member States;
- drafting a single Treaty and eliminating the pillars;
- applying the Community method to various aspects of justice and home affairs;
- creating an EU foreign affairs minister;
- integrating specific provisions for the implementation of foreign, security and defence policy.

1.2. Introduction to the European Institutions

Common policies, such as the common social policy, are the fruit of intensive negotiations among the parties of the multinational integration set. In order to be acceptable to all parties, the conception of a common policy must try to satisfy all national interests and, therefore, all parties must participate in the decision-making process. Their participation, however, may be direct or indirect. Decisions on fundamental common policies, requiring new transfers of national sovereignties to the shared sovereignty, are taken by the participating governments and are outlined in treaties, signed by those governments and ratified by them after authorisation by the national parliaments. Decisions on secondary common policies, which take the form of legal acts such as the ones we examine in this book, are normally taken by the common institutions set up by the treaty, according to procedures and following the legal forms agreed in this treaty. Clearly, the governments of the member states are the managers of the play, but, following the rules of multinational integration, they leave the stage to the actors appointed by them and by their citizens.

The principal actors of European integration are the **five institutional organs** of the Community, whose tasks are set down in Articles 189 to 248 of the EC Treaty and **two consultative organs**. We examine below the role of these actors in the order in which each intervenes in the decision-making process of the Union: the European Council, which sets the goals of the common policies; the European Commission, which makes the proposals for the decisions to be taken; the Economic and Social Committee and the Committee of the Regions, both of which give their opinion on these decisions; the European Parliament and the Council of Ministers, which take the decisions; and the Court of Justice and the Court of Auditors, which control the legality of these decisions [see annex 1.3.].

The **European Council** consists of the Heads of State (the President of the French Republic, responsible for foreign and European affairs) or of Government (the Prime Ministers) of the Community Member States and the President of the European Commission. The European Council is the architect of European construction. It provides the Union with the necessary impetus for its development; it defines the general political guidelines thereof and resolves the most important problems of the construction. At those meetings the Heads of State or Government and the President of the Commission are assisted by the Ministers of Foreign Affairs and one Member of the Commission. The European Council meets in principle four times a year (twice every six months) and, in exceptional circumstances, it may hold an extraordinary meeting. European Council meetings are prepared by the General Affairs and External Relations Council, which coordinates all the preparatory work and draws up the agenda. The Presidency ensures that meetings proceed smoothly.

The **European Commission**, usually referred to simply as the Commission, is the driving force for European integration. Under the Community decision-making process provided for in the European Community Treaty, it alone has the initiative to make proposals with a view to the taking of Community decisions. No other body and no individual State can replace the Commission in this task. It alone can amend its proposal, with the sole exception of there being unanimity in the Council to do so. The Commission is the guardian of the Treaties and of the "acquis communautaire" (i.e., all the Community's legislation). One of its main tasks is to ensure fulfilment of the obligations of the Member States and/or proper application by them of the provisions of the Treaties and of secondary legislation (Art 226 TEC). The Commission is also the executive body of the Community and plays, therefore, an administrative role. The Treaties confer upon the Commission extensive powers of execution to ensure the attainment of the objectives set out in them. It is the Commission, which implements the decisions of the legislative bodies (the Council and the Parliament) and manages the Community budget and in particular the various Community Funds[1] [see section 3.3.2.], including the European Social Fund. Finally, the Commission plays a representative role by ensuring the representation of the European Union in third countries and in many international organisations.

The **Economic and Social Committee (ESC)** is the official body, which enables the Community institutions to evaluate and take into account in the conception of common policies the interests of the various economic and social groups. Its 222 members are proposed by the governments of the Member States and are appointed by the Council after consulting the Commission. They must provide a wide representation of the various categories of economic and social life (Art. 257-262 TEC) and divide voluntarily into three groups: the Employers' Group (known as "Group I"), which is made up of representatives of industry, banking or financial institutions, transport operators' federations, etc.; the Workers' Group (known as "Group II"), mainly composed of representatives of trade union organisations; and the Various Interests Group (known as "Group III"), which comprises representatives of agriculture, skilled trades, small and medium-sized enterprises, the professions, consumers' associations and organisations representing various interests, such as the families or ecological movements.

The **Committee of the Regions** is made up of representatives of regional and local bodies (Art. 263-265 TEC). The 222 members of the Committee and an equal number of alternate members (with the same national distribution as the members of the ESC) are proposed by the governments of the Member States and appointed for four years by the Council, acting unanimously. The Committee of the Regions must be consulted by the Council or the Commission on matters relating notably to employment guidelines, legislation on social matters, environment, education,

[1] Regulation 1105/2003, OJ L 158, 27.06.2003.

vocational training, culture, public health, European networks and the Structural Funds. It may be consulted in all other cases considered appropriate by one of the two institutions, in particular those which concern cross-border cooperation. It can also issue an own-initiative opinion when it considers that specific regional interests are at stake (Art. 265 TEC). The Committee of the Regions thus involves regional and local authorities in the decision-making process and expresses their views on all common policies concerning them.

The **European Parliament (EP)** plays an increasingly important role in the European integration process. In fact, although under the original Treaties the Parliament's role was purely advisory, it has kept growing, by virtue of the increasing political influence it has gradually managed to secure. At present it exercises four functions: legislative, political, supervisory and budgetary. The legislative function of the Parliament was considerably increased with the Treaty of Amsterdam. Article 192 (TEC) provides, in fact, for the participation of the European Parliament in the process leading up to the adoption of Community acts through exercise of its powers under the procedures laid down in Articles 251 and 252 (co-decision and cooperation). The political function of the Parliament is also essential. As it represents 375 million citizens (in the EU of the 15) and is the European forum par excellence, the Parliament is the virtual contractor for European construction. Indeed, the Treaty gives it the right to request that the Commission submit any appropriate proposals on matters on which it considers a Community act is required (Art. 192 TEC). The monitoring function of the Parliament is exercised in particular vis-à-vis the Commission. Under the Treaties the Commission is answerable to the Parliament alone, so as to obviate its bowing before the will of the national governments or of some of their number. The Commission has to account to the European Parliament, defend its position before parliamentary commissions and in plenary sessions. The Parliament has to give its agreement to any major decision involving expenditure to be borne by the Community budget. It is effectively the Parliament which, at the end of a conciliation procedure with the Council, adopts or rejects the budget proposed by the Commission. Thus, it exercises a democratic control on the own resources of the Community.

The **Council of the European Union**, composed of Ministers of Member States and usually called the Council of Ministers or simply the Council, is the Union's main decision-making body. It alone, in some cases, or with the European Parliament, in a growing number of areas, adopts the instruments of secondary legislation on proposals from the Commission. In practice, important decisions are taken either unanimously, in which case the vote of the smallest country weighs as much as that of the largest and any country can block the integration process, or by a qualified majority, notably in the areas where there is participation of the Parliament in the decision-making process. Although "the Council" is referred to in the abstract, it consists in fact of nine specialised configurations regrouping several related areas: agriculture and fisheries; economic and financial affairs; employment, social policy, health and consumer affairs; etc[1]. The Council Presidency changes every six months to another country in alphabetical order, and it is therefore the Minister of the country holding the Presidency who chairs each Council meeting. The draft Constitution suggests the abolishment of the practice of alternating presidencies and the institution of a permanent president of the Council.

The **Court of Justice and to the Court of First Instance** ensure that the Community law is observed in a uniform manner in the interpretation and application of the Treaty, of the legal acts and of the decisions adopted by the Council and the Parliament or by the Commission (Art. 220 to 245 TEC). Being the supreme court of the Communities, the Court of Justice not only gives a coherent and uniform interpretation of Community law, but it ensures that all the Member States and their citizens comply with it. Apart from the tendency of States to interpret Community law

[1] Decision 2000/396, OJ L 149, 23.06.2000.

in their interest, it is new law and not always well known. The national judges, who are the judges of first instance of the rules and behaviour relative to Community law, may turn to the Court of Justice by means of a referral for a preliminary ruling to ask it to adopt a position on the interpretation or evaluation of the validity of Community provisions. Through its judgments and interpretations, the Court of Justice promotes the emergence of a genuine European law to which all are subject: European institutions, Member States, national courts and citizens. The decision-making authorities often amend the ambiguous provisions of the Community law in order to heed the case law of the Court of Justice, which plays therefore an important role in the European integration process.

The **Court of Auditors** examines the accounts of all administrative expenditure and revenue of the Community and of all the bodies set up by the Community. It verifies that revenue has been received and expenditure incurred in a lawful and regular manner and makes observations on the financial management of the Community budget, especially by the Commission. The Court of Auditors may also submit observations on specific questions and deliver an opinion at the request of a European institution. Lastly, it may carry out audits based on records and, if necessary, on the spot in the other institutions of the Community as well as in the Member States in respect of operations which the latter carry out on behalf of the Union.

1.3. Introduction to the common policies of the Union

The **multinational integration process** may de defined as the voluntary establishment by treaty, concluded between independent states, of common institutions and the gradual development by them of common policies pursuing common goals and serving common interests. The primary goal of multinational integration is the achievement of peace and security among the member states as well as between them and the rest of the world. But, unlike a military alliance where this goal is pursued by various pledges of political and military nature, a multinational integration scheme is built gradually by means of a large number of common policies, cementing common interests and creating a real solidarity among the member states. The Treaty establishing the European Community (TEC) clearly declares in its Article 2 that "the Community shall have as its task, by establishing a common market and an economic and monetary union and by implementing common policies or activities referred to in Articles 3 and 4, to promote throughout the Community a harmonious, balanced and sustainable development of economic activities...". Articles 3 and 4 of the TEC serve, in fact, as legal bases for common policies in a great number of sectors or for common measures in some other fields (the distinction between common policies and common measures being quantitative rather than qualitative).

A common policy, as far as multinational integration is concerned, is defined as a set of decisions, rules, measures and codes of conduct adopted by the common institutions set up by a group of states. Common policies develop when, where and to the extent that the governments, representing the parties to a treaty, believe that the individual interests of their states are better served by them than by national policies. Decisions on fundamental common policies, affecting national sovereignties, are taken by the participating governments and are outlined in treaties, signed by those governments and ratified after agreement of the parliaments of the Member States. Decisions on secondary common policies, including guidelines and legal acts based on a treaty, are normally taken by the common institutions set up by the treaty, according to procedures and following the legal forms agreed in the treaty.

In EC/EU usage, "**common policies**" are the ones that take the place of the essential elements of national policies (agriculture, fisheries, foreign trade). The policies that support and supplement national policies, such as the social ones, are called "**Community policies**". But, in fact, the distinction, between the two categories is not at all clear-cut. Indeed, all common policies, whether called thus by the Treaties or by Community practice, are in a process of development. They start as mere objectives set specifically or in more general terms by the Treaties or the institutions and are gradually built up by common or "Community" legal acts. In this book, the terms "common policy" and "Community policy" are used alternatively, as the latter is taken to mean "the common policy of the Community" in a certain field. Hence, by "common social policy" we mean the common policy of the Community and of the Member States in the social field. This policy provides a common framework for the social policies of the Member States.

Common policies, as all other public policies, are there to answer societal needs which arise in a defined community at a certain time. Therefore, not only the objectives that the member states set for each common policy, but also the means that they give to the common institutions to attain them and the measures that the latter adopt in order to implement them change in accordance with the economic, political and social needs that the states, which take part in the process, experience at a certain time. In the case of the EC/EU, the common policies are in permanent evolution, demonstrated, for all of them, by the constant amendment of the Community laws (regulations, directives, etc.) that form them, and, for some of them (e.g., agricultural, regional, social and research policies), by the several fundamental reforms that they have undergone since their inception. Moreover, a common policy tends to spill over into the area of other common policies, produce needs, cause reactions and nourish their development.

1.4. Introduction to the European legal system

Inherent in the concept of a common policy is its binding force on the member states. The latter must give the common institutions the legal means to implement common policies and to enforce their decisions on all the parties concerned and on their citizens. Hence, common policies are shaped by legal acts ordained by the common institutions, implemented by the member states and/or the common institutions and controlled by the common institutions. The national laws of the member states are harmonised in a great number of fields in the context of common policies. A special law, based on the treaties and called acquis communautaire, is thus built to bring into being common policies, a law that is superimposed and takes precedence over national law, even the constitutional law, of the Member States, whether national legislation predates or postdates Community legislation.

The legal acts, which substantiate the common policies, may be undertaken by the competent institutions with legal effect only if they are empowered to do so by the European Treaties (principle of attribution of powers). Article 249 of the EC Treaty provides for five forms of legal act, each with a different effect on the Member States' legal systems: some are directly applicable in place of national legislation, while others permit the progressive adjustment of that legislation to Community provisions.

The **regulation** has a general scope, is binding in all its elements and is directly applicable in each Member State. Just like a national law, it gives rise to rights and obligations directly applicable to the citizens of the European Union[1]. Regulations enter into force on a date which they lay down or, where they do not set a date, on the twentieth day following their publication in the Official Journal of the European Union. The regulation substitutes European law for national law and is therefore the most effective legal instrument provided for by the EC Treaty. As "European

[1] See on this subject, notably, the judgments of the Court of Justice of 14.12.1971, case 43/71, Politi, ECR 1971, p. 1049 and of 7.2.1973, case 39/72, Commission v Italy, ECR 1973, pp. 114-115.

laws", regulations must be complied with fully by those to whom they are addressed (individuals, Member States, European institutions).

The **directive** binds any Member State to which it is addressed with regard to the result to be achieved, while allowing the national authorities competency as to the form and methods used. It is a sort of Community framework law and lends itself particularly well to the harmonisation of national laws. It defines the objective or objectives to be attained by a common policy and leaves it to the Member States to choose the forms and instruments necessary for complying with it. Since the Member States are only bound by the objectives laid down in directives, they have some discretion, in transposing them into national law, in taking into account of special national circumstances. They must, however, "ensure fulfilment of the obligations arising out of the Treaty or resulting from action taken by the institutions of the Community" (Art. 10 TEC). Although they are generally published in the Official Journal, Directives take effect by virtue of being notified to the Member States to which they are addressed. The latter are obliged to adopt the national measures necessary for implementation of the Directive within time-limits set by it, failing which they are infringing Community legislation.

The **decision** is binding on the addressees it indicates, who may be one, several, or even all the Member States or one or more natural or legal persons. This variety of potential addressees is coupled with a variety in the scope of its contents, which may extend from a quasi regulation or a quasi directive to a specific administrative decision. It takes effect on its communication to the addressees rather than on its publication in the Official Journal. In any case, according to the Court of Justice, a decision can produce direct effects creating for the individuals rights that national jurisdictions must safeguard[1].

In addition to the above binding acts, which form the Community law, the Council and the Commission can adopt **recommendations** suggesting a certain line of conduct or outlining the goals of a common policy and opinions assessing a current situation or certain facts in the Community or the Member States. Furthermore, the Council and the European Parliament adopt **resolutions**, which are also not binding, suggesting a political desire to act in a given area. These instruments enable the Community institutions to suggest guidelines for coordination of national legislations or administrative practices in a non-binding manner, i.e. without any legal obligations for the addressees - Member States and/or citizens.

While resolutions and opinions are published in the "C" series (communications) of the **Official Journal of the European Union (OJ)**, binding acts and recommendations are published in the "L" series (legislation) of the OJ. It is the binding instruments (regulations, directives and decisions) that constitute derivative Community law, known as the "acquis communautaire", that is, the law adopted by the institutions in order to pursue the objectives of the European Treaties, giving certain rights and obligations to the citizens and obliging the Member States to adapt their legislation and/or the administrative practices.

[1] Judgment of 6 October 1970, case 9/70, Grad, ECR 1970, p. 838 and judgment of 12 December 1990, joined cases 100/89 and 101/89, ECR 1990, p. I-4647.

Annex 1

INTRODUCTION TO EUROPEAN INTEGRATION

Annex 1.1. European Community and European Union

Image of the European Union in three pillars

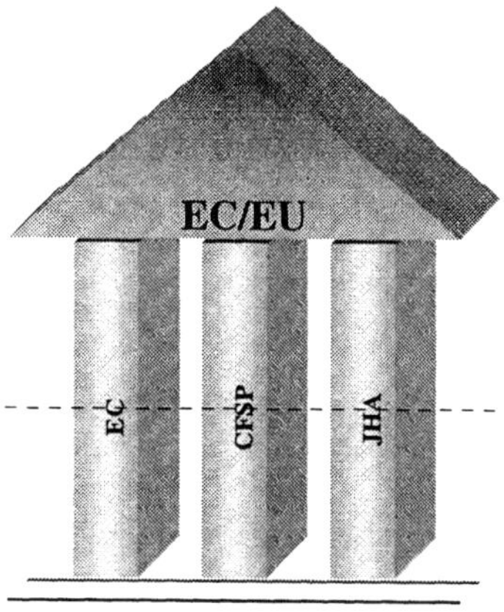

Mis en forme : Anglais États-Unis

Image of the European Union as an edifice

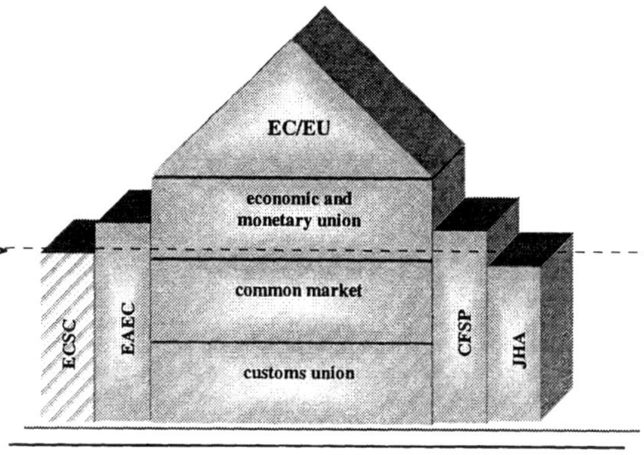

Mis en forme : Anglais États-Unis

Annnex 1.2. The European Treaties

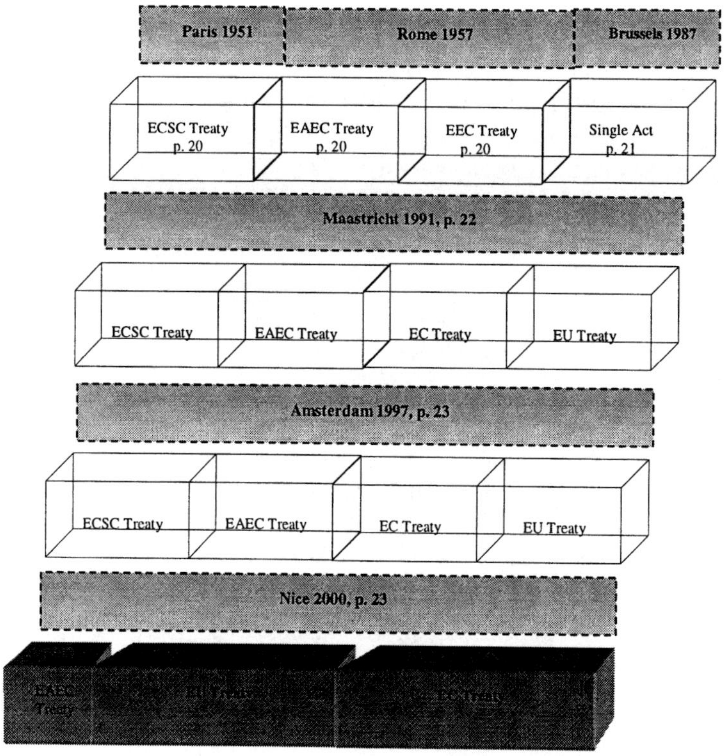

Annex 1.3. The European institutions

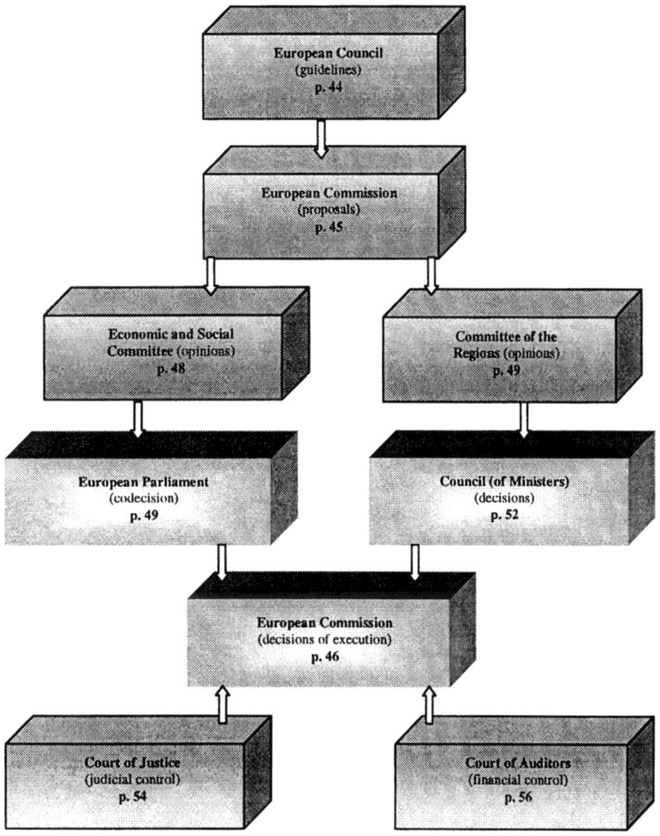

Chapter 2

THE LEGAL FRAMEWORK OF THE COMMON SOCIAL POLICY

Given the varied economic structures of the Community Member States, their social problems were at the launch of the European integration process quite different. They still are, as a result, in particular, of successive enlargements. It would not have been possible at the start - and that still holds true - to entrust the common social policy with the task of solving all the Member States' social problems. Such a solution depends to a great extent upon economic policy, which is still to a large degree in the hands of the individual governments. But as European integration advances and the Member States delegate significant economic and monetary policy instruments to the European Union, the latter commits itself increasingly to the advancement of social progress for all the peoples who make it up. Thus, whilst the Treaty of Rome aimed mainly at the free movement of workers and relied above all on the functioning of the common market to improve living and working conditions in all Member States, the Treaty of Maastricht assigned to the Community the task of actively promoting economic and social cohesion in its Member States. Going a step further, the Treaty of Amsterdam set the objective of promoting a common employment policy. The common social policy thus progresses in step with multinational integration.

2.1. The need for social cohesion

With growing European integration, the Union increasingly shares responsibility with the Member States for the maintenance of the **European model of society**. This model reflects the values of the social market economy, which seeks to combine a system of economic organisation based on market forces, freedom of opportunity and enterprise with a commitment to the values of solidarity and access for all members of society to social protection and services of general interest. Therefore, the policies of economic and social cohesion, which are linked with the objectives of the European model of society, are considered to be a factor in strengthening the productivity of European society and contributing to economic and social wellbeing.

Economic and social cohesion is an objective of the Community (Art. 2 and 3 TEC). Whereas the common regional policy deals mainly with economic cohesion, the common social policy tries to strengthen social cohesion. Article 136 of the EC Treaty declares that the Community and the Member States, having in mind fundamental social rights such as those set out in the European Social Charter signed at Turin on 18 October 1961 and in the 1989 Community Charter of the Fundamental Social Rights of Workers [see section 4.1.], have as their objectives the promotion of employment, improved living and working conditions, so as to make possible their harmonisation while the improvement is being maintained, proper social protection, dialogue between management and labour and the development of human resources [see annex 2.1.]. This last goal entails effectual education and training policies. Article 136 states also that the objectives of social progress and cohesion that it sets should ensue not only from the functioning of the common market, which will favour the harmonisation of social systems, but also from the procedures provided for in the Treaty and from the approximation of provisions laid down by law, regulation or administrative action (particularly in the context of the single market). However, the measures taken by the Community and the Member States to attain the objectives of Article 136 must take account of the diverse forms of national practices, in particular in the field of contractual relations, and the need to maintain the competitiveness of the Community economy.

To attain social cohesion in the Union minimum social standards are needed, having regard to differing national systems and needs, and to the relative economic strengths of the Member States. The establishment of a framework of basic minimum standards guarantees acceptable social and physical security conditions to all the workers in the Union. At the same time, it provides a bulwark against reducing social standards to increase the competitiveness of the businesses of one Member State and, hence, against using low social standards as an instrument of unfair economic competition. These basic standards should not over-stretch the economically weaker Member States, but they should not prevent the more developed Member States from implementing higher standards.

2.2. The objectives of the social policy

The objectives of the common social policy are very close to those of the common regional policy. The latter is directed towards improving the lot of the least-favoured regions of the European Union, the social policy that of its poorest citizens. Both seek to even out the economic and social imbalances in the Union and to ensure that the advantages ensuing from the functioning of the common market are shared amongst all the countries and all the citizens. Several of their measures are complementary, and their financial instruments are closely coordinated in order to put them into effect.

A Community social policy, which was necessary for the social cohesion of the Community as early as the stage of the progressive implementation of the common market, was provided for in **vague terms in the EEC Treaty**. Although its signatories stated that they were resolved to ensure social progress by common action and affirmed as the essential objective the improvement of the living and working conditions of their peoples, they remained entirely independent in the field of social policies. They placed their faith above all in the automatic improvement of social conditions, relying on the knock-on effect that economic integration would produce. They were not wrong in that, but they were not completely right either.

It is certain that the progressive integration of the economies in itself promotes the convergence of the social conditions of the States of the Community. The most characteristic social features of the Community during the first forty years of its existence have been the moderate growth of the population, increased life expectancy and shorter working life, the widespread extension of compulsory education and the mass entry of women into economic activities. In addition to those general phenomena there have been structural changes within sectors and sectoral movements from agriculture to industry and from the latter to the service industries. Thus, it is not by chance that the problems of employment, social security and the vocational training of certain categories of workers (the young, the old and women) are priorities in every Member State. It is, therefore, true that the closer the economic conditions become in a multinational integration scheme, the more the social problems of the member states become similar and more similar, not to say common, solutions become necessary. Likewise, the free movement of workers and transnational trade union contacts have promoted a degree of upward levelling of wages, social benefits and social protection.

Increased prosperity brought about largely by European integration, did not, however, resolve all the Community's social problems. It even made some of them more acute or gave rise to new ones, viz. problems of disadvantaged regions and categories of persons who do not participate fully in the general progress; problems of structural unemployment; problems relating to the distribution of income and wealth; contradictions between economic and social values and, on occasion, dramatic changes in lifestyle with negative consequences for the behaviour of young people. Since the Treaty on the European Community actually calls for a social model based on the market economy, democracy and pluralism, respect of individual rights, free collective bargaining, equality of opportunity for all, social welfare and solidarity, it instructs the common institutions to strive to attain those objectives.

The effort to complete the single market at the end of the 1980s was to mean a fresh start for the Community's social policy and its financial instrument, the European Social Fund (ESF) [see section 6.3.]. The **Single European Act** [see section 1.1.] gave new impetus to social policy, especially in the areas of health and safety at work, dialogue with the social partners and economic and social cohesion. The Single Act and, later on, the Maastricht Treaty stated that "in order to promote its overall harmonious development, the Community shall develop and pursue its actions leading to the strengthening of its economic and social cohesion" (Art. 158 TEC). The Structural Funds, and especially the European Social Fund (ESF), represent the main instruments for promoting social cohesion within the Union [see section 3.3.2.]. The ESF contributes to the attainment of the Objectives set out set out in the context of the Community structural policy, namely of Objective 3 [see section 3.3.3.].

The **Treaty of Maastricht** had taken social policy one step forward with the adoption of the Protocol on Social Policy, signed by the twelve countries which were Member States at the time and annexed to the Treaty on European Union, noting that eleven Member States (all except the United Kingdom) wished to continue to make significant progress in this field. The Protocol authorised them, by means of an Agreement on social policy, "to have recourse to the institutions, procedures and mechanisms of the Treaty for the purposes of taking among themselves and applying as far as they are concerned the acts and decisions required for giving effect to the abovementioned Agreement". However, it was not very satisfactory to have two legal bases for social policy.

The **Treaty of Amsterdam** restored unity and coherence to social policy by incorporating into the EC Treaty the Agreement referred to above (see annex 2.1, Chapter 1 of the new Title XI, new Articles 136 to 145). The Treaty of Nice, which succeeded the Treaty of Amsterdam [see section 1.1.], consolidates the mechanisms set in place by the Maastricht Treaty and promotes a series of social policy priorities at Community level, especially in the area of employment. Moreover, the new Article 13 of the EC Treaty, introduced by the Treaty of Amsterdam, refers to the adoption of provisions on non-discrimination, and authorises the Council, acting unanimously, to take appropriate action to combat any discrimination based on sex, race, ethnic origin, religion or belief, disability, age or sexual orientation.

The EC Treaty also confirms the recognition, already introduced by the Single Act, of the key role of the social partners. This recognition takes effect at two levels: at national level, since Member States may entrust management and labour with the implementation of the aforementioned directives (Article 137(4) of the EC Treaty); and at Community level, since the Commission has the task of promoting the consultation of management and labour and taking any relevant measure to facilitate their dialogue by ensuring balanced support for the parties (Article 138(1).

With the entry into force of the **Amsterdam Treaty**, the promotion of employment has been added to the list of Community objectives, becoming a "matter of common concern" (Article 2 of the EC Treaty). The new objective consists in reaching a "high level of employment" without undermining competitiveness. In order to attain this objective, the Community is given a new area of responsibility to complement the activities of the Member States, involving the development of a "coordinated strategy" for employment. The main element of this strategy is formed by common guidelines, modelled on those which were adopted by the Essen European Council. The new Title VIII on employment (new Articles 125 to 130), which takes effect immediately following a decision of the Amsterdam European Council, specifies what the objectives are and how to attain them. It also provides for the establishment of an Employment Committee [see annex 2.1.].

Article 136 (TEC) confirms that social policy falls under the joint responsibility of the European Community and the Member States. The objectives of social policy are set out, following the example of the European Social Charter signed at Turin on 18 October 1961 and of the Community Charter of the fundamental social rights of workers of 1989. These objectives are the promotion of employment, improved living and working conditions, proper social protection, dialogue between management and labour, the development of human resources with a view to lasting high employment and the combating of exclusion (formerly Article 1 of the Agreement).

In order to achieve these objectives, the Community supports and complements the activities of the Member States. **Article 137 (TEC)** provides that the Council may first of all, by adopting directives by qualified majority in codecision with Parliament and after consulting the Economic and Social Committee and the Committee of the Regions, act or reinforce its action in the following areas:

- workers' health and safety;
- working conditions;
- the integration of persons excluded from the labour market;
- the information and consultation of workers; and
- equality between men and women with regard to labour market opportunities and treatment at work [see annex 2.1.].

Under the same procedure, the Council may also adopt measures designed to encourage the combating of social exclusion. However, **unanimity in the Council** remains the norm in the following areas:

- social security and social protection of workers;
- protection of workers where their employment contract is terminated;
- representation and collective defence of the interests of workers and employers, including co-determination subject to paragraph 6;
- conditions of employment for third country nationals legally residing in Community territory; and
- financial contributions for promotion of employment and job creation.

The salaried workers wages, the right of association, the right to strike and the right to impose lockouts are still excluded from Community competence (paragraph 6).

Education and training are the bases of the European social model. In accordance with Articles 149 and 150 of the EC Treaty, the Community's role is to contribute to the development of quality education by encouraging cooperation between Member States and, if necessary, by supporting and supplementing their action. The main purpose of this is to develop the European dimension in education, encourage mobility and promote cooperation between schools and universities. Under the principle of subsidiarity[1] every Member State of the European Union retains full responsibility for the content of teaching and the organisation of its own education system.

At the **Lisbon European Council**, in March 2000, the European Union, in response to the challenges of globalisation and the information society, set out its new strategic objective for the coming decade, viz.: becoming the most competitive and dynamic knowledge-based economy in the world capable of sustainable economic growth with more and better jobs and greater social cohesion [see section 6.2.]. This implies efforts to strengthen cooperation on education and training policy to be implemented by the "open method of coordination" between Member States, which was also defined in Lisbon. This method provides a cooperation framework for the Member States with a view to convergence of national policies and the attainment of certain objectives shared by everyone. It is based essentially on:

- identifying and defining jointly the objectives to be attained;
- commonly-defined yardsticks (statistics, indicators) enabling Member States to know where they stand and to assess progress towards the objectives set;
- comparative cooperation tools to stimulate innovation, the quality and relevance of teaching and training programmes (dissemination of "best practice", pilot projects, etc).

The Barcelona European Council, in March 2002, underlined that Europe's education systems should become a "world quality reference" by 2010. In response to the Barcelona declaration, the "**Bruges process**" of increased cooperation in vocational education and training, supports the development of transparency and mutual trust as the principles underpinning improved recognition of qualifications and competences, as well as the quality of European vocational education and training.

The social policy agenda, proposed by the Commission and approved by the Nice European Council in December 2000, provides the roadmap for employment and social policy, in the period from 2000 to 2006, translating the policy objectives of the Lisbon strategy for economic and social renewal into concrete measures[2] [see section 2.1.]. In short, the Union aims at social progress and cohesion through the specific policies for employment, education and professional training, as well as through the promotion and improvement of living and working conditions, including social protection and social inclusion.

2.3. The social policy and other common policies

A dynamic social policy is essential for an efficient **industrial policy**. Adequate vocational training for workers and the improvement of the occupational and geographical mobility of labour are prerequisites for the efficiency of European industry. Technological progress and improved training lead to the strengthening of the requirements as regards social justice, to worker participation and to the improvement of the quality of life and of work. At the same time, however, technological progress gives rise to numerous structural changes accompanied by tension on the labour market. A common approach must be taken to these phenomena so as not to give rise to distortions of competition within the common market. In fact, given the increasing economic interdependence of the member countries, any one of their number which decided to carry out a social reform on its own might handicap some of its industrial sectors or even its economy in general.

1 Moussis (2004), section 3.2.
2 COM (2000) 379 and COM (2003) 312, 2 June 2003.

The general Regulation on the **Structural Funds** specifies that the Commission and the Member States must ensure that the operations of the Funds are consistent with other Community policies and operations [see section 3.3.]. Indeed, several common policies favour by their nature the process of integration and cohesion. Thus, the common social policy has an important impact on labour law, health and security at work, free movement of workers and equal opportunities for men and women in the poor regions of the Union. Community research programmes develop research capabilities in weaker Member States strengthening their scientific and technological base and accelerating innovation and economic development. The common agricultural policy has also a positive cohesion effect, with the cohesion countries receiving net transfers through it.

Article 153 (TEC), gives the Community the task of contributing to the **protection of health**, safety and economic interests of consumers, as well to the promotion of their right to information, education and to organise themselves in order to safeguard their interests. The attainment of those objectives should be pursued through: (a) measures adopted pursuant to Article 95 (harmonisation of legislations) in the context of the completion of the internal market; and (b) measures which support, supplement and monitor the policy pursued by the Member States. The protection of health and safety of consumers obviously interacts with the objectives of the common social policy [see section 9.3.].

The activities of the common **research policy** carried out under the theme "life sciences, genomics and biotechnology for health" are intended to help Europe exploit, by means of an integrated research effort, breakthroughs achieved in decoding the genomes of living organisms, more particularly for the benefit of public health and citizens. They may culminate in numerous applications in various health-related sectors, and notably in the development of new diagnostic tools and new treatments capable of helping to combat diseases that are not at present under control. This research may thus have implications on the common social policy.

At the dawn of the 21st century, the European societies are faced with new common challenges. The **globalisation** of trade and production, the impact of new technologies on work, society and individuals, the high level of unemployment of some categories and the ageing of the population are all combining to put severe strains on the social fabric of all the Member States. While the basic responsibility in these areas lies with the Member States, full cooperation between them, within the Union, plays an important role in ensuring that the national systems of social protection do not develop in ways which conflict with overall Union employment objectives or standards, distort conditions of competition, or inhibit the free movement of people within the Union.

THE LEGAL FRAMEWORK OF THE COMMON SOCIAL POLICY

Annex 2.1.

Consolidated versions of the Treaty on European Union and of the Treaty establishing the European Community
Official Journal C 325 of 24 December 2002

RELEVANT PROVISIONS OF THE TREATY ESTABLISHING THE EUROPEAN COMMUNITY

TITLE VIII - EMPLOYMENT

Article 125
Member States and the Community shall, in accordance with this title, work towards developing a coordinated strategy for employment and particularly for promoting a skilled, trained and adaptable workforce and labour markets responsive to economic change with a view to achieving the objectives defined in Article 2 of the Treaty on European Union and in Article 2 of this Treaty.

Article 126
1. Member States, through their employment policies, shall contribute to the achievement of the objectives referred to in Article 125 in a way consistent with the broad guidelines of the economic policies of the Member States and of the Community adopted pursuant to Article 99(2).

2. Member States, having regard to national practices related to the responsibilities of management and labour, shall regard promoting employment as a matter of common concern and shall coordinate their action in this respect within the Council, in accordance with the provisions of Article 128.

Article 127
1. The Community shall contribute to a high level of employment by encouraging cooperation between Member States and by supporting and, if necessary, complementing their action. In doing so, the competences of the Member States shall be respected.
2. The objective of a high level of employment shall be taken into consideration in the formulation and implementation of Community policies and activities.

Article 128
1. The European Council shall each year consider the employment situation in the Community and adopt conclusions thereon, on the basis of a joint annual report by the Council and the Commission.
2. On the basis of the conclusions of the European Council, the Council, acting by a qualified majority on a proposal from the Commission and after consulting the European Parliament, the Economic and Social Committee, the Committee of the Regions and the Employment Committee referred to in Article 130, shall each year draw up guidelines which the Member States shall take into account in their employment policies. These guidelines shall be consistent with the broad guidelines adopted pursuant to Article 99(2).
3. Each Member State shall provide the Council and the Commission with an annual report on the principal measures taken to implement its employment policy in the light of the guidelines for employment as referred to in paragraph 2.
4. The Council, on the basis of the reports referred to in paragraph 3 and having received the views of the Employment Committee, shall each year carry out an examination of the implementation of the employment policies of the Member States in the light of the guidelines for employment. The Council, acting by a qualified majority on a recommendation from the Commission, may, if it considers it appropriate in the light of that examination, make recommendations to Member States.

5. On the basis of the results of that examination, the Council and the Commission shall make a joint annual report to the European Council on the employment situation in the Community and on the implementation of the guidelines for employment.

Article 129
The Council, acting in accordance with the procedure referred to in Article 251 and after consulting the Economic and Social Committee and the Committee of the Regions, may adopt incentive measures designed to encourage cooperation between Member States and to support their action in the field of employment through initiatives aimed at developing exchanges of information and best practices, providing comparative analysis and advice as well as promoting innovative approaches and evaluating experiences, in particular by recourse to pilot projects.
Those measures shall not include harmonisation of the laws and regulations of the Member States.

Article 130
The Council, after consulting the European Parliament, shall establish an Employment Committee with advisory status to promote coordination between Member States on employment and labour market policies. The tasks of the Committee shall be:
- to monitor the employment situation and employment policies in the Member States and the Community,
- without prejudice to Article 207, to formulate opinions at the request of **either the Council** or the Commission or on its own initiative, and to contribute to the preparation of the Council proceedings referred to in Article 128.
In fulfilling its mandate, the Committee shall consult management and labour.
Each Member State and the Commission shall appoint two members of the Committee.

TITLE XI - SOCIAL POLICY, EDUCATION, VOCATIONAL TRAINING AND YOUTH

CHAPTER 1 - SOCIAL PROVISIONS

Article 136
The Community and the Member States, having in mind fundamental social rights such as those set out in the European Social Charter signed at Turin on 18 October 1961 and in the 1989 Community Charter of the Fundamental Social Rights of Workers, shall have as their objectives the promotion of employment, improved living and working conditions, so as to make possible their harmonisation while the improvement is being maintained, proper social protection, dialogue between management and labour, the development of human resources with a view to lasting high employment and the combating of exclusion.
To this end the Community and the Member States shall implement measures which take account of the diverse forms of national practices, in particular in the field of contractual relations, and the need to maintain the competitiveness of the Community economy.
They believe that such a development will ensue not only from the functioning of the common market, which will favour the harmonisation of social systems, but also from the procedures provided for in this Treaty and from the approximation of provisions laid down by law, regulation or administrative action.

Article 137
1. With a view to achieving the objectives of Article 136, the Community shall support and complement the activities of the Member States in the following fields:
(a) improvement in particular of the working environment to protect workers' health and safety;
(b) working conditions;
(c) social security and social protection of workers;
(d) protection of workers where their employment contract is terminated;
(e) the information and consultation of workers;
(f) representation and collective defence of the interests of workers and employers, including co-determination, subject to paragraph 5;
(g) conditions of employment for third-country nationals legally residing in Community territory;
(h) the integration of persons excluded from the labour market, without prejudice to Article 150;
(i) equality between men and women with regard to labour market opportunities and treatment at work;
(j) the combating of social exclusion;
(k) the modernisation of social protection systems without prejudice to point (c).

2. To this end, the Council:

(a) may adopt measures designed to encourage cooperation between Member States through initiatives aimed at improving knowledge, developing exchanges of information and best practices, promoting innovative approaches and evaluating experiences, excluding any harmonisation of the laws and regulations of the Member States;
(b) may adopt, in the fields referred to in paragraph 1(a) to (i), by means of directives, minimum requirements for gradual implementation, having regard to the conditions and technical rules obtaining in each of the Member States. Such directives shall avoid imposing administrative, financial and legal constraints in a way which would hold back the creation and development of small and medium-sized undertakings.
The Council shall act in accordance with the procedure referred to in Article 251 after consulting the Economic and Social Committee and the Committee of the Regions, except in the fields referred to in paragraph 1(c), (d), (f) and (g) of this article, where the Council shall act unanimously on a proposal from the Commission, after consulting the European Parliament and the said Committees. The Council, acting unanimously on a proposal from the Commission, after consulting the European Parliament, may decide to render the procedure referred to in Article 251 applicable to paragraph 1(d), (f) and (g) of this article.

3. A Member State may entrust management and labour, at their joint request, with the implementation of directives adopted pursuant to paragraph 2.
In this case, it shall ensure that, no later than the date on which a directive must be transposed in accordance with Article 249, management and labour have introduced the necessary measures by agreement, the Member State concerned being required to take any necessary measure enabling it at any time to be in a position to guarantee the results imposed by that directive.

4. The provisions adopted pursuant to this article:
- shall not affect the right of Member States to define the fundamental principles of their social security systems and must not significantly affect the financial equilibrium thereof,
- shall not prevent any Member State from maintaining or introducing more stringent protective measures compatible with this Treaty.

5. The provisions of this article shall not apply to pay, the right of association, the right to strike or the right to impose lock-outs.

Article 138
1. The Commission shall have the task of promoting the consultation of management and labour at Community level and shall take any relevant measure to facilitate their dialogue by ensuring balanced support for the parties.
2. To this end, before submitting proposals in the social policy field, the Commission shall consult management and labour on the possible direction of Community action.
3. If, after such consultation, the Commission considers Community action advisable, it shall consult management and labour on the content of the envisaged proposal. Management and labour shall forward to the Commission an opinion or, where appropriate, a recommendation.
4. On the occasion of such consultation, management and labour may inform the Commission of their wish to initiate the process provided for in Article 139. The duration of the procedure shall not exceed nine months, unless the management and labour concerned and the Commission decide jointly to extend it.

Article 139
1. Should management and labour so desire, the dialogue between them at Community level may lead to contractual relations, including agreements.
2. Agreements concluded at Community level shall be implemented either in accordance with the procedures and practices specific to management and labour and the Member States or, in matters covered by Article 137, at the joint request of the signatory parties, by a Council decision on a proposal from the Commission.
The Council shall act by qualified majority, except where the agreement in question contains one or more provisions relating to one of the areas for which unanimity is required pursuant to Article 137(2). In that case, it shall act unanimously.

Article 140
With a view to achieving the objectives of Article 136 and without prejudice to the other provisions of this Treaty, the Commission shall encourage cooperation between the Member States and facilitate the coordination of their action in all social policy fields under this chapter, particularly in matters relating to:
- employment,
- labour law and working conditions,
- basic and advanced vocational training,

- social security,
- prevention of occupational accidents and diseases,
- occupational hygiene,
- the right of association and collective bargaining between employers and workers.

To this end, the Commission shall act in close contact with Member States by making studies, delivering opinions and arranging consultations both on problems arising at national level and on those of concern to international organisations.

Before delivering the opinions provided for in this article, the Commission shall consult the Economic and Social Committee.

Article 141

1. Each Member State shall ensure that the principle of equal pay for male and female workers for equal work or work of equal value is applied.
2. For the purpose of this article, "pay" means the ordinary basic or minimum wage or salary and any other consideration, whether in cash or in kind, which the worker receives directly or indirectly, in respect of his employment, from his employer.

Equal pay without discrimination based on sex means:

(a) that pay for the same work at piece rates shall be calculated on the basis of the same unit of measurement;

(b) that pay for work at time rates shall be the same for the same job.

3. The Council, acting in accordance with the procedure referred to in Article 251, and after consulting the Economic and Social Committee, shall adopt measures to ensure the application of the principle of equal opportunities and equal treatment of men and women in matters of employment and occupation, including the principle of equal pay for equal work or work of equal value.
4. With a view to ensuring full equality in practice between men and women in working life, the principle of equal treatment shall not prevent any Member State from maintaining or adopting measures providing for specific advantages in order to make it easier for the underrepresented sex to pursue a vocational activity or to prevent or compensate for disadvantages in professional careers.

Article 142

Member States shall endeavour to maintain the existing equivalence between paid holiday schemes.

Article 143

The Commission shall draw up a report each year on progress in achieving the objectives of Article 136, including the demographic situation in the Community. It shall forward the report to the European Parliament, the Council and the Economic and Social Committee.

The European Parliament may invite the Commission to draw up reports on particular problems concerning the social situation.

Article 144

The Council, after consulting the European Parliament, shall establish a Social Protection Committee with advisory status to promote cooperation on social protection policies between Member States and with the Commission. The tasks of the Committee shall be:

- to monitor the social situation and the development of social protection policies in the Member States and the Community,
- to promote exchanges of information, experience and good practice between Member States and with the Commission,
- without prejudice to Article 207, to prepare reports, formulate opinions or undertake other work within its fields of competence, at the request of either the Council or the Commission or on its own initiative.

In fulfilling its mandate, the Committee shall establish appropriate contacts with management and labour.

Each Member State and the Commission shall appoint two members of the Committee.

Article 145

The Commission shall include a separate chapter on social developments within the Community in its annual report to the European Parliament.

The European Parliament may invite the Commission to draw up reports on any particular problems concerning social conditions.

CHAPTER 2 - THE EUROPEAN SOCIAL FUND

Article 146
In order to improve employment opportunities for workers in the internal market and to contribute thereby to raising the standard of living, a European Social Fund is hereby established in accordance with the provisions set out below; it shall aim to render the employment of workers easier and to increase their geographical and occupational mobility within the Community, and to facilitate their adaptation to industrial changes and to changes in production systems, in particular through vocational training and retraining.

Article 147
The Fund shall be administered by the Commission.
The Commission shall be assisted in this task by a Committee presided over by a Member of the Commission and composed of representatives of governments, trade unions and employers' organisations.

Article 148
The Council, acting in accordance with the procedure referred to in Article 251 and after consulting the Economic and Social Committee and the Committee of the Regions, shall adopt implementing decisions relating to the European Social Fund.

CHAPTER 3 - EDUCATION, VOCATIONAL TRAINING AND YOUTH

Article 149
1. The Community shall contribute to the development of quality education by encouraging cooperation between Member States and, if necessary, by supporting and supplementing their action, while fully respecting the responsibility of the Member States for the content of teaching and the organisation of education systems and their cultural and linguistic diversity.
2. Community action shall be aimed at:
- developing the European dimension in education, particularly through the teaching and dissemination of the languages of the Member States,
- encouraging mobility of students and teachers, by encouraging inter alia, the academic recognition of diplomas and periods of study,
- promoting cooperation between educational establishments,
- developing exchanges of information and experience on issues common to the education systems of the Member States,
- encouraging the development of youth exchanges and of exchanges of socioeducational instructors,
- encouraging the development of distance education.
3. The Community and the Member States shall foster cooperation with third countries and the competent international organisations in the field of education, in particular the Council of Europe.
4. In order to contribute to the achievement of the objectives referred to in this Article, the Council:
- acting in accordance with the procedure referred to in Article 251, after consulting the Economic and Social Committee and the Committee of the Regions, shall adopt incentive measures, excluding any harmonisation of the laws and regulations of the Member States,
- acting by a qualified majority on a proposal from the Commission, shall adopt recommendations.

Article 150
1. The Community shall implement a vocational training policy which shall support and supplement the action of the Member States, while fully respecting the responsibility of the Member States for the content and organisation of vocational training.
2. Community action shall aim to:
- facilitate adaptation to industrial changes, in particular through vocational training and retraining,
- improve initial and continuing vocational training in order to facilitate vocational integration and reintegration into the labour market,
- facilitate access to vocational training and encourage mobility of instructors and trainees and particularly young people,
- stimulate cooperation on training between educational or training establishments and firms,
- develop exchanges of information and experience on issues common to the training systems of the Member States.
3. The Community and the Member States shall foster cooperation with third countries and the competent international organisations in the sphere of vocational training.

4. The Council, acting in accordance with the procedure referred to in Article 251 and after consulting the Economic and Social Committee and the Committee of the Regions, shall adopt measures to contribute to the achievement of the objectives referred to in this article, excluding any harmonisation of the laws and regulations of the Member States.

TITLE XIII - PUBLIC HEALTH

Article 152
1. A high level of human health protection shall be ensured in the definition and implementation of all Community policies and activities.
Community action, which shall complement national policies, shall be directed towards improving public health, preventing human illness and diseases, and obviating sources of danger to human health. Such action shall cover the fight against the major health scourges, by promoting research into their causes, their transmission and their prevention, as well as health information and education.
The Community shall complement the Member States' action in reducing drugs-related health damage, including information and prevention.
2. The Community shall encourage cooperation between the Member States in the areas referred to in this Article and, if necessary, lend support to their action.
Member States shall, in liaison with the Commission, coordinate among themselves their policies and programmes in the areas referred to in paragraph 1. The Commission may, in close contact with the Member States, take any useful initiative to promote such coordination.
3. The Community and the Member States shall foster cooperation with third countries and the competent international organisations in the sphere of public health.
4. The Council, acting in accordance with the procedure referred to in Article 251 and after consulting the Economic and Social Committee and the Committee of the Regions, shall contribute to the achievement of the objectives referred to in this article through adopting:
(a) measures setting high standards of quality and safety of organs and substances of human origin, blood and blood derivatives; these measures shall not prevent any Member State from maintaining or introducing more stringent protective measures;
(b) by way of derogation from Article 37, measures in the veterinary and phytosanitary fields which have as their direct objective the protection of public health;
(c) incentive measures designed to protect and improve human health, excluding any harmonisation of the laws and regulations of the Member States.
The Council, acting by a qualified majority on a proposal from the Commission, may also adopt recommendations for the purposes set out in this article.
5. Community action in the field of public health shall fully respect the responsibilities of the Member States for the organisation and delivery of health services and medical care. In particular, measures referred to in paragraph 4(a) shall not affect national provisions on the donation or medical use of organs and blood.

TITLE XIV - CONSUMER PROTECTION

Article 153
1. In order to promote the interests of consumers and to ensure a high level of consumer protection, the Community shall contribute to protecting the health, safety and economic interests of consumers, as well as to promoting their right to information, education and to organise themselves in order to safeguard their interests.
2. Consumer protection requirements shall be taken into account in defining and implementing other Community policies and activities.
3. The Community shall contribute to the attainment of the objectives referred to in paragraph 1 through:
(a) measures adopted pursuant to Article 95 in the context of the completion of the internal market;
(b) measures which support, supplement and monitor the policy pursued by the Member States.
4. The Council, acting in accordance with the procedure referred to in Article 251 and after consulting the Economic and Social Committee, shall adopt the measures referred to in paragraph 3(b).
5. Measures adopted pursuant to paragraph 4 shall not prevent any Member State from maintaining or introducing more stringent protective measures. Such measures must be compatible with this Treaty. The Commission shall be notified of them.

TITLE XVII - ECONOMIC AND SOCIAL COHESION

Article 158

In order to promote its overall harmonious development, the Community shall develop and pursue its actions leading to the strengthening of its economic and social cohesion.
In particular, the Community shall aim at reducing disparities between the levels of development of the various regions and the backwardness of the least favoured regions or islands, including rural areas.

Article 159
Member States shall conduct their economic policies and shall coordinate them in such a way as, in addition, to attain the objectives set out in Article 158. The formulation and implementation of the Community's policies and actions and the implementation of the internal market shall take into account the objectives set out in Article 158 and shall contribute to their achievement. The Community shall also support the achievement of these objectives by the action it takes through the Structural Funds (European Agricultural Guidance and Guarantee Fund, Guidance Section; European Social Fund; European Regional Development Fund), the European Investment Bank and the other existing Financial Instruments.
The Commission shall submit a report to the European Parliament, the Council, the Economic and Social Committee and the Committee of the Regions every three years on the progress made towards achieving economic and social cohesion and on the manner in which the various means provided for in this Article have contributed to it. This report shall, if necessary, be accompanied by appropriate proposals.
If specific actions prove necessary outside the Funds and without prejudice to the measures decided upon within the framework of the other Community policies, such actions may be adopted by the Council acting in accordance with the procedure referred to in Article 251 and after consulting the Economic and Social Committee and the Committee of the Regions.

Article 160
The European Regional Development Fund is intended to help to redress the main regional imbalances in the Community through participation in the development and structural adjustment of regions whose development is lagging behind and in the conversion of declining industrial regions.

Article 161
Without prejudice to Article 162, the Council, acting unanimously on a proposal from the Commission and after obtaining the assent of the European Parliament and consulting the Economic and Social Committee and the Committee of the Regions, shall define the tasks, priority objectives and the organisation of the Structural Funds, which may involve grouping the Funds. The Council, acting by the same procedure, shall also define the general rules applicable to them and the provisions necessary to ensure their effectiveness and the coordination of the Funds with one another and with the other existing Financial Instruments.
A Cohesion Fund set up by the Council in accordance with the same procedure shall provide a financial contribution to projects in the fields of environment and trans-European networks in the area of transport infrastructure.
From 1 January 2007, the Council shall act by a qualified majority on a proposal from the Commission after obtaining the assent of the European Parliament and after consulting the Economic and Social Committee and the Committee of the Regions if, by that date, the multiannual financial perspective applicable from 1 January 2007 and the Interinstitutional Agreement relating thereto have been adopted. If such is not the case, the procedure laid down by this paragraph shall apply from the date of their adoption.

Article 162
Implementing decisions relating to the European Regional Development Fund shall be taken by the Council, acting in accordance with the procedure referred to in Article 251 and after consulting the Economic and Social Committee and the Committee of the Regions.
With regard to the European Agricultural Guidance and Guarantee Fund, Guidance Section, and the European Social Fund, Articles 37 and 148 respectively shall continue to apply.

Chapter 3

THE ECONOMIC AND SOCIAL COHESION OF THE UNION

The wide European market reinforces the polarisation of pre-existing economic activities and thus accelerates the agglomeration and concentration process. If measures were not taken at national and European level, the completion of the internal market would tend further to widen existing inequalities in the distribution of economic activities throughout the territory of the EU. That is why, the objective of economic and social cohesion, implying the desire to reduce disparities between the various regions of the Community, was introduced by the Single European Act [see section 1.1.].

3.1. The effect of economic integration on social conditions

On top of the single market, the achievement of **economic and monetary union** promises enhanced prospects for the developed and the less favoured regions alike. The reduction of trans-frontier transaction costs and the elimination of exchange rate risk may promote regional specialisation and intra-Community trade in goods and services. The weaker regions can benefit from this specialisation by exploiting more fully their comparative advantages. Furthermore, increased capital mobility in EMU, supported by the single currency and the tendency towards quasi-uniform inflation rates, tends to equalise interest rates for any given level of risk, which should favour the less developed regions where capital is often relatively scarce and capital costs, therefore, relatively high.

At the same time, however, Member States participating in the euro-zone lose certain fiscal and monetary policy options as well as the ability to adjust the exchange rate. Exchange rate flexibility is important in that, in principle, it enables a country, through devaluation, to offset a loss in international competitiveness in a relatively painless manner. As such, it facilitates short-term adjustment to general, or country-specific economic shocks. The removal of the possibility of exchange rate adjustment, therefore, represents a more important loss to the least developed countries of the euro-zone, which are the ones that must carry out the most important structural changes. Those countries must invest most, while spending least so as to conform to the Maastricht criteria and to the requirements of the Stability Pact[1].

In addition, those countries could **lose the advantage of lower labour costs**. As long as markets were protected by customs and other barriers, salaries in certain countries were much lower than in others, compensating for the lower productivity of a labour force that was not very qualified. But in a common market, and even more in an economic and monetary union, freedom of movement for workers, better information on respective situations, and trade union demands tend to align revenues towards the levels already attained in the more prosperous regions. This may be a positive outcome from a social point of view but it is one which engenders inflationist

---

[1] Moussis (2004), section 7.2.4. and 7.3.2.

tendencies and creates difficulties for businesses in areas where productivity is low. If these businesses have to shut down, the workers lose their jobs and their revenue increase is merely an illusion.

From both an economic and social point of view, neither the weakest member countries nor the European Union can tolerate a substantial part of their patrimony being left to underdevelopment because of economic integration. The prosperity of certain areas of the union cannot be paid for by the decline or stagnation of other areas. **Wide disparities are intolerable in a community**, if the term is to have any meaning at all. Furthermore, disparities do not just imply a poorer quality of life for the disadvantaged regions, but indicate a failure to take advantage of economic opportunities that could benefit the Union as a whole.

For the reasons mentioned above, the Treaty on the European Union states in its Article 2 that the strengthening of **economic and social cohesion is a fundamental objective of the Union**. Article 158 (TEC) specifies that in order to promote its overall harmonious development, the Community shall develop and pursue its actions leading to the strengthening of its economic and social cohesion, aiming, in particular, at reducing disparities between the levels of development of the various regions and the backwardness of the least-favoured regions, including rural areas. Although all Community policies can contribute to reinforcing economic and social cohesion, as is stated in Article 159 (TEC), a major role is, certainly, played by the Structural Funds (Art. 161 TEC). In the Community terminology "**Structural Funds**" or simply "Funds" mean the European Regional Development Fund (ERDF), the European Social Fund (ESF), the European Agricultural Guidance and Guarantee Fund (EAGGF) - Guidance Section, and the Financial Instrument for Fisheries Guidance (FIFG).

3.2. The Cohesion Fund

The situation in which certain Member States find themselves necessitates special efforts to promote economic and social cohesion and thus enable them to comply with the convergence criteria required inside the EMU. Indeed, among these criteria is, in particular, the one on curbing public deficits[1]. In order to satisfy this condition, the less wealthy countries must apply very strict budgetary disciplines, whereas they need, at the same time, pursue and even increase public investments in order to close the prosperity gap with the other Member States.

In order to cope with these contradictory requirements, Article 161 (TEC) and a Protocol annexed to the Treaty of Maastricht [see section 1.1.] have provided for the creation of the **Cohesion Fund**. This must contribute financially to projects in the fields of the environment and transport infrastructure for trans-European networks[2] in Member States whose per capita GNP is less than 90% of the Community average (Greece, Spain, Portugal and Ireland) and which are implementing a programme aiming to fulfil the conditions of economic convergence announced in Article 104 of the EC Treaty[3] [see annexes 3.1. and 3.2.]. In conjunction with the fulfilment of the conditions of economic convergence as set out in Article 104 of the Treaty and with the need for sound management of the government deficit, conditionality in the granting of the Fund's financial assistance takes account of the obligations of the beneficiary Member States with regard to excessive government deficits, the Resolution of the European Council on the Stability and Growth Pact[4] and the stability of the euro.

---

1 Moussis (2004), section 7.3.2.
2 Moussis (2004), section 6.8.
3 Regulation 1164/94, OJ L 130, 25.05.1994 and Regulations 1264/1999 and 1265/1999, OJ L 161, 26.06.1999.
4 Moussis (2004), sections 7.2.4. and 7.3.2.

The objective of economic and social cohesion means a great deal more than the mere redistribution of funds to the poorest Member States and regions. It requires coherent action through a coordination of national and common economic policies. Therefore, the common regional policy has two wings. Firstly, it seeks to **coordinate national regional policies** by formulating guidelines and establishing certain principles in order to avoid distortion of competition between Member States through their regional aid schemes. Secondly, it **coordinates the various policies and financial instruments of the EU** to give them a "regional dimension" and thus more impact on regions most in need of care.

The Commission has established a series of guidelines regarding the Cohesion Fund indicating that its assistance should be subject to a coordinated strategic approach and framed within programmes identifying the main priorities for assistance in the different sectors of application selected and looking for better coordination with other Community financial instruments[1]. An indicative allocation of the total resources of the Cohesion Fund is made on the basis of precise and objective criteria, principally population, surface area and per capita GNP taking account of the improvement in national prosperity attained over the previous period. For the period 2000 to 2006, the indicative allocation of the total resources of the Cohesion Fund among the beneficiary Member States is the following:

- Spain: 61 % to 63,5 % of the total;
- Greece: 16 % to 18 % of the total;
- Portugal: 16 % to 18 % of the total;
- Ireland: 2 % to 6 % of the total.

In its communication of 15 July 1997, called "**Agenda 2000**", dealing with the outlook of the European Union in the beginning of the 21st century, the Commission advocated greater geographical concentration, reducing from over 50% to below 40% the population qualifying for structural aid. The Berlin European Council on 25 March 1999 reached an overall agreement on Agenda 2000 based broadly on the guidelines laid down by the Commission. It allocated a total of EUR 213 billion for structural and cohesion policies (EUR 195 billion for the Structural Funds and EUR 18 billion for the Cohesion Fund). The Structural Funds were again reformed in 1999 and an Instrument for Structural Policies for Pre-accession (ISPA) was established to contribute to the preparation for accession to the European Union of ten applicant countries in the area of economic and social cohesion, concerning environmental measures and transport infrastructure[2] [see annex 3.7.].

3.3. The common structural policy

By assisting the problem regions build up their infrastructure networks, the Member States and the Union can help them to both develop their markets for the benefit of all and better balance the European economy in the light of future changes. Of course, each Member State carries out its own regional policy, which generally aims at favouring the development of the national territory's less prosperous regions by means of transferring resources from wealthier regions. The means normally used by Member States to remedy regional problems are of two types: firstly, improving the infrastructure and the social and cultural development of backward regions, and secondly, various premiums, subsidies and tax incentives for attracting private investment in these regions. The general objective of these measures is to create or re-establish a better distribution of eco-

1 COM (2001) 602, 22 October 2001.
2 Regulation 3906/89, OJ L 375, 23.12.1989, Regulations 1266/1999, 1267/1999 and 1268/1999, OJ L 161, 26.06.1999.

nomic activities and population over the national territory. To do this, certain governments also try to discourage investments in highly developed regions. The advantages of such measures are twofold: favouring the transfer of resources towards poor regions while halting the disproportionate expansion of congested regions.

Certainly, it is primarily up to the national authorities to solve the problems of their regions, namely by promoting infrastructures or giving incentives to businesses to attract their investments in disadvantaged regions. The scale of the effort required to stimulate economic activity in the least advanced regions means that public funds must be used in conjunction with private investment. Regional aid, when judiciously applied, is a vital instrument to regional development and to continued and balanced expansion within the European Union. But given the possibility of competition inside a single market between the various regions in order to attract Community and foreign investments (including those from partner countries), the advantages granted can go beyond compensation for material difficulties faced by investors in the areas to be promoted. Thus, part of the aid granted would merely serve a reciprocal neutralisation. The national regional actions would simply be more expensive and grant unwarranted profits to benefiting undertakings[1]. Therefore, the prime objective of EU regional policy is to coordinate national regional policies by formulating guidelines and setting priorities at European level, which effectively help close the gap between regions.

In addition, the EU has a common interest in regional development through structural change. The very essence of economic integration is the **optimisation of the market mechanism** at a European scale. But a market policy based on some sort of spontaneous balance between the various economic parameters essentially benefits rich regions. Indeed, prior to the creation of the common market, economic activities had developed in a national context; certain activities usually grouped in certain regions were protected from international competition by customs barriers. With the opening of borders, European and foreign (American, Japanese...) companies wanting to set up business in the EU market are normally attracted in European regions where infrastructure is most developed, where labour is most qualified, and where the economic environment is most adapted to their activities. Economic concentration invites more concentration. The common regional policy strives to make up for this tendency in order to achieve a better-balanced growth within the common market. Its goals and mechanisms are coordinated and interact with those of other common policies, notably social, enterprise, environment, agricultural and fisheries policies.

Recently, **innovation** has evolved into a continuous process requiring the rapid introduction of new technological advances and therefore a constant interaction between research laboratories and businesses either developing or using new technology. Hence, the economic success of a region depends to a large extent on the possibilities available for securing access to research and technological development (RTD) on an ongoing basis. The problem for weaker regions is that their productive base consists largely of small and medium-sized enterprises (SMEs), usually working in traditional sectors and lacking an outward-looking perspective[2]. In many regions, highly qualified people are in short supply and ancillary services, such as banking, are inadequate, thus inhibiting innovation. In fact, most factors which favour RTD and innovation (organisation, management, commercial, financial and technical skills required introducing a new or improved product or process onto the market) are almost always found in developed regions.

3.3.1. Priority regions of the Union

[1] Moussis (2004), section 15.5.
[2] Moussis (2004), section 17.1.4.

The Economic and Social Cohesion of the European Union

All the Member States of the European Union are experiencing disparities in the levels of development and living standards from one region to another and the gaps are wider still when measured across the Union as a whole. At the beginning of the 1990s, some 52% of the total population of the Union (EU-12) lived in **problem regions**. The per capita gross domestic product (GDP) in the ten poorest regions of the Union was only about one quarter of that in the ten richest regions. Unemployment in the ten regions worst hit was up to seven times greater than in the ten most fortunate regions. From one country to another the ratio of young people receiving vocational training was about 1 to 2, the ratio for basic infrastructure about 1 to 3 and the ratio for grants for research and technology about 1 to 7.

Since the beginning of the 21st century, the Community regional policy recognises **two main types of "priority" regions and areas**: regions whose development is lagging behind and areas facing structural difficulties. The identification of the priority regions and areas at Community level is based on the common system of classification of the regions, referred to as the "Nomenclature of Territorial Statistical Units (NUTS)", established by the Statistical Office of the European Communities in cooperation with the national institutes for statistics and ensuring that these non-administrative units correspond to comparable economic, social, geographical and environmental circumstances[1].

In 1999, per capita GDP, expressed in terms of purchasing power standards in the 211 "NUTS 2" regions of the EU, ranged from 51% of the EU average in the French regions of Réunion and Guyana and in Ipeiros in Greece to 242% of the average in the Inner London region of the United Kingdom. The European Union had 22 regions above 125% of the EU average and 46 below 75%. The feature, which these regions have in common, is their excessive dependence on a limited range of traditional economic activities that can no longer provide sufficient productivity, employment and income. The consequences are common to all these regions, namely per capita GDP below the Community average, high and prolonged unemployment and a continuous outward population flow.

Regions whose development is lagging behind, termed "Objective 1 regions" in Community jargon are basically regions corresponding to level II of the Nomenclature of Territorial Statistical Units (NUTS level II) whose per capita gross domestic product (GDP) is less than 75% of the Community average. The outermost regions (the French overseas departments, the Azores, the Canary Islands and Madeira), which are all below the 75% threshold, and the areas with very low population density (less than 8 inhabitants per square kilometre), which are situated in the north and east of Finland and the northern half of Sweden[2]. The exact list of regions eligible under Objective 1 was drawn up by the Commission and is valid for seven years from 1 January 2000[3] [see annex 3.4.].

The Objective 1 regions are faced with a combination of handicaps: insufficient or rundown infrastructure - transport, energy or telecommunications; weak or outdated industrial structures whose production methods often fall short of the mark and whose products are ill-adapted to the marketplace; agriculture where archaic structures prevail; population exodus combined with urban decay; and high rates of unemployment particularly among young people and unqualified or poorly qualified workers. All of the regions whose development is lagging behind are situated at the periphery of the country to which they belong and/or of the European Union. A quarter of the population of these regions live on islands, some of which are very small (Greek islands[4]) or very

---

1 Regulation 1059/2003, OJ L 154, 21.06.2003.
2 Decision 502/99, OJ L 194, 27.07.1999.
3 Decision 502/99, OJ L 194, 27.07.1999.
4 Regulation 2019/93, OJ L 184, 27.07.1993.

far from the heart of the Union (Canaries, Azores, Madeira, Overseas Departments). This is an additional development handicap, for remoteness from the main centres of economic activity and the main centres of consumption renders their products less competitive and makes them less attractive to private investment.

The **regions with structural problems** whose socio-economic conversion is supported under Objective 2 of the structural policy include in particular: areas undergoing socio-economic change in the industrial and service sectors; declining rural areas; urban areas in difficulty; and depressed areas dependent on fisheries. According to the Regulation laying down general provisions on the Structural Funds [see section 3.3.3.], these regions constitute about 10% of the population of the Community in the case of the industrial areas, 5% in the case of the rural areas, 2% in the case of the urban areas and 1% in the case of the fisheries areas. The total population of the Objective 2 regions must not exceed 18% of the total population of the Community. Accordingly, the Commission set a population ceiling for each Member State on the basis of certain criteria fixed by the Regulation laying down general provisions on the Structural Funds [see section 3.3.3.].

The **areas undergoing socio-economic change**, eligible under Objective 2, must belong to a NUTS level III territorial unit which satisfies the following criteria:

- an average rate of unemployment over the last three years above the Community average;
- a percentage share of industrial employment in total employment equal to or greater than the Community average in any reference year from 1985 onwards;
- an observable fall in industrial employment compared with the reference year chosen in accordance with (b).

The **rural areas** covered by Objective 2 must represent or belong to a NUTS level III territorial unit, which satisfies the following criteria:

- either a population density of less than 100 people per km2, or a percentage share of agricultural employment in total employment which is equal to, or higher than, twice the Community average in any reference year from 1985;
- either an average unemployment rate over the last three years above the Community average, or a decline in population since 1985.

The **urban areas** eligible for assistance must be densely populated areas, which also meet at least one of the following criteria:

- a rate of long-term unemployment higher than the Community average;
- a high level of poverty, including precarious housing conditions;
- a particularly damaged environment;
- a high crime and delinquency rate;
- a low level of education among the population.

The **areas dependent on fisheries**, covered by Objective 2, mean coastal areas in which the number of jobs in the fisheries industry as a percentage of total employment is significant and which are facing structural socio-economic problems relating to the restructuring of the fisheries sector which result in a significant reduction in the number of jobs in that sector.

Community assistance **may extend to areas** whose population or area is significant, which fall into one of the following categories:

- areas meeting the relevant criteria and which are adjacent to an industrial area, to a rural area or to a region covered by Objective 1;
- rural areas with socio-economic problems arising either from the ageing or decline of the agricultural working population;
- areas facing or threatened by serious structural problems on account of relevant, verifiable characteristics, or a high level of unemployment arising from an ongoing or planned restructuring of one or more activities in the agricultural, industrial or service sector.

3.3.2. The Structural Funds and the EIB

The European Community uses four Structural Funds for its structural measures of various common policies:

- the European Regional Development Fund (ERDF) contributes mainly to assisting the regions whose development is lagging behind and those undergoing economic conversion or experiencing structural difficulties [see annex 3.6.];
- the European Social Fund (ESF) mainly provides assistance under the European employment strategy [see section 6.3.];
- the European Agricultural Guidance and Guarantee Fund (EAGGF) Guidance Section helps in both the development and the structural adjustment of rural areas whose development is lagging behind by improving the efficiency of their structures for producing, processing and marketing agricultural and forest products;
- the Financial Instrument for Fisheries Guidance (FIFG) supports restructuring in the fisheries sector.

According to Article 10 of the general Regulation on the Structural Funds[1] [see annex 3.3.], coordination between the various Funds must be carried out in particular through:

- the plans, the Community support frameworks, the operational programmes and the single programming documents;
- the monitoring and evaluation of assistance under an Objective; and
- the indicative guidelines published by the Commission that help the competent national and regional authorities to draw up development plans and to carry out any revision of the assistance.

In order to maximise the stimulus provided by the budget resources deployed, making use of appropriate financial instruments, the Community assistance provided in the form of grants may be combined in an appropriate way with loans and guarantees of the **European Investment Bank (EIB)**. The latter is the longest standing regional development instrument, for the Treaty of Rome called upon it to ensure a balanced and smooth development of the common market in the interests of the Community (Art. 267 TEC). Almost 75% of EIB financing in the Community contribute to regional development, although they pursue other objectives such as those of promoting SMEs and trans-European networks. The EIB notably supplies long-term capital for the financing of infrastructure projects in the fields of transport, energy and telecommunications.

According to Article 267 (TEC) the task of the EIB is to contribute, by having recourse to the capital market and utilising its own resources, to the balanced and steady development of the Community and the implementation of its policies. Thanks to its high credit rating, the Bank bor-

[1] Regulation 1260/1999, OJ L 161, 26.06.1999

rows on the best terms on the capital markets world-wide and on-lends to the Member States and their financial institutions - which distribute these global loans to SMEs. Since the EIB is a bank, it does not grant interest-rate reductions, but the financial institutions in the Member States and notably those whose vocation is regional development can borrow from the Bank and on-lend at more favourable terms. Some of the loans do have interest-rate subsidies attached, funded by the Community budget.

Article 267 of the EC Treaty confirms that the loans and guarantees of the EIB will facilitate projects for developing less-developed regions, for modernising or converting undertakings or for developing fresh activities as well as for projects of common interest to several Member States. This Article makes specific reference to the desired interaction between EIB operations and Structural Funds measures, stating that "in carrying out its task, the Bank shall facilitate the financing of investment programmes in conjunction with assistance from the Structural Funds and other Community financial instruments", which concern regions whose development is lagging behind and declining industrial areas. The Bank also plays an active role in the financing of trans-European networks and thus in the implementation of the support instruments financed by the Community budget: interest rate subsidies on its own loans, co-financing of feasibility studies and co-financing of guarantee funds.

3.3.3. The objectives and methods of the Structural Funds

According to Article 159 (TEC), the "Structural Funds", i.e. the European Regional Development Fund (ERDF), the European Social Fund (ESF), the European Agricultural Guidance and Guarantee Fund (EAGGF) - Guidance Section, and the Financial Instrument for Fisheries Guidance (FIFG), should participate in a coordinated way to the attainment of the objective of economic and social cohesion in the Community. To this end, the Regulation laying down general provisions on the Structural Funds ascribes to the Funds the attainment of the following three priority objectives for the period 2000-2006[1] [see annex 3.3.]:

- **Objective 1** promotes the development and structural adjustment of regions whose development is lagging behind, i.e. whose average per capita GDP is below 75% of the European Union average, through funds coming from the ERDF, ESF and EAGGF-Guidance and FIFG. Almost 70% of the total funding is reserved for the Objective 1 regions and almost 20% of the Union's total population should benefit from the measures taken under this Objective. This Objective also covers the most remote regions (the French overseas départements, the Azores, Madeira and the Canary Islands) as well as the areas eligible under the former Objective 6 created pursuant to the Act of Accession of Austria, Finland and Sweden [see annex 3.4.];

- **Objective 2** supports, through all four Structural Funds, the economic and social conversion of areas facing structural difficulties and in particular areas undergoing socio-economic change in the industrial and service sectors, declining rural areas, urban areas in difficulty and depressed areas dependent on fisheries. 11,5% of the funding goes to these regions, which account for some 18% of the Union's population;

- **Objective 3** contributes to the adaptation and modernisation of policies and systems of education, training and employment outside the regions covered by Objective 1 and provides a policy frame of reference for all measures promoting human resource development. Objective 3 is, in fact, the reference framework for the measures taken under the Title on employment

[1] Regulation 1260/1999, OJ L 161, 26.06.1999

in the EC Treaty and under the European Employment Strategy [see section 6.2.]. The ESF alone is responsible for this Objective and disposes of a little over 12% of the Structural Funds.

The Commission is responsible for making indicative breakdowns by Member State of the commitment appropriations available for the programming period 2000 to 2006, taking full account, for Objectives 1 and 2, of one or more objective criteria, namely: eligible population, regional prosperity, national prosperity and the relative severity of the structural problems, especially the level of unemployment[1] [see annex 3.4.]. For Objective 3, the breakdown by Member State is based principally on the eligible population, the employment situation and the severity of the problems, such as social exclusion, education and training levels, and participation of women in the labour market[2] [see annex 3.5.].

Under Objective 1 two specific programmes were established: a PEACE programme in support of the peace process in Northern Ireland for the years 2000 to 2004 for the benefit of Northern Ireland and the border areas of Ireland; and a special programme of assistance from 2000 to 2006 for certain Swedish regions meeting specific criteria.

3.3.4. The organisation of structural operations

In order to attain the objectives stated above, the work of the Structural Funds is based on four principles: the **concentration** of measures on those objectives; **programming**, which results in multiannual development programmes; additionality; and partnership. These specific principles of structural operations are compatible with the general principle of **subsidiarity**[3], according to which the implementation of assistance is the responsibility of the Member States without prejudice to the powers vested in the Commission, notably for managing the general budget of the European Communities[4].

Programming means the organising, decision-making and financing process carried out in a number of stages to implement on a multiannual basis the joint action of the Community and the Member States to attain the Objectives mentioned above. **Additionality** means that Community action is viewed as a complement to the corresponding national action or a contribution to it; it must not replace but rather bring added value to national initiatives.

Programming is based upon **partnership** between the Commission, the Member State in question and the authorities and competent bodies designated by it, namely the regional, local and other competent public authorities, the economic and social partners and any other relevant competent bodies. Partnership focuses upon preparation, including the financing of preparatory research, financing of action, follow-up, including the financing of in-the-field technical assistance, and evaluation of its impact. Technical assistance of various forms can be given at any stage of a programme and include any measure allowing the Member States to use the Structural Funds in an optimal way. As requested by Regulation 1260/1999, the Commission adopted broad, indicative guidelines to help the national and regional authorities to prepare their programming strategies[5]. Likewise, the Commission fixed an indicative allocation by Member State of the commitment appropriations for Objectives 1, 2 and 3, and drew up the list of eligible regions for Objectives 1 and 2[6] [see annexes 3.4 and 3.5.].

---

1 Decision 1999/502, OJ L 194, 27.07.1999.
2 Decision 1999/505, OJ L 194, 27.07.1999.
3 Moussis (2004), section 3.2.
4 Moussis (2004), section 3.4.
5 OJ C 267, 22.09.1999, p. 2-21.
6 Decisions 1999/500-505, OJ L 194, 27.07.1999.

The Commission evaluates the plans and action proposed by the Member States and draws up, with the agreement of the national authorities, the **Community Support Framework (CSF)** for Community structural operations in a certain region. This Framework includes:

- a statement of the strategy and priorities for joint Community and national action; their specific objectives; evaluation of the expected impact; the economic policies, the strategy for developing employment and the regional policies of the Member State concerned;
- an indication of the nature and the duration of the operational programmes not decided at the same time as the Community support framework, including their specific aims and the priorities selected;
- an indicative financing plan specifying, for each priority and each year, the financial allocation envisaged for the contribution of each Fund, where appropriate the EIB and the other financial instruments.

Instead of a CSF, the Commission may, at the request of the State concerned, adopt a **Single Programming Document (SPD)**, which is produced by a simplified procedure whereby the strategic priorities, programming procedures and aid granted are all included in a single document. Hence, an SPD contains the same information to be found in a Community support framework and operational programme, notably: (a) the strategy and priorities for joint Community and national action; (b) a summary description of the measures planned to implement the priorities; (c) an indicative financing plan; and (d) the provisions for implementing the SPD. SPDs are generally employed in respect of Objectives 2 and 3. They are exceptionally employed in respect of Objective 1, where the Community allocation does not exceed EUR 1000 million. Each CSF or SPD is supervised by a Monitoring Committee set up by the Member State.

With the aim of simplifying and accelerating the programming procedure, the Member States submit to the Commission their draft operational programmes along with their regional development plans. The latter incorporate a description of the current situation and of the appropriate strategy to attain the objectives of the Structural Funds, an indication of the planned use and form of the financial contribution from the Funds and an account of arrangements made to consult partners. The plan submitted under Objective 3 is, in fact, a policy frame of reference, i.e. a document which sets the context for assistance concerning employment and human-resource development throughout the territory of each Member State, and which identifies the relationship with the priorities set out in the National Action Plan for Employment [see section 6.2. and annex 3.5.].

Community financial instruments can either co-finance the operational programmes of appropriate aid systems or projects or can grant a global grant managed by an intermediary appointed by the Member State with the approval of the Commission. An **operational programme** is a document approved by the Commission comprising a collection of multi-annual measures that can be implemented through use of one or several Community financial instruments. It allows the financing of actions and projects selected by national or regional authorities. The **global grant**, for its part, is used notably to assist local development initiatives and is entrusted to an intermediary organisation, such as a local authority, a regional development body or a non-governmental organisation. It can help the introduction of various services for businesses operating in the industrial, craft, agricultural or tourism sectors and can smooth SME access to the capital market. It can cover all financial engineering operations which are of particular interest to SMEs.

3.3.5. The European Regional Development Fund

The **European Regional Development Fund (ERDF)** has been reformed four times since its creation in 1975, demonstrating both the Community's growing commitment to regional development and its increased experience on this matter. The new ERDF Regulation is characterised by considerable flexibility at operational level. The Fund can make use of all forms of financial operation, such as co-financing of regional operational programmes, regional aid systems and major projects for infrastructures and productive investments, the granting of global subsidies to assist local development initiatives and support for technical assistance and for preparation and assessment measures[1] [see annex 3.6.].

The Regulation laying down general provisions on the Structural Funds provides that the main task of the ERDF is to contribute to the **attainment of Objectives 1 and 2** defined by that Regulation[2] [see annex 3.3.]. In addition, in the regions designated under Objective 1, the ERDF may contribute towards the financing of **investment in education and health** that is beneficial to the region's structural adjustment. It also contributes to the implementation of the **Community initiatives** for cross-border, transnational and inter-regional cooperation ("INTERREG") and for economic and social regeneration of cities and urban neighbourhoods in crisis ("URBAN") [see section 3.3.6.]. Finally, the ERDF contributes to the financing of **innovative measures**, notably studies, pilot projects and exchanges of experience.

As part of its tasks, the ERDF contributes namely towards the financing of:

(a) **productive investment** to create and safeguard sustainable jobs;
(b) **investment in infrastructure**; and
(c) **the development of endogenous potential** by measures which encourage and support local development and employment initiatives and the activities of small and medium-sized enterprises (SMEs)[3], involving in particular:
- assistance towards services for enterprises, in particular in the fields of management, market studies and research and services common to several enterprises;
- financing the transfer of technology, including in particular the collection and dissemination of information, common organisation between enterprises and research establishments and financing the implementation of innovation in enterprises;
- improvement of access by enterprises to finance and loans, by creating and developing appropriate financing instruments;
- direct aid to investment where no aid scheme exists;
- the provision of infrastructure on a scale appropriate to local and employment development;
- aid for structures providing neighbourhood services to create new jobs but excluding measures financed by the European Social Fund (ESF) [see section 6.3.];
- technical assistance measures.

3.3.6. Community Initiatives

Outside the CSFs and the SPDs [see section 3.3.4.], the Structural Funds operate individually or collectively to support **programmes of common interest called Community initiatives**. Whereas Community Support Frameworks are underpinned by national development plans, Community initiatives are transnational programmes whose objectives are the same for all of the

1 Regulation 1783/1999, OJ L 213, 13.08.1999.
2 Regulation 1260/1999, OJ L 161, 26.06.1999.
3 Moussis (2004), section 17.1.4.

eligible regions as they aim to resolve problems which have a particular relevance for the Community. However, by way of application of the principles of partnership and subsidiarity, national, regional or local authorities are deeply involved in drawing up and implementing Community initiatives, in particular through the operational programmes which they submit to the Commission.

Community initiatives are, in fact, operations of Community interest carried out at the initiative of the Commission to supplement those implemented under the priority objectives. These Community initiatives should concentrate on promoting cross-border, transnational and interregional cooperation, economic and social regeneration of cities and urban neighbourhoods in crisis, rural development and the development of human resources in the context of equal opportunities.

The four Community initiatives in operation for the period 2000 to 2006 are:

- **INTERREG**, financed by the ERDF, is concerned with transnational and interregional cooperation intended to encourage the harmonious, balanced and sustainable development of the whole of the Community area;

- **URBAN**, financed by the ERDF, is geared to the economic and social regeneration of cities and urban neighbourhoods in crisis, so as to promote sustainable urban development [see section 8.6.];

- **LEADER**, financed by the EAGGF-Guidance Section, is aimed at rural development[1];

- **EQUAL**, financed by the European Social Fund, is focusing on transnational cooperation for new means of combating all forms of discrimination and inequalities in relation to the labour market [see sections 4.2 and 6.3.].

At least 2,5 % of the Structural Funds commitment appropriations shall be allocated to Interreg, under which due attention should be given to cross-border activities, in particular in the perspective of enlargement, and for Member States which have extensive frontiers with the applicant countries, as well as to improved coordination with the PHARE, TACIS and MEDA programmes[2]. Due attention shall also be given to cooperation with the outermost regions. In the framework of EQUAL due account must be taken of the social and vocational integration of asylum seekers.

The Commission publishes guidelines describing, for each initiative, the aims, scope and the appropriate method of implementation. On the basis of proposals drawn up by the Member States in accordance with these guidelines, the Commission decides on Community initiative programmes, which cover a period of seven years, beginning on 1 January 2000, but may be reexamined and amended where required.

---

[1] Moussis (2004), section 21.5.4.

[2] Moussis (2004), sections 25.2., 25.4. and 25.5.

THE ECONOMIC AND SOCIAL COHESION OF THE UNION

Annex 3.1.

Council Regulation (EC) No 1164/94 of 16 May 1994 **establishing a Cohesion Fund.**
Official Journal L 130 , 25/05/1994 P. 0001 - 0013

MAIN PROVISIONS

Article 1
Definition and objective
1. A Cohesion Fund, hereinafter referred to as 'the Fund', is hereby established.
2. The Fund shall contribute to the strengthening of the economic and social cohesion of the Community and shall operate according to the provisions set out in this Regulation.
3. The Fund may contribute to the financing of:
- projects, or
- stages of a project which are technically and financially independent, or
- groups of projects linked to a visible strategy which form a coherent whole.

Article 2
Scope 1. The Fund shall provide financial contributions to projects, which contribute to achieving the objectives laid down in the Treaty on European Union, in the fields of the environment and trans-European transport infrastructure networks in Member States with a per capita gross national product (GNP), measured in purchasing power parities, of less than 90 % of the Community average which have a programme leading to the fulfilment of the conditions of economic convergence referred to in Article 104c of the Treaty.
2. Until the end of 1999, only the four Member States which currently meet the criterion regarding per capita GNP referred to in paragraph 1 shall be eligible for assistance from the Fund. Those Member States are Greece, Spain, Ireland and Portugal.
3. With regard to the GNP criterion referred to in paragraph 1, the Member States referred to in paragraph 2 shall continue to be eligible for assistance from the Fund provided that, after a mid-term review in 1996, their GNP remains below 90 % of the Community average. Any eligible Member State whose GNP exceeds the 90 % threshold at that time shall lose its entitlement to assistance from the Fund for new projects or, in the case of important projects split into several technically and financially separate stages, for new stages of a project.

Article 3
Eligible measures 1. The Fund may provide assistance for the following:
- environmental projects contributing to the achievement of the objectives of Article 130r of the Treaty, including projects resulting from measures adopted pursuant to Article 130s of the Treaty and, in particular, projects in line with the priorities conferred on Community environmental policy by the Fifth Programme of Policy and Action in relation to the Environment and Sustainable Development,
- transport infrastructure projects of common interest, financed by Member States, which are identified within the framework of the guidelines referred to in Article 129c of the Treaty; however, other transport infrastructure projects contributing to the achievement of the objectives of Article 129b of the Treaty may be financed until appropriate guidelines have been adopted by the Council.
2. Assistance may also be granted for:
- preliminary studies related to eligible projects, including those necessary for their implementation,

- technical support measures, particularly:
(a) horizontal measures such as comparative studies to assess the impact of Community assistance;
(b) measures and studies which contribute to the appraisal, monitoring or evaluation, of projects, and to strengthening and ensuring the coordination and consistency of projects, particularly their consistency with other Community policies;
(c) measures and studies helping to make the necessary adjustments to the implementation of projects.
Article 4
Financial resources For the period 1993 to 1999, the total resources available for commitment for the Fund under this Regulation and Regulation (EEC) No 792/93, as set out in the Interinstitutional Agreement of 29 October 1993, shall be ECU 15 150 million at 1992 prices.
The financial perspectives established with regard to the commitment appropriations available for each year of the period under the Regulations referred to in the first paragraph are as follows:
- 1993: ECU 1 500 million,
- 1994: ECU 1 750 million,
- 1995: ECU 2 000 million,
- 1996: ECU 2 250 million,
- 1997: ECU 2 500 million,
- 1998: ECU 2 550 million,
- 1999: ECU 2 600 million.

Article 5
Indicative allocation An indicative allocation of the total resources of the Fund shall be made on the basis of precise and objective criteria, principally population, per capita GNP and surface area; it shall also take account of other socio-economic factors such as deficiencies in transport infrastructure.
The indicative allocation of the total resources resulting from the application of those criteria is set out in Annex I.

Article 6
Conditional assistance 1. In the event of the Council deciding, in accordance with Article 104c (6) of the Treaty, that an excessive government deficit exists in a Member State, and if that decision is not abrogated in accordance with Article 104c (12) of the Treaty within one year or any other period specified for correcting the deficit in a recommendation under Article 104c (7), no new projects or, in the case of large multi-stage projects, no new stages of a project shall be financed from the Fund for that Member State.
2. Exceptionally, in the case of projects directly affecting more than one Member State, the Council, acting by a qualified majority on a recommendation from the Commission, may decide to defer suspension of financing.
3. Suspension of financing shall not take effect less than two years after the entry into force of the Treaty on European Union.
4. The suspension of financing shall cease when the Council, in accordance with Article 104c (12) of the Treaty, abrogates its decision adopted in accordance with Article 104c (6) of the Treaty.

Article 7
Rate of assistance 1. The rate of Community assistance granted by the Fund shall be 80 % to 85 % of public or equivalent expenditure, including expenditure by bodies whose activities are undertaken within an administrative or legal framework by virtue of which they may be deemed to be equivalent to public bodies. The actual rate of assistance shall be fixed according to the type of operation to be carried out.
2. Where assistance is granted for a project which generates revenue, the amount of the expenditure on which the calculation of the assistance from the Fund is based shall be established by the Commission, taking account of revenue where it constitutes substantial net revenue for the promoters and in close collaboration with the beneficiary Member State.
'Project which generates revenue' means:
- infrastructures the use of which involves fees borne directly by users,
- productive investments in the environment sector.
3. The beneficiary Member States may submit proposals for preparatory studies and technical support measures.
4. Preliminary studies and technical support measures, including those undertaken at the Commission's initiative, may be financed exceptionally at 100 % of the total cost.
Total expenditure carried out pursuant to this paragraph may not exceed 0,5 % of the total allocation to the Fund.

Article 8
Coordination and compatibility with Community policies 1. Projects financed by the Fund shall be in keeping

with the provisions of the Treaties, with the instruments adopted pursuant thereto and with Community policies, including those concerning environmental protection, transport, trans-European networks, competition and the award of public contracts.
2. The Commission shall ensure coordination and consistency between projects undertaken pursuant to this Regulation and measures undertaken with contributions from the Community budget, the European Investment Bank (EIB) and the other financial instruments of the Community.
Article 9
Cumulation and overlapping 1. No item of expenditure may benefit both from the Fund and from the European Agricultural Guidance and Guarantee Fund, the European Social Fund, the European Regional Development Fund or the financial instrument of fisheries guidance.
2. The combined assistance of the Fund and other Community aid for a project shall not exceed 90 % of the total expenditure relating to that project.

Article 10
Approval of projects 1. The projects to be financed by the Fund shall be adopted by the Commission in agreement with the beneficiary Member State.
2. A suitable balance shall be struck between projects in the field of the environment and projects relating to transport infrastructure. This balance shall take account of Article 130s (5) of the Treaty.
3. Applications for assistance for projects under Article 3 (1) shall be submitted by the beneficiary Member State. Projects, including groups of related projects, shall be of a sufficient scale to have a significant impact in the field of environmental protection or in the improvement of trans-European transport infrastructure networks. In any event, the total cost of projects or groups of projects may in principle not be less than ECU 10 million. Projects or groups of projects costing less than this may be approved in duly justified cases.
4. Applications shall contain the following information: the body responsible for implementation, the nature of the investment and a description thereof, its costs and location, including, where applicable, an indication of projects of common interest situated on the same transport axis, the timetable for implementation of the work, a cost-benefit analysis, including the direct and indirect effects on employment, information enabling possible impact on the environment to be assessed, information on public contracts, the financing plan including, where possible, information on the economic viability of the project, and the total financing the Member State is seeking from the Fund and any other Community source.
They shall also contain all relevant information providing the required proof that the projects comply with the Regulation and with the criteria set out in paragraph 5, and particularly that there are medium-term economic and social benefits commensurate with the resources deployed.
5. The following criteria shall be applied to ensure the high quality of projects:
- their medium-term economic and social benefits, which shall be commensurate with the resources deployed; an assessment shall be made in the light of a cost-benefit analysis,
- the priorities established by the beneficiary Member States,
- the contribution which projects can make to the implementation of Community policies on the environment and trans-European networks,
- the compatibility of projects with Community policies and their consistency with other Community structural measures,
- the establishment of an appropriate balance between the fields of the environment and transport infrastructure.
6. Subject to Article 6 and to the availability of commitment appropriations, the Commission shall decide on the grant of assistance from the Fund provided that the requirements of this Article are fulfilled, as a general rule within three months of receipt of the application. Commission decisions approving projects, stages of projects or groups of related projects shall determine the amount of financial support and lay down a financing plan together with all the provisions and conditions necessary for the implementation of the projects.
7. The key details of the Commission's decisions shall be published in the Official Journal of the European Communities.

Article 11
Financial provisions 1. The commitment appropriations entered in the budget shall be granted on the basis of the decisions approving the measures concerned, in accordance with Article 10.
2. Assistance relating to the projects referred to in Article 3 (1) shall as a general rule be committed by annual instalments. However, in appropriate cases, the Commission may commit the total amount of the assistance granted when it adopts the decision granting the assistance.
3. Expenditure within the meaning of Article 7 (1) shall not be deemed eligible for assistance from the Fund if incurred by the beneficiary Member State before the date on which the Commission receives the relevant application.
4. Payments made after an initial advance must be closely and transparently linked to progress made in the

implementation of the projects.
5. Payments shall be made in ecus and shall be subject to the specific provisions set out in Annex II.

Article 12
Financial checks 1. In order to guarantee successful completion of the projects financed by the Fund, Member States shall take the necessary measures:
- to verify on a regular basis that operations financed by the Community have been properly carried out,
- to prevent irregularities and take action against them,
- to recover any amounts lost as a result of irregularity or negligence. Except where the Member State and/or the implementing authority provide proof that they were not responsible for the irregularity or negligence, the Member State shall be liable in the alternative for reimbursement of any sums unduly paid.
2. Member States shall inform the Commission of the measures taken for those purposes and, in particular, shall notify the Commission of the description of the management and control systems established to ensure the efficient implementation of operations. They shall regularly inform the Commission of the progress of administrative and judicial proceedings. In that context, the Member States and the Commission shall take the necessary steps to ensure that the information exchanged remains confidential.
3. Member States shall make available to the Commission any appropriate national control reports on the projects concerned.
4. Without prejudice to checks carried out by Member States in accordance with national laws, regulations and administrative provisions and without prejudice to Article 188a of the Treaty or to any inspection arranged on the basis of Article 209 (c) of the Treaty, the Commission may, through its officials or agents, carry out on-the-spot checks, including sample checks, in respect of projects financed by the Fund, and may examine the control arrangements and measures established by the national authorities, which shall inform the Commission of measures taken to that end.
5. As soon as this Regulation enters into force, the Commission shall adopt detailed rules for the application of this Article and shall inform the European Parliament thereof.

Article 13
Appraisal, monitoring and evaluation 1. The Member States and the Commission shall ensure that the implementation of projects under this Regulation is effectively monitored and evaluated. Projects must be adjusted on the basis of the results of monitoring and evaluation.
2. In order to ensure the effectiveness of Community assistance, the Commission and the beneficiary Member States shall, in cooperation with the EIB where appropriate, carry out a systematic appraisal and evaluation of projects.
3. On receipt of a request for assistance and before approving a project, the Commission shall carry out a thorough appraisal in order to assess the project's consistency with the criteria laid down in Article 10 (5). The Commission shall invite the EIB to contribute to the assessment of projects as necessary.
4. During the implementation of projects and after their completion, the Commission and the beneficiary Member States shall evaluate the manner in which they have been carried out and the potential and actual impact of their implementation in order to assess whether the original objectives can be, or have been, achieved. This evaluation shall, inter alia, address the environmental impact of the projects, in compliance with the existing Community rules.
5. In vetting individual applications for assistance, the Commission shall take into account the findings of appraisals and evaluations made in accordance with this Article.
6. The detailed rules for monitoring and evaluation, as provided for in paragraph 4, shall be laid down in the decisions approving projects.

Annex 3.2.

Council Regulation (EC) No 1265/1999 of 21 June 1999 **amending Annex II** to Regulation (EC) No 1164/94 establishing a Cohesion Fund
Official Journal L 161 , 26/06/1999 P. 0062 - 0067

MAIN PROVISIONS

Council Regulation (EC) No 1260/1999 of 21 June 1999 laying down **general provisions on the Structural Funds**
Official Journal L 161 , 26/06/1999 P. 0001 - 0042

MAIN PROVISIONS

TITLE I - GENERAL PRINCIPLES

CHAPTER I - OBJECTIVES AND TASKS

Article 1: Objectives

Community action through the Structural Funds, the Cohesion Fund, the European Agricultural Guidance and Guarantee Fund (EAGGF), Guarantee Section, the European Investment Bank (EIB) and the other existing financial instruments shall support the achievement of the general objectives set out in Articles 158 and 160 of the Treaty. The Structural Funds, the EIB and the other existing financial instruments shall each contribute in appropriate fashion to the attainment of the following three priority objectives:

1. promoting the development and structural adjustment of regions whose development is lagging behind, hereinafter referred to as "Objective 1";
2. supporting the economic and social conversion of areas facing structural difficulties, hereinafter referred to as "Objective 2";
3. supporting the adaptation and modernisation of policies and systems of education, training and employment, hereinafter referred to as "Objective 3". This objective shall provide financial assistance outside the regions covered by Objective 1 and provide a policy frame of reference for all measures to promote human resources in a national territory without prejudice to the specific features of each region.

In pursuing these objectives, the Community shall contribute to the harmonious, balanced and sustainable development of economic activities, the development of employment and human resources, the protection and improvement of the environment, and the elimination of inequalities, and the promotion of equality between men and women.

Article 2: Means and tasks

1. For the purposes of this Regulation, "Structural Funds" shall mean the European Regional Development Fund (ERDF), the European Social Fund (ESF), the European Agricultural Guidance and Guarantee Fund (EAGGF), Guidance Section, and the Financial Instrument for Fisheries Guidance (FIFG), hereinafter referred to as "the Funds".
2. In accordance with Articles 33, 146 and 160 of the Treaty, the Funds shall contribute, each according to the specific provisions governing its operations, to the attainment of Objectives 1, 2 and 3, as follows:
(a) Objective 1: ERDF, ESF, EAGGF Guidance Section and FIFG;
(b) Objective 2: ERDF and ESF;
(c) Objective 3: ESF.
3. The FIFG shall contribute to structural actions in the fisheries sector outside Objective 1 regions in accordance with Council Regulation (EC) No 1263/1999 of 21 June 1999 on the financial instrument for fisheries guidance(12).
The EAGGF Guarantee Section shall contribute to the attainment of Objective 2 in accordance with Regulation (EC) No 1257/1999.

4. The Funds shall contribute to financing Community initiatives and to supporting innovative measures and technical assistance.
Technical assistance measures shall be carried out within the framework of the programming defined in Articles 13 to 27 or at the initiative of the Commission under Article 23.
5. The other resources of the Community budget which may be used to attain the Objectives referred to in Article 1 are in particular those allocated to other structural measures and to the Cohesion Fund.
The Commission and the Member States shall ensure that the operations of the Funds are consistent with other Community policies and operations, in particular in the areas of employment, equality between men and women, social policy and vocational training, the common agricultural policy, the common fisheries policy, transport, energy and the trans-European networks and the incorporation of the requirements of environmental protection into the definition and implementation of the operations of the Funds.
6. The EIB shall cooperate in attaining the objectives set out in Article 1, in accordance with the procedures laid down in its Statute.
The other existing financial instruments which may contribute, each according to the specific provisions governing its operations, to attaining the Objectives referred to in Article 1 include the European Investment Fund and the European Atomic Energy Community (Euratom) (loans, guarantees), hereinafter "the other financial instruments".

CHAPTER II - GEOGRAPHICAL ELIGIBILITY FOR THE PRIORITY OBJECTIVES

Article 3: Objective 1

1. The regions covered by Objective 1 shall be regions corresponding to level II of the Nomenclature of Territorial Statistical Units (NUTS level II) whose per capita GDP, measured in purchasing power parities and calculated on the basis of Community figures for the last three years available on 26 March 1999, is less than 75 % of the Community average.
The outermost regions (the French overseas departments, the Azores, the Canary Islands and Madeira), which are all below the 75 % threshold, and the areas eligible under Objective 6 for the period 1995 to 1999 pursuant to Protocol 6 to the Act of Accession of Austria, Finland and Sweden shall also be covered by this Objective.
2. The Commission shall draw up the list of regions covered by Objective 1 strictly in accordance with the first subparagraph of paragraph 1, without prejudice to Article 6(1) and Article 7(4), second subparagraph.
This list shall be valid for seven years from 1 January 2000.

Article 4: Objective 2

1. The regions covered by Objective 2 shall be those with structural problems whose socio-economic conversion is to be supported in accordance with Article 1(2) and whose population or area is sufficiently substantial. They shall include in particular areas undergoing socio-economic change in the industrial and service sectors, declining rural areas, urban areas in difficulty and depressed areas dependent on fisheries.
2. The Commission and the Member States shall seek to ensure that assistance is genuinely concentrated on the areas most seriously affected and at the most appropriate geographical level. The population of the areas referred to in paragraph 1 shall not exceed 18 % of the total population of the Community. Accordingly, the Commission shall lay down a population ceiling for each Member State on the basis of the following factors:
(a) the total population in the NUTS III areas of each Member State which meet the criteria referred to in paragraphs 5 and 6;
(b) the severity of the structural problems at national level in each Member State as compared with the other Member States concerned. Such severity shall be assessed on the basis of total unemployment and long-term unemployment outside the regions eligible under Objective 1;
(c) the need to ensure that each Member State makes a fair contribution to the overall concentration effort as defined in this subparagraph; the maximum reduction in the population covered by Objective 2 shall not exceed one third compared to the population covered by Objectives 2 and 5b as set out in Regulation (EEC) No 2052/88, in 1999.
The Commission shall provide the Member States with all the information it has available about the criteria set out in paragraphs 5 and 6.
3. Subject to the ceilings referred to in paragraph 2, the Member States shall propose to the Commission a list of significant areas representing:
(a) the NUTS level III regions, or the most seriously affected areas within those regions, which satisfy either the criteria set out in paragraph 5 or those set out in paragraph 6;
(b) the areas satisfying the criteria referred to in paragraph 7 or paragraph 8 or Member States' specific criteria referred to in paragraph 9.

The Member States shall provide the statistics and other information, at the most appropriate geographical level, which the Commission requires to evaluate these proposals.
4. On the basis of the information referred to in paragraph 3, the Commission, in close concertation with the Member State concerned, shall draw up the list of areas eligible under Objective 2 with due regard to national priorities, without prejudice to Article 6(2).
The areas meeting the criteria in paragraphs 5 and 6 must contain at least 50 % of the population covered by Objective 2 in each Member State, except where duly justified by objective circumstances.
5. The areas undergoing socio-economic change referred to in paragraph 1 shall represent or belong to a NUTS level III territorial unit which satisfies the following criteria:
(a) an average rate of unemployment over the last three years above the Community average;
(b) a percentage share of industrial employment in total employment equal to or greater than the Community average in any reference year from 1985 onwards;
(c) an observable fall in industrial employment compared with the reference year chosen in accordance with (b).
6. The rural areas referred to in paragraph 1 must represent or belong to a NUTS level III territorial unit which satisfies the following criteria:
(a) either a population density of less than 100 people per km2, or a percentage share of agricultural employment in total employment which is equal to, or higher than, twice the Community average in any reference year from 1985;
(b) either an average unemployment rate over the last three years above the Community average, or a decline in population since 1985.
7. The urban areas referred to in paragraph 1 shall mean densely populated areas which also meet at least one of the following criteria:
(a) a rate of long-term unemployment higher than the Community average;
(b) a high level of poverty, including precarious housing conditions;
(c) a particularly damaged environment;
(d) a high crime and delinquency rate;
(e) a low level of education among the population.
8. The areas dependent on fisheries referred to in paragraph 1 shall mean coastal areas in which the number of jobs in the fisheries industry as a percentage of total employment is significant and which are facing structural socio-economic problems relating to the restructuring of the fisheries sector which result in a significant reduction in the number of jobs in that sector.
9. Community assistance may extend to areas whose population or area is significant which fall into one of the following categories:
(a) areas meeting the criteria set out in paragraph 5 which are adjacent to an industrial area, areas meeting the criteria set out in paragraph 6 which are adjacent to a rural area, areas which meet either the criteria set out in paragraph 5 or those set out in paragraph 6 which are adjacent to a region covered by Objective 1;
(b) rural areas with socio-economic problems arising either from the ageing or decline of the agricultural working population;
(c) areas facing or threatened by serious structural problems on account of relevant, verifiable characteristics, or a high level of unemployment arising from an ongoing or planned restructuring of one or more activities in the agricultural, industrial or service sector.
10. Any one area may be eligible for assistance under only one of Objectives 1 or 2.
11. The list of areas shall be valid for seven years from 1 January 2000.
Where there is a serious crisis in a region, the Commission, acting on a proposal from a Member State, may amend the list of areas during 2003 in accordance with paragraphs 1 to 10 without increasing the proportion of the population within each region referred to in Article 13(2).

Article 5: Objective 3
The areas eligible for financing under Objective 3 shall be those not covered by Objective 1.

Article 6: Transitional support

1. Notwithstanding Article 3, the regions covered by Objective 1 in 1999 pursuant to Regulation (EEC) No 2052/88 which are not referred to in the second subparagraph of Article 3(1) and (2) of this Regulation shall continue to receive support from the Funds under Objective 1 on a transitional basis from 1 January 2000 to 31 December 2005.
At the time of adoption of the list referred to in Article 3(2), the Commission shall draw up in accordance with Article 4(5) and (6) the list of the NUTS level III areas belonging to those regions which are to receive support from the Funds under Objective 1 on a transitional basis in 2006.
However, within the limit of the population of the areas referred to in the second subparagraph and in

conformity with the provisions of Article 4(4), second subparagraph, the Commission may on a proposal from a Member State, substitute these areas by areas at or smaller than NUTS level III belonging to those regions which satisfy the criteria of Article 4(5) to (9).
The areas of the regions not on the list referred to in the second and third subparagraphs shall continue to receive support in 2006 from the ESF, FIFG and the EAGGF Guidance Section only, within the same form of assistance.
2. Notwithstanding Article 4, the regions covered by Objectives 2 and 5(b) in 1999 pursuant to Regulation (EEC) No 2052/88 which are not on the list referred to in Article 4(4) of this Regulation shall receive support from the ERDF, from 1 January 2000 to 31 December 2005, under Objective 2 pursuant to this Regulation, on a transitional basis.
Such areas shall receive support from 1 January 2000 to 31 December 2006 from the ESF under Objective 3 on the same basis as Objective 3 areas, the EAGGF Guarantee Section under its support to rural development and from the FIFG under its structural measures in the fisheries sector outside of Objective 1.

CHAPTER III - FINANCIAL PROVISIONS

Article 7: Resources and concentration

1. The resources available for commitment from the Funds for the period 2000 to 2006 shall be EUR 195 billion at 1999 prices.
The annual breakdown of those resources is shown in the Annex.
2. The breakdown of budgetary resources between objectives shall be such as to achieve a significant concentration on Objective 1 regions.
69,7 % of the Structural Funds will be allocated to Objective 1, including 4,3 % for transitional support (i.e. a total of EUR 135,9 billion).
11,5 % of the Structural Funds will be allocated to Objective 2, including 1,4 % for transitional support (i.e. a total of EUR 22,5 billion).
12,3 % of the Structural Funds will be allocated to Objective 3 (i.e. a total of EUR 24,05 billion).
The figures stated for Objectives 1, 2 and 3 do not include the financial resources referred to in paragraph 6 nor the financing for FIFG outside Objective 1.
3. Using transparent procedures, the Commission shall make indicative breakdowns by Member State of the commitment appropriations available for the programming referred to in Articles 13 to 19, taking full account, for Objectives 1 and 2, of one or more objective criteria similar to those covered by Regulation (EEC) No 2052/88, namely: eligible population, regional prosperity, national prosperity and the relative severity of the structural problems, especially the level of unemployment.
For Objective 3, the breakdown by Member State shall be based principally on the eligible population, the employment situation and the severity of the problems, such as social exclusion, education and training levels, and participation of women in the labour market.
For Objectives 1 and 2, these breakdowns shall distinguish allocations of appropriations to regions and areas benefiting from transitional support. These allocations shall be determined in accordance with the criteria referred to in the first subparagraph. The annual breakdown of these appropriations shall be degressive from 1 January 2000 and shall be lower in 2000 than in 1999. The profile of transitional support may be tailored to the specific needs of individual regions, in agreement with the Commission, provided the financial allocation for each region is respected.
Using transparent procedures, the Commission shall also make indicative breakdowns by Member State of the commitment appropriations available for the structural actions in the fisheries sector outside Objective 1 regions, as referred to in Article 2(3), first subparagraph.
4. Under Objective 1, a PEACE programme in support of the peace process in Northern Ireland shall be established for the years 2000 to 2004 for the benefit of Northern Ireland and the border areas of Ireland.
Under Objective 1, a special programme of assistance for the period 2000 to 2006 shall be established for the Swedish NUTS-II regions which are not covered by the list referred to in Article 3(2) and which meet the criteria laid down in Article 2 of Protocol 6 to the Act of Accession for Austria, Sweden and Finland.
5. 4 % of commitment appropriations under each national indicative breakdown referred to in paragraph 3 shall be allocated in accordance with Article 44.
6. For the period referred to in paragraph 1, 5,35 % of the commitment appropriations for the Structural Funds referred to in paragraph 1 shall be devoted to funding the Community initiatives.
0,65 % of the appropriations referred to in paragraph 1 shall be devoted to funding innovative measures and technical assistance as defined in Articles 22 and 23.
7. For the purpose of their programming and subsequent inclusion in the general budget of the European Communities, the sums referred to in paragraph 1 shall be indexed as from 1 January 2000 at 2 % per year.

Indexation of the allocations for 2004 to 2006 shall be reviewed, if necessary, by 31 December 2003 at the latest for technical adjustment by the Commission on the basis of the latest economic information available. The difference relative to the initial programming shall be reallocated for inclusion in the sum referred to in paragraph 5.
8. Total annual receipts in any Member State from the Structural Funds pursuant to this Regulation - in combination with assistance provided under the Cohesion Fund - should not exceed 4 % of national GDP.

CHAPTER IV - ORGANISATION

Article 8: Complementarity and partnership

1. Community actions shall complement or contribute to corresponding national operations. They shall be drawn up in close consultation, hereinafter referred to as the "partnership", between the Commission and the Member State, together with the authorities and bodies designated by the Member State within the framework of its national rules and current practices, namely:
- the regional and local authorities and other competent public authorities,
- the economic and social partners,
- any other relevant competent bodies within this framework.

The partnership shall be conducted in full compliance with the respective institutional, legal and financial powers of each of the partners as defined in the first subparagraph.
In designating the most representative partnership at national, regional, local or other level, the Member State shall create a wide and effective association of all the relevant bodies, according to national rules and practice, taking account of the need to promote equality between men and women and sustainable development through the integration of environmental protection and improvement requirements.
All the designated parties, hereinafter referred to as the "partners", shall be partners pursuing a common goal.
2. Partnership shall cover the preparation, financing, monitoring and evaluation of assistance. Member States shall ensure the association of the relevant partners at the different stages of programming, taking account of the time limit for each stage.
3. In application of the principle of subsidiarity, the implementation of assistance shall be the responsibility of the Member States, at the appropriate territorial level according to the arrangements specific to each Member State, and without prejudice to the powers vested in the Commission, notably for implementing the general budget of the European Communities.
4. Member States shall cooperate with the Commission to ensure that Community Funds are used in accordance with the principles of sound financial management.
5. Each year, the Commission shall consult the European-level organisations representing the social partners about the structural policy of the Community.

Article 9: Definitions

For the purposes of this Regulation:
(a) programming: means the organising, decision-making and financing process carried out in a number of stages to implement on a multiannual basis the joint action of the Community and the Member States to attain the Objectives referred to in Article 1;
(b) development plan (hereinafter referred to as "the plan": means the analysis of the situation prepared by a Member State in the light of the objectives referred to in Article 1 and the priority needs for attaining those objectives, together with the strategy, the planned action priorities, their specific goals and the related indicative financial resources;
(c) Objective 3 policy frame of reference: means a document which sets the context for assistance concerning employment and human-resource development throughout the territory of each Member State, and which identifies the relationship with the priorities set out in the National Action Plan for Employment;
(d) Community support framework: means the document approved by the Commission, in agreement with the Member State concerned, following appraisal of the plan submitted by a Member State and containing the strategy and priorities for action of the Funds and the Member State, their specific objectives, the contribution of the Funds and the other financial resources. This document shall be divided into priorities and implemented by means of one or more operational programmes;
(e) assistance: means the forms of assistance provided by the Funds, i.e.:
(i) operational programmes or single programming documents;

(ii) Community initiative programmes;
(iii) support for technical assistance and innovative measures;
(f) operational programme: means the document approved by the Commission to implement a Community support framework and comprising a consistent set of priorities comprising multiannual measures and which may be implemented through recourse to one or more Funds, to one or more of the other existing financial instruments and to the EIB. An integrated operational programme means an operational programme financed by more than one Fund;
(g) single programming document: means a single document approved by the Commission and containing the same information to be found in a Community support framework and operational programme;
(h) priority: means one of the priorities of the strategy adopted in a Community support framework or assistance; to it is assigned a contribution from the Funds and other financial instruments and the relevant financial resources of the Member State and a set of specified targets;
(i) global grant: means that part of assistance the implementation and management of which may be entrusted to one or more approved intermediaries in accordance with Article 27(1), including local authorities, regional development bodies or non-governmental organisations, used preferably to assist local development initiatives. The decision to employ a global grant shall be taken in agreement with the Commission by the Member State or, in agreement with the Member State, by the managing authority.
In the case of Community initiative programmes and innovative measures, the Commission may decide to employ a global grant for all or part of the assistance. In the case of Community initiatives, this decision may only be taken with the prior agreement of the Member States concerned.
(j) measure: means the means by which a priority is implemented over several years which enable operations to be financed. Any aid scheme pursuant to Article 87 of the Treaty or any aid granted by bodies designated by the Member States, or any group of aid schemes or aid grants of this type or any combination thereof which have the same purpose and are defined as a measure;
(k) operation: means any project or action carried out by the final beneficiaries of assistance;
(l) final beneficiaries: means the bodies and public or private firms responsible for commissioning operations. In the case of aid schemes pursuant to Article 87 of the Treaty and in the case of aid granted by bodies designated by the Member States, the final beneficiaries are the bodies which grant the aid;
(m) programme complement: means the document implementing the assistance strategy and priorities and containing detailed elements at measure level, as set out in Article 18(3), drawn up by the Member State or managing authority and revised as necessary in accordance with Article 34(3). It is sent to the Commission for information;
(n) managing authority: means any public or private authority or body at national, regional or local level designated by the Member State, or the Member State when it is itself carrying out this function, to manage assistance for the purposes of this Regulation. If the Member State designates a managing authority other than itself, it shall determine all the modalities of its relationship with the managing authority and of the latter's relationship with the Commission. If the Member State so decides, the managing authority may be the same body as the paying authority for the assistance concerned;
o) paying authority: means one or more national, regional or local authorities or bodies designated by the Member States for the purposes of drawing up and submitting payment applications and receiving payments from the Commission. The Member State shall determine all the modalities of its relationship with the paying authority and of the latter's relationship with the Commission.

Article 10: Coordination

1. Coordination between the various Funds shall be carried out in particular through:
(a) the plans, the Community support frameworks, the operational programmes and the single programming documents (as defined in Article 9) including the frame of reference where relevant in accordance with Article 9(1)(c);
(b) the monitoring and evaluation of assistance under an Objective;
(c) the guidelines referred to in paragraph 3.
2. The Commission and Member State shall, in a manner consistent with the principle of partnership, ensure coordination of assistance from the different Funds between the Funds and with assistance from the EIB and other existing financial instruments.
In order to maximise the stimulus provided by the budget resources deployed, making use of appropriate financial instruments, the Community assistance provided in the form of grants may be combined in an appropriate way with loans and guarantees. This combination may be determined in conjunction with the EIB when the Community support framework or single programming document is being drawn up. It may take account of the balance in the proposed financing plan, the contribution from the Funds and the development goals pursued.

3. No later than one month from the entry into force of this Regulation and subsequently before the mid-term review referred to in Article 42, and on each occasion after consulting all Member States, the Commission shall publish broad, indicative guidelines on relevant and agreed Community policies in relation to the objectives referred to in Article 1, to help the competent national and regional authorities to draw up development plans and to carry out any revision of the assistance. This guidance shall be published in the Official Journal of the European Communities.

Article 11: Additionality

1. In order to achieve a genuine economic impact, the appropriations of the Funds may not replace public or other equivalent structural expenditure by the Member State.
2. For this purpose, the Commission and the Member State concerned shall determine the level of public or equivalent structural expenditure that the Member State is to maintain in the sum of its regions covered by Objective 1 during the programming period.
For Objectives 2 and 3 taken together, the Commission and the Member State concerned shall determine the level of expenditure on the active labour-market policy and, where justified, other actions designed to make it possible to achieve the goals of those two Objectives which the Member State is to maintain at national level during the programming period.
Such expenditure shall be determined by the Member State and the Commission, taking account of the provisions of the fourth subparagraph, in advance of the Commission decision approving any Community support framework or single programming documents relating to the Member State concerned and shall be integrated into those documents.
As a general rule, the level of expenditure referred to in the first and second subparagraphs shall be at least equal to the amount of average annual expenditure in real terms achieved in the previous programming period and shall be determined in the light of the general macroeconomic circumstances in which the funding takes place, although account should be taken of certain specific economic situations, namely privatisations, an exceptional level of public structural effort or equivalent effort on the part of the Member State during the previous programming period and national economic trends.
Account shall also be taken of any reduction in Structural Fund expenditure when compared to the period 1994 to 1999.
3. Additionality shall be verified at the territorial level set out in paragraph 2 at three points during the programming period:
(a) an ex-ante verification as described in the third subparagraph of paragraph 2, to provide a frame of reference for the whole programming period;
(b) a mid-term verification no later than three years after approval of the Community support framework or the single programming documents and as a general rule no later than 31 December 2003, following which the Commission and the Member State may agree to revise the level of structural expenditure to be attained if the economic situation has resulted in developments in public revenue or employment in the Member State concerned significantly different from those expected at the time of the ex-ante verification;
(c) a verification by 31 December 2005.
To that end, the Member State shall provide the Commission with appropriate information at the time when the plans are submitted and when the mid-term verification and the verification before 31 December 2005 are made. Where necessary, methods of statistical estimation shall be used.
Independently of these verifications, the Member State shall inform the Commission at any point during the programming period of developments likely to call into question its ability to maintain the level of expenditure referred to in paragraph 2.

Article 12: Compatibility

Operations financed by the Funds or receiving assistance from the EIB or from another financial instrument shall be in conformity with the provisions of the Treaty, with instruments adopted under it and with Community policies and actions, including the rules on competition, on the award of public contracts, on environmental protection and improvement and on the elimination of inequalities and the promotion of equality between men and women.

TITLE II - PROGRAMMING

CHAPTER I - GENERAL PROVISIONS CONCERNING OBJECTIVES 1, 2 AND 3

Article 13: Geographical coverage

1. Plans submitted under Objective 1 shall be drawn up at the geographical level deemed by the Member State concerned to be most appropriate but shall, as a general rule, cover a single region at NUTS level II. However, Member States may submit a general development plan covering some or all of their regions included in the list referred to in Article 3(2), Article 6(1) and Article 7(4), provided that such plan contains the features listed in Article 16.
2. Plans submitted under Objective 2 shall be drawn up at the geographical level deemed by the Member State concerned to be most appropriate, but shall as a general rule comprise all the areas covered by a single NUTS level II region, included in the list referred to in Article 4(4) and Article 6(2). However, the Member States may submit a plan covering certain or all of their regions included in the list referred to in Article 4(4) and in Article 6(2), provided that such plan contains the features listed in Article 16. Where plans cover regions other than those eligible under Objective 2, they shall distinguish between operations in regions or areas covered by Objective 2 and operations elsewhere.
3. Plans submitted under Objective 3 shall cover the territory of a Member State in respect of assistance outside the regions covered by Objective 1 and, taking into account the general needs of areas facing structural problems of socio-economic conversion, shall provide, for the whole of the national territory, a framework of reference for developing human resources.

Article 14: Duration and revision

1. Each plan, Community support framework, operational programme and single programming document shall cover a period of seven years, without prejudice to Article 6 and Article 7(4), first subparagraph.
The programming period shall begin on 1 January 2000.
2. Community support frameworks, operational programmes and single programming documents shall be re-examined and, if necessary, adapted at the initiative of the Member State or the Commission in agreement with the Member State, in accordance with this Title following the mid-term evaluation referred to in Article 42 and the allocation of the performance reserve referred to in Article 44.
They may also be revised in the event of significant changes in the socio-economic situation and the labour market.

Article 15: Preparation and approval

1. In respect of Objectives 1, 2 and 3, Member States shall submit a plan to the Commission. That plan shall be drawn up by the competent authorities designated by the Member State at national, regional and other level. In cases where assistance is to take the form of a single programming document, the plan shall be dealt with as a draft single programming document.
In respect of Objective 1, Community support frameworks shall be employed for all regions covered by Objective 1; however, where the Community allocation is less than or does not substantially exceed EUR 1000 million, the Member States shall, as a general rule, submit a draft single programming document.
In respect of Objectives 2 and 3, single programming documents shall as a general rule be employed; however, Member States may elect to have a Community support framework drawn up.
2. The plans shall be submitted by the Member State to the Commission after consultation with the partners, who shall express their views within a period of time consistent with the deadline set in the second subparagraph.
Unless otherwise agreed with the Member State concerned, plans shall be submitted not later than four months after the list of eligible regions referred to in Article 3(2) and Article 4(4) have been drawn up.
3. The Commission shall appraise these plans to determine whether they are consistent with the aims of this Regulation, taking account of the framework of reference referred to in Article 9(1)(c), other Community policies and Article 41(2).
The Commission shall also appraise each Objective 3 plan proposed in the light of the consistency of the measures envisaged with the national plan for implementing the European employment strategy in accordance with Article 16(1)(b) and having regard to the manner in which and the degree to which the general needs of areas facing structural problems of socio-economic conversion are taken into account.
4. Where applicable as provided in paragraph 1, the Commission shall draw up the Community support frameworks in agreement with the Member State concerned and following the procedures laid down in Articles 48 to 51. The EIB may be involved in the preparation of the Community support frameworks. The Commission shall take a decision on the contribution from the Funds not later than five months after receiving the relevant plan or plans provided they contain all the features listed in Article 16.
The Commission shall appraise the proposed operational programmes submitted by the Member State to determine whether they are consistent with the aims of the corresponding Community support framework and

compatible with other Community policies. It shall adopt a decision on the contribution of the Funds in accordance with Article 28(1) and in agreement with the Member State concerned, provided that the proposals contain all the features listed in Article 18(2).
In order to expedite the examination of applications and the implementation of programmes, the Member States may submit, at the same time as their plans, draft operational programmes. When adopting its decision on a Community support framework, the Commission shall also approve, in accordance with Article 28(1), the operational programmes submitted at the same time as the plans provided they include all the features listed in Article 18(2).
5. Where applicable as provided in paragraph 1 on the basis of the plans, the Commission shall take a decision on the single programming documents in agreement with the Member State concerned, following the procedures laid down in Articles 48 to 51. The EIB may be involved in the preparation of the single programming documents. The Commission shall take a single decision on the single programming document and the contribution of the Funds pursuant to Article 28(1) not later than five months after having received the relevant plan, provided that it contains all the features listed in Article 19(3).
6. The Member State or the managing authority shall adopt the programme complement defined in Article 9(m) after the agreement of the Monitoring Committee if the programme complement is drawn up after the Commission decision on the contribution of the Funds, or after consulting the relevant partners if it is drawn up before the decision on the contribution of the Funds. In the latter case, the Monitoring Committee shall either confirm the programme complement or request an adjustment in accordance with Article 34(3).
Within three months of the Commission decision approving an operational programme or single programming document, the Member State shall send the programme complement to the Commission in a single document for information.
7. The Commission decisions on a Community support framework or single programming document shall be published in the Official Journal of the European Communities. At the request of the European Parliament, the Commission shall transmit to it, for information, these decisions and the Community support framework and single programming documents it has approved.

CHAPTER II - CONTENT OF THE PROGRAMMING FOR OBJECTIVES 1, 2 AND 3

Article 16: Plans

1. The plans submitted under Objectives 1, 2 and 3 shall be based on appropriate national and regional priorities and shall take account of the indicative guidance referred to in Article 10(3) and shall include:
(a) a description, quantified where it lends itself to quantification, of the current situation either with regard to disparities, gaps and potential for development in the regions covered by Objective 1, or in terms of conversion in the areas covered by Objective 2, or in terms of developing human resources and employment policy in the Member State and the areas covered by Objective 3; also, a description of the financial resources deployed and the main results of operations undertaken in the previous programming period with regard to the evaluation results available;
(b) a description of an appropriate strategy to attain the objectives referred to in Article 1 and the priorities selected for the sustainable development and conversion of regions and areas, including rural areas, and the related development of human resources and the adaptation and modernisation of policies and systems for education, training and employment.
In addition to the other items listed in this point, Member States shall demonstrate in each Objective 3 plan that the priorities planned are consistent with the prevailing national employment plan, by reference to a description of the main aims of the strategy and the main means of attaining them.
Similarly, Member States shall demonstrate that the activities provided for in each Objective 2 plan on human resources and employment to be assisted by the ESF are integrated into the conversion strategy, coordinated with the other Funds and consistent with the ex-ante evaluation relating to human resources and employment as referred to in Article 41(2). If these needs do not amount to a significant sum, they shall be covered by Objective 3;
(c) an indication of the planned use and form of the financial contribution from the Funds and, where appropriate, the EIB and the other financial instruments including, for information, the total amount from the EAGGF Guarantee Section for the measures referred to in Article 33 of Regulation (EC) No 1257/1999; the expected requirement for technical assistance; an indication as regards additionality in accordance with Article 11(2), whereby for Objective 1 this should take the form of an indicative overall financing table summarising the public or equivalent and, where appropriate, estimated private resources and the Community structural resources allocated corresponding to each priority proposed in the plan.
In any case, the plans shall distinguish between the financial envelopes allocated to areas receiving transitional support and those allocated to other areas covered by Objective 1 or 2.

In the case of ESF assistance under Objective 2 or 3, the percentage contribution may be higher in Objective 2 areas than in others.
In the case of Objective 3, this financing plan shows the concentration of appropriations planned for the areas facing structural problems of economic and social conversion;
(d) an account of arrangements made to consult partners.
2. For regions covered by Objective 1, the plans shall include all relevant measures for economic and social conversion, the development of human resources, having regard to the frame of reference referred to in Article 9(1)(c), and rural development and fisheries structures.
Where a Member State is covered in its entirety by Objective 1, the plan shall cover the points in the second subparagraph of paragraph (1)(b).
3. Member States shall indicate the particulars relating to each Fund, including the amount of the financial contribution requested and an outline of the operational programmes planned with particular regard to their specific aims and the main types of actions planned.

Article 17: Community support frameworks

1. The Community support framework shall provide coordination of all Community structural assistance in the regions concerned, including, in accordance with Article 1(3), assistance for the development of human resources.
2. Each Community support framework shall include:
(a) a statement of the strategy and priorities for joint Community and national action; their specific objectives, quantified where they lend themselves to quantification; evaluation of the expected impact in accordance with Article 41(2); an indication of how this strategy and these priorities have taken account of the indicative guidance referred to in Article 10(3), the economic policies, the strategy for developing employment through improving the adaptability and skills of people and, where appropriate, the regional policies of the Member State concerned;
(b) an indication of the nature and the duration of the operational programmes not decided at the same time as the Community support framework, including their specific aims and the priorities selected;
(c) an indicative financing plan specifying, in accordance with Articles 28 and 29, for each priority and each year, the financial allocation envisaged for the contribution of each Fund, where appropriate the EIB, the other financial instruments - including, for information, the total amount from the EAGGF Guarantee Section for the measures referred to in Article 33 of Regulation (EC) No 1257/1999 - where they contribute directly to the financing plan concerned and the total amount of eligible public and estimated private funding relating to the contribution of each Fund.
In the case of Objective 3, that financing plan shall show the concentration of appropriations planned for the areas facing structural problems of economic and social conversion.
This financing plan shall distinguish the funding planned for the regions receiving transitional support.
The total contribution of the Funds planned for each year for each Community support framework shall be compatible with the relevant financial perspective, taking account of the degressivity referred to in the third subparagraph of Article 7(3);
(d) the provisions for implementing a Community support framework including:
- designation by the Member State of a managing authority within the meaning of Article 9(n) responsible for managing the Community support framework in accordance with Article 34,
- arrangements for involving the partners in the Monitoring Committees described in Article 35;
(e) where appropriate, information on the appropriations required for preparing, monitoring and evaluating assistance.
In accordance with Article 11, the Community support frameworks shall include the ex-ante verification of additionality and the appropriate information concerning the transparency of financial flows, in particular from the Member State concerned to the beneficiary regions.

Article 18: Operational programmes

1. Assistance covered by a Community support framework shall as a general rule be provided in the form of an integrated operational programme by region, as defined in Article 9.
2. Each operational programme shall contain:
(a) the priorities of the programme, their consistency with the relevant Community support framework, their specific targets, quantified where they lend themselves to quantification, and an evaluation of the impact expected, in accordance with Article 41(2);
(b) a summary description of the measures planned to implement the priorities, including the information needed to check compliance with aid schemes pursuant to Article 87 of the Treaty; where appropriate, the nature

of the measures required to prepare, monitor and evaluate the operational programme;
(c) an indicative financing plan specifying for each priority and each year, in accordance with Articles 28 and 29, the financial allocation envisaged for the contribution of each Fund, the EIB where appropriate, and the other financial instruments - including, for information, the total amount from the EAGGF Guarantee Section for the measures referred to in Article 33 of Regulation (EC) No 1257/1999 - in so far as they contribute directly to the financing plan, as well as the total amount of eligible public and estimated private funding relating to the contribution of each Fund.
This financing plan shall distinguish in the total contribution of the various Funds the funding planned for the regions receiving transitional support.
The total contribution of the Funds planned for each year shall be compatible with the relevant financial perspective, taking account of the degressivity referred to in the third subparagraph of Article 7(3);
(d) the provisions for implementing an operational programme shall include:
(i) designation by the Member State of a managing authority within the meaning of Article 9(n) responsible for managing the operational programme in accordance with Article 34;
(ii) a description of the arrangements for managing the operational programme;
(iii) a description of the systems for monitoring and evaluation, including the role of the Monitoring Committee;
(iv) a definition of the procedures concerning the mobilisation and circulation of financial flows to ensure their transparency;
(v) a description of the specific arrangements and procedures for checking on the operational programme.
3. The programme complement shall contain:
(a) the measures implementing the corresponding priorities in the operational programme; ex-ante evaluation, in accordance with Article 41(3), of quantified measures, where they lend themselves to quantification; the relevant monitoring indicators in accordance with Article 36;
(b) the definition of the types of final beneficiary of measures;
(c) the financing plan specifying for each measure, in accordance with Articles 28 and 29, the financial allocation envisaged for the contribution of the Fund concerned, the EIB where appropriate, and the other existing financial instruments and the amount of eligible public or equivalent funding and estimated private funding relating to the contribution of the Funds; the percentage contribution of a Fund to a measure shall be determined in accordance with Article 29 and the total amount of Community funds allocated to the priority concerned.
This financing plan shall distinguish the funding planned for the regions receiving transitional support.
The financing plan shall be accompanied by a description of the arrangements for providing the co-financing for measures, taking account of the institutional, legal and financial systems of the Member State concerned;
(d) measures intended to publicise the operational programme in accordance with Article 46;
(e) a description of arrangements agreed between the Commission and the Member State concerned for the computerised exchange, where possible, of the data required to fulfil the management, monitoring and evaluation requirements of this Regulation.

Article 19: Single programming documents
1. Assistance under Objectives 2 and 3, and under Objective 1 as specified in Article 15(1), shall, as a general rule, take the form of single programming documents. In the case of Objectives 2 and 3, Article 15(1)(c) shall apply.
2. An Objective 1 single programming document shall include all relevant measures for economic and social conversion, the development of employment through improving adaptability and skills of people, having regard to the frame of reference referred to in Article 9(1)(c) and rural development and fisheries structures.
An Objective 2 single programming document shall provide coordination of all Community structural assistance including, in accordance with Article 41(2) of Regulation (EC) No 1257/1999, the coordination of rural development measures pursuant to Article 33 of that Regulation, but excluding assistance for developing human resources granted under Objective 3, in all the areas covered by Objective 2.
An Objective 3 single programming document shall provide coordination of all Community structural assistance for the development of human resources in the areas referred to in Article 5, excluding aid in this area granted under Objective 2.
3. Each single programming document shall contain the following elements:
(a) a statement of the strategy and priorities for joint Community and national action; their specific objectives, quantified where they lend themselves to quantification; an evaluation of the expected impact, including on the environmental situation, in accordance with Article 41(2); an indication of how this strategy and these priorities have taken account of the indicative guidelines referred to in Article 10(3), the economic policies, the strategy for developing employment through improving the adaptability and skills of people and, where appropriate, the regional policies of the Member State concerned;
(b) a summary description of the measures planned to implement the priorities, including the information

needed to check the compliance with aid schemes pursuant to Article 87 of the Treaty; where appropriate, the nature of the measures required to prepare, monitor and evaluate the single programming document;
(c) an indicative financing plan specifying for each priority and each year, in accordance with Articles 28 and 29, the financial allocation envisaged for the contribution of each Fund, the EIB where appropriate, and the other financial instruments - including, for information, the total amount from the EAGGF Guarantee Section for the measures referred to in Article 33 of Regulation (EC) No 1257/1999 - in so far as they contribute directly to the financing plan, as well as the total amount of eligible public or equivalent and estimated private funding relating to the contribution of each Fund.
This financing plan shall distinguish the funding planned for the regions receiving transitional support.
The total contribution of the Funds planned for each year shall be compatible with the relevant financial perspective, taking account of the degressivity referred to in the third subparagraph of Article 7(3).
In the case of Objective 3, the financing plan shall indicate the concentration of appropriations planned for the areas facing structural, economic and social reconversion problems;
(d) the provisions for implementing a single programming document shall include:
(i) the designation by the Member State of a managing authority within the meaning of Article 9 responsible for managing the single programming document in accordance with Article 34;
(ii) a description of the arrangements for managing the single programming document;
(iii) a description of the systems for monitoring and evaluation, including the role of the Monitoring Committee;
(iv) a definition of the procedures concerning the mobilisation and circulation of funding to ensure that flows are transparent;
(v) a description of the specific arrangements and procedures for checking on the single programming document;
(e) where appropriate, information on the resources required for preparing, monitoring and evaluating assistance.
In accordance with Article 11, the single programming document shall include the ex-ante verification of additionality for the relevant objective or objectives agreed between the Member State and the Commission and appropriate information concerning the transparency of financial flows, in particular from the Member State concerned to the beneficiary regions.
4. Each single programming document shall be supplemented by a programme complement as defined in Article 9(m) and described in Article 18(3).

CHAPTER III - COMMUNITY INITIATIVES

Article 20: Content

1. The Community initiatives shall cover the following fields:
(a) cross-border, transnational and interregional cooperation intended to encourage the harmonious, balanced and sustainable development of the whole of the Community area ("Interreg");
(b) economic and social regeneration of cities and of urban neighbourhoods in crisis with a view to promoting a sustainable urban development ("URBAN");
(c) rural development ("Leader");
(d) transnational cooperation to promote new means of combating all forms of discrimination and inequalities in connection with the labour market ("EQUAL").
2. At least 2,5 % of the Structural Funds commitment appropriations referred to in Article 7(1) shall be allocated to Interreg, under which due attention should be given to cross-border activities, in particular in the perspective of enlargement, and for Member States which have extensive frontiers with the applicant countries, as well as to improved coordination with the PHARE, TACIS and MEDA programmes. Due attention shall also be given to cooperation with the outermost regions.
Due account shall be taken of the social and vocational integration of asylum seekers in the framework of EQUAL.
3. Programmes approved within the framework of the Community initiatives may cover areas other than those referred to in Articles 3 and 4.

Article 21: Preparation, approval and implementation

1. In accordance with the procedures referred to in Articles 48 to 51 and after notifying them for information to the European Parliament, the Commission shall lay down guidelines describing, for each initiative, the aims, scope and the appropriate method of implementation. Those guidelines shall be published in the Official Journal of the European Communities.
2. Each area referred to in Article 20(1) shall be financed by a single Fund: the area referred to in paragraph 1(a)

and (b) from the ERDF, the area referred to in paragraph 1(c) from the EAGGF Guidance Section and the area referred to in paragraph 1(d) from the ESF. The decision on the contribution of a Fund may amplify the scope of each Fund as defined in the Regulations specific to each Fund, but without broadening it, to include all measures required to implement the Community initiative programme concerned.
3. On the basis of proposals drawn up in accordance with the guidelines referred to in paragraph 1 and with Article 41(2) and submitted by the Member State(s), the Commission shall decide on Community initiative programmes in accordance with Article 28.
4. The Community initiative programmes shall be re-examined following the mid-term evaluation referred to in Article 42 and amended where required on application by the Member State(s) concerned or by the Commission by agreement with the Member State(s).
5. The Community initiative programmes shall cover a period of seven years, beginning on 1 January 2000.

CHAPTER IV - INNOVATIVE ACTIONS AND TECHNICAL ASSISTANCE

Article 22 - Innovative actions

1. At the initiative of the Commission and following consultation of the committees referred to in Articles 48 to 51 on the guidelines for the various types of innovative actions, subject to a ceiling of 0,40 % of their respective annual funding, the Funds may finance innovative actions at Community level. These shall include studies, pilot projects and exchanges of experience.
Such innovative actions shall contribute to the preparation of innovative methods and practices designed to improve the quality of assistance under Objectives 1, 2 and 3. They shall be implemented in a simple, transparent fashion and in accordance with the principles of sound financial management.
2. Each field of action for pilot projects shall be financed by one fund only. The decision on the contribution of a fund may amplify the scope of each fund as defined in the Regulations specific to each fund, but without broadening it, to include all measures required to implement the pilot project concerned.

Article 23 - Technical assistance

At the initiative or on behalf of the Commission and following consultation of the committees referred to in Articles 48 to 51 on the different types of measures, subject to a ceiling of 0,25 % of their respective annual allocation, the Funds may finance the preparatory, monitoring, evaluation and checking measures necessary for implementing this Regulation. These shall include:
(a) studies, including studies of a general nature, concerning the operations of the Funds;
(b) measures of technical assistance, the exchange of experience and information aimed at the partners, the final beneficiaries of assistance from the Funds and the general public;
(c) the installation, operation and interconnection of computerised systems for management, monitoring and evaluation;
(d) improvements in evaluation methods and exchange of information on practices in this field.

Article 24: Approval of innovative actions and technical assistance

1. Making use of information on innovative actions from the Member States concerned, the Commission shall appraise applications for a contribution from the Funds pursuant to Articles 22 and 23 on the basis of the following details:
(a) a description of the proposed assistance, its scope, including geographical coverage, and specific aims;
(b) the bodies to be responsible for implementing the assistance and the beneficiaries;
(c) the timetable and financing plan, including contributions from any other source of Community finance;
(d) provisions to ensure efficient and correct implementation;
(e) any other information necessary to verify compatibility with Community policies and with the guidelines referred to in Article 10(3).
The Commission shall approve the contribution of the Funds when this information enables it to appraise the application.
2. The Member States concerned shall be immediately notified by the Commission following approval of an application.
3. The financial liability of the Member States within the meaning of this Regulation shall not be engaged for the innovative actions referred to in Article 22 or the technical assistance measures referred to in Article 23, without prejudice to their obligations arising out of the institutional arrangements specific to each Member State.

CHAPTER V - MAJOR PROJECTS

Article 25: Definition

As part of any assistance, the Funds may finance expenditure in respect of major projects, i.e. those:
(a) which comprise an economically indivisible series of works fulfilling a precise technical function and which have clearly identified aims; and
(b) whose total cost taken into account in determining the contribution of the Funds exceeds EUR 50 million.

Article 26: Approval and implementation
1. During the implementation of assistance, where a Member State or managing authority envisages the Funds contributing to a major project, it shall inform the Commission in advance and provide the following information:
(a) the body to be responsible for implementation;
(b) the nature of the investment and a description of it, its financial volume and location;
(c) the timetable for implementing the project;
(d) a cost-benefit analysis, including financial costs and benefits, a risk assessment and information on the economic viability of the project;
(e) plus:
- in the case of investment in infrastructure: the analysis of the costs and the socio-economic benefits of the project, including an indication of the anticipated rate of use, the foreseeable impact on the development or conversion of the region concerned, and the application of Community rules on public contracting,
- in the case of investment in production facilities: the analysis of the market prospects in the sector concerned and the anticipated return on the project,
(f) the direct and indirect effects on the employment situation, as far as possible in the Community;
(g) information allowing an evaluation to be made of the environmental impact and the implementation of the precautionary principle and the principles that preventive action should be taken, that environmental damage should as a priority be rectified at source and that the polluter should pay and compliance with the Community rules on the environment;
(h) information needed to assess compliance with competition rules, inter alia rules on State aids;
(i) an indication of the influence of the contribution of the Funds on whether the project will be implemented;
(j) the financing plan and the total financial resources expected from the contribution of the Funds and any other source of Community finance.
2. The Commission shall appraise the project, consulting the EIB if necessary, in the light of the following factors:
(a) the type of investment planned and, where applicable, the revenue expected;
(b) the results of the cost-benefit analysis;
(c) the result of the evaluation of the impact on the environment;
(d) consistency with the priorities in the corresponding assistance;
(e) compliance with other Community policies;
(f) the expected economic and social benefits, particularly in terms of employment, having regard to the financial resources deployed;
(g) the coordination of the financial instruments and the combination of assistance and loans referred to in Article 10(2).
3. Within two months of receipt of the information referred to in paragraph 1 or three months where consultation of the EIB proves necessary, the Commission shall decide to confirm or amend the level of Community assistance. If it considers that the project appears not to justify either part or all of the contribution from the Funds, it may decide to withhold part or all of that contribution, stating the reasons for so doing.

CHAPTER VI - GLOBAL GRANTS

Article 27: Global grants

1. Where implementation or management of part of assistance has been entrusted to intermediaries in accordance with Article 9(i), such intermediaries must provide guarantees of their solvency and proven competence and experience in administrative and financial management. They must normally be established or represented in the region or regions concerned but may, in limited and justified circumstances, be established outside. They must have several years' experience in the relevant field, operate in the public interest and adequately involve the socio-economic interests directly affected by the implementation of the planned

measures.
2. The choice of a global grant shall appear in the corresponding decision on the contribution of the Funds as a special implementing provision as defined in Article 18(2)(d) and Article 19(3)(d). The procedures for the use of global grants shall be the subject of an agreement between the Member State or managing authority and the intermediary body concerned.
In the case of Community initiative programmes and innovative measures, the procedures for the use of global grants shall be the subject of an agreement between the Commission and the intermediary body concerned. In the case of Community initiative programmes, these procedures must also be agreed with the Member States concerned. The programme complement referred to in Article 18 shall not relate to that part of the assistance bearing on the global grant.
3. The procedures for the use of the global grant shall detail in particular:
(a) the measures to be implemented;
(b) the criteria for choosing beneficiaries;
(c) the conditions and rates of assistance from the Funds, including the use of any interest accruing;
(d) the arrangements for monitoring, evaluating and ensuring the financial control of the global grant;
(e) where applicable, any use of a bank guarantee, in which case the Commission must be informed.

TITLE III - CONTRIBUTIONS AND FINANCIAL MANAGEMENT BY THE FUNDS

CHAPTER I: FINANCIAL CONTRIBUTIONS BY THE FUNDS

Article 28: Decision on the contributions from the Funds

1. Provided that all the requirements of this Regulation are fulfilled, the Commission shall adopt in a single decision the contributions of all the Funds within five months of receipt of the application for assistance. The decision shall distinguish clearly the regions and areas receiving transitional support, where applicable.
A maximum contribution from the Funds shall be set for each priority in the assistance.
For a given period, a measure may not receive a financial contribution from more than one fund at a time.
A measure or operation may benefit from a contribution from a Structural Fund under only one of the objectives referred to in Article 1 at a time.
No operation may benefit simultaneously from a contribution from a Fund under Objective 1, 2 or 3 and under a Community initiative.
No operation may benefit simultaneously from a contribution from a Fund under Objective 1, 2 or 3 and under the EAGGF Guarantee Section.
No operation may benefit simultaneously from a contribution from a Fund under a Community initiative and under the EAGGF Guarantee Section.
2. The contribution of the Funds to operational programmes undertaken in implementing a Community support framework shall be consistent with the financing plan laid down in the corresponding Community support framework, as set out in Article 17(2)(c).
3. In implementing measures, the contribution of the Funds shall principally take the form of non-repayable direct assistance (hereinafter referred to as "direct assistance"), as well as other forms, such as repayable assistance, an interest-rate subsidy, a guarantee, an equity holding, a venture-capital holding or another form of finance.
Assistance repaid to the managing authority or to another public authority shall be reallocated to the same purpose.

Article 29: Differentiation of the rates of contribution

1. The contribution of the Funds shall be differentiated in the light of the following:
(a) the gravity of the specific problems, in particular of a regional or social nature, to be tackled by the assistance;
(b) the financial capacity of the Member State concerned, taking into account in particular its relative prosperity and the need to avoid excessive increases in budget expenditure;
(c) within the framework of the objectives of the Funds set out in Article 1, the importance attaching to the assistance and the priorities from the Community viewpoint, where appropriate, for the elimination of inequalities and the promotion of equality between men and women and for the protection and improvement of the environment, principally through the application of the precautionary principle, of the principle of preventive action, and the polluter-pays principle;
(d) the importance attaching to the assistance and priorities from the regional and national viewpoint;
(e) the particular characteristics of the type of assistance and priority concerned, to take account of the needs

identified by the ex-ante evaluation, in particular with regard to human resources and employment;
(f) the optimum utilisation of financial resources in the financing plans, including the combination of public and private resources, the use made of appropriate financial instruments in accordance with Article 10(2), and the choice of forms of financing as set out in Article 28(3).
Where the contribution of the ESF is differentiated in accordance with Article 16(1), this shall be done taking account of the needs identified by the ex-ante evaluation, notably in the field of human resources and employment.
2. The contribution from the Funds shall be calculated in relation to either the total eligible cost, or the total public or similar eligible expenditure (national, regional or local, and Community) under each assistance.
3. The contribution of the Funds shall be subject to the following ceilings:
(a) a maximum of 75 % of the total eligible cost and, as a general rule, at least 50 % of eligible public expenditure in the case of measures carried out in the regions covered by Objective 1. Where the regions are located in a Member State covered by the Cohesion Fund, the Community contribution may rise, in exceptional and duly justified cases, to a maximum of 80 % of the total eligible cost and to a maximum of 85 % of the total eligible cost for the outermost regions and for the outlying Greek islands which are under a handicap due to their distant location;
(b) a maximum of 50 % of the total eligible cost and, as a general rule, at least 25 % of eligible public expenditure in the case of measures carried out in areas covered by Objective 2 or 3.
In the case of investment in firms, the contribution of the Funds shall comply with the ceilings on the rate of aid and on combinations of aid set in the field of State aids.
4. Where the assistance concerned entails the financing of revenue-generating investments, the contribution from the Funds to these investments shall be determined in the light of their intrinsic characteristics, including the size of the gross self-financing margin which would normally be expected for the class of investments concerned in the light of the macro-economic circumstances in which the investments are to be implemented, and without there being any increase in the national budget effort as a result of the contribution by the Funds.
In any event, the contribution of the Funds shall be subject to the following ceilings:
(a) in the case of investment in infrastructure generating substantial net revenue, the contribution may not exceed:
(i) 40 % of the total eligible cost in the regions covered by Objective 1, which may be increased by not more than an extra 10 % in the Member States covered by the Cohesion Fund;
(ii) 25 % of the total eligible cost in the areas covered by Objective 2;
(iii) these rates may be increased by an amount for forms of finance other than direct assistance, provided that this increase does not exceed 10 % of the total eligible cost;
(b) in the case of investments in firms, the contribution may not exceed:
(i) 35 % of the total eligible cost in the regions covered by Objective 1;
(ii) 15 % of the total eligible cost in the areas covered by Objective 2;
(iii) in the case of investments in small and medium-sized undertakings, these rates may be increased by an amount for forms of finance other than direct assistance, provided that this increase does not exceed 10 % of the total eligible cost.
5. References in paragraphs 3 and 4 to the regions and areas covered by Objectives 1 and 2 shall also be construed as references to regions or areas receiving on the one hand transitional support pursuant to Article 6(1) and support pursuant to Article 7(4) and on the other hand pursuant to Article 6(2) respectively.
6. The measures carried out on the Commission's initiative referred to in Articles 22 and 23 may be financed at a rate of 100 % of the total cost. The measures carried out on behalf of the Commission referred to in Article 23 shall be financed at a rate of 100 % of the total cost.
7. The rates in this Article shall apply to technical assistance measures within the framework of programming and to the Community initiatives.

Article 30: Eligibility

1. Expenditure in respect of operations shall be eligible for a contribution from the Funds only if these operations form part of the assistance concerned.
2. Expenditure may not be considered eligible for a contribution from the Funds if it has actually been paid by the final beneficiary before the date on which the application for assistance reaches the Commission. That date shall constitute the starting point for the eligibility of expenditure.
The final date for the eligibility of expenditure shall be laid down in the decision to grant a contribution from the Funds. It shall relate to payments made by the final beneficiaries. It may be extended by the Commission at the duly justified request of the Member State in accordance with Articles 14 and 15.
3. The relevant national rules shall apply to eligible expenditure except where, as necessary, the Commission lays down common rules on the eligibility of expenditure in accordance with the procedure referred to in Article

53(2).
4. The Member States shall ensure that an operation retains the contribution from the Funds only if that operation does not, within five years of the date of the decision of the competent national authorities or the managing authority on the contribution of the Funds, undergo a substantial modification:
(a) affecting its nature or its implementation conditions or giving to a firm or a public body an undue advantage; and
(b) resulting either from a change in the nature of ownership in an item of infrastructure or a cessation or change of location in a productive activity.
The Member States shall inform the Commission of any such modification. Where such a modification occurs, Article 39 shall apply.

CHAPTER II - FINANCIAL MANAGEMENT

Article 31: Budget commitments

1. Community budget commitments shall be made on the basis of the decision to grant a contribution from the Funds.
2. Commitments in respect of assistance to be carried out over a period of two or more years shall be as a general rule effected annually. The first commitment shall be made when the Commission lays down its decision approving the assistance. Subsequent commitments shall be effected as a general rule by 30 April each year.
The Commission shall automatically decommit any part of a commitment which has not been settled by the payment on account or for which it has not received an acceptable payment application, as defined in Article 32(3), by the end of the second year following the year of commitment or, where appropriate and for the amounts concerned, following the date of a subsequent Commission decision necessary in order to authorise a measure or an operation or by the end of the deadline for the transmission of the final report referred to in Article 37(1); the contribution from the Funds to that assistance shall be reduced by that amount.
The period for automatic decommitment referred to in the second subparagraph shall cease to run for the part of the commitment corresponding to operations which, at the specified date of decommitment, are the subject of a judicial procedure, or an administrative appeal having suspensory effects, subject to the Commission receiving prior information giving reasons from the Member State concerned and to information being issued by the Commission.
In any case, the Commission shall in good time inform the Member State and the paying authority whenever there is a risk of application of the automatic decommitment provided for in the second subparagraph.
If this Regulation enters into force after 1 January 2000, the period for automatic decommitment referred to in the second subparagraph shall be extended for the first commitment by the number of months between 1 January 2000 and the date of the decision on the contributions from the Funds referred to in Article 28.
3. For assistance to be carried out over a period of less than two years the total amount of the contribution from the Funds shall be committed when the Commission adopts its decsion granting a contribution from the Funds.

Article 32: Payments

1. Payment by the Commission of the contribution from the Funds shall be made, in accordance with the corresponding budget commitments, to the paying authority as defined in Article 9(o).
Payments shall be posted to the earliest open commitment made pursuant to Article 31.
Payments may take the form of payments on account, interim payments or payments of the final balance.
Interim payments and payments of the balance shall relate to expenditure actually paid out, which must correspond to payments effected by the final beneficiaries, supported by receipted invoices or accounting documents of equivalent probative value.
Subject to available funding, the Commission shall make interim payments within no more than two months of receipt of an acceptable payment application, as described in paragraph 3.
The paying authority shall ensure that final beneficiaries receive payment of their contribution from the Funds as quickly as possible and in full. No deduction, retention or further specific charge which would reduce these amounts shall be made.
2. When the first commitment is made, the Commission shall make a payment on account to the paying authority. This payment on account shall be 7 % of the contribution from the Funds to the assistance in question. In principle, it may be subdivided over two budget years at most depending on the availability of budget funds.
Throughout the lifetime of assistance, the paying authority shall use the payment on account to pay the Community contribution to expenditure relating to this assistance.
All or part of a payment on account, depending on progress towards implementation of the assistance, shall be

repaid to the Commission by the paying authority if no payment application is sent to the Commission within 18 months of its decision to grant a contribution from the Funds. If any interest is earned on the payment on account it shall be allocated by the paying authority to the form of assistance concerned.
3. Interim payments shall be made by the Commission to reimburse expenditure actually paid under the Funds as certified by the paying authority. Such payments shall be made at the level of each assistance and calculated at the level of measures contained in the financing plan of the programme complement. They shall be subject to the following conditions:
(a) the programme complement containing the information specified in Article 18(3) has been presented to the Commission;
(b) the latest annual implementation report due, containing the information specified in Article 37 has been forwarded to the Commission;
(c) the mid-term evaluation of the assistance referred to in Article 42, when due, has been forwarded to the Commission;
(d) decisions taken by the managing authority and the Monitoring Committee are consistent with the total amount of the contribution from the Funds granted to the priorities concerned;
(e) any recommendations as referred to in Article 34(2) have been acted upon within the specified period, or reasons have been communicated by the Member State to explain why no measure has been taken, where those recommendations are intended to remedy serious shortcomings in the monitoring or management system which undermine proper financial management of the assistance; any requests for corrective measures as referred to in Article 38(4) have been acted upon, if the application relates to the measure or measures concerned;
(f) no suspension of payments under the first subparagraph of Article 39(2) has been decided, and no decision has been taken by the Commission to embark on an infringement procedure within the meaning of Article 226 of the Treaty concerning the measure(s) that is or are the subject of the application in question.
The Member State and the paying authority shall be informed immediately by the Commission if one of these conditions is not fulfilled and the payment application is therefore not acceptable and they shall take the necessary steps to remedy the situation.
Member States shall ensure that, as far as possible, applications for interim payments are presented to the Commission in batches three times a year, the last application being presented no later than 31 October. Applications for interim payments shall distinguish, for each priority, the expenditure incurred in regions and areas receiving transitional support.
The combined total of the payments referred to in paragraph 2 and in this paragraph which are made in respect of an assistance shall not exceed 95 % of the contribution from the Funds to that assistance.
4. The final balance of the assistance shall be paid if:
(a) the paying authority submits to the Commission within six months of the deadline for payment laid down in the decision granting a contribution from the Funds, a certified statement of expenditure actually paid;
(b) the final report on implementation has been submitted to and approved by the Commission;
(c) the Member State has sent the Commission the statement referred to in Article 38(1)(f).
5. The final payment of the balance may no longer be corrected at the request of the Member State if the paying authority has not sent an application to the Commission within nine months from the date of transfer of the final balance.
6. The Member States shall designate the authorities empowered to issue the certificates and declarations referred to in paragraphs 3 and 4.
7. No later than 30 April of each year, the Member States shall send the Commission their updated forecasts of applications for payment for the current year and the forecast for the following year.
8. The Commission shall lay down appropriate payment procedures, consistent with the objectives of these provisions, for the innovative measures referred to in Article 22 and the measures referred to in Article 23 and inform the committees referred to in Articles 48 to 51.

Article 33: Use of the euro

Commission decisions, commitments and payments shall be denominated and carried out in euro in accordance with the arrangements to be drawn up by the Commission under the procedure referred to in Article 53(2).

TITLE IV - EFFECTIVENESS OF ASSISTANCE FROM THE FUNDS

CHAPTER I: MONITORING

Article 34
Management by the managing authority
1. Without prejudice to Article 8(3), the managing authority as defined in Article 9(n) shall be responsible for

the efficiency and correctness of management and implementation, and in particular for:
(a) setting up a system to gather reliable financial and statistical information on implementation, for the monitoring indicators referred to in Article 36, and for evaluation in compliance with Articles 42 and 43; and for forwarding this data in accordance with arrangements agreed between the Member State and the Commission, using where possible computer systems permitting the exchange of data with the Commission, as defined in Article 18(3)(e);
(b) adjustment in accordance with paragraph 3 and the implementation of the programme complement within the meaning of Article 18(3), without prejudice to Article 35;
(c) drawing up and, after obtaining the approval of the Monitoring Committee, submitting to the Commission the annual implementation report;
(d) organising, in cooperation with the Commission and the Member State, the mid-term evaluation referred to in Article 42;
(e) ensuring that those bodies taking part in the management and implementation of the assistance maintain either a separate accounting system or an adequate accounting code for all transactions relating to the assistance;
(f) ensuring the correctness of operations financed under the assistance, particularly by implementing internal controls in keeping with the principles of sound financial management and acting in response to any observations or requests for corrective measures adopted pursuant to Article 38(4), first subparagraph, or recommendations for adjustment made under paragraph 2 of this Article in accordance with the provisions of those Articles;
(g) ensuring compliance with Community policies as stipulated in Article 12; in the context of the application of Community rules on the award of public contracts, notices sent for publication in the Official Journal of the European Communities shall specify those projects in respect of which a contribution from the Funds has been applied for or granted;
(h) compliance with the obligations concerning information and publicity referred to in Article 46.
Without prejudice to the provisions of this Regulation, in carrying out its tasks the managing authority shall act in full compliance with the institutional, legal and financial systems of the Member State concerned.
2. Every year, when the annual implementation report referred to in Article 37 is submitted, the Commission and the managing authority shall review the main outcomes of the previous year, in accordance with arrangements to be defined by agreement with the Member State and the managing authority concerned.
After this review, the Commission may make comments to the Member State and the managing authority. The Member State shall inform the Commission of the action taken on these comments. Where in duly substantiated cases the Commission considers that the measures taken are inadequate, it may make recommendations to the Member State and the managing authority for adjustments aimed at improving the effectiveness of the monitoring or management arrangements for the assistance, together with the reasons for any such recommendations. If it receives any such recommendations, the managing authority shall subsequently demonstrate the steps taken to improve the monitoring or management arrangements or it shall explain why it has not taken any.
3. The managing authority shall, at the request of the Monitoring Committee or on its own initiative, adjust the programme complement, without changing the total amount of the contribution from the Funds granted to the priority concerned nor its specific targets. After approval by the Monitoring Committee, it shall inform the Commission of the adjustment within one month.
Any amendments to the elements contained in the decision on the contribution of the Funds shall be decided by the Commission, in agreement with the Member State concerned, within four months of delivery of the Monitoring Committee's approval.

Article 35: Monitoring Committees

1. Each Community support framework or single programming document and each operational programme shall be supervised by a Monitoring Committee.
Monitoring Committees shall be set up by the Member State, in agreement with the managing authority after consultation with the partners. The partners shall promote the balanced participation of women and men.
The Monitoring Committees shall be set up no more than three months after the decision on the contribution of the Funds. The Monitoring Committees shall act under the authority and within the legal jurisdiction of the Member State.
2. A representative of the Commission and, where appropriate, of the EIB, shall participate in the work of the Monitoring Committee in an advisory capacity.
The Monitoring Committee shall draw up its own rules of procedure within the institutional, legal and financial framework of the Member State concerned and agree them with the managing authority.
In principle, the Monitoring Committee shall be chaired by a representative of the Member State or the managing authority.

3. The Monitoring Committee shall satisfy itself as to the effectiveness and quality of the implementation of assistance. To that end:
(a) pursuant to Article 15, it shall confirm or adjust the programme complement, including the physical and financial indicators to be used to monitor the assistance. Its approval must be obtained before any further adjustment is made;
(b) it shall consider and approve the criteria for selecting the operations financed under each measure within six months of approval of the assistance;
(c) it shall periodically review progress made towards achieving the specific objectives of the assistance;
(d) it shall examine the results of implementation, particularly achievement of the targets set for the different measures and the mid-term evaluation referred to in Article 42;
(e) it shall consider and approve the annual and final implementation reports before they are sent to the Commission;
(f) it shall consider and approve any proposal to amend the contents of the Commission decision on the contribution of the Funds;
(g) it may in any event propose to the managing authority any adjustment or review of the assistance likely to make possible the attainment of the objectives referred to in Article 1 or to improve the management of assistance, including in respect of financial management. Any adjustment to the assistance shall be made in accordance with Article 34(3).

Article 36: Monitoring indicators

1. The managing authority and the Monitoring Committee shall carry out the monitoring by reference to physical and financial indicators specified in the operational programme, single programming document, or programme complement. In drawing up their indicators, they should take into account the indicative methodology and list of examples of indicators published by the Commission, as well as a categorisation of fields of intervention to be proposed by the Commission upon entry into force of this Regulation. The indicators shall relate to the specific character of the assistance concerned, its objectives and the socio-economic, structural and environmental situation of the Member State concerned and its regions, as appropriate, and shall take account, where appropriate, of the existence of regions or areas receiving transitional support. These indicators shall include, in particular, those used for allocating the reserve referred to in Article 44.
2. These indicators shall show, for the assistance in question:
(a) the specific targets, quantified where they lend themselves to quantification, for the measures and priorities, and their mutual consistency;
(b) the stage reached in the assistance in terms of physical implementation, results and, as soon as practicable, its impact at the appropriate level (priority or measure);
(c) the progress of the financing plan.
Where the nature of the assistance permits, the statistics shall be broken down by sex and by the size of the recipient undertakings.
3. The financial and progress indicators shall be such that the information set out in paragraph 2(a), (b) and (c) can be identified separately for major projects.

Article 37: Annual and final implementation reports

1. For multiannual assistance, the managing authority shall, within six months of the end of each full calendar year of implementation, submit to the Commission an annual implementation report as provided for in Article 34(1)(c). A final report shall be submitted to the Commission at the latest six months after the final date of eligibility of the expenditure.
For all assistance to be implemented over a period of less than two years, the managing authority shall submit only a final report to the Commission. This shall be submitted within six months of the last payment made by the paying authority.
The report shall be examined and approved by the Monitoring Committee before it is sent to the Commission. Once the Commission has received an annual implementation report, it shall indicate within a period of two months if the report is considered unsatisfactory, giving its reasons; otherwise, the report shall be deemed to be accepted. In the case of a final report the Commission shall respond within a period of five months from its receipt of the report.
2. All annual and final implementation reports shall include the following information:
(a) any change in general conditions which is of relevance to the implementation of the assistance, in particular the main socio-economic trends, changes in national, regional or sectoral policies or in the frame of reference referred to in Article 9(c) and, where applicable, their implications for the mutual consistency of assistance from the different Funds and consistency between Fund assistance and that from other financial instruments;

(b) the progress in the implementation of priorities and measures for each of the Funds in relation to their specific targets, with a quantification, wherever and whenever they lend themselves to quantification, of the physical indicators and indicators of results and of impact referred to in Article 36 at the appropriate level (priority or measure);
(c) the financial implementation of the assistance, summarising for each measure the total expenditure actually paid out by the paying authority and a record of the total payments received from the Commission and quantifying the financial indicators referred to in Article 36(2)(c); financial implementation in the areas receiving transitional support shall be presented separately in respect of each priority; financial implementation of the EAGGF Guarantee Section for the measures referred to in Article 33 of Regulation (EC) No 1257/1999 shall be presented at the level of the total amount of the financial implementation;
(d) the steps taken by the managing authority and the Monitoring Committee to ensure the quality and effectiveness of implementation, in particular:
(i) monitoring, financial control and evaluation measures, including data collection arrangements;
(ii) a summary of any significant problems encountered in managing the assistance and any measures taken, including action on recommendations for adjustments made pursuant to Article 34(2) or requests for corrective measures pursuant to Article 38(4);
(iii) the use made of technical assistance;
(iv) the measures taken to ensure publicity for the assistance in accordance with Article 46;
(e) the steps taken to ensure compatibility with Community policies as stipulated in Article 12 and to ensure coordination of all the Community structural assistance referred to in Article 17(1) and the second subparagraph of Article 19(2);
(f) a separate section, where appropriate, on the progress and financing of major projects and global grants.

CHAPTER II - FINANCIAL CONTROL

Article 38: General provisions

1. Without prejudice to the Commission's responsibility for implementing the general budget of the European Communities, Member States shall take responsibility in the first instance for the financial control of assistance. To that end, the measures they take shall include:
(a) verifying that management and control arrangements have been set up and are being implemented in such a way as to ensure that Community funds are being used efficiently and correctly;
(b) providing the Commission with a description of these arrangements;
(c) ensuring that assistance is managed in accordance with all the applicable Community rules and that the funds placed at their disposal are used in accordance with the principles of sound financial management;
(d) certifying that the declarations of expenditure presented to the Commission are accurate and ensuring that they result from accounting systems based on verifiable supporting documents;
(e) preventing, detecting and correcting irregularities, notifying these to the Commission, in accordance with the rules, and keeping the Commission informed of the progress of administrative and legal proceedings;
(f) presenting to the Commission, when each assistance is wound up, a declaration drawn up by a person or department having a function independent of the designated managing authority. This declaration shall summarise the conclusions of the checks carried out during previous years and shall assess the validity of the application for payment of the final balance and the legality and regularity of the transactions covered by the final certificate of expenditure. The Member States may attach their own opinion to this certificate if they consider it necessary;
(g) cooperating with the Commission to ensure that Community funds are used in accordance with the principles of sound financial management;
(h) recovering any amounts lost as a result of an irregularity detected and, where appropriate, charging interest on late payments.
2. The Commission in its responsibility for the implementation of the general budget of the European Communities shall ensure that Member States have smoothly functioning management and control systems so that Community funds are efficiently and correctly used.
To that end, without prejudice to checks carried out by the Member States in accordance with national laws, regulations and administrative provisions, Commission officials or servants may, in accordance with arrangements agreed with the Member State in the framework of cooperation described in paragraph 3, carry out on-the-spot checks, including sample checks, on the operations financed by the Funds and on management and control systems with a minimum of one working day's notice. The Commission shall give notice to the Member State concerned with a view to obtaining all the assistance necessary. Officials or servants of the Member State concerned may take part in such checks.
The Commission may require the Member State concerned to carry out an on-the-spot check to verify the

correctness of one or more transactions. Commission officials or servants may take part in such checks.
3. The Commission and the Member States shall on the basis of bilateral administrative arrangements cooperate to coordinate plans, methods and implementation of checks so as to maximise the usefulness of those carried out. They shall immediately exchange the results of the checks carried out.
At least once a year and, in any event, before the annual review provided for in Article 34(2) the following shall be examined and evaluated:
(a) the results of the checks carried out by the Member State and the Commission;
(b) any comments made by other national or Community control bodies or institutions;
(c) the financial impact of the irregularities noted, the steps already taken or still required to correct them and, where necessary, adjustments to the management and control systems.
4. Following this examination and evaluation and without prejudice to the measures to be taken immediately by the Member State under this Article and Article 39, the Commission may make observations, particularly regarding the financial impact of any irregularities detected. These observations shall be addressed to the Member State and the managing authority of the assistance concerned. The observations shall be accompanied, where necessary, by requests for corrective measures to remedy the management shortcomings found and correct those irregularities detected which have not already been corrected. The Member State shall have the opportunity to comment on these observations.
Where, following or in the absence of comments from the Member State, the Commission adopts conclusions, the Member State shall take the necessary steps within the deadline set to comply with the Commission's requests and inform the Commission of its actions.
5. Without prejudice to this Article, the Commission, after due verification, may suspend all or part of an interim payment if it finds that the expenditure concerned is linked to a serious irregularity which has not been corrected and that immediate action is needed. The Commission shall inform the Member State concerned of the action taken and the reasons for it. If, after five months, the reasons for the suspension remain or the Member State concerned has not notified the Commission of the measures taken to correct the serious irregularity, the provisions laid down under Article 39 shall apply.
6. For a period of three years, unless otherwise decided in the bilateral administrative arrangements, following the payment by the Commission of the final balance in respect of any assistance, the responsible authorities shall keep available for the Commission all the supporting documents (either the originals or versions certified to be in conformity with the originals on commonly accepted data carriers) regarding expenditure and checks on the assistance concerned. This period shall be interrupted either in the case of legal proceedings or at the duly motivated request of the Commission.

Article 39: Financial corrections

1. The Member States shall, in the first instance, bear the responsibility for investigating irregularities, acting upon evidence of any major change affecting the nature or conditions for the implementation or supervision of assistance and making the financial corrections required.
The Member State shall make the financial corrections required in connection with the individual or systemic irregularity. The corrections made by the Member State shall consist in cancelling all or part of the Community contribution. The Community funds released in this way may be re-used by the Member State for the assistance concerned, in compliance with the arrangements to be defined pursuant to Article 53(2).
2. If, after completing the necessary verifications, the Commission concludes that:
(a) a Member State has not complied with its obligations under paragraph 1; or
(b) all or part of an operation justifies neither part nor the whole of the contribution from the Funds; or
(c) there are serious failings in the management or control systems which could lead to systemic irregularities;
the Commission shall suspend the interim payments in question and, stating its reasons, request that the Member State submit its comments and, where appropriate, carry out any corrections, within a specified period of time.
If the Member State objects to the observations made by the Commission, the Member State shall be invited to a hearing by the Commission, in which both sides in cooperation based on the partnership make efforts to reach an agreement about the observations and the conclusions to be drawn from them.
3. At the end of the period set by the Commission, the Commission may, if no agreement has been reached and the Member State has not made the corrections and taking account of any comments made by the Member State, decide within three months to:
(a) reduce the payment on account referred to in Article 32(2); or
(b) make the financial corrections required by cancelling all or part of the contribution of the Funds to the assistance concerned.
The Commission shall when deciding the amount of a correction take account, in compliance with the principle of proportionality, of the type of irregularity or change and the extent and financial implications of the shortcomings found in the management or control systems of the Member States.

In the absence of a decision to do either (a) or (b) the interim payments shall immediately cease to be suspended.
4. Any sum received unduly and to be recovered shall be repaid to the Commission, together with interest on account of late payment.
5. This Article shall apply without prejudice to Article 32.

CHAPTER III - EVALUATION

Article 40: General provisions

1. In order to gauge its effectiveness, Community structural assistance shall be the subject of ex-ante, mid-term and ex-post evaluation designed to appraise its impact with respect to the objectives set out in Article 1 and to analyse its effects on specific structural problems.
2. The effectiveness of the operations of the Funds shall be measured by the following criteria:
(a) their overall impact on the goals set out in Article 158 of the Treaty, and in particular the strengthening of the economic and social cohesion of the Community;
(b) the impact of the priorities proposed in the development plans and of the priorities incorporated in each Community support framework and in each case of assistance.
3. The competent authorities of the Member States and the Commission shall assemble the appropriate resources and collect the data required to ensure that this evaluation can be carried out in the most effective manner. In this connection, evaluation shall make use of the various particulars that the monitoring arrangements may yield, supplemented where necessary by the gathering of information to improve its relevance.
On the initiative of the Member States or the Commission, after informing the Member State concerned, supplementary evaluations, if appropriate on a specific topic, may be launched with a view to identifying transferable experience.
4. The results of the evaluation shall be made available to the public, on request. As regards the results of the evaluation provided for in Article 42, the Monitoring Committee's agreement shall be required according to the institutional arrangements of each Member State.
5. The evaluation procedures shall be laid down in the Community support frameworks and forms of assistance.

Article 41: ex-ante evaluation

1. The purpose of ex-ante evaluation shall be to provide a basis for preparing the development plans, assistance and programme complement of which it shall form part.
Ex-ante evaluation shall be the responsibility of the authorities responsible for preparing the plans, assistance and programme complement.
2. For the preparation of plans and assistance ex-ante evaluation shall involve an analysis of the strengths, weaknesses and potential of the Member State, region or sector concerned. In the light of the criteria listed in Article 40(2)(a) it shall assess the consistency of the strategy and targets selected with the specific features of the regions or areas concerned, including demographic trends, and the expected impact of the planned priorities for action, quantifying their specific targets in relation to the starting situation, where they lend themselves thereto.
The ex-ante evaluation shall take into account, amongst other things, the situation in terms of competitiveness and innovation, small and medium-sized enterprises, employment and the labour market having regard to the European employment strategy, the environment and equality between men and women, and it shall include in particular:
(a) an ex-ante evaluation of the social and economic situation, mainly trends in the national labour market, including regions encountering particular employment problems and of the overall strategy in the field of human resource development and the way in which this strategy is linked to the national employment strategy as set out in the national action plans;
(b) an ex-ante evaluation of the environmental situation of the region concerned, in particular of those environmental sectors which will presumably be considerably affected by the assistance; the arrangements to integrate the environmental dimension into the assistance and how far they fit in with existing short- and long-term national, regional and local objectives (e.g. environmental management plans); the arrangements for ensuring compliance with the Community rules on the environment. The ex-ante evaluation shall give a description, quantified as far as possible, of the existing environmental situation and an estimate of the expected impact of the strategy and assistance on the environmental situation;
(c) an ex-ante evaluation of the situation in terms of equality between men and women with regard to labour market opportunities and treatment at work, including the specific constraints on each group; an estimate of the expected impact of the strategy and assistance, particularly on the integration of women and men into the labour market, on education and vocational training, on the establishment of women in business and on the

reconciliation of family and working life.
The ex-ante evaluation shall verify the relevance of the proposed implementing and monitoring arrangements, consistency with Community policies and how far the indicative guidance referred to in Article 10(3) has been taken into account.
It shall take account of results from evaluations of earlier programming periods.
3. evaluation of the measures in the programme complement shall demonstrate consistency with the aims of the corresponding priorities, quantify their specific targets where the priorities lend themselves thereto, and subsequently verify the relevance of the selection criteria, as provided for pursuant to Article 35(3)(b).

Article 42: Mid-term evaluation

1. Mid-term evaluation shall examine, in the light of the ex-ante evaluation, the initial results of the asssistance, their relevance and the extent to which the targets have been attained. It shall also assess the use made of financial resources and the operation of monitoring and implementation.
2. Mid-term evaluation shall be carried out under the responsibility of the managing authority, in cooperation with the Commission and the Member State. It shall cover each Community support framework and each assistance. It shall be carried out by an independent assessor, be submitted to the Monitoring Committee for the Community support framework or assistance concerned in accordance with Article 35(3), and then sent to the Commission, as a general rule three years after adoption of the Community support framework or assistance, and no later than 31 December 2003, with a view to the revision referred to in Article 14(2).
3. The Commission shall examine the relevance and quality of the evaluation on the basis of criteria defined beforehand by the Commission and the Member State in partnership, with a view to reviewing the assistance and allocating the reserve referred to in Article 44.
4. As a continuation of mid-term evaluation, it shall be updated for each Community support framework and assistance and completed no later than 31 December 2005 in order to prepare for subsequent assistance operations.

Article 43: ex-post evaluation

1. On the basis of the evaluation results already available, ex-post evaluation shall cover the utilisation of resources and the effectiveness and efficiency of the assistance and its impact and shall draw conclusions regarding policy on economic and social cohesion. It shall cover the factors contributing to the success or failure of implementation and the achievements and results, including their sustainability.
2. Ex-post evaluation shall be the responsibility of the Commission, in collaboration with the Member State and the managing authority. It shall cover the assistance and be carried out by independent assessors. It shall be completed not later than three years after the end of the programming period.

CHAPTER IV - PERFORMANCE RESERVE

Article 44: Allocation of the performance reserve

1. Each Member State, in close consultation with the Commission, shall assess under each objective and not later than 31 December 2003 the performance of each of their operational programmes or single programming documents on the basis of a limited number of monitoring indicators reflecting effectiveness, management and financial implementation and measuring the mid-term results in relation to their specific initial targets.
These indicators shall be decided by the Member State in close consultation with the Commission taking account of all or part of an indicative list of indicators proposed by the Commission and shall be quantified in the existing different annual implementation reports as well as the mid-term evaluation report. The Member States shall be responsible for their application.
2. At mid-term and not later than 31 March 2004, the Commission shall allocate, in close consultation with the Member States concerned, under each objective, on the basis of proposals from each Member State, taking account of its specific institutional features and their corresponding programming, the commitment appropriations referred to in Article 7(5) to the operational programmes or single programming documents or their priorities which are considered to be successful. The operational programmes or single programming documents shall be adapted in accordance with Articles 14 and 15.

TITLE V - REPORTS AND PUBLICITY

Article 45: Reports

1. Pursuant to Article 159 of the Treaty, the Commission shall submit a report at three-yearly intervals to the European Parliament, the Council, the Economic and Social Committee and the Committee of the Regions on the progress made towards economic and social cohesion and the contribution made to this by the Funds, the Cohesion Fund, the EIB and other financial instruments. This report shall review in particular:
(a) progress in achieving economic and social cohesion, including the socio-economic situation of the regions and any changes observed, and an analysis of direct investment flows and their impact on the Community employment situation;
(b) the role of the Funds, the Cohesion Fund, the EIB and other financial instruments as well as the impact of other Community and national policies in accomplishing this process;
(c) any proposals concerning Community measures and policies which may need to be adopted in order to strengthen economic and social cohesion.
2. Before 1 November of each year, the Commission shall forward to the European Parliament, the Council, the Economic and Social Committee and the Committee of the Regions a report on the implementation of this Regulation during the preceding year. This report shall review in particular:
(a) the activities of each fund, the utilisation of their budget resources and the concentration of assistance, the deployment of the other financial instruments for which the Commission has responsibility and the concentration of their resources; this review shall include:
- an annual breakdown by Member State of appropriations committed and paid in respect of each fund, including Community initiatives;
- an annual evaluation of innovative actions and technical assistance;
(b) the coordination of assistance from the Funds among themselves and with the assistance granted by the EIB and the other existing financial instruments;
(c) as soon as they are available, the results of the evaluations referred to in Article 42 - indicating any adjustments to the assistance - and in Article 43, and an evaluation of the consistency of measures taken by the Funds with the Community policies referred to in Article 12;
(d) a list of the major projects to which the Funds have contributed;
(e) the results of checks carried out by the Commission in accordance with Article 38(2) and the lessons to be drawn from them, including an indication of the number of recorded irregularities, the amounts in question and the financial corrections made in respect of Article 39(2);
(f) information on the opinions of committees delivered in accordance with Articles 48 to 51.

Article 46: Information and publicity

1. For the purposes of consultation as referred to in Article 15(1), Member States shall ensure that publicity is given to development plans.
2. Without prejudice to Article 23(1), the managing authority shall be responsible for ensuring that publicity is given to the package and particularly for informing:
(a) potential final beneficiaries, trade and professional bodies, the economic and social partners, bodies promoting equality between men and women and the relevant non-governmental organisations about the opportunities afforded by the assistance;
(b) the general public about the role played by the Community in the assistance concerned and its results.
3. The Member States shall consult the Commission and in accordance with Article 37(2) inform it each year of the initiatives taken for the purposes set out in paragraphs 1 and 2 of this Article.

TITLE VI - COMMITTEES

Article 47: General provisions

1. In implementing this Regulation, the Commission shall be assisted by four committees:
(a) the Committee on the Development and Conversion of Regions;
(b) the Committee pursuant to Article 147 of the Treaty;
(c) the Committee on Agricultural Structures and Rural Development;
(d) the Committee on Structures for Fisheries and Aquaculture.
2. Where the Committees mentioned in paragraph 1(a), (c) and (d) are acting as Consultative Committees pursuant to Articles 48, 50 and 51 respectively, the following procedure applies:
- the Commission representative shall submit to the committee a draft of the measure to be taken,
- the committee shall deliver its opinion on this draft within a time limit which the chairman may lay down according to the urgency of the matter; the matter may be put to a vote where appropriate,
- its opinions shall be entered in the minutes; each Member State shall in addition have the right to ask for its

position to be included in the minutes,
- the Commission shall take the utmost account of the opinions delivered by the committee. It shall inform the committee of the manner in which it takes account of its opinions.
3. Where the committees mentioned in paragraph 1(a), (c) and (d) are acting as Management Committees pursuant to Articles 48, 50 and 51 respectively, the following procedure applies:
- the Commission representative shall submit to the committee a draft of the measure to be taken,
- the committee shall deliver its opinion on this draft within a time limit which the chairman may lay down according to the urgency of the matter under consideration. The opinion shall be delivered by the majority stipulated in Article 205(2) of the Treaty in the case of decisions which the Council is requested to adopt on a proposal from the Commission. When a matter is put to the vote within the committee, the votes of the Member States' representatives shall be weighted as provided for in the said Article. The chairman shall not vote,
- the Commission shall adopt measures which shall apply immediately. However, if they are not in accordance with the opinion delivered by the committee, they shall be communicated forthwith by the Commission to the Council. In that event:
- the Commission may defer application of the measure which it has decided for a period of not more than one month from the date of such communication,
- the Council, acting by a qualified majority, may take a different decision within the time limit provided for in the above sub-indent.
4. The Commission shall refer the reports referred to in Article 45 to the committees. It may seek the opinion of a Committee on any matter concerning assistance under the Funds, other than assistance provided for in this Title. This includes matters primarily dealt with by other committees.
5. Each committee's opinions shall be brought to the attention of the other committees referred to in this Title.
6. Each committee shall draw up its rules of procedure.
7. The European Parliament shall be regularly informed of the work of the committees.

Article 48: Committee on the Development and Conversion of Regions

1. A Committee on the Development and Conversion of Regions, made up of Member States' representatives and chaired by a Commission representative, is hereby set up under the auspices of the Commission. The EIB shall appoint a non-voting representative.
2. The committee shall act as a Management Committee according to the procedure laid down in Article 47(3) when it deals with:
(a) the implementing rules referred to in Article 53(2).
Other committees shall be consulted under their consultative competence on the abovementioned implementing rules, in so far as they are concerned;
(b) the implementing rules referred to in Article 5 of Regulation (EC) No 1261/1999 of the European Parliament and of the Council of 21 June 1999 on the European Regional Development Fund (ERDF)(13);
(c) the guidelines relating to the Community initiatives referred to in Article 20(1)(a) ("Interreg") and 20(1)(b) ("Urban");
(d) the guidelines for the different types of innovative measures provided for in application of Article 22, in the case of support from the ERDF.
3. The committee acts as a consultative committee according to the procedure laid down in Article 47(2) when it discusses the following matters:
(a) establishment and revision of the list of areas eligible under Objective 2;
(b) the Community support frameworks and the corresponding information contained in the single programming documents, under Objectives 1 and 2;
(c) the types of technical-assistance measure in accordance with Article 23 in the case of support from the ERDF;
(d) any other questions concerning Articles 20 to 22.

Article 49: Committee pursuant to Article 147 of the Treaty

1. The committee set up pursuant to Article 147 of the Treaty shall be composed of two government representatives, two representatives of the workers' organisations and two representatives of the employers' organisations from each Member State. The Member of the Commission responsible for chairing the committee may delegate that responsibility to a senior Commission official.
For each Member State, an alternate shall be appointed for each category of representative mentioned in the first paragraph. In the absence of one or both members, the alternate shall be automatically entitled to take part in the proceedings.
The members and alternates shall be appointed by the Council, acting on a proposal from the Commission, for a

period of three years. They may be reappointed. The Council shall, as regards the composition of the committee, endeavour to ensure fair representation of the different groups concerned. For the items on the agenda affecting it, the EIB shall appoint a non-voting representative.
2. The committee shall:
(a) deliver opinions on the draft Commission decisions relating to single programming documents and to Community support frameworks under Objective 3 as well as on the Community support frameworks and corresponding information contained in the single programming documents, under Objectives 1 and 2, in the case of support from the ESF;
(b) deliver its opinion on the implementing rules provided for in Article 53(2);
(c) be consulted on the implementing rules referred to in Article 8 of Regulation (EC) No 1262/1999 of the European Parliament and of the Council of 21 June 1999 on the European Social Fund (ESF)(14);
(d) deliver opinions on draft Commission guidelines relating to the Community initiative referred to in Article 20(1)(d) ("EQUAL") and for the various types of innovative measure in the context of Article 22 in the case of support from the ESF. The Commission may also refer further questions to it within the meaning of Articles 20 to 22;
(e) be consulted on the types of technical-assistance measure in accordance with Article 23 in the case of support from the ESF.
3. For their adoption, the opinions of the committee shall require an absolut majority of the votes validly cast. The Commission shall inform the committee of the manner in which it has taken account of its opinions.

Article 50: Committee on Agricultural Structures and Rural Development

1. A Committee on Agricultural Structures and Rural Development, made up of Member States' representatives and chaired by a Commission representative, is hereby set up under the auspices of the Commission. The EIB shall appoint a non-voting representative.
2. The Committee acts as a Management Committee according to the procedure laid down in Article 47(3) when it deals with:
(a) the implementing rules and transitional rules referred to in Articles 34, 50 and 53 of Regulation (EC) No 1257/1999;
(b) the guidelines relating to the Community initiative referred to in Article 20(1)(c) ("Leader").
3. The committee acts as a Consultative Committee according to the procedure laid down in Article 47(2) when it discusses the following matters:
(a) the establishment and revision of the list of areas eligible under Objective 2;
(b) the parts of the intervention concerning agricultural structures and rural development included in the draft Commission decisions relating to the Community support frameworks and corresponding information contained in the single programming documents, for the regions under Objectives 1 and 2;
(c) the implementing rules referred to in Article 53(2);
(d) the types of technical-assistance measure in accordance with Article 23 in the case of support from the EAGGF;
(e) any other questions concerning Articles 20 to 22.

Article 51: Committee on Structures for Fisheries and Aquaculture

1. A Committee on Structures for Fisheries and Aquaculture, made up of Member States' representatives and chaired by a Commission representative, is hereby set up under the auspices of the Commission. The EIB shall appoint a non-voting representative.
2. The committee shall act as a Management Committee according to the procedure laid down in Article 47(3) when it deals with:
(a) the implementing rules referred to in Article 4 of Regulation (EC) No 1263/1999;
(b) the guidelines for the different types of innovative measures provided for in application of Article 22, in the case of support from the FIFG.
3. The committee shall act as a Consultative Committee according to the procedure laid down in Article 47(2) when it discusses the following matters:
(a) the establishment and revision of the list of areas eligible under Objective 2;
(b) the parts of the intervention concerning fisheries structures included in the draft Commission Decision relating to the Community support frameworks and corresponding information contained in the single programming documents under Objective 1;
(c) the implementing rules provided for in Article 53(2);
(d) the types of technical-assistance measure in accordance with Article 23 in the case of support from the FIFG;

(e) any other questions concerning Article 22.

Annex 3.4.

1999/502/EC: Commission Decision of 1 July 1999 drawing up the **list of regions covered by Objective 1 of the Structural Funds** for the period 2000 to 2006 (notified under document number C(1999) 1770)
Official Journal L 194 , 27/07/1999 P. 0053 - 0057

MAIN PROVISIONS

Article 1
The regions covered by Objective 1 shall be those listed in Annex I.
This list shall be valid from 1 January 2000 to 31 December 2006.

Article 2
The regions and areas to receive transitional support under Objective 1 shall be those listed in Annex II.
This list shall be valid from 1 January 2000 to 31 December 2005 or 31 December 2006, respectively, for the regions listed therein.

ANNEX I

List of NUTS II regions covered by Objective 1 of the Structural Funds for the period from 1 January 2000 to 31 December 2006

Germany
Brandenburg
Mecklenburg-Vorpommern
Chemnitz
Dresden
Leipzig
Dessau
Halle
Magdeburg
Thüringen

Greece
Anatoliki Makedonia, Thraki
Kentriki Makedonia
Dytiki Makedonia
Thessalia
Ipiros
Ionia Nisia
Dytiki Ellada
Sterea Ellada
Peloponnisos
Attiki
Vorio Aigaio
Notio Aigaio
Kriti

Spain
Galicia
Principado de Asturias
Castilla y León
Castilla-La Mancha
Extremadura
Comunidad Valenciana
Andalucía
Región de Murcia

Ceuta y Melilla
Canarias

France
Guadeloupe
Martinique
Guyane
Réunion

Ireland
Border Midlands and Western

Italy
Campania
Puglia
Basilicata
Calabria
Sicilia
Sardegna

Austria
Burgenland

Portugal
Norte
Centro
Alentejo
Algarve
Açores
Madeira

Finland
Itä-Suomi
Väli-Suomi(1)
Pohjois-Suomi(2)

Sweden
Norra Mellansverige(3)
Mellersta Norrland(4)
Övre Norrland(5)

United Kingdom
South Yorkshire
West Wales and The Valleys
Cornwall and Isles of Scilly
Merseyside

(1) Only the areas listed in Annex I to Protocol 6 annexed to the Act of Accession of Austria, Finland and Sweden.
(2) Only the areas listed in Annex I to Protocol 6 annexed to the Act of Accession of Austria, Finland and Sweden.
(3) Only the areas listed in Annex I to Protocol 6 annexed to the Act of Accession of Austria, Finland and Sweden.
(4) Only the areas listed in Annex I to Protocol 6 annexed to the Act of Accession of Austria, Finland and Sweden.
(5) Only the areas listed in Annex I to Protocol 6 annexed to the Act of Accession of Austria, Finland and Sweden.

Annex 3.5.

1999/505/EC: Commission decision of 1 July 1999 fixing an indicative allocation by Member State of the **commitment appropriations for Objective 3** of the Structural Funds for the period 2000 to 2006
Official Journal L 194 , 27/07/1999 P. 0053 - 0057

MAIN PROVISIONS

Article 1
The indicative amounts per Member State of the commitment appropriations for Objective 3 for 2000 to 2006 shall be as set out in the Annex.

Article 2
This Decision is addressed to the Member States.
Done at Brussels, 1 July 1999.
For the Commission
Pádraig FLYNN
Member of the Commission
(1) OJ L 161, 26.6.1999, p. 1.
EN Official Journal of the European Communities 27. 7. 1999 L 194/64

ANNEX
Indicative allocation by Member State of the commitment appropriationsfor Objective 3 of the Structural Funds
for the period 2000 to 2006 - *(EUR million (1999 prices))*

Member State Appropriations:

Belgium 737
Denmark 365
Germany 4581
Greece —
Spain 2140
France 4540
Ireland —
Italy 3744
Luxembourg 38
Netherlands 1686
Austria 528
Portugal —
Finland 403
Sweden 720
United Kingdom 4568
Total 24 050

Annex 3.6.

Regulation (EC) No 1783/1999 of the European Parliament and of the Council of 12 June 1999 on the **European Regional Development Fund**
Official Journal L 213 , 13/08/1999 p. 0001 - 0004

MAIN PROVISIONS

Article 1: Tasks

Pursuant to Article 160 of the Treaty and Regulation (EC) No 1260/1999, the European Regional Development Fund (ERDF) shall contribute towards the financing of assistance as defined in Article 9 of that Regulation to promote economic and social cohesion by correcting the main regional imbalances and participating in the development and conversion of regions.
To that end, the ERDF shall also contribute to promoting sustainable development and the creation of sustainable jobs.

Article 2: Scope

1. As part of its tasks as defined in Article 1, the ERDF shall contribute towards the financing of:
(a) productive investment to create and safeguard sustainable jobs;
(b) investment in infrastructure:
(i) which, in regions covered by Objective 1, helps to increase the economic potential, development, structural adjustment and creation or maintenance of sustainable jobs in those regions, including investment in infrastructure contributing to the establishment and development of trans-European networks in the areas of transport, telecommunications and energy infrastructures taking into account the need to link to the central regions of the Community regions suffering from a structural handicap because of their insular, landlocked or peripheral status;
(ii) which, in regions and areas covered by Objectives 1 and 2 or the Community initiatives referred to in Article 20(1)(a) and (b) of Regulation (EC) No 1260/1999, concerns the diversification of economic sites and industrial areas suffering from decline, the renewal of depressed urban areas and the revitalisation of and improved access to rural areas and areas dependent on fisheries; instruments in infrastructure where modernisation or regeneration is a prerequisite for the creation or development of job-creating economic activities, including infrastructure links on which the development of such activities depends;
(c) the development of endogenous potential by measures which encourage and support local development and employment initiatives and the activities of small and medium-sized enterprises, involving in particular:
(i) assistance towards services for enterprises, in particular in the fields of management, market studies and research and services common to several enterprises,
(ii) financing the transfer of technology, including in particular the collection and dissemination of information, common organisation between enterprises and research establishments and financing the implementation of innovation in enterprises,
(iii) improvement of access by enterprises to finance and loans, by creating and developing appropriate financing instruments, as referred to in Article 28 of Regulation (EC) No 1260/1999,
(iv) direct aid to investment as defined in Article 28(3) of Regulation (EC) No 1260/1999 where no aid scheme exists,
(v) the provision of infrastructure on a scale appropriate to local and employment development,
(vi) aid for structures providing neighbourhood services to create new jobs but excluding measures financed by the European Social Fund (ESF);
(d) technical assistance measures as referred to in the second subparagraph of Article 2(4) of Regulation (EC) No 1260/1999.
In the regions designated under Objective 1, the ERDF may contribute towards the financing of investment in education and health that is beneficial to the regions' structural adjustment.
2. In application of paragraph 1, the financial contribution of the ERDF shall support, inter alia, the following:
(a) the productive environment, in particular to increase competitiveness and sustainable investment by firms, especially the small and medium-sized enterprises, and to make regions more attractive, particularly by improving the standard of their infrastructure;
(b) research and technological development with a view to promoting the introduction of new technologies and innovation and the strengthening of research and technological development capacities contributing to regional development;
(c) the development of the information society;

(d) the development of tourism and cultural investment, including the protection of cultural and natural heritage, provided that they are creating sustainable jobs;
(e) the protection and improvement of the environment, in particular taking account of the principles of precaution and preventative action in support of economic development, the clean and efficient utilisation of energy and the development of renewable energy sources;
(f) equality between women and men in the field of employment, principally through the establishment of firms and through infrastructure or services enabling the reconciliation of family and working life;
(g) transnational, cross-border and inter-regional cooperation on sustainable regional and local development.

Article 3: Community initiative

1. Pursuant to Article 20 of Regulation (EC) No 1260/1999, the ERDF shall, in accordance with Article 21 of that Regulation, contribute to the implementation of the Community initiative for cross-border, transnational and inter-regional cooperation intended to encourage the harmonious, balanced and sustainable development of the whole of the Community's territory ("Interreg") as well as to the implementation of the Community initiative for economic and social regeneration of cities and urban neighbourhoods in crisis with a view to promoting sustainable urban development ("URBAN").
2. In accordance with Article 21(2) of Regulation (EC) No 1260/1999, the scope laid down in paragraph 1 of this Article shall be extended by the decision on the Funds' contribution to the financing of measures eligible under Regulations (EC) No 1784/1999(8), (EC) No 1257/1999(9) and (EC) No 1263/1999(10) with a view to implementing all the measures set out in the Community initiative programme concerned.

Article 4: Innovative measures

1. In accordance with Article 22(1) of Regulation (EC) No 1260/1999, the ERDF may also contribute to financing:
(a) studies initiated by the Commission to identify and analyse regional development problems and solutions, particularly with a view to the harmonious, balanced and sustainable development of the whole of the Community's territory, including the European Spatial Development Perspective;
(b) pilot projects to identify or test new regional and local development solutions with a view to their inclusion in assistance after demonstration of their feasibility;
(c) exchanges of experience relating to innovation with the aim of turning to account and transferring experience gained in the regional or local development field.
2. In accordance with Article 22(2) of Regulation (EC) No 1260/1999, the scope laid down in paragraph 1 of this Article shall be extended by the decision on the Funds' contribution to the financing of measures eligible under Regulations (EC) No 1784/1999, (EC) No 1257/1999 and (EC) No 1263/1999 with a view to implementing all the measures in the pilot project concerned.

Article 5: Implementing rules

Any detailed implementing rules for this Regulation shall be adopted by the Commission in accordance with the procedure laid down in Article 48 of Regulation (EC) No 1260/1999.

Article 6: Repeal

Regulation (EEC) No 4254/88 shall be repealed with effect from 1 January 2000.
References to the repealed Regulation shall be construed as references to this Regulation.

Article 7: Review clause

On a proposal from the Commission, the European Parliament and the Council shall review this Regulation by 31 December 2006.
They shall act on this proposal in accordance with the procedure laid down in Article 162 of the Treaty.

Annex 3.7.

Council Regulation (EC) No 1267/1999 of 21 June 1999 establishing an **Instrument for Structural Policies for Pre-accession**
Official Journal L 161 , 26/06/1999 P. 0073 - 0086

MAIN PROVISIONS

Article 1: Definition and objective

1. The Instrument for Structural Policies for Pre-accession, hereinafter referred to as "ISPA" is hereby established.
ISPA shall provide assistance to contribute to the preparation for accession to the European Union of the following applicant countries: Bulgaria, Czech Republic, Estonia, Hungary, Latvia, Lithuania, Poland, Romania, Slovakia and Slovenia, hereinafter referred to as the "beneficiary countries", in the area of economic and social cohesion, concerning environment and transport policies in accordance with the provisions of this Regulation.
2. The Community assistance granted under ISPA shall contribute to the objectives laid down in the Accession Partnership for each beneficiary country and to corresponding national programmes for the improvement of the environment and of transport infrastructure networks.

Article 2: Eligible measures

1. The Community assistance financed under ISPA shall include projects, stages of a project which are technically and financially independent, groups of projects or project schemes in the field of environment or transport, hereinafter referred to collectively as "measures". A stage of a project may also cover preliminary, feasibility and technical studies needed for carrying out a project.
2. The Community shall provide assistance under ISPA in the light of the objectives mentioned in Article 1 for the following:
(a) environmental measures enabling the beneficiary countries to comply with the requirements of Community environmental law and with the objectives of the Accession Partnerships;
(b) transport infrastructure measures which promote sustainable mobility, and in particular those that constitute projects of common interest based on the criteria of Decision No 1692/96/EC and those which enable the beneficiary countries to comply with the objectives of the Accession Partnerships; this includes interconnection and interoperability of national networks as well as with the trans-European networks together with access to such networks.
Measures shall be of a sufficient scale to have a significant impact in the field of environmental protection or in the improvement of transport infrastructure networks. The total cost of each measure shall in principle not be less than EUR 5 million. In duly justified cases, taking into account the specific circumstances concerned, the total cost of a measure may be less than EUR 5 million.
3. A balance shall be struck between measures in the field of the environment and measures relating to transport infrastructure.
4. Assistance may also be granted for:
(a) preliminary studies related to eligible measures, including those necessary for their implementation, and
(b) technical support measures, including information and publicity actions, particularly:
(i) horizontal measures such as comparative studies to assess the impact of Community assistance;
(ii) measures and studies which contribute to the appraisal, monitoring, evaluation or control of projects and to strengthening and ensuring the coordination and consistency of projects with the Accession Partnerships, and
(iii) measures and studies to ensure effective project management and implementation and to make any necessary adjustments.

Article 3: Financial resources

Community assistance under ISPA shall be granted during the period from 2000 to 2006.
The annual appropriations shall be authorised by the budgetary authority within the limits of the financial perspectives.

Article 4: Indicative allocation

An indicative allocation between beneficiary countries of the total Community assistance under ISPA shall be made by the Commission, acting in accordance with the procedure laid down in Article 14, on the basis of the

criteria of population, per capita GDP in purchasing power parities and surface area.
This allocation may be adjusted to take account of the performance in previous years of each of the beneficiary countries in implementing ISPA measures. Due account shall also be taken of the countries' respective deficiencies in environment and transport infrastructure.

Article 5: Compatibility with Community policies

1. Measures financed by the Community under ISPA shall comply with the provisions set out in the Europe Agreements, including the implementing rules for the application of the provisions on State aids, and shall contribute to the achievement of Community policies, particularly those concerning environmental protection and improvement, transport and trans-European networks.
2. The Commission shall ensure coordination and consistency between measures undertaken pursuant to this Regulation and measures undertaken with contributions from the Community budget, including contributions from Community initiatives for cross-border transnational and interregional cooperation, the operations of the European Investment Bank (EIB), including through its pre-accession facility as well as the other financial instruments of the Community and inform the Committee established under Article 14 hereof.
3. The Commission shall seek coordination and consistency between measures undertaken in the beneficiary countries pursuant to this Regulation and the operations of the European Bank for Reconstruction and Development (EBRD), the World Bank and other such financial institutions and inform the Committee established under Article 14 hereof.

Article 6: Forms and rate of assistance

1. Community assistance under ISPA may take the form of non-repayable direct assistance, repayable assistance or any other form of assistance.
Assistance repaid to the managing authority or to another public authority shall be reapplied for the same purpose.
2. The rate of Community assistance granted under ISPA may be up to 75 % of public or equivalent expenditure, including expenditure by bodies whose activities are undertaken within an administrative or legal framework by virtue of which they are regarded as equivalent to public bodies. The Commission may decide, in accordance with the procedure laid down in Article 14, to increase this rate to up to 85 %, in particular where it considers that a rate higher than 75 % is required for realising projects essential for achieving the general objectives of ISPA.
Save in the case of repayable assistance or when there is a substantial Community interest, the rate of assistance shall be reduced to take into account:
(a) the availability of co-financing;
(b) the measure's capacity to generate revenues, and
(c) an appropriate application of the polluter-pays principle.
3. Measures which generate revenues in accordance with paragraph 2(b) shall be those concerning:
(a) infrastructure the use of which involves fees borne by users;
(b) productive investments in the environment sector.
4. Preliminary studies and technical support measure, may be financed exceptionally at 100 % of the total cost. Total expenditure carried out at the Commission's initiative or on behalf of the Commission pursuant to this paragraph may not exceed 2 % of the total allocation to ISPA.

Article 7: Appraisal and approval of measures

1. The Commission shall adopt decisions on the measures to be financed under ISPA in accordance with the procedure laid down in Article 14.
2. The beneficiary countries shall submit applications for assistance to the Commission. However, the Commission may grant assistance pursuant to Article 2(4) on its own initiative, where there is an overriding Community interest.
3. Applications shall contain:
(a) the information set out in Annex I;
(b) all relevant information proving that the measures comply with this Regulation and with the criteria set out in Annex II, and in particular that there are medium-term economic and social benefits commensurate with the resources deployed.
4. On receipt of an application for assistance and before approving a measure, the Commission shall carry out a thorough appraisal in order to assess the measure's compliance with the criteria set out in Annex II.
5. Commission decisions approving measures shall determine the amount of financial assistance and lay down a

financing plan together with all the provisions and conditions necessary for the implementation of the measures.
6. The combined assistance under ISPA and other Community aid for a measure shall not exceed 90 % of the total expenditure relating to that measure.
7. The Commission shall adopt common rules for the eligibility of expenditure in accordance with the procedure laid down in Article 14.

Article 8: Commitments and payments

1. The Commission shall implement expenditure under ISPA in accordance with the Financial Regulation applicable to the general budget of the European Communities on the basis of the financing memorandum to be drawn up between the Commission and the beneficiary country.
However, annual budgetary commitments in respect of assistance granted to measures shall be carried out in one of the following two ways:
(a) commitments in respect of the measures referred to in Article 2(2) to be carried out over a period of two or more years shall, as a general rule and subject to point (b), be effected in annual instalments.
The commitments in respect of the first annual instalment shall be made when the financing memorandum is drawn up. Commitments in respect of subsequent annual instalments shall be based on the initial or revised financing plan for the measure and in principle be granted at the start of each financial year and at the latest by 1 April of the year in question according to forecast expenditure for this year;
(b) for measures with a duration of less than two years or for which the Community assistance does not exceed EUR 20 million a first commitment of up to 80 % of the assistance granted may take place when the financing memorandum is drawn up. The remainder will be committed subject to the state of the implementation of the measure.
2. Except in duly justified cases, assistance granted to a measure where substantial work has not begun within the specified contractual period shall be cancelled.
3. Payments of financial assistance for measures may take the form either of advances or of intermediate payments or payments of balances in respect of expenditure certified and actually paid.
The Commission shall adopt detailed rules on payments in accordance with the procedure laid down in Article 14.
4. The details of the payment mechanism for measures shall be laid down in the financing memorandum with each beneficiary country.

Article 9: Management and control

1. The Commission shall require the beneficiary countries:
(a) to establish as from 1 January 2000 and in any event not later than 1 January 2002, management and control systems which ensure:
(i) the proper implementation of the assistance granted under this Regulation in accordance with the principles of sound financial management,
(ii) the separation of the functions of management and control,
(iii) that expenditure declarations presented to the Commission are accurate and emanate from accounting systems based on supporting documents which are open to verification;
(b) to verify on a regular basis that the measures financed by the Community have been properly carried out;
(c) to prevent irregularities and take action against them;
(d) to recover any amounts lost as a result of irregularity or negligence.
2. Without prejudice to checks carried out by beneficiary countries, the Commission and the Court of Auditors may, through their own staff or duly authorised representatives, carry out on-the-spot technical or financial audits, including sample checks and final audits.
3. The detailed implementing provisions of the principles established in paragraphs 1 and 2 shall be contained in the financing memorandum, together with arrangements for cooperation and for coordination of programming and methodology of control between the Commission and the beneficiary country. The Commission shall inform the Committee established under Article 14 hereof.
4. The financing memorandum shall also contain provisions concerning the reduction, suspension and cancellation of assistance where the implementation of a measure does not justify either a part or the whole of the assistance allocated.
5. In implementing this Regulation, the Commission shall ensure that the principles of sound financial management are adhered to, with particular reference to the elements set out in Annex III.

Article 10: Use of the euro

1. The amounts in the applications for assistance, together with the relevant financing plan, shall be expressed in euro.
2. The amounts of assistance and the financing plans approved by the Commission shall be expressed in euro.
3. Declarations of expenditure in support of the corresponding payment applications shall be expressed in euro.
4. Payments of financial assistance by the Commission shall be made in euro to the authority designated by the beneficiary country to receive such payments.

Article 11: Monitoring and ex-post evaluation

The beneficiary countries and the Commission shall ensure that the implementation of measures under this Regulation is monitored and evaluated in accordance with the provisions in Annex IV.

Article 12: Annual report

The Commission shall present an annual report on Community assistance granted under ISPA to the European Parliament, the Council, the Economic and Social Committee and the Committee of the Regions. The annual report shall contain the information set out in Annex V.
The European Parliament shall deliver an opinion on the report within three months. The Commission shall report on the manner in which that opinion has been taken into account.
The Commission shall ensure that the beneficiary countries are regularly informed of the activities of ISPA.

Article 13: Information and publicity

1. The beneficiary countries responsible for implementing measures for which the Community has granted financial assistance under ISPA shall ensure that adequate publicity is given to the measure with a view to:
(a) making the general public aware of the role played by the Community in relation to the measures;
(b) making potential beneficiaries and professional organisations aware of the possibilities afforded by the measures.
Beneficiary countries shall ensure, in particular, that directly visible display panels are erected showing that the measures are being co-financed by the Community, together with the Community logo, and that representatives of the Community institutions are duly involved in the most important public activities connected with Community assistance granted under ISPA.
They shall inform the Commission annually of the initiatives taken under this paragraph.
2. The Commission shall adopt detailed rules on information and publicity acting in accordance with the procedure laid down in Article 14.
It shall inform the European Parliament thereof and shall publish them in the Official Journal of the European Communities.

Article 14: Committee

1. The Commission shall be assisted by a Management committee composed of the representatives of the Member States and chaired by the representative of the Commission, hereinafter referred to as "the Committee". The European Investment Bank shall appoint a non-voting representative.
2. The representative of the Commission shall submit to the Committee a draft of the measures to be taken. The Committee shall deliver its opinion on the draft, within a time limit which the Chairman may lay down, according to the urgency of the matter. The opinion shall be delivered by the majority laid down in Article 205(2) of the Treaty in the case of decisions which the Council is required to adopt on a proposal from the Commission. The votes of the representatives of the Member States within the Committee shall be weighted in the manner set out in that Article. The Chairman shall not vote.
3. (a) The Commission shall adopt measures which shall apply immediately.
(b) However, if these measures are not in accordance with the opinion of the Committee, they shall be communicated by the Commission to the Council forthwith. In that event:
- the Commission shall defer application of the measures which it has decided for a period to be laid down in each act adopted by the Council but which may in no case exceed three months from the date of communication,
- the Council, acting by a qualified majority, may take a differnet decision within the time-limit referred to in the preceding indent.
4. The Committee may examine any question relating to the implementation of this Regulation which is put to it by its Chairman, including at the request of the representative of a Member State.

5. The Committee shall adopt its rules of procedure by a qualified majority.

Article 15: Reallocation of resources

On accession to the European Union, a country shall lose its entitlement to support under this Regulation. Resources made available as a result of an applicant country acceding to the European Union shall be reallocated to other applicant countries listed in Article 1(1). Reallocation shall be based on applicant countries' need and capacity for absorbing assistance and on the criteria laid down in Article 4.
The Council, acting by qualified majority on a proposal from the Commission, shall take a decision outlining the general approach for reallocation.
In the light of the decision referred to in the second paragraph by the Council, the Commission shall decide on the reallocation of available resources among the other beneficiaries in accordance with the procedure laid down in Article 14.

Article 16: Final and transitional provisions

The Council, acting on a proposal from the Commission, shall re-examine this Regulation by 31 December 2006. It shall act on the proposal in accordance with the procedure laid down in Article 308 of the Treaty.

Chapter 4

THE RIGHTS OF EU WORKERS AND CITIZENS

In their great majority citizens ignore the many rights that they have acquired thanks to European integration, some of which are founded directly on the EC and EU Treaties, while most are based on the policies and the legislation derived from them[1]. The fact is that, since the economic activities of the Member States are considerably guided by European law, the activities of individual citizens are influenced and administered to a large extent by the European policies which dictate that law.

4.1. Fundamental rights of workers

The Treaty of Rome aimed mainly at the free movement of workers and relied above all on the functioning of the common market to improve living and working conditions in all Member States. In line with the reform of the Structural Funds, which constituted the financial side of economic and social cohesion, the European Council, despite the opposition of Mrs. Thatcher, who was then Prime Minister of the United Kingdom, agreed in December 1989 on the Community Charter of the fundamental rights of workers, which represented the legal side of social cohesion and stressed particularly the alignment of social standards in the Member States: social protection; freedom of association and of collective bargaining; equal treatment for men and women; information, consultation and participation of workers; the protection of health and safety at the workplace; and the protection of children and adolescents, the elderly and the disabled. The Commission, which had proposed the Charter, proposed immediately after its adoption by the majority of heads of State of Government, a series of Community laws in order to implement it. But due to the unanimity rule required and the negative position of the United Kingdom, very few social measures were adopted before the completion of the internal market, which they should in principle follow in step. In order to get out of the impasse, eleven (out of the then twelve Member States), on the one hand, and the United Kingdom, on the other, signed at Maastricht a Social Protocol allowing the former to adopt alone the social measures that they deemed useful.

However, the anomaly of a common policy where one Member State did not share the others' objectives was corrected at Amsterdam, in June 1997, when the Labour British Government decided to accede to the social provisions of the new Treaty and to accept the Directives that had already been agreed under the Social Agreement. Protocol N° 14 on social policy annexed to the TEC and the Agreement on social policy attached thereto were repealed. The new Chapter 4 on Social Policy of the TEC incorporates most of the provisions of the Maastricht Social Agreement, notably: the objectives of the Community Charter of the Fundamental Social Rights of Workers and the measures to achieve those objectives.

[1] Moussis (2004), chapter 9.

It should be noted that the Community Charter of the Fundamental Social Rights of Workers of 1989 was surpassed by the Charter of Fundamental Rights of the European Union solemnly proclaimed in Nice, on 7 December 2000, by the European Parliament, the Council and the Commission [see section 4.2.]. The 2000 Charter exceeds the 1989 Charter, on the one hand, because it guarantees not only social rights but all rights and freedoms of the citizens of the Union and, on the other, because it is an official document agreed by all Member States whereas, as seen above, the Social Charter was not agreed by the United Kingdom.

4.2. Fundamental rights of citizens

Article 6 of the TEU states that the Union is founded on the principles of liberty, democracy, respect for human rights and fundamental freedoms, and the rule of law. While respecting the national identities of its Member States, the Union must respect fundamental rights, as they result from the constitutional traditions common to the Member States, as general principle of Community law. The EC Treaty explicitly acknowledges that human rights include economic and social rights, and lays down the principle of equal rights for citizens without discrimination based on sex, racial or ethnic origin, religion or belief, disability, age or sexual orientation (Art. 13 TEC). Upon a proposal from one-third of the Member States, the Parliament or the Commission, the Council, acting by a four-fifths majority of its members and with the assent of Parliament, can declare that a clear danger exists of a Member State committing a serious breach of fundamental rights and address to that Member State appropriate recommendations.

Protection of fundamental rights is a founding principle of the Union and an indispensable prerequisite for its legitimacy. The Cologne European Council (3 and 4 June 1999) concluded that there was a need to establish a charter of fundamental rights in order to make their overriding importance and relevance more visible to the Union's citizens. The charter, which was officially proclaimed at the Nice European Council (7-9 December 2000) by the European Parliament, the Council and the Commission, is divided into chapters dealing with the universal values of human dignity, freedom, equality, solidarity, citizenship and justice[1] [see annex 4.1.]. It is designed to make more visible and explicit to the European Union's citizens the fundamental rights, which are already derived from a variety of international and Community sources, such as the European Convention on Human Rights, the Community Treaties and the case-law of the Court of Justice. Alongside the standard civil and political rights and the rights of citizens deriving from the Community Treaties, the charter incorporates fundamental social and economic rights, such as the rights of workers to collective bargaining, to take strike action and to be informed and consulted. The charter is likely to become mandatory through the Court of Justice's interpretation of it as belonging to the general principles of Community law[2].

The Treaty of Nice (following the Treaty of Amsterdam) establishes the citizenship of the Union, which is complementary to national citizenship. Every person holding the nationality of a Member State is a citizen of the Union. Citizens of the Union, thus defined, enjoy the rights conferred by the Treaty and are subject to the duties imposed thereby (Art. 17 TEC). Every citizen of the Union is, in the territory of a third country in which the Member State of which he or she is a national is not represented, entitled to protection by the diplomatic or consular authorities of any Member State, on the same conditions as the nationals of that State (Art. 20 TEC). Two Decisions specify the **right to diplomatic protection**[3]. This right is not negligible, as there are many cases where one Member State is not represented in a third country. It includes assistance in the event

[1] Solemn proclamation, OJ C 364, 18.12.2000.
[2] COM(2000) 644, 11 October 2000.
[3] Decision 95/553/EC, OJ L 314, 28.12.1995.

of death, illness or serious accident, arrest, detention or assault as well as help and repatriation in the event of difficulty. In practical terms, EU nationals whose passport or travel document is lost, stolen or temporarily unavailable in a country where their own Member State has no representation, may obtain an **emergency travel document**, from the diplomatic or consular representation of another Member State[1].

In addition, every citizen of the Union residing in a Member State of which he or she is not a national has the right to vote and to stand as a candidate at European and municipal elections in the Member State in which he resides, under the same conditions as nationals of that State (Art. 19 TEC). Community directives lay down arrangements for the exercise of the right to vote and to stand as a candidate in elections to the European Parliament in the Member State of residence[2]. While including provisions to ensure freedom of choice and to prevent individuals from voting or standing for election in two constituencies at once, the Directive is based on the principles of equality and non-discrimination and is designed to facilitate the exercise by the citizens of the Union of their right to vote and to stand for election in the Member State where they reside.

With the emergence of information systems spanning the entire internal market, the European Union has increasingly to concentrate on the **protection of the personal data** of its citizens. Thus a Directive aims at the development of the information society and the service sector in the EU, while guaranteeing individuals a high level of protection with regard to the processing of personal data (safe harbour privacy principles)[3] [see annex 4.2.]. Accordingly, it imposes obligations on data controllers such as public authorities, companies and associations, and establishes rights for data subjects, such as the right to be informed of processing carried out, the right of access to data and the right to ask for data to be corrected. In any event, the Directive prohibits the processing of sensitive data, such as data revealing racial or ethnic origin, political opinions, religious or philosophical beliefs, or state of health, except in certain circumstances that are exhaustively listed, in particular when the data subject has given his explicit consent or where a substantial public interest requires such processing (e.g. medical or scientific research). Community legal acts on the protection of individuals with regard to the processing of personal data and the free movement of such data apply to Community institutions and bodies[4]. An independent supervisory body, the European Data Protection Supervisor, monitors the application of the relevant rules[5].

Publicly available electronic communications services over the Internet open new possibilities for users but also new risks for their personal data and privacy, in particular with regard to the increasing capacity for automated storage and processing of data relating to subscribers and users. Therefore, a Directive on **privacy and electronic communications** harmonises the provisions of the Member States required to ensure an equivalent level of protection of fundamental rights and freedoms, and in particular the right to privacy, with respect to the processing of personal data in the electronic communication sector and to ensure the free movement of such data and of electronic communication equipment and services in the Community[6].

The average citizen may think that fundamental freedoms are a normal attribute of any democratic State; not particularly of the European Union. This is certainly right, but the EU guarantees that a State that does not respect the fundamental freedoms of its citizens cannot become a member and that the government of a Member State cannot injure its citizens' rights, if it does not want to exclude its country from the Union. Indeed, Article 49 of the TEU makes membership of

1 Decision 96/409/CFSP, OJ L 168, 06.07.1996.
2 Directive 93/109, OJ L 329, 30.12.1993.
3 Directive 95/46, OJ L 281, 23.11.1995.
4 Regulation 45/2001, OJ L 8, 12.01.2001.
5 Decision 1247/2002, OJ L 183, 12.07.2002.
6 Directive 2002/58, OJ L 201, 31.07.2002.

the Union conditional upon the respect of the principles set out in Article 6 and Article 7 (TEU) provides action in the event of a breach by a Member State of the principles on which the Union is founded. The Council, in the composition of the Heads of State or Government, acting by unanimity, but without taking into account the vote of the representative of the Member State concerned, may determine the existence of a serious and persistent breach by a Member State of those principles. Where such a determination has been made, the Council, acting by a qualified majority, may decide to suspend certain of the rights deriving from the application of the Treaty to the State in question, including its voting rights in the Council. In view of the strong upward tendency of extremist movements in some countries, these precautionary measures of the Union are not at all superfluous or theoretical.

4.3. Other rights of EU citizens

In addition to the fundamental rights, as defined in the Charter of the Union and in the European Convention for the Protection of Human Rights and Fundamental Freedoms signed in Rome on 4 November 1950, the citizens of the European Union have many rights, some of which they are not even aware of because they appear obvious. Their self-evident nature is a consequence of the existence of the Union and the membership of their State of origin to it. The Court of Justice has established that Community law, independent from the legislation of the Member States, can create obligations and rights for individuals[1]. These rights are so numerous that it would be tedious to list them all here. **Almost all the provisions of Community law create rights** and obligations for the citizens of the EU's Member States, particularly as regards professional activities. The weight of this law is growing as European integration marches forward. It is superimposed on national law and in many cases simply replaces it. It therefore has growing influence over the professional and day-to-day lives of European citizens.

Some examples may illustrate the importance of Community law for the **professional activities** of citizens. Traders have the right to consider the entire European Union as a potential market and therefore to purchase in any of the Member States and sell anywhere in the Union without any import duties or quantitative restrictions[2]. Workers have the right to seek employment anywhere they wish in the Union, set up home with their family in the country where they are working and remain there even after they have lost their job [see sections 4.2 and 5.1.]; they have the right to exactly the same social benefits as the citizens of the Member State in which they are residing [see section 5.1.2.]. Businessmen and non salaried workers have the right to be treated without discrimination by the public authorities of all Member States concerning all their professional activities, including the procedures for the award of public supply or works contracts. Farmers have the right to guaranteed prices for their produce and therefore to a certain guarantee of income. Members of the professions - lawyers, architects, doctors and so on - have the right to set up a practice and to work in any Member State [see section 5.2.1.]. Women have the right for equal treatment with men in their professional life [see section 8.5.].

Some Community policies influence not only the professional life, but also the **everyday life** of citizens. Thus, important measures for the citizens in the fields of employment, vocational training, security at work and public health have their origin in the Community social policy. Furthermore, obligations imposed on industrialists by the Community policies of environment and consumers' protection have important effects on the quality of life of citizens. Likewise, the citizens have the right to use any banking, insurance, telecommunications and audiovisual services offered in the large European market. They have the right to be treated by the administrative or

---

1 Judgment of 5 February 1963, case 26/62, van Gend en Loos, ECR 1963, p. 1.

2 Moussis (2004), sections 5.1. and 6.2.

judicial authorities of a country of the Union in the same way as the nationals of that country, i.e. without any discrimination on grounds of nationality (Art 12 TEC). This right covers a wide range of situations and human relations such as financial, contractual, family or student, which fall within the scope of Community law[1].

One of the most important rights of European Union citizens is that of being able to **travel freely** throughout the Community. By virtue of Article 18 of the EC Treaty, every citizen of the Union has the right to move and reside freely within the territory of the Member States, subject to the conditions laid down in the Treaty and to the measures adopted to give them effect. This right has become such standard practice for the European citizen that it is forgotten that it did not exist as recently as the 1950s and still does not exist for citizens of many of the world's countries. Moreover, to ensure its effective exercise, this right has to be shored up by a range of secondary rights, guarantees of safety, simplifications of all kinds and removal of all administrative red tape. These rights and facilitations are provided by EU legislation. Thus, in the event of illness or accident in a Member State other than that of residence, EU citizens are covered by the social security system of the host country on presentation of an "E111" form, which proves their entitlement to social security cover in the country of residence [see section 5.1.2.]. Citizens of the Member States can carry a near limitless sum of currency on their intra-Community trips, whereas, before the liberalisation of capital movements they could take only limited tourist allowance. Cash dispensers in the Member States can be used by holders of cards issued by banks in other Member States and automatic dispensers of petrol, drinks, etc. accept the euro coins issued in any country of the euro zone. In the ports and airports of the Member States, special channels exist for citizens of the European Union who possess a uniform passport[2]. Checks on the car insurance green card were abolished, as were the disembarkment cards upon arrival in a partner country.

There is much overlapping between the provisions on the free movement of workers and of self-employed persons [see sections 5.1.1 and 5.2.1.] and those on the **free movement of citizens** established by the Schengen agreement and now by the EU Treaty. In fact, many EU countries signed, on June 19, 1990, the **Schengen agreement** for the abolition of border checks at the frontiers between them, the reinforcement of controls at external borders and the cooperation among their administrations. A Protocol annexed to the Treaty of Amsterdam integrates the Schengen "acquis" - i.e., the existing legislation - into the framework of the European Union[3] and allows the signatories to the Schengen Convention (the Member States of the Union minus the United Kingdom and Ireland plus Norway and Iceland[4]) to initiate between them, within the legal and institutional framework of the Union, cooperation in the areas covered by the Convention. Ireland participates in all aspects of the Schengen acquis with the exception of those elements linked to border controls, notably cross-border surveillance and hot pursuit[5]. The United Kingdom participates in cooperation in police, judicial and criminal matters, drug trafficking and the Schengen information system[6]. Persons passing internal frontiers in the Schengen area have not to go through a passport control[7]. The movement of owners of pet animals within the EU is greatly facilitated[8].

EU citizens must feel at home in all the Member States of the Union. As a consequence, the right to travel freely throughout the Union is backed up by the **right to reside** where they choose in the EU. Council Directives establish the right of workers to keep their residence in the country

1 Judgment of 12 May 1998, Case C-85/96, ECR 1998 I-2691.
2 Resolutions, OJ C 241, 19.09.1981, p. 1-7, OJ C 185, 24.07.1986, p. 1 and OJ C 200, 04.08.1995, p. 1.
3 Decisions 1999/435 and 1999/436, OJ L 176, 10.07.1999.
4 Agreement, OJ L 149, 23.06.2000.
5 Decision 2002/192, OJ L 64, 07.03.2002.
6 Decision 2000/365, OJ L 131, 01.06.2000.
7 Decision 2000/586, OJ L 248, 03.10.2000.
8 Regulation 998/2003, OJ L 146, 13.06.2003.

where they are living at the time of ceasing their professional activity and the right for members of their family to remain in this country even after the death of the worker[1]. Other directives guarantee the right of residence of employees and self-employed persons who have ceased their occupational activity, students and other Community nationals not yet covered by a Community right of residence[2] [see annex 5.10.]. By virtue of these Directives, nationals from the Member States enjoy right of residence provided that they satisfy certain conditions, notably if they themselves and the members of their families have sickness insurance covering all the risks in the host Member State. The right of residence in any Member State is made tangible by a number of Community Regulations abolishing work permits and guaranteeing migrant workers and members of their families entitlement to social security and trade union rights, vocational training, free education for their children and, in general, the same treatment as national workers [see section 5.1.]. It has been teamed up with a number of practical measures such as the mutual recognition of driving licences[3].

4.4. The defence of citizens' rights

Citizens should be conscious of their rights, some of which were mentioned above, to be able to defend them when they think that a Member State is not respecting them. They should also know that they are entitled to **defend their rights** acquired through Community law. They can do so by taking their case to the national courts, which can either issue a ruling or turn to the Court of Justice for a preliminary ruling[4], or by simply and inexpensively lodging a complaint with the Commission or a petition with the European Parliament (Art. 21 and 194 TEC). The Parliament has a Committee on Petitions which examines the complaints of citizens, mainly relating to social security, the recognition of professional qualifications or environment protection[5]. If the complaint concerns instances of mismanagement in the activities of the Community institutions or bodies, the citizen may address himself or herself to the **Ombudsman** appointed by the European Parliament (Art. 21 and 195 TEC)[6].

Regardless of whether they are lodged with it or with the Parliament, the Commission is obliged to examine the **grievances of citizens**, which number around one thousand per year. Sometimes they are not justified and the Commission must explain to the citizen why this is the case. Not infrequently, however, they are justified and the Commission must address the Member State in question and ask it for explanations. If it does not get a good answer it must formally ask the Member State to correct its legislation or administrative practices which are causing injury to one or several citizens either of the State in question or of another Member State. If the Member State does not come into step with Community law as requested by the Commission, the latter must take the State to the Court of Justice, which will give a final ruling on the obligations of the Member State. According to the Court, the Member States are obliged to compensate for damage caused to individuals by violations of Community law attributable to them[7]. The citizens of the European Union therefore have powerful means at their disposal to obtain justice under Community law. They are sometimes more favoured than if they were just citizens of an individual State, for they can go beyond national judicial bodies to international ones in order to defend their rights and interests.

---

1 Directive 68/360, OJ L 257, 19.10.1968.
2 Directives 90/364, 90/365 and 90/366, OJ L 180, 13.07.1990 and Directive 93/96, OJ L 317, 18.12.1993.
3 Directive 91/439, OJ L 237, 24.08.1991 and Directive 2003/59, OJ L 226, 10.09.2003.
4 Judgment of 25 July 2002, Case C-50/00 P, Unión de Pequeños Agricultores v Council, ECR 2002, p. I-6677.
5 Resolution, OJ C 175, 16.07.1990, p. 214.
6 Decision 94/114, OJ L 54, 25.02.1994, Decision 94/262, OJ L 113, 04.05.1994 and Decision 2002/262, OJ L 92, 09.04.2002.
7 Judgment of November 19, 1991 in the joint cases C-6/90 and C-9/90, Francovich, ECR 1991, p. I-5357.

It goes without saying that if they are to defend these rights, they must be aware of them. The fact is that the vast majority of the citizens of the Member States are not **aware of their rights as citizens** of the European Union. The task of informing them therefore falls both to national and Community authorities, which are not very active in this area. The **information deficit**, which is a serious problem of the European Union[1], weakens the defence of citizens' rights. On the contrary, the multinational human networks, which are growing in number and influence in the Union[2], may, among other things, defend the rights of citizens of different Member States.

[1] Moussis (2004), section 10.1.2.
[2] Ibid, section 9.4.

THE RIGHTS OF EU WORKERS AND CITIZENS

Annex 4.1.

Charter of fundamental rights of the European Union
Official Journal C 364 , 18/12/2000 P. 0001 - 0022

PREAMBLE

The peoples of Europe, in creating an ever closer union among them, are resolved to share a peaceful future based on common values.
Conscious of its spiritual and moral heritage, the Union is founded on the indivisible, universal values of human dignity, freedom, equality and solidarity; it is based on the principles of democracy and the rule of law. It places the individual at the heart of its activities, by establishing the citizenship of the Union and by creating an area of freedom, security and justice.
The Union contributes to the preservation and to the development of these common values while respecting the diversity of the cultures and traditions of the peoples of Europe as well as the national identities of the Member States and the organisation of their public authorities at national, regional and local levels; it seeks to promote balanced and sustainable development and ensures free movement of persons, goods, services and capital, and the freedom of establishment.
To this end, it is necessary to strengthen the protection of fundamental rights in the light of changes in society, social progress and scientific and technological developments by making those rights more visible in a Charter.
This Charter reaffirms, with due regard for the powers and tasks of the Community and the Union and the principle of subsidiarity, the rights as they result, in particular, from the constitutional traditions and international obligations common to the Member States, the Treaty on European Union, the Community Treaties, the European Convention for the Protection of Human Rights and Fundamental Freedoms, the Social Charters adopted by the Community and by the Council of Europe and the case-law of the Court of Justice of the European Communities and of the European Court of Human Rights.
Enjoyment of these rights entails responsibilities and duties with regard to other persons, to the human community and to future generations.
The Union therefore recognises the rights, freedoms and principles set out hereafter.

CHAPTER I - DIGNITY

Article 1: Human dignity

Human dignity is inviolable. It must be respected and protected.

Article 2: Right to life

1. Everyone has the right to life.
2. No one shall be condemned to the death penalty, or executed.

Article 3: Right to the integrity of the person

1. Everyone has the right to respect for his or her physical and mental integrity.
2. In the fields of medicine and biology, the following must be respected in particular:
- the free and informed consent of the person concerned, according to the procedures laid down by law,
- the prohibition of eugenic practices, in particular those aiming at the selection of persons,
- the prohibition on making the human body and its parts as such a source of financial gain,
- the prohibition of the reproductive cloning of human beings.

Article 4

Prohibition of torture and inhuman or degrading treatment or punishment
No one shall be subjected to torture or to inhuman or degrading treatment or punishment.

Article 5

Prohibition of slavery and forced labour
1. No one shall be held in slavery or servitude.
2. No one shall be required to perform forced or compulsory labour.
3. Trafficking in human beings is prohibited.

CHAPTER II - FREEDOMS

Article 6: Right to liberty and security

Everyone has the right to liberty and security of person.

Article 7: Respect for private and family life

Everyone has the right to respect for his or her private and family life, home and communications.

Article 8: Protection of personal data
1. Everyone has the right to the protection of personal data concerning him or her.
2. Such data must be processed fairly for specified purposes and on the basis of the consent of the person concerned or some other legitimate basis laid down by law. Everyone has the right of access to data which has been collected concerning him or her, and the right to have it rectified.
3. Compliance with these rules shall be subject to control by an independent authority.

Article 9: Right to marry and right to found a family

The right to marry and the right to found a family shall be guaranteed in accordance with the national laws governing the exercise of these rights.

Article 10: Freedom of thought, conscience and religion

1. Everyone has the right to freedom of thought, conscience and religion. This right includes freedom to change religion or belief and freedom, either alone or in community with others and in public or in private, to manifest religion or belief, in worship, teaching, practice and observance.
2. The right to conscientious objection is recognised, in accordance with the national laws governing the exercise of this right.

Article 11: Freedom of expression and information

1. Everyone has the right to freedom of expression. This right shall include freedom to hold opinions and to receive and impart information and ideas without interference by public authority and regardless of frontiers.
2. The freedom and pluralism of the media shall be respected.

Article 12: Freedom of assembly and of association

1. Everyone has the right to freedom of peaceful assembly and to freedom of association at all levels, in particular in political, trade union and civic matters, which implies the right of everyone to form and to join trade unions for the protection of his or her interests.
2. Political parties at Union level contribute to expressing the political will of the citizens of the Union.

Article 13: Freedom of the arts and sciences

The arts and scientific research shall be free of constraint. Academic freedom shall be respected.

Article 14: Right to education

1. Everyone has the right to education and to have access to vocational and continuing training.
2. This right includes the possibility to receive free compulsory education.
3. The freedom to found educational establishments with due respect for democratic principles and the right of parents to ensure the education and teaching of their children in conformity with their religious, philosophical and pedagogical convictions shall be respected, in accordance with the national laws governing the exercise of such freedom and right.

Article 15: Freedom to choose an occupation and right to engage in work

1. Everyone has the right to engage in work and to pursue a freely chosen or accepted occupation.
2. Every citizen of the Union has the freedom to seek employment, to work, to exercise the right of establishment and to provide services in any Member State.
3. Nationals of third countries who are authorised to work in the territories of the Member States are entitled to working conditions equivalent to those of citizens of the Union.

Article 16: Freedom to conduct a business

The freedom to conduct a business in accordance with Community law and national laws and practices is recognised.

Article 17: Right to property

1. Everyone has the right to own, use, dispose of and bequeath his or her lawfully acquired possessions. No one may be deprived of his or her possessions, except in the public interest and in the cases and under the conditions provided for by law, subject to fair compensation being paid in good time for their loss. The use of property may be regulated by law in so far as is necessary for the general interest.
2. Intellectual property shall be protected.

Article 18: Right to asylum

The right to asylum shall be guaranteed with due respect for the rules of the Geneva Convention of 28 July 1951 and the Protocol of 31 January 1967 relating to the status of refugees and in accordance with the Treaty establishing the European Community.

Article 19: Protection in the event of removal, expulsion or extradition

1. Collective expulsions are prohibited.
2. No one may be removed, expelled or extradited to a State where there is a serious risk that he or she would be subjected to the death penalty, torture or other inhuman or degrading treatment or punishment.

CHAPTER III - EQUALITY

Article 20: Equality before the law

Everyone is equal before the law.

Article 21: Non-discrimination

1. Any discrimination based on any ground such as sex, race, colour, ethnic or social origin, genetic features, language, religion or belief, political or any other opinion, membership of a national minority, property, birth, disability, age or sexual orientation shall be prohibited.
2. Within the scope of application of the Treaty establishing the European Community and of the Treaty on European Union, and without prejudice to the special provisions of those Treaties, any discrimination on grounds of nationality shall be prohibited.

Article 22: Cultural, religious and linguistic diversity

The Union shall respect cultural, religious and linguistic diversity.

Article 23: Equality between men and women

Equality between men and women must be ensured in all areas, including employment, work and pay.
The principle of equality shall not prevent the maintenance or adoption of measures providing for specific advantages in favour of the under-represented sex.

Article 24: The rights of the child

1. Children shall have the right to such protection and care as is necessary for their well-being. They may express their views freely. Such views shall be taken into consideration on matters which concern them in accordance with their age and maturity.
2. In all actions relating to children, whether taken by public authorities or private institutions, the child's best interests must be a primary consideration.
3. Every child shall have the right to maintain on a regular basis a personal relationship and direct contact with both his or her parents, unless that is contrary to his or her interests.

Article 25: The rights of the elderly

The Union recognises and respects the rights of the elderly to lead a life of dignity and independence and to participate in social and cultural life.

Article 26: Integration of persons with disabilities

The Union recognises and respects the right of persons with disabilities to benefit from measures designed to ensure their independence, social and occupational integration and participation in the life of the community.

CHAPTER IV - SOLIDARITY

Article 27: Workers' right to information and consultation within the undertaking

Workers or their representatives must, at the appropriate levels, be guaranteed information and consultation in good time in the cases and under the conditions provided for by Community law and national laws and practices.

Article 28: Right of collective bargaining and action

Workers and employers, or their respective organisations, have, in accordance with Community law and national laws and practices, the right to negotiate and conclude collective agreements at the appropriate levels and, in cases of conflicts of interest, to take collective action to defend their interests, including strike action.

Article 29: Right of access to placement services

Everyone has the right of access to a free placement service.

Article 30: Protection in the event of unjustified dismissal

Every worker has the right to protection against unjustified dismissal, in accordance with Community law and national laws and practices.

Article 31: Fair and just working conditions

1. Every worker has the right to working conditions which respect his or her health, safety and dignity.
2. Every worker has the right to limitation of maximum working hours, to daily and weekly rest periods and to an annual period of paid leave.

Article 32: Prohibition of child labour and protection of young people at work

The employment of children is prohibited. The minimum age of admission to employment may not be lower than the minimum school-leaving age, without prejudice to such rules as may be more favourable to young people and except for limited derogations.
Young people admitted to work must have working conditions appropriate to their age and be protected against economic exploitation and any work likely to harm their safety, health or physical, mental, moral or social development or to interfere with their education.

Article 33: Family and professional life

1. The family shall enjoy legal, economic and social protection.
2. To reconcile family and professional life, everyone shall have the right to protection from dismissal for a reason connected with maternity and the right to paid maternity leave and to parental leave following the birth or adoption of a child.

Article 34: Social security and social assistance

1. The Union recognises and respects the entitlement to social security benefits and social services providing protection in cases such as maternity, illness, industrial accidents, dependency or old age, and in the case of loss of employment, in accordance with the rules laid down by Community law and national laws and practices.
2. Everyone residing and moving legally within the European Union is entitled to social security benefits and social advantages in accordance with Community law and national laws and practices.
3. In order to combat social exclusion and poverty, the Union recognises and respects the right to social and housing assistance so as to ensure a decent existence for all those who lack sufficient resources, in accordance with the rules laid down by Community law and national laws and practices.

Article 35: Health care

Everyone has the right of access to preventive health care and the right to benefit from medical treatment under the conditions established by national laws and practices. A high level of human health protection shall be ensured in the definition and implementation of all Union policies and activities.

Article 36: Access to services of general economic interest

The Union recognises and respects access to services of general economic interest as provided for in national laws and practices, in accordance with the Treaty establishing the European Community, in order to promote the social and territorial cohesion of the Union.

Article 37: Environmental protection

A high level of environmental protection and the improvement of the quality of the environment must be integrated into the policies of the Union and ensured in accordance with the principle of sustainable development.

Article 38: Consumer protection

Union policies shall ensure a high level of consumer protection.

CHAPTER V - CITIZENS' RIGHTS

Article 39: Right to vote and to stand as a candidate at elections to the European Parliament

1. Every citizen of the Union has the right to vote and to stand as a candidate at elections to the European Parliament in the Member State in which he or she resides, under the same conditions as nationals of that State.
2. Members of the European Parliament shall be elected by direct universal suffrage in a free and secret ballot.

Article 40: Right to vote and to stand as a candidate at municipal elections
Every citizen of the Union has the right to vote and to stand as a candidate at municipal elections in the Member State in which he or she resides under the same conditions as nationals of that State.

Article 41:Right to good administration

1. Every person has the right to have his or her affairs handled impartially, fairly and within a reasonable time by the institutions and bodies of the Union.
2. This right includes:
- the right of every person to be heard, before any individual measure which would affect him or her adversely is taken;
- the right of every person to have access to his or her file, while respecting the legitimate interests of confidentiality and of professional and business secrecy;
- the obligation of the administration to give reasons for its decisions.
3. Every person has the right to have the Community make good any damage caused by its institutions or by its servants in the performance of their duties, in accordance with the general principles common to the laws of the Member States.
4. Every person may write to the institutions of the Union in one of the languages of the Treaties and must have an answer in the same language.

Article 42: Right of access to documents

Any citizen of the Union, and any natural or legal person residing or having its registered office in a Member State, has a right of access to European Parliament, Council and Commission documents.

Article 43: Ombudsman

Any citizen of the Union and any natural or legal person residing or having its registered office in a Member State has the right to refer to the Ombudsman of the Union cases of maladministration in the activities of the Community institutions or bodies, with the exception of the Court of Justice and the Court of First Instance acting in their judicial role.

Article 44: Right to petition

Any citizen of the Union and any natural or legal person residing or having its registered office in a Member State has the right to petition the European Parliament.

Article 45: Freedom of movement and of residence

1. Every citizen of the Union has the right to move and reside freely within the territory of the Member States.
2. Freedom of movement and residence may be granted, in accordance with the Treaty establishing the European Community, to nationals of third countries legally resident in the territory of a Member State.

Article 46: Diplomatic and consular protection
Every citizen of the Union shall, in the territory of a third country in which the Member State of which he or she is a national is not represented, be entitled to protection by the diplomatic or consular authorities of any Member State, on the same conditions as the nationals of that Member State.

CHAPTER VI - JUSTICE

Article 47: Right to an effective remedy and to a fair trial

Everyone whose rights and freedoms guaranteed by the law of the Union are violated has the right to an effective remedy before a tribunal in compliance with the conditions laid down in this Article.
Everyone is entitled to a fair and public hearing within a reasonable time by an independent and impartial tribunal previously established by law. Everyone shall have the possibility of being advised, defended and represented.
Legal aid shall be made available to those who lack sufficient resources in so far as such aid is necessary to ensure effective access to justice.

Article 48: Presumption of innocence and right of defence

1. Everyone who has been charged shall be presumed innocent until proved guilty according to law.
2. Respect for the rights of the defence of anyone who has been charged shall be guaranteed.

Article 49: Principles of legality and proportionality of criminal offences and penalties

1. No one shall be held guilty of any criminal offence on account of any act or omission which did not constitute a criminal offence under national law or international law at the time when it was committed. Nor shall a heavier penalty be imposed than that which was applicable at the time the criminal offence was committed. If, subsequent to the commission of a criminal offence, the law provides for a lighter penalty, that penalty shall be applicable.
2. This Article shall not prejudice the trial and punishment of any person for any act or omission which, at the time when it was committed, was criminal according to the general principles recognised by the community of nations.
3. The severity of penalties must not be disproportionate to the criminal offence.

Article 50: Right not to be tried or punished twice in criminal proceedings for the same criminal offence

No one shall be liable to be tried or punished again in criminal proceedings for an offence for which he or she has already been finally acquitted or convicted within the Union in accordance with the law.

CHAPTER VII - GENERAL PROVISIONS

Article 51: Scope

1. The provisions of this Charter are addressed to the institutions and bodies of the Union with due regard for the principle of subsidiarity and to the Member States only when they are implementing Union law. They shall therefore respect the rights, observe the principles and promote the application thereof in accordance with their respective powers.
2. This Charter does not establish any new power or task for the Community or the Union, or modify powers and tasks defined by the Treaties.

Article 52: Scope of guaranteed rights
1. Any limitation on the exercise of the rights and freedoms recognised by this Charter must be provided for by law and respect the essence of those rights and freedoms. Subject to the principle of proportionality, limitations may be made only if they are necessary and genuinely meet objectives of general interest recognised by the Union or the need to protect the rights and freedoms of others.
2. Rights recognised by this Charter which are based on the Community Treaties or the Treaty on European Union shall be exercised under the conditions and within the limits defined by those Treaties.
3. In so far as this Charter contains rights which correspond to rights guaranteed by the Convention for the Protection of Human Rights and Fundamental Freedoms, the meaning and scope of those rights shall be the

same as those laid down by the said Convention. This provision shall not prevent Union law providing more extensive protection.

Article 53: Level of protection

Nothing in this Charter shall be interpreted as restricting or adversely affecting human rights and fundamental freedoms as recognised, in their respective fields of application, by Union law and international law and by international agreements to which the Union, the Community or all the Member States are party, including the European Convention for the Protection of Human Rights and Fundamental Freedoms, and by the Member States' constitutions.

Article 54: Prohibition of abuse of rights

Nothing in this Charter shall be interpreted as implying any right to engage in any activity or to perform any act aimed at the destruction of any of the rights and freedoms recognised in this Charter or at their limitation to a greater extent than is provided for herein.

Annex 4.2.

Directive 95/46/EC of the European Parliament and of the Council of 24 October 1995 on the protection of individuals with regard to the **processing of personal data** and on the free movement of such data
Official Journal L 281 , 23/11/1995 P. 0031 - 0050

MAIN PROVISIONS

Article 1: Object of the Directive

1. In accordance with this Directive, Member States shall protect the fundamental rights and freedoms of natural persons, and in particular their right to privacy with respect to the processing of personal data.
2. Member States shall neither restrict nor prohibit the free flow of personal data between Member States for reasons connected with the protection afforded under paragraph 1.

Article 2: Definitions

For the purposes of this Directive:
(a) 'personal data' shall mean any information relating to an identified or identifiable natural person ('data subject'); an identifiable person is one who can be identified, directly or indirectly, in particular by reference to an identification number or to one or more factors specific to his physical, physiological, mental, economic, cultural or social identity;
(b) 'processing of personal data' ('processing') shall mean any operation or set of operations which is performed upon personal data, whether or not by automatic means, such as collection, recording, organization, storage, adaptation or alteration, retrieval, consultation, use, disclosure by transmission, dissemination or otherwise making available, alignment or combination, blocking, erasure or destruction;
(c) 'personal data filing system' ('filing system') shall mean any structured set of personal data which are accessible according to specific criteria, whether centralized, decentralized or dispersed on a functional or geographical basis;
(d) 'controller' shall mean the natural or legal person, public authority, agency or any other body which alone or jointly with others determines the purposes and means of the processing of personal data; where the purposes and means of processing are determined by national or Community laws or regulations, the controller or the specific criteria for his nomination may be designated by national or Community law;
(e) 'processor' shall mean a natural or legal person, public authority, agency or any other body which processes personal data on behalf of the controller;
(f) 'third party' shall mean any natural or legal person, public authority, agency or any other body other than the data subject, the controller, the processor and the persons who, under the direct authority of the controller or the processor, are authorized to process the data;
(g) 'recipient' shall mean a natural or legal person, public authority, agency or any other body to whom data are disclosed, whether a third party or not; however, authorities which may receive data in the framework of a particular inquiry shall not be regarded as recipients;
(h) 'the data subject's consent' shall mean any freely given specific and informed indication of his wishes by which the data subject signifies his agreement to personal data relating to him being processed.

Article 3: Scope

1. This Directive shall apply to the processing of personal data wholly or partly by automatic means, and to the processing otherwise than by automatic means of personal data which form part of a filing system or are intended to form part of a filing system.
2. This Directive shall not apply to the processing of personal data:
- in the course of an activity which falls outside the scope of Community law, such as those provided for by Titles V and VI of the Treaty on European Union and in any case to processing operations concerning public security, defence, State security (including the economic well-being of the State when the processing operation relates to State security matters) and the activities of the State in areas of criminal law,
- by a natural person in the course of a purely personal or household activity.

Article 4: National law applicable

1. Each Member State shall apply the national provisions it adopts pursuant to this Directive to the processing of

personal data where:
(a) the processing is carried out in the context of the activities of an establishment of the controller on the territory of the Member State; when the same controller is established on the territory of several Member States, he must take the necessary measures to ensure that each of these establishments complies with the obligations laid down by the national law applicable;
(b) the controller is not established on the Member State's territory, but in a place where its national law applies by virtue of international public law;
(c) the controller is not established on Community territory and, for purposes of processing personal data makes use of equipment, automated or otherwise, situated on the territory of the said Member State, unless such equipment is used only for purposes of transit through the territory of the Community.
2. In the circumstances referred to in paragraph 1 (c), the controller must designate a representative established in the territory of that Member State, without prejudice to legal actions which could be initiated against the controller himself.

CHAPTER II - GENERAL RULES ON THE LAWFULNESS OF THE PROCESSING OF PERSONAL DATA

Article 5
Member States shall, within the limits of the provisions of this Chapter, determine more precisely the conditions under which the processing of personal data is lawful.

SECTION I: PRINCIPLES RELATING TO DATA QUALITY

Article 6
1. Member States shall provide that personal data must be:
(a) processed fairly and lawfully;
(b) collected for specified, explicit and legitimate purposes and not further processed in a way incompatible with those purposes. Further processing of data for historical, statistical or scientific purposes shall not be considered as incompatible provided that Member States provide appropriate safeguards;
(c) adequate, relevant and not excessive in relation to the purposes for which they are collected and/or further processed;
(d) accurate and, where necessary, kept up to date; every reasonable step must be taken to ensure that data which are inaccurate or incomplete, having regard to the purposes for which they were collected or for which they are further processed, are erased or rectified;
(e) kept in a form which permits identification of data subjects for no longer than is necessary for the purposes for which the data were collected or for which they are further processed. Member States shall lay down appropriate safeguards for personal data stored for longer periods for historical, statistical or scientific use.
2. It shall be for the controller to ensure that paragraph 1 is complied with.

SECTION II: CRITERIA FOR MAKING DATA PROCESSING LEGITIMATE

Article 7
Member States shall provide that personal data may be processed only if:
(a) the data subject has unambiguously given his consent; or
(b) processing is necessary for the performance of a contract to which the data subject is party or in order to take steps at the request of the data subject prior to entering into a contract; or
(c) processing is necessary for compliance with a legal obligation to which the controller is subject; or
(d) processing is necessary in order to protect the vital interests of the data subject; or
(e) processing is necessary for the performance of a task carried out in the public interest or in the exercise of official authority vested in the controller or in a third party to whom the data are disclosed; or
(f) processing is necessary for the purposes of the legitimate interests pursued by the controller or by the third party or parties to whom the data are disclosed, except where such interests are overridden by the interests for fundamental rights and freedoms of the data subject which require protection under Article 1 (1).

SECTION III: SPECIAL CATEGORIES OF PROCESSING

Article 8: The processing of special categories of data
1. Member States shall prohibit the processing of personal data revealing racial or ethnic origin, political opinions, religious or philosophical beliefs, trade-union membership, and the processing of data concerning health or sex life.

2. Paragraph 1 shall not apply where:
(a) the data subject has given his explicit consent to the processing of those data, except where the laws of the Member State provide that the prohibition referred to in paragraph 1 may not be lifted by the data subject's giving his consent; or
(b) processing is necessary for the purposes of carrying out the obligations and specific rights of the controller in the field of employment law in so far as it is authorized by national law providing for adequate safeguards; or
(c) processing is necessary to protect the vital interests of the data subject or of another person where the data subject is physically or legally incapable of giving his consent; or
(d) processing is carried out in the course of its legitimate activities with appropriate guarantees by a foundation, association or any other non-profit-seeking body with a political, philosophical, religious or trade-union aim and on condition that the processing relates solely to the members of the body or to persons who have regular contact with it in connection with its purposes and that the data are not disclosed to a third party without the consent of the data subjects; or
(e) the processing relates to data which are manifestly made public by the data subject or is necessary for the establishment, exercise or defence of legal claims.
3. Paragraph 1 shall not apply where processing of the data is required for the purposes of preventive medicine, medical diagnosis, the provision of care or treatment or the management of health-care services, and where those data are processed by a health professional subject under national law or rules established by national competent bodies to the obligation of professional secrecy or by another person also subject to an equivalent obligation of secrecy.
4. Subject to the provision of suitable safeguards, Member States may, for reasons of substantial public interest, lay down exemptions in addition to those laid down in paragraph 2 either by national law or by decision of the supervisory authority.
5. Processing of data relating to offences, criminal convictions or security measures may be carried out only under the control of official authority, or if suitable specific safeguards are provided under national law, subject to derogations which may be granted by the Member State under national provisions providing suitable specific safeguards. However, a complete register of criminal convictions may be kept only under the control of official authority.
Member States may provide that data relating to administrative sanctions or judgements in civil cases shall also be processed under the control of official authority.
6. Derogations from paragraph 1 provided for in paragraphs 4 and 5 shall be notified to the Commission.
7. Member States shall determine the conditions under which a national identification number or any other identifier of general application may be processed.

Article 9: Processing of personal data and freedom of expression

Member States shall provide for exemptions or derogations from the provisions of this Chapter, Chapter IV and Chapter VI for the processing of personal data carried out solely for journalistic purposes or the purpose of artistic or literary expression only if they are necessary to reconcile the right to privacy with the rules governing freedom of expression.

SECTION IV: INFORMATION TO BE GIVEN TO THE DATA SUBJECT

Article 10: Information in cases of collection of data from the data subject

Member States shall provide that the controller or his representative must provide a data subject from whom data relating to himself are collected with at least the following information, except where he already has it:
(a) the identity of the controller and of his representative, if any;
(b) the purposes of the processing for which the data are intended;
(c) any further information such as
- the recipients or categories of recipients of the data,
- whether replies to the questions are obligatory or voluntary, as well as the possible consequences of failure to reply,
- the existence of the right of access to and the right to rectify the data concerning him

in so far as such further information is necessary, having regard to the specific circumstances in which the data are collected, to guarantee fair processing in respect of the data subject.

Article 11: Information where the data have not been obtained from the data subject

1. Where the data have not been obtained from the data subject, Member States shall provide that the controller

or his representative must at the time of undertaking the recording of personal data or if a disclosure to a third party is envisaged, no later than the time when the data are first disclosed provide the data subject with at least the following information, except where he already has it:
(a) the identity of the controller and of his representative, if any;
(b) the purposes of the processing;
(c) any further information such as
- the categories of data concerned,
- the recipients or categories of recipients,
- the existence of the right of access to and the right to rectify the data concerning him
in so far as such further information is necessary, having regard to the specific circumstances in which the data are processed, to guarantee fair processing in respect of the data subject.
2. Paragraph 1 shall not apply where, in particular for processing for statistical purposes or for the purposes of historical or scientific research, the provision of such information proves impossible or would involve a disproportionate effort or if recording or disclosure is expressly laid down by law. In these cases Member States shall provide appropriate safeguards.

SECTION V: THE DATA SUBJECT'S RIGHT OF ACCESS TO DATA

Article 12: Right of access

Member States shall guarantee every data subject the right to obtain from the controller:
(a) without constraint at reasonable intervals and without excessive delay or expense:
- confirmation as to whether or not data relating to him are being processed and information at least as to the purposes of the processing, the categories of data concerned, and the recipients or categories of recipients to whom the data are disclosed,
- communication to him in an intelligible form of the data undergoing processing and of any available information as to their source,
- knowledge of the logic involved in any automatic processing of data concerning him at least in the case of the automated decisions referred to in Article 15 (1);
(b) as appropriate the rectification, erasure or blocking of data the processing of which does not comply with the provisions of this Directive, in particular because of the incomplete or inaccurate nature of the data;
(c) notification to third parties to whom the data have been disclosed of any rectification, erasure or blocking carried out in compliance with (b), unless this proves impossible or involves a disproportionate effort.

SECTION VI: EXEMPTIONS AND RESTRICTIONS

Article 13: Exemptions and restrictions

1. Member States may adopt legislative measures to restrict the scope of the obligations and rights provided for in Articles 6 (1), 10, 11 (1), 12 and 21 when such a restriction constitutes a necessary measures to safeguard:
(a) national security;
(b) defence;
(c) public security;
(d) the prevention, investigation, detection and prosecution of criminal offences, or of breaches of ethics for regulated professions;
(e) an important economic or financial interest of a Member State or of the European Union, including monetary, budgetary and taxation matters;
(f) a monitoring, inspection or regulatory function connected, even occasionally, with the exercise of official authority in cases referred to in (c), (d) and (e);
(g) the protection of the data subject or of the rights and freedoms of others.
2. Subject to adequate legal safeguards, in particular that the data are not used for taking measures or decisions regarding any particular individual, Member States may, where there is clearly no risk of breaching the privacy of the data subject, restrict by a legislative measure the rights provided for in Article 12 when data are processed solely for purposes of scientific research or are kept in personal form for a period which does not exceed the period necessary for the sole purpose of creating statistics.

SECTION VII: THE DATA SUBJECT'S RIGHT TO OBJECT

Article 14: The data subject's right to object:

Member States shall grant the data subject the right:
(a) at least in the cases referred to in Article 7 (e) and (f), to object at any time on compelling legitimate grounds relating to his particular situation to the processing of data relating to him, save where otherwise provided by national legislation. Where there is a justified objection, the processing instigated by the controller may no longer involve those data;
(b) to object, on request and free of charge, to the processing of personal data relating to him which the controller anticipates being processed for the purposes of direct marketing, or to be informed before personal data are disclosed for the first time to third parties or used on their behalf for the purposes of direct marketing, and to be expressly offered the right to object free of charge to such disclosures or uses.
Member States shall take the necessary measures to ensure that data subjects are aware of the existence of the right referred to in the first subparagraph of (b).

Article 15: Automated individual decisions

1. Member States shall grant the right to every person not to be subject to a decision which produces legal effects concerning him or significantly affects him and which is based solely on automated processing of data intended to evaluate certain personal aspects relating to him, such as his performance at work, creditworthiness, reliability, conduct, etc.
2. Subject to the other Articles of this Directive, Member States shall provide that a person may be subjected to a decision of the kind referred to in paragraph 1 if that decision:
(a) is taken in the course of the entering into or performance of a contract, provided the request for the entering into or the performance of the contract, lodged by the data subject, has been satisfied or that there are suitable measures to safeguard his legitimate interests, such as arrangements allowing him to put his point of view; or
(b) is authorized by a law which also lays down measures to safeguard the data subject's legitimate interests.

SECTION VIII: CONFIDENTIALITY AND SECURITY OF PROCESSING

Article 16: Confidentiality of processing

Any person acting under the authority of the controller or of the processor, including the processor himself, who has access to personal data must not process them except on instructions from the controller, unless he is required to do so by law.

Article 17: Security of processing

1. Member States shall provide that the controller must implement appropriate technical and organizational measures to protect personal data against accidental or unlawful destruction or accidental loss, alteration, unauthorized disclosure or access, in particular where the processing involves the transmission of data over a network, and against all other unlawful forms of processing.
Having regard to the state of the art and the cost of their implementation, such measures shall ensure a level of security appropriate to the risks represented by the processing and the nature of the data to be protected.
2. The Member States shall provide that the controller must, where processing is carried out on his behalf, choose a processor providing sufficient guarantees in respect of the technical security measures and organizational measures governing the processing to be carried out, and must ensure compliance with those measures.
3. The carrying out of processing by way of a processor must be governed by a contract or legal act binding the processor to the controller and stipulating in particular that:
- the processor shall act only on instructions from the controller,
- the obligations set out in paragraph 1, as defined by the law of the Member State in which the processor is established, shall also be incumbent on the processor.
4. For the purposes of keeping proof, the parts of the contract or the legal act relating to data protection and the requirements relating to the measures referred to in paragraph 1 shall be in writing or in another equivalent form.

SECTION IX: NOTIFICATION

Article 18: Obligation to notify the supervisory authority

1. Member States shall provide that the controller or his representative, if any, must notify the supervisory authority referred to in Article 28 before carrying out any wholly or partly automatic processing operation or set of such operations intended to serve a single purpose or several related purposes.
2. Member States may provide for the simplification of or exemption from notification only in the following cases and under the following conditions:
- where, for categories of processing operations which are unlikely, taking account of the data to be processed, to affect adversely the rights and freedoms of data subjects, they specify the purposes of the processing, the data or categories of data undergoing processing, the category or categories of data subject, the recipients or categories of recipient to whom the data are to be disclosed and the length of time the data are to be stored, and/or
- where the controller, in compliance with the national law which governs him, appoints a personal data protection official, responsible in particular:
- for ensuring in an independent manner the internal application of the national provisions taken pursuant to this Directive
- for keeping the register of processing operations carried out by the controller, containing the items of information referred to in Article 21 (2),

thereby ensuring that the rights and freedoms of the data subjects are unlikely to be adversely affected by the processing operations.
3. Member States may provide that paragraph 1 does not apply to processing whose sole purpose is the keeping of a register which according to laws or regulations is intended to provide information to the public and which is open to consultation either by the public in general or by any person demonstrating a legitimate interest.
4. Member States may provide for an exemption from the obligation to notify or a simplification of the notification in the case of processing operations referred to in Article 8 (2) (d).
5. Member States may stipulate that certain or all non-automatic processing operations involving personal data shall be notified, or provide for these processing operations to be subject to simplified notification.

Article 19: Contents of notification

1. Member States shall specify the information to be given in the notification. It shall include at least:
(a) the name and address of the controller and of his representative, if any;
(b) the purpose or purposes of the processing;
(c) a description of the category or categories of data subject and of the data or categories of data relating to them;
(d) the recipients or categories of recipient to whom the data might be disclosed;
(e) proposed transfers of data to third countries;
(f) a general description allowing a preliminary assessment to be made of the appropriateness of the measures taken pursuant to Article 17 to ensure security of processing.
2. Member States shall specify the procedures under which any change affecting the information referred to in paragraph 1 must be notified to the supervisory authority.

Article 20: Prior checking

1. Member States shall determine the processing operations likely to present specific risks to the rights and freedoms of data subjects and shall check that these processing operations are examined prior to the start thereof.
2. Such prior checks shall be carried out by the supervisory authority following receipt of a notification from the controller or by the data protection official, who, in cases of doubt, must consult the supervisory authority.
3. Member States may also carry out such checks in the context of preparation either of a measure of the national parliament or of a measure based on such a legislative measure, which define the nature of the processing and lay down appropriate safeguards.

Article 21:Publicizing of processing operations

1. Member States shall take measures to ensure that processing operations are publicized.
2. Member States shall provide that a register of processing operations notified in accordance with Article 18 shall be kept by the supervisory authority.

The register shall contain at least the information listed in Article 19 (1) (a) to (e).
The register may be inspected by any person.
3. Member States shall provide, in relation to processing operations not subject to notification, that controllers or another body appointed by the Member States make available at least the information referred to in Article 19 (1) (a) to (e) in an appropriate form to any person on request.
Member States may provide that this provision does not apply to processing whose sole purpose is the keeping of a register which according to laws or regulations is intended to provide information to the public and which is open to consultation either by the public in general or by any person who can provide proof of a legitimate interest.

CHAPTER III - JUDICIAL REMEDIES, LIABILITY AND SANCTIONS

Article 22: Remedies

Without prejudice to any administrative remedy for which provision may be made, inter alia before the supervisory authority referred to in Article 28, prior to referral to the judicial authority, Member States shall provide for the right of every person to a judicial remedy for any breach of the rights guaranteed him by the national law applicable to the processing in question.

Article 23: Liability

1. Member States shall provide that any person who has suffered damage as a result of an unlawful processing operation or of any act incompatible with the national provisions adopted pursuant to this Directive is entitled to receive compensation from the controller for the damage suffered.
2. The controller may be exempted from this liability, in whole or in part, if he proves that he is not responsible for the event giving rise to the damage.

Article 24: Sanctions

The Member States shall adopt suitable measures to ensure the full implementation of the provisions of this Directive and shall in particular lay down the sanctions to be imposed in case of infringement of the provisions adopted pursuant to this Directive.

CHAPTER IV - TRANSFER OF PERSONAL DATA TO THIRD COUNTRIES

Article 25:Principles

1. The Member States shall provide that the transfer to a third country of personal data which are undergoing processing or are intended for processing after transfer may take place only if, without prejudice to compliance with the national provisions adopted pursuant to the other provisions of this Directive, the third country in question ensures an adequate level of protection.
2. The adequacy of the level of protection afforded by a third country shall be assessed in the light of all the circumstances surrounding a data transfer operation or set of data transfer operations; particular consideration shall be given to the nature of the data, the purpose and duration of the proposed processing operation or operations, the country of origin and country of final destination, the rules of law, both general and sectoral, in force in the third country in question and the professional rules and security measures which are complied with in that country.
3. The Member States and the Commission shall inform each other of cases where they consider that a third country does not ensure an adequate level of protection within the meaning of paragraph 2.
4. Where the Commission finds, under the procedure provided for in Article 31 (2), that a third country does not ensure an adequate level of protection within the meaning of paragraph 2 of this Article, Member States shall take the measures necessary to prevent any transfer of data of the same type to the third country in question.
5. At the appropriate time, the Commission shall enter into negotiations with a view to remedying the situation resulting from the finding made pursuant to paragraph 4.
6. The Commission may find, in accordance with the procedure referred to in Article 31 (2), that a third country ensures an adequate level of protection within the meaning of paragraph 2 of this Article, by reason of its domestic law or of the international commitments it has entered into, particularly upon conclusion of the negotiations referred to in paragraph 5, for the protection of the private lives and basic freedoms and rights of individuals. Member States shall take the measures necessary to comply with the Commission's decision.

Article 26: Derogations

1. By way of derogation from Article 25 and save where otherwise provided by domestic law governing particular cases, Member States shall provide that a transfer or a set of transfers of personal data to a third country which does not ensure an adequate level of protection within the meaning of Article 25 (2) may take place on condition that:
(a) the data subject has given his consent unambiguously to the proposed transfer; or
(b) the transfer is necessary for the performance of a contract between the data subject and the controller or the implementation of precontractual measures taken in response to the data subject's request; or
(c) the transfer is necessary for the conclusion or performance of a contract concluded in the interest of the data subject between the controller and a third party; or
(d) the transfer is necessary or legally required on important public interest grounds, or for the establishment, exercise or defence of legal claims; or
(e) the transfer is necessary in order to protect the vital interests of the data subject; or
(f) the transfer is made from a register which according to laws or regulations is intended to provide information to the public and which is open to consultation either by the public in general or by any person who can demonstrate legitimate interest, to the extent that the conditions laid down in law for consultation are fulfilled in the particular case.
2. Without prejudice to paragraph 1, a Member State may authorize a transfer or a set of transfers of personal data to a third country which does not ensure an adequate level of protection within the meaning of Article 25 (2), where the controller adduces adequate safeguards with respect to the protection of the privacy and fundamental rights and freedoms of individuals and as regards the exercise of the corresponding rights; such safeguards may in particular result from appropriate contractual clauses.
3. The Member State shall inform the Commission and the other Member States of the authorizations it grants pursuant to paragraph 2.
If a Member State or the Commission objects on justified grounds involving the protection of the privacy and fundamental rights and freedoms of individuals, the Commission shall take appropriate measures in accordance with the procedure laid down in Article 31 (2).
Member States shall take the necessary measures to comply with the Commission's decision.
4. Where the Commission decides, in accordance with the procedure referred to in Article 31 (2), that certain standard contractual clauses offer sufficient safeguards as required by paragraph 2, Member States shall take the necessary measures to comply with the Commission's decision.

CHAPTER V - CODES OF CONDUCT

Article 27
1. The Member States and the Commission shall encourage the drawing up of codes of conduct intended to contribute to the proper implementation of the national provisions adopted by the Member States pursuant to this Directive, taking account of the specific features of the various sectors.
2. Member States shall make provision for trade associations and other bodies representing other categories of controllers which have drawn up draft national codes or which have the intention of amending or extending existing national codes to be able to submit them to the opinion of the national authority.
Member States shall make provision for this authority to ascertain, among other things, whether the drafts submitted to it are in accordance with the national provisions adopted pursuant to this Directive. If it sees fit, the authority shall seek the views of data subjects or their representatives.
3. Draft Community codes, and amendments or extensions to existing Community codes, may be submitted to the Working Party referred to in Article 29. This Working Party shall determine, among other things, whether the drafts submitted to it are in accordance with the national provisions adopted pursuant to this Directive. If it sees fit, the authority shall seek the views of data subjects or their representatives. The Commission may ensure appropriate publicity for the codes which have been approved by the Working Party.

CHAPTER VI - SUPERVISORY AUTHORITY AND WORKING PARTY ON THE PROTECTION OF INDIVIDUALS WITH REGARD TO THE PROCESSING OF PERSONAL DATA

Article 28: Supervisory authority

1. Each Member State shall provide that one or more public authorities are responsible for monitoring the application within its territory of the provisions adopted by the Member States pursuant to this Directive. These authorities shall act with complete independence in exercising the functions entrusted to them.
2. Each Member State shall provide that the supervisory authorities are consulted when drawing up

administrative measures or regulations relating to the protection of individuals' rights and freedoms with regard to the processing of personal data.
3. Each authority shall in particular be endowed with:
- investigative powers, such as powers of access to data forming the subject-matter of processing operations and powers to collect all the information necessary for the performance of its supervisory duties,
- effective powers of intervention, such as, for example, that of delivering opinions before processing operations are carried out, in accordance with Article 20, and ensuring appropriate publication of such opinions, of ordering the blocking, erasure or destruction of data, of imposing a temporary or definitive ban on processing, of warning or admonishing the controller, or that of referring the matter to national parliaments or other political institutions,
- the power to engage in legal proceedings where the national provisions adopted pursuant to this Directive have been violated or to bring these violations to the attention of the judicial authorities.
Decisions by the supervisory authority which give rise to complaints may be appealed against through the courts.
4. Each supervisory authority shall hear claims lodged by any person, or by an association representing that person, concerning the protection of his rights and freedoms in regard to the processing of personal data. The person concerned shall be informed of the outcome of the claim.
Each supervisory authority shall, in particular, hear claims for checks on the lawfulness of data processing lodged by any person when the national provisions adopted pursuant to Article 13 of this Directive apply. The person shall at any rate be informed that a check has taken place.
5. Each supervisory authority shall draw up a report on its activities at regular intervals. The report shall be made public.
6. Each supervisory authority is competent, whatever the national law applicable to the processing in question, to exercise, on the territory of its own Member State, the powers conferred on it in accordance with paragraph 3. Each authority may be requested to exercise its powers by an authority of another Member State.
The supervisory authorities shall cooperate with one another to the extent necessary for the performance of their duties, in particular by exchanging all useful information.
7. Member States shall provide that the members and staff of the supervisory authority, even after their employment has ended, are to be subject to a duty of professional secrecy with regard to confidential information to which they have access.

Article 29: Working Party on the Protection of Individuals with regard to the Processing of Personal Data

1. A Working Party on the Protection of Individuals with regard to the Processing of Personal Data, hereinafter referred to as 'the Working Party', is hereby set up.
It shall have advisory status and act independently.
2. The Working Party shall be composed of a representative of the supervisory authority or authorities designated by each Member State and of a representative of the authority or authorities established for the Community institutions and bodies, and of a representative of the Commission.
Each member of the Working Party shall be designated by the institution, authority or authorities which he represents. Where a Member State has designated more than one supervisory authority, they shall nominate a joint representative. The same shall apply to the authorities established for Community institutions and bodies.
3. The Working Party shall take decisions by a simple majority of the representatives of the supervisory authorities.
4. The Working Party shall elect its chairman. The chairman's term of office shall be two years. His appointment shall be renewable.
5. The Working Party's secretariat shall be provided by the Commission.
6. The Working Party shall adopt its own rules of procedure.
7. The Working Party shall consider items placed on its agenda by its chairman, either on his own initiative or at the request of a representative of the supervisory authorities or at the Commission's request.

Article 30
1. The Working Party shall:
(a) examine any question covering the application of the national measures adopted under this Directive in order to contribute to the uniform application of such measures;
(b) give the Commission an opinion on the level of protection in the Community and in third countries;
(c) advise the Commission on any proposed amendment of this Directive, on any additional or specific measures to safeguard the rights and freedoms of natural persons with regard to the processing of personal data and on any other proposed Community measures affecting such rights and freedoms;
(d) give an opinion on codes of conduct drawn up at Community level.

2. If the Working Party finds that divergences likely to affect the equivalence of protection for persons with regard to the processing of personal data in the Community are arising between the laws or practices of Member States, it shall inform the Commission accordingly.
3. The Working Party may, on its own initiative, make recommendations on all matters relating to the protection of persons with regard to the processing of personal data in the Community.
4. The Working Party's opinions and recommendations shall be forwarded to the Commission and to the committee referred to in Article 31.
5. The Commission shall inform the Working Party of the action it has taken in response to its opinions and recommendations. It shall do so in a report which shall also be forwarded to the European Parliament and the Council. The report shall be made public.
6. The Working Party shall draw up an annual report on the situation regarding the protection of natural persons with regard to the processing of personal data in the Community and in third countries, which it shall transmit to the Commission, the European Parliament and the Council. The report shall be made public.

CHAPTER VII - COMMUNITY IMPLEMENTING MEASURES

Article 31: The Committee

1. The Commission shall be assisted by a committee composed of the representatives of the Member States and chaired by the representative of the Commission.
2. The representative of the Commission shall submit to the committee a draft of the measures to be taken. The committee shall deliver its opinion on the draft within a time limit which the chairman may lay down according to the urgency of the matter.
The opinion shall be delivered by the majority laid down in Article 148 (2) of the Treaty. The votes of the representatives of the Member States within the committee shall be weighted in the manner set out in that Article. The chairman shall not vote.
The Commission shall adopt measures which shall apply immediately. However, if these measures are not in accordance with the opinion of the committee, they shall be communicated by the Commission to the Council forthwith. It that event:
- the Commission shall defer application of the measures which it has decided for a period of three months from the date of communication,
- the Council, acting by a qualified majority, may take a different decision within the time limit referred to in the first indent.

FINAL PROVISIONS

Article 32
1. Member States shall bring into force the laws, regulations and administrative provisions necessary to comply with this Directive at the latest at the end of a period of three years from the date of its adoption.
When Member States adopt these measures, they shall contain a reference to this Directive or be accompanied by such reference on the occasion of their official publication. The methods of making such reference shall be laid down by the Member States.
2. Member States shall ensure that processing already under way on the date the national provisions adopted pursuant to this Directive enter into force, is brought into conformity with these provisions within three years of this date.
By way of derogation from the preceding subparagraph, Member States may provide that the processing of data already held in manual filing systems on the date of entry into force of the national provisions adopted in implementation of this Directive shall be brought into conformity with Articles 6, 7 and 8 of this Directive within 12 years of the date on which it is adopted. Member States shall, however, grant the data subject the right to obtain, at his request and in particular at the time of exercising his right of access, the rectification, erasure or blocking of data which are incomplete, inaccurate or stored in a way incompatible with the legitimate purposes pursued by the controller.
3. By way of derogation from paragraph 2, Member States may provide, subject to suitable safeguards, that data kept for the sole purpose of historical research need not be brought into conformity with Articles 6, 7 and 8 of this Directive.
4. Member States shall communicate to the Commission the text of the provisions of domestic law which they adopt in the field covered by this Directive.

Annex 4.3.

Directive 2002/58/EC of the European Parliament and of the Council of 12 July 2002 concerning the processing of personal data and the protection of privacy in the electronic communications sector (Directive on privacy and electronic communications) *Official Journal L 201 , 31/07/2002 P. 0037 - 0047*

MAIN PROVISIONS

Article 1
Scope and aim
1. This Directive harmonises the provisions of the Member States required to ensure an equivalent level of protection of fundamental rights and freedoms, and in particular the right to privacy, with respect to the processing of personal data in the electronic communication sector and to ensure the free movement of such data and of electronic communication equipment and services in the Community.
2. The provisions of this Directive particularise and complement Directive 95/46/EC for the purposes mentioned in paragraph 1. Moreover, they provide for protection of the legitimate interests of subscribers who are legal persons.
3. This Directive shall not apply to activities which fall outside the scope of the Treaty establishing the European Community, such as those covered by Titles V and VI of the Treaty on European Union, and in any case to activities concerning public security, defence, State security (including the economic well-being of the State when the activities relate to State security matters) and the activities of the State in areas of criminal law.

Article 2
Definitions
Save as otherwise provided, the definitions in Directive 95/46/EC and in Directive 2002/21/EC of the European Parliament and of the Council of 7 March 2002 on a common regulatory framework for electronic communications networks and services (Framework Directive)(8) shall apply.
The following definitions shall also apply:
(a) "user" means any natural person using a publicly available electronic communications service, for private or business purposes, without necessarily having subscribed to this service;
(b) "traffic data" means any data processed for the purpose of the conveyance of a communication on an electronic communications network or for the billing thereof;
(c) "location data" means any data processed in an electronic communications network, indicating the geographic position of the terminal equipment of a user of a publicly available electronic communications service;
(d) "communication" means any information exchanged or conveyed between a finite number of parties by means of a publicly available electronic communications service. This does not include any information conveyed as part of a broadcasting service to the public over an electronic communications network except to the extent that the information can be related to the identifiable subscriber or user receiving the information;
(e) "call" means a connection established by means of a publicly available telephone service allowing two-way communication in real time;
(f) "consent" by a user or subscriber corresponds to the data subject's consent in Directive 95/46/EC;
(g) "value added service" means any service which requires the processing of traffic data or location data other than traffic data beyond what is necessary for the transmission of a communication or the billing thereof;
(h) "electronic mail" means any text, voice, sound or image message sent over a public communications network which can be stored in the network or in the recipient's terminal equipment until it is collected by the recipient.

Article 3
Services concerned
1. This Directive shall apply to the processing of personal data in connection with the provision of publicly available electronic communications services in public communications networks in the Community.
2. Articles 8, 10 and 11 shall apply to subscriber lines connected to digital exchanges and, where technically possible and if it does not require a disproportionate economic effort, to subscriber lines connected to analogue exchanges.
3. Cases where it would be technically impossible or require a disproportionate economic effort to fulfil the requirements of Articles 8, 10 and 11 shall be notified to the Commission by the Member States.

Article 4
Security
1. The provider of a publicly available electronic communications service must take appropriate technical and organisational measures to safeguard security of its services, if necessary in conjunction with the provider of the public communications network with respect to network security. Having regard to the state of the art and the cost of their implementation, these measures shall ensure a level of security appropriate to the risk presented.
2. In case of a particular risk of a breach of the security of the network, the provider of a publicly available electronic communications service must inform the subscribers concerning such risk and, where the risk lies outside the scope of the measures to be taken by the service provider, of any possible remedies, including an indication of the likely costs involved.

Article 5
Confidentiality of the communications
1. Member States shall ensure the confidentiality of communications and the related traffic data by means of a public communications network and publicly available electronic communications services, through national legislation. In particular, they shall prohibit listening, tapping, storage or other kinds of interception or surveillance of communications and the related traffic data by persons other than users, without the consent of the users concerned, except when legally authorised to do so in accordance with Article 15(1). This paragraph shall not prevent technical storage which is necessary for the conveyance of a communication without prejudice to the principle of confidentiality.
2. Paragraph 1 shall not affect any legally authorised recording of communications and the related traffic data when carried out in the course of lawful business practice for the purpose of providing evidence of a commercial transaction or of any other business communication.
3. Member States shall ensure that the use of electronic communications networks to store information or to gain access to information stored in the terminal equipment of a subscriber or user is only allowed on condition that the subscriber or user concerned is provided with clear and comprehensive information in accordance with Directive 95/46/EC, inter alia about the purposes of the processing, and is offered the right to refuse such processing by the data controller. This shall not prevent any technical storage or access for the sole purpose of carrying out or facilitating the transmission of a communication over an electronic communications network, or as strictly necessary in order to provide an information society service explicitly requested by the subscriber or user.

Article 6
Traffic data
1. Traffic data relating to subscribers and users processed and stored by the provider of a public communications network or publicly available electronic communications service must be erased or made anonymous when it is no longer needed for the purpose of the transmission of a communication without prejudice to paragraphs 2, 3 and 5 of this Article and Article 15(1).
2. Traffic data necessary for the purposes of subscriber billing and interconnection payments may be processed. Such processing is permissible only up to the end of the period during which the bill may lawfully be challenged or payment pursued.
3. For the purpose of marketing electronic communications services or for the provision of value added services, the provider of a publicly available electronic communications service may process the data referred to in paragraph 1 to the extent and for the duration necessary for such services or marketing, if the subscriber or user to whom the data relate has given his/her consent. Users or subscribers shall be given the possibility to withdraw their consent for the processing of traffic data at any time.
4. The service provider must inform the subscriber or user of the types of traffic data which are processed and of the duration of such processing for the purposes mentioned in paragraph 2 and, prior to obtaining consent, for the purposes mentioned in paragraph 3.
5. Processing of traffic data, in accordance with paragraphs 1, 2, 3 and 4, must be restricted to persons acting under the authority of providers of the public communications networks and publicly available electronic communications services handling billing or traffic management, customer enquiries, fraud detection, marketing electronic communications services or providing a value added service, and must be restricted to what is necessary for the purposes of such activities.
6. Paragraphs 1, 2, 3 and 5 shall apply without prejudice to the possibility for competent bodies to be informed of traffic data in conformity with applicable legislation with a view to settling disputes, in particular interconnection or billing disputes.

Article 7
Itemised billing
1. Subscribers shall have the right to receive non-itemised bills.
2. Member States shall apply national provisions in order to reconcile the rights of subscribers receiving itemised bills with the right to privacy of calling users and called subscribers, for example by ensuring that sufficient alternative privacy enhancing methods of communications or payments are available to such users and subscribers.

Article 8
Presentation and restriction of calling and connected line identification
1. Where presentation of calling line identification is offered, the service provider must offer the calling user the possibility, using a simple means and free of charge, of preventing the presentation of the calling line identification on a per-call basis. The calling subscriber must have this possibility on a per-line basis.
2. Where presentation of calling line identification is offered, the service provider must offer the called subscriber the possibility, using a simple means and free of charge for reasonable use of this function, of preventing the presentation of the calling line identification of incoming calls.
3. Where presentation of calling line identification is offered and where the calling line identification is presented prior to the call being established, the service provider must offer the called subscriber the possibility, using a simple means, of rejecting incoming calls where the presentation of the calling line identification has been prevented by the calling user or subscriber.
4. Where presentation of connected line identification is offered, the service provider must offer the called subscriber the possibility, using a simple means and free of charge, of preventing the presentation of the connected line identification to the calling user.
5. Paragraph 1 shall also apply with regard to calls to third countries originating in the Community. Paragraphs 2, 3 and 4 shall also apply to incoming calls originating in third countries.
6. Member States shall ensure that where presentation of calling and/or connected line identification is offered, the providers of publicly available electronic communications services inform the public thereof and of the possibilities set out in paragraphs 1, 2, 3 and 4.

Article 9
Location data other than traffic data
1. Where location data other than traffic data, relating to users or subscribers of public communications networks or publicly available electronic communications services, can be processed, such data may only be processed when they are made anonymous, or with the consent of the users or subscribers to the extent and for the duration necessary for the provision of a value added service. The service provider must inform the users or subscribers, prior to obtaining their consent, of the type of location data other than traffic data which will be processed, of the purposes and duration of the processing and whether the data will be transmitted to a third party for the purpose of providing the value added service. Users or subscribers shall be given the possibility to withdraw their consent for the processing of location data other than traffic data at any time.
2. Where consent of the users or subscribers has been obtained for the processing of location data other than traffic data, the user or subscriber must continue to have the possibility, using a simple means and free of charge, of temporarily refusing the processing of such data for each connection to the network or for each transmission of a communication.
3. Processing of location data other than traffic data in accordance with paragraphs 1 and 2 must be restricted to persons acting under the authority of the provider of the public communications network or publicly available communications service or of the third party providing the value added service, and must be restricted to what is necessary for the purposes of providing the value added service.

Article 10
Exceptions
Member States shall ensure that there are transparent procedures governing the way in which a provider of a public communications network and/or a publicly available electronic communications service may override:
(a) the elimination of the presentation of calling line identification, on a temporary basis, upon application of a subscriber requesting the tracing of malicious or nuisance calls. In this case, in accordance with national law, the data containing the identification of the calling subscriber will be stored and be made available by the provider of a public communications network and/or publicly available electronic communications service;
(b) the elimination of the presentation of calling line identification and the temporary denial or absence of consent of a subscriber or user for the processing of location data, on a per-line basis for organisations dealing with emergency calls and recognised as such by a Member State, including law enforcement agencies,

ambulance services and fire brigades, for the purpose of responding to such calls.

Article 11
Automatic call forwarding
Member States shall ensure that any subscriber has the possibility, using a simple means and free of charge, of stopping automatic call forwarding by a third party to the subscriber's terminal.

Article 12
Directories of subscribers
1. Member States shall ensure that subscribers are informed, free of charge and before they are included in the directory, about the purpose(s) of a printed or electronic directory of subscribers available to the public or obtainable through directory enquiry services, in which their personal data can be included and of any further usage possibilities based on search functions embedded in electronic versions of the directory.
2. Member States shall ensure that subscribers are given the opportunity to determine whether their personal data are included in a public directory, and if so, which, to the extent that such data are relevant for the purpose of the directory as determined by the provider of the directory, and to verify, correct or withdraw such data. Not being included in a public subscriber directory, verifying, correcting or withdrawing personal data from it shall be free of charge.
3. Member States may require that for any purpose of a public directory other than the search of contact details of persons on the basis of their name and, where necessary, a minimum of other identifiers, additional consent be asked of the subscribers.
4. Paragraphs 1 and 2 shall apply to subscribers who are natural persons. Member States shall also ensure, in the framework of Community law and applicable national legislation, that the legitimate interests of subscribers other than natural persons with regard to their entry in public directories are sufficiently protected.

Article 13
Unsolicited communications
1. The use of automated calling systems without human intervention (automatic calling machines), facsimile machines (fax) or electronic mail for the purposes of direct marketing may only be allowed in respect of subscribers who have given their prior consent.
2. Notwithstanding paragraph 1, where a natural or legal person obtains from its customers their electronic contact details for electronic mail, in the context of the sale of a product or a service, in accordance with Directive 95/46/EC, the same natural or legal person may use these electronic contact details for direct marketing of its own similar products or services provided that customers clearly and distinctly are given the opportunity to object, free of charge and in an easy manner, to such use of electronic contact details when they are collected and on the occasion of each message in case the customer has not initially refused such use.
3. Member States shall take appropriate measures to ensure that, free of charge, unsolicited communications for purposes of direct marketing, in cases other than those referred to in paragraphs 1 and 2, are not allowed either without the consent of the subscribers concerned or in respect of subscribers who do not wish to receive these communications, the choice between these options to be determined by national legislation.
4. In any event, the practice of sending electronic mail for purposes of direct marketing disguising or concealing the identity of the sender on whose behalf the communication is made, or without a valid address to which the recipient may send a request that such communications cease, shall be prohibited.
5. Paragraphs 1 and 3 shall apply to subscribers who are natural persons. Member States shall also ensure, in the framework of Community law and applicable national legislation, that the legitimate interests of subscribers other than natural persons with regard to unsolicited communications are sufficiently protected.

Article 14
Technical features and standardisation
1. In implementing the provisions of this Directive, Member States shall ensure, subject to paragraphs 2 and 3, that no mandatory requirements for specific technical features are imposed on terminal or other electronic communication equipment which could impede the placing of equipment on the market and the free circulation of such equipment in and between Member States.
2. Where provisions of this Directive can be implemented only by requiring specific technical features in electronic communications networks, Member States shall inform the Commission in accordance with the procedure provided for by Directive 98/34/EC of the European Parliament and of the Council of 22 June 1998 laying down a procedure for the provision of information in the field of technical standards and regulations and of rules on information society services(9).
3. Where required, measures may be adopted to ensure that terminal equipment is constructed in a way that is compatible with the right of users to protect and control the use of their personal data, in accordance with

Directive 1999/5/EC and Council Decision 87/95/EEC of 22 December 1986 on standardisation in the field of information technology and communications(10).

Article 15

Application of certain provisions of Directive 95/46/EC

1. Member States may adopt legislative measures to restrict the scope of the rights and obligations provided for in Article 5, Article 6, Article 8(1), (2), (3) and (4), and Article 9 of this Directive when such restriction constitutes a necessary, appropriate and proportionate measure within a democratic society to safeguard national security (i.e. State security), defence, public security, and the prevention, investigation, detection and prosecution of criminal offences or of unauthorised use of the electronic communication system, as referred to in Article 13(1) of Directive 95/46/EC. To this end, Member States may, inter alia, adopt legislative measures providing for the retention of data for a limited period justified on the grounds laid down in this paragraph. All the measures referred to in this paragraph shall be in accordance with the general principles of Community law, including those referred to in Article 6(1) and (2) of the Treaty on European Union.

2. The provisions of Chapter III on judicial remedies, liability and sanctions of Directive 95/46/EC shall apply with regard to national provisions adopted pursuant to this Directive and with regard to the individual rights derived from this Directive.

3. The Working Party on the Protection of Individuals with regard to the Processing of Personal Data instituted by Article 29 of Directive 95/46/EC shall also carry out the tasks laid down in Article 30 of that Directive with regard to matters covered by this Directive, namely the protection of fundamental rights and freedoms and of legitimate interests in the electronic communications sector.

Article 16

Transitional arrangements

1. Article 12 shall not apply to editions of directories already produced or placed on the market in printed or off-line electronic form before the national provisions adopted pursuant to this Directive enter into force.

2. Where the personal data of subscribers to fixed or mobile public voice telephony services have been included in a public subscriber directory in conformity with the provisions of Directive 95/46/EC and of Article 11 of Directive 97/66/EC before the national provisions adopted in pursuance of this Directive enter into force, the personal data of such subscribers may remain included in this public directory in its printed or electronic versions, including versions with reverse search functions, unless subscribers indicate otherwise, after having received complete information about purposes and options in accordance with Article 12 of this Directive.

Article 17

Transposition

1. Before 31 October 2003 Member States shall bring into force the provisions necessary to comply with this Directive. They shall forthwith inform the Commission thereof.

When Member States adopt those provisions, they shall contain a reference to this Directive or be accompanied by such a reference on the occasion of their official publication. The methods of making such reference shall be laid down by the Member States.

2. Member States shall communicate to the Commission the text of the provisions of national law which they adopt in the field governed by this Directive and of any subsequent amendments to those provisions.

Chapter 5

FREE MOVEMENT AND ESTABLISHMENT

Although the free movement of workers has advantages, it also has disadvantages such as, the impoverishment of regions of emigration in terms of their most dynamic human capital and an overloading of the social services in the areas of immigration. The free movement of labour within the European Union is therefore no panacea. It has to be channelled and supported by social measures in favour of migrant workers and their families. It has above all to be coupled with an efficient regional policy capable of creating jobs in the less favoured regions of the Union to provide employment for the labour available in situ [see section 3.1.]. Under these conditions, the freedoms of movement and establishment are acquired rights of EU salaried and non salaried-workers.

5.1. Free movement of salaried workers

One of the great achievements of European integration has been the transformation of economic migratory movements of the post-war period into free movement of workers. The freedom of movement of workers allows EU citizens to seek, within the Union, better living and working conditions than are available to them in their region of origin. It therefore boosts greatly the chances of improving the standards of living of the individual. At the same time, freedom of movement reduces social pressure in the poorest regions of the European Union and allows the living conditions of those remaining to improve. In the EU in general it facilitates the adjustment of the labour supply to the variations in the demand of undertakings and opens the way for more coherent and more effective economic policies at a European level. Thus, freedom of movement of workers contributes to the attainment of the objectives of the common market as well as to the flexibility and efficiency of the labour market.

Free movement is not restricted to workers. Article 18 of the EC Treaty, which has direct effect[1], gives every citizen of the Union the right to move and reside freely within the territory of the Member States. A citizen of the European Union who no longer enjoys a right of residence as a migrant worker in the host Member State can, as a citizen of the Union, enjoy there a right of residence by direct application of Article 18(1) EC[2]. The same right is enjoyed by his spouse, their descendants under the age of 21 and their dependent relatives in the ascending line. This right contributes to a concrete and practical expression of European citizenship [see section 4.2.]. Freedom of movement may contribute to the attainment of the objectives of the common market, while giving more flexibility and thus greater efficiency to the labour market. The challenge to the Union now is, however, to create a real European mobility area, in which freedom of movement becomes not only a legal entitlement but also a daily reality for people across Europe. This

1 Moussis (2004), section 3.3.
2 Judgment of 17 September 2002, Case C-413/99, Baumbast and R v Secretary of State for the Home Department, ECR 2002, p. I-07091.

calls for a complex interaction of common policies.

5.1.1. The common labour market

Article 69 of the **ECSC Treaty** [see section 1.1.] committed the Member States to removing any restriction based on nationality upon the employment in the coal and steel industries of workers who were nationals of Member States and had "recognised qualifications in a coal-mining or steel-making occupation", subject to the limitations imposed by the basic requirements of health and public policy. That provision was repeated in virtually the same terms in Articles 96 of the **EAEC Treaty (Euratom)**, although the latter also called upon the Council to adopt a directive on free access to skilled employment in the field of nuclear energy, which it duly did in July 1962[1]. Limiting free movement to skilled labour was logical for the sectoral Treaties, which could only deal with economic activities that they governed.

The **EEC Treaty** had the objective, as regards workers, of creating a common labour market, which meant the free movement of labour within the Community and the abolition of any discrimination based on nationality between workers of the Member States as regards employment, remuneration and other conditions of work and employment. Under Article 39 of the EC Treaty (former Art. 48 EEC), freedom of movement of workers entails the right, subject to limitations justified on grounds of public policy, public security or public health to accept offers of employment actually made, to move freely within the territory of Member States for this purpose, to stay in a Member State for the purpose of employment and to remain in the territory of that Member State after having been employed in it. The Community legislation that materialised those principles was completed in 1968 and, thus, freedom of movement of workers was achieved, from the legal point of view, at the same time as customs union [see annex 5.1.]. This freedom was extended to all the workers in the European Economic Area in 1994[2]. The worker can continue to reside, in the country in which he or she has settled after the termination of his or her employment. That takes specific form in the automatic renewal of the residence permit held by the person concerned as an employed person. The members of the family resident with him or her enjoy that right even after the worker's death. Nowadays, all persons residing legally in a Member State have equal rights of movement and residence in the other states of the Union.

The **principle of the free movement of workers** applies equally to nationals of third countries, who stay lawfully in a Member State. Indeed, according to a Judgment of the Court of Justice, a firm established in a member country, which employs lawfully and habitually non-member country nationals, may detach them in another Member State in order to provide services[3]. The principle of free movement applies also to all cases of **posting of workers** taking place in the framework of a transnational provision of services. Thus, workers posted to another Member State by their employers enjoy at least the terms and conditions compulsory in the host Member State[4] [see annex 5.2.].

Article 39(4) of the EC Treaty excludes employment in the national public service from the principle of the free movement of workers. However, according to the Commission and the Court of Justice, this exception from the general principle of free movement does not concern jobs, which, even if they are funded by the State, are not public service as such, e.g. bodies responsible for administering commercial services, public health care services, teaching in State educational establishments and research for non-military purposes in public establishments[5]. Moreover, according to the Court of Justice, given the fundamental character of the principles of free movement and of equal treatment, the derogations based on Article 39.4 (ex article 48.4) should not

1 Directive OJ L 57, 09.07.1962, p. 1650-1652.
2 Regulation 1612/68, OJ L 257, 19.10.1968 and Agreement on the EEA, OJ L 1, 03.01.1994, pp. 325, 572.
3 Judgment given on 9 August 1994 in Case C-43/93, Vander Elst v OMI, ECR 1994, p. I-3803.
4 Directive 96/71, OJ L 18, 21.01.1997.
5 See Judgment of 12 March 1998, Commission v Hellenic Republic, Case C-187/96, ECR 1998 p. I-1095.

exceed the aims of this exception to the rule[1] and should not contravene the principle of non-discrimination[2].

A directive implementing the principle of equal treatment between persons irrespective of racial or ethnic origin, provided in Article 13 of the EC Treaty, seeks to prohibit discrimination throughout the Community in different areas such as employment, education, social security, health care and access to goods and services[3] [see annex 5.3.]. It defines the concepts of direct and indirect discrimination, gives right of redress to victims of discrimination, imposes an obligation on the employer to prove that the principle of equal treatment has not been breached, and offers protection against harassment and victimisation in all the Member States.

The Community has set up a general **framework for combating discrimination** on grounds of religion or belief, disability, age or sexual orientation as regards employment and occupation[4] [see annex 5.4.]. A Community **action programme to combat discrimination** (2001-06) aims to promote measures to combat all forms of discrimination except that based on sex, which is the subject of specific Community action[5] [see annex 5.5.]. The objective is to change practices and attitudes by mobilising the players involved and fostering the exchange of information and good practice. In particular, the programme seeks to set up databases and promote the networking of those involved.

The Court of Justice has consistently held that the rules on equal treatment prohibit not only overt discrimination but also any form of concealed discrimination, which is based on various distinction criteria but has the same effect[6]. However, discrimination exists only where different rules are applied to comparable situations or the same rule is applied to different situations. For instance, where direct taxes are concerned, the Court has ruled that the provisions of the free movement of workers do not in principle preclude the application of national rules under which a non-resident working as an employed person in a Member State is taxed more heavily on his income than a resident in the same employment[7].

The principle of free movement of workers cannot be hindered by the rules of **sports associations**. In the Bosman judgment, which revolutionised European sport customs, the Court of Justice held, indeed, that Article 48 EEC (Art. 39 TEC) applied to the collective rules adopted by private sports associations since the exercise of sport as an economic activity was covered by Community law[8] [see section 7.1.]. In particular, the Court held that by preventing or deterring nationals of a Member State from leaving their country of origin the transfer rules constituted an obstacle to the free movement of workers. According to the Court, the rules in question are not likely to provide encouragement and financing for small clubs training young players, since there was no guarantee that they would collect such fees and since the amount of the fees bore no relation to the costs actually incurred for the training. The Court also held that under Article 48 (EEC) no rules could require clubs to field, for a given match, only a limited number of professional players who were nationals of other Member States, but it admitted that the nationality requirement was justified in the case of matches between the national teams of different countries.

However, the Court judgment did not definitely solve the question of the free movement of football and other players. In fact, following complaints by European football associations, the Commission had initiated proceedings in 1999 on the grounds that the International Federation of Football Associations (FIFA) rules were illegal because they denied players the right to negotiate the termination of their contract. The Commission's aim was to strike a balance between the players' fundamental right to free movement and the equally legitimate objective of the integrity of

1 Judgment of 12 February 1974, case 152/73, Sotgiu, ECR 1974, p. 153.
2 Judgment of 12 March 1998, Case C-187/96, ECR 1998, I-1095.
3 Directive 2000/43, OJ L 180, 19.07.2000.
4 Directive 2000/78, OJ L 303, 02.12.2000.
5 Decision 2000/750, OJ L 303, 02.12.2000.
6 See, e.g., case 65/81, ECR 1982, p. 33 and case 137/84, ECR 1985, p. 2681.
7 Judgment of 14 February 1995, case C-279/93, Finanzamt Köln-Altstadt v R. Schumacker, ECR 1995, p. I-0225.
8 Judgment of 15 December 1995, case C-415/93, Jean-Marc Bosman, ECR 1995, p. I-4921.

the sport and the stability of the championships. Following discussions between FIFA and the Commission, FIFA's Executive Committee drew up satisfactory rules and application regulations, which were adopted in Buenos Aires on 5 July 2001.

5.1.2. Social security and other measures for migrant workers

Adequate protection by European **provisions in the field of social security** is necessary for the effective use of the right of the citizens of one Member State to stay and work in another State of the Union. Without such protection, persons moving across borders to work or to look for a job, would risk losing all or part of their rights acquired or in the process of being acquired under national legislation (concerning, for example pensions, health insurance, unemployment benefits or family benefits). Article 42 of the EC Treaty (Art. 51 EEC) provides for the adoption of the measures necessary for that purpose through arrangements to secure for migrant workers and their dependents: (a) aggregation, for the purpose of acquiring and retaining the right to benefit, of all periods taken into account under the laws of several countries, and (b) payment of benefits to persons resident in the territories of Member States. The system required by the Treaty was in fact adopted in 1958, but it has undergone many changes and improvements since then.

On the basis of Regulations 1408/71 and 574/72, **pensions of similar nature** acquired in the various Member States may be aggregated, but the person concerned may not obtain total benefits in excess of the highest pension he or she would have obtained if he or she had spent his or her whole insurance career under the legislation of any one of the States in which he or she had been employed[1] [see annexes 5.6 and 5.7.]. This legislation covers also **students** moving within the Community, taking account of their specific situation and of the special features of the schemes under which they are insured. **Civil servants** and persons treated as such have equal treatment as regards general statutory pension rights and special schemes for civil servants prevailing in the Member States[2] [see annex 5.8.]. The supplementary pension rights of employed and self-employed persons moving within the European Union are equally guaranteed[3]. Rights and obligations comparable to those applying to EU citizens are granted to nationals of third countries who are legally resident in the Community and who satisfy the other conditions laid down in Regulations 1408/71 and 574/72[4].

The **unemployed person** who leaves for another Member State to seek employment receives, for a maximum period of three months from the date of departure, the benefits of the country in which he or she was last employed, to be paid for by that country. Repayments in respect of health care provided for members of the family resident in a Member State other than that in which the worker is employed and insured are made entirely to the institutions of the country of residence. Family allowances are granted under the legislation of, and at the rate laid down in, the country of employment. According to the Court of Justice, such allowances are not subject to requirements as to minimum period of residence[5].

Similar arrangements cover **self-employed persons** and their families[6] as well as employed persons or self-employed persons pursuing activities in the territories of two or more Member States[7]. Any insured person staying temporarily in a Member State other than the one in which he or she is insured, for tourist or employment purposes, may be admitted to hospital or receive refunds in respect of urgent medical care in the host State on presentation of a **special form (E 111)**. Indeed, various **E-FORMS** help transfer social rights within the European Union and the European Economic Area. A new European health insurance card should soon replace all the cur-

1 Regulation 1408/71, OJ L 149, 05.07.1971, Regulation 574/72, OJ L 74, 27.03.1972 and Regulation 631/2004, JO L 100, 06.04.2004.
2 Regulation 1606/98, OJ L 209, 25.07.1998.
3 Regulation 1223/98, OJ L 168, 13.06.1998.
4 Regulation 859/2003, OJ L 124, 20.05.2003.
5 Judgment given on 10 March 1993, Case C-111/91, Commission v Luxembourg, ECR 1993, I-840.
6 Regulation 1390/81, OJ L 143, 29.05.1981.
7 Regulation 3811/86, OJ L 355, 16.12.1986.

rent paper forms needed for health treatment in another Member State and should also simplify procedures without changing existing rights and obligations[1].

For the effective functioning of a common labour market, it is also necessary that potential migrant workers have at their disposal adequate information regarding the number and nature of jobs available in the Community and the qualifications required. This is the task of the **European Employment Service (EURES)**, a network of some 400 "Euroadvisers" from the national employment services, employer organisations, trade unions, regional administrations and universities, specially trained to deal with the needs of transnational job-seekers and job-providers[2] [see annex 5.11.].

The core of the **EURES network** is a computerised databank providing information on transnational job and recruitment opportunities, as well as information on living and working conditions in the countries of the Union, from accommodation to contract law and taxation. The European Commission ensures the coordination of the network. EURES serves both as an employment service at the scale of Europe, having as task to inform, counsel and place job seekers on the territory of the European Economic Area, and as a forum for the examination, at operational level, of all questions relating to employment in Europe. By encouraging trans-border recruitment and acquisition of qualifications, this network makes a real contribution to the creation of a European labour market. More than half a million people seek the EURES services every year. An Internet site on the Europa server is a key source of information for job-seekers and employers as regards living and working conditions in the different Member States, providing access to the EURES database of job vacancies (around 10 000) and links to all the Internet sites of the participating public employment services (http://europa.eu.int/jobs/eures).

To facilitate the mobility of workers within the Community it was also necessary to ensure and encourage the **education of the children** of migrant workers. That was achieved in a Council Directive, which obliges the Member States to treat the children of migrant workers in the same way as the children of national workers, including as regards the aid granted by the public authorities to school pupils and to students[3] [see annex 5.9.]. Two Council Resolutions on school provision for gypsy and traveller children and on school provision for children of occupational travellers respectively, provide for measures to be taken by the Community and the Member States to resolve the specific problems of those poorly educated people[4].

Concerning **sickness insurance** covered by Regulation 1408/71, the Court of Justice has established that, when an insured person has been authorised by the competent institution to go to another Member State for treatment, the institution of the place where the treatment is provided is required to provide him with benefits in kind in accordance with the rules on assumption of the costs of health care which the latter administers, as if the person concerned were registered with it[5]. An authorisation can be refused on the ground of lack of medical necessity, only if the same or equally effective treatment can be obtained without undue delay at an establishment having a contractual arrangement with the insured person's sickness insurance fund[6].

5.1.3. Common treatment of nationals of third countries

The Member States of the EU are all subject to **migration pressures** from many - and often new - sources to which they have to respond by finding the balance between economic and humanitarian considerations in line with Community legislation and key international agreements. The abolition of internal border controls and the notion of a common external border reinforces the desirability for the Union to develop more common approaches and closer cooperation in the

---

1 COM (2003) 73, 17 Februqry 2003.
2 Decision2003/8, OJ L 5, 10.01.2003.
3 Directive 77/486, OJ L 199, 06.08.1977.
4 OJ C 153, 21.06.1989.
5 Judgment of 12 July 2001, Case C-368/98 Vanbraekel, ECR 2001, p. I-05363.
6 Judgment of 12 July 2001, Case C-157/99, Geraets-Smits, ECR 2001, p. I-05473.

immigration policy area. These are new concerns for the Community which emerged with the completion of the single market and which are taken into account by the Treaty on European Union. Hence, the common policy on the treatment of nationals of third countries is a spillover effect of the single market legislation.

In fact, the **abolition of checks at internal borders** of the Community is effective both for the citizens of the Member States and for third country nationals, once they have crossed the external frontiers of a Member State. In other words, freedom of movement applies to all those within the territory of the Community. This is why the Member States must have common rules for the crossing of their borders by foreigners and for the treatment of foreigners within their territory. This common need has led to the adoption of common policies in the fields of visas, immigration, the right of asylum, the status of refugees and extradition. The ARGO programme (2002-2006) is designed to help promote administrative cooperation in the fields of external borders, visas, asylum and immigration, particularly from the point of view of implementing and properly applying the relevant Community rules[1].

Visa policy is now under Community competence. A Council regulation established a uniform format for visas for nationals of third countries[2]. This single, clearly identifiable visa is issued by the Member States and includes all the necessary information. It meets the highest technical standards, notably as regards safeguards against counterfeiting and falsification. It guarantees, however, protection of the personal data involved. Another regulation determined the third countries whose nationals are subject to the visa requirement for crossing the external borders of the European Union, and those whose nationals are exempt from that requirement[3]. A regulation facilitates the free movement within the EU territory of holders of long-stay visas pending the issue of their residence permit[4] [see annex 5.12.]. An EC Directive harmonised financial penalties imposed on carriers transporting into the territory of the Member States third-country nationals lacking the documents necessary for admission[5]. Several measures were adopted in the context of cooperation in the field of the **justice and home affairs (JHA) policy**, notably: a joint action on airport transit arrangements[6]; consular cooperation regarding visas[7]; the organisation of pre-frontier assistance and training assignments to airports outside the Union[8]; and a system for exchanging information with a view to facilitating the detection of false and stolen documents[9].

Immigration policy has entered the Community arena through the prior consultation procedure on migratory policies towards third countries, in place since 1988[10]. The European Monitoring Centre on Racism and Xenophobia in Vienna was set up in order to provide objective, reliable and comparable data and improve the exchange of information and experience in these fields[11]. A regulation laid down a uniform format for residence permits for third-country nationals with high technology specifications, including enhanced anti-forgery, counterfeiting and falsification standards[12]. On the contrary, in the framework of intergovernmental cooperation in the fields of JHA were adopted: the Council recommendations on harmonising means of combating illegal immigration and illegal employment and on concerted action in carrying out expulsion measures[13]; the Council resolution on the status of third-country nationals residing on a long-term basis in the territory of the Member States[14]; a joint action on a uniform format for residence permits to facili-

1 Decision 2002/463, OJ L 161, 19.06.2002.
2 Regulation 1683/95, OJ L 164, 14.07.1995 and Regulation 334/2002, OJ L 53, 23.02.2002.
3 Regulation 539/2001, OJ L 81, 21.03.2001 and Regulation 453/2003, OJ L 69, 13.03.2003..
4 Regulation 1091/2001, OJ L 150, 06.06.2001.
5 Directive 2001/51, OJ L 187, 10.07.2001.
6 Joint Action 96/197/JHA, OJ L 63, 13.03.1996.
7 OJ C 80, 18.03.1996, p. 1.
8 Joint Position 96/622/JHA, OJ L 281, 31.10.1996.
9 Decision 2000/261/JHA, OJ L 81, 01.04.2000.
10 Decision 88/384, OJ L 183, 14.07.1988.
11 Regulation 1035/97, OJ L 151, 10.06.1997.
12 Regulation 1030/2002, OJ L 157, 15.06.2002.
13 OJ C 5, 10.01.1996, p. 1-7.
14 OJ C 80, 18.03.1996, p. 2-4.

tate inspection by the competent authorities[1]; a joint action to combat racism and xenophobia in the field of judicial cooperation[2]; and the Resolution encouraging the Member States to deter marriages of convenience concluded with the sole aim of circumventing the rules on entry and residence of third-country nationals[3].

A directive provides a definition of the facilitation of **illegal immigration** and approximates legal provisions concerning precise definition of the infringement in question and exemptions[4] [see annex 5.13.]. A framework decision aims at strengthening of the penal framework to prevent the facilitation of unauthorised entry, transit and residence by defining minimum rules for penalties, liability of legal persons and jurisdiction[5]. According to the Commission, the fight against illegal immigration should include: promoting actions in, and supporting actions of, countries of origin and transit, taking account of human rights policy; stepping up surveillance; intensifying administrative cooperation and information exchanges; harmonising the concept of adequate sanctions against promoters of illegal immigration; addressing the problem of undeclared work of illegal residents; strengthening police cooperation and the role of Europol[6]. In a Green Paper on a Community return policy on illegal residents, the Commission considers this policy as a part of a comprehensive immigration policy[7].

A particularly difficult area, in view of different traditions, but essential for the smooth operation of the internal market is that of the **right of asylum**. Of course, the Dublin asylum Convention, which came into force on 1 September 1997, commits all signatories to examining all asylum demands deposited by a citizen of a third country at the frontier or on the territory of Member States and exchanging individualised information on all such demands[8]. But this Convention does not harmonise national legislations on asylum and, therefore, it does not create a Community refugee status. Nevertheless, the Community set up, in June 1992, a Centre for Information, Research and Exchange on Asylum matters (CIREA). A Council resolution deals with minimum guarantees that asylum procedures must present to ensure that they comply with the Geneva Convention of 28 July 1951 on the **Status of Refugees**. Joint positions deal with: the harmonised application of the term "refugee" in Article 1 of the Geneva Convention; the establishment of an alert and emergency procedure for burden-sharing with regard to the admission and residence of displaced persons on a temporary basis[9]; and the financing of specific projects in favour of displaced persons (asylum seekers and refugees) who have found temporary protection in the Member States[10].

Several **means of the asylum policy** were adopted in the Community context. A directive aims to give the European Union the means to act in the event of a mass influx of displaced persons by means of a mechanism for immediate protection, establishing minimum standards for giving this protection and for ensuring a balance of efforts between the Member States in receiving refugees and displaced persons[11]. The range of instruments available on EU asylum policy include: the exchange of information concerning assistance for the voluntary repatriation of third-country nationals[12]; the monitoring of the implementation by the Member States of measures adopted concerning asylum[13]; minimum standards on information, documentation, health, accommodation, clothing and money on the reception of applicants for asylum[14]; minimum stan-

1 Joint Action 97/11/JHA, OJ L 7, 10.01.1997 and Decision 98/701/JHA, OJ L 333, 09.12.1998.
2 Joint Action 96/443/JHA, OJ L 185, 24.07.1996.
3 OJ C 382, 16.12.1997, p. 1-2.
4 Directive 2002/90, OJ L 328, 05.12.2002.
5 Decision 2002/946, OJ L 328, 05.12.2002.
6 COM (2001) 672, 15 November 2001.
7 Commission communication, COM (2002) 175, 10 April 2002.
8 OJ C 254, 19.08.1997, p. 1-12 and OJ C 191, 23.06.1997, p. 27-28.
9 Joint Position 96/196/JHA, OJ L 63, 13.03.1996.
10 Joint Actions 97/477/JHA and 97/478/JHA, OJ L 205, 31.07.1997 and Joint Actions 98/304/JHA and 98/305/JHA, OJ L 138, 09.05.1998.
11 Directive 2001/55, OJ L 212, 07.08.2001.
12 Decision 97/340/CFSP, OJ L 147, 05.06.1997.
13 Decision 97/420/CFSP, OJ L 178, 07.07.1997.
14 COM (2001) 181, OJ C 213 , 31.07.2001.

dards for the reception of asylum seekers in Member States[1] [see annex 5.14.]; and criteria and mechanisms for determining the Member State responsible for examining an application for asylum lodged in one of the Member States by a third-country national, incorporating the related Dublin Convention into the Community framework[2]. The resources of the European Refugee Fund are divided among the Member States in proportion to the number of asylum-seekers they receive and the number of refugees they accommodate on their territory[3]. A centralised system, "Eurodac", was set up for processing, comparing and transmitting in digital format fingerprints of asylum seekers and certain other third-country nationals[4]. The principle of mutual recognition covers an **expulsion** decision issued by a competent authority in one Member State against a third-country national[5].

5.2. Freedom of establishment and recognition of diplomas

Freedom of establishment means the free movement of self-employed persons. For them, as for salaried workers, the basic principle is equality of treatment of all Community citizens, i.e. the abolition of discriminations based on nationality. **Freedom of establishment includes** the right to take up and pursue activities as self-employed persons and to set up and manage undertakings, in particular companies or firms within the meaning of the second paragraph of Article 48 (TEC), i.e., companies established under the conditions laid down for its own nationals by the law of the country where such establishment is effected. The freedom of establishment of companies extends to what is known as freedom of secondary establishment, i.e. the setting up of agencies, branches or subsidiaries (Art. 43 TEC).

Under Article 46 (TEC), the principle of freedom of establishment does not concern national provisions providing for special treatment for foreign nationals on **grounds of public policy, public security or public health.** A Council Directive of 1964 contains an enumeration of the circumstances, which cannot be invoked as grounds for refusal of entry or deportation and a series of rules concerning the procedure, which must be followed where nationals of Member States may be refused entry or deported[6]. In order to take into account the concept of citizenship of the EU introduced by the Treaty of Amsterdam [see section 1.1.], as well as the case law of the Court of Justice, the Commission has laid down guidelines for correctly interpreting and applying the directive[7].

5.2.1. Right of establishment

Whereas, freedom to provide services chiefly concerns the pursuit of an economic activity by a person in another Member State without having the principal or secondary place of business in that State, **right of establishment entails** permanent installation in a Member State in order to pursue an economic activity in that State. In fact, the situation of the person who establishes himself is characterised by the fact that he creates a permanent link with the country of establishment, unlike somebody who provides services in a country other then that of his permanent establishment.

The right for nationals of EU Member States to work or pursue activities as self-employed persons in the Member States means the **right to enter and to reside** in the member country in

[1] Directive 2003/9, OJ L 31, 06.02.2003.
[2] Regulation 343/2003, OJ L 50, 25.02.2003.
[3] Decision 2000/596, OJ L 252, 06.10.2000.
[4] Regulation 2725/2000, OJ L 316, 15.12.2000 and Regulation 407/2002, OJ L 62, 05.03.2002.
[5] Directive 2001/40, OJ L 149, 02.06.2001.
[6] Directive 64/221, OJ 56, 04.04.1964 and OJ L 14, 20.01.1975.
[7] COM (1999) 372, 19 July 1999.

which they wish to work or pursue those activities. This right is extended to their spouses, children and other members of their families[1] [see annex 5.15.]. Nationals of one Member State have the right to remain in the territory of a Member State after having pursued activities as self-employed persons in that State[2] [see annex 5.16.]. The right of residence is certified, for those concerned, by a residence permit for a national of a Member State of the European Community, which is issued by the authorities of the country of residence on presentation, by the interested party, of an identity card or passport[3].

In Articles 54 and 63, the EEC Treaty stipulated that the Council would, acting on proposals from the Commission, draw up programmes for the **abolition of restrictions** on freedom of establishment and freedom to provide services. Indeed, on 18 December 1961 the Council adopted two general programmes for the abolition of restrictions on freedom of establishment and freedom to provide services respectively. However, through its judgment of 21 June 1974 in the Reyners case (Dutch legal practitioner wishing to pursue his profession in Belgium), the Court established the **direct effect** of Article 52 EEC (Art. 43 TEC)[4]. It held that any individual may, on the basis of Article 52 of the EEC Treaty (43 TEC), demand directly the same treatment as is applied to nationals[5]. After that judgment, the abolition of discriminatory practices is based directly on the provisions of the Treaty.

5.2.2. Recognition of diplomas

After removing obvious discriminatory practices, there could, however, remain other obstacles to the freedom of establishment, i.e. the numerous requirements of the Member States with regard to the training of employed and self-employed persons, and the detailed arrangements for pursuing industrial and commercial activities. Even though these requirements were not in themselves discriminatory, they could impede the free establishment, if they differed from country to country and obliged the interested person to **take a new examination** for the recognition of his or her professional competence. That is why Article 47 of the EC Treaty empowers the Council and the Parliament to issue directives for the mutual recognition of diplomas, certificates and other evidence of formal qualifications and for the coordination of national provisions concerning the taking up and pursuit of activities as self-employed persons.

Such directives have in fact been adopted, in order to establish the comparability and the mutual recognition of **diplomas and qualifications for certain professions**. A series of Council Decisions set up advisory committees on training, and a series of Directives aimed at the mutual recognition of diplomas, certificates and other evidence of formal qualifications, comprising measures to facilitate the effective exercise of freedom of establishment and freedom to provide services in respect of: nurses[6], dental practitioners[7], veterinarians[8], midwives[9], architects[10], pharmacists[11] and doctors[12]. In parallel the Council decided to lay down provisions relating to the comparability of vocational training qualifications in the hotel-restaurant, motor vehicle repair and construction sectors[13] [see annex 5.17]. A Directive facilitates practice of the profession of lawyer on a permanent basis in a Member State other than that in which the qualification was obtained without an aptitude test or adaptation period[14] [see annex 18]. The Directive has not abol-

1 Directive 73/148, OJ L 172, 28.06.1973.
2 Directive 75/34, OJ L 14, 20.01.1975.
3 Directive 90/364, OJ L 180, 13.07.1990.
4 Moussis (2004), section 3.3.
5 Judgment of 21 June 1974, Case 2/74, ECR 1974, p. 631.
6 Directives 77/452 and 77/453, OJ L 176, 15.07.1977 and Directive 2001/19, OJ L 206, 31.07.2001.
7 Directives 78/686 and 78/687, OJ L 233, 24.08.1978 and Directive 2001/19, OJ L 206, 31.07.2001.
8 Directives 78/1026 and 78/1027, OJ L 362, 23.12.1978 and Directive 2001/19, OJ L 206, 31.07.2001.
9 Directives 80/154 and 80/155, OJ L 33, 11.02.1980 and Directive 2001/19, OJ L 206, 31.07.2001.
10 Directive 85/384, OJ L 223, 21.08.1985 and Directive 2001/19, OJ L 206, 31.07.2001.
11 Directives 85/432 and 85/433, OJ L 253, 24.09.1985 and Directive 2001/19, OJ L 206, 31.07.2001.
12 Directive 93/16, OJ L 167, 30.06.1975 and Directive 2001/19, OJ L 206, 31.07.2001.
13 Decision 85/368, OJ L 199, 31.07.1985.
14 Directive 98/5, OJ L 77, 14.03.1998.

ished the requirement that the lawyer concerned should know the national law applicable in the cases he handles but has simply released him from the obligation to prove that knowledge in advance[1].

However, the issuing of Directives aimed at the mutual recognition of diplomas, certificates and other evidence of formal qualification is not necessary any more, since the Community has adopted a **general system for the recognition of higher-education diplomas** awarded on completion of professional education and training of at least three years' duration[2] [see annex 5.19.]. The salient features of this system are the following: the principle of mutual trust amongst the Member States; the principle of the comparability of university studies between Member States; the mutual recognition of diplomas without prior harmonisation of the conditions for taking up and pursuing occupations, and lastly the principle that any divergence between Member States, in particular as regards training, should be offset by vocational experience. This system means, provided that the persons pursuing a profession fulfil certain minimum conditions as to qualifications, experience and professional education, that their qualifications will be recognised in all Member States and they will be authorised to pursue their activities without restriction.

A similar system relates to diplomas and certificates awarded on completion of **professional education and training of fewer than three years** of higher education or not covered by higher education. It covers two training levels: higher education or post-secondary diplomas where course duration is less than three years and secondary education diplomas. It also applies to certain non-graduates who have acquired professional experience[3] [see annex 5.20.]. There is provision for link-up between the two systems in order to cover professions that fall under the first system in one Member State and under the second in another.

A simple mechanism exists also for **recognising qualifications for professional activities** outside the scope of the general systems above, notably in the distributive trade and craft sectors. The directive that establishes it is based on the principle of the equivalence of qualifications[4] [see annex 5.21.]. A Member State may not, on the grounds of inadequate qualifications, refuse to permit a national of another Member State to take up or pursue any of the activities listed in the directive, without having first compared the knowledge and skills certified by the diplomas, certificates or other evidence of formal qualifications obtained by the beneficiary with those required under its own national rules. Where, the comparative examination shows a substantial difference, the host Member State must give the beneficiary the opportunity, either to demonstrate that he or she has acquired the knowledge and skills which were lacking or to undergo an adaptation period. According to the Court, all qualifications and experience must be taken into account, that is to say, both those acquired in another Member State and those acquired in a non-member country[5].

With these general systems for the recognition of diplomas and qualifications, any EU national has the right to have vocational qualifications obtained in another Member State **recognised in respect of any host Member State** which regulates any activity whatsoever in its territory. However, in order to enable the holders of vocational training qualifications to have certificates which are valid in all the Member States and the employers to check that these certificates are relevant to their needs, the Council, in July 1996, called on the Member States to indicate in the certificates the content of the training and the nature of the qualifications. It also called on them to promote measures for vocational training certificates to be issued in other Community languages[6].

---

1 Judgment of 7 November 2000, Case C-168/98 Luxembourg v Parliament and Council, ECR 2000, p. I-9131.
2 Directive 89/48, OJ L 19, 24.01.1989 and Directive 2001/19, OJ L 206, 31.07.2001.
3 Directive 92/51, OJ L 209, 24.07.1992 and Directive 2001/19, OJ L 206, 31.07.2001.
4 Directive 1999/42, OJ L 201, 31.07.1999.
5 Judgment of 14 September 2000, Case C-238/98, Hocsman, ECR 2000, p. I-6623.
6 OJ C 224, 01.08.1996, p. 7-8.

FREE MOVEMENT AND ESTABLISHMENT

Annex 5.1.

Regulation (EEC) No 1612/68 of the Council of 15 October 1968 on **freedom of movement for workers** within the Community
Official Journal L 257 , 19/10/1968 P. 0002 - 0012

MAIN PROVISIONS

PART I: EMPLOYMENT AND WORKERS' FAMILIES

TITLE I Eligibility for employment

Article 1
1. Any national of a Member State, shall, irrespective of his place of residence, have the right to take up an activity as an employed person, and to pursue such activity, within the territory of another Member State in accordance with the provisions laid down by law, regulation or administrative action governing the employment of nationals of that State.
2. He shall, in particular, have the right to take up available employment in the territory of another Member State with the same priority as nationals of that State.

Article 2
Any national of a Member State and any employer pursuing an activity in the territory of a Member State may exchange their applications for and offers of employment, and may conclude and perform contracts of employment in accordance with the provisions in force laid down by law, regulation or administrative action, without any discrimination resulting therefrom.

Article 3
1. Under this Regulation, provisions laid down by law, regulation or administrative action or administrative practices of a Member State shall not apply: - where they limit application for and offers of employment, or the right of foreign nationals to take up and pursue employment or subject these to conditions not applicable in respect of their own nationals ; or
- where, though applicable irrespective of nationality, their exclusive or principal aim or effect is to keep nationals of other Member States away from the employment offered.

This provision shall not apply to conditions relating to linguistic knowledge required by reason of the nature of the post to be filled.
2. There shall be included in particular among the provisions or practices of a Member State referred to in the first subparagraph of paragraph 1 those which: (a) prescribe a special recruitment procedure for foreign nationals;
(b) limit or restrict the advertising of vacancies in the press or through any other medium or subject it to conditions other than those applicable in respect of employers pursuing their activities in the territory of that Member State;
(c) subject eligibility for employment to conditions of registration with employment offices or impede recruitment of individual workers, where persons who do not reside in the territory of that State are concerned.

Article 4
1. Provisions laid down by law, regulation or administrative action of the Member States which restrict by number or percentage the employment of foreign nationals in any undertaking, branch of activity or region, or at

a national level, shall not apply to nationals of the other Member States.
2. When in a Member State the granting of any benefit to undertakings is subject to a minimum percentage of national workers being employed, nationals of the other Member States shall be counted as national workers, subject to the provisions of the Council Directive of 15 October 1963.2 1 OJ No L 257, 19.10.1968, p. 1. 2 OJ No 159, 2.11.1963, p. 2661/63.

Article 5
A national of a Member State who seeks employment in the territory of another Member State shall receive the same assistance there as that afforded by the employment offices in that State to their own nationals seeking employment.

Article 6
1. The engagement and recruitment of a national of one Member State for a post in another Member State shall not depend on medical, vocational or other criteria which are discriminatory on grounds of nationality by comparison with those applied to nationals of the other Member State who wish to pursue the same activity.
2. Nevertheless, a national who holds an offer in his name from an employer in a Member State other than that of which he is a national may have to undergo a vocational test, if the employer expressly requests this when making his offer of employment.

TITLE II Employment and equality of treatment

Article 7
1. A worker who is a national of a Member State may not, in the territory of another Member State, be treated differently from national workers by reason of his nationality in respect of any conditions of employment and work, in particular as regards remuneration, dismissal, and should he become unemployed, reinstatement or re-employment;
2. He shall enjoy the same social and tax advantages as national workers.
3. He shall also, by virtue of the same right and under the same conditions as national workers, have access to training in vocational schools and retraining centres.
4. Any clause of a collective or individual agreement or of any other collective regulation concerning eligibility for employment, employment, remuneration and other conditions of work or dismissal shall be null and void in so far as it lays down or authorises discriminatory conditions in respect of workers who are nationals of the other Member States.

Article 8
1. A worker who is a national of a Member State and who is employed in the territory of another Member State shall enjoy equality of treatment as regards membership of trade unions and the exercise of rights attaching thereto, including the right to vote ; he may be excluded from taking part in the management of bodies governed by public law and from holding an office governed by public law. Furthermore, he shall have the right of eligibility for workers' representative bodies in the undertaking. The provisions of this Article shall not affect laws or regulations in certain Member States which grant more extensive rights to workers coming from the other Member States.
2. This Article shall be reviewed by the Council on the basis of a proposal from the Commission which shall be submitted within not more than two years.

Article 9
1. A worker who is a national of a Member State and who is employed in the territory of another Member State shall enjoy all the rights and benefits accorded to national workers in matters of housing, including ownership of the housing he needs.
2. Such worker may, with the same right as nationals, put his name down on the housing lists in the region in which he is employed, where such lists exist ; he shall enjoy the resultant benefits and priorities.
If his family has remained in the country whence he came, they shall be considered for this purpose as residing in the said region, where national workers benefit from a similar presumption.

TITLE III Workers' families

Article 10
1. The following shall, irrespective of their nationality, have the right to install themselves with a worker who is a national of one Member State and who is employed in the territory of another Member State: (a) his spouse and their descendants who are under the age of 21 years or are dependants;

(b) dependent relatives in the ascending line of the worker and his spouse.

2. Member States shall facilitate the admission of any member of the family not coming within the provisions of paragraph 1 if dependent on the worker referred to above or living under his roof in the country whence he comes.
3. For the purposes of paragraphs 1 and 2, the worker must have available for his family housing considered as normal for national workers in the region where he is employed ; this provision, however must not give rise to discrimination between national workers and workers from the other Member States.

Article 11
Where a national of a Member State is pursuing an activity as an employed or self-employed person in the territory of another Member State, his spouse and those of the children who are under the age of 21 years or dependent on him shall have the right to take up any activity as an employed person throughout the territory of that same State, even if they are not nationals of any Member State.

Article 12
The children of a national of a Member State who is or has been employed in the territory of another Member State shall be admitted to that State's general educational, apprenticeship and vocational training courses under the same conditions as the nationals of that State, if such children are residing in its territory.
Member States shall encourage all efforts to enable such children to attend these courses under the best possible conditions.

PART II CLEARANCE OF VACANCIES AND APPLICATIONS FOR EMPLOYMENT

TITLE I Co-operation between the Member States and with the Commission

Article 13
1. The Member States or the Commission shall instigate or together undertake any study of employment or unemployment which they consider necessary for securing freedom of movement for workers within the Community.
The central employment services of the Member States shall co-operate closely with each other and with the Commission with a view to acting jointly as regards the clearing of vacancies and applications for employment within the Community and the resultant placing of workers in employment.
2. To this end the Member States shall designate specialist services which shall be entrusted with organising work in the fields referred to above and co-operating with each other and with the departments of the Commission.
The Member States shall notify the Commission of any change in the designation of such services ; the Commission shall publish details thereof for information in the Official Journal of the European Communities.

Article 14
1. The Member States shall send to the Commission information on problems arising in connection with the freedom of movement and employment of workers and particulars of the state and development of employment by region and by branch of activity.
2. In co-operation with the Technical Committee, the Commission shall determine the manner in which the information referred to in paragraph 1 shall be drawn up and the intervals at which it shall be communicated. To assess the state of their labour markets, the Member States shall use uniform criteria established by the Commission in accordance with the results of the work of the Technical Committee carried out in pursuance of Article 33 (d), after having obtained the Opinion of the Advisory Committee.
3. In accordance with the procedure laid down by the Commission in agreement with the Technical Committee, the specialist service of each Member State shall send to the specialist services of the other Member States and to the European Co-ordination Office such information concerning living and working conditions and the state of the labour market as is likely to be of guidance to workers from the other Member States. Such information shall be brought up to date regularly.
The specialist services of the other Member States shall ensure that wide publicity is given to such information, in particular by circulating it among the appropriate employment services and by all suitable means of communication for informing the workers concerned.

TITLE II Machinery for vacancy clearance

Article 15
1. At least once a month the specialist service of each Member State shall send to the specialist services of the other Member States and to the European Co-ordination Office a return showing by occupation and by region:
(a) vacancies unfilled or unlikely to be filled by manpower from the national labour market;
(b) applicants for employment who have declared themselves actually ready and able to accept employment in another country.
The specialist service of each Member State shall forward such information to the appropriate employment services and agencies.
2. The returns referred to in paragraph 1 shall be circulated according to a uniform system to be established by the European Co-ordination Office in collaboration with the Technical Committee, within eighteen months following the entry into force of this Regulation.

Article 16
1. Any vacancy communicated to the employment services of a Member State which cannot be filled from the national labour market and which, on the basis of the returns referred to in Article 15, can be cleared within the Community, shall be notified to the competent employment services of the Member State which has indicated that it has manpower available in the same occupation.
2. Such services shall forward to the services of the first Member State the details of suitable applications. For a period of 18 days from receipt of the communication of the vacancy to the services of the second Member State, such applications shall be submitted to employers with the same priority as that granted to national workers over nationals of non-Member States. During the above-mentioned period, vacancies shall be notified to non-Member States only if the Member State having such vacancies considers that for the occupations corresponding to such vacancies there are insufficient workers available who are nationals of the Member States.
3. The provisions of paragraph 1 shall not apply to vacancies offered to workers who are nationals of non-Member States where:
(a) such an offer is made to a named worker and is of a special nature in view of: (i) the requirement of specialist qualifications or the confidential nature of the post offered or previous occupational ties;
(ii) the existence of family ties either between the employer and the worker asked for, or between the latter and a worker who has been employed regularly for at least a year in the undertaking.
Items (i) and (ii) shall be applied in accordance with the provisions set out in the Annex;
(b) such vacancies are for the recruitment of homogeneous groups of seasonal workers of whom at least one named member has been offered a vacancy;
(c) such vacancies are offered by employers to workers resident in regions adjacent to either side of the frontier between a Member State and a non-Member State;
(d) vacancies are offered expressly to workers from non-Member States by the employer for reasons connected with the smooth running of the undertaking, where the employment services, having intervened for the purposes of securing the employment of national workers or workers from the other Member States of the Community, are of the opinion that such reasons are justified.

Article 17
1. The provisions of Article 16 shall be implemented by the specialist services. However, in so far as they have been authorised by the central services and in so far as the organisation of the employment services of a Member State and the placing techniques employed make it possible:
(a) the regional employment services of the Member States shall: (i) on the basis of the returns referred to in Article 15, on which appropriate action will be taken, directly bring together and clear vacancies and applications for employment;
(ii) establish direct relations for clearance: - of vacancies offered to a named worker;
- of individual applications for employment sent either to a specific employment service or to an employer pursuing his activity within the area covered by such a service;
- where the clearing operations concern seasonal workers who must be recruited as quickly as possible;
(b) the services territorially responsible for the border regions of two or more Member States shall regularly exchange data relating to vacancies and applications for employment outstanding in their area and, acting in accordance with their arrangements with the other employment services of their countries, shall directly bring together and clear vacancies and applications for employment;
(c) official employment services which specialise in certain occupations or specific categories of persons shall cooperate directly with each other.

2. The Member States concerned shall forward to the Commission the list, drawn up by common accord, of

services referred to in paragraph 1 ; the Commission shall publish such list, and any amendment thereto, in the Official Journal of the European Communities.

Article 18
Adoption of recruiting procedures as applied by the implementing bodies provided for under agreements concluded between two or more Member States shall not be obligatory.

TITLE III Measures for controlling the balance of the labour market

Article 19
1. Twice a year, on the basis of a report from the Commission drawn up from information supplied by the Member States, the latter and the Commission shall together analyse: - the results of Community arrangements for vacancy clearance;
- the number of placings of nationals of non-Member States;
- the foreseeable developments in the state of the labour market and, as far as possible, the movements of manpower within the Community.
2. The Member States shall examine with the Commission all the possibilities of giving priority to nationals of Member States when filling employment vacancies in order to achieve a balance between vacancies and applications for employment within the Community. They shall adopt all measures necessary for this purpose.

Article 20
1. When a Member State undergoes or foresees disturbances on its labour market which could seriously threaten the standard of living or level of employment in a given region or occupation, that State shall inform the Commission and the other Member States thereof and shall supply them with all relevant particulars.
2. The Member States and the Commission shall take all suitable measures to inform Community workers so that they shall not apply for employment in that region or occupation.
3. Without prejudice to the application of the Treaty and of the Protocols annexed thereto, the Member State referred to in paragraph 1 may request the Commission to state that, in order to restore to normal the situation in that region or occupation, the operation of the clearance machinery provided for in Articles 15, 16 and 17 should be partially or totally suspended.
The Commission shall decide on the suspension as such and on the duration thereof not later than two weeks after receiving such request. Any Member State may, within a strict time limit of two weeks, request the Council to annul or amend any such decision. The Council shall act on any such request within two weeks.
4. Where such suspension does take place, the employment services of the other Member States which have indicated that they have workers available shall not take any action to fill vacancies notified directly to them by employers in the Member States referred to in paragraph 1.

TITLE IV European Co-ordination Office

Article 21
The European Office for Co-ordinating the Clearance of Vacancies and Applications for Employment, established within the Commission (called in this Regulation the "European Co-ordination Office"), shall have the general task of promoting vacancy clearance at Community level. It shall be responsible in particular for all the technical duties in this field which, under the provisions of this Regulation, are assigned to the Commission, and especially for assisting the national employment services.
It shall summarise the information referred to in Articles 14 and 15 and the data arising out of the studies and research carried out pursuant to Article 13, so as to bring to light any useful facts about foreseeable developments on the Community labour market ; such facts shall be communicated to the specialist services of the Member States and to the Advisory and Technical Committees.

Article 22
1. The European Co-ordination Office shall be responsible, in particular, for: (a) co-ordinating the practical measures necessary for vacancy clearance at Community level and for analysing the resulting movements of workers;
(b) contributing to such objectives by implementing, in co-operation with the Technical Committee, joint methods of action at administrative and technical levels;
(c) carrying out, where a special need arises, and in agreement with the specialist services, the bringing together of vacancies and applications for employment for clearance by these specialist services.

2. It shall communicate to the specialist services vacancies and applications for employment sent directly to the

Commission, and shall be informed of the action taken thereon.

Article 23
The Commission may, in agreement with the competent authority of each Member State, and in accordance with the conditions and procedures which it shall determine on the basis of the Opinion of the Technical Committee, organise visits and assignments for officials of other Member States, and also advanced programmes for specialist personnel.

PART III COMMITTEES FOR ENSURING CLOSE COOPERATION BETWEEN THE MEMBER STATES IN MATTERS CONCERNING THE FREEDOM OF MOVEMENT OF WORKERS AND THEIR EMPLOYMENT

TITLE I The Advisory Committee

Article 24
The Advisory Committee shall be responsible for assisting the Commission in the examination of any questions arising from the application of the Treaty and measures taken in pursuance thereof, in matters concerning the freedom of movement of workers and their employment.

Article 25
The Advisory Committee shall be responsible in particular for:
(a) examining problems concerning freedom of movement and employment within the framework of national manpower policies, with a view to co-ordinating the employment policies of the Member States at Community level, thus contributing to the development of the economies and to an improved balance of the labour market;
(b) making a general study of the effects of implementing this Regulation and any supplementary measures;
(c) submitting to the Commission any reasoned proposals for revising this Regulation;
(d) delivering, either at the request of the Commission or on its own initiative, reasoned opinions on general questions or on questions of principle, in particular on exchange of information concerning developments in the labour market, on the movement of workers between Member States, on programmes or measures to develop vocational guidance and vocational training which are likely to increase the possibilities of freedom of movement and employment, and on all forms of assistance to workers and their families, including social assistance and the housing of workers.

Article 26
1. The Advisory Committee shall be composed of six members for each Member State, two of whom shall represent the government, two the trade unions and two the employers' associations.
2. For each of the categories referred to in paragraph 1, one alternate member shall be appointed by each Member State.
3. The term of office of the members and their alternates shall be two years. Their appointments shall be renewable.
On expiry of their term of office, the members and their alternates shall remain in office until replaced or until their appointments are renewed.

Article 27
The members of the Advisory Committee and their alternates shall be appointed by the Council which shall endeavour, when selecting representatives of trade unions and employers' associations, to achieve adequate representation on the Committee of the various economic sectors concerned.
The list of members and their alternates shall be published by the Council for information in the Official Journal of the European Communities.

Article 28
The Advisory Committee shall be chaired by a member of the Commission or his alternate. The Chairman shall not vote. The Committee shall meet at least twice a year. It shall be convened by its Chairman, either on his own initiative, or at the request of at least one third of the members. Secretarial services shall be provided for the Committee by the Commission.

Article 29
The chairman may invite individuals or representatives of bodies with wide experience in the field of employment or movement of workers to take part in meetings as observers or as experts. The Chairman may be assisted by expert advisers.

Article 30
1. An opinion delivered by the Committee shall not be valid unless two-thirds of the members are present.
2. Opinions shall state the reasons on which they are based ; they shall be delivered by an absolute majority of the votes validly cast ; they shall be accompanied by a written statement of the views expressed by the minority, when the latter so requests.

Article 31
The Advisory Committee shall establish its working methods by rules of procedure which shall enter into force after the Council, having received an opinion from the Commission, has given its approval. The entry into force of any amendment that the Committee decides to make thereto shall be subject to the same procedure.

TITLE II The Technical Committee

Article 32
The Technical Committee shall be responsible for assisting the Commission to prepare, promote and follow up all technical work and measures for giving effect to this Regulation and any supplementary measures.

Article 33
The Technical Committee shall be responsible in particular for:
(a) promoting and advancing co-operation between the public authorities concerned in the Member States on all technical questions relating to freedom of movement of workers and their employment;
(b) formulating procedures for the organisation of the joint activities of the public authorities concerned;
(c) facilitating the gathering of information likely to be of use to the Commission and for the studies and research provided for in this Regulation, and encouraging exchange of information and experience between the administrative bodies concerned;
(d) investigating at a technical level the harmonisation of the criteria by which Member States assess the state of their labour markets.

Article 34
1. The Technical Committee shall be composed of representatives of the Governments of the Member States. Each Government shall appoint as member of the Technical Committee one of the members who represent it on the Advisory Committee.
2. Each government shall appoint an alternate from among its other representatives - members or alternates - on the Advisory Committee.

Article 35
The Technical Committee shall be chaired by a member of the Commission or his representative. The Chairman shall not vote. The Chairman and the members of the Committee may be assisted by expert advisers. Secretarial services shall be provided for the Committee by the Commission.

Article 36
The proposals and opinions formulated by the Technical Committee shall be submitted to the Commission, and the Advisory Committee shall be informed thereof. Any such proposals and opinions shall be accompanied by a written statement of the views expressed by the various members of the Technical Committee, when the latter so request.

Article 37
The Technical Committee shall establish its working methods by rules of procedure which shall enter into force after the Council, having received an opinion from the Commission, has given its approval. The entry into force of any amendment which the Committee decides to make thereto shall be subject to the same procedure.

PART IV TRANSITIONAL AND FINAL PROVISIONS

TITLE I Transitional provisions

Article 38
Until the adoption by the Commission of the uniform system referred to in Article 15 (2), the European Co-ordination Office shall propose any measures likely to be of use in drawing up and circulating the returns referred to in Article 15 (1).

Article 39
The rules of procedure of the Advisory Committee and the Technical Committee in force at the time of entry into force of this Regulation shall continue to apply.

Article 40
Until the entry into force of the measures to be taken by Member States in pursuance of the Council Directive of 15 October 19681 and where, under the measures taken by the Member States in pursuance of the Council Directive of 25 March 19642 the work permit provided for in Article 22 of Regulation No 38/64/EEC is necessary to determine the period of validity and extension of the residence permit, written confirmation of engagement from the employer or a certificate of employment stating the period of employment may be substituted for such work permit. Any written confirmation by the employer or certificate of employment showing that the worker has been engaged for an indefinite period shall have the same effect as that of a permanent work permit. 1 OJ No L 257, 19.10.1968, p. 13. 2 OJ No 62, 17.4.1964, p. 981/64.

Article 41
If, by reason of the abolition of the work permit, a Member State can no longer compile certain statistics on the employment of foreign nationals, such Member State may, for statistical purposes, retain the work permit in respect of nationals of the other Member States until new statistical methods are introduced, but no later than 31 December 1969. The work permit must be issued automatically and must be valid until the actual abolition of work permits in such Member State.

TITLE II Final provisions

Article 42
1. This Regulation shall not affect the provisions of the Treaty establishing the European Coal and Steel Community which relate to workers with recognised qualifications in coalmining or steelmaking, nor those of the Treaty establishing the European Atomic Energy Community which deal with eligibility for skilled employment in the field of nuclear energy, nor any measures taken in pursuance of those Treaties.
Nevertheless, this Regulation shall apply to categories of workers referred to in the first subparagraph and to members of their families in so far as their legal position is not governed by the above-mentioned Treaties or measures.
2. This Regulation shall not affect measures taken in accordance with Article 51 of the Treaty.
3. This Regulation shall not affect the obligations of Member States arising out of: - special relations or future agreements with certain non-European countries or territories, based on institutional ties existing at the time of the entry into force of this Regulation ; or
- agreements in existence at the time of the entry into force of this Regulation with certain non-European countries or territories, based on institutional ties between them.
Workers from such countries or territories who, in accordance with this provision, are pursuing activities as employed persons in the territory of one of those Member States may not invoke the benefit of the provisions of this Regulation in the territory of the other Member States.

Article 43
Member States shall, for information purposes, communicate to the Commission the texts of agreements, conventions or arrangements concluded between them in the manpower field between the date of their being signed and that of their entry into force.

Article 44
The Commission shall adopt measures pursuant to this Regulation for its implementation. To this end it shall act in close co-operation with the central public authorities of the Member States.

Article 45
The Commission shall submit to the Council proposals aimed at abolishing, in accordance with the conditions of the Treaty, restrictions on eligibility for employment of workers who are nationals of Member States, where the absence of mutual recognition of diplomas, certificates or other evidence of formal qualifications may prevent freedom of movement for workers.

Annex 5.2.

Directive 96/71/EC of the European Parliament and of the Council of 16 December 1996 concerning **the posting of workers** in the framework of the provision of services
Official Journal L 018 , 21/01/1997 P. 0001 - 0006

MAIN PROVISIONS

Article 1: Scope

1. This Directive shall apply to undertakings established in a Member State which, in the framework of the transnational provision of services, post workers, in accordance with paragraph 3, to the territory of a Member State.
2. This Directive shall not apply to merchant navy undertakings as regards seagoing personnel.
3. This Directive shall apply to the extent that the undertakings referred to in paragraph 1 take one of the following transnational measures:
(a) post workers to the territory of a Member State on their account and under their direction, under a contract concluded between the undertaking making the posting and the party for whom the services are intended, operating in that Member State, provided there is an employment relationship between the undertaking making the posting and the worker during the period of posting; or
(b) post workers to an establishment or to an undertaking owned by the group in the territory of a Member State, provided there is an employment relationship between the undertaking making the posting and the worker during the period of posting; or
(c) being a temporary employment undertaking or placement agency, hire out a worker to a user undertaking established or operating in the territory of a Member State, provided there is an employment relationship between the temporary employment undertaking or placement agency and the worker during the period of posting.
4. Undertakings established in a non-member State must not be given more favourable treatment than undertakings established in a Member State.

Article 2: Definition

1. For the purposes of this Directive, 'posted worker` means a worker who, for a limited period, carries out his work in the territory of a Member State other than the State in which he normally works.
2. For the purposes of this Directive, the definition of a worker is that which applies in the law of the Member State to whose territory the worker is posted.

Article 3: Terms and conditions of employment

1. Member States shall ensure that, whatever the law applicable to the employment relationship, the undertakings referred to in Article 1 (1) guarantee workers posted to their territory the terms and conditions of employment covering the following matters which, in the Member State where the work is carried out, are laid down:
- by law, regulation or administrative provision, and/or
- by collective agreements or arbitration awards which have been declared universally applicable within the meaning of paragraph 8, insofar as they concern the activities referred to in the Annex:
(a) maximum work periods and minimum rest periods;
(b) minimum paid annual holidays;
(c) the minimum rates of pay, including overtime rates; this point does not apply to supplementary occupational retirement pension schemes;
(d) the conditions of hiring-out of workers, in particular the supply of workers by temporary employment undertakings;
(e) health, safety and hygiene at work;
(f) protective measures with regard to the terms and conditions of employment of pregnant women or women who have recently given birth, of children and of young people;
(g) equality of treatment between men and women and other provisions on non-discrimination.
For the purposes of this Directive, the concept of minimum rates of pay referred to in paragraph 1 (c) is defined by the national law and/or practice of the Member State to whose territory the worker is posted.
2. In the case of initial assembly and/or first installation of goods where this is an integral part of a contract for the supply of goods and necessary for taking the goods supplied into use and carried out by the skilled and/or

specialist workers of the supplying undertaking, the first subparagraph of paragraph 1 (b) and (c) shall not apply, if the period of posting does not exceed eight days.
This provision shall not apply to activities in the field of building work listed in the Annex.
3. Member States may, after consulting employers and labour, in accordance with the traditions and practices of each Member State, decide not to apply the first subparagraph of paragraph 1 (c) in the cases referred to in Article 1 (3) (a) and (b) when the length of the posting does not exceed one month.
4. Member States may, in accordance with national laws and/or practices, provide that exemptions may be made from the first subparagraph of paragraph 1 (c) in the cases referred to in Article 1 (3) (a) and (b) and from a decision by a Member State within the meaning of paragraph 3 of this Article, by means of collective agreements within the meaning of paragraph 8 of this Article, concerning one or more sectors of activity, where the length of the posting does not exceed one month.
5. Member States may provide for exemptions to be granted from the first subparagraph of paragraph 1 (b) and (c) in the cases referred to in Article 1 (3) (a) and (b) on the grounds that the amount of work to be done is not significant.
Member States availing themselves of the option referred to in the first subparagraph shall lay down the criteria which the work to be performed must meet in order to be considered as 'non-significant`.
6. The length of the posting shall be calculated on the basis of a reference period of one year from the beginning of the posting.
For the purpose of such calculations, account shall be taken of any previous periods for which the post has been filled by a posted worker.
7. Paragraphs 1 to 6 shall not prevent application of terms and conditions of employment which are more favourable to workers.
Allowances specific to the posting shall be considered to be part of the minimum wage, unless they are paid in reimbursement of expenditure actually incurred on account of the posting, such as expenditure on travel, board and lodging.
8. 'Collective agreements or arbitration awards which have been declared universally applicable` means collective agreements or arbitration awards which must be observed by all undertakings in the geographical area and in the profession or industry concerned.
In the absence of a system for declaring collective agreements or arbitration awards to be of universal application within the meaning of the first subparagraph, Member States may, if they so decide, base themselves on:
- collective agreements or arbitration awards which are generally applicable to all similar undertakings in the geographical area and in the profession or industry concerned, and/or
- collective agreements which have been concluded by the most representative employers' and labour organizations at national level and which are applied throughout national territory,
provided that their application to the undertakings referred to in Article 1 (1) ensures equality of treatment on matters listed in the first subparagraph of paragraph 1 of this Article between those undertakings and the other undertakings referred to in this subparagraph which are in a similar position.
Equality of treatment, within the meaning of this Article, shall be deemed to exist where national undertakings in a similar position:
- are subject, in the place in question or in the sector concerned, to the same obligations as posting undertakings as regards the matters listed in the first subparagraph of paragraph 1, and
- are required to fulfil such obligations with the same effects.
9. Member States may provide that the undertakings referred to in Article 1 (1) must guarantee workers referred to in Article 1 (3) (c) the terms and conditions which apply to temporary workers in the Member State where the work is carried out.
10. This Directive shall not preclude the application by Member States, in compliance with the Treaty, to national undertakings and to the undertakings of other States, on a basis of equality of treatment, of:
- terms and conditions of employment on matters other than those referred to in the first subparagraph of paragraph 1 in the case of public policy provisions,
- terms and conditions of employment laid down in the collective agreements or arbitration awards within the meaning of paragraph 8 and concerning activities other than those referred to in the Annex.

Article 4: Cooperation on information

1. For the purposes of implementing this Directive, Member States shall, in accordance with national legislation and/or practice, designate one or more liaison offices or one or more competent national bodies.
2. Member States shall make provision for cooperation between the public authorities which, in accordance with national legislation, are responsible for monitoring the terms and conditions of employment referred to in Article 3. Such cooperation shall in particular consist in replying to reasoned requests from those authorities for

information on the transnational hiring-out of workers, including manifest abuses or possible cases of unlawful transnational activities.
The Commission and the public authorities referred to in the first subparagraph shall cooperate closely in order to examine any difficulties which might arise in the application of Article 3 (10).
Mutual administrative assistance shall be provided free of charge.
3. Each Member State shall take the appropriate measures to make the information on the terms and conditions of employment referred to in Article 3 generally available.
4. Each Member State shall notify the other Member States and the Commission of the liaison offices and/or competent bodies referred to in paragraph 1.

Article 5: Measures

Member States shall take appropriate measures in the event of failure to comply with this Directive.
They shall in particular ensure that adequate procedures are available to workers and/or their representatives for the enforcement of obligations under this Directive.

Article 6: Jurisdiction

In order to enforce the right to the terms and conditions of employment guaranteed in Article 3, judicial proceedings may be instituted in the Member State in whose territory the worker is or was posted, without prejudice, where applicable, to the right, under existing international conventions on jurisdiction, to institute proceedings in another State.

Annex 5.3.

Council Directive 2000/43/EC of 29 June 2000 **implementing the principle of equal treatment** between persons irrespective of racial or ethnic origin
Official Journal L 180 , 19/07/2000 P. 0022 - 0026

MAIN PROVISIONS

CHAPTER I - GENERAL PROVISIONS

Article 1
Purpose
The purpose of this Directive is to lay down a framework for combating discrimination on the grounds of racial or ethnic origin, with a view to putting into effect in the Member States the principle of equal treatment.

Article 2
Concept of discrimination
1. For the purposes of this Directive, the principle of equal treatment shall mean that there shall be no direct or indirect discrimination based on racial or ethnic origin.
2. For the purposes of paragraph 1:
(a) direct discrimination shall be taken to occur where one person is treated less favourably than another is, has been or would be treated in a comparable situation on grounds of racial or ethnic origin;
(b) indirect discrimination shall be taken to occur where an apparently neutral provision, criterion or practice would put persons of a racial or ethnic origin at a particular disadvantage compared with other persons, unless that provision, criterion or practice is objectively justified by a legitimate aim and the means of achieving that aim are appropriate and necessary.
3. Harassment shall be deemed to be discrimination within the meaning of paragraph 1, when an unwanted conduct related to racial or ethnic origin takes place with the purpose or effect of violating the dignity of a person and of creating an intimidating, hostile, degrading, humiliating or offensive environment. In this context, the concept of harassment may be defined in accordance with the national laws and practice of the Member States.
4. An instruction to discriminate against persons on grounds of racial or ethnic origin shall be deemed to be discrimination within the meaning of paragraph 1.

Article 3
Scope
1. Within the limits of the powers conferred upon the Community, this Directive shall apply to all persons, as regards both the public and private sectors, including public bodies, in relation to:
(a) conditions for access to employment, to self-employment and to occupation, including selection criteria and recruitment conditions, whatever the branch of activity and at all levels of the professional hierarchy, including promotion;
(b) access to all types and to all levels of vocational guidance, vocational training, advanced vocational training and retraining, including practical work experience;
(c) employment and working conditions, including dismissals and pay;
(d) membership of and involvement in an organisation of workers or employers, or any organisation whose members carry on a particular profession, including the benefits provided for by such organisations;
(e) social protection, including social security and healthcare;
(f) social advantages;
(g) education;
(h) access to and supply of goods and services which are available to the public, including housing.
2. This Directive does not cover difference of treatment based on nationality and is without prejudice to provisions and conditions relating to the entry into and residence of third-country nationals and stateless persons on the territory of Member States, and to any treatment which arises from the legal status of the third-country nationals and stateless persons concerned.

Article 4
Genuine and determining occupational requirements
Notwithstanding Article 2(1) and (2), Member States may provide that a difference of treatment which is based on a characteristic related to racial or ethnic origin shall not constitute discrimination where, by reason of the nature of the particular occupational activities concerned or of the context in which they are carried out, such a

characteristic constitutes a genuine and determining occupational requirement, provided that the objective is legitimate and the requirement is proportionate.

Article 5
Positive action
With a view to ensuring full equality in practice, the principle of equal treatment shall not prevent any Member State from maintaining or adopting specific measures to prevent or compensate for disadvantages linked to racial or ethnic origin.

Article 6
Minimum requirements
1. Member States may introduce or maintain provisions which are more favourable to the protection of the principle of equal treatment than those laid down in this Directive.
2. The implementation of this Directive shall under no circumstances constitute grounds for a reduction in the level of protection against discrimination already afforded by Member States in the fields covered by this Directive.

CHAPTER II - REMEDIES AND ENFORCEMENT

Article 7
Defence of rights
1. Member States shall ensure that judicial and/or administrative procedures, including where they deem it appropriate conciliation procedures, for the enforcement of obligations under this Directive are available to all persons who consider themselves wronged by failure to apply the principle of equal treatment to them, even after the relationship in which the discrimination is alleged to have occurred has ended.
2. Member States shall ensure that associations, organisations or other legal entities, which have, in accordance with the criteria laid down by their national law, a legitimate interest in ensuring that the provisions of this Directive are complied with, may engage, either on behalf or in support of the complainant, with his or her approval, in any judicial and/or administrative procedure provided for the enforcement of obligations under this Directive.
3. Paragraphs 1 and 2 are without prejudice to national rules relating to time limits for bringing actions as regards the principle of equality of treatment.

Article 8
Burden of proof
1. Member States shall take such measures as are necessary, in accordance with their national judicial systems, to ensure that, when persons who consider themselves wronged because the principle of equal treatment has not been applied to them establish, before a court or other competent authority, facts from which it may be presumed that there has been direct or indirect discrimination, it shall be for the respondent to prove that there has been no breach of the principle of equal treatment.
2. Paragraph 1 shall not prevent Member States from introducing rules of evidence which are more favourable to plaintiffs.
3. Paragraph 1 shall not apply to criminal procedures.
4. Paragraphs 1, 2 and 3 shall also apply to any proceedings brought in accordance with Article 7(2).
5. Member States need not apply paragraph 1 to proceedings in which it is for the court or competent body to investigate the facts of the case.

Article 9
Victimisation
Member States shall introduce into their national legal systems such measures as are necessary to protect individuals from any adverse treatment or adverse consequence as a reaction to a complaint or to proceedings aimed at enforcing compliance with the principle of equal treatment.

Article 10
Dissemination of information
Member States shall take care that the provisions adopted pursuant to this Directive, together with the relevant provisions already in force, are brought to the attention of the persons concerned by all appropriate means throughout their territory.

Article 11
Social dialogue
1. Member States shall, in accordance with national traditions and practice, take adequate measures to promote the social dialogue between the two sides of industry with a view to fostering equal treatment, including through the monitoring of workplace practices, collective agreements, codes of conduct, research or exchange of experiences and good practices.
2. Where consistent with national traditions and practice, Member States shall encourage the two sides of the industry without prejudice to their autonomy to conclude, at the appropriate level, agreements laying down anti-discrimination rules in the fields referred to in Article 3 which fall within the scope of collective bargaining. These agreements shall respect the minimum requirements laid down by this Directive and the relevant national implementing measures.

Article 12
Dialogue with non-governmental organisations
Member States shall encourage dialogue with appropriate non-governmental organisations which have, in accordance with their national law and practice, a legitimate interest in contributing to the fight against discrimination on grounds of racial and ethnic origin with a view to promoting the principle of equal treatment.

CHAPTER III - BODIES FOR THE PROMOTION OF EQUAL TREATMENT

Article 13
1. Member States shall designate a body or bodies for the promotion of equal treatment of all persons without discrimination on the grounds of racial or ethnic origin. These bodies may form part of agencies charged at national level with the defence of human rights or the safeguard of individuals' rights.
2. Member States shall ensure that the competences of these bodies include:
- without prejudice to the right of victims and of associations, organisations or other legal entities referred to in Article 7(2), providing independent assistance to victims of discrimination in pursuing their complaints about discrimination,
- conducting independent surveys concerning discrimination,
- publishing independent reports and making recommendations on any issue relating to such discrimination.

CHAPTER IV - FINAL PROVISIONS

Article 14
Compliance
Member States shall take the necessary measures to ensure that:
(a) any laws, regulations and administrative provisions contrary to the principle of equal treatment are abolished;
(b) any provisions contrary to the principle of equal treatment which are included in individual or collective contracts or agreements, internal rules of undertakings, rules governing profit-making or non-profit-making associations, and rules governing the independent professions and workers' and employers' organisations, are or may be declared, null and void or are amended.

Article 15
Sanctions
Member States shall lay down the rules on sanctions applicable to infringements of the national provisions adopted pursuant to this Directive and shall take all measures necessary to ensure that they are applied. The sanctions, which may comprise the payment of compensation to the victim, must be effective, proportionate and dissuasive. The Member States shall notify those provisions to the Commission by 19 July 2003 at the latest and shall notify it without delay of any subsequent amendment affecting them.

Article 16
Implementation
Member States shall adopt the laws, regulations and administrative provisions necessary to comply with this Directive by 19 July 2003 or may entrust management and labour, at their joint request, with the implementation of this Directive as regards provisions falling within the scope of collective agreements. In such cases, Member States shall ensure that by 19 July 2003, management and labour introduce the necessary measures by agreement, Member States being required to take any necessary measures to enable them at any time to be in a position to guarantee the results imposed by this Directive. They shall forthwith inform the Commission thereof. When Member States adopt these measures, they shall contain a reference to this Directive or be accompanied

by such a reference on the occasion of their official publication. The methods of making such a reference shall be laid down by the Member States.

Article 17
Report
1. Member States shall communicate to the Commission by 19 July 2005, and every five years thereafter, all the information necessary for the Commission to draw up a report to the European Parliament and the Council on the application of this Directive.
2. The Commission's report shall take into account, as appropriate, the views of the European Monitoring Centre on Racism and Xenophobia, as well as the viewpoints of the social partners and relevant non-governmental organisations. In accordance with the principle of gender mainstreaming, this report shall, inter alia, provide an assessment of the impact of the measures taken on women and men. In the light of the information received, this report shall include, if necessary, proposals to revise and update this Directive.

Annex 5.4.

Council Directive 2000/78/EC of 27 November 2000 establishing a general framework for **equal treatment in employment and occupation**
Official Journal L 303 , 02/12/2000 P. 0016 - 0022

MAIN PROVISIONS

CHAPTER I - GENERAL PROVISIONS

Article 1
Purpose
The purpose of this Directive is to lay down a general framework for combating discrimination on the grounds of religion or belief, disability, age or sexual orientation as regards employment and occupation, with a view to putting into effect in the Member States the principle of equal treatment.

Article 2
Concept of discrimination
1. For the purposes of this Directive, the "principle of equal treatment" shall mean that there shall be no direct or indirect discrimination whatsoever on any of the grounds referred to in Article 1.
2. For the purposes of paragraph 1:
(a) direct discrimination shall be taken to occur where one person is treated less favourably than another is, has been or would be treated in a comparable situation, on any of the grounds referred to in Article 1;
(b) indirect discrimination shall be taken to occur where an apparently neutral provision, criterion or practice would put persons having a particular religion or belief, a particular disability, a particular age, or a particular sexual orientation at a particular disadvantage compared with other persons unless:
(i) that provision, criterion or practice is objectively justified by a legitimate aim and the means of achieving that aim are appropriate and necessary, or
(ii) as regards persons with a particular disability, the employer or any person or organisation to whom this Directive applies, is obliged, under national legislation, to take appropriate measures in line with the principles contained in Article 5 in order to eliminate disadvantages entailed by such provision, criterion or practice.
3. Harassment shall be deemed to be a form of discrimination within the meaning of paragraph 1, when unwanted conduct related to any of the grounds referred to in Article 1 takes place with the purpose or effect of violating the dignity of a person and of creating an intimidating, hostile, degrading, humiliating or offensive environment. In this context, the concept of harassment may be defined in accordance with the national laws and practice of the Member States.
4. An instruction to discriminate against persons on any of the grounds referred to in Article 1 shall be deemed to be discrimination within the meaning of paragraph 1.
5. This Directive shall be without prejudice to measures laid down by national law which, in a democratic society, are necessary for public security, for the maintenance of public order and the prevention of criminal offences, for the protection of health and for the protection of the rights and freedoms of others.

Article 3
Scope
1. Within the limits of the areas of competence conferred on the Community, this Directive shall apply to all persons, as regards both the public and private sectors, including public bodies, in relation to:
(a) conditions for access to employment, to self-employment or to occupation, including selection criteria and recruitment conditions, whatever the branch of activity and at all levels of the professional hierarchy, including promotion;
(b) access to all types and to all levels of vocational guidance, vocational training, advanced vocational training and retraining, including practical work experience;
(c) employment and working conditions, including dismissals and pay;
(d) membership of, and involvement in, an organisation of workers or employers, or any organisation whose members carry on a particular profession, including the benefits provided for by such organisations.
2. This Directive does not cover differences of treatment based on nationality and is without prejudice to provisions and conditions relating to the entry into and residence of third-country nationals and stateless persons in the territory of Member States, and to any treatment which arises from the legal status of the third-country nationals and stateless persons concerned.
3. This Directive does not apply to payments of any kind made by state schemes or similar, including state social security or social protection schemes.

4. Member States may provide that this Directive, in so far as it relates to discrimination on the grounds of disability and age, shall not apply to the armed forces.

Article 4
Occupational requirements
1. Notwithstanding Article 2(1) and (2), Member States may provide that a difference of treatment which is based on a characteristic related to any of the grounds referred to in Article 1 shall not constitute discrimination where, by reason of the nature of the particular occupational activities concerned or of the context in which they are carried out, such a characteristic constitutes a genuine and determining occupational requirement, provided that the objective is legitimate and the requirement is proportionate.
2. Member States may maintain national legislation in force at the date of adoption of this Directive or provide for future legislation incorporating national practices existing at the date of adoption of this Directive pursuant to which, in the case of occupational activities within churches and other public or private organisations the ethos of which is based on religion or belief, a difference of treatment based on a person's religion or belief shall not constitute discrimination where, by reason of the nature of these activities or of the context in which they are carried out, a person's religion or belief constitute a genuine, legitimate and justified occupational requirement, having regard to the organisation's ethos. This difference of treatment shall be implemented taking account of Member States' constitutional provisions and principles, as well as the general principles of Community law, and should not justify discrimination on another ground.
Provided that its provisions are otherwise complied with, this Directive shall thus not prejudice the right of churches and other public or private organisations, the ethos of which is based on religion or belief, acting in conformity with national constitutions and laws, to require individuals working for them to act in good faith and with loyalty to the organisation's ethos.

Article 5
Reasonable accommodation for disabled persons
In order to guarantee compliance with the principle of equal treatment in relation to persons with disabilities, reasonable accommodation shall be provided. This means that employers shall take appropriate measures, where needed in a particular case, to enable a person with a disability to have access to, participate in, or advance in employment, or to undergo training, unless such measures would impose a disproportionate burden on the employer. This burden shall not be disproportionate when it is sufficiently remedied by measures existing within the framework of the disability policy of the Member State concerned.

Article 6
Justification of differences of treatment on grounds of age
1. Notwithstanding Article 2(2), Member States may provide that differences of treatment on grounds of age shall not constitute discrimination, if, within the context of national law, they are objectively and reasonably justified by a legitimate aim, including legitimate employment policy, labour market and vocational training objectives, and if the means of achieving that aim are appropriate and necessary.
Such differences of treatment may include, among others:
(a) the setting of special conditions on access to employment and vocational training, employment and occupation, including dismissal and remuneration conditions, for young people, older workers and persons with caring responsibilities in order to promote their vocational integration or ensure their protection;
(b) the fixing of minimum conditions of age, professional experience or seniority in service for access to employment or to certain advantages linked to employment;
(c) the fixing of a maximum age for recruitment which is based on the training requirements of the post in question or the need for a reasonable period of employment before retirement.
2. Notwithstanding Article 2(2), Member States may provide that the fixing for occupational social security schemes of ages for admission or entitlement to retirement or invalidity benefits, including the fixing under those schemes of different ages for employees or groups or categories of employees, and the use, in the context of such schemes, of age criteria in actuarial calculations, does not constitute discrimination on the grounds of age, provided this does not result in discrimination on the grounds of sex.

Article 7
Positive action
1. With a view to ensuring full equality in practice, the principle of equal treatment shall not prevent any Member State from maintaining or adopting specific measures to prevent or compensate for disadvantages linked to any of the grounds referred to in Article 1.
2. With regard to disabled persons, the principle of equal treatment shall be without prejudice to the right of Member States to maintain or adopt provisions on the protection of health and safety at work or to measures

aimed at creating or maintaining provisions or facilities for safeguarding or promoting their integration into the working environment.

Article 8
Minimum requirements
1. Member States may introduce or maintain provisions which are more favourable to the protection of the principle of equal treatment than those laid down in this Directive.
2. The implementation of this Directive shall under no circumstances constitute grounds for a reduction in the level of protection against discrimination already afforded by Member States in the fields covered by this Directive.

CHAPTER II - REMEDIES AND ENFORCEMENT

Article 9
Defence of rights
1. Member States shall ensure that judicial and/or administrative procedures, including where they deem it appropriate conciliation procedures, for the enforcement of obligations under this Directive are available to all persons who consider themselves wronged by failure to apply the principle of equal treatment to them, even after the relationship in which the discrimination is alleged to have occurred has ended.
2. Member States shall ensure that associations, organisations or other legal entities which have, in accordance with the criteria laid down by their national law, a legitimate interest in ensuring that the provisions of this Directive are complied with, may engage, either on behalf or in support of the complainant, with his or her approval, in any judicial and/or administrative procedure provided for the enforcement of obligations under this Directive.
3. Paragraphs 1 and 2 are without prejudice to national rules relating to time limits for bringing actions as regards the principle of equality of treatment.

Article 10
Burden of proof
1. Member States shall take such measures as are necessary, in accordance with their national judicial systems, to ensure that, when persons who consider themselves wronged because the principle of equal treatment has not been applied to them establish, before a court or other competent authority, facts from which it may be presumed that there has been direct or indirect discrimination, it shall be for the respondent to prove that there has been no breach of the principle of equal treatment.
2. Paragraph 1 shall not prevent Member States from introducing rules of evidence which are more favourable to plaintiffs.
3. Paragraph 1 shall not apply to criminal procedures.
4. Paragraphs 1, 2 and 3 shall also apply to any legal proceedings commenced in accordance with Article 9(2).
5. Member States need not apply paragraph 1 to proceedings in which it is for the court or competent body to investigate the facts of the case.

Article 11
Victimisation
Member States shall introduce into their national legal systems such measures as are necessary to protect employees against dismissal or other adverse treatment by the employer as a reaction to a complaint within the undertaking or to any legal proceedings aimed at enforcing compliance with the principle of equal treatment.

Article 12
Dissemination of information
Member States shall take care that the provisions adopted pursuant to this Directive, together with the relevant provisions already in force in this field, are brought to the attention of the persons concerned by all appropriate means, for example at the workplace, throughout their territory.

Article 13
Social dialogue
1. Member States shall, in accordance with their national traditions and practice, take adequate measures to promote dialogue between the social partners with a view to fostering equal treatment, including through the monitoring of workplace practices, collective agreements, codes of conduct and through research or exchange of experiences and good practices.
2. Where consistent with their national traditions and practice, Member States shall encourage the social

partners, without prejudice to their autonomy, to conclude at the appropriate level agreements laying down anti-discrimination rules in the fields referred to in Article 3 which fall within the scope of collective bargaining. These agreements shall respect the minimum requirements laid down by this Directive and by the relevant national implementing measures.

Article 14
Dialogue with non-governmental organisations
Member States shall encourage dialogue with appropriate non-governmental organisations which have, in accordance with their national law and practice, a legitimate interest in contributing to the fight against discrimination on any of the grounds referred to in Article 1 with a view to promoting the principle of equal treatment.

CHAPTER III - PARTICULAR PROVISIONS

Article 15
Northern Ireland
1. In order to tackle the under-representation of one of the major religious communities in the police service of Northern Ireland, differences in treatment regarding recruitment into that service, including its support staff, shall not constitute discrimination insofar as those differences in treatment are expressly authorised by national legislation.
2. In order to maintain a balance of opportunity in employment for teachers in Northern Ireland while furthering the reconciliation of historical divisions between the major religious communities there, the provisions on religion or belief in this Directive shall not apply to the recruitment of teachers in schools in Northern Ireland in so far as this is expressly authorised by national legislation.

CHAPTER IV- FINAL PROVISIONS

Article 16
Compliance
Member States shall take the necessary measures to ensure that:
(a) any laws, regulations and administrative provisions contrary to the principle of equal treatment are abolished;
(b) any provisions contrary to the principle of equal treatment which are included in contracts or collective agreements, internal rules of undertakings or rules governing the independent occupations and professions and workers' and employers' organisations are, or may be, declared null and void or are amended.

Article 17
Sanctions
Member States shall lay down the rules on sanctions applicable to infringements of the national provisions adopted pursuant to this Directive and shall take all measures necessary to ensure that they are applied. The sanctions, which may comprise the payment of compensation to the victim, must be effective, proportionate and dissuasive. Member States shall notify those provisions to the Commission by 2 December 2003 at the latest and shall notify it without delay of any subsequent amendment affecting them.

Article 18
Implementation
Member States shall adopt the laws, regulations and administrative provisions necessary to comply with this Directive by 2 December 2003 at the latest or may entrust the social partners, at their joint request, with the implementation of this Directive as regards provisions concerning collective agreements. In such cases, Member States shall ensure that, no later than 2 December 2003, the social partners introduce the necessary measures by agreement, the Member States concerned being required to take any necessary measures to enable them at any time to be in a position to guarantee the results imposed by this Directive. They shall forthwith inform the Commission thereof.
In order to take account of particular conditions, Member States may, if necessary, have an additional period of 3 years from 2 December 2003, that is to say a total of 6 years, to implement the provisions of this Directive on age and disability discrimination. In that event they shall inform the Commission forthwith. Any Member State which chooses to use this additional period shall report annually to the Commission on the steps it is taking to tackle age and disability discrimination and on the progress it is making towards implementation. The Commission shall report annually to the Council.
When Member States adopt these measures, they shall contain a reference to this Directive or be accompanied by such reference on the occasion of their official publication. The methods of making such reference shall be laid down by Member States.

Annex 5.5.

2000/750/EC: Council Decision of 27 November 2000 establishing a Community **action programme to combat discrimination** (2001 to 2006)
Official Journal L 303 , 02/12/2000 p. 0023 - 0028

MAIN PROVISIONS

Article 1
Establishment of the programme
This Decision establishes a Community action programme, hereinafter referred to as "the programme", to promote measures to combat direct or indirect discrimination based on racial or ethnic origin, religion or belief, disability, age or sexual orientation, for the period from 1 January 2001 to 31 December 2006.

Article 2
Objectives
Within the limits of the Community's powers, the programme shall support and supplement the efforts at Community level and in the Member States to promote measures to prevent and combat discrimination whether based on one or on multiple factors, taking account, where appropriate, of future legislative developments. It shall have the following objectives:
(a) to improve the understanding of issues related to discrimination through improved knowledge of this phenomenon and through evaluation of the effectiveness of policies and practice;
(b) to develop the capacity to prevent and address discrimination effectively, in particular by strengthening organisations' means of action and through support for the exchange of information and good practice and networking at European level, while taking into account the specific characteristics of the different forms of discrimination;
(c) to promote and disseminate the values and practices underlying the fight against discrimination, including through the use of awareness-raising campaigns.

Article 3
Community actions
1. With a view to achieving the objectives set out in Article 2, the following actions may be implemented within a transnational framework:
(a) analysis of factors related to discrimination, including through studies and the development of qualitative and quantitative indicators and benchmarks, in accordance with national law and practices, and the evaluation of anti-discrimination legislation and practice, with a view to assessing its effectiveness and impact, with effective dissemination of the results;
(b) transnational cooperation and the promotion of networking at European level between partners active in the prevention of, and the fight against, discrimination, including non-governmental organisations;
(c) awareness-raising, in particular to emphasise the European dimension of the fight against discrimination and to publicise the results of the programme, in particular through communications, publications, campaigns and events.
2. Arrangements for the implementation of the Community actions described in paragraph 1 are set out in the Annex.

Article 4
Implementation of the programme and cooperation with the Member States
1. The Commission shall:
(a) ensure the implementation of the Community actions covered by the programme in conformity with the Annex;
(b) have a regular exchange of views with representatives of non-governmental organisations and the social partners at European level on the design, implementation and follow-up of the programme and on related policy orientations. To that end the Commission shall make the relevant information available to the non-governmental organisations and the social partners. The Commission shall inform the committee established under Article 6 of their exchange of views.
2. The Commission, in cooperation with the Member States, shall take the necessary steps to:
(a) promote the involvement in the programme of all the parties concerned, including non-governmental organisations of all sizes;
(b) promote active partnership and dialogue between all the partners involved in the programme, inter alia to encourage an integrated and coordinated approach to the fight against discrimination;

(c) ensure the dissemination of the results of the actions undertaken within the framework of the programme;
(d) provide accessible information and appropriate publicity and follow-up with regard to actions supported by the programme.

Article 5
Implementing measures
1. The measures necessary for the implementation of this Decision relating to the matters referred to below shall be adopted in accordance with the management procedure referred to in Article 6(2):
(a) the general guidelines for the implementation of the programme;
(b) the annual plan of work for the implementation of the programme's actions, including the possibility of adapting or supplementing the programme themes;
(c) the financial support to be supplied by the Community;
(d) the annual budget and the breakdown of the funds among different actions of the programme;
(e) the arrangements for selecting actions and organisations for Community support and the draft list of actions and organisations submitted by the Commission for such support;
(f) the criteria for monitoring and evaluating the programme and, in particular, its cost-effectiveness and the arrangements for disseminating and transferring the results.
2. The measures necessary for the implementation of this Decision relating to all other matters shall be adopted in accordance with the advisory procedure referred to in Article 6(3).

Article 6
Committee
1. The Commission shall be assisted by a committee.
2. Where reference is made to this paragraph, Articles 4 and 7 of Decision 1999/468/EC shall apply.
The period laid down in Article 4(3) of Decision 1999/468/EC shall be set at two months.
3. Where reference is made to this paragraph, Articles 3 and 7 of Decision 1999/468/EC shall apply.
4. The committee shall adopt its rules of procedure.

Article 7
Cooperation with other committees
To ensure the consistency and complementarity of the programme with other measures referred to in Article 8, the Commission shall keep the Committee regularly informed of other Community action contributing to the fight against discrimination. Where appropriate, the Commission shall establish regular and structured cooperation between this Committee and the monitoring committees established for other relevant policies, instruments and actions.

Article 8
Consistency and complementarity
1. The Commission shall, in cooperation with the Member States, ensure overall consistency with other Union and Community policies, instruments and actions, in particular by establishing appropriate mechanisms to coordinate the activities of the programme with relevant activities relating to research, employment, equality between women and men, social inclusion, culture, education, training and youth policy and in the field of the Community's external relations.
2. The Commission and the Member States shall ensure consistency and complementarity between action undertaken under the programme and other relevant Union and Community action, in particular under the Structural Funds and the Community initiative Equal.
3. Member States shall make all possible efforts to ensure consistency and complementarity between activities under the programme and those carried out at national, regional and local levels.

Article 9
Participation of the EFTA/EEA countries, the associated countries of Central and Eastern Europe, Cyprus, Malta and Turkey
The programme shall be open to the participation of:
(a) the EFTA/EEA countries in accordance with the conditions established in the EEA Agreement;
(b) the candidate countries of central and eastern Europe (CCEE) in accordance with the conditions established in the Europe Agreements, in their additional protocols and in the decisions of the respective Association Councils;
(c) Cyprus, Malta and Turkey, funded by additional appropriations in accordance with procedures to be agreed with these countries;

Article 10
Funding
1. The financial reference amount for the implementation of the programme for the period 2001 to 2006 is hereby set at EUR 98,4 million.
2. The annual appropriations shall be authorised by the budgetary authority within the limits of the financial perspective.

Article 11
Monitoring and evaluation
1. The Commission shall regularly monitor the programme in cooperation with the Member States, in accordance with the procedures set out in Article 6(2) or 6(3).
2. The programme shall be evaluated by the Commission with the assistance of independent experts. This evaluation shall assess the relevance, the effectiveness and the cost/effectiveness ratios of actions implemented with regard to the objectives referred to in Article 2. It shall also examine the impact of the programme as a whole.
The evaluation will also examine the complementarity between action under the programme and that pursued under other relevant Community policies, instruments and actions.
3. The Commission shall submit to the European Parliament, the Council, the Economic and Social Committee and the Committee of the Regions an evaluation report on the implementation of the programme by 31 December 2005.

Article 12
Entry into force
This Decision shall enter into force on the date of its publication in the Official Journal of the European Communities.

Done at Brussels, 27 November 2000.

For the Council
The President
É. Guigou

(1) Opinion delivered 5.10.2000 (Not yet published in the Official Journal).
(2) OJ C 204, 18.7.2000, p. 82.
(3) OJ C 226, 8.8.2000, p. 1.
(4) OJ L 184, 17.7.1999, p. 23.
(5) OJ C 172, 18.6.1999, p. 1.

ANNEX

INDICATIONS FOR THE IMPLEMENTATION OF THE PROGRAMME
I. Areas of action
The programme may operate in the following areas, within the limits of the powers conferred by the Treaty upon the Community:
(a) non-discrimination within and by public administrations;
(b) non-discrimination within and by the media;
(c) equal participation in political, economic and social decision-making;
(d) equal access to, and supply of, goods and services which are available to the public, including housing, transport, culture, leisure and sport;
(e) effective monitoring of discrimination, including multiple discrimination;
(f) effective dissemination of information about rights to equal treatment and non-discrimination;
(g) the mainstreaming of anti-discriminatory policies and practices.
In all its activities, the programme will respect the principle of gender mainstreaming.
In carrying out the programme, the Commission may, for the mutual benefit of the Commission and of the beneficiaries, have recourse to technical and/or administrative assistance in the identification, preparation, management, monitoring, audit and control of the programme or projects.
The Commission may also carry out studies, organise meetings of experts, conduct information campaigns and launch publications directly related to the objective of this programme.
II. Access to the programme

Under the conditions and arrangements for implementation specified in this Annex, access to this programme shall be open to public and/or private bodies and institutions involved in the fight against discrimination, in particular:
(a) Member States;
(b) local and regional authorities;
(c) bodies for the promotion of equal treatment;
(d) social partners;
(e) non-governmental organisations;
(f) universities and research institutes;
(g) national statistical offices;
(h) the media.

III. Actions

Strand 1 - Analysis and evaluation
The following measures may be supported:
1. the development and dissemination of comparable statistical series on the scale of discrimination in the Community in accordance with national law and practices;
2. the development and dissemination of methodologies and indicators for evaluating the effectiveness of anti-discrimination policy and practice (benchmarking) in accordance with national law and practices;
3. the analysis, by means of annual reports, of anti-discrimination legislation and practice, with a view to evaluating its effectiveness and disseminating lessons learned;
4. thematic studies within the framework of the priority themes comparing and contrasting approaches within and across the different grounds of discrimination.
In implementing this Strand, the Commission will in particular ensure consistency and complementarity with the activities of the European Monitoring Centre on Racism and Xenophobia, the Community framework programme for research, technological development and demonstration activities and the Community statistical programme.

Strand 2 - Capacity building
The following measures may be supported in order to improve the capacity and effectiveness of target actors involved in combating discrimination in the fields covered by this programme:
1. Transnational exchange actions involving a range of actors from at least three Member States, consisting of the transfer of information, lessons learned and good practice. Activities may include a comparison of the effectiveness of processes, methods and tools related to the chosen themes, the mutual transfer and application of good practice, exchanges of personnel, the joint development of products, processes, strategy and methodology, the adaptation to different contexts of the methods, tools and processes identified as good practices and/or the common dissemination of results, visibility materials and events. The process of selecting applications for funding under the programme will take account of the diverse nature of discrimination;
2. Core funding for relevant European-level non-governmental organisations with experience of fighting discrimination and acting as advocates of people exposed to discrimination in order to promote the development of an integrated and coordinated approach to the fight against discrimination.
Core funding will be capped at 90 % of the expenditure eligible for support.
The procedures for selecting such organisations may take account of the diverse and heterogeneous nature of the groups facing discrimination.

Strand 3 - Awareness-raising
The following measures may be supported:
1. the organisation of conferences, seminars and events at European level;
2. the organisation of seminars by the Member States in support of the implementation of Community law in the field of non-discrimination, and the promotion of a European dimension to events organised at national level;
3. the organisation of European media campaigns and events to support the transnational exchange of information and the identification and dissemination of good practice, including the award of prizes to successful actions under Strand 2, to strengthen the visibility of the fight against discrimination;
4. the publication of materials to disseminate the results of the programme, including through the construction of an Internet Site providing examples of good practice, a forum for the exchange of ideas and a database of potential partners for transnational exchange actions.

IV. Method of presenting applications for support

Strand 1: this Strand will be implemented mainly through calls for tender. For cooperation with National Statistical Offices, the EUROSTAT procedures will apply.

Strand 2: Strands 2, Point 1 and 2, Point 2 will be implemented in response to calls for proposals which will be submitted to the Commission.

Strand 3: this Strand will be implemented, in general, in response to calls for tender. However, action under Strands 3, Point 2 and 3, Point 3 may be subsidised in response to requests for subsidies, for example from the Member States.

Annex 5.6.

Regulation (EEC) No 1408/71 of the Council of 14 June 1971 on the **application of social security schemes** to employed persons and their families moving within the Community
Official Journal L 149 , 05/07/1971 P. 0002 - 0050

MAIN PROVISIONS

TITLE I - GENERAL PROVISIONS

Article 1
Definitions
For the purpose of this Regulation:
(a) 'worker' means:
(i) subject to the restrictions set out in Annex V, any person who is insured, compulsorily or on an optional continued basis, for one or more of the contingencies covered by the branches of a social security scheme for employed persons;
(ii) any person who is compulsorily insured for one or more of the contingencies covered by the branches of social security dealt with in this Regulation, under a social security scheme for all residents or for the whole working population if such person:
- can be identified as an employed person by virtue of the manner in which such scheme is administered or financed, or
- failing such criteria, is insured for some other contingency specified in Annex V under a scheme for employed persons, either compulsorily or on an optional continued basis;
(iii) any person who is voluntarily insured for one or more of the contingencies covered by the branches dealt with in this Regulation, under a social security scheme of a Member State for employed persons or for all residents or for certain categories of residents if such person has previously been compulsorily insured for the same contingency under a scheme for employed persons of the same Member State;
(b) 'frontier worker' means any worker employed in the territory of a Member State and residing in the territory of another Member State to which he returns as a rule daily or at least once a week; however, a frontier worker who is posted elsewhere in the territory of the same or another Member State by the undertaking to which he is normally attached and is prevented on account of such posting from returning daily or at least once a week to the place where he resides shall nevertheless retain the status of frontier worker for a period not exceeding four months;
(c) 'seasonal worker' means any worker who goes to the territory of a Member State other than the one in which he is resident to do work there of a seasonal nature for an undertaking or an employer of that State for a period which may on no account exceed eight months, and who stays in the territory of the said State for the duration of his work; work of a seasonal nature shall be taken to mean work which, being dependent on the succession of the seasons, automatically recurs each year;
(d) 'refugee' shall have the meaning assigned to it in Article 1 of the Convention on the Status of Refugees, signed at Geneva on 28 July 1951;
(e) 'stateless person' shall have the meaning assigned to it in Article 1 of the Convention on the Status of Stateless Persons, signed in New York on 28 September 1954;
(f) 'member of the family' means any person defined or recognised as a member of the family or designated as a member of the household by the legislation under which benefits are provided or, in the cases referred to in Article 22 (1) (a) and Article 39, by the legislation of the Member State in whose territory such person resides; where, however, the said legislations regard as a member of the family or a member of the household only a person living under the same roof as the worker, this condition shall be considered satisfied if the person in question is mainly dependent on that worker;
(g) 'survivor' means any person defined or recognised as such by the legislation under which the benefits are granted; where, however, the said legislation regards as a survivor only a person who was living under the same roof as the deceased worker, this condition shall be considered satisfied if such person was mainly dependent on the deceased worker;
(h) 'residence' means habitual residence;
(i) 'stay' means temporary residence;
(j) 'legislation' means all the laws, regulations, and other provisions and all other present or future implementing measures of each Member State relating to the branches and schemes of social security covered by Article 4 (1) and (2);
This term excludes provisions of existing or future industrial agreements, whether or not they have been the

subject of a decision by the authorities rendering them compulsory or extending their scope. However, where such industrial agreements serve to implement an insurance requirement under the laws or regulations referred to in the preceding subparagraph, this restriction may at any time be lifted by a declaration by the Member State concerned, specifying the schemes of such a kind to which this Regulation applies. Notification shall be given of such declaration, which shall be published in accordance with the provisions of Article 96. The provisions of the preceding subparagraph shall not have the effect of exempting from application of this Regulation the schemes to which Regulation No 3 has been applied;
(k) 'social security convention' means any bilateral or multilateral instrument which binds or will bind two or more Member States exclusively, and any other multilateral instrument which binds or will bind at least two Member States and one or more other States in the field of social security, for all or part of the branches and schemes set out in Article 4 (1) and (2), together with agreements, of whatever kind, concluded pursuant to the said instruments;
(l) 'competent authority' means, in respect of each Member State, the Minister, Ministers or other equivalent authority responsible for social security schemes throughout or in any part of the territory of the State in question;
(m) 'Administrative Commission' means the Commission referred to in Article 80;
(n) 'institution' means, in respect of each Member State, the body or authority responsible for administering all or part of the legislation;
(o) 'competent institution' means:
(i) the institution with which the person concerned is insured at the time of the application for benefit, or
(ii) the institution from which the person concerned is entitled or would be entitled to benefits if he or a member or members of his family were resident in the territory of the Member State in which the institution is situated, or
(iii) the institution designated by the competent authority of the Member State concerned, or
(iv) in the case of a scheme relating to an employer's liability in respect of the benefits set out in Article 4 (1), either the employer or the insurer involved or, in default thereof, a body or authority designated by the competent authority of the Member State concerned;
(p) 'institution of the place of residence' and 'institution of the place of stay' mean respectively the institution which is competent to provide benefits in the place where the person concerned resides and the institution which is competent to provide benefits in the place where the person concerned is staying, under the legislation administered by that institution or, where no such institution exists, the institution designated by the competent authority of the Member State in question;
(q) 'competent State' means the Member State in whose territory the competent institution is situated;
(r) 'insurance periods' means contribution periods or periods of employment as defined or recognised as insurance periods by the legislation under which they were completed or considered as completed, and all periods treated as such, where they are regarded by the said legislation as equivalent to insurance periods;
(s) 'periods of employment' means periods defined or recognised as such by the legislation under which they were completed, and all periods treated as such, where they are regarded by the said legislation as equivalent to periods of employment;
(t) 'benefits' and 'pensions' mean all benefits and pensions, including all elements thereof payable out of public funds, revalorisation increases and supplementary allowances, subject to the provisions of Title III, as also lump-sum benefits which may be paid in lieu of pensions, and payments made by way of reimbursement of contributions;
(u) (i) 'family benefits' means all benefits in kind or in cash intended to meet family expenses under the legislation provided for in Article 4 (1) (h), excluding the special childbirth allowances mentioned in Annex I;
(ii) 'family allowances' means periodical cash benefits granted exclusively by reference to the number and, where appropriate, the age of members of the family;
(v) 'death grants' means any once-for-all payment in, the event of death, exclusive of the lump-sum benefits referred to in subparagraph (t).

Article 2
Persons covered
1. This Regulation shall apply to workers who are or have been subject to the legislation of one or more Member States and who are nationals of one of the Member States or who are stateless persons or refugees residing within the territory of one of the Member States, as also to the members of their families and their survivors.
2. In addition, this Regulation shall apply to the survivors of workers who have been subject to the legislation of one or more Member States, irrespective of the nationality of such workers, where their survivors are nationals of one of the Member States, or stateless persons or refugees residing within the territory of one of the Member States.
3. This Regulation shall apply to civil servants and to persons who, in accordance with the legislation

applicable, are treated as such, where they are or have been subject to the legislation of a Member State to which this Regulation applies.

Article 3
Equality of treatment
1. Subject to the special provisions of this Regulation, persons resident in the territory of one of the Member States to whom this Regulation applies shall be subject to the same obligations and enjoy the same benefits under the legislation of any Member State as the nationals of that State.
2. The provisions of paragraph 1 shall apply to the right to elect members of the organs of social security institutions or to participate in their nomination, but shall not affect the legislative provisions of any Member State relating to eligibility or methods of nomination.
3. Save as provided in Annex II, social security conventions which remain in force pursuant to Article 7 (2) (c) and conventions concluded pursuant to Article 8 (1), shall apply to all persons to whom this Regulation applies.

Article 4
Matters covered
1. This Regulation shall apply to all legislation concerning the following branches of social security:
(a) sickness and maternity benefits;
(b) invalidity benefits, including those intended for the maintenance or improvement of earning capacity;
(c) old-age benefits;
(d) survivors' benefits;
(e) benefits in respect of accidents at work and occupational diseases;
(f) death grants;
(g) unemployment benefits;
(h) family benefits.
2. This Regulation shall apply to all general and special social security schemes, whether contributory or non-contributory, and to schemes concerning the liability of an employer or ship owner in respect of the benefits referred to in paragraph 1.
3. The provisions of Title III of this Regulation shall not, however, affect the legislative provisions of any Member State concerning a ship owner's liability.
4. This Regulation shall not apply to social and medical assistance, to benefit schemes for victims of war or its consequences, or to special schemes for civil servants and persons treated as such.

Article 5
Declarations of Member States on the scope of this Regulation
The Member States shall specify the legislation and schemes referred to in Article 4 (1) and (2), the minimum benefits referred to in Article 50 and the benefits referred to in Articles 77 and 78 in declarations to be notified and published in accordance with Article 96.

Article 6
Social security conventions replaced by this Regulation
Subject to the provisions of Articles 7, 8 and 46 (4) this Regulation shall, as regards persons and matters which it covers, replace the provisions of any social security convention binding either;
(a) two or more Member States exclusively, or
(b) at least two Member States and one or more other States, where settlement of the cases concerned does not involve any institution of one of the latter States.

Article 7
International provisions not affected by this Regulation
1. This Regulation shall not affect obligations arising from:
(a) any convention adopted by the International Labour Conference which, after ratification by one or more Member States, has entered into force;
(b) the European Interim Agreements on Social Security of 11 December 1953 concluded between the Member States of the Council of Europe.
2. The provisions of Article 6 notwithstanding, the following shall continue to apply:
(a) the Agreement of 27 July 1950 concerning social security for Rhine boatmen, revised on 13 February 1961;
(b) the European Convention of 9 July 1956 concerning social security for workers in international transport;
(c) the social security conventions listed in Annex II.

Article 8
Conclusion of conventions between Member States
1. Two or more Member States may, as need arises, conclude conventions with each other based on the principles and in the spirit of this Regulation.
2. Each Member State shall notify, in accordance with Article 96 (1), any convention concluded with another Member State pursuant to paragraph 1.

Article 9
Admission to voluntary or optional continued insurance
1. The legislative provisions of any Member State which make admission to voluntary or optional continued insurance conditional upon residence in the territory of that State shall not apply to workers to whom this Regulation applies and who are resident in the territory of another Member State, provided that at some time in their past working life they were subject to the legislation of the first State.
2. Where, under the legislation of a Member State, admission to voluntary or optional continued insurance is conditional upon completion of insurance periods, any such periods completed under the Legislation of another Member State shall be taken into account, to the extent required, as if they were completed under the legislation of the first State.

Article 10
Waiving of residence clauses - Effect of compulsory insurance on reimbursement of contributions
1. Save as otherwise provided in this Regulation, invalidity, old-age or survivors' cash benefits, pensions for accidents at work or occupational diseases and death grants acquired under the legislation of one or more Member States shall not be subject to any reduction, modification, suspension, withdrawal or confiscation by reason of the fact that the recipient resides in the territory of a Member State other than that in which the institution responsible for payment is situated.
The preceding subparagraph shall also apply to lump-sum benefits granted in cases of remarriage of a surviving spouse who was entitled to a survivor's pension.
2. Where under the legislation of a Member State reimbursement of contributions is conditional upon the person concerned having ceased to be subject to compulsory insurance, this condition shall not be considered satisfied as long as the person concerned is subject to compulsory insurance as a worker under the legislation of another Member State.

Article 11
Revalorisation of benefits
Rules for revalorisation provided by the legislation of a Member State shall apply to benefits due under that legislation by virtue of the provisions of this Regulation.
Article 12
Prevention of overlapping of benefits
1. This Regulation can neither confer nor maintain the right to several benefits of the same kind for one and the same period of compulsory insurance. However, this provision shall not apply to benefits in respect of invalidity, old age, death (pensions) or occupational disease which are awarded by the institutions of two or more Member States, in accordance with Article 41, Article 43 (2) and (3), Articles 46, 50 and 51 or Article 60 (1) (b).
2. The legislative provisions of a Member State for reduction, suspension or withdrawal of benefit in cases of overlapping with other social security benefits or other income may be invoked even though the right to such benefits was acquired under the legislation of another Member State or such income arises in the territory of another Member State. However, this provision shall not apply when the person concerned receives benefits of the same kind in respect of invalidity, old age, death (pensions) or occupational disease which are awarded by the institutions of two or more Member States in accordance with Articles 46, 50, 51 or Article 60 (1) (b).
3. The legislative provisions of a Member State for reduction, suspension or withdrawal of benefit in the case of a person in receipt of invalidity benefits or anticipatory old-age benefits pursuing a professional or trade activity may be invoked against such person even though he is pursuing his activity in the territory of another Member State.
4. An invalidity pension payable under Netherlands legislation shall, in a case where the Netherlands institution is bound under Article 57 (3) (c) or Article 60 (2) (a) to contribute also to the cost of benefits for occupational disease granted under the legislation of another Member State, be reduced by the amount payable to the institution of the other Member State which is responsible for granting the benefits for occupational disease.

TITLE II - DETERMINATION OF THE LEGISLATION APPLICABLE

Article 13
General rules
1. A worker to whom this Regulation applies shall be subject to the legislation of a single Member State only. That legislation shall be determined in accordance with the provisions of this Title.
2. Subject to the provisions of Articles 14 to 17:
(a) a worker employed in the territory of one Member State shall be subject to the legislation of that State even if he resides in the territory of another Member State or if the registered office or place of business of the undertaking or individual employing him is situated in the territory of another Member State;
(b) a worker employed on board a vessel flying the flag of a Member State shall be subject to the legislation of that State;
(c) civil servants and persons treated as such shall be subject to the legislation of the Member State to which the administration employing them is subject;
(d) a worker called up or recalled for service in the armed forces of a Member State shall retain the status of worker, and shall be subject to the legislation of that State; if entitlement under that legislation is subject to the completion of insurance period before entry into or release from such service, insurance periods completed under the legislation of any other Member State shall be taken into account, to the extent necessary, as if they were insurance periods completed under the legislation of the first State.

Article 14
Special rules
1. Article 13 (2) (a) shall apply subject to the following exceptions or circumstances:
(a) (i) A worker employed in the territory of a Member State by an undertaking to which he is normally attached who is posted by that undertaking to the territory of another Member State to perform work there for that undertaking shall continue to be subject to the legislation of the first Member State, provided that the anticipated duration of that work does not exceed twelve months and that he is not sent to replace another worker who has completed his term of posting;
(ii) if the duration of the work to be done extends beyond the duration originally anticipated, owing to unforesecable circumstances, and exceeds twelve months, the legislation of the first State shall continue to apply until the completion of such work, provided that the competent authority of the State in whose territory the worker is posted or the body designated by that authority gives its consent; such consent must be requested before the end of the initial twelve month period. Such consent cannot, however, be given for a period exceeding twelve months;
(b) a worker employed in international transport in the territory of two or more Member States as a member of travelling or flying personnel and who is working for an undertaking which, for hire or reward or on own account, operates transport services for passengers or goods by rail, road, air or inland waterway and has its registered office or place of business in the territory of a Member State, shall be subject to the legislation of the latter State, with the following restrictions:
(i) where the said undertaking has a branch or permanent representation in the territory of a Member State other than that in which it has its registered office or place of business, a worker employed by such branch or agency shall be subject to the legislation of the Member State in whose territory such branch or permanent representation is situated;
(ii) where a worker is employed principally in the territory of the Member State in which he resides, he shall be subject to the legislation of that State, even if the undertaking which employs him has no registered office or place of business or branch or permanent representation in that territory;
(c) a worker, other than one employed in international transport, who normally pursues his activity in the territory of two or more Member States shall be subject:
(i) to the legislation of the Member State in whose territory he resides, if he pursues his activity partly in that territory or if he is attached to several undertakings or several employers who have their registered offices or places of business in the territory of different Member States;
(ii) to the legislation of the Member State in whose territory is situated the registered office or place of business of the undertaking or individual employing him, if he does not reside in the territory of any of the Member States where he is pursuing his activity;
(d) a worker who is employed in the territory of one Member State by an undertaking which has its registered office or place of business in the territory of another Member State and which straddles the common frontier of these States shall be subject to the legislation of the Member State in whose territory the undertaking has its registered office or place of business.
2. Article 13 (2) (b) shall apply subject to the following exceptions and circumstances:
(a) a worker employed by an undertaking to which he is normally attached, either in the territory of a Member

State or on board a vessel flying the flag of a Member State, who is posted by that undertaking on board a vessel flying the flag of another Member State to perform work there for that undertaking shall, subject to the conditions provided in paragraph 1 (a), continue to be subject to the legislation of the first Member State;
(b) a worker who, while not being habitually employed at sea, is employed in the territorial waters or in a port of a Member State on a vessel flying the flag of another Member State, but is not a member of the crew, shall be subject to the legislation of the first State;
(c) a worker employed on board a vessel flying the flag of a Member State and remunerated for such employment by an undertaking or a person whose registered office or place of business is in the territory of another Member State shall be subject to the legislation of the latter State if he is resident in the territory of that State; the undertaking or person paying the remuneration shall be considered as the employer for the purposes of the said legislation.
3. The legistative provisions of a Member State under which a pensioner who is pursuing a professional or trade activity is not subject to compulsory insurance in respect of such activity shall also apply to a pensioner whose pension was acquired under the legislation of another Member State.

Article 15
Rules concerning voluntary insurance or optional continued insurance
1. The provisions of Articles 13 and 14 shall not apply to voluntary insurance or optional continued insurance.
2. Where application of the legislations of two or more Member States entails overlapping of insurance:
- under a compulsory insurance scheme and one or more voluntary or optional continued insurance schemes, the person concerned shall be subject exclusively to the compulsory insurance schemes;
- under two or more voluntary or optional continued insurance schemes, the person concerned may join only the voluntary or optional continued insurance scheme for which he has opted.
3. However, in respect of invalidity, old age and death (pensions), the person concerned may join the voluntary or optional continued insurance scheme of a Member State, even if he is compulsorily subject to the legislation of another Member State, to the extent that such overlapping is explicitly or implicitly admitted in the first Member State.
The person concerned who applies to join a voluntary or optional continued insurance scheme in a Member State whose legislation provides, in addition to such insurance, for complementary optional insurance may only join the latter.

Article 16
Special rules regarding persons employed by diplomatic missions and consular posts, and auxiliary staff of the European Communties
1. Article 13 (2) (a) shall apply to persons employed by diplomatic missions and consular posts and to the private domestic staff of agents of such missions or posts.
2. However, workers covered by paragraph 1 who are nationals of the Member State which is the accrediting or sending State may opt to be subject to the legislation of that State. Such right of option may be renewed at the end of each calendar year and shall not have retrospective effect.
3. Auxiliary staff of the European Communities may opt to be subject to the legislation of the Member State in whose territory they are employed, to the legislation of the Member State to which they were last subject or to the legislation of the Member State whose nationals they are, in respect of provisions other than those relating to family allowances, the granting of which is governed by the conditions of employment applicable to such staff. This right of option, which may be exercised once only, shall take effect from the date of entry into employment.

Article 17
Exceptions to the provisions of Articles 13 to 16
Two or more Member States or the competent authorities of those States may, by common agreement, provide for exceptions to the provisions of Articles 13 to 16 in the interest of certain workers or categories of workers.

TITLE III - SPECIAL PROVISIONS RELATING TO THE VARIOUS CATEGORIES OF BENEFITS

CHAPTER 1: SICKNESS AND MATERNITY
Section 1: Common provisions

Article 18
Aggregation of insurance periods
1. The competent institution of a Member State whose legislation makes the acquisition, retention or recovery of the right to benefits conditional upon the completion of insurance periods shall, to the extent necessary, take

account of insurance periods completed under the legislation of any other Member State as if they were periods completed under its own legislation.
2. The provisions of paragraph 1 shall apply to seasonal workers, even in respect of periods prior to any break in insurance exceeding the period allowed by the legislation of the competent State, provided however that the worker concerned has not ceased to be insured for a period exceeding four months.

Section 2: Workers and members of their families

Article 19
Residence in a Member State other than the competent State - General rules
1. A worker residing in the territory of a Member State other than the competent State, who satisfies the conditions of the legislation of the competent State for entitlement to benefits, taking account where appropriate of the provisions of Article 18, shall receive in the State in which he is resident:
(a) benefits in kind provided on behalf of the competent institution by the institution of the place of residence in accordance with the legislation administered by that institution as though he were insured with it;
(b) cash benefits provided by the competent institution in accordance with the legislation which it administers. However, by agreement between the competent institution and the institution of the place of residence, such benefits may be provided by the latter institution on behalf of the former, in accordance with the legislation of the competent State.
2. The provisions of paragraph 1 (a) shall apply by analogy to members of the family who are residing in the territory of a Member State other than the competent State, where they are not entitled to such benefits under the legislation of the State in whose territory they reside.

Article 20
Frontier workers and members of their families - Special rules
A frontier worker may also obtain benefits in the territory of the competent State. Such benefits shall be provided by the competent institution in accordance with the legislation of that State, as though the worker were resident there. Members of his family may receive benefits in kind under the same conditions; however, receipt of such benefits shall, except in urgent cases, be conditional upon an agreement between the States concerned or between the competent authorities of those States or, in its absence, on prior authorisation by the competent institution.

Article 21
Stay in or transfer of residence to the competent State
1. A worker and members of his family referred to in Article 19 who are staying in the territory of the competent State shall receive benefits in accordance with the legislation of that State as though they were resident there even if they have already received benefits for the same case of sickness or maternity before their stay. This provision shall not, however, apply to frontier workers and members of their families.
2. A worker and members of his family referred to in Article 19 who transfer their residence to the territory of the competent State, shall receive benefits in accordance with the legislation of that State, even if they have already received benefits for the same case of sickness or maternity before transferring their residence.

Article 22
Stay outside the competent State - Return to or transfer of residence to another Member State during sickness or maternity - Need to go to another Member State in order to receive appropriate treatment
1. A worker who satisfies the conditions of the legislation of the competent State for entitlement to benefits, taking account where appropriate of the provisions of Article 18, and:
(a) whose condition necessitates immediate benefits during a stay in the territory of another Member State, or
(b) who, having become entitled to benefits chargeable to the competent institution, is authorised by that institution to return to the territory of the Member State where he resides, or to transfer his residence to the territory of another Member State, or
(c) who is authorised by the competent institution to go to the territory of another Member State to receive there the treatment appropriate to his condition, shall be entitled:
(i) to benefits in kind provided on behalf of the competent institution by the institution of the place of stay or residence in accordance with the legislation which it administers, as though he were insured with it; the length of the period during which benefits are provided shall be governed however by the legislation of the competent State;
(ii) to cash benefits provided by the competent institution in accordance with the legislation which it administers. However, by agreement between the competent institution and the institution of the place of stay or residence, such benefits may be provided by the latter institution on behalf of the former, in accordance with the

legislation of the competent State.
2. The authorisation required under paragraph 1 (b) may be refused only if it is established that movement of the person concerned would be prejudicial to his state of health or the receipt of medical treatment.
The authorisation required under paragraph 1 (c) may not be refused where the treatment in question cannot be provided for the person concerned within the territory of the Member State in which he resides.
3. The provisions of paragraphs 1 and 2 shall apply to members of a worker's family in respect of benefits in kind.
4. The fact that the provisions of paragraph 1 apply to a worker shall not affect the right to benefit of members of his family.

Article 23
Calculation of cash benefits
1. The competent institution of a Member State whose legislation provides that the calculation of cash benefits shall be based on an average wage or salary, shall determine that average wage or salary exclusively by reference to wages or salaries confirmed as having been paid during the periods completed under the said legislation.
2. The competent institution of a Member State whose legislation provides that the calculation of cash benefits shall be based on a standard wage or salary, shall take account exclusively of the standard wage or salary or, where appropriate, of the average of the standard wages or salaries for the periods completed under the said legislation.
3. The competent institution of a Member State under whose legislation the amount of cash benefits varies with the number of members of the family, shall also take into account the members of the family of the person concerned who are resident in the territory of another Member State as if they were resident in the territory of the competent State.

Article 24
Substantial benefits in kind
1. Where the right of a worker or a member of his family to a prosthesis, a major appliance or other substantial benefits in kind has been recognised by the institution of a Member State before be becomes insured with the institution of another Member State, the said worker shall receive such benefits at the expense of the first institution, even if they are granted after he becomes insured with the second institution.
2. The Administrative Commission shall draw up the list of benefits to which the provisions of paragraph 1 apply.

Section 3: Unemployed persons and members of their families

Article 25
1. An unemployed person, to whom Article 69 (1) and the second sentence of Article 71 (1) (b) (ii) apply, and who satisfies the conditions of the legislation of the competent State for entitlement to benefits in kind and in cash, taking account where appropriate of the provisions of Article 18, shall receive for the period provided under Article 69 (1) (c):
(a) benefits in kind provided on behalf of the competent institution by the institution of the Member State in which he seeks employment in accordance with the legislation of the latter institution, as though he were insured with it;
(b) cash benefits provided by the competent institution in accordance with the legislation which it administers. However, by agreement between the competent institution and the institution of the Member State in which the unemployed person seeks employment, benefits may be provided by the latter institution on behalf of the former institution in accordance with the legislation of the competent State. Unemployment benefits under Article 69 (1) shall not be granted for the period during which cash benefits are received.
2. A totally unemployed person to whom the provisions of Article 71 (1) (a) (ii) or the first sentence of Article 71 (1) (b) (ii) apply shall receive benefits in kind and in cash in accordance with the legislation of the Member State in whose territory he resides, as though he had been subject to that legislation during his last employment, taking account where appropriate of the provisions of Article 18; the cost of such benefits shall be met by the institution of the country of residence.
3. Where an unemployed person satisfies the conditions of the legislation of the Member State which is responsible for the cost of unemployment benefits for entitlement to benefits in kind, taking account where appropriate of the provisions of Article 18, the members of his family shall receive such benefits, irrespective of the Member State in whose territory they reside or are staying. Such benefits shall be provided by the institution of the place of residence or of stay, in accordance with the legislation which it administers on behalf of the competent institution of the Member State which is responsible for the cost of unemployment benefits.

4. Without prejudice to any legislative provisions of a Member State which permit an extension of the period during which sickness benefits may be granted, the period provided for in paragraph 1 may, in cases of force majeure, be extended by the competent institution within the limit fixed by the legislation administered by the institution.

Section 4: Pension claimants and members of their families

Article 26
Right to benefits in kind in cases of cessation of the right to benefits from the institution which was last competent
1. A worker, members of his family or his survivors who, during the investigation of a claim, cease to be entitled to benefits in kind under the legislation of the Member State last competent, shall nevertheless receive such benefits under the following conditions: benefits in kind shall be provided in accordance with the legislation of the Member State in whose territory the person or persons concerned reside, provided that they are entitled to such benefits under that legislation or would be entitled to them under the legislation of another Member State if they were residing in the territory of that State, taking account where appropriate of the provisions of Article 18.
2. A pension claimant who is entitled to benefits in kind under the legislation of a Member State which obliges the person concerned to pay sickness insurance contributions himself during the investigation of his pension claim shall cease to be entitled to benefits in kind at the end of the second month for which he has not paid the contributions due.
3. Benefits in kind provided pursuant to paragraph 1 shall be chargeable to the institution which has collected contributions pursuant to paragraph 2; where no contributions are payable under paragraph 2, the institution responsible for the cost of the benefits in kind shall, after awarding the pension pursuant to Article 28, refund the amount of the benefits provided to the institution of the place of residence.

Section 5: Pensioners and members of their families

Article 27
Pensions payable under the legislation of several States where a right to benefits in kind is enjoyed in the country of residence
A pensioner who is entitled to draw pensions under the legislation of two or more Member States and who is entitled to benefits in kind under the legislation of the Member State in whose territory he resides, taking account where appropriate of the provisions of Article 18 and Annex V, shall, with the members of his family, receive such benefits from the institution of the place of residence and at the expense of that institution as though he were a pensioner whose pension was payable solely under the legislation of the latter State.

Article 28
Pensions payable under the legislation of one or more States where no right to benefits in kind is enjoyed in the country of residence
1. A pensioner who is entitled to draw a pension or pensions under the legislation of one or more Member States and who is not entitled to benefits in kind under the legislation of the Member State in whose territory he resides, shall nevertheless receive such benefits for himself and members of his family if, taking account where appropriate of the provisions of Article 18 and Annex V, he would be entitled thereto under the legislation of the Member State, or of at least one of the Member States, competent in respect of pensions if he were resident in the territory of such State. The benefits shall be provided on behalf of the institution referred to in paragraph 2 by the institution of the place of residence as though the person concerned were a pensioner under the legislation of the State in whose territory he resides and were entitled to benefits in kind.
2. In the cases covered by paragraph 1, the cost of benefits in kind shall be borne by the institution determined according to the following rules:
(a) where the pensioner is entitled to the said benefits under the legislation of a single Member State, the cost shall be borne by the competent institution of that State;
(b) where the pensioner is entitled to the said benefits under the legislations of two or more Member States, the cost thereof shall be borne by the competent institution of the Member State under whose legislation the pensioner has completed the longest period of insurance; should the application of this rule result in several institutions being responsible for the cost of benefits, cost shall be borne by the institution with which the pensioner was last insured.

Article 29
Residence of members of the family in a State other than the one in which the pensioner resides - Transfer of

residence to the State where the pensioner resides
1. Members of the family of a pensioner entitled to draw a pension or pensions under the legislation of one or more Member States who reside in the territory of a Member State other than the one in which the pensioner resides shall where he is entitled under the legislation of a Member State to benefits in kind, receive such benefits as though the pensioner were resident in the same territory as them. Such benefits shall be provided by the institution of the place of residence of the members of the family, in accordance with the legislation which that institution administers and shall be chargeable to the institution of the pensioner's place of residence.
2. Members of the family referred to in paragraph 1 who transfer their residence to the territory of the Member State where the pensioner resides, shall receive benefits under the legislation of that State, even if they have already received benefits for the same case of sickness or maternity before transferring their residence.

Article 30
Substantial benefits in kind
The provisions of Article 24 shall apply by analogy to pensioners.

Article 31
A pensioner and/or member of his family staying in a State other than the State in which they reside
A pensioner entitled to draw a pension or pensions under the legislation of one or more Member States who is also entitled to benefits in kind under the legislation of one of those States shall, with members of his family, receive such benefits while staying in the territory of a Member State other than the one in which they reside. Such benefits shall be provided by the institution of the place of stay in accordance with the legislation which it administers and shall be chargeable to the institution of the pensioner's place of residence.

Article 32
Special provisions concerning responsibility for the cost of benefits provided for former frontier workers, members of their families or their survivors
The cost of benefits with which a pensioner who is a former frontier worker or the survivor of a frontier worker is provided under Article 27, and the cost of benefits with which members of his family are provided under Article 27 or 31 shall, where the frontier worker was working as such for the three months immediately preceding the date on which the pension became payable on the date of his death, be divided equally between the institution of the pensioner's place of residence and that with which he was last insured.

Article 33
Contributions payable by pensioners
The institution responsible for payment of a pension, and belonging to a Member State whose legislation provides for deductions from pensions in respect of contributions payable by a pensioner to cover benefits in kind, shall be authorised to make such deductions from the pension payable by such institution, calculated in accordance with the legislation concerned, to the extent that the cost of the benefits in kind under Articles 27, 28, 31 and 32 are to be borne by an institution of the said Member State.

Article 34
General provision
The provisions of Articles 27 to 33 shall not apply to a pensioner or to members of his family who are entitled to benefits in kind under the legislation of a Member State as a result of pursuing a professional or trade activity. In such a case the person concerned shall for the purposes of this Chapter, be considered as a worker or as a member of a worker's family.

CHAPTER 2 - INVALIDITY

Section 1: Workers subject only to legislations under which the amount of invalidity benefits is independent of the duration of insurance periods

Article 37
General provisions
1. A worker who has been successively or alternately subject to the legislations of two or more Member States and who has completed insurance periods exclusively under legislations according to which the amount of invalidity benefits is independent of the duration of insurance periods, shall receive benefits in accordance with Article 39. This Article shall not affect pension increases or supplements in respect of children, granted in accordance with the provisions of Chapter 8.
2. Annex III lists legislations of the kind mentioned in paragraph 1 which are in force in the territory of each of

the Member States concerned.

Article 38
Aggregation of insurance periods
1. The competent institution of a Member State whose legislation makes the acquisition, retention or recovery of the right to benefit conditional upon the completion of insurance periods shall take account to the extent necessary of insurance periods completed under the legislation of any other Member States, as though they had been completed under its own legislation.
2. Where the legislation of a Member State makes the granting of certain benefits conditional upon the insurance periods having been completed in an completion of insurance periods shall take account to where appropriate, in a specific employment, insurance periods completed under the legislations of other Member States shall be taken into account for the granting of these benefits only if completed under a corresponding scheme or, failing this, in the same occupation or, where appropriate, in the same employment. If, account having been taken of the periods thus completed, the person concerned does not satisfy the conditions for receipt of these benefits, these periods shall be taken into account for the granting of the benefits under the general scheme or, failing this, under the scheme applicable to manual or clerical workers, as appropriate.

Article 39
Award of benefits
1. The institution of the Member State whose legislation was applicable at the time when incapacity for work followed by invalidity occurred, shall determine, in accordance with that legislation, whether the person concerned satisfies the conditions for entitlement to benefits, taking account where appropriate of the provisions of Article 38.
2. A person who satisfies the conditions referred to in paragraph 1 shall obtain the benefits exclusively from the said institution, in accordance with the legislation which it administers.
3. A person who does not satisfy the conditions referred to in paragraph 1 shall receive the benefits to which he is still entitled under the legislation of another Member State, taking account where appropriate of the provisions of Article 38.
4. If the legislation applicable under paragraph 2 or 3 provides that the amount of the benefits shall be determined taking into account the existence of members of the family other than the children, the competent institution shall also take into consideration the members of the family of the person concerned who are residing in the territory of another Member State, as if they were residing in the territory of the competent State.

CHAPTER 3 - OLD AGE AND DEATH (PENSIONS)

Article 44
General provisions for the award of benefits when a worker has been subject to the legislation of two or more Member States
1. The rights to benefits of a worker who has been subject to the legislation of two or more Member States, or of his survivors, shall be determined in accordance with the provisions of this Chapter.
2. Subject to the provisions of Article 49, when a claim for the award of a benefit is lodged, such award must be made having regard to all the legislations to which the worker has been subject. Exception shall be made to this rule if the person concerned expressly asks for postponement of the award of old age benefits to which he would be entitled under the legislation of one or more Member States, provided that the periods completed under that legislation or those legislations are not taken into account for the purpose of acquiring the right to benefit in another Member State.
3. This Chapter shall not apply to increases in or supplements to pensions in respect of children, or to orphans' pensions granted pursuant to Chapter 8.

Article 45
Consideration of insurance periods completed under the legislations to which a worker has been subject for the acquisition, retention or recovery of the right to benefits
1. An institution of a Member State whose legislation makes the acquisition, retention or recovery of the right to benefits conditional upon the completion of insurance period shall take into account, to the extent necessary, insurance periods completed under the legislation of any Member State as though they had been completed under the legislation which it administers.
2. Where the legislation of am Member State makes the granting of certain benefits conditional upon the insurance periods having been completed in an occupation subject to a special scheme or, where appropriate, in a specific employment, periods completed under the legislations of other Member States shall bei taken into account for the granting of such benefits only if completed under such a scheme or, failing this, in the same

occupation or, where appropriate, in the same employment. If, taking into account periods thus completed, the person concerned does not satisfy the conditions for receipt of these benefits, those periods shall be taken into account for the granting of benefits under the general scheme or, failing this, under the scheme applicable to manual or clerical workers, as appropriate.
3. Where the legislation of am Member State which makes the granting of benefits conditional upon a worker being subject to its legislation at the time when the risk materialises has no requirements as to the length of insurance periods either for entitlement to or calculation of benefits, any worker who ist no longer subject to that legislation shall for the purposes of this Chapter, be deemed to be stil so subject at the time when the risk materialises, if at that time he is subject to the legislation of another Member State or, failing this, can establish a claim to benefits under the legislation of another Member State. However, this latter condition shall bedeemed to be satisfied in the case referred to in Article 48 (1).

Article 46
Award of benefits
1. Where a worker has been subject to the legislation of a Member State and where he satisfies its conditions for entitlement to benefits, without application of the provisions of Article 45 being necessary, the competent institution of that Member State shall, in accordance with the legislation which it administers, determine the amount of benefit corresponding to the total length of the insurance periods to be taken into account in pursuance of such legislation.
This institution shall also calculate the amount of benefit which would be obtained by applying the rules laid down in paragraph (2) (a) and (b). Only the higher of these two amounts shall be taken into consideration.
2. Where a worker has been subject to the legislation of am Member State and does not satisfy the conditions for entitlement to benefits unless account is taken of the provisions of Article 45, the competent institution of that Member State shall apply the following rules:
(a) the institution shall calculate the theoretical amount of benefit that the person concerned could claim if all the insurance periods completed under the legislations of the Member States to which he has been subject had been completed in the State in question and under the legislation administered by it on the date the benefit is awarded. If, under that legislation, the amount of the benefit does not depend on the length of the insurance periods, then that amount shall be taken as the theoretical amount referred to in this subparagraph;
(b) the institution shall then establish the actual amount of the benefit on the basis of the theoretical amount referred to in the preceding subparagraph and in the ratio which the length of the insurance periods completed before the materialisation of the risk under the legislation administered by that institution, bears to the total length of the insurance periods completed before materialisation of the risk under the legislations of all the Member States concerned;
(c) if the total length of the insurance periods completed under the legislations of all the Member States concerned before the materialisation of the risk is longer than the maximum period required by the legislation of one of these States for receipt of full benefit, the competent institution of that State shall, when applying the provisions of this paragraph, take into consideration this maximum period instead of the total length of the periods completed; this method of calculation must not result in the imposition on that institution of the costs of a benefit greater than the full benefit provided for by the legislation which it administers;
(d) the procedure for taking into account duplicate periods when applying the rules of calculation laid down in this paragraph, shall be laid down in the implementing Regulation referred to in Article 97.
3. The person concerned shall be entitled to the total sum of the benefits calculated in accordance with the provisions of paragraphs 1 and 2, within the limit of the highest theoretical amount of benefits calculated according to paragraph 2 (a).
Where the amount referred to in the preceding subparagraph is exceeded, any institution applying paragraph 1 shall adjust its benefit by an amount corresponding to the proportion which the amount of the benefit concerned bears to the total of the benefits determined in accordance with paragraph 1.
4. When in a case of invalidity, old age or survivors' pensions, the total of the benefits due from two or more Member States, under the provisions of a multilateral social security convention referred to in Article 6 (b), is lower than the total which would be due from such Member States under paragraphs 1 and 3, the person concerned shall benefit from the provisions of this Chapter.

CHAPTER 4 - ACCIDENTS AT WORK AND OCCUPATIONAL DISEASES

Section 1: Right to benefits

Article 52
Residence in a Member State other than the competent State - General Rules
A worker who sustains an accident at work or contracts an occupational disease, and who is residing in the

territory of a Member State other than the competent State, shall receive in the State in which he is residing:
(a) benefits in kind, provided on behalf of the competent institution by the institution of his place of residence in accordance with the legislation which it administers as if he were insured with it;
(b) cash benefits provided by the competent institution in accordance with the legislation which it administers. However, by agreement between the competent institution and the institution of the place of residence, these benefits may be provided by the latter institution on behalf of the former in accordance with the legislation of the competent State.

Article 53
Frontier workers - Special rule
A frontier worker may also obtain benefits in the territory of the competent State. Such benefits shall be provided by the competent institution in accordance with the legislation of that State, as if the worker were residing there.

Article 60
1. In the event of aggravation of an occupational disease for which a worker has received or is receiving benefit under the legislation of a Member State, the following rules shall apply:
(a) if the worker has not, while in receipt of benefits, been in employment under the legislation of another Member State likely to cause or aggravate the disease in question, the competent institution of the first Member State shall be bound to meet the cost of the benefits under the legislation which it administers taking into account the aggravation;
(b) if the worker, while in receipt of benefits, has been in such employment under the legislation of another Member State, the competent institution of the first State shall be bound to meet the cost of the benefits under the legislation which it administers without taking into account the aggravation. The competent institution of the second Member State shall grant a supplement to the worker, the amount of which shall be determined according to the legislation which it administers and shall be equal to the difference between the amount of benefits due after the aggravation and the amount which would have been due prior to the aggravation under the legislation which it administers if the disease in question had occurred under the legislation of that State;
(c) if in cases covered by subparagraph (b) a worker suffering from sclerogenic pneumoconiosis or from a disease determined under Article 57 (4) is not entitled to benefits under the legislation of the second State, the competent institution of the first State shall be bound to provide benefits under the legislation which it administers, taking into account the aggravation. The institution of the second State shall, however, meet the cost of the difference between the amount of cash benefits, including pensions, due from the competent institution of the first State, taking into account the aggravation and the amount of the corresponding benefits which were due prior to the aggravation.

CHAPTER 5 - DEATH GRANTS

Article 64
Aggregation of insurance periods
The competent institution of a Member State whose legislation makes the acquisition, retention or recovery of the right to death grants subject to the completion of insurance periods shall take account, to the extent necessary, of insurance periods completed under the legislation of any other Member State as though they had been completed under the legislation which it administers.

Article 65
Right to grants where death occurs in, or where the person entitled resides in, a Member State other than the competent State
1. When a worker, a pensioner or a pension claimant, or a member of his family, dies in the territory of a Member State other than the competent State, the death shall be deemed to have occurred in the territory of the competent State.
2. The competent institution shall be obliged to award death grants payable under the legislation which it administers, even if the person entitled resides in the territory of a Member State other than the competent State.
3. The provisions of paragraphs 1 and 2 shall also apply when the death is the result of an accident at work or an occupational disease.

Article 66
Provision of benefits in the event of the death of a pensioner who had resided in a Member state other than the one whose institutions was responsible for providing benefits in kind
In the event of the death of a pensioner who was entitled to draw a pension or pensions under the legislation of

one or more Member states, when such pensioner was residing in the territory of a Member States other than the one whose institution was responsible for providing him with benefits in kind under Article 28, the death grants payable under the legislation administrated by that instituion shall be provided by the institution at its own expense as though the pensioner had been residing in the territory of the Member States of that institution at the time of his death.
The provisions of the preceding paragraph shall apply by analogy to the members of a pensioner's family.

CHAPTER 6 - UNEMPLOYMENT

Section 1: Common provisions

Article 67
Aggregation of periods of insurance or employment
1. The competent institution of a Member State whose legislation makes the acquiçsition, retention or recovery of the right to benefits subject to the completion of insurance periods shall takes into account, to the extent necessary, periods of insurance or employment completed under the legislation of any other Member States, as though they were periods completed under the legislation with it administers, provided, however, that the periods of employment would have been counted as insurance periods had they been completed under that legislation.
2. The competent institution of a Member State whose legislation makes the acquisition, retention or recovery of the right to benefits subject to the completion of periods of employment shall take into account, to the extent necessary, periods of insurance or employment completed under the legislation of any other Member State, as though they were periods of employment completed under the legislation which it administers.
3. Except in the cases referred to in Article 71 (1) (a) (ii) and (b) (ii), application of the provisions of paragraphs 1 and 2 shall be subject to the condition that the person concerned should have completed lastly:

Article 68
Calculation of benefits
1. The competent institution of a Member State whose legislation provides that the calculation of benefits should be based on the amount of the previous wage or salary shall take into account exclusively the wage or salary received by the person concerned in respect of his last employment in the territory of that State. However, if the person concerned had been in his last employment in that territory for less than four weeks, the benefits shall be calculated on the basis of the normal wage or salary corresponding, in the place where the unemployment person is residing or staying, to an equivalent or similar employment to his last employment in the territory of another Member State.
2. The competent institution of a Member State whose legislation provides that the amount of benefits varies with the number of members of the family, shall take into account also members of the family of the person concerned who are residing in the territory of another Member State, as though they were residing in the territory of the competent State. This provision shall not apply if, in the country of residence of the members of the family, another person is entitled to unemployment benefits for the calculation of which the members of the family are taken into consideration.
Section 2
Unemployment persons going to a Member State other than the competent State

Article 69
Conditions and limits for the retention of the right to benefits
1. A worker whos is wholly unemployed and who satisfies the conditions of the legislation of a Member State for entitlement to benefits and who goes to one or more other Member States in order to seek employment there shall retain his entitlement to such benefits under the conditions and within the limits hereinafter indicated:
(a) before his departure, he must have been registered with the employment services of the competent State as a person seeking work and must have remained available for at least four weeks after becoming unemployed. However, the competent services or institutions may authorise his departure before such time has expired;
(b) he must register as a person seeking work with the employment services of each of the Member States to which he goes and be subject to the control procedure organised therein. This condition shall be considered satisfied for the period before registration if the person concerend registered within seven days of the date when he ceased to be available to the employment services of the State he left. In exceptional cases, this period may be extended by the competent services or institutions;
(c) entitlement to benefits shall continue for a maximum period of three months from the date when the person concerned ceased to be available to the employment services of the State which he left, provided that the total duration of the benefits does not exceed the duration of the period of benefits he was entitled to under the

legislation of the State. In the case of a seasonal worker such duration shall, moreover, be limited to the period remaining until the end of the season for which he was engaged.
2. If the person concerned returns to the competent State before the expiry of the period during which he is entitled to benefits under paragraph 1 (c), he shall continue to be entitled to benefits under the legislation of that State; he shall lose all entitlement to benefits under the legislation of the competent State if he does not return there before the expiry of that period. In exceptional cases, this time limit may be extended by the competent services or institutions.

Article 70
Provision of benefits and reimbursements
1. In the case referred to in Article 69 (1), benefits shall be provided by the institution of each of the States to which an unemployed person goes to seek employment.
The competent institution of the Member State to whose legislation a worker was subject at the time of his last employment shall be obliged to reimburse the amount of such benefits.
2. The reimbursements referred to in paragraph 1 shall be determined and made in accordance with the procedure laid down by the implementing Regulation referred to in Article 97, on proof of actual expenditure, or by lump sum payments.
3. Two or more Member States, or the competent authorities of those States, may provide for other methods of reimbursements or payment, or may waive all reimbursement between the institutions coming under their jurisdiction.

Section 3: Unemployment persons who during their last employment, were residing in a Member State other than the competent State

Article 71
1. An unemployed person who, during his last employment, was residing in the territory of a Member State other the competent State shall receive benefits in accordance with the following provisions:
(a) (i) a frontier worker who is partially or intermittently unemployed in the undertaking which employs him, shall receive benefits in accordance with the legislation of the competent State as if he were residing in the territory of that State; these benefits shall be provided by the competent institution;
(ii) a frontier worker who is wholly unemployed shall receive benefits in accordance with the legislation of the Member State in whose territory he resides as though he had been subject to that legislation while last employed the institution of the place of residence shall provide such benefits at its own expense;
(b) (i) a worker, other than a frontier worker, who is partially, intermittently or wholly unemplyed and who remains available to his employer or to the employment services in the territory of the competent State shall receive benefits in accordance with the legislation of that State as though he were residing in its territory; these benefits shall be provided by the competent institution;
(ii) a worker, other than a frontier worker, who is wholly unemployed and who makes himself available for work to the employment services in the territory of the Member State in which he resides, or who returns to that territory, shall receive benefits in accordance with the legislation of that State as if he had last been employed there; the institution of the place of residence shall provide such benefits at its own expense However, if such worker has become entitled to benefits at the expense of the competent institution of the Member State to whose legislation he was last subject, he shall receive benefits under the provisions of Article 69. Receipt of benefits under the legislation of the State in which he resides shall be suspended for any period during which the unemployed person may, under Article 69, make a claim for benefits under the legislation to which he was last subject.
2. An unemployed person may not claim benefits under the legislation of the Member State in whose territory he resides while he is entitled to benefits under paragraph 1 (a) (i) or (b) (i).

CHAPTER 7 - FAMILY BENEFITS AND FAMILY ALLOWANCES FOR EMPLOYED AND UNEMPLOYED PERSONS

Section 1: Common Provision

Article 72
Aggregation of periods of employment
Where the legislation of one Member State makes acquisition of the right to benefits conditional upon the completion of periods of employment, the competent institution of that State shall take into account, to the extent necessary, periods of employment completed in the territory of any other Member State, as if they had

been completed under its own legislation.

Article 73
Workers
1. A worker subject to the legislation of a Member State other than France shall be entitled to the family benefits provided for by the legislation of the first Member State for members of his family residing in the territory of another Member State, as though they were residing in the residing in the territory of the first State.
2. A worker subject to French legislation shall be entitled, in respect of members of his family residing in the territory of a Member State other than France, to the family allowances provided for by the legislation of such Member State; the worker must satisfy the conditions regarding employment on which French legislation bases entitlement to such benefits.
3. However, a worker who is subject to French legislation by virtue of the provisions of Article 14 (1) (a) shall be entitled to the family benefits provided for by French legislation and set out in Annex V in respect of members of his family who accompany him to the territory of the Member State where he is posted.

Article 74
Unemployed persons
1. An unemployed person drawing unemployment benefits under the legislation of a Member State other than France shall be entitled to the family benefits provided for by the legislation of the first Member State for members of his family residing in the territory of another Member State as though they were residing in the territory of the first State.
2. An unemployed person drawing unemployment benefits under French legislation shall be entitled, in respect of members of his family residing in the territory of a Member State other than France, to the family allowances provided for by legislation of the State in whose territory those members of the family are residing.

Article 75
Provision of benefits and reimbursements
1. (a) Family benefits shall be provided, in the cases referred to in Article 73 (1) and (3), by the competent institution of the State to whose legislation to worker is subject and, in the case referred to in Article 74 (1), by the competent institution of the State under whose legislation the unemployed worker is receiving unemployement benefits. They shall be provided in accordance with the provisions administered by such institutions, whether the natural or legal person to whom such benefits are payable is staying, residing or situated in the territory of the competent State or in that of another Member State;
(b) however, if the family benefits are not applied by the person to whom they should be provided for the maintenance of the members of the family, the competent institution shall discharge its legal obligations by providing the said benefits to the natural or legal person actually maintaining the members of the family, on application by and through the agency of the institution of their place of residence or of the institution or body appointed to that end by the competent authority of their country of residence;
(c) two or more Member States may agree, in accordance with Article 8, that the competent institution shall provide the family benefits due under the legislation of one or more of those States to the natural or legal person actually maintaining the members of the family, either directly, or through the agency of the institution of their place of residence.
2. (a) family allowances shall be provided, in the cases referred to in Articles 73 (2) and 74 (2), by the institution of the place of residence of the members of the family, in accordance with the legislation administered by that institution;
(b) however, if, under that legislation, the allowances must be provided to the worker, the institution referred to in the preceding subparagraph shall pay such allowances to the natural or legal person actually maintaining the members of the family in their place of residence or, where appropriate, directly to the members of the family;
(c) the competent institution shall reimburse the full amount of the allowances provided in accordance with the preceding subparagraphs. The reimbursements shall be determined and made in accordance with the procedures laid down by the implementing Regulation referred to in Article 97.

CHAPTER 8 - BENEFITS FOR DEPENDENT CHILDREN OF PENSIONERS AND FOR ORPHANS

Article 77
Dependent children of pensioners
1. The term 'benefits', for the purposes of this Article, shall mean family allowances for persons receiving pensions for old age, invalidity or an accident at work or occupational disease, and increases or supplements to such pensions in respect of the children of such pensioners, with the exception of supplements granted under insurance schemes for accidents at work and occupational diseases.

2. Benefits shall be granted in accordance with the following rules, irrespective of the Member State in whose territory the pensioner or the children are residing;
(a) to a pensioner who draws a pension under the legislation of one Member State only, in accordance with the legislation of the Member State responsible for the pension;
(b) to a pensioner who draws pensions under the legislation of more than one Member State:
(i) in accordance with the legislation of whichever of these States he resides in provided that, taking into account where appropriate Article 79 (1) (a), a right to one of the benefits referred to in paragraph 1 is acquired under the legislation of that State, or
ii) in other cases, in accordance with that legislation under which he has completed the longest insurance period, provided that, taking into account where appropriate Article 79 (1) (a), a right to one of the benefits referred to in paragraph (i) is acquired under such legislation; if no right to benefit is acquired under such legislation, the conditions for the acquisition of such right under the legislations of the other States concerned shall be examined in decreasing order of the length of insurance periods completed under the legislation of those States.

Article 78
Orphans
1. The term 'benefits', for the purposes of this Article, means family allowances and, where appropriate, supplementary or special allowances for orphans and orphans' pensions except those granted under insurance schemes for accidents at work and occupational diseases.
2. Orphans' benefits shall be granted in accordance with the following rules, irrespective of the Member State in whose territory the orphan or the natural or legal person actually maintaining him is resident or situated;
(a) for the orphan of a deceased worker who was subject to the legislation of one Member State only in accordance with the legislation of that State;
(b) for the orphan of a deceased worker who was subject to the legislation of several Member States:
(i) in accordance with the legislation of the Member State in whose territory the orphan resides provided that, taking into account where appropriate Article 79 (1) (a), a right to one of the benefits referred to in paragraph 4 is acquired under the legislation of that State, or
(ii) in other cases, in accordance with the legislation of the Member State under which the deceased worker had completed the longest insurance period provided that, taking into account where appropriate Article 79 (1) (a), the right to one of the benefits referred to in paragraph 1 is acquired under the legislation of that State; if no right is acquired under that legislation, the conditions for the acquisition of such right under the legislations of the other States in question shall be examined in decreasing order of the length of insurance periods completed under the legislation of these States.

Annex 5.7.

Regulation (EEC) No 574/72 of the Council of 21 March 1972 fixing the procedure for **implementing Regulation (EEC) No 1408/71 on the application of social security schemes** to employed persons and their families moving within the Community
Official Journal L 074 , 27/03/1972 P. 0001 - 0083

MAIN PROVISIONS

TITLE I GENERAL PROVISIONS

Article 1
Definitions For the purposes of this Regulation:
(a) 'Regulation' means Regulation (EEC) No 1408/71;
(b) 'Implementing Regulation' means this Regulation;
(c) the definitions in Article 1 of the Regulation have the meaning assigned to them in the said Article.

Article 2
Printed model forms - Information on legislations - Guides 1. Models of certificates, certified statements, declarations, applications and other documents necessary for the application of the Regulation and of the Implementing Regulation shall be drawn up by the Administrative Commission. Two Member States or their competent authorities may, by mutual agreement and having received the Opinion of the Administrative Commission, adopt simplified forms for use between them.
2. For the benefit of the competent authorities of each Member State, the Administrative Commission may assemble information on the provisions of national legislations which come within the scope of the Regulation.
3. The Administrative Commission shall prepare guides for the purpose of advising persons concerned of their rights and of the administrative formalities to be completed for the exercise of those rights.
The Advisory Committee shall be consulted before such guides are drawn up.

Article 3
Liaison bodies - Communications between institutions and between beneficiaries and institutions 1. The competent authorities may designate liaison bodies which may communicate directly with each other.
2. Any institution of a Member State, and any person residing or staying in the territory of a Member State, may make application to the institution of another Member State, either directly or through the liaison bodies.

Article 4
Annexes 1. The competent authority or authorities of each Member State are given in Annex 1.
2. The competent institutions of each Member State are listed in Annex 2.
3. The institutions of the place of residence and the place of stay of each Member State are listed in Annex 3.
4. The liaison bodies appointed pursuant to Article 3 (1) of the Implementing Regulation are listed in Annex 4.
5. The provisions referred to in Articles 5, 53 (3), 104, 105 (2), 116 and 120 of the Implementing Regulation are set out in Annex 5.
6. The procedure for the payment of benefits chosen by the institutions responsible for payment in each Member State, in accordance with Article 53 (1) of the Implementing Regulation, is set out in Annex 6.
7. The names and seats of the banks referred to in Article 55 (1) of the Implementing Regulation are listed in Annex 7.
8. The Member States for whom the provisions of Article 10 (2) (d) of the Implementing Regulation apply in their dealings with each other are specified in Annex 8.
9. The schemes to be taken into consideration when calculating the average annual cost of benefits in kind, in accordance with Article 94 (3) (a) and Article 95 (3) (a) of the Implementing Regulation, are listed in Annex 9.
10. The institutions or bodies appointed by the competent authorities pursuant, in particular, to the following Articles of the Implementing Regulation: Article 6 (1), Article 11 (1), Article 13 (2) and (3), Article 14 (1), (2) and (3), Article 38 (1), Article 70 (1), Article 80 (2), Article 81, Article 82 (2), Article 85 (2), Article 89 (1), Article 91 (2), Article 102 (2), Article 110, Article 113 (2), are listed in Annex 10.

TITLE II - IMPLEMENTATION OF THE GENERAL PROVISIONS OF THE REGULATION
Implementation of Articles 6 and 7 of the Regulation

Article 5
Replacement of the arrangements the implementing of convention by the Implementing Regulation The provisions of the Implementing Regulation shall replace those of the arrangements for implementing the conventions referred to in Article 6 of the Regulation; they shall also replace the provisions relating to the implementation of the provisions of the conventions referred to in Article 7 (2) (c) of the Regulation providing that they are not set out in Annex 5 of the Regulation.
Implementation of Article 9 of the Regulation

Article 6
Admission to voluntary or optional continued insurance 1. If, by virtue of Articles 9 and 15 (3) of the Regulation, a person satisfies the conditions for joining a voluntary or optional continued insurance scheme in respect of invalidity, old age and death (pensions) under the legislation of one Member State, and if he has not been subject to compulsory insurance under one of those schemes by virtue of his last employment he may, under the said Articles, join the voluntary or optional continued insurance scheme specified by the legislation of that Member State or, failing that, the scheme of his choice.
2. In order to invoke the provisions of Article 9 (2) of the Regulation, a person shall submit to the institution of the Member State in question a certified statement relating to the insurance periods completed under the legislation of any other Member State. Such certified statement shall be issued, at the request of the person concerned, by the institution or institutions who administer the legislations under which he has completed those insurance periods.
Implementation of Article 12 of the Regulation

Article 7
General rules for the implementation of provisions dealing with the prevention of overlapping of benefits - Application of those provisions to benefits in respect of invalidity, old age and death (pensions) 1. Where a person entitled to a benefit due under the legislation of one Member State is also entitled to benefits under the legislation of one or more of the other Member States, the following rules shall apply:
(a) if the application of Article 12 (2) or (3) of the Regulation entails the reduction or the concurrent suspension of those benefits, none of them may be reduced or suspended by an amount greater than the amount obtained by dividing the sum which is subject to reduction or suspension under the legislation under which the benefit is due by the number of benefits subject to reduction or suspension to which the person concerned is entitled;
(b) as regards benefits in respect of invalidity, old age or death (pensions) awarded under Article 46 (2) of the Regulation by the institution of a Member State, that institution shall take into account any benefits of a different kind and any income or remuneration likely to entail the reduction or suspension of the benefit due from that institution, not for the calculation of the theoretical amount referred to in Article 46 (2) (a) of the Regulation but exclusively for the reduction or suspension of the amount referred to in Article 46 (2) (b) of the Regulation. However, only a fraction of the total amount of such benefit, income or remuneration shall be taken into account, and that fraction shall be determined in proportion to the duration of the insurance periods completed, in accordance with Article 46 (2) (b) of the Regulation.
(c) As regards benefits in respect of invalidity, old age or death (pensions) awarded under the first subparagraph of Article 46 (1) of the Regulation by the institution of a Member State, that institution shall, where the provisions of Article 46 (3) of the Regulation apply, take into account any benefits of a different kind and any income or remuneration likely to entail the reduction or suspension of the benefit due from that institution, not for the calculation of the amount referred to in Article 46 (1) of the Regulation, but exclusively for the reduction or suspension of the amount resulting from the application of Article 46 (3) of the Regulation. However, only a fraction of the amount of those benefits, income or remuneration shall be taken into account; such fraction shall be obtained by applying to that amount a coefficient equal to the ratio between the amount of benefit resulting from the application of Article 46 (3) of the Regulation and the amount resulting from the application of the first subparagraph of Article 46 (1) of the Regulation.
2. For the purposes of Article 12 (2), (3) and (4) of the Regulation, the competent institutions concerned shall, on request, exchange all requisite information.

Article 8
Rules applicable in the case of overlapping of rights to maternity benefits under the legislation of several Member States If a worker or a member of his family is entitled to claim maternity benefits under the legislations of two or more Member States, those benefits shall be granted exclusively under the legislation of the Member State in whose territory the confinement took place or, if the confinement did not take place in the

territory of one of these Member States, exclusively under the legislation of the Member State to which the worker was last subject.

Article 9
Rules applicable in the case of overlapping of rights to death grants under the legislations of several Member States 1. Where the death occurs in the territory of a Member State, the right to a death grant acquired under the legislation of that Member State only shall be maintained, whilst the right acquired under the legislation of any other Member State shall lapse.
2. Where the death occurs in the territory of one Member State when the right to a death grant has been acquired under the legislation of two or more other Member States, or where the death occurs outside the territory of the Member States and the said right has been acquired under the legislation of two or more Member States, only the right acquired under the legislation of the Member State under which the worker completed his last period of insurance shall be maintained, whilst the right acquired under the legislation of any other Member State shall lapse.

Article 10
Rules applicable in the case of overlapping of rights to family benefits or family allowances or when, during the same period or part of a period, the worker is successively subject to the legislation of several Member States 1. If during the same period family benefits or family allowances are due to two persons in respect of the same member of the family, under Article 73 (1) or (2) or Article 74 (1) or (2) of the Regulation and under the legislation of the country of residence of that member of the family, the provisions to be applied in respect of the overlapping of rights to familiy allowances or family benefits shall be those provided for by the legislation of the country of residence of the member of the family. To this end, the right to family benefits or family allowances under Article 73 (1) or (2) or Article 74 (1) or (2) of the Regulation shall be taken into account as if it were a right acquired under the legislation of the country of residence of the member of the family in question.
2. If a worker has been subject successively to the legislation of two Member States during the period separating two dates for the payment of family benefits or family allowances as provided for by the legislation of one or both of the Member States concerned, the following rules shall apply:
(a) the family benefits or family allowances which such worker may claim under the legislation of each one of these States shall correspond to the number of daily benefits or allowances due under the relevant legislation. Where these legislations do not provide for daily benefits or allowances, the family benefits or family allowances shall be granted in proportion to the length of time during which such worker has been subject to the legislation of each one of the Member States in relation to the period fixed by the legislation concerned;
(b) where the family benefits or family allowances have been provided by an institution during a period when they should have been provided by another institution, there shall be an adjustment of accounts between the said institutions;
(c) for the purposes of subparagraphs (a) and (b) where periods of employment completed under the legislation of one Member State are expressed in units different from those which are used in the calculation of family benefits or family allowances under the legislation of another Member State to which the worker has also been subject during the same period, the conversion shall be carried out in accordance with Article 15 (3) of the Implementing Regulation;
(d) notwithstanding the provisions of subparagraph (a), in respect of dealings between the Member States specified in Annex 8 to the Implementing Regulation, the institution bearing the costs of the family benefits or family allowances by reason of the first employment during the period concerned, shall bear their cost throughout the whole of the current period.
3. If the members of the family of a worker subject to French legislation, or of an unemployed person in receipt of unemployment benefits under French legislation, transfer their residence from the territory of one Member State to the territory of another Member State during the same calendar month, the institution responsible for providing the family allowances at the beginning of that month shall continue to provide them throughout the whole of the current month.

TITLE III - IMPLEMENTATION OF THE PROVISIONS OF THE REGULATION FOR DETERMINING THE LEGISLATION APPLICABLE
Implementation of Articles 13 to 16 of the Regulation

Article 11
Formalities in the case of posting elsewhere 1. In cases referred to in Article 14 (1) (a) and (2) (a) of the Regulation, the institution designated by the competent authority of the Member State whose legislation remains applicable shall issue to the worker, at his own or his employer's request, and if the required conditions are fulfilled, a certificate of posting testifying that he shall remain subject to that legislation up to a specified date.

2. The consent provided for in Article 14 (1) (a) (ii) of the Regulation shall be requested by the employer.

Article 12
Special provisions concerning insurance under the German social security scheme 1. Where, under the terms of Article 14 (1) (b) and (c) or 2 (a) of the Regulation, German legislation applies to a worker employed by an undertaking or employer whose registered office or place of business is not situated in German territory, this legislation shall apply as if the worker were employed in his place of residence in German territory.
2. When contributions are paid for a fixed period, pursuant to the legislation of a Member State other than Germany, under a compulsory scheme for invalidity, old age, or death (pensions), supplementary contributions for additional insurance under German legislation (Hoeherversicherung) may also be paid for the same period.

Article 13
Exercise of the right of option by persons employed by diplomatic missions and consular posts 1. The right of option provided for in Article 16 (2) of the Regulation must be exercised in the first instance within the three months following the date on which the worker was engaged by the diplomatic mission or consular post concerned, or on which he entered into employment with agents of such mission or post. The option shall take effect on the date of entry into employment.
When a worker renews his right of option at the end of the calendar year, the option shall take effect on the first day of the following calendar year.
2. A worker who exercises his right of option shall inform the institution designated by the competent authority of the Member State for whose legislation he has opted, at the same time notifying his employer thereof. The said institution shall, where necessary, forward such information to all other institutions of the same Member State, in accordance with to him directives issued by the competent authority of that Member State.
3. The institution designated by the competent authority of the Member State for whose legislation a worker has opted, shall issue him with a certificate testifying that he is subject to the legislation of that Member State while he is employed by the diplomatic mission or consular post in question, by agents of such mission or post.
4. Where a worker has opted for German legislation to be applied the provisions of such legislation shall be applied as though that worker were employed in the place where the German Government has its seat. The competent authority shall nominate the competent sickness insurance institution.

Article 14
Exercise of the right of option by auxiliary staff of the European Communities 1. The right of option provided for in Article 16 (3) of the Regulation must be exercised at the time when the contract of employment is concluded. The authority empowered to conclude such contract shall inform the institution designated by the competent authority of the Member State for whose legislation the auxiliary staff member has opted. The said institution shall, where necessary, transmit such information to all other institutions of the same Member State.
2. The institution designated by the competent authority of the Member State for whose legislation the auxiliary staff member has opted, shall issue to him a certificate testifying that he is subject to the legislation of that Member State while he is employed by the European Communities as an auxiliary staff member.
3. The competent authorities of the Member States shall, where necessary, designate the institutions competent in respect of members of the auxiliary staff of the European Communities.
4. Where an auxiliary staff member, employed in the territory of a Member State other than Germany, has opted to have German legislation applied to him, the provisions of that legislation shall be applied as though that auxiliary staff member were employed in the place where the German Government has its seat. The competent authority shall designate the competent sickness insurance institution.

TITLE IV - IMPLEMENTATION OF THE PROVISIONS OF THE REGULATION DEALING WITH THE DIFFERENT CATEGORIES OF BENEFITS

CHAPTER 1: GENERAL RULES FOR THE AGGREGATION OF INSURANCE PERIODS

Article 15
1. In the cases referred to in Articles 18 (1), 38, 45 (1) and (2), 64, and 67 (1) and (2) of the Regulation, aggregation of insurance periods shall be effected in accordance with the following rules:
(a) to insurance periods completed under the legislation of one Member State shall be added insurance periods completed under the legislation of any other Member State, to the extent that it is necessary to have recourse thereto in order to supplement insurance periods completed under the legislation of the first Member State for the purpose of acquiring, retaining, or recovering the rights to benefits, provided that such insurance periods do not overlap. Where benefits in respect of invalidity, old age or death (pensions) are to be awarded by the institutions of two or more Member States in accordance with Article 46 (2) of the Regulation, each of the

institutions concerned shall effect a separate aggregation, by taking into account the whole of the insurance periods completed by the worker under the legislations of all the Member States to which he has been subject, without prejudice, where appropriate, to the provisions of Article 45 (2) and Article 46 (2) (c) of the Regulation;
(b) when a period of compulsory insurance completed under the legislation of one Member State coincides with a period of voluntary or optional continued insurance under the legislation of another Member State, only the former shall be taken into account;
(c) when an insurance period other than a period treated as such, completed under the legislation of one Member State coincides with a period treated as an insurance period under the legislation of another Member State, only the former shall be taken into account;
(d) any period treated as an insurance period under the legislations of two or more Member States, shall be taken into account only by the institution of the Member State under whose legislation the insured person was last compulsorily insured prior to the said period; where the insured person has not been compulsorily insured under the legislation of a Member State before the said period, the latter shall be taken into account by the institution of the Member State under whose legislation he was compulsorily insured for the first time after the said period;
(e) where it is not possible to accurately determine the period of time in which certain insurance periods were completed under the legislation of one Member State, such insurance periods shall be presumed not to overlap with insurance periods completed under the legislation of another Member State and shall, where advantageous, be taken into account.
(f) where, under the legislation of one Member State, certain insurance periods are taken into account only if they have been completed within a specified period of time, the institution which administers such legislation shall:
(i) take into account insurance periods completed under the legislation of another Member State only if they were completed within the said period of time; or
(ii) extend such period of time for the duration of insurance periods completed wholly or partly within the said time limit under the legislation of another Member State, where the insurance periods involved under legislation of the second Member State give rise only to the suspension of the period of time within which the insurance periods must be completed.
2. Insurance periods completed under legislation of a Member State to which the Regulation does not apply, but which are taken into account under legislation of that Member State to which the Regulation does apply, shall be considered as insurance periods to be taken into account for the purposes of aggregation.
3. When insurance periods completed under the legislation of one Member State are expressed in units different from those used by the legislation of another Member State, the conversion necessary for the purposes of aggregation shall be carried out according to the following rules:
(a) where the worker has been subject to a six day week:
(i) one day shall be equivalent to eight hours and vice versa;
(ii) six days shall be equivalent to one week and vice versa;
(iii) twenty-six days shall be equivalent to one month and vice versa;
(iv) three months or thirteen weeks or seventy-eight days shall be equivalent to one quarter and vice versa;
(v) for the conversion of weeks into months and vice versa the weeks and months shall be converted into days;
(vi) the application of the preceding rules shall not have the effect of producing, for the sum total of the insurance periods completed during one calendar year, a total exceeding three hundred and twelve days or fifty-two weeks or twelve months or four quarters;
(b) Where the worker has been subject to a five day week:
(i) one day shall be equivalent to nine hours and vice versa;
(ii) five days shall be equivalent to one week and vice versa;
(iii) twenty-two days shall be equivalent to one month and vice versa;
(iv) three months or thirteen weeks or sixty-six days shall be equivalent to one quarter and vice versa;
(v) for the conversion of weeks into months and vice versa, the weeks and the months shall be converted into days;
(vi) the application of the preceding rules shall not have the effect of producing, for the sum total of the insurance periods completed during one calendar year, a total exceeding two-hundred and sixty-four days or fifty-two weeks or twelve months or four quarters.

CHAPTER 2 - SICKNESS AND MATERNITY
Implementation of Article 18 of the Regulation

Article 16
Certification of insurance periods 1. In order to invoke the provisions of Article 18 of the Regulation, a worker shall submit to the competent institution a certified statement specifying the insurance periods completed under the legislation to which he was last subject.

2. This certified statement shall be issued at the request of the worker by the institution or institutions of the Member State to whose legislation he was last subject. If he does not submit the said certified statement, the competent institution shall obtain it directly from the institution or institutions concerned.
3. The provisions of paragraphs (1) and (2) shall apply by analogy, if it is necessary to take into account insurance periods previously completed under the legislation of any other Member State in order to satisfy the conditions of the legislation of the competent State.
Implementation of Article 19 of the Regulation

Article 17
Benefits in kind in the case of residence in a Member State other than the competent State 1. In order to receive benefits in kind under Article 19 of the Regulation, a worker must register himself and the members of his family with the institution of his place of residence by submitting a certified statement testifying that he and the members of his family are entitled to the said benefits. Such certified statement shall be issued by the competent institution, if need be in the light of information furnished by the employer. If the worker or the members of his family do not submit the said certified statement the institution of the place of residence shall obtain it directly from the competent institution.
2. This certified statement shall remain valid until the institution of the place of residence is notified of its cancellation. However, when the said certified statement is issued by a French institution, it shall be valid for a period of three months only following the date of issue, and it must be renewed every three months.
3. If the worker is a seasonal worker, the certified statement referred to in paragraph 1 shall be valid for the whole anticipated period of the seasonal work unless, in the meanwhile, the competent institution notifies the institution of the place of residence of its cancellation.
4. The institution of the place of residence shall inform the competent institution of every registration effected in accordance with paragraph 1.
5. When applying for any benefits in kind, the person concerned shall submit the documentary evidence required for the granting of benefits in kind under the legislation of the Member State in whose territory he is residing.
6. In the case of hospitalization, the institution of the place of residence shall notify the competent institution, within three days following the date on which it became aware of the hospitalization, of the date of entry into hospital, the probable duration of hospitalization and the date of leaving hospital. Notification shall be unnecessary, however, when the costs of the benefits in kind are repaid in a lump sum to the institution of the place of residence.
7. The institution of the place of residence shall inform the competent institution in advance of every decision relating to the granting of benefits in kind included in the list referred to in Article 24 (2) of the Regulation. The competent institution shall have fifteen days from the day on which such information is sent within which to raise any objection and to state the reasons on which such objection is based; if, on the expiry of that period, no such objection has been raised, the institution of the place of residence shall grant the benefits in kind. Where such benefits have to be granted in a case of extreme urgency, the institution of the place of residence shall forthwith inform the competent institution thereof. However, notification of its objection, stating the reasons on which such objection is based, shall be unnecessary when the costs of the benefits in kind are to be repaid in a lump sum to the institution of the place of residence.
8. The worker or the members of his family shall inform the institution of the place of residence of any change in their situation which is likely to alter their entitlement to benefits in kind, in particular any cessation of, or change in, employment by the worker or any transfer of residence or stay of that worker or of a member of his family. Likewise, should the worker cease to be insured or cease to be entitled to benefits in kind, the competent institution shall inform the institution of the place of residence accordingly. The institution of the place of residence may, at any time, request the competent institution to supply it with any information relating to the worker's insurance or to his entitlement to benefits in kind.
9. Two or more Member States or the competent authorities of those Member States may, having received the Opinion of the Administrative Commission, agree on other implementing provisions.

Article 18
Cash benefits in the case of residence in a Member State other than the competent State 1. In order to draw cash benefits under Article 19 (1) (b) of the Regulation a worker shall, within three days of commencement of the incapacity for work, apply to the institution of the place of residence by submitting a notification of having ceased work or, if the legislation administered by the competent institution or by the institution of the place of residence so provides, a certificate of incapacity for work issued by the doctor treating the worker concerned.
2. Where the doctors treating the worker concerned in the country of residence do not issue certificates of incapacity for work, the worker shall apply directly to the institution of the place of residence within the time limit fixed by the legislation which it administers.

That institution shall forthwith have the incapacity for work medically confirmed and the certificate referred to in paragraph 1 drawn up. Such a certificate shall state the probable duration of the incapacity and shall be forwarded to the competent institution forthwith.
3. In cases where paragraph 2 does not apply, the institution of the place of residence shall, as soon as possible and in any event within the three days following the date on which the worker applied to it, have the worker medically examined as if he were insured with that institution. The report of the examining doctor shall indicate, in particular, the probably duration of the incapacity for work, and shall be forwarded to the competent institution by the institution of the place of residence within the three days following the date of the examination.
4. The institution of the place of residence shall subsequently carry out any necessary administrative checks or medical examinations of the worker as if he were insured with that institution. As soon as it establishes that the worker is fit to resume work, it shall forthwith notify the worker and the competent institution thereof, stating the date on which the worker's incapacity ceased. Without prejudice to the provisions of paragraph 6, the notification to the worker shall be treated as a decision taken on behalf of the competent institution.
5. In all cases the competent institution shall reserve the right to have the worker examined by a doctor of its own choice.
6. If the competent institution decides to withhold the cash benefits because the worker has not completed the formalities laid down by the legislation of the country of residence, or if it establishes that the worker is fit to resume work, it shall notify the worker of its decision and shall simultaneously send a copy of such decision to the institution of the place of residence.
7. When the worker resumes work, he shall notify the competent institution accordingly, if such notification is required by the legislation administered by that institution.
8. The competent institution shall pay cash benefits by the appropriate method, in particular by international money order, and shall inform the institution of the place of residence and the worker accordingly. Where cash benefits are paid by the institution of the place of residence on behalf of the competent institution, the latter shall inform the worker of his rights and shall notify the institution of the place of residence of the amount of the cash benefits, the dates for payment, and the maximum period during which they should be granted, in accordance with the legislation of the competent State.
9. Two or more Member States, or the competent authorities of those States may, having received the Opinion of the Administrative Commission, agree on other implementing provisions.
Implementation of Article 20 of the Regulation

Article 19
Special provisions for frontier workers and members of their families In the case of frontier workers or members of their families, medicinal products, bandages, spectacles and small appliances may be issued, and laboratory analyses and tests carried out, only in the Member State in whose territory they were prescribed or recommended, in accordance with the legislation of that Member State.
Implementation of Article 22 of the Regulation

Article 20
Benefits in kind in the case of a stay in a Member State other than the competent State - Special case of workers posted elsewhere and workers employed in international transport and members of their families 1. In order to receive benefits in kind for himself or for members of his family who accompany him at the time of his posting, a worker covered by Article 14 (1) (a) (i) or 2 (a) of the Regulation shall submit to the institution of the place of stay the certificate provided for in Article 11 of the Implementing Regulation. A worker who has submitted such certificate shall be presumed to have satisfied the conditions for the acquisition of the right to benefits in kind.
2. In order to receive benefits in kind for himself or for members of his family who accompany him, a worker employed in international transport, covered by Article 14 (1) (b) of the Regulation, who in the course of his employment goes to the territory of a Member State other than the competent State shall, as soon as possible, submit to the institution of the place of stay a special certified statement issued by the employer or by his agent during the current calendar month or during the two calendar months preceding its submission. Such certified statement shall state in particular the date from which the worker has been employed by the said employer, and the name and address of the competent institution; if, however, under the legislation of the competent State the employer is not required to know the competent institution, the worker shall provide in writing the name and address of that institution when submitting his application to the institution of the place of stay. A worker who has submitted the certified statement shall be presumed to have satisfied the conditions for aquisition of the right to benefits in kind. If a worker is unable to contact the institution of the place of stay before receiving medical treatment, he shall nevertheless receive such treatment on presentation of the said certified statement as if he were insured with that institution.
3. The institution of the place of stay shall, within three days, inquire of the competent institution whether the

person concerned satisfies the conditions for acquisition of the right to benefits in kind. That institution shall provide benefits in kind until it receives a reply from the competent institution, but for not more than thirty days.
4. The competent institution shall send its reply to the institution of the place of stay within ten days of the receipt of the request from that institution. If the reply is in the affirmative, the competent institution shall indicate, if necessary, the maximum period during which the benefits in kind may be granted, in accordance with the legislation which it administers, and the institution of the place of stay shall continue to provide the said benefits.
5. In place of the certificate or certified statement provided for in paragraphs 1 and 2 respectively, workers covered by those paragraphs may submit to the institution of the place of stay a certified statement testifying that the conditions for acquisition of the right to benefits in kind have been satisfied. This certified statement, which shall be issued by the competent institution, shall specify in particular, where necessary, the maximum period during which benefits in kind may be granted in accordance with the legislation of the competent State. In such a case paragraphs 1, 2, 3 and 4 shall not apply.
6. Paragraphs 6, 7 and 9 of Article 17 of the Implementing Regulation shall apply by analogy.
7. Benefits in kind provided by virtue of the presumption made in paragraphs 1 or 2 shall be reimbursed as provided for in Article 36 (1) of the Regulation.

Article 21
Benefits in kind in the case of a stay in a Member State other than the competent State - Workers other than those covered by Article 20 of the Implementing Regulation 1. In order to receive benefits in kind under Article 22 (1) (a) (1) of the Regulation, save in the cases referred to in Article 20 of the Implementing Regulation, a worker shall submit to the institution of the place of stay a certified statement testifying that he is entitled to benefits in kind. Such certified statement, which shall be issued by the competent institution at the worker's request, if possible before he leaves the territory of the Member State in which he resides, shall specify in particular, where necessary, the maximum period during which benefits in kind may be granted, in accordance with the legislation of the competent State. If the worker does not submit the said certified statement, the institution of the place of stay shall obtain it directly from the competent institution.
2. Article 17 (6) (7) and (9) of the Implementing Regulation shall apply by analogy.

Article 22
Benefits in kind for workers in the case of transfer of residence or return to the country of residence, and for workers authorized to go to another Member State for medical treatment 1. In order to receive benefits in kind under Article 22 (1) (b) (i) of the Regulation, a worker shall submit to the institution of the place of residence a certified statement testifying that he is entitled to continue receiving the said benefits. This certified statement, which shall be issued by the competent institution, shall specify in particular, where necessary, the maximum period during which such benefits may continue to be provided, in accordance with the legislation of the competent State. The certified statement may, at the worker's request, be issued after his departure if, for reasons of force majeure, it cannot be drawn up beforehand.
2. Paragraphs 6, 7 and 9 of Article 17 of the Implementing Regulation shall apply by analogy.
3. Paragraphs 1 and 2 shall apply by analogy in respect of the provisions of benefits in kind in the case referred to in Article 22 (1) (c) (i) of the Regulation.

Article 23
Benefits in kind for members of the family The provisions of Article 21 or Article 22 of the Implementing Regulation, as appropriate, shall apply by analogy in respect of the granting of benefits in kind to members of the family as provided for in Article 23 (3) of the Regulation.

Article 24
Cash benefits for workers in the case of a stay in a Member State other than the competent State The provisions of Article 18 of the Implementing Regulation shall apply by analogy in respect of the drawing of cash benefits under Article 22 (1) (a) (ii) of the Regulation. However, without prejudice to the requirement to submit a certificate of incapacity for work, a worker who is staying in the territory of a Member State, but not pursuing any professional or trade activity there, shall not be required to submit the notification of having ceased work referred to in Article 18 (1) of the Implementing Regulation.
Implementation of Article 23 (3) of the Regulation

Article 25
Certified statement relating to the members of the family to be taken into account in the calculation of cash benefits 1. In order to draw benefits under Article 23 (3) of the Regulation, a worker shall submit to the competent institution a certified statement relating to the members of his family who are resident in the territory

of a Member State other than that wherein the said institution is situated.
2. This certified statement shall be issued by the institution of the place of residence of the members of the family.
It shall be valid for the twelve months following the date of its issue. It may be renewed; in such a case, it shall be valid from the date of its renewal.
The worker shall immediately notify the competent institution of any occurrence necessitating an amendment to the said certified statement. Such amendment shall take effect from the date of such occurrence.
3. In place of the certified statement provided for in paragraph 1, the competent institution may require the worker to produce recent civil status documents relating to the members of his family who are resident in the territory of a Member State other than that wherein the said institution is situated.
Implementation of Article 25 (1) of the Regulation

Article 26
Benefits to unemployed persons who go to a Member State other than the competent State in order to seek employment there 1. In order to receive benefits in cash and in kind under Article 25 (1) of the Regulation for himself and for the members of his family, an unemployed person shall submit to the sickness insurance institution of the place where he has gone a certified statement which he should have applied for, prior to his departure, from the competent sickness insurance institution. If he does not submit the said certified statement, the institution of the place to which he has gone shall obtain it from the competent institution.
This certified statement must testify the existence of the right to the said benefits under the conditions set out in Article 69 (1) (a) of the Regulation; indicate the duration of such right, taking into account Article 69 (1) (c) of the Regulation; and specify the amount of cash benefits to be provided, where appropriate, by way of sickness insurance during the abovementioned period, in the case of incapacity for work or hospitalization.
2. The unemployment insurance institution of the place where the unemployed person has gone shall testify on a copy of the certified statement referred to in Article 83 of the Implementing Regulation, which shall be sent to the sickness insurance institution of that same place, that the conditions laid down in Article 69 (1) (b) of the Regulation have been fulfilled and shall specify the date from which they were fulfilled, and the date from which the unemployed person qualifies for unemployment insurance benefits at the expense of the competent institution.
This certified statement shall be valid for the period laid down in Article 69 (1) (c) of the Regulation, for as long as the conditions are fulfilled. The unemployment insurance institution of the place where the unemployed person has gone shall, within three days inform the said sickness insurance institution if the conditions are no longer satisfied.
3. Article 17 (6) and (7) of the Implementing Regulation shall apply by analogy.
Implementation of Article 25 (3) of the Regulation

Article 27
Benefits in kind for members of the family of unemployed persons in the case of residence in a Member State other than the competent State Article 17 of the Implementing Regulation shall apply by analogy in respect of the granting of benefits in kind to the members of the family of unemployed persons when such members of the family are resident in the territory of a Member State other than the competent State. At the time of the registration of the members of the family of unemployed persons drawing benefits under Article 69 (1) of the Regulation, the certified statement referred to in Article 26 (1) of the Implementing Regulation must be produced. This certified statement shall be valid for the period of time during which the benefits may be granted under Article 69 (1) of the Regulation.
Implementation of Article 26 of the Regulation

Article 28
Benefits in kind for pension claimants and for members of their families 1. In order to receive benefits in kind in the territory of the Member State in which he resides, under Article 26 (1) of the Regulation, a claimant and the members of his family shall register with the institution of the place of residence by submitting a certified statement testifying that he is entitled under the legislation of another Member State to the said benefits for himself and for the members of his family. This certified statement shall be issued by the institution of that other Member State which is responsible for benefits in kind.
2. The institution of the place of residence shall inform the institution which has issued the certified statement of every registration effected in accordance with paragraph 1.
Implementation of Article 28 of the Regulation

Article 29
Benefits in kind for pensioners and members of their families who are not resident in a Member State under

whose legislation they are entitled to benefits 1. In order to receive benefits in kind in the territory of the Member State in which he resides, under Article 28 (1) of the Regulation, a pensioner and the members of his family shall register with the institution of the place of residence by submitting a certified statement testifying that he is entitled to the said benefits for himself and for the members of his family, under the legislation or one of the legislations under which a pension is payable.
2. This certified statement shall be issued, at the request of the pensioner, by the institution or one of the institutions responsible for payment of the pension or, where appropriate, by the institution empowered to determine entitlement to benefits in kind, as soon as the pensioner satisfies the conditions for acquisition of the right to such benefits. If the pensioner does not submit the certified statement, the institution of the place of residence shall obtain it directly from the institution or institutions responsible for payment of the pension or, where appropriate, from the institution empowered to issue such certified statement. Whilst awaiting the receipt of this certified statement, the institution of the place of residence may, in the light of the documentary evidence accepted by it, register the pensioner and the members of his family provisionally. This registration shall not be applied by the institution responsible for the payment of benefits in kind until the institution of the place of residence has delivered the certified statement provided for in paragraph 1.
3. The institution of the place of residence shall inform the institution which has issued the certified statement provided for in paragraph 1 of every registration effected in accordance with the provisions of the said paragraph.
4. When making any application for benefits in kind the pensioner must prove to the institution of the place of residence, by means of the receipt or the counterfoil of the money order of the last payment made, that he is still entitled to a pension.
5. The pensioner or the members of his family shall inform the institution of the place of residence of any change in their situation which might alter their entitlement to benefits in kind, in particular any suspension or withdrawal of the pension and any transfer of their residence. The institutions responsible for the pension shall also inform the institution of the pensioner's place of residence of any such change.
6. The Administrative Commission shall, to the extent necessary, fix the procedure for determining the institution which shall bear the cost of the payment of benefits in kind, in the case referred to in Article 28 (2) (b) of the Regulation.
Implementation of Article 29 of the Regulation

Article 30
Benefits in kind for members of the family who are resident in a Member State other than the State in which the pensioner is resident 1. In order to receive benefits in kind in the territory of the Member State in which they reside, under Article 29 (1) of the Regulation, the members of the family shall register with the institution of their place of residence by submitting the documentary evidence required by the legislation which that institution administers for the granting of such benefits to members of a pensioner's family, together with a certified statement testifying that the pensioner is entitled to benefits in kind for himself and for the members of his family. This certified statement, which shall be issued by the institution of the pensioner's place of residence, shall remain valid as long as the institution of his family's place of residence has not been notified of its cancellation. When, however, the said certified statement is issued by a French institution, it shall only be valid for a period of twelve months from the date of issue and must be renewed yearly.
2. When making an application for benefits in kind, the members of the family shall submit to the institution of their place of residence the certified statement referred to in paragraph 1, if the legislation which that institution administers provides that such an application must be accompanied by evidence of entitlement to a pension.
3. The institution of the pensioner's place of residence shall inform the institution of the place of residence of the members of the family of the suspension or withdrawal of the pension, and of any transfer of residence of the pensioner. The institution of the place of residence of the members of the family may, at any time, request the institution of the pensioner's place of residence to furnish it with any information relating to entitlement to benefits in kind.
4. The members of the family shall inform the institution of the place of their residence of any change in their situation which is likely to alter their entitlement to benefits in kind, in particular any transfer of residence.
Implementation of Article 31 of the Regulation

Article 31
Benefits in kind for pensioners and members of their families staying in a Member State other than the one in which they are resident 1. in order to receive benefits in kind under Article 31 of the Regulation, a pensioner shall submit to the institution of the place of stay a certified statement testifying that he is entitled to the said benefits. This certified statement, which shall be issued by the institution of the pensioner's place of residence, if possible before he leaves the territory of the Member State where he resides, shall indicate in particular, where appropriate, the maximum period during which benefits in kind may be granted, in accordance with the

legislation of that Member State. If the pensioner does not submit the said certified statement, the institution of the place of stay shall obtain it directly from the institution of the place of residence.
2. Paragraphs 6, 7 and 9 of Article 17 of the Implementing Regulation shall apply by analogy. In such a case, the institution of the pensioner's place of residence shall be considered to be the competent institution.
3. Paragraphs 1 and 2 shall apply by analogy in respect of the granting of benefits in kind to the members of the family covered by Article 31 of the Regulation.
Implementation of Article 35 (1) of the Regulation

Article 32
Institutions to which workers in mines and similar undertakings and members of their families can apply when staying or residing in a Member State other than the competent State 1. In the cases referred to in Article 35 (1) of the Regulation and where, in the country of stay or residence, the benefits provided under the sickness or maternity insurance scheme covering manual workers in the steel industry are equivalent to those provided under the special scheme for workers in mines and similar undertakings, workers belonging to such category and members of their families may apply to the nearest institution in the territory of the Member State in which they are staying or residing, specified in Annex 3 of the Implementing Regulation, even if the latter is an institution administering the scheme covering manual workers in the steel industry, and the said institution shall then be required to provide the benefits.
2. Where the benefits provided under the special scheme for workers in mines and similar undertakings are more advantageous, such workers or the members of their families shall have the option of applying either to the institution responsible for the administration of that scheme, or to the nearest institution in the territory of the Member State in which they are staying or residing which administers the scheme for manual workers in the steel industry. In the latter case, the institution in question shall draw the attention of the person concerned to the fact that by applying to the institution responsible for the administration of the abovementioned special scheme, he will obtain more advantageous benefits; it should, furthermore, inform him of the name and address of such institution.
Implementation of Article 35 (3) of the Regulation

Article 33
Taking into account of the period during which benefits have already been provided by the institution of another Member State For the purposes of implementing Article 35 (3) of the Regulation, the institution of a Member State called upon to provide benefits may request the institution of another Member State to send information relating to the period during which the latter institution has already provided benefits for the same case of sickness or maternity.
Refund by the competent institution of one Member State of expenses incurred during a stay in another Member State

Article 34
1. If it is not possible during a worker's stay in a Member State other than the competent State to complete the formalities provided for in Article 20 (1), (2) and (5), and Articles 21, 23 and 31 of the Implementing Regulation, his expenses shall, upon his application, be refunded by the competent institution of the place of stay.
2. The institution of the place of stay shall, at the request of the competent institution, supply it with the necessary information about such rates.

CHAPTER 3 - INVALIDITY, OLD AGE AND DEATH (PENSIONS)
Submission and investigation of claims for benefits

Article 35
Claims for invalidity benefits where the worker has been insured exclusively under the legislations specified in Annex III of the Regulation, and in the case referred to in Article 40 (2) of the Regulation 1. In order to receive benefits under Articles 37, 38 and 39 of the Regulation, including the cases referred to in Articles 40 (2), 42 (1) and 42 (2) of the Regulation, a worker shall submit a claim either to the institution of the Member State to whose legislation he was subject at the time of the occurrence of the incapacity for work followed by invalidity or the aggravation of such invalidity, or to the institution of the place of residence, which shall then forward the claim to the first institution, indicating the date on which it was submitted; this date shall be regarded as the date of the submission of the claim to the first institution. However, if sickness insurance cash benefits have been granted, the date on which such cash benefits ceased to be granted shall, where appropriate, be regarded as the date of submission of the pension claim.
2. In the case referred to in Article 41 (1) (b) of the Regulation, the institution with which the claimant was last

insured shall notify the amount and the operative date of the benefits due under the legislation which it administers to the institution initially responsible for payment of the benefits. With effect from that date, the benefits due prior to the aggravation of the invalidity shall be cancelled or reduced to an amount not exceeding the supplement referred to in Article 41 (1) (c) of the Regulation.
3. Paragraph 2 shall not apply in the case referred to in Article 41 (1) (d) of the Regulation. In this case, the institution with which the claimant was last insured shall apply to the Netherlands institution in order to ascertain the amount due from that institution.

Article 36
Claims for old age and survivors' benefits (excluding orphans' benefits) and invalidity benefits in cases not referred to in Article 35 of the Implementing Regulation 1. In order to receive benefits under Articles 40 to 51 of the Regulation, except in the cases referred to in Article 35 of the Implementing Regulation, the person concerned shall submit a claim to the institution of the place of residence in accordance with the procedure provided for by the legislation administered by that institution. If the worker has not completed insurance periods under that legislation, the institution of the place of residence shall forward the claim to the institution of the Member State to whose legislation the claimant was last subject, indicating the date on which the claim was submitted. That date shall be regarded as the date on which the claim was submitted to the latter institution.
2. Where a claimant resides in the territory of a Member State under whose legislation the worker has not completed insurance periods, he may send his claim to the institution of the Member State to whose legislation the worker was last subject.
3. Where a claimant resides in the territory of a State which is not a Member State, he shall submit his claim to the competent institution of that Member State to whose legislation the worker was last subject.
Should the claimant send his claim to the institution of the Member State of which he is a national, the latter shall forward such claim to the competent institution.
4. A claim for benefits sent to the institution of one Member State shall automatically involve the concurrent award of benefits under the legislation of all the Member States in question whose conditions the claimant satisfies except where, under Article 44 (2) of the Regulation, the claimant asks for postponement of any old age benefits to which he would be entitled.

Article 37
Documents and information which should accompany claims to the benefits referred to in Article 36 of the implementing Regulation The submission of the claims under Article 36 of the Implementing Regulation shall be subject to the following rules:
(a) the claim must be accompanied by the requisite supporting documents and must be drawn up on the form provided for by the legislation,
(i) of the Member State in whose territory the claimant resides, in the case referred to in Article 36 (1);
(ii) of the Member State to which the worker was last subject, in the cases referred to in Article 36 (2) and (3);
(b) the accuracy of the information supplied by the claimant must be proved by official documents attached to the claim form, or confirmed by the competent bodies of the Member State in whose territory the claimant resides;
(c) the claimant must indicate, in so far as is possible, either the institution or institutions administering insurance in respect of invalidity, old age or death (pensions) of any Member State with which the worker has been insured, or the employer or employers for whom he has worked in the territory of any Member State, by producing any employment certificates which he may have in his possession;
(d) if, under Article 44 (2) of the Regulation, the claimant asks for the postponement of the award of any old age benefits to which he would be entitled under the legislation of one or more Member States he may specify the legislation under which he is claiming benefits.

Article 38
Certified statements relating to the members of the family to be taken into account when establishing the amount of the benefit 1. In order to draw benefits under Article 39 (4) or Article 47 (3) of the Regulation, the claimant shall submit a certified statement relating to the members of his family, his children excepted, who are residing in the territory of a Member State other than that in which the institution responsible for the award of benefits is situated.
This certified statement shall be issued by the sickness insurance institution of the place of residence of the members of the family, or by another institution designated by the competent authority of the Member State in whose territory they are resident. The second and third subparagraphs of Article 25 (2) of the Implementing Regulation shall apply by analogy.
In place of the certified statement provided for in the first paragraph, the institution responsible for the award of benefits may require the claimant to supply recent civil status documents relating to the members of his family,

his children excepted, who are residing in the territory of a Member State other than the State in which the said institution is situated.
2. In the case referred to in paragraph 1, if the legislation administered by the institution in question requires that the members of the family should live under the same roof as the pensioner, the fact that such members of the family who do not satisfy that condition are, nevertheless, mainly dependent on the claimant must be established by documents proving that the claimant is regularly sending them a part of his earnings.

Article 39
Investigation of claims for invalidity benefits in the case where the worker has been insured exclusively under the legislations specified in Annex III of the Regulation 1. If a worker has submitted a claim for invalidity benefits, and the institution establishes that the provisions of Article 37 (1) of the Regulation apply, that institution shall, where necessary, obtain from the institution with which the worker was last insured a certified statement of the insurance periods completed by him under the legislation administered by that last institution.
2. Where it is necessary to take into account insurance periods previously completed under the legislation of any other Member State in order to satisfy the conditions of the legislation of the competent State, the provisions of paragraph 1 shall apply by analogy.
3. In the case referred to in Article 39 (3) of the Regulation, the institution which has investigated the claimant's case shall forward his file to the institution with which the worker was last insured.
4. Articles 41 to 50 of the Implementing Regulation shall not apply to the investigation of claims referred to in paragraphs 1, 2 and 3.

Article 40
Determination of the degree of invalidity In order to determine the degree of invalidity, the institution of the Member State shall take into consideration the documents and medical reports and the information of an administrative nature obtained by the institution of any other Member State. Each institution shall, however, retain the right to have the claimant examined by a doctor of its own choice except where Article 40 (3) of the Regulation applies.
Investigation of claims for benefits in respect of invalidity, old age and survivors in the cases referred to in Article 36 of the Implementing Regulation

Article 41
Determination of the investigating institution
1. Claims for benefit shall be investigated by the institution (hereinafter called the 'investigating institution') to which they have been sent or forwarded in accordance with Article 36 of the Implementing Regulation.
2. The investigating institution shall forthwith notify claims for benefits to all the institutions concerned on a special form, so that the claims may be investigated simultaneously and without delay by all these institutions.

Article 42
Forms to be used for the investigation of claims for benefits 1. When investigating claims for benefits, the investigating institution shall use a form which will include, in particular, a statement and a summary of the insurance periods completed by the worker under the legislations of all the Member States concerned.
2. These forms, when forwarded to the institution of any other Member State, shall take the place of supporting documents.

Article 43
Procedure to be followed by the institutions concerned in the investigation of a claim 1. The investigating institution shall enter on the form provided for in Article 42 (1) of the Implementing Regulation the insurance periods completed under the legislation which it administers and it shall forward a copy of that form to the institution administering insurance in respect of invalidity, old age or death (pensions) of any Member State with which the worker has been insured enclosing, where appropriate, any employment certificates produced by the claimant.
2. Where only one other institution is involved, that institution shall complete the said form by indicating:
(a) the insurance periods completed under the legislation which it administers;
(b) the amount of benefit which the claimant could claim in respect of those insurance periods only;
(c) the theoretical amount and the actual amount of benefits calculated in accordance with Article 46 (2) of the Regulation.
The form, thus completed, shall be returned to the investigating institution.
If a right to benefits is acquired taking into account only the insurance periods completed under the legislation administered by the institution of the second Member State, and if the amount of benefit corresponding to those insurance periods can be established without delay, whereas the calculation procedure referred to in (c) requires

an appreciably longer period of time, the form shall be returned to the investigating institution with the information referred to in (a) and (b); the information referred to in (c) shall be forwarded to the investigating institution as soon as possible.
3. If two or more other institutions are involved, each one of those institutions shall complete the said form by indicating the insurance periods completed under the legislation which it administers, and shall return it to the investigating institution.
If a right to benefit is acquired taking into account only the insurance periods completed under the legislation administered by one or more of those institutions, and if the amount of benefit corresponding to those insurance periods can be determined without delay, the investigating institution shall be simultaneously notified of that amount and of the insurance periods; if the determination of the amount involves some delay, the investigating institution shall be notified of that amount as soon as it has been determined.
On receipt of all the forms giving information concerning insurance periods and, where applicable, the amount or amounts due under the legislation of one or more of the Member States concerned, the investigating institution shall forward a copy of the forms thus completed to each one of the institutions concerned; each such institution shall specify thereon the theoretical amount and the actual amount of the benefits, calculated in accordance with Article 46 (2) of the Regulation, and shall return the form to the investigating institution.
4. As soon as the investigating institution, upon receipt of the information referred to in paragraphs 2 or 3, establishes the fact that Articles 40 (2) or 48 (2) or (3) of the Regulation should be applied, it shall inform the other institutions concerned accordingly.
5. In the case provided for in Article 37 (d) of the Implementing Regulation, the institutions of the Member States to whose legislation the claimant has been subject but to whom he has applied for postponement of the award of the benefits, shall enter on the form provided for in Article 42 (1) of the Implementing Regulation only the insurance periods completed by the claimant under the legislation which they administer.

CHAPTER 6 - UNEMPLOYMENT BENEFITS
Implementation of Article 67 of the Regulation

Article 80
Certified statement of periods of insurance or employment 1. In order to invoke the provisions of Article 67 (1), (2) or (4) of the Regulation, the claimant shall submit to the competent institution a certified statement specifying the periods of insurance or employment completed previously under the legislation to which he was last subject, together with any further information required by the legislation administered by that institution.
2. This certified statement shall be issued, at the request of the person concerned, either by the institution competent in matters of unemployment of the Member State to whose legislation he was last subject, or by another institution designated by the competent authority of the said Member State. If he does not submit the said certified statement, the competent institution shall obtain it from one or other of the aforementioned institutions.
3. Where it is necessary to take into account periods of insurance or employment previously completed under the legislation of any other Member State in order to satisfy the conditions of the legislation of the competent State, paragraphs 1 and 2 shall apply by analogy.
Implementation of Article 68 of the Regulation

Article 81
Certified statement for the calculation of benefits Where the responsibility for the calculation of benefits rests upon an institution covered by Article 68 (1) of the Regulation, and where a person has followed his last occupation for less than four weeks in the territory of the Member State in which that institution is situated, he shall submit to the said institution a certified statement indicating the nature of the last occupation followed for at least four weeks in the territory of another Member State, and the branch of the economy in which that occupation was followed. If the person concerned does not submit this certified statement, the said institution shall obtain it either from the institution competent in respect of unemployment of the latter Member State with which he was last insured, or from another institution designated by the competent authority of that Member State.

Article 82
Certified statement relating to the members of the family to be taken into consideration for the calculation of benefits 1. In order to invoke the provisions of Article 68 (2) of the Regulation, a person shall submit to the competent institution a certified statement relating to the members of his family who are resident in the territory of a Member State other than the one in which the said institution is situated.
2. This certified statement shall be issued by the institution designated by the competent authority of the Member State in whose territory those members of the family reside. It must certify that the members of the

family are not taken into consideration for the calculation of unemployment benefits due to another person under the legislation of the said Member State. The certified statement shall be valid for the twelve months following the date of its issue. It may be renewed; in such case, it shall be valid as from the date of its renewal. The person concerned shall notify the competent institution forthwith of any occurrence necessitating a modification of the said certified statement; such modification shall take effect as from the day of the occurrence.
Implementation of Article 69 of the Regulation

Article 83
Conditions and limits for the retention of the right to benefits when an unemployed person goes to another Member State 1. In order to retain the right to benefits, an unemployed person covered by Article 69 (1) of the Regulation shall submit to the institution of the place to which he has gone a certified statement in which the competent institution shall certify that he is still entitled to benefits under the conditions laid down in paragraph 1 (b) of the said Article. The competent institution shall specify in particular in this certified statement:
(a) the amount of benefit to be paid to the unemployed person under the legislation of the competent State;
(b) the date on which the unemployed person ceased to be available to the employment services of the competent State;
(c) the time limit under Article 69 (1) (b) of the Regulation for registration as a person seeking work in the Member State to which the unemployed person has gone;
(d) the maximum period, in accordance with Article (69 (1) (c) of the Regulation, during which the right to benefit may be retained;
(e) facts which might alter entitlement to benefit.
2. An unemployed person who intends to go to another Member State in order to seek employment there shall, before his departure, apply for the certified statement referred to in paragraph 1. If the unemployed person does not submit the said certified statement, the institution of the place to which he has gone shall obtain it from the competent institution. The employment services of the competent State must ensure that the unemployed person has been informed of his obligations under Article 69 of the Regulation and under the present Article.
3. The institution of the place to which the unemployed person has gone shall notify the competent institution of the date on which the unemployed person registered and the date on which payment of benefits was commenced and shall pay out the benefits of the competent State in accordance with the procedure provided for by the legislation of the Member State to which the unemployed person has gone.
The institution of the place to which the unemployed person has gone shall carry out a check or arrange for one to be carried out as if it were dealing with an unemployed person entitled to benefits under the legislation which it administers. It shall inform the competent institution of any occurrence coming within paragraph 1 (e) above as soon as the same comes to its knowledge and, in cases where the benefit has to be suspended or withdrawn, it shall immediately discontinue payment of the benefit. The competent institution shall forthwith inform it to what extent, and from what date, the unemployed person's entitlement to benefit is affected by that fact. Payment of benefits may only be resumed, where appropriate, after receipt of such information. Where the benefit has to be reduced, the institution of the place to which the unemployed person has gone shall continue to pay him a reduced amount of benefit, subject to adjustment, after receipt of the reply from the competent institution.
4. Two or more Member States or the competent authorities of those Member States may, having received the Opinion of the Administrative Commission, agree to introduce other implementing provisions.
Implementation of Article 71 of the Regulation

Article 84
Unemployed persons who, during their last employment, were residing in a Member State other than the competent State 1. In the cases referred to in Article 71 (1) (a) (ii) and in the first sentence of Article 71 (1) (b) (ii) of the Regulation, the institution of the place of residence shall be considered to be the competent institution, for the purposes of applying Article 80 of the Implementing Regulation.
2. In order to claim benefits under Article 71 (1) (b) (ii) of the Regulation, an unemployed person shall submit to the institution of his place of residence, in addition to the certified statement provided for in Article 80 of the Implementing Regulation, a certified statement from the institution of the Member State to whose legislation he was last subject, indicating that he has no right to benefit under Article 69 of the Regulation.
3. For the purposes of Article 71 (2) of the Regulation, the institution of the place of residence shall ask the competent institution for any information relating to the unemployed person's entitlements from the latter institution.

CHAPTER 7 - FAMILY BENEFITS AND FAMILY ALLOWANCES
Implementation of Article 72 of the Regulation

Article 85
Certified statement of periods of employment
1. In order to invoke the provisions of Article 72 of the Regulation a person shall submit to the competent institution a certified statement specifying the periods of employment completed under the legislation to which he was last subject.
2. That certified statement shall be issued, at the request of the person concerned, either by the institution competent in respect of family benefits of the Member State with which he was last insured, or by another institution designated by the competent authority of the said Member State. If the claimant does not submit the said certified statement, the competent institution shall obtain it from one or other of the abovementioned institutions unless the sickness insurance institution is able to forward him a copy of the certified statement provided for in Article 16 (1) of the Implementing Regulation.
3. Where it is necessary to take into account periods of employment completed previously under the legislation of any other Member State in order to satisfy the conditions of the legislation of the competent State, paragraphs 1 and 2 shall apply by analogy.
Implementation of Article 73 (1) and Article 75 (1) (a) and (b) of the Regulation

Article 86
Workers subject to the legislation of a Member State other than France 1. In order to draw family benefits under Article 73 (1) of the Regulation, a worker shall submit a claim to the competent institution, where necessary through his employer.
2. In support of his claim, the worker shall submit, a declaration of family status, issued by the authorities competent in civil status matters in the country of residence of the members of the family. Such declaration must be renewed once a year.
3. Where the legislation of the competent State provides that the family benefits may or must be paid to a person other than the worker, the worker shall also submit in support of his claim, information identifying the individual to whom the family benefits are to be paid in the country of residence (name, forename, full address).
4. The competent authorities of two or more Member States may agree on special procedures for the payment of family benefits, in particular with a view to facilitating the implementation of Article 75 (1) (a) and (b) of the Regulation. Such agreements shall be communicated to the Administrative Commission.
5. A worker shall inform the competent institution, where necessary through his employer:
- of any change in the situation of the members of his family which might alter entitlement to family benefits;
- of any change in the number of members of his family for whom family benefits are due;
- of any transfer of residence or stay of such members of the family;
- of any pursuit of a professional or trade activity by virtue of which family benefits are also due under the legislation of the Member State in whose territory the members of the family are resident.
Implementation of Article 73 (2) of the Regulation

Article 87
Workers subject to French legislation 1. In order to draw family allowances under Article 73 (2) of the Regulation, a worker shall submit a claim to the competent institution which shall issue him with a certified statement testifying that he satisfies the conditions of employment which govern the acquisition of the right to family allowances under French legislation. At the same time, the worker shall sign a declaration certifying that he has no right to family allowances under the legislation of the country of residence of the members of the family, by virtue of a professional or trade activity.
Where French legislation provides for entitlement to family allowances to last for a period corresponding to the duration of the periods of employment, the certified statement shall specify the duration of employment completed in the course of the period concerned.
The members of the family shall be registered with the institution of their place of residence on presentation of that certified statement and of the supporting documents required by the legislation administered by that institution for the granting of family allowances.
If the members of the family do not submit the said certified statement, the institution of the place of residence shall obtain it from the competent institution.
2. The certified statement provided for in paragraph 1 shall remain valid for a period of three months following the date of its issue, and must be renewed automatically every three months by the competent institution.
3. In the case of a seasonal worker, the certified statement provided for in paragraph 1 shall be valid for the expected duration of seasonal work unless, in the meantime, the competent institution notifies to the institution of the place of residence of its cancellation.

4. If the legislation of a Member State in whose territory the members of the family reside provides for the monthly or quarterly granting of family allowances, while French legislation provides for entitlement to family allowances to last for a period corresponding to the duration of employment, the family allowances shall be granted in the ratio which that duration bears to the duration laid down by the legislation of the country of residence of the members of the family.
5. If the legislation of the Member State in whose territory the members of the family reside provides for the granting of allowances for a number of days corresponding to the number of days of employment, while French legislation provides for entitlement to family allowances to last for one month, then the family allowances shall be granted for one month.
6. In the cases referred to in paragraphs 4 and 5, when the periods of employment completed under French legislation are expressed in units different from those which are used for the calculation of family allowances under the legislation of the Member State in whose territory the members of the family reside, the conversion shall be carried out in accordance with the provisions of Article 15 (3) of the Implementing Regulation.
7. The competent institution shall forthwith inform the institution of the place of residence of the members of the family of the date on which the worker ceases to be entitled to family allowances or on which he transfers his residence from the territory of one Member State to that of another Member State.
The institution of the place of residence of the members of the family may, at any time, ask the competent institution to supply it with any information relating to the worker's entitlement to family allowances.
If the competent institution considers it necessary, the institution of the place of residence shall, at its request, verify the declaration referred to in the first subparagraph of paragraph 1.
8. The members of the family shall be required to inform the institution of their place of residence of any change in their situation which might alter their entitlement to family allowances, in particular any change of residence.
Implementation of Article 74 (1) of the Regulation

Article 88
Unemployed persons subject to the legislation of a Member State other than France Article 86 of the Implementing Regulation shall apply by analogy to unemployed persons covered by Article 74 (1) of the Regulation.
Implementation of Article 74 (2) of the Regulation

Article 89
Unemployed persons subject to French legislation 1. In order to draw family allowances in the territory of the Member State where they reside, the members of the family covered by Article 74 (2) of the Regulation shall submit to the institution of their place of residence a certified statement testifying that the unemployed person is drawing unemployment benefits under French legislation.
This certified statement shall be issued by the French institution competent in respect of unemployment matters or by the institution designated by the competent French authority, at the request of the unemployed person who shall sign a declaration certifying that he has no right to family allowances under the legislation of the country of residence of the members of the family by virtue of a professional or trade activity.
If the members of the family do not submit the said certified statement the institution of the place of residence shall obtain it from the competent institution.
2. Article 87 (2) to (8) of the Implementing Regulation shall apply by analogy.

CHAPTER 8 - BENEFITS FOR DEPENDENT CHILDREN OF PENSIONERS AND FOR ORPHANS
Implementation of Articles 77, 78 and 79 of the Regulation

Article 90
1. In order to receive benefits under Article 77 or 78 of the Regulation, a claimant shall submit a claim to the institution of his place of residence, in accordance with the procedures laid down by the legislation administered by that institution.
2. If, however, the claimant does not reside in the territory of the Member State in which the competent institution is situated, he may submit his claim either to the competent institution or to the institution of his place of residence which shall then forward the claim to the competent institution, indicating the date on which it was submitted. That date shall be considered as the date of submission of the claim to the competent institution.
3. If the competent institution referred to in paragraph 2 finds that there is no entitlement under the legislation which it administers, it shall forward that claim forthwith, together with all necessary documents and information, to the institution of the Member State under whose legislation the worker completed his longest insurance period.
Where necessary the matter may have to be referred back, under the same conditions, to the institution of the Member State under whose legislation the worker completed his shortest insurance period.

4. The Administrative Commission shall, where necessary, lay down any supplementary procedures required for tihe submission of claims for benefits.

Annex 5.8.

Council Regulation (EC) No 1606/98 of 29 June 1998 amending Regulation (EEC) No 1408/71 on the application of social security schemes to employed persons, to self-employed persons and to members of their families moving within the Community and Regulation (EEC) No 574/72 laying down the procedure for implementing Regulation (EEC) No 1408/71 with a view to extending them to cover **special schemes for civil servants**

Official Journal L 209 , 25/07/1998 P. 0001 - 0015

MAIN PROVISIONS

Article 1

Regulation (EEC) No 1408/71 is hereby amended as follows:

(1) Article 1 shall be amended as follows:

(a) point (a)(i) shall be replaced by the following:

'(i) any person who is insured, compulsorily or on an optional continued basis, for one or more of the contingencies covered by the branches of a social security scheme for employed or self-employed persons or by a special scheme for civil servants; `

(b) the following point shall be added after point (j):

'(ja) "special scheme for civil servants" means any social security scheme which is different from the general social security scheme applicable to employed persons in the Member States concerned and to which all, or certain categories of, civil servants or persons treated as such are directly subject; `

(c) the following shall be added to point (r):

'periods completed under a special scheme for civil servants are also considered as periods of insurance; `

(d) the following shall be added to point (s):

'periods completed under a special scheme for civil servants are also considered as periods of employment; `

(2) Article 2(3) shall be deleted;

(3) in Article 4(4), the words 'or to special schemes for civil servants and persons treated as such` shall be deleted;

(4) Article 13(1) shall be replaced by the following:

'1. Subject to Articles 14c and 14f, persons to whom this Regulation applies shall be subject to the legislation of a single Member State only. That legislation shall be determined in accordance with the provisions of this Title;

(5) Article 14d(1) shall be replaced by the following:

'1. The person referred to in Article 14(2) and (3), Article 14a(2), (3) and (4), Article 14c(a) and Article 14e shall be treated, for the purposes of application of the legislation laid down in accordance with these provisions, as if he pursued all his professional activity or activities in the territory of the Member State concerned.`

(6) in Title II, the following Articles shall be inserted:

'Article 14e

Special rules applicable to persons insured in a special scheme for civil servants who are simultaneously employed and/or self-employed in the territory of one or more other Member States

A person who is simultaneously employed as a civil servant or a person treated as such and insured in a special scheme for civil servants in one Member State and who is employed and/or self-employed in the territory of one or more other Member States shall be subject to the legislation of the Member State in which he is insured in a special scheme for civil servants.

Article 14f

Special rules applicable to civil servants simultaneously employed in more than one Member State and insured in one of these States in a special scheme

A person who is simultaneously employed in two or more Member States as a civil servant or person treated as such and insured in at least one of those Member States in a special scheme for civil servants shall be subject to the legislation of each of these Member States.`

(7) in Chapter 2 of Title III, the following section shall be added:

'Section 5

Persons covered by a special scheme for civil servants

Article 43a

1. The provisions of Articles 37, 38(1), 39 and Sections 2, 3 and 4 shall apply by analogy to persons covered by a special scheme for civil servants.

2. However, if the legislation of a Member State makes the acquisition, liquidation, retention or recovery of the rights to benefits under a special scheme for civil servants subject to the condition that all periods of insurance

have been completed under one or more special schemes for civil servants in that Member State, or are regarded by the legislation of that Member State as equivalent to such periods, account shall be taken only of the periods which can be recognised under the legislation in that Member State.
If, account having been taken of the periods thus completed, the person concerned does not satisfy the conditions for the receipt of these benefits, these periods shall be taken into account for the granting of the benefits under the general scheme or, failing that, the scheme applicable to manual or clerical workers, as the case may be.
3. Where, under the legislation of a Member State, benefits are calculated on the basis of the last salary or salaries received during a reference period, the competent institution of that State shall take into account for the purposes of the calculation only those salaries, duly revalued, received during the period or periods for which the person concerned was subject to that legislation.`
(8) Chapter 3 of Title III shall be amended as follows:
(a) Article 44(3) shall be replaced by the following:
'3. Save as otherwise provided for in Article 79a, this Chapter shall not apply to increases in pensions or to supplements for pensions in respect of children or to orphan's pensions granted in accordance with the provisions of Chapter 8.`
(b) the following Article shall be added:
'Article 51a
Persons covered by a special scheme for civil servants
1. The provisions of Article 44, Article 45(1), (5) and (6) and Articles 46 to 51 shall apply by analogy to persons covered by a special scheme for civil servants.
2. However, if the legislation of a Member State makes the acquisition, liquidation, retention or recovery of the rights to benefits under a special scheme for civil servants subject to the condition that all periods of insurance have been completed under one or more special schemes for civil servants in that Member State, or are regarded by the legislation of that Member State as equivalent to such periods, account shall be taken only of the periods which can be recognised under the legislation in that Member State.
If, account having been taken of the periods thus completed, the person concerned does not satisfy the conditions for the receipt of these benefits, these periods shall be taken into account for the granting of the benefits under the general scheme or, failing that, the scheme applicable to manual or clerical workers, as the case may be.
3. Where, under the legislation of a Member State, benefits are calculated on the basis of the last salary or salaries received during a reference period, the competent institution of that State shall take into account for the purposes of the calculation only those salaries, duly revalued, received during the period or periods for which the person concerned was subject to that legislation.`
(9) in Chapter 6 of Title III, the following section shall be added:
'Section 4
Persons covered by a special scheme for civil servants
Article 71a
1. The provisions of Sections 1 and 2 shall apply by analogy to persons covered by a special unemployment scheme for civil servants.
2. The provisions of Section 3 shall not apply to persons covered by a special unemployment scheme for civil servants. An unemployed person who is covered by a special unemployment scheme for civil servants, who is partially or wholly unemployed, and who, during his last employment, was residing in the territory of a Member State other than the competent State, shall receive benefits in accordance with the provisions of the legislation of the competent State as if he were residing in the territory of that State; these benefits shall be provided by the competent institution, at its expense.`
(10) the following Article shall be inserted:
'Article 79a
Provisions relating to benefits for orphans entitled to benefits under a special scheme for civil servants
1. Notwithstanding the provisions of Article 78, orphans' pensions drawn under a special scheme for civil servants shall be calculated in accordance with the provisions of Chapter 3.
2. Where, in a case provided for in paragraph 1, periods of insurance, employment, self-employment or residence have also been completed under a general scheme, then benefits due under that general scheme shall be paid in accordance with the provisions of Chapter 8. Periods of insurance, self-employment or employment completed in accordance with the legislation of a special scheme for civil servants or periods which are regarded by the legislation of that Member State as equivalent to such periods, shall, where appropriate, be taken into account for the acquisition, retention or recovery of the rights to benefit in accordance with the legislation of that general scheme.`

Annex 5.9.

Council Directive 77/486/EEC of 25 July 1977 on the **education of the children of migrant workers**
Official Journal L 199 , 06/08/1977 P. 0032 - 0033

MAIN PROVISIONS

Article 1
This Directive shall apply to children for whom school attendance is compulsory under the laws of the host State, who are dependants of any worker who is a national of another Member State, where such children are resident in the territory of the Member State in which that national carries on or has carried on an activity as an employed person.

Article 2
Member States shall, in accordance with their national circumstances and legal systems, take appropriate measures to ensure that free tuition to facilitate initial reception is offered in their territory to the children referred to in Article 1, including, in particular, the teaching - adapted to the specific needs of such children - of the official language or one of the official languages of the host State.
Member States shall take the measures necessary for the training and further training of the teachers who are to provide this tuition.

Article 3
Member States shall, in accordance with their national circumstances and legal systems, and in cooperation with States of origin, take appropriate measures to promote, in coordination with normal education, teaching of the mother tongue and culture of the country of origin for the children referred to in Article 1. (1)OJ No C 280, 8.12.1975, p. 48. (2)OJ No C 45, 27.2.1976, p. 6. (3)OJ No C 13, 12.2.1974, p. 1.

Article 4
The Member States shall take the necessary measures to comply with this Directive within four years of its notification and shall forthwith inform the Commission thereof.
The Member States shall also inform the Commission of all laws, regulations and administrative or other provisions which they adopt in the field governed by this Directive.

Article 5
The Member States shall forward to the Commission within five years of the notification of this Directive, and subsequently at regular intervals at the request of the Commission, all relevant information to enable the Commission to report to the Council on the application of this Directive.

Annex 5.10.

Council Directive 93/96/EEC of 29 October 1993 on the **right of residence for students**
Official Journal L 317 , 18/12/1993 P. 0059 - 0060

MAIN PROVISIONS

Article 1
In order to lay down conditions to facilitate the exercise of the right of residence and with a view to guaranteeing access to vocational training in a non-discriminatory manner for a national of a Member State who has been accepted to attend a vocational training course in another Member State, the Member States shall recognize the right of residence for any student who is a national of a Member State and who does not enjoy that right under other provisions of Community law, and for the student's spouse and their dependent children, where the student assures the relevant national authority, by means of a declaration or by such alternative means as the student may choose that are at least equivalent, that he has sufficient resources to avoid becoming a burden on the social assistance system of the host Member State during their period of residence, provided that the student is enrolled in a recognized educational establishment for the principal purpose of following a vocational training course there and that he is covered by sickness insurance in respect of all risks in the host Member State.

Article 2
1. The right of residence shall be restricted to the duration of the course of studies in question.
The right of residence shall be evidenced by means of the issue of a document known as a 'residence permit for a national of a Member State of the Community', the validity of which may be limited to the duration of the course of studies or to one year where the course lasts longer; in the latter event it shall be renewable annually.
Where a member of the family does not hold the nationality of a Member State, he or she shall be issued with a residence document of the same validity as that issued to the national on whom he or she depends.
For the purpose of issuing the residence permit or document, the Member State may require only that the applicant present a valid identity card or passport and provide proof that he or she meets the conditions laid down in Article 1.
2. Articles 2, 3 and 9 of Directive 68/360/EEC shall apply mutatis mutandis to the beneficiaries of this Directive.
The spouse and the dependent children of a national of a Member State entitled to the right of residence within the territory of a Member State shall be entitled to take up any employed or self-employed activity anywhere within the territory of that Member State, even if they are not nationals of a Member State.
Member States shall not derogate from the provisions of this Directive save on grounds of public policy, public security or public health; in that event, Articles 2 to 9 of Directive 64/221/EEC shall apply.

Article 3
This Directive shall not establish any entitlement to the payment of maintenance grants by the host Member State on the part of students benefiting from the right of residence.

Article 4
The right of residence shall remain for as long as beneficiaries of that right fulfil the conditions laid down in Article 1.

Article 5
The Commission shall, not more than three years after the date of implementation of this Directive, and at three-yearly intervals thereafter, draw up a report on the application of this Directive and submit it to the European Parliament and the Council.
The Commission shall pay particular attention to any difficulties to which the implementation of Article 1 might give rise in the Member States; it shall, if appropriate, submit proposals to the Council with the aim of remedying such difficulties.

Article 6
Member States shall bring into force the laws, regulations and administrative provisions necessary to comply with this Directive not later than 31 December 1993. They shall forthwith inform the Commission thereof.
For the period preceding that date, the effects of Directive 90/366/EEC shall be maintained.
When Member States adopt those measures, they shall contain a reference to this Directive or shall be accompanied by such a reference on the occasion of their official publication. The methods of making such references shall be laid down by the Member States.

Annex 5.11.

2003/8/EC: Commission Decision of 23 December 2002 implementing Council Regulation (EEC) No 1612/68 as regards the **clearance of vacancies and applications for employment** (Text with EEA relevance) (notified under document number C(2002) 5236)
Official Journal L 005 , 10/01/2003 P. 0016 - 0019

MAIN PROVISIONS

Article 1
The EURES network
The Commission, the employment services of the Member States and any further national partners which they may have, shall create a European network of services, designated EURES (EURopean Employment Services) responsible for developing the exchange of information and cooperation provided for in Part II of Regulation (EEC) No 1612/68.

Article 2
Objectives
EURES contributes to the coordinated implementation of provisions of Part II of Regulation (EEC) No 1612/68. It supports the European Employment Strategy and contributes to the strengthening of the European Single market.
In particular, for the benefit of job seekers, workers and employers, EURES shall seek to promote:
(a) the development of European labour markets open and accessible for all;
(b) the transnational, interregional and cross-border exchange of vacancies and job applications;
(c) transparency and information exchange on the European labour markets, including on living conditions and on the opportunities for acquisition of skills;
(d) the development of methodologies and indicators for this purpose.

Article 3
Composition
EURES shall comprise the following categories:
(a) the EURES members, which shall be the specialist services appointed by the Member States in accordance with Article 13(2) of Regulation (EEC) No 1612/68, and the European Coordination Office, in accordance with Articles 21, 22 and 23 of that Regulation; and
(b) the EURES partners, as provided for in Article 17(1) of Regulation (EEC) No 1612/68; namely:
(i) regional employment services of the Member States;
(ii) employment services responsible for border regions;
(iii) specialised employment services that have been notified to the Commission in accordance with Article 17(2) of Regulation (EEC) No 1612/68.
These categories shall include the trades union and employer organisations designated by the EURES members.

Article 4
Role of the European Coordination Office
The Directorate-General for Employment and Social Affairs of the Commission is responsible for managing the European Coordination Office.
The European Coordination Office (hereinafter referred to as the EURES Coordination Office) shall oversee compliance with the provisions of Part II of Regulation (EEC) No 1612/68 and shall assist the network in carrying out its activities.
It shall, in particular, undertake:
(a) the analysis of geographic and occupational mobility and the development of a general approach to mobility in accordance with the European Employment Strategy;
(b) the formulation of a coherent overall approach and of appropriate arrangements to promote cooperation and coordination between Member States;
(c) overall monitoring and evaluation of EURES activity, and action to check that it is carried out in accordance with Regulation (EEC) No 1612/68 and with this Decision.

Article 5
EURES logo
The acronym EURES shall be used exclusively for activities within EURES. It shall be illustrated by a standard

logo, defined by a graphic design scheme.
The logo shall be registered as a Community trade mark at the Office for Harmonization in the Internal Market (OHIM). It may be used by the EURES members and partners.

Article 6
High Level Strategy Group
A High Level Strategy Group is hereby created, composed of the Heads of the EURES members and chaired by a representative of the Commission. It shall assist the Commission in promoting and overseeing the development of EURES.
The Commission shall consult the High Level Strategy Group on questions concerning the strategic planning, development, implementation, monitoring and evaluation of the services and activities referred to in this Decision, including:
(a) the EURES Charter, in accordance with Article 8(2);
(b) the EURES guidelines, in accordance with Article 9(1);
(c) the Commission's draft annual report provided for by Article 19(1) of Regulation (EEC) No 1612/68;
(d) the Commission's two-yearly report to the European Parliament, the Council and the Economic and Social Committee required by Article 19(3) of Regulation (EEC) No 1612/68.
The Heads of the European social partners' organisations shall be invited to participate in the meetings of the Group.
The Group shall establish its working methods and rules of procedure. As a general rule, it shall be convened twice a year by the chairperson. It shall deliver its opinions by simple majority.
The EURES Coordination Office shall provide secretarial support.

Article 7
Working party
In order to assist it in the development, implementation and monitoring of EURES activities, the EURES Coordination Office shall institute a Working Party composed of EURES managers, each one representing a EURES member. The EURES Coordination Office shall invite representatives of the European social partners and, when appropriate, representatives of other EURES partners and experts, to attend the meetings of the Working Party.

Article 8
EURES Charter
1. The EURES Coordination Office shall adopt the EURES Charter in accordance with the procedures set out in Article 14(2), Article 15(2), Article 22(1)(a), (b) and (c), and Article 23 of Regulation (EEC) No 1612/68, after consultation of the EURES High Level Strategy Group established by Article 6 of this Decision.
2. On the basis of the principle that all vacancies and applications for employment that are made public by any of the EURES members and partners must be accessible throughout the Community, the EURES Charter shall, in particular, establish:
(a) descriptions of the activities that the EURES members and partners shall carry out, including:
(i) job-matching services, including personalised counselling and advice to customers, whether they be job seekers, workers or employers;
(ii) the development of transnational and cross-border cooperation, including employment and social services, the social partners and other institutions concerned, with a view to the improvement of the functioning of the labour markets, their integration and improved mobility;
(iii) the promotion of coordinated monitoring and assessment of obstacles to mobility, skills surpluses and shortages and migration flows;
(b) the operational objectives of the EURES system, the quality standards to be applied as well as the obligations of the EURES members and partners, which include:
(i) the integration of members' relevant databases of job vacancies, with the EURES vacancy exchange mechanism, by a deadline to be specified;
(ii) the kind of information, such as labour market information, information on living and working conditions, information on job offers and requests, and obstacles to mobility, which they have to supply to their customers and to the rest of the network;
(iii) the training and qualifications required for EURES personnel and conditions and procedures for the organisation of visits and assignments for officials;
(iv) the drawing up, submission to the EURES Coordination Office and execution of activity plans, including specific rules for the EURES cross-border activities;
(v) the conditions governing the use of the EURES logo by the members and partners;
(vi) principles for monitoring and evaluating EURES activities;

(c) procedures to set up a uniform system and common models for the exchange of labour market and mobility-related information within the EURES network, as provided for in Articles 14, 15 and 16 of Regulation (EEC) No 1612/68, including information on jobs and on learning opportunities in the European Union to be incorporated into an integrated job mobility information website.

Article 9
Guidelines and Activity Plans
1. In line with the EURES Charter provided for in Article 8, and after consulting the EURES High Level Strategy Group provided for in Article 6, the EURES Coordination Office shall establish guidelines for the activities of EURES covering a three-year period.
The guidelines shall include the conditions for any financial assistance which the Community may provide in accordance with paragraph 4.
2. On the basis of the guidelines, EURES members shall present their respective activity plans for the period covered by the guidelines to the EURES Coordination Office. The activity plan shall specify:
(a) the main activities to be undertaken by the EURES member within the framework of the network, including the transnational, cross-border and sectoral activities provided for in Article 17 of Regulation (EEC) No 1612/68;
(b) the human and financial resources allocated for the implementation of Part II of Regulation (EEC) No 1612/68;
(c) the arrangements for monitoring and evaluation of the activities planned, including the information to be sent to the Commission on an annual basis.
The activity plans shall also include an assessment of the activities and progress achieved during the previous period.
3. The EURES Coordination Office shall examine the activity plans and the information sent on their implementation with a view to assessing their consistency with the guidelines and the provisions of Part II of Regulation (EEC) No 1612/68. The results of this assessment shall be analysed jointly with the EURES members on an annual basis, in accordance with Article 19(1) of that Regulation, and shall be included in the Commission's two-yearly report to the European Parliament, the Council and the Economic and Social Committee required by Article 19(3) of that Regulation.
4. The Commission may grant financial assistance for the implementation of the activity plans subject to the rules governing the relevant budgetary resources.

Annex 5.12.

Council Regulation (EC) No 1091/2001 of 28 May 2001 on **freedom of movement with a long-stay visa**
Official Journal L 150 , 06/06/2001 P. 0004 - 0005

MAIN PROVISIONS

Article 1
Article 18 of the Convention implementing the Schengen Agreement shall be replaced by the following:
"Article 18
Visas for stays exceeding three months shall be national visas issued by one of the Member States in accordance with its national law. For a period of not more than three months from their initial date of validity such visas shall be valid concurrently as uniform short-stay visas, provided that they were issued in accordance with the common conditions and criteria adopted under or pursuant to the relevant provisions of Chapter 3, section 1 and their holders fulfil the entry conditions referred to in Article 5(1)(a), (c), (d) and (e). Otherwise, such visas shall merely enable their holders to transit through the territories of the other Member States in order to reach the territory of the Member State which issued the visa, unless the holders do not fulfil the entry conditions referred to in Article 5(1)(a), (d) and (e) or are on the national list of alerts of the Member State through whose territory they seek to transit."

Article 2
Section 2.2 of Part I of the Common Consular Instructions on Visas shall be replaced by the following: "2.2. Long-stay visas
Visas for visits exceeding three months shall be national visas issued by one of the Member States in accordance with its national legislation.
However, such visas shall, for a period of not more than three months from their initial date of validity, be valid concurrently as uniform short-stay visas, provided that they were issued in accordance with the common conditions and criteria adopted under or pursuant to the relevant provisions of Chapter 3, section 1 of the Convention implementing the Schengen Agreement and their holders fulfil the entry conditions referred to in Article 5(1)(a), (c), (d) and (e) of the said Convention and reproduced in Part IV of these Instructions.
Otherwise, such visas shall merely enable their holders to transit through the territories of the other Contracting Parties in order to reach the territory of the Member State which issued the visa, unless the holders do not fulfil the entry conditions referred to in Article 5(1)(a), (d) and (e) of the Convention implementing the Schengen Agreement or are on the national list of alerts of the Member State through whose territory they seek to transit."

Annex 5.13.

Council Directive 2002/90/EC of 28 November 2002 defining the **facilitation of unauthorised entry, transit and residence**
Official Journal L 328 , 05/12/2002 P. 0017 - 0018

MAIN PROVISIONS

Article 1
General infringement
1. Each Member State shall adopt appropriate sanctions on:
(a) any person who intentionally assists a person who is not a national of a Member State to enter, or transit across, the territory of a Member State in breach of the laws of the State concerned on the entry or transit of aliens;
(b) any person who, for financial gain, intentionally assists a person who is not a national of a Member State to reside within the territory of a Member State in breach of the laws of the State concerned on the residence of aliens.
2. Any Member State may decide not to impose sanctions with regard to the behaviour defined in paragraph 1(a) by applying its national law and practice for cases where the aim of the behaviour is to provide humanitarian assistance to the person concerned.

Article 2
Instigation, participation and attempt
Each Member State shall take the measures necessary to ensure that the sanctions referred to in Article 1 are also applicable to any person who:
(a) is the instigator of,
(b) is an accomplice in, or
(c) attempts to commit
an infringement as referred to in Article 1(1)(a) or (b).

Article 3
Sanctions
Each Member State shall take the measures necessary to ensure that the infringements referred to in Articles 1 and 2 are subject to effective, proportionate and dissuasive sanctions.

Article 4
Implementation
1. Member States shall bring into force the laws, regulations and administrative provisions necessary to comply with this Directive before 5 December 2004. They shall forthwith inform the Commission thereof.
When Member States adopt these measures, they shall contain a reference to this Directive or shall be accompanied by such reference on the occasion of their official publication. The methods of making such a reference shall be laid down by the Member States.
2. Member States shall communicate to the Commission the text of the main provisions of their national law which they adopt in the field covered by this Directive, together with a table showing how the provisions of this Directive correspond to the national provisions adopted. The Commission shall inform the other Member States thereof.

Article 5
Repeal
Article 27(1) of the 1990 Schengen Convention shall be repealed as from 5 December 2004. Where a Member State implements this Directive pursuant to Article 4(1) in advance of that date, the said provision shall cease to apply to that Member State from the date of implementation.

Annex 5.14.

Council Directive 2003/9/EC of 27 January 2003 laying down **minimum standards for the reception of asylum seekers**
Official Journal L 031 , 06/02/2003 P. 0018 - 0025

MAIN PROVISIONS

CHAPTER I - PURPOSE, DEFINITIONS AND SCOPE

Article 1
Purpose
The purpose of this Directive is to lay down minimum standards for the reception of asylum seekers in Member States.

Article 2
Definitions
For the purposes of this Directive:
(a) "Geneva Convention" shall mean the Convention of 28 July 1951 relating to the status of refugees, as amended by the New York Protocol of 31 January 1967;
(b) "application for asylum" shall mean the application made by a third-country national or a stateless person which can be understood as a request for international protection from a Member State, under the Geneva Convention. Any application for international protection is presumed to be an application for asylum unless a third-country national or a stateless person explicitly requests another kind of protection that can be applied for separately;
(c) "applicant" or "asylum seeker" shall mean a third country national or a stateless person who has made an application for asylum in respect of which a final decision has not yet been taken;
(d) "family members" shall mean, in so far as the family already existed in the country of origin, the following members of the applicant's family who are present in the same Member State in relation to the application for asylum:
(i) the spouse of the asylum seeker or his or her unmarried partner in a stable relationship, where the legislation or practice of the Member State concerned treats unmarried couples in a way comparable to married couples under its law relating to aliens;
(ii) the minor children of the couple referred to in point (i) or of the applicant, on condition that they are unmarried and dependent and regardless of whether they were born in or out of wedlock or adopted as defined under the national law;
(e) "refugee" shall mean a person who fulfils the requirements of Article 1(A) of the Geneva Convention;
(f) "refugee status" shall mean the status granted by a Member State to a person who is a refugee and is admitted as such to the territory of that Member State;
(g) "procedures" and "appeals", shall mean the procedures and appeals established by Member States in their national law;
(h) "unaccompanied minors" shall mean persons below the age of eighteen who arrive in the territory of the Member States unaccompanied by an adult responsible for them whether by law or by custom, and for as long as they are not effectively taken into the care of such a person; it shall include minors who are left unaccompanied after they have entered the territory of Member States;
(i) "reception conditions" shall mean the full set of measures that Member States grant to asylum seekers in accordance with this Directive;
(j) "material reception conditions" shall mean the reception conditions that include housing, food and clothing, provided in kind, or as financial allowances or in vouchers, and a daily expenses allowance;
(k) "detention" shall mean confinement of an asylum seeker by a Member State within a particular place, where the applicant is deprived of his or her freedom of movement;
(l) "accommodation centre" shall mean any place used for collective housing of asylum seekers.

Article 3
Scope
1. This Directive shall apply to all third country nationals and stateless persons who make an application for asylum at the border or in the territory of a Member State as long as they are allowed to remain on the territory as asylum seekers, as well as to family members, if they are covered by such application for asylum according to the national law.
2. This Directive shall not apply in cases of requests for diplomatic or territorial asylum submitted to

representations of Member States.
3. This Directive shall not apply when the provisions of Council Directive 2001/55/EC of 20 July 2001 on minimum standards for giving temporary protection in the event of a mass influx of displaced persons and on measures promoting a balance of efforts between Member States in receiving such persons and bearing the consequences thereof(5) are applied.
4. Member States may decide to apply this Directive in connection with procedures for deciding on applications for kinds of protection other than that emanating from the Geneva Convention for third-country nationals or stateless persons who are found not to be refugees.

Article 4
More favourable provisions
Member States may introduce or retain more favourable provisions in the field of reception conditions for asylum seekers and other close relatives of the applicant who are present in the same Member State when they are dependent on him or for humanitarian reasons insofar as these provisions are compatible with this Directive.

CHAPTER II - GENERAL PROVISIONS ON RECEPTION CONDITIONS

Article 5
Information
1. Member States shall inform asylum seekers, within a reasonable time not exceeding fifteen days after they have lodged their application for asylum with the competent authority, of at least any established benefits and of the obligations with which they must comply relating to reception conditions.
Member States shall ensure that applicants are provided with information on organisations or groups of persons that provide specific legal assistance and organisations that might be able to help or inform them concerning the available reception conditions, including health care.
2. Member States shall ensure that the information referred to in paragraph 1 is in writing and, as far as possible, in a language that the applicants may reasonably be supposed to understand. Where appropriate, this information may also be supplied orally.

Article 6
Documentation
1. Member States shall ensure that, within three days after an application is lodged with the competent authority, the applicant is provided with a document issued in his or her own name certifying his or her status as an asylum seeker or testifying that he or she is allowed to stay in the territory of the Member State while his or her application is pending or being examined.
If the holder is not free to move within all or a part of the territory of the Member State, the document shall also certify this fact.
2. Member States may exclude application of this Article when the asylum seeker is in detention and during the examination of an application for asylum made at the border or within the context of a procedure to decide on the right of the applicant legally to enter the territory of a Member State. In specific cases, during the examination of an application for asylum, Member States may provide applicants with other evidence equivalent to the document referred to in paragraph 1.
3. The document referred to in paragraph 1 need not certify the identity of the asylum seeker.
4. Member States shall adopt the necessary measures to provide asylum seekers with the document referred to in paragraph 1, which must be valid for as long as they are authorised to remain in the territory of the Member State concerned or at the border thereof.
5. Member States may provide asylum seekers with a travel document when serious humanitarian reasons arise that require their presence in another State.

Article 7
Residence and freedom of movement
1. Asylum seekers may move freely within the territory of the host Member State or within an area assigned to them by that Member State. The assigned area shall not affect the unalienable sphere of private life and shall allow sufficient scope for guaranteeing access to all benefits under this Directive.
2. Member States may decide on the residence of the asylum seeker for reasons of public interest, public order or, when necessary, for the swift processing and effective monitoring of his or her application.
3. When it proves necessary, for example for legal reasons or reasons of public order, Member States may confine an applicant to a particular place in accordance with their national law.
4. Member States may make provision of the material reception conditions subject to actual residence by the applicants in a specific place, to be determined by the Member States. Such a decision, which may be of a

general nature, shall be taken individually and established by national legislation.
5. Member States shall provide for the possibility of granting applicants temporary permission to leave the place of residence mentioned in paragraphs 2 and 4 and/or the assigned area mentioned in paragraph 1. Decisions shall be taken individually, objectively and impartially and reasons shall be given if they are negative.
The applicant shall not require permission to keep appointments with authorities and courts if his or her appearance is necessary.
6. Member States shall require applicants to inform the competent authorities of their current address and notify any change of address to such authorities as soon as possible.

Article 8
Families
Member States shall take appropriate measures to maintain as far as possible family unity as present within their territory, if applicants are provided with housing by the Member State concerned. Such measures shall be implemented with the asylum seeker's agreement.

Article 9
Medical screening
Member States may require medical screening for applicants on public health grounds.

Article 10
Schooling and education of minors
1. Member States shall grant to minor children of asylum seekers and to asylum seekers who are minors access to the education system under similar conditions as nationals of the host Member State for so long as an expulsion measure against them or their parents is not actually enforced. Such education may be provided in accommodation centres.
The Member State concerned may stipulate that such access must be confined to the State education system.
Minors shall be younger than the age of legal majority in the Member State in which the application for asylum was lodged or is being examined. Member States shall not withdraw secondary education for the sole reason that the minor has reached the age of majority.
2. Access to the education system shall not be postponed for more than three months from the date the application for asylum was lodged by the minor or the minor's parents. This period may be extended to one year where specific education is provided in order to facilitate access to the education system.
3. Where access to the education system as set out in paragraph 1 is not possible due to the specific situation of the minor, the Member State may offer other education arrangements.

Article 11
Employment
1. Member States shall determine a period of time, starting from the date on which an application for asylum was lodged, during which an applicant shall not have access to the labour market.
2. If a decision at first instance has not been taken within one year of the presentation of an application for asylum and this delay cannot be attributed to the applicant, Member States shall decide the conditions for granting access to the labour market for the applicant.
3. Access to the labour market shall not be withdrawn during appeals procedures, where an appeal against a negative decision in a regular procedure has suspensive effect, until such time as a negative decision on the appeal is notified.
4. For reasons of labour market policies, Member States may give priority to EU citizens and nationals of States parties to the Agreement on the European Economic Area and also to legally resident third-country nationals.

Article 12
Vocational training
Member States may allow asylum seekers access to vocational training irrespective of whether they have access to the labour market.
Access to vocational training relating to an employment contract shall depend on the extent to which the applicant has access to the labour market in accordance with Article 11.

Article 13
General rules on material reception conditions and health care
1. Member States shall ensure that material reception conditions are available to applicants when they make their application for asylum.
2. Member States shall make provisions on material reception conditions to ensure a standard of living adequate

for the health of applicants and capable of ensuring their subsistence.
Member States shall ensure that that standard of living is met in the specific situation of persons who have special needs, in accordance with Article 17, as well as in relation to the situation of persons who are in detention.
3. Member States may make the provision of all or some of the material reception conditions and health care subject to the condition that applicants do not have sufficient means to have a standard of living adequate for their health and to enable their subsistence.
4. Member States may require applicants to cover or contribute to the cost of the material reception conditions and of the health care provided for in this Directive, pursuant to the provision of paragraph 3, if the applicants have sufficient resources, for example if they have been working for a reasonable period of time.
If it transpires that an applicant had sufficient means to cover material reception conditions and health care at the time when these basic needs were being covered, Member States may ask the asylum seeker for a refund.
5. Material reception conditions may be provided in kind, or in the form of financial allowances or vouchers or in a combination of these provisions.
Where Member States provide material reception conditions in the form of financial allowances or vouchers, the amount thereof shall be determined in accordance with the principles set out in this Article.

Article 14
Modalities for material reception conditions
1. Where housing is provided in kind, it should take one or a combination of the following forms:
(a) premises used for the purpose of housing applicants during the examination of an application for asylum lodged at the border;
(b) accommodation centres which guarantee an adequate standard of living;
(c) private houses, flats, hotels or other premises adapted for housing applicants.
2. Member States shall ensure that applicants provided with the housing referred to in paragraph 1(a), (b) and (c) are assured:
(a) protection of their family life;
(b) the possibility of communicating with relatives, legal advisers and representatives of the United Nations High Commissioner for Refugees (UNHCR) and non-governmental organisations (NGOs) recognised by Member States.
Member States shall pay particular attention to the prevention of assault within the premises and accommodation centres referred to in paragraph 1(a) and (b).
3. Member States shall ensure, if appropriate, that minor children of applicants or applicants who are minors are lodged with their parents or with the adult family member responsible for them whether by law or by custom.
4. Member States shall ensure that transfers of applicants from one housing facility to another take place only when necessary. Member States shall provide for the possibility for applicants to inform their legal advisers of the transfer and of their new address.
5. Persons working in accommodation centres shall be adequately trained and shall be bound by the confidentiality principle as defined in the national law in relation to any information they obtain in the course of their work.
6. Member States may involve applicants in managing the material resources and non-material aspects of life in the centre through an advisory board or council representing residents.
7. Legal advisors or counsellors of asylum seekers and representatives of the United Nations High Commissioner for Refugees or non-governmental organisations designated by the latter and recognised by the Member State concerned shall be granted access to accommodation centres and other housing facilities in order to assist the said asylum seekers. Limits on such access may be imposed only on grounds relating to the security of the centres and facilities and of the asylum seekers.
8. Member States may exceptionally set modalities for material reception conditions different from those provided for in this Article, for a reasonable period which shall be as short as possible, when:
- an initial assessment of the specific needs of the applicant is required,
- material reception conditions, as provided for in this Article, are not available in a certain geographical area,
- housing capacities normally available are temporarily exhausted,
- the asylum seeker is in detention or confined to border posts.
These different conditions shall cover in any case basic needs.

Article 15
Health care
1. Member States shall ensure that applicants receive the necessary health care which shall include, at least, emergency care and essential treatment of illness.
2. Member States shall provide necessary medical or other assistance to applicants who have special needs.

CHAPTER III - REDUCTION OR WITHDRAWAL OF RECEPTION CONDITIONS

Article 16
Reduction or withdrawal of reception conditions
1. Member States may reduce or withdraw reception conditions in the following cases:
(a) where an asylum seeker:
- abandons the place of residence determined by the competent authority without informing it or, if requested, without permission, or
- does not comply with reporting duties or with requests to provide information or to appear for personal interviews concerning the asylum procedure during a reasonable period laid down in national law, or
- has already lodged an application in the same Member State.
When the applicant is traced or voluntarily reports to the competent authority, a duly motivated decision, based on the reasons for the disappearance, shall be taken on the reinstallation of the grant of some or all of the reception conditions;
(b) where an applicant has concealed financial resources and has therefore unduly benefited from material reception conditions.
If it transpires that an applicant had sufficient means to cover material reception conditions and health care at the time when these basic needs were being covered, Member States may ask the asylum seeker for a refund.
2. Member States may refuse conditions in cases where an asylum seeker has failed to demonstrate that the asylum claim was made as soon as reasonably practicable after arrival in that Member State.
3. Member States may determine sanctions applicable to serious breaching of the rules of the accommodation centres as well as to seriously violent behaviour.
4. Decisions for reduction, withdrawal or refusal of reception conditions or sanctions referred to in paragraphs 1, 2 and 3 shall be taken individually, objectively and impartially and reasons shall be given. Decisions shall be based on the particular situation of the person concerned, especially with regard to persons covered by Article 17, taking into account the principle of proportionality. Member States shall under all circumstances ensure access to emergency health care.
5. Member States shall ensure that material reception conditions are not withdrawn or reduced before a negative decision is taken.

CHAPTER IV -PROVISIONS FOR PERSONS WITH SPECIAL NEEDS

Article 17
General principle
1. Member States shall take into account the specific situation of vulnerable persons such as minors, unaccompanied minors, disabled people, elderly people, pregnant women, single parents with minor children and persons who have been subjected to torture, rape or other serious forms of psychological, physical or sexual violence, in the national legislation implementing the provisions of Chapter II relating to material reception conditions and health care.
2. Paragraph 1 shall apply only to persons found to have special needs after an individual evaluation of their situation.

Article 18
Minors
1. The best interests of the child shall be a primary consideration for Member States when implementing the provisions of this Directive that involve minors.
2. Member States shall ensure access to rehabilitation services for minors who have been victims of any form of abuse, neglect, exploitation, torture or cruel, inhuman and degrading treatment, or who have suffered from armed conflicts, and ensure that appropriate mental health care is developed and qualified counselling is provided when needed.

Article 19
Unaccompanied minors
1. Member States shall as soon as possible take measures to ensure the necessary representation of unaccompanied minors by legal guardianship or, where necessary, representation by an organisation which is responsible for the care and well-being of minors, or by any other appropriate representation. Regular assessments shall be made by the appropriate authorities.
2. Unaccompanied minors who make an application for asylum shall, from the moment they are admitted to the territory to the moment they are obliged to leave the host Member State in which the application for asylum was made or is being examined, be placed:

(a) with adult relatives;
(b) with a foster-family;
(c) in accommodation centres with special provisions for minors;
(d) in other accommodation suitable for minors.
Member States may place unaccompanied minors aged 16 or over in accommodation centres for adult asylum seekers.
As far as possible, siblings shall be kept together, taking into account the best interests of the minor concerned and, in particular, his or her age and degree of maturity. Changes of residence of unaccompanied minors shall be limited to a minimum.
3. Member States, protecting the unaccompanied minor's best interests, shall endeavour to trace the members of his or her family as soon as possible. In cases where there may be a threat to the life or integrity of the minor or his or her close relatives, particularly if they have remained in the country of origin, care must be taken to ensure that the collection, processing and circulation of information concerning those persons is undertaken on a confidential basis, so as to avoid jeopardising their safety.
4. Those working with unaccompanied minors shall have had or receive appropriate training concerning their needs, and shall be bound by the confidentiality principle as defined in the national law, in relation to any information they obtain in the course of their work.

Article 20
Victims of torture and violence
Member States shall ensure that, if necessary, persons who have been subjected to torture, rape or other serious acts of violence receive the necessary treatment of damages caused by the aforementioned acts.

Annex 5.15.

Council Directive 73/148/EEC of 21 May 1973 on the **abolition of restrictions on movement and residence** within the Community for nationals of Member States with regard to establishment and the provision of services
Official Journal L 172 , 28/06/1973 P. 0014 - 0016

MAIN PROVISIONS

Article 1
1. The Member States shall, acting as provided in this Directive, abolish restrictions on the movement and residence of: (1)OJ No 2, 15.1.1962, p. 32/62 and 36/62. (2)OJ No C 19, 28.2.1972, p. 5. (3)OJ No C 67, 24.6.1972, p. 7. (4)OJ No 56, 4.4.1964, p. 845/64. (5)OJ No L 257, 19.10.1968, p. 13. (6)OJ No 62, 17.4.1964, p. 981/64. (7)OJ No 56, 4.4.1964, p. 850/64. (a) nationals of a Member State who are established or who wish to establish themselves in another Member State in order to pursue activities as self-employed persons, or who wish to provide services in that State;
(b) nationals of Member States wishing to go to another Member State as recipients of services;
(c) the spouse and the children under twenty-one years of age of such nationals, irrespective of their nationality;
(d) the relatives in the ascending and descending lines of such nationals and of the spouse of such nationals, which relatives are dependent on them, irrespective of their nationality.

2. Member States shall favour the admission of any other member of the family of a national referred to in paragraph 1 (a) or (b) or of the spouse of that national, which member is dependent on that national or spouse of that national or who in the country of origin was living under the same roof.

Article 2
1. Member States shall grant the persons referred to in Article 1 the right to leave their territory. Such right shall be exercised simply on production of a valid identity card or passport. Members of the family shall enjoy the same right as the national on whom they are dependent.
2. Member States shall, acting in accordance with their laws, issue to their nationals, or renew, an identity card or passport, which shall state in particular the holder's nationality.
3. The passport must be valid at least for all Member States and for countries through which the holder must pass when travelling between Member States. Where a passport is the only document on which the holder may lawfully leave the country, its period of validity shall be not less than five years.
4. Member States may not demand from the persons referred to in Article 1 any exit visa or any equivalent requirement.

Article 3
1. Member States shall grant to the persons referred to in Article 1 right to enter their territory merely on production of a valid identity card or passport.
2. No entry visa or equivalent requirement may be demanded save in respect of members of the family who do have the nationality of a Member State. Member States shall afford to such persons every facility for obtaining any necessary visas.

Article 4
1. Each Member State shall grant the right of permanent residence to nationals of other Member States who establish themselves within its territory in order to pursue activities as self-employed persons, when the restrictions on these activities have been abolished pursuant to the Treaty.
As proof of the right of residence, a document entitled "Residence Permit for a National of a Member State of the European Communities" shall be issued. This document shall be valid for not less than five years from the date of issue and shall be automatically renewable.
Breaks in residence not exceeding six consecutive months and absence on military service shall not affect the validity of a residence permit.
A valid residence permit may not be withdrawn from a national referred to in Article 1 (1) (a) solely on the grounds that he is no longer in employment because he is temporarily incapable of work as a result of illness or accident.
Any national of a Member State who is not specified in the first subparagraph but who is authorized under the laws of another Member State to pursue an activity within its territory shall be granted a right of abode for a period not less than that of the authorization granted for the pursuit of the activity in question.
However, any national referred to in subparagraph 1 and to whom the provisions of the preceding subparagraph

apply as a result of a change of employment shall retain his residence permit until the date on which it expires.
2. The right of residence for persons providing and receiving services shall be of equal duration with the period during which the services are provided.
Where such period exceeds three months, the Member State in the territory of which the services are performed shall issue a right of abode as proof of the right of residence.
Where the period does not exceed three months, the identity card or passport with which the person concerned entered the territory shall be sufficient to cover his stay. The Member State may, however, require the person concerned to report his presence in the territory.
3. A member of the family who is not a national of a Member State shall be issued with a residence document which shall have the same validity as that issued to the national on whom he is dependent.

Article 5
The right of residence shall be effective throughout the territory of the Member State concerned.

Article 6
An applicant for a residence permit or right of abode shall not be required by a Member State to produce anything other than the following, namely: (a) the identity card or passport with which he or she entered its territory;
(b) proof that he or she comes within one of the classes of person referred to in Articles 1 and 4.

Article 7
1. The residence documents granted to nationals of a Member State shall be issued and renewed free of charge or on payment of an amount not exceeding the dues and taxes charged for the issue of identity cards to nationals. These provisions shall also apply to documents and certificates required for the issue and renewal of such residence documents.
2. The visas referred to in Article 3 (2) shall be free of charge.
3. Member States shall take the necessary steps to simplify as much as possible the formalities and the procedure for obtaining the documents mentioned in paragraph 1.

Article 8
Member States shall not derogate from the provisions of this Directive save on grounds of public policy, public security or public health.

Annex 5.16.

Council Directive 75/34/EEC of 17 December 1974 concerning the right of nationals of a Member State to remain in the territory of another Member State after having pursued therein an **activity in a self-employed capacity**
Official Journal L 014 , 20/01/1975 P. 0010 - 0013

MAIN PROVISIONS

Article 1
Member States shall, under the conditions laid down in this Directive, abolish restrictions on the right to remain in their territory in favour of nationals of another Member State who have pursued activities as self-employed persons in their territory, and members of their families, as defined in Article 1 of Directive No 73/148/EEC.

Article 2
1. Each Member State shall recognize the right to remain permanently in its territory of: (a) any person who, at the time of termination of his activity, has reached the age laid down by the law of that State for entitlement to an old-age pension and who has pursued his activity in that State for at least the previous twelve months and has resided there continuously for more than three years.
Where the law of that Member State does not grant the right to an old-age pension to certain categories of self-employed workers, the age requirement shall be considered as satisfied when the beneficiary reaches 65 years of age;
(b) any person who, having resided continuously in the territory of that State for more than two years, ceases to pursue his activity there as a result of permanent incapacity to work.
If such incapacity is the result of an accident at work or an occupational illness entitling him to a pension which is payable in whole or in part by an institution of that State no condition shall be imposed as to length of residence;
(c) any person who, after three years' continuous activity and residence in the territory of that State, pursues his activity in the territory of another Member State, while retaining his residence in the territory of the first State, to which he returns, as a rule, each day or at least once a week.

Periods of activity so completed in the territory of the other Member State shall, for the purposes of entitlement to the rights referred to in (a) and (b), be considered as having been completed in the territory of the State of residence.
2. The conditions as to length of residence and activity laid down in paragraph 1 (a) and the condition as to length of residence laid down in paragraph 1 (b) shall not apply if the spouse of the self-employed person is a national of the Member State concerned or has lost the nationality of that State by marriage to that person.

Article 3
1. Each Member State shall recognize the right of the members of the self-employed person's family referred to in Article 1 who are residing with him in the territory of that State to remain there permanently, if the person concerned has acquired the right to remain in the territory of that State in accordance with Article 2. This provision shall continue to apply even after the death of the person concerned.
2. If, however, the self-employed person dies during his working life and before having acquired the right to remain in the territory of the State concerned, that State shall recognize the right of the members of his family to remain there permanently on condition that: - the person concerned, on the date of his decease, had resided continuously in its territory for at least two years ; or
- his death resulted from an accident at work or an occupational illness ; or
- the surviving spouse is a national of that State or lost such nationality by marriage to the person concerned.

Article 4
1. Continuity of residence as provided for in Articles 2 (1) and 3 (2) may be attested by any means of proof in use in the country of residence. It may not be affected by temporary absences not exceeding a total of three months per year, nor by longer absences due to compliance with the obligations of military service.
2. Periods of inactivity due to circumstances outside the control of the person concerned or of inactivity owing to illness or accident must be considered as periods of activity within the meaning of Article 2 (1).

Article 5
1. Member States shall allow the person entitled to the right to remain to exercise such right within two years from the time of becoming entitled thereto pursuant to Article 2 (1) (a) and (b) and Article 3. During this period

the beneficiary must be able to leave the territory of the Member State without adversely affecting such right.
2. Member States shall not require the person concerned to comply with any particular formality in order to exercise the right to remain.

Article 6
1. Member States shall recognize the right of persons having the right to remain in their territory to a residence permit, which must: (a) be issued and renewed free of charge or on payment of a sum not exceeding the dues and taxes payable by nationals for the issue or renewal of identity cards;
(b) by valid throughout the territory of the Member State issuing it;
(c) be valid for five years and renewable automatically.

2. Periods of non-residence not exceeding six consecutive months and longer absences due to compliance with the obligations of military service may not affect the validity of a residence permit.

Article 7
Member States shall apply to persons having the right to remain in their territory the right of equality of treatment recognized by the Council Directives on the abolition of restrictions on freedom of establishment pursuant to Title III of the General Programme which provides for such abolition.

Article 8
1. This Directive shall not affect any provisions laid down by law, regulation or administrative action of any Member State which would be more favourable to nationals of other Member States.
2. Member States shall facilitate re-admission to their territories of self-employed persons who left those territories after having resided there permanently for a long period while pursuing an activity there and who wish to return when they have reached retirement age as defined in Article 2 (1) (a) or are permanently incapacitated for work.

Article 9
Member States may not derogate from the provisions of this Directive save on grounds of public policy, public security or public health.

Annex 5.17.

85/368/EEC: Council Decision of 16 July 1985 on the **comparability of vocational training qualifications** between the Member States of the European Community
Official Journal L 199 , 31/07/1985 p. 0056 - 0059

MAIN PROVISIONS

Article 1
The aim of enabling workers to make better use of their qualifications, in particular for the purposes of obtaining suitable employment in another Member State, shall require, for features of job descriptions mutually agreed by the Member States on behalf of workers, within the meaning of Article 128 of the Treaty, expedited common action by the Member States and the Commission to establish the comparability of vocational training qualifications in the Community and improved information on the subject.

Article 2
1. The Commission, in close cooperation with the Member States, shall undertake work to fulfil the aims set out in Article 1 on the comparability of vocational training qualifications between the various Member States, in respect of specific occupations or groups of occupations.
2. The work may use as a reference the structure of training levels drawn up by the Commission with the help of the Advisory Committee for Vocational Training.
The text of the said structure is attached to this Decision for information purposes.
3. The work referred to in paragraph 2 shall first and foremost concentrate on the occupational qualifications of skilled workers in mutually agreed occupations or groups of occupations.
4. The scope of this Decision may subsequently be extended to permit work to be undertaken, on a proposal from the Commission, at other levels of training.
5. The SEDOC register, used in connection with the European system for the international clearing of vacancies and applications for employment, shall, whenever possible, be used as the common frame of reference for vocational classifications.

Article 3
The following working procedure shall be employed by the Commission in establishing the comparability of vocational training qualifications in close cooperation with the Member States and the organizations of workers and employers at Community level:
- selection of the relevant occupations or groups of occupations on a proposal from the Member States or the competent employer or worker organizations at Community level;
- drawing up mutually agreed Community job descriptions for the occupations or groups of occupations referred to in the first indent;
- matching the vocational training qualifications recognized in the various Member States with the job descriptions referred to in the second indent;
- establishing tables incorporating information on:
(a) the SEDOC and national classification codes;
(b) the level of vocational training;
(c) for each Member State, the vocational title and corresponding vocational training qualifications;
(d) the organizations and institutions responsible for dispensing vocational training;
(e) the authorities and organizations competent to issue or to validate diplomas, certificates, or other documents certifying that vocational training has been acquired;
- publication of the mutually agreed Community job descriptions and the comparative tables in the Official Journal of the European Communities;
- establishment, within the meaning of Article 4 (3), of a standard information sheet for each occupation or group of occupations, to be published in the Official Journal of the European Communities;
- dissemination of information on the established comparabilities to all appropriate bodies at national, regional and local levels, as well as throughout the occupational sectors concerned.
This action could be supported by the creation of a Community-wide data base, if experience shows the need for such a base.

Article 4
1. Each Member State shall designate a coordination body, based wherever possible on existing structures, which shall be responsible for ensuring - in close collaboration with the social partners and the occupational sectors concerned - the proper dissemination of information to all interested bodies. The Member States shall

also designate the body responsible for contacts with the coordination bodies in other Member States and with the Commission. 2. The coordination bodies of the Member States shall be competent to establish appropriate arrangements with regard to vocational training information for their competent national, regional or local bodies as well as for their own nationals wishing to work in other Member States and for workers who are nationals of other Member States, on established cases of comparable vocational qualifications.
3. The bodies referred to in paragraph 2 may supply on request in all Member States an information sheet drawn up in accordance with the model provided for in the sixth indent of Article 3, which the worker may present to the employer together with his national certificate.
4. The Commission is to continue studying the introduction of the European vocational training pass advocated by the Committee for a People's Europe in paragraph 21 of its report of 29 and 30 March 1985.
5. The Commission shall give the bodies referred to in paragraph 2, on request, all necessary assistance and advice concerning the preparation and setting up of the arrangements provided for in paragraph 2, including the adaptation and checking of the relevant technical documents.

Article 5
The Commission shall, in close liaison with the national coordination bodies designated by the Member States,
- review and update at appropriate, regular intervals, in close cooperation with the Member States and the organizations of workers and employers at Community level, the mutually agreed Community job descriptions and the comparative tables relating to the comparability of vocational training qualifications,
- where necessary, formulate proposals for a more efficient operation of the system including other measures likely to improve the situation as regards the comparability of vocational qualification certificates,
- where necessary, assist in the case of technical difficulties encountered by the national authorities or specialized bodies concerned.

Article 6
Each Member State shall submit to the Commission, for the first time two years after adoption of this Decision, and therefore every four years, a national report on the implementation of this Decision and the results obtained. The Commission shall, at appropriate intervals, submit a report on its own work and on the application of this Decision in the Member States.

Article 7
This Decision is addressed to the Member States and the Commission.

Done at Brussels, 16 July 1985.
For the Council
The President
M. FISCHBACH
(1) OJ No 63, 20. 4. 1963, p. 1338/63.
(2) OJ No C 77, 19. 3. 1984, p. 11.
(3) OJ No C 35, 9. 2. 1984, p. 12.
(4) OJ No C 98, 20. 8. 1974, p. 1.
(5) OJ No C 193, 20. 7. 1983, p. 2.

ANNEX
Training-level structure referred to in Article 2 (2)

LEVEL 1
Training providing access to this level: compulsory education and professional initiation
This professional initiation is acquired at an educational establishment, in an out-of-school training programme, or at the undertaking. The volume of theoretical knowledge and practical capabilities involved is very limited. This form of training must primarily enable the holder to perform relatively simple work and may be fairly quickly acquired.

LEVEL 2
Training providing access to this level: compulsory education and vocational training (including, in particular, apprenticeships)
This level corresponds to a level where the holder is fully qualified to engage in a specific activity, with the capacity to use the instruments and techniques relating thereto.
This activity involves chiefly the performance of work which may be independent within the limits of the relevant techniques.

LEVEL 3
Training providing access to this level: compulsory education and/or vocational training and additional technical training or technical educational training or other secondary-level training
This form of training involves a greater fund of theoretical knowledge than level 2. Activity involves chiefly technical work which can be performed independently and/or entail executive and coordination duties.

LEVEL 4
Training providing access to this level: secondary training (general or vocational) and post-secondary technical training
This form of training involves high-level technical training acquired at or outside educational establishments. The resultant qualification covers a higher level of knowledge and of capabilities. It does not generally require mastery of the scientific bases of the various areas concerned. Such capabilities and knowledge make it possible in a generally autonomous or in an independent way to assume design and/or management and/or administrative responsibilities.

LEVEL 5
Training providing access to this level: secondary training (general or vocational) and complete higher training
This form of training generally leads to an autonomously pursued vocational activity - as an employee or as self-employed person - entailing a mastery of the scientific bases of the occupation. The qualifications required for engaging in a vocational activity may be integrated at these various levels.

Annex 5.18.

Directive 98/5/EC of the European Parliament and of the Council of 16 February 1998 to **facilitate practice of the profession of lawyer** on a permanent basis in a Member State other than that in which the qualification was obtained
Official Journal L 077 , 14/03/1998 P. 0036 - 0043

MAIN PROVISIONS

Article 1
Object, scope and definitions
1. The purpose of this Directive is to facilitate practice of the profession of lawyer on a permanent basis in a self-employed or salaried capacity in a Member State other than that in which the professional qualification was obtained.
2. For the purposes of this Directive:
(a) 'lawyer` means any person who is a national of a Member State and who is authorised to pursue his professional activities.
(b) 'home Member State` means the Member State in which a lawyer acquired the right to use one of the professional titles referred to in (a) before practising the profession of lawyer in another Member State;
(c) 'host Member State` means the Member State in which a lawyer practises pursuant to this Directive;
(d) 'home-country professional title` means the professional title used in the Member State in which a lawyer acquired the right to use that title before practising the profession of lawyer in the host Member State;
(e) 'grouping` means any entity, with or without legal personality, formed under the law of a Member State, within which lawyers pursue their professional activities jointly under a joint name;
(f) 'relevant professional title` or 'relevant profession` means the professional title or profession governed by the competent authority with whom a lawyer has registered under Article 3, and 'competent authority` means that authority.
3. This Directive shall apply both to lawyers practising in a self-employed capacity and to lawyers practising in a salarial capacity in the home Member State and, subject to Article 8, in the host Member State.
4. Practice of the profession of lawyer within the meaning of this Directive shall not include the provision of services, which is covered by Directive 77/249/EEC.

Article 2
Right to practise under the home-country professional title
Any lawyer shall be entitled to pursue on a permanent basis, in any other Member State under his home-country professional title, the activities specified in Article 5.
Integration into the profession of lawyer in the host Member State shall be subject to Article 10.

Article 3
Registration with the competent authority
1. A lawyer who wishes to practise in a Member State other than that in which he obtained his professional qualification shall register with the competent authority in that State.
2. The competent authority in the host Member State shall register the lawyer upon presentation of a certificate attesting to his registration with the competent authority in the home Member State. It may require that, when presented by the competent authority of the home Member State, the certificate be not more than three months old. It shall inform the competent authority in the home Member State of the registration.
3. For the purpose of applying paragraph 1:
- in the United Kingdom and Ireland, lawyers practising under a professional title other than those used in the United Kingdom or Ireland shall register either with the authority responsible for the profession of barrister or advocate or with the authority responsible for the profession of solicitor,
- in the United Kingdom, the authority responsible for a barrister from Ireland shall be that responsible for the profession of barrister or advocate, and the authority responsible for a solicitor from Ireland shall be that responsible for the profession of solicitor,
- in Ireland, the authority responsible for a barrister or an advocate from the United Kingdom shall be that responsible for the profession of barrister, and the authority responsible for a solicitor from the United Kingdom shall be that responsible for the profession of solicitor.
4. Where the relevant competent authority in a host Member State publishes the names of lawyers registered with it, it shall also publish the names of lawyers registered pursuant to this Directive.

Article 4
Practice under the home-country professional title
1. A lawyer practising in a host Member State under his home-country professional title shall do so under that title, which must be expressed in the official language or one of the official languages of his home Member State, in an intelligible manner and in such a way as to avoid confusion with the professional title of the host Member State.
2. For the purpose of applying paragraph 1, a host Member State may require a lawyer practising under his home-country professional title to indicate the professional body of which he is a member in his home Member State or the judicial authority before which he is entitled to practise pursuant to the laws of his home Member State. A host Member State may also require a lawyer practising under his home-country professional title to include a reference to his registration with the competent authority in that State.

Article 5
Area of activity
1. Subject to paragraphs 2 and 3, a lawyer practising under his home-country professional title carries on the same professional activities as a lawyer practising under the relevant professional title used in the host Member State and may, inter alia, give advice on the law of his home Member State, on Community law, on international law and on the law of the host Member State. He shall in any event comply with the rules of procedure applicable in the national courts.
2. Member States which authorise in their territory a prescribed category of lawyers to prepare deeds for obtaining title to administer estates of deceased persons and for creating or transferring interests in land which, in other Member States, are reserved for professions other than that of lawyer may exclude from such activities lawyers practising under a home-country professional title conferred in one of the latter Member States.
3. For the pursuit of activities relating to the representation or defence of a client in legal proceedings and insofar as the law of the host Member State reserves such activities to lawyers practising under the professional title of that State, the latter may require lawyers practising under their home-country professional titles to work in conjunction with a lawyer who practises before the judicial authority in question and who would, where necessary, be answerable to that authority or with an 'avoué` practising before it.
Nevertheless, in order to ensure the smooth operation of the justice system, Member States may lay down specific rules for access to supreme courts, such as the use of specialist lawyers.

Article 6
Rules of professional conduct applicable
1. Irrespective of the rules of professional conduct to which he is subject in his home Member State, a lawyer practising under his home-country professional title shall be subject to the same rules of professional conduct as lawyers practising under the relevant professional title of the host Member State in respect of all the activities he pursues in its territory.
2. Lawyers practising under their home-country professional titles shall be granted appropriate representation in the professional associations of the host Member State. Such representation shall involve at least the right to vote in elections to those associations' governing bodies.
3. The host Member State may require a lawyer practising under his home-country professional title either to take out professional indemnity insurance or to become a member of a professional guarantee fund in accordance with the rules which that State lays down for professional activities pursued in its territory. Nevertheless, a lawyer practising under his home-country professional title shall be exempted from that requirement if he can prove that he is covered by insurance taken out or a guarantee provided in accordance with the rules of his home Member State, insofar as such insurance or guarantee is equivalent in terms of the conditions and extent of cover. Where the equivalence is only partial, the competent authority in the host Member State may require that additional insurance or an additional guarantee be contracted to cover the elements which are not already covered by the insurance or guarantee contracted in accordance with the rules of the home Member State.

Article 7
Disciplinary proceedings
1. In the event of failure by a lawyer practising under his home-country professional title to fulfil the obligations in force in the host Member State, the rules of procedure, penalties and remedies provided for in the host Member State shall apply.
2. Before initiating disciplinary proceedings against a lawyer practising under his home-country professional title, the competent authority in the host Member State shall inform the competent authority in the home Member State as soon as possible, furnishing it with all the relevant details.
The first subparagraph shall apply mutatis mutandis where disciplinary proceedings are initiated by the

competent authority of the home Member State, which shall inform the competent authority of the host Member State(s) accordingly.

3. Without prejudice to the decision-making power of the competent authority in the host Member State, that authority shall cooperate throughout the disciplinary proceedings with the competent authority in the home Member State. In particular, the host Member State shall take the measures necessary to ensure that the competent authority in the home Member State can make submissions to the bodies responsible for hearing any appeal.

4. The competent authority in the home Member State shall decide what action to take, under its own procedural and substantive rules, in the light of a decision of the competent authority in the host Member State concerning a lawyer practising under his home-country professional title.

5. Although it is not a prerequisite for the decision of the competent authority in the host Member State, the temporary or permanent withdrawal by the competent authority in the home Member State of the authorisation to practise the profession shall automatically lead to the lawyer concerned being temporarily or permanently prohibited from practising under his home-country professional title in the host Member State.

Article 8

Salaried practice

A lawyer registered in a host Member State under his home-country professional title may practise as a salaried lawyer in the employ of another lawyer, an association or firm of lawyers, or a public or private enterprise to the extent that the host Member State so permits for lawyers registered under the professional title used in that State.

Article 9

Statement of reasons and remedies

Decisions not to effect the registration referred to in Article 3 or to cancel such registration and decisions imposing disciplinary measures shall state the reasons on which they are based.

A remedy shall be available against such decisions before a court or tribunal in accordance with the provisions of domestic law.

Article 10

Like treatment as a lawyer of the host Member State

1. A lawyer practising under his home-country professional title who has effectively and regularly pursued for a period of at least three years an activity in the host Member State in the law of that State including Community law shall, with a view to gaining admission to the profession of lawyer in the host Member State, be exempted from the conditions set out in Article 4(1)(b) of Directive 89/48/EEC, 'Effective and regular pursuit` means actual exercise of the activity without any interruption other than that resulting from the events of everyday life.

It shall be for the lawyer concerned to furnish the competent authority in the host Member State with proof of such effective regular pursuit for a period of at least three years of an activity in the law of the host Member State. To that end:

(a) the lawyer shall provide the competent authority in the host Member State with any relevant information and documentation, notably on the number of matters he has dealt with and their nature;

(b) the competent authority of the host Member State may verify the effective and regular nature of the activity pursued and may, if need be, request the lawyer to provide, orally or in writing, clarification of or further details on the information and documentation mentioned in point (a).

Reasons shall be given for a decision by the competent authority in the host Member State not to grant an exemption where proof is not provided that the requirements laid down in the first subparagraph have been fulfilled, and the decision shall be subject to appeal under domestic law.

2. A lawyer practising under his home-country professional title in a host Member State may, at any time, apply to have his diploma recognised in accordance with Directive 89/48/EEC with a view to gaining admission to the profession of lawyer in the host Member State and practising it under the professional title corresponding to the profession in that Member State.

3. A lawyer practising under his home-country professional title who has effectively and regularly pursued a professional activity in the host Member State for a period of at least three years but for a lesser period in the law of that Member State may obtain from the competent authority of that State admission to the profession of lawyer in the host Member State and the right to practise it under the professional title corresponding to the profession in that Member State, without having to meet the conditions referred to in Article 4(1)(b) of Directive 89/48/EEC, under the conditions and in accordance with the procedures set out below:

(a) The competent authority of the host Member State shall take into account the effective and regular professional activity pursued during the abovementioned period and any knowledge and professional experience of the law of the host Member State, and any attendance at lectures or seminars on the law of the host Member State, including the rules regulating professional practice and conduct.

(b) The lawyer shall provide the competent authority of the host Member State with any relevant information and documentation, in particular on the matters he has dealt with. Assessment of the lawyer's effective and regular activity in the host Member State and assessment of his capacity to continue the activity he has pursued there shall be carried out by means of an interview with the competent authority of the host Member State in order to verify the regular and effective nature of the activity pursued.
Reasons shall be given for a decision by the competent authority in the host Member State not to grant authorisation where proof is not provided that the requirements laid down in the first subparagraph have been fulfilled, and the decision shall be subject to appeal under domestic law.
4. The competent authority of the host Member State may, by reasoned decision subject to appeal under domestic law, refuse to allow the lawyer the benefit of the provisions of this Article if it considers that this would be against public policy, in a particular because of disciplinary proceedings, complaints or incidents of any kind.
5. The representatives of the competent authority entrusted with consideration of the application shall preserve the confidentiality of any information received.
6. A lawyer who gains admission to the profession of lawyer in the host Member State in accordance with paragraphs 1, 2 and 3 shall be entitled to use his home-country professional title, expressed in the official language or one of the official languages of his home Member State, alongside the professional title corresponding to the profession of lawyer in the host Member State.

Article 11
Joint practice
Where joint practise is authorised in respect of lawyers carrying on their activities under the relevant professional title in the host Member State, the following provisions shall apply in respect of lawyers wishing to carry on activities under that title or registering with the competent authority:
(1) One or more lawyers who belong to the same grouping in their home Member State and who practise under their home-country professional title in a host Member State may pursue their professional activities in a branch or agency of their grouping in the host Member State. However, where the fundamental rules governing that grouping in the home Member State are incompatible with the fundamental rules laid down by law, regulation or administrative action in the host Member State, the latter rules shall prevail insofar as compliance therewith is justified by the public interest in protecting clients and third parties.
(2) Each Member State shall afford two or more lawyers from the same grouping or the same home Member State who practise in its territory under their home-country professional titles access to a form of joint practice. If the host Member State gives its lawyers a choice between several forms of joint practice, those same forms shall also be made available to the aforementioned lawyers. The manner in which such lawyers practise jointly in the host Member State shall be governed by the laws, regulations and administrative provisions of that State.
(3) The host Member State shall take the measures necessary to permit joint practice also between:
(a) several lawyers from different Member States practising under their home-country professional titles;
(b) one or more lawyers covered by point (a) and one or more lawyers from the host Member State.
The manner in which such lawyers practice jointly in the host Member State shall be governed by the laws, regulations and administrative provisions of that State.
(4) A lawyer who wishes to practise under his home-country professional title shall inform the competent authority in the host Member State of the fact that he is a member of a grouping in his home Member State and furnish any relevant information on that grouping.
(5) Notwithstanding points 1 to 4, a host Member State, insofar as it prohibits lawyers practising under its own relevant professional title from practising the profession of lawyer within a grouping in which some persons are not members of the profession, may refuse to allow a lawyer registered under his home-country professional title to practice in its territory in his capacity as a member of his grouping. The grouping is deemed to include persons who are not members of the profession if
- the capital of the grouping is held entirely or partly, or
- the name under which it practises is used, or
- the decision-making power in that grouping is exercised, de facto or de jure,
by persons who do not have the status of lawyer within the meaning of Article 1(2).
Where the fundamental rules governing a grouping of lawyers in the home Member State are incompatible with the rules in force in the host Member State or with the provisions of the first subparagraph, the host Member State may oppose the opening of a branch or agency within its territory without the restrictions laid down in point (1).

Article 12
Name of the grouping
Whatever the manner in which lawyers practise under their home-country professional titles in the host Member State, they may employ the name of any grouping to which they belong in their home Member State.
The host Member State may require that, in addition to the name referred to in the first subparagraph, mention be made of the legal form of the grouping in the home Member State and/or of the names of any members of the grouping practising in the host Member State.

Article 13
Cooperation between the competent authorities in the home and host Member States and confidentiality
In order to facilitate the application of this Directive and to prevent its provisions from being misapplied for the sole purpose of circumventing the rules applicable in the host Member State, the competent authority in the host Member State and the competent authority in the home Member State shall collaborate closely and afford each other mutual assistance.
They shall preserve the confidentiality of the information they exchange.

Article 14
Designation of the competent authorities
Member States shall designate the competent authorities empowered to receive the applications and to take the decisions referred to in this Directive by 14 March 2000. They shall communicate this information to the other Member States and to the Commission.

Article 15
Report by the Commission
Ten years at the latest from the entry into force of this Directive, the Commission shall report to the European Parliament and to the Council on progress in the implementation of the Directive.
After having held all the necessary consultations, it shall on that occasion present its conclusions and any amendments which could be made to the existing system.

Article 16
Implementation
1. Member States shall bring into force the laws, regulations and administrative provisions necessary to comply with this Directive by 14 March 2000. They shall forthwith inform the Commission thereof.
When Member States adopt these measures, they shall contain a reference to this Directive or shall be accompanied by such reference on the occasion of their official publication. The methods of making such reference shall be adopted by Member States.
2. Member States shall communicate to the Commission the texts of the main provisions of domestic law which they adopt in the field covered by this Directive.

Annex 5.19.

Council Directive 89/48/EEC of 21 December 1988 on a **general system for the recognition of higher-education diplomas** awarded on completion of professional education and training of at least three years' duration
Official Journal L 019 , 24/01/1989 P. 0016 - 0023

MAIN PROVISIONS

Article 1
For the purposes of this Directive the following definitions shall apply:
(a) diploma: any diploma, certificate or other evidence of formal qualifications or any set of such diplomas, certificates or other evidence:
- which has been awarded by a competent authority in a Member State, designated in accordance with its own laws, regulations or administrative provisions;
- which shows that the holder has successfully completed a post-secondary course of at least three years' duration, or of an equivalent duration part-time, at a university or establishment of higher education or another establishment of similar level and, where appropriate, that he has successfully completed the professional training required in addition to the post-secondary course, and
- which shows that the holder has the professional qualifications required for the taking up or pursuit of a regulated profession in that Member State,
provided that the education and training attested by the diploma, certificate or other evidence of formal qualifications were received mainly in the Community, or the holder thereof has three years' professional experience certified by the Member State which recognized a third-country diploma, certificate or other evidence of formal qualifications.
The following shall be treated in the same way as a diploma, within the meaning of the first subparagraph: any diploma, certificate or other evidence of formal qualifications or any set of such diplomas, certificates or other evidence awarded by a competent authority in a Member State if it is awarded on the successful completion of education and training received in the Community and recognized by a competent authority in that Member State as being of an equivalent level and if it confers the same rights in respect of the taking up and pursuit of a regulated profession in that Member State;
(b) host Member State: any Member State in which a national of a Member State applies to pursue a profession subject to regulation in that Member State, other than the State in which he obtained his diploma or first pursued the profession in question;
(c) a regulated profession: the regulated professional activity or range of activities which constitute this profession in a Member State;
(d) regulated professional activity: a professional activity, in so far as the taking up or pursuit of such activity or one of its modes of pursuit in a Member State is subject, directly or indirectly by virtue of laws, regulations or administrative provisions, to the possession of a diploma. The following in particular shall constitute a mode of pursuit of a regulated professional activity:
- pursuit of an activity under a professional title, in so far as the use of such a title is reserved to the holders of a diploma governed by laws, regulations or administrative provisions,
- pursuit of a professional activity relating to health, in so far as remuneration and/or reimbursement for such an activity is subject by virtue of national social security arrangements to the possession of a diploma.
Where the first subparagraph does not apply, a professional activity shall be deemed to be a regulated professional activity if it is pursued by the members of an association or organization the purpose of which is, in particular, to promote and maintain a high standard in the professional field concerned and which, to achieve that purpose, is recognized in a special form by a Member State and:
- awards a diploma to its members,
- ensures that its members respect the rules of professional conduct which it prescribes, and
- confers on them the right to use a title or designatory letters, or to benefit from a status corresponding to that diploma.
A non-exhaustive list of associations or organizations which, when this Directive is adopted, satisfy the conditions of the second subparagraph is contained in the Annex. Whenever a Member State grants the recognition referred to in the second subparagraph to an association or organization, it shall inform the Commission thereof, which shall publish this information in the Official Journal of the European Communities.
(e) professional experience: the actual and lawful pursuit of the profession concerned in a Member State;
(f) adaptation period: the pursuit of a regulated profession in the host Member State under the responsibility of a qualified member of that profession, such period of supervised practice possibly being accompanied by further

training. This period of supervised practice shall be the subject of an assessment. The detailed rules governing the adaptation period and its assessment as well as the status of a migrant person under supervision shall be laid down by the competent authority in the host Member States;
(g) aptitude test: a test limited to the professional knowledge of the applicant, made by the competent authorities of the host Member State with the aim of assessing the ability of the applicant to pursue a regulated profession in that Member State.
In order to permit this test to be carried out, the competent authorities shall draw up a list of subjects which, on the basis of a comparison of the education and training required in the Member State and that received by the applicant, are not covered by the diploma or other evidence of formal qualifications possessed by the applicant. The aptitude test must take account of the fact that the applicant is a qualified professional in the Member State of origin or the Member State from which he comes. It shall cover subjects to be selected from those on the list, knowledge of which is essential in order to be able to exercise the profession in the host Member State. The test may also include knowledge of the professional rules applicable to the activities in question in the host Member State. The detailed application of the aptitude test shall be determined by the competent authorities of that State with due regard to the rules of Community law.
The status, in the host Member State, of the applicant who wishes to prepare himself for the aptitude test in that State shall be determined by the competent authorities in that State.

Article 2
This Directive shall apply to any national of a Member State wishing to pursue a regulated profession in a host Member State in a self-employed capacity or as an employed person.
This Directive shall not apply to professions which are the subject of a separate Directive establishing arrangements for the mutual recognition of diplomas by Member States.
(1) OJ No C 217, 28. 8. 1985, p. 3, and
OJ No C 143, 10. 6. 1986, p. 7.
(2) OJ No C 345, 31. 12. 1985, p. 80, and
OJ No C 309, 5. 12. 1988.
(3) OJ No C 75, 3. 4. 1986, p. 5.

Article 3
Where, in a host Member State, the taking up or pursuit of a regulated profession is subject to possession of a diploma, the competent authority may not, on the grounds of inadequate qualifications, refuse to authorize a national of a Member State to take up or pursue that profession on the same conditions as apply to its own nationals:
(a) if the applicant holds the diploma required in another Member State for the taking up or pursuit of the profession in question in its territory, such diploma having been awarded in a Member State; or
(b) if the applicant has pursued the profession in question full-time for two years during the previous ten years in another Member State which does not regulate that profession, within the meaning of Article 1 (c) and the first subparagraph of Article 1 (d), and possesses evidence of one or more formal qualifications:
- which have been awarded by a competent authority in a Member State, designated in accordance with the laws, regulations or administrative provisions of such State,
- which show that the holder has successfully completed a post-secondary course of at least three years' duration, or of an equivalent duration part-time, at a university or establishment of higher education or another establishment of similar level of a Member State and, where appropriate, that he has successfully completed the professional training required in addition to the post-secondary course and
- which have prepared the holder for the pursuit of his profession.
The following shall be trated in the same way as the evidence of formal qualifications referred to in the first subparagraph: any formal qualifications or any set of such formal qualifications awarded by a competent authority in a Member State if it is awarded on the successful completion of training received in the Community and is recognized by that Member State as being of an equivalent level, provided that the other Member States and the Commission have been notified of this recognition.

Article 4
1. Notwithstanding Article 3, the host Member State may also require the applicant:
(a) to provide evidence of professional experience, where the duration of the education and training adduced in support of his application, as laid down in Article 3 (a) and (b), is at least one year less than that required in the host Member State. In this event, the period of professional experience required:
- may not exceed twice the shortfall in duration of education and training where the shortfall relates to post-secondary studies and/or to a period of probationary practice carried out under the control of a supervising professional person and ending with an examination,

- may not exceed the shortfall where the shortfall relates to professional practice acquired with the assistance of a qualified member of the profession.
In the case of diplomas within the meaning of the last subparagraph of Article 1 (a), the duration of education and training recognized as being of an equivalent level shall be determined as for the education and training defined in the first subparagraph of Article 1 (a).
When applying these provisions, account must be taken of the professional experience referred to in Article 3 (b).
At all events, the professional experience required may not exceed four years;
(b) to complete an adaptation period not exceeding three years or take an aptitude test:
- where the matters covered by the education and training he has received as laid down in Article 3 (a) and (b), differ substantially from those covered by the diploma required in the host Member State, or
- where, in the case referred to in Article 3 (a), the profession regulated in the host Member State comprises one or more regulated professional activities which are not in the profession regulated in the Member State from which the applicant originates or comes and that difference corresponds to specific education and training required in the host Member State and covers matters which differ substantially from those covered by the diploma adduced by the applicant, or
- where, in the case referred to in Article 3 (b), the profession regulated in the host Member State comprises one or more regulated professional activities which are not in the profession pursued by the applicant in the Member State from which he originates or comes, and that difference corresponds to specific education and training required in the host Member State and covers matters which differ substantially from those covered by the evidence of formal qualifications adduced by the applicant.
Should the host Member State make use of this possibility, it must give the applicant the right to choose between an adaptation period and an aptitude test. By way of derogation from this principle, for professions whose practice requires precise knowledge of national law and in respect of which the provision of advice and/or assistance concerning national law is an essential and constant aspect of the professional activity, the host Member State may stipulate either an adaptation period or an aptitude test. Where the host Member State intends to introduce derogations for other professions as regards an applicant's right to choose, the procedure laid down in Article 10 shall apply.
2. However, the host Member State may not apply the provisions of paragraph 1 (a) and (b) cumulatively.

Article 5
Without prejudice to Articles 3 and 4, a host Member State may allow the applicant, with a view to improving his possibilities of adapting to the professional environment in that State, to undergo there, on the basis of equivalence, that part of his professional education and training represented by professional practice, acquired with the assistance of a qualified member of the profession, which he has not undergone in his Member State of origin or the Member State from which he has come.

Article 6
1. Where the competent authority of a host Member State requires of persons wishing to take up a regulated profession proof that they are of good character or repute or that they have not been declared bankrupt, or suspends or prohibits the pursuit of that profession in the event of serious professional misconduct or a criminal offence, that State shall accept as sufficient evidence, in respect of nationals of Member States wishing to pursue that profession in its territory, the production of documents issued by competent authorities in the Member State of origin or the Member State from which the foreign national comes showing that those requirements are met.
Where the competent authorities of the Member State of origin or of the Member State from which the foreign national comes do not issue the documents referred to in the first subparagraph, such documents shall be replaced by a declaration on oath - or, in States where there is no provision for declaration on oath, by a solemn declaration - made by the person concerned before a competent judicial or administrative authority or, where appropriate, a notary or qualified professional body of the Member State of origin or the Member State from which the person comes; such authority or notary shall issue a certificate attesting the authenticity of the declaration on oath or solemn declaration.
2. Where the competent authority of a host Member State requires of nationals of that Member State wishing to take up or pursue a regulated profession a certificate of physical or mental health, that authority shall accept as sufficient evidence in this respect the production of the document required in the Member State of origin or the Member State from which the foreign national comes.
Where the Member State of origin or the Member State from which the foreign national comes does not impose any requirements of this nature on those wishing to take up or pursue the profession in question, the host Member State shall accept from such nationals a certificate issued by a competent authority in that State corresponding to the certificates issued in the host Member State.
3. The competent authorities of host Member States may require that the documents and certificates referred to

in paragraphs 1 and 2 are presented no more than three months after their date of issue.
4. Where the competent authority of a host Member State requires nationals of that Member State wishing to take up or pursue a regulated profession to take an oath or make a solemn declaration and where the form of such oath or declaration cannot be used by nationals of other Member States, that authority shall ensure that an appropriate and equivalent form of oath or declaration is offered to the person concerned.

Article 7
1. The competent authorities of host Member States shall recognize the right of nationals of Member States who fulfil the conditions for the taking up and pursuit of a regulated profession in their territory to use the professional title of the host Member State corresponding to that profession.
2. The competent authorities of host Member States shall recognize the right of nationals of Member States who fulfil the conditions for the taking up and pursuit of a regulated profession in their territory to use their lawful academic title and, where appropriate, the abbreviation thereof deriving from their Member State of origin or the Member State from which they come, in the language of that State. Host Member State may require this title to be followed by the name and location of the establishment or examining board which awarded it.
3. Where a profession is regulated in the host Member State by an association or organization referred to in Article 1 (d), nationals of Member States shall only be entitled to use the professional title or designatory letters conferred by that organization or association on proof of membership.
Where the association or organization makes membership subject to certain qualification requirements, it may apply these to nationals of other Member States who are in possession of a diploma within the meaning of Article 1 (a) or a formal qualification within the meaning of Article 3 (b) only in accordance with this Directive, in particular Articles 3 and 4.

Article 8
1. The host Member State shall accept as proof that the conditions laid down in Articles 3 and 4 are satisfied the certificates and documents issued by the competent authorities in the Member States, which the person concerned shall submit in support of his application to pursue the profession concerned.
2. The procedure for examining an application to pursue a regulated profession shall be completed as soon as possible and the outcome communicated in a reasoned decision of the competent authority in the host Member State not later than four months after presentation of all the documents relating to the person concerned. A remedy shall be available against this decision, or the absence thereof, before a court or tribunal in accordance with the provisions of national law.

Article 9
1. Member States shall designate, within the period provided for in Article 12, the competent authorities empowered to receive the applications and take the decisions referred to in this Directive. They shall communicate this information to the other Member States and to the Commission.
2. Each Member State shall designate a person responsible for coordinating the activities of the authorities referred to in paragraph 1 and shall inform the other Member States and the Commission to that effect. His role shall be to promote uniform application of this Directive to all the professions concerned. A coordinating group shall be set up under the aegis of the Commission, composed of the coordinators appointed by each Member State or their deputies and chaired by a representative of the Commission.
The task of this group shall be:
- to facilitate the implementation of this Directive,
- to collect all useful information for its application in the Member States.
The group may be consulted by the Commission on any changes to the existing system that may contemplated.
3. Member States shall take measures to provide the necessary information on the recognition of diplomas within the framework of this Directive. They may be assisted in this task by the information centre on the academic recognition of diplomas and periods of study established by the Member States within the framework of the Resolution of the Council and the Ministers of Education meeting within the Council of 9 February 1976 (1), and, where appropriate, the relevant professional associations or organizations. The Commission shall take the necessary initiatives to ensure the development and coordination of the communication of the necessary information.

Article 10
1. If, pursuant to the third sentence of the second subparagraph of Article 4 (1) (b), a Member State proposes not to grant applicants the right to choose between an adaptation period and an aptitude test in respect of a profession within the meaning of this Directive, it shall immediately communicate to the Commission the corresponding draft provision. It shall at the same time notify the Commission of the grounds which make the enactment of such a provision necessary.

The Commission shall immediately notify the other Member States of any draft it has received; it may also consult the coordinating group referred to in Article 9 (2) of the draft.
2. Without prejudice to the possibility for the Commission and the other Member States of making comments on the draft, the Member State may adopt the provision only if the Commission has not taken a decision to the contrary within three months.
3. At the request of a Member State or the Commission, Member States shall communicate to them, without delay, the definitive text of a provision arising from the application of this Article.

Article 11
Following the expiry of the period provided for in Article 12, Member States shall communicate to the Commission, every two years, a report on the application of the system introduced.
In addition to general remarks, this report shall contain a statistical summary of the decisions taken and a description of the main problems arising from application of the Directive.

Article 12
Member States shall take the measures neccessary to comply with this Directive within two years of its notification (2). They shall forthwith inform the Commission thereof.
Member States shall communicate to the Commission the texts of the main provisions of national law which they adopt in the field governed by this Directive.

Article 13
Five years at the latest following the date specified in Article 12, the Commission shall report to the European Parliament and the Council on the state of application of the general system for the recognition of higher-education diplomas awarded on completion of professional education and training of at least three years' duration.
After conducting all necessary consultations, the Commission shall, on this occasion, present its conclusions as to any changes that need to be made to the system as it stands. At the same time the Commission shall, where appropriate, submit proposals for improvements in the present system in the interest of further facilitating the freedom of movement, right of establishment and freedom to provide services of the persons covered by this Directive.

Article 14
This Directive is addressed to the Member States.

Done at Brussels, 21 December 1988.
For the Council
The President
V. PAPANDREOU
(1) OJ No C 38, 19. 2. 1976, p. 1.
(2) This Directive was notified to Member States on 4 January 1989.

ANNEX
List of professional associations or organizations which satisfy the conditions of the second subparagraph of Article 1 (d)

IRELAND (1)
1. The Institute of Chartered Accountants in Ireland (2)
2. The Institute of Certified Public Accountants in Ireland (2)
3. The Association of Certified Accountants (2)
4. Institution of Engineers of Ireland
5. Irish Planning Institute

UNITED KINGDOM
1. Institute of Chartered Accountants in England and Wales
2. Institute of Chartered Accountants of Scotland
3. Institute of Chartered Accountants in Ireland
4. Chartered Association of Certified Accountants
5. Chartered Institute of Loss Adjusters
6. Chartered Institute of Management Accountants
7. Institute of Chartered Secretaries and Administrators

8. Chartered Insurance Institute
9. Institute of Actuaries
10. Faculty of Actuaries
11. Chartered Institute of Bankers
12. Institute of Bankers in Scotland
13. Royal Institution of Chartered Surveyors
14. Royal Town Planning Institute
15. Chartered Society of Physiotherapy
16. Royal Society of Chemistry
17. British Psychological Society
18. Library Association
19. Institute of Chartered Foresters
20. Chartered Institute of Building
21. Engineering Council
22. Institute of Energy
23. Institution of Structural Engineers
24. Institution of Civil Engineers
25. Institution of Mining Engineers
26. Institution of Mining and Metallurgy

(1) Irish nationals are also members of the following United Kingdom chartered bodies:
Institute of Chartered Accountants in England and Wales
Institute of Chartered Accountants of Scotland
Institute of Actuaries
Faculty of Actuaries
The Chartered Institute of Management Accountants
Institute of Chartered Secretaries and Administrators
Royal Town Planning Institute
Royal Institution of Chartered Surveyors
Chartered Institute of Building.

(2) For the purposes of the activity of auditing only.
STATEMENT BY THE COUNCIL AND THE COMMISSION
Re Article 9 (1)
'The Council and the Commission agree that professional bodies and higher-education establishments should be consulted or be involved in an appropriate way in the decision-making process.'.

Annex 5.20.

Council Directive 92/51/EEC of 18 June 1992 on a **second general system for the recognition of professional education and training** to supplement Directive 89/48/EEC
Official Journal L 209 , 24/07/1992 P. 0025 - 0045

MAIN PROVISIONS

CHAPTER I
Definitions

Article 1
For the purposes of this Directive, the following definitions shall apply:
(a) diploma: any evidence of education and training or any set of such evidence:
- which has been awarded by a competent authority in a Member State, designated in accordance with the laws, regulations or administrative provisions of that State,
- which shows that the holder has successfully completed:

(i) either a post-secondary course other than that referred to in the second indent of Article 1 (a) of Directive 89/48/EEC, of at least one year's duration or of equivalent duration on a part-time basis, one of the conditions of entry of which is, as a general rule, the successful completion of the secondary course required to obtain entry to university or higher education, as well as the professional training which may be required in addition to that post-secondary course;

(ii) or one of the education and training courses in Annex C, and

- which shows that the holder has the professional qualifications required for the taking up or pursuit of a regulated profession in that Member State,

provided that the education and training attested by this evidence was received mainly in the Community, or outside the Community at teaching establishments which provide education and training in accordance with the laws, regulations or administrative provisions of a Member State, or that the holder thereof has three years' professional experience certified by the Member State which recognized third-country evidence of education and training.

The following shall be treated in the same way as a diploma within the meaning of the first subparagraph: any evidence of education and training or any set of such evidence awarded by a competent authority in a Member State if it is awarded on the successful completion of education and training received in the Community and recognized by a competent authority in that member State as being of an equivalent level and if it confers the same rights in respect of the taking up and pursuit of a regulated profession in that Member State;

(b) certificate: any evidence of education and training or any set of such evidence:

- which has been awarded by a competent authority in a Member State, designated in accordance with the laws, regulations or administrative provisions of that State,

- which shows that the holder, after having followed a secondary course, has completed:

either a course of education or training other than courses referred to in point (a), provided at an educational or training establishment or on the job, or in combination at an educational or training establishment and on the job, and complemented, where appropriate, by the probationary or professional practice required in addition to this course,

or the probationary or professional practice required in addition to this secondary course, or

- which shows that the holder, after having followed a secondary course of a technical or vocational nature has completed, where necessary,

either a course of education or training as referred to in the previous indent, or the probationary or professional practice required in addition to this secondary course of a technical or vocational nature and

- which shows that the holder has the professional qualifications required for the taking up or pursuit of a regulated profession in that Member State,

provided that the education and training attested by this evidence was received mainly in the Community, or outside the Community at teaching establishments which provide education and training in accordance with the laws, regulations or administrative provisions of a Member State, or that the holder thereof has two years' professional experience certified by the Member State which recognized third-country evidence of education and training.

The following shall be treated in the same was as a certificate, within the meaning of the first subparagraph: any evidence of education and training or any set of such evidence awarded by a competent authority in a Member State if it is awarded on the successful completion of education and training received in the Community and recognized by a competent authority in a Member State as being of an equivalent level and if it confers the same rights in respect of the taking up and pursuit of a regulated profession in that Member State;

(c) attestation of competence: any evidence of qualifications:

- attesting to education and training not forming part of a set constituting a diploma within the meaning of Directive 89/48/EEC or a diploma or certificate within the meaning of this Directive, or

- awarded following an assessment of the personal qualities, aptitudes or knowledge which it is considered essential that the applicant have for the pursuit of a profession by an authority designated in accordance with the laws, regulations or administrative provisions of a Member State, without proof of prior education and training being required;

(d) host Member State: any Member State in which a national of a Member State applies to pursue a profession subject to regulation in that Member State, other than the State in which he obtained his evidence of education and training or attestation of competence or first pursued the profession in question;

(e) regulated profession: the regulated professional activity or range of activities which constitute this profession in a Member State;

(f) regulated professional activity: a professional activity the taking up or pursuit of which, or one of its modes of pursuit in a Member State, is subject, directly or indirectly, by virtue of laws, regulations or administrative provisions, to the possession of evidence of education and training or an attestation of competence. The following in particular shall constitute a mode of pursuit of a regulated professional activity:

- pursuit of an activity under a professional title, in so far as the use of such a title is reserved to the holders of evidence of education and training or an attestation of competence governed by laws, regulations or administrative provisions,

- pursuit of a professional activity relating to health, in so far as remuneration and/or reimbursement for such an activity is subject by virtue of national social security arrangements to the possession of evidence of education and training or an attestation of competence.

Where the first subparagraph does not apply, a professional activity shall be deemed to be a regulated professional activity if it is pursued by the members of an association or organization the purpose of which is, in particular, to promote and maintain a high standard in the professional field concerned and which, to achieve that purpose, is recognized in a special form by a Member State and:

- awards evidence of education and training to its members,

- ensures that its members respect the rules of professional conduct which it prescribes, and

- confers on them the right to use a professional title or designatory letters, or to benefit from a status corresponding to that education and training.

Whenever a Member State grants the recognition referred to in the second subparagraph to an association or organization which satisfies the conditions of that subparagraph, it shall inform the Commission thereof;

(g) regulated education and training: any education and training which:

- is specifically geared to the pursuit of a given profession, and

- comprises a course or courses complemented, where appropriate, by professional training or probationary or professional practice, the structure and level of which are determined by the laws, regulations or administrative provisions of that Member State or which are monitored or approved by the authority designated for that purpose;

(h) professional experience: the actual and lawful pursuit of the profession concerned in a Member State;

(i) adaptation period: the pursuit of a regulated profession in the host Member State under the responsibility of a qualified member of that profession, such period of supervised practice possibly being accompanied by further education and training. This period of supervised practice shall be the subject of an assessment. The detailed rules governing the adaptation period and its assessment shall be laid down by the competent authorities in the host Member State.

The status enjoyed in the host Member State by the person undergoing the period of supervised practice, in particular in the matter of right of residence as well as of obligations, social rights and benefits, allowances and remuneration, shall be established by the competent authorities in that Member State in accordance with applicable Community law;

(j) aptitude test: a test limited to the professional knowledge of the applicant, made by the competent authorities of the host Member State with the aim of assessing the ability of the applicant to pursue a regulated profession in that Member State.

In order to permit this test to be carried out, the competent authorities shall draw up a list of subjects which, on the basis of a comparison of the education and training required in the Member State and that received by the applicant, are not

covered by the evidence of education and training possessed by the applicant. These subjects may cover both theoretical knowledge and practical skills required for the pursuit of the profession.

This aptitude test must take account of the fact that the applicant is a qualified professional in the Member State of origin or the Member State from which he comes. It shall cover subjects to be selected from those on the list referred to in the second subparagraph, knowledge of which is essential to the pursuit of the profession in the host Member State. The test may also include knowledge of the professional rules applicable to the activities in question in the host Member State. The detailed application of the aptitude test shall be determined by the competent authorities of that State.

The status in the host Member State of the applicant who wishes to prepare himself for the aptitude test in that State shall be determined by the competent authorities in that State, in accordance with applicable Community law.

CHAPTER II
Scope

Article 2
This Directive shall apply to any national of a Member State wishing to pursue a regulated profession in a host Member State in a self-employed capacity or as an employed person.

This Directive shall apply to neither professions which are the subject of a specific Directive establishing arrangements for the mutual recognition of diplomas by Member States, nor activities covered by a Directive listed in Annex A.

The Directives listed in Annex B shall be made applicable to the pursuit as an employed person of the activities covered by those Directives.

CHAPTER III

System for recognition where a host Member State requires possession of a diploma within the meaning of this Directive or Directive 89/48/EEC

Article 3
Without prejudice to Directive 89/48/EEC, where, in a host Member State, the taking up or pursuit of a regulated profession is subject to possession of a diploma, as defined in this Directive or in Directive 89/48/EEC, the competent authority may not, on the grounds of inadequate qualifications, refuse to authorize a national of a Member State to take up or pursue that profession on the same conditions as those which apply to its own nationals:

(a) if the applicant holds the diploma, as defined in this Directive or in Directive 89/48/EEC, required in another Member State for the taking up or pursuit of the profession in question in its territory, such diploma having been awarded in a Member State; or

(b) if the applicant has pursued the profession in question full-time for two years, or for an equivalent period on a part-time basis, during the previous 10 years in another Member State which does not regulate that profession within the meaning of either Article 1 (e) and the first subparagraph of Article 1 (f) of this Directive or Article 1 (c) and the first subparagraph of Article 1 (d) of Directive 89/48/EEC, and possesses evidence of education and training which:

- has been awarded by a competent authority in a Member State, designated in accordance with the laws, regulations or administrative provisions of that State, and

- either shows that the holder has successfully completed a post-secondary course, other than that referred to in the second indent of Article 1 (a) of Directive 89/48/EEC, of at least one year's duration, or of equivalent duration on a part-time basis, one of the conditions of entry of which is, as a general rule, the successful completion of the secondary course required to obtain entry to university or higher education, as well as any professional training which is an integral part of that post-secondary course,

- or attests to regulated education and training referred to in Annex D, and

- has prepared the holder for the pursuit of his profession.

However, the two years' professional experience referred to above may not be required where the evidence of education and training held by the applicant and referred to in this point is awarded on completion of regulated education and training.

The following shall be treated in the same way as the evidence of education and training referred to in the first subparagraph of this point: any evidence of education and training or any set of such evidence awarded by a competent authority in a Member State if it is awarded on the completion of education and training received in the Community and is recognized by that Member State as being of an equivalent level, provided that the other Member States and the Commission have been notified of this recognition.

By way of derogation from the first subparagraph of this Article, the host Member State is not required to apply this Article where the taking up or pursuit of a regulated profession is subject in its country to possession of a diploma as defined in Directive 89/48/EEC, one of the conditions for the issue of which shall be the completion of a post-secondary course of more than four years duration.

Article 4
1. Notwithstanding Article 3, the host Member State may also require the applicant:

(a) to provide evidence of professional experience, where the duration of the education and training adduced in support of his application, as laid down in points (a) and (b) of the first subparagraph of Article 3, is at least one year less than that required in the host Member State. In this event, the period of professional experience required may not exceed:

- twice the shortfall in duration of education and training where the shortfall relates to a post-secondary course and/or to a period of probationary practice carried out under the control of a supervising professional person and ending with an examination,

- the shortfall where the shortfall relates to professional practice acquired with the assistance of a qualified member of the profession concerned.

In the case of diplomas within the meaning of the second subparagraph of Article 1 (a), the duration of education and training recognized as being of an equivalent level shall be determined as for the education and training defined in the first subparagraph of Article 1 (a).

When these provisions are applied, account must be taken of the professional experience referred to in point (b) of the first subparagraph of Article 3.

In any event, the professional experience required may not exceed four years.

Professional experience may not, however, be required of an applicant holding a diploma attesting to a post-secondary course as referred to in the second indent of Article 1 (a) or a diploma as defined in Article 1 (a) of Directive 89/48/EEC who wishes to pursue his profession in a host Member State which requires the possession of a diploma or evidence of education and training attesting to one of the courses of education and training as referred to in Annexes C and D;

(b) to complete an adaptation period not exceeding three years or take an aptitude test where:

- the theoretical and/or practical matters covered by the education and training which he has received as laid down in points (a) or (b) of the first subparagraph of Article 3 differ substantially from those covered by the diploma, as defined in this Directive or in Directive 89/48/EEC, required in the host Member State, or

- in the case referred to in point (a) of the first subparagraph of Article 3, the profession regulated in the host Member State comprises one or more regulated professional activities which do not form part of the profession regulated in the Member State from which the applicant originates or comes and that difference corresponds to specific education and training required in the host Member State and covers theoretical and/or practical matters which differ substantially from those covered by the diploma, as defined in this Directive or in Directive 89/48/EEC, adduced by the applicant, or

- in the case referred to in point (b) of the first subparagraph of Article 3, the profession regulated in the host Member State comprises one or more regulated professional activities which do not form part of the profession pursued by the applicant in the Member State from which he originates or comes, and that difference corresponds to specific education and training required in the host Member State and covers theoretical and/or practical matters which differ substantially from those covered by the evidence of education and training adduced by the applicant.

Should the host Member State make use of this possibility, it must give the applicant the right to choose between an adaptation period and an aptitude test. Where the host Member State, which requires a diploma as defined in Directive 89/48/EEC or in this Directive, intends to introduce derogations from an applicant's right to choose, the procedure laid down in Article 14 shall apply.

By way of derogation from the second subparagraph of this point, the host Member State may reserve the right to choose between the adaptation period and the aptitude test if

- a profession is involved the pursuit of which requires a precise knowledge of national law and in respect of which the provision of advice and/or assistance concerning national law is an essential and constant feature of the professional activity, or

- where the host Member State makes access to the profession or its pursuit subject to the possession of a diploma as defined in Directive 89/48/EEC, one of the conditions for the award of which is the completion of a post-secondary course of at least three years' duration or an equivalent period on a part-time basis and the applicant holds either a diploma as defined in this Directive or evidence of education and training within the meaning of point (b) of the first subparagraph of Article 3 and not covered by Article 3 (b) of Directive 89/48/EEC.

2. However, the host Member State may not apply the provisions of paragraph 1 (a) and (b) cumulatively.

CHAPTER IV

System for recognition where a host Member State requires possession of a diploma and the applicant is the holder of a certificate or has received corresponding education and training

Article 5
Where, in a host Member State, the taking up or pursuit of a regulated profession is subject to possession of a diploma, the competent authority may not, on the grounds of inadequate qualifications, refuse to authorize a national of a Member State to take up or pursue that profession on the same conditions as those which apply to its own nationals:

(a) if the applicant holds the certificate required in another Member State for the taking up or pursuit of the same profession in its territory, such certificate having been awarded in a Member State; or

(b) if the applicant has pursued the same profession full-time for two years during the previous 10 years in another Member State which does not regulate that profession, within the meaning of Article 1 (e) and the first subparagraph of Article 1 (f), and possesses evidence of education and training:

- which was been awarded by a competent authority in a Member State, designated in accordance with the laws, regulations or administrative provisions of that State, and

- which shows that the holder, after having followed a secondary course, has completed:

either a course of professional education or training other than courses referred to in point (a), provided at an educational or training establishment or on the job, or in combination at an educational or training establishment and on the job and complemented, where appropriate, by the probationary or professional practice which is an integral part of that training course,

or the probationary or professional practice which is an integral part of that secondary course, or

- which shows that the holder, after having followed a secondary course of a technical or vocational nature has completed, where necessary,

either a course of professional education or training as referred to in the previous indent,

or the period of probationary or professional practice which is an integral part of that secondary course of a technical or vocational nature and

- which has prepared the holder for the pursuit of this profession.

However, the two years' professional experience referred to above may not be required where the evidence of education and training held by the applicant and referred to in this point is awarded on completion of regulated education and training.

Nevertheless, the host Member State may require the applicant to undergo an adaptation period not exceeding three years or take an aptitude test. The host Member State must give the applicant the right to choose between an adaptation period and an aptitude test.

Where the host Member State intends to introduce derogations from an applicant's right to choose, the procedure laid down in Article 14 shall apply.

CHAPTER V

System for recognition where a host Member State requires possession of a certificate

Article 6
Where, in the host Member State, the taking up or pursuit of a regulated profession is subject to possession of a certificate, the competent authority may not, on the grounds of inadequate qualifications, refuse to authorize a national of a Member State to take up or pursue that profession on the same conditions as those which apply to its own nationals:

(a) if the applicant holds the diploma, as defined in this Directive or in Directive 89/48/EEC, or the certificate required in another Member State for the taking up or pursuit of the profession in question in its territory, such diploma having been awarded in a Member State; or

(b) if the applicant has pursued the profession in question full-time for two years or for an equivalent period on a part-time basis during the previous 10 years in another Member State which does not regulate that profession, within the meaning of Article 1 (e) and the first subparagraph of Article 1 (f), and possesses evidence of education and training:

- which has been awarded by a competent authority in a Member State, designated in accordance with the laws, regulations or administrative provisions of that State, and

- which shows that the holder has successfully completed a post-secondary course other than that referred to in the second indent of Article 1 (a) of Directive 89/48/EEC, of at least one year's duration or of equivalent duration on a part-time basis, one of the conditions of entry of which is, as a general rule, the completion of the secondary course required to obtain entry to university or higher education, as well as any professional training which is an integral part of that post-secondary course, or

- which shows that the holder, after having followed a secondary course, has completed:

either a course of education or training for a profession other than courses referred to in point (a), provided at an educational establishment or on the job, or in combination at an educational establishment and on the job and complemented, where appropriate, by the probationary or professional practice which is an integral part of that training course,

or the probationary or professional practice which is an integral part of that secondary course, or

- which shows that the holder, after having followed a secondary course of a technical or vocational nature has completed, where necessary,

either a course of education or training for a profession as referred to in the previous indent,

or the period of probationary or professional practice which is an integral part of that secondary course of a technical or vocational nature and

- which has prepared the holder for the pursuit of this profession.

However, the two years' professional experience referred to above may not be required where the evidence of education and training held by the applicant and referred to in this point is awarded on completion or regulated education and training.

(c) if the applicant who does not hold any diploma, certificate or other evidence of education and training within the meaning of Article 3 (b) or of point (b) of this Article has pursued the profession in question full-time for three consecutive years, or for an equivalent period on a part-time basis, during the previous 10 years in another Member State which does not regulate that profession within the meaning of Article 1 (e) and the first subparagraph of Article 1 (f).

The following shall be treated in the same way as the evidence of education and training referred to under (b) in the first subparagraph: any evidence of education and training or any set of such evidence awarded by a competent authority in a Member State if it is awarded on the completion of education and training received in the Community and is recognized by that Member State as being of an equivalent level, provided that the other Member States and the Commission have been notified of this recognition.

Article 7
Without prejudice to Article 6, a host Member State may also require the applicant to:

(a) complete an adaptation period not exceeding two years or to take an aptitude test when the education and training which he received in accordance with points (a) or (b) of the first subparagraph of Article 5 relates to theoretical or practical matters differing substantially from those covered by the certificate required in the host Member State, or where there are differences in the fields of activity characterized in the host Member State by specific education and training relating to theoretical or practical matters differing substantially from those covered by the applicant's evidence of formal qualifications.

Should the host Member State make use of this possibility, it must give the applicant the right to choose between an adaptation period and an aptitude test. Where the host Member State which requires a certificate intends to introduce derogations as regards an applicant's right to choose, the procedure laid down in Article 14 shall apply;

(b) undergo an adaptation period not exceeding two years or take an aptitude test where, in the instance referred to in point (c) of the first subparagraph of Article 6, he does not hold a diploma, certificate or other evidence of education and training. The host Member State may reserve the right to choose between an adaptation period and an aptitude test.

CHAPTER VI

Special systems for recognition of other qualifications

Article 8
Where, in the host Member State, the taking up or pursuit of a regulated profession is subject to possession of

an attestation of competence, the competent authority may not, on the grounds of inadequate qualifications, refuse to authorize a national of a Member State to take up or pursue that profession on the same conditions as those which apply to its own nationals:

(a) if the applicant holds the attestation of competence required in another Member State for the taking up or pursuit of the same profession in its territory, such attestation having been awarded in a Member State; or

(b) if the applicant provides proof of qualifications obtained in other Member States,

and giving guarantees, in particular in the matter of health, safety, environmental protection and consumer protection, equivalent to those required by the laws, regulations or administrative provisions of the host Member State.

If the applicant does not provide proof of such an attestation or of such qualifications the laws, regulations or administrative provisions of the host Member State shall apply.

Article 9
Where, in the host Member State, the taking up or pursuit of a regulated profession is subject only to possession of evidence of education attesting to general education at primary or secondary school level, the competent authority may not, on the grounds of inadequate qualifications, refuse to authorize a national of a Member State to take up or pursue that profession on the same conditions as those which apply to its own nationals if the applicant possesses formal qualifications of the corresponding level, awarded in another Member State.

This evidence of formal qualifications must have been awarded by a competent authority in that Member State, designated in accordance with its own laws, regulations or administrative provisions.

CHAPTER VII

Other measures to facilitate the effective exercise of the right of establishment, freedom to provide services and freedom of movement of employed persons

Article 10
1. Where the competent authority of the host Member State requires of persons wishing to take up a regulated profession proof that they are of good character or repute or that they have not been declared bankrupt, or suspends or prohibits the pursuit of that profession in the event of serious professional misconduct or a criminal offence, that State shall accept as sufficient evidence, in respect of nationals of Member States wishing to pursue that profession in its territory, the production of documents issued by competent authorities in the Member State of origin or the Member State from which the foreign national comes showing that those requirements are met. Where the competent authorities of the Member State of origin or of the Member State from which the foreign national comes do not issue the documents referred to in the first subparagraph, such documents shall be

replaced by a declaration on oath - or, in Member States where there is no provision for declaration on oath, by a solemn declaration - made by the person concerned before a competent judicial or administrative authority or, where appropriate, a notary or qualified professional body of the Member State of origin or the Member State from which the person comes; such authority or notary shall issue written confirmation attesting the authenticity of the declaration on oath or solemn declaration.

2. Where the competent authority of the host Member State requires of nationals of that Member State wishing to take up or pursue a regulated profession a statement of physical of mental health, that authority shall accept as sufficient evidence in this respect the production of the document required in the Member State of origin or the Member State from which the foreign national comes.

Where the Member State of origin or the Member State from which the foreign national comes does not impose any requirements of this nature on those wishing to take up or pursue the profession in question, the host Member State shall accept from such nationals a statement issued by a competent authority in that State corresponding to the statement issued in the host Member State.

3. The competent authority of the host Member State may require that the documents and statements referred to in paragraphs 1 and 2 are presented no more than three months after their date of issue.

4. Where the competent authority of the host Member State requires nationals of that Member State wishing to take up or pursue a regulated profession to take an oath or make solemn declaration and where the form of such oath or declaration cannot be used by nationals of other Member States, that authority shall ensure that an appropriate and equivalent form of oath or declaration is offered to the person concerned.

Article 11

1. The competent authorities of host Member States shall recognize the right of nationals of Member States who fulfil the conditions for the taking up and pursuit of a regulated profession in their territory to use the professional title of the host Member State corresponding to that profession.

2. The competent authority of the host Member State shall recognize the right of nationals of Member States who fulfil the conditions for the taking up and pursuit of a regulated profession in the territory to use their lawful academic title and, where appropriate, the abbreviation thereof deriving from their Member State of origin or the Member State from which they come, in the language of that State. The host Member State may require this title to be followed by the name and location of the establishment or examining board which awarded it.

3. Where a profession is regulated in the host Member State by an association or organization referred to in Article 1 (f), nationals of Member States shall be entitled to use the professional title or designatory letters conferred by that organization or association only on proof of membership.

Where the association or organization makes membership subject to certain qualification requirements, it may apply these to nationals of other Member States who are in possession of a diploma within the meaning of Article 1 (a), a certificate within the meaning of Article 1 (b) or evidence of education and training or qualification within the meaning of point (b) of the first subparagraph of Article 3, point (b) of the first subparagraph of Article 5 or Article 9 in accordance only with this Directive, in particular Articles 3, 4 and 5.

Article 12

1. The host Member State shall accept as means of proof that the conditions laid down in Articles 3 to 9 are satisfied the documents issued by the competent authorities in the Member States, which the person concerned shall submit in support of his application to pursue the profession concerned.

2. The procedure for examining an application to pursue a regulated profession shall be completed as soon as possible and the outcome communicated in a reasoned decision of the competent authority in the host Member State not later than four months after presentation of all the documents relating to the person concerned. A remedy shall be available against this decision or the absence thereof, before a court or tribunal in accordance with the provisions of national law.

CHAPTER VIII
Procedure for coordination

Article 13
1. Member States shall designate, within the period provided for in Article 17, the competent authorities empowered to receive the applications and take the decisions referred to in this Directive. They shall communicate this information to the other Member States and to the Commission.

2. Each Member State shall designate a person responsible for coordinating the activities of the authorities referred to in paragraph 1 and shall inform the other Member States and the Commission to that effect. His role shall be to promote uniform application of this Directive to all the professions concerned. This coordinator shall be a member of the coordinating group set up under the aegis of the Commission by Article 9 (2) of Directive 89/48/EEC.

The coordinating group set up under the aforementioned provision of Directive 89/48/EEC shall also be required to:
- facilitate the implementation of this Directive,
- collect all useful information for its application in the Member States, particularly information relating to the establishment of an indicative list of regulated professions and to the disparities between the qualifications awarded in the Member States with a view to assisting the competent authorities of the Member States in their task of assessing whether substantial differences exist.
The group may be consulted by the Commission on any changes to the existing system which may be contemplated.

3. The Member States shall take measures to provide the necessary information on the recognition of diplomas and certificates and on other conditions governing the taking up of the regulated professions within the framework of this Directive. To carry out this task they may call upon the existing information networks and, where appropriate, the relevant professional associations or organizations. The Commission shall take the necessary initiatives to ensure the development and coordination of the communication of the necessary information.

CHAPTER IX
Procedure for derogating from the right to choose between adaptation period and aptitude test

Article 14
1. If, pursuant to the second sentence of the second subparagraph of Article 4 (1) (b), the third subparagraph of Article 5, or the second sentence of the second subparagraph of Article 7 (a), a Member State proposes not to grant applicants the right to choose between an adaptation period and an aptitude test, it shall immediately communicate to the Commission the corresponding draft provision. It shall at the same time notify the Commission of the grounds which make the enactment of such a provision necessary.

The Commission shall immediately notify the other Member States of any draft which it has received; it may also consult the coordinating group referred to in Article 13 (2) on the draft.

2. Without prejudice to the possibility for the Commission and the other Member States to make comments on the draft, the Member State may adopt the provision only if the Commission has not taken a decision to the contrary within three months.

3. At the request of a Member State or the Commission, Member States shall communicate to them, without delay, the definitive text of any provision arising from the application of this Article.

CHAPTER X
Procedure for amending Annexes C and D

Article 15
1. The lists of education and training courses set out in Annexes C and D may be amended on the basis of a reasoned request from any Member State concerned to the Commission. All appropriate information and in particular the text of the relevant provisions of national law shall accompany the request. The Member State making the request shall also inform the other Member States.

2. The Commission shall examine the education and training course in question and those required in the other Member States. It shall verify in particular whether the qualification resulting from the course in question confers on the holder:

- a level of professional education or training of a comparably high level to that of the post-secondary course referred to in point (i) of the second indent of the first subparagraph of Article 1 (a),
- a similar level of responsibility and activity.

3. The Commission shall be assisted by a committee composed of the representatives of the Member States and chaired by the representative of the Commission.

4. The representative of the Commission shall submit to the committee a draft of the measures to be taken. The committee shall deliver its opinion on the draft within a time limit which the chairman may lay down according to the urgency of the matter. The opinion shall be delivered by the majority laid down in Article 148 (2) of the Treaty in the case of decisions which the Council is required to adopt on a proposal from the Commission. The votes of the representatives of the Member States within the committee shall be weighted in the manner set out in that Article. The chairman shall not vote.

5. The Commission shall adopt measures which shall apply immediately. However, if these measures are not in accordance with the opinion of the committee, they shall be communicated by the Commission to the Council forthwith. In that event, the Commission shall defer for a period of two months the application of the measures which it has decided.

6. The Council, acting by a qualified majority, may take a different decision within the time limit referred to in the previous paragraph.

7. The Commission shall inform the Member State concerned of the decision and shall, where appropriate, publish the amended list in the Official Journal of the European Communities.

Annex 5.21.

Directive 1999/42/EC of the European Parliament and of the Council of 7 June 1999 establishing a **mechanism for the recognition of qualifications** in respect of the professional activities covered by the Directives on liberalisation and transitional measures and supplementing the general systems for the recognition of qualifications *Official Journal L 201 , 31/07/1999 P. 0077 - 0093.*

MAIN PROVISIONS

TITLE I
Scope

Article 1
1. Member States shall adopt the measures defined in this Directive in respect of establishment or provision of services in their territories by natural persons and companies or firms covered by Title I of the General Programmes for the abolition of restrictions on freedom to supply services(7) and on freedom of establishment(8) (hereinafter called "beneficiaries") who wish to pursue the activities listed in Annex A.
2. This Directive shall apply to the activities listed in Annex A which nationals of Member States wish to pursue in a host Member State in a self-employed or employed capacity.

Article 2
Member States in which the taking-up or pursuit of any activity referred to in Annex A is subject to possession of certain qualifications shall ensure that any beneficiaries who apply therefor be provided, before they establish themselves or before they begin to provide services, with information as to the rules governing the occupation which they propose to pursue.

TITLE II
Recognition of formal qualifications awarded by another Member State

Article 3
1. Without prejudice to Article 4, a Member State may not, on the grounds of inadequate qualifications, refuse to permit a national of another Member State to take up or pursue any of the activities listed in Part One of Annex A on the same conditions as apply to its own nationals, without having first compared the knowledge and skills certified by the diplomas, certificates or other evidence of formal qualifications obtained by the beneficiary with a view to pursuing the same activity elsewhere in the Community with those required under its own national rules. Where the comparative examination shows that the knowledge and skills certified by a diploma, certificate or other evidence of formal qualifications awarded by another Member State correspond to those required by the national rules, the host Member State cannot refuse the holder the right to pursue the activity in question. Where, however, the comparative examination shows a substantial difference, the host Member State shall give the beneficiary the opportunity to demonstrate that he has acquired the knowledge and skills which were lacking. In this case, the host Member State shall give the applicant the right to choose between an adaptation period and an aptitude test by analogy with Directives 89/48/EEC and 92/51/EEC.
By way of derogation from this rule, the host Member State may require an adaptation period or an aptitude test if the migrant envisages exercising professional activities in a self-employed capacity or as a manager of an undertaking which are covered by Part One of Annex A and which require the knowledge and the application of the specific national rules in force, provided that knowledge and application of those rules are required by the competent authorities of the host Member State for access to such activities by its own nationals.
Member States shall endeavour to take into consideration the beneficiary's preference as between those alternatives.
2. Applications for recognition within the meaning of paragraph 1 shall be examined within the shortest possible time, and the competent authority in the host Member State shall state its reasons when giving a decision, which shall be taken no later than four months from the date on which the application and comprehensive supporting documentation were submitted. There shall be a right to appeal under national law against a decision or against the absence of such decision.

TITLE III
Recognition of professional qualifications on the basis of professional experience acquired in another Member State

Article 4
Where, in a Member State, the taking-up or pursuit of any activity listed in Annex A is subject to possession of general, commercial or professional knowledge and ability, that Member State shall accept as sufficient evidence of such knowledge and ability the fact that the activity in question has been pursued in another Member State. Where the activity is mentioned in Part One of Annex A, it must have been pursued:
1. in the case of the activities in List I:
(a) for six consecutive years in either a self-employed capacity or as a manager of an undertaking; or
(b) for three consecutive years in a self-employed capacity or as a manager of an undertaking where the beneficiary proves that he has received at least three years' prior training for the activity in question, attested by a nationally recognised certificate or regarded by a competent professional or trade body as fully satisfying its requirements; or
(c) for three consecutive years in a self-employed capacity where the beneficiary proves that he has pursued the activity in question for at least five years in an employed capacity; or
(d) for five consecutive years in a managerial capacity of which at least three years were spent in technical posts with responsibility for one or more departments of the undertaking where the beneficiary proves that he has received at least three years' prior training for the activity in question, attested by a nationally recognised certificate or regarded by a competent professional or trade body as fully satisfying its requirements.
In the cases referred to in (a) and (c), pursuit of the activity shall not have ceased more than ten years before the date on which the application under Article 8 is made;
2. in the case of the activities in List II:
(a) for six consecutive years in either a self-employed capacity or as a manager of an undertaking; or
(b) - for three consecutive years in a self-employed capacity or as a manager of an undertaking where the beneficiary proves that he has received at least three years' prior training for the activity in question, attested by a nationally recognised certificate or regarded by a competent professional or trade body as fully satisfying its requirements, or
- for four consecutive years in a self-employed capacity or as a manager of an undertaking where the beneficiary proves that he has received at least two years' prior training for the activity in question, attested by a nationally recognised certificate or regarded by a competent professional or trade body as fully satisfying its requirements, or
(c) for three consecutive years in a self-employed capacity or as a manager of an undertaking where the beneficiary proves that he has pursued the activity in question for at least five years in an employed capacity; or
(d) - for five consecutive years in an employed capacity where the beneficiary proves that he has received at least three years' prior training for the activity in question, attested by a nationally recognised certificate or regarded by a competent professional or trade body as fully satisfying its requirements, or
- for six consecutive years in an employed capacity where the beneficiary proves that he has received at least two years' prior training for the activity in question, attested by a nationally recognised certificate or regarded by a competent professional or trade body as fully satisfying its requirements.
In the cases referred to in (a) and (c), pursuit of the activity shall not have ceased more than ten years before the date on which the application provided for in Article 8 is made;
3. in the case of the activities in List III:
(a) for six consecutive years in either a self-employed capacity or as a manager of an undertaking; or
(b) for three consecutive years in a self-employed capacity or as a manager of an undertaking, where the beneficiary proves that he has received at least three years' prior training for the activity in question, attested by a nationally recognised certificate or regarded by a competent professional or trade body as fully satisfying its requirements; or
(c) for three consecutive years in a self-employed capacity where the beneficiary proves that he has pursued the activity in question for at least five years in an employed capacity.
In the cases referred to in (a) and (c), pursuit of the activity shall not have ceased more than ten years before the date on which the application provided for in Article 8 is made;
4. in the case of the activities in List IV:
(a) for five consecutive years in either a self-employed capacity or as a manager of an undertaking; or
(b) for two consecutive years in a self-employed capacity or as a manager of an undertaking where the beneficiary proves that he has received at least three years' prior training for the activity in question, attested by a nationally recognised certificate or regarded by a competent professional or trade body as fully satisfying its requirements; or
(c) for three consecutive years in a self-employed capacity or as a manager of an undertaking where the beneficiary proves that he has received at least two years' prior training for the activity in question, attested by a nationally recognised certificate or regarded by a competent professional or trade body as fully satisfying its requirements; or
(d) for two consecutive years in a self-employed capacity or as a manager of an undertaking where the

beneficiary proves that he has pursued the activity in question for at least three years in an employed capacity; or
(e) for three consecutive years in an employed capacity where the beneficiary proves that he has received at least two years' previous training for the activity in question, attested by a nationally recognised certificate or regarded by a competent professional or trade body as fully satisfying its requirements;
5. in the case of the activities in List V(a) and (b):
(a) for three years in a self-employed capacity or as a manager of an undertaking, provided that pursuit of the activity in question did not cease more than two years before the date on which the application provided for in Article 8 is made;
(b) for three years in a self-employed capacity or as a manager of an undertaking, provided that pursuit of the activity in question did not cease more than two years before the date on which the application provided for in Article 8 is made, unless the host Member State permits its nationals to interrupt their pursuit of that activity for a longer period; or
6. in the case of the activities in List VI:
(a) for three consecutive years in either a self-employed capacity or as a manager of an undertaking; or
(b) for two consecutive years in a self-employed capacity or as a manager of an undertaking where the beneficiary proves that he has received prior training for the activity in question, attested by a nationally recognised certificate or regarded by a competent professional or trade body as fully satisfying its requirements; or
(c) for two consecutive years in a self-employed capacity or as a manager of an undertaking where the beneficiary proves that he has pursued the activity in question for at least three years in an employed capacity; or
(d) for three consecutive years in an employed capacity where the beneficiary proves that he has received previous training for the activity in question, attested by a nationally recognised certificate or regarded by a competent professional or trade body as fully satisfying its requirements.
In the cases referred to in (a) and (c), pursuit of the activity shall not have ceased more than 10 years before the date on which the application provided for in Article 8 is made.

Article 5
Where a beneficiary holds a nationally recognised certificate obtained in a Member State attesting to knowledge of and ability in the activity in question equivalent to at least two or three years, as appropriate, of professional training, that certificate may be treated by the host Member State in the same way as a certificate attesting to training of the duration required by Article 4(1)(b) and (d), (2)(b) and (d), (3)(b) and (4)(b), (c) and (e).

Article 6
Where the duration of the training of the beneficiary is at least two years and less than three years, the requirements of Article 4 shall be satisfied if the duration of professional experience in a self-employed capacity or as a manager specified in Article 4(1)(b) and (d), (2)(b), first indent, (3)(b) and (4)(b) or in an employed capacity specified in Article 4(2)(d), first indent is extended in the same proportion to cover the difference in the duration of the training.

Article 7
A person shall be regarded as having pursued an activity as a manager of an undertaking within the meaning of Article 4 if he has pursued such an activity in an undertaking in the occupational field in question:
(a) as a manager of an undertaking or a manager of a branch of an undertaking; or
(b) as a deputy to the proprietor or the manager of an undertaking where that post involves responsibility equivalent to that of the proprietor or manager represented; or
(c) in a managerial post with duties of a commercial and/or technical nature and with responsibility for one or more departments of the undertaking.

Article 8
Proof that the conditions laid down in Article 4 are satisfied shall be established by a certificate concerning the nature and duration of the activity issued by the competent authority or body in the home Member State or in the Member State from where the beneficiary comes which the beneficiary must submit in support of his application for authorisation to pursue the activity or activities in question in the host Member State.

TITLE IV
Recognition of other professional qualifications obtained in another Member State

Article 9
1. Where a host Member State requires its own nationals wishing to take up any activity referred to in Article 1(2) to furnish proof of good character and proof that they are not and have not previously been declared bankrupt, or proof of either of these, it shall accept as sufficient evidence, in respect of nationals of other Member States, the production of an extract from the "judicial record" or, failing this, of an equivalent document issued by a competent judicial or administrative authority in the home Member State or in the Member State from where the beneficiary comes showing that these requirements are satisfied.
2. Where a host Member State imposes on its own nationals wishing to take up any activity referred to in Article 1(2) certain requirements as to good character and requires them to prove that they are not and have not previously been declared bankrupt and have not previously been the subject of professional or administrative disciplinary measures (for example, withdrawal of the right to hold certain offices, suspension from practice or striking-off), but proof cannot be obtained from the document referred to in paragraph 1 of this Article, it shall accept as sufficient evidence in respect of nationals of other Member States a certificate issued by a competent judicial or administrative authority in the home Member State or in the Member State from where the beneficiary comes attesting that the requirements are satisfied. Such certificate shall relate to the specific facts regarded as relevant by the host Member State.
3. Where the home Member State or the Member State from where the beneficiary comes does not issue the documents referred to in paragraphs 1 and 2, such documents shall be replaced by a declaration on oath - or, in those Member States where there is no provision for such declaration on oath, by a solemn declaration - made by the person concerned before a competent judicial or administrative authority or, where appropriate, a notary in that Member State; such authority or notary shall issue a certificate attesting the authenticity of the declaration on oath or solemn declaration. The declaration of no previous bankruptcy may also be made before a competent professional or trade body in that Member State.
4. Where a host Member State requires proof of financial standing, it shall regard certificates issued by banks in the home Member State or in the Member State from where the beneficiary comes as equivalent to those issued in its own territory.
5. Where a host Member State requires its own nationals wishing to take up or pursue any activity referred to in Article 1(2) to furnish proof that they are insured against the financial risks arising from their professional liability, it shall accept certificates issued by the insurance undertakings of other Member States as equivalent to those issued in its own territory. Such certificates shall state that the insurer has complied with the laws and regulations in force in the host Member State regarding the terms and extent of cover.
6. At the time of their production, the documents referred to in paragraphs 1, 2, 3 and 5 may not date from more than three months after their date of issue.

TITLE V
Procedural provisions

Article 10
1. Member States shall designate, within the period stipulated in Article 14, the authorities and bodies responsible for issuing the certificates referred to in Articles 8 and 9(1), (2) and (3) and shall communicate this information forthwith to the other Member States and to the Commission.
2. Each Member State may nominate a coordinator for the activities of the authorities and bodies referred to in paragraph 1 to the coordinating group set up under Article 9(2) of Directive 89/48/EEC. The tasks of the coordinating group shall also be as follows:
- facilitating the implementation of this Directive;
- collecting all useful information for its application in the Member States and especially gathering and comparing information on the different professional qualifications in the areas of activity falling within the scope of this Directive.

TITLE VI
Final provisions

Article 11
1. The Directives listed in Annex B are hereby repealed.
2. References to the repealed Directives shall be construed as references to this Directive.

Article 12
As from 1 January 2001, Member States shall communicate to the Commission every two years a report on the application of the system introduced.
In addition to general remarks, that report shall contain a statistical summary of the decisions taken and a description of the main problems arising from the application of this Directive.

Article 13
Not later than five years after the date referred to in Article 14, the Commission shall report to the European Parliament and the Council on the state of application of this Directive, and in particular of Article 5, in the Member States.
After undertaking all the necessary hearings, especially of the coordinators, the Commission shall submit its conclusions regarding any changes to the existing arrangement. If necessary, the Commission shall also submit proposals for improving the existing arrangements with the aim of facilitating free movement of persons, the right of establishment and freedom to provide services.

Article 14
1. Member States shall bring into force the laws, regulations and administrative provisions necessary to comply with this Directive before 31 July 2001. They shall immediately inform the Commission thereof.
When Member States adopt these measures, they shall contain a reference to this Directive or shall be accompanied by such reference on the occasion of their official publication. The methods of making such a reference shall be laid down by the Member States.
2. Member States shall communicate to the Commission the text of the main provisions of national law which they adopt in the field covered by this Directive.

Annexes - Chapter 5: Free Movement and Establishment

Chapter 6

COMMON EMPLOYMENT POLICY

Unemployment became a matter of serious concern for all the countries of the Community around the mid-1970s. Until then employment problems in the Community merely consisted of structural and regional imbalances in a general context of full employment. A series of very variable economic factors led to the **rapid deterioration of the employment situation** in the Community, viz.: the inflation and economic recession of the late 1970s and early 1980s, resulting from monetary and energy crises[1], lively competition from recently industrialised countries in Asia with cheap labour, a degree of saturation of demand in Europe for industrial goods and the evolution of the economy and of European companies towards a post-industrial stage. Many jobs thus became superfluous and disappeared. Others were created, but required new qualifications which most of the unemployed did not possess. At the same time, women, most of who had previously stayed at home, joined the labour market in force.

Averaging more than 10% of the active population of the Member States (with important differences between them), in the beginning of the 21st century, the unemployment rate of the European Union is seen as **its gravest social problem**. The economic and social costs of this unemployment are enormous. They include not only the direct expenditure on providing social security support for the unemployed, but also: the loss of tax revenue which the unemployed would pay out of their income if they were working; the increased burden on social services; rising poverty, crime and ill-health. Special concern focuses on the lack of prospects for new entrants to the labour market, especially young people and women and for people excluded from regular work [see section 8.5.]. Under the pressure of these problems was endorsed the employment strategy of the Union.

6.1. Institutional machinery for employment policy

Thanks to a **levy system** on the production of the industries concerned, the ECSC was better placed than the EEC to cope with the employment problems. Article 56 of the **ECSC Treaty** [see section 1.1.] contained provisions on employment in the coal and steel industries. Useful lessons can probably be learned from experience gained with the ECSC, which has operated in exceptionally close association with the social partners and with co-financing redeployment aid for the workers losing their jobs from the industries concerned. This system has cushioned the social impact of tremendous job losses over the past thirty years in these industries. After the expiry of the ECSC Treaty in July 2002, the ownership, management and destination of funds from the ECSC were transferred to the European Community, represented by the Commission[2].

Unlike the ECSC Treaty, the EEC Treaty did not prepare the Community Institutions sufficiently to cope with the employment problems which started plaguing the Community since the

[1] Moussis (2004), sections 7.2.1. and 19.1.1.
[2] Decisions 2003/76 and 2003/77, OJ L 29, 05.02.2003.

mid-1970s. Of course Article 118 of that Treaty gave the Commission the task of promoting close cooperation between States in the social field with regard to employment *inter alia.* To do so, however, it could act, in accordance with that Article, only by making studies, delivering opinions and arranging consultations. The Commission has used and is still using those means, which were supplemented by the new means developed thanks to the EC Treaty.

In view of mutual information and coordination, the Commission set up a programme of employment statistics, and publishes reports on employment forecasts for each sector, based on national work and containing homogeneous quantitative data[1]. It keeps a continuous inventory of the measures taken in the countries of the Community to tackle the employment problems.

In collaboration with the national administrations, the European Commission has prepared an information system on employment policies - the **European Employment Observatory** - whose main task is to run a network between Member States and the Commission with a view to pooling information. The Observatory provides services to the public in the form of periodic publications and regularly updated databases. It also prepares comparative political analyses and tenders advice. In its current form the Observatory relies on three information networks.

- **MISEP** (Mutual Information System on Employment Policies) is a network of representatives of the national administrations responsible for employment in the Member States and the Commission. MISEP's chief task is to exchange and disseminate information in the field of employment policies;
- **SYSDEM** (System of Documentation, Evaluation and Monitoring of Employment Policies) is a network of independent labour market experts (one per Member State) which produces comparative and thematic studies of employment policies and labour market policies throughout the EU;
- **RESEARCH** is a high-level group that tenders advice on employment policy and labour market policy issues and produces assessment reports on the employment situation and on employability.

The Commission examines the information thus obtained, studies the trends which affect employment in the Member States and publishes reports and bulletins assessing the rapid changes currently taking place in the Union's labour market[2]. It communicates this information to the **Standing Committee on Employment** (made up of representatives of the Commission, the Council and the social partners at European level) to provide them with an opportunity of discussing the employment situation, the measures taken in each country and the coordination of employment strategy at Community level[3]. The main task of this Committee is to ensure that there is continuous dialogue, coordination and consultation between the Council, the Commission and the social partners in order to enable the social partners to contribute to the coordinated employment strategy and to facilitate coordination by the Member States of their policies in this field reflected in both the Employment Guidelines and the Broad Economic Policy Guidelines[4].

The Standing Committee on Employment should not be confused with the **Employment Committee**, made up of representatives of the Member States, whose main tasks are to monitor the employment situation and employment policies in the Member States and the Community; and to formulate opinions at the request of either the Council or the Commission or on its own initiative, and to contribute to the preparation of the Council proceedings referred to in Article 128 of the EC Treaty[5].

---

[1] Regulation 371/91, OJ L 351, 20.12.1991.
[2] See, e.g., COM (95) 465, 11 October 1995.
[3] Decision 1999/207, OJ L 72, 18.03.1999.
[4] Moussis (2004), sections 13.3.2 and 7.3.1.
[5] Decision 2000/98, OJ L 29, 04.02.2000.

6.2. The employment strategy of the Union

On the basis of Article 118 EEC, which enjoined it to promote a close cooperation among the Member States in the field of employment without having recourse to formal legislation, the Commission, in the 1990s, led the Council adopt guidelines for a Community labour market policy[1] and a series of Community **Resolutions and programmes in the field of employment**. These Council Resolutions aimed at:

- a Community action to combat unemployment[2];
- the promotion of employment for young people[3];
- combating unemployment amongst women[4];
- the contribution of local employment initiatives to combating unemployment[5];
- action to combat long-term unemployment[6];
- promoting the integration or reintegration of women in active life[7]; and
- assisting the long-term unemployed[8].

Despite their non-compulsory character [see section 1.4.], these Resolutions have had some practical effects. Thus, the Resolution on the promotion of employment for young people gave rise to many initiatives of the European Social Fund, whether measures in favour of young people establishing undertakings (companies, businesses), innovative practices on the part of undertakings or aid for the integration of disadvantaged young people. The Resolution on long-term unemployment led to a job creation programme being adopted for specific groups of long-term unemployed (**ERGO**). Likewise, local job-creation schemes formed the subject of an important action programme for the local development of employment (**LEDA**) aimed at pinpointing and removing the obstacles to those schemes. The Commission also set up a system for exchanges of information for local employment initiatives (**ELISE**) and a support programme for innovative local or regional job creation schemes (**SPEC**).

On the basis of these last experiences, the Commission presented in a communication the elements of a European strategy for encouraging **local development and employment initiatives (LDEI)**[9]. These are viewed in terms of local projects calling for a legal and financial partnership between the public and private sectors and geared to meeting new needs such as, home-help services, child care, assistance for young people facing difficulties, cultural heritage, crafts and tourism, waste management, protection and conservation of natural areas. The proliferation of LDEIs has created a major dynamic impetus affecting the entire territory of the European Union and combining entrepreneurial spirit, employment and local diversity.

These first experiences of the Community could not, of course, by themselves combat unemployment on a large scale. In the 1990s it has become clear that reducing unemployment necessarily requires **pro-active labour market policies**. A radical new look is needed at the whole range of available instruments, which can influence the employment environment, whether these be regulatory, fiscal or social security incentives. The educational system, labour laws, work contracts, contractual negotiation systems, the social security system and business management form the pillars of the "employment environment" in each Member State and combine to give each of them a distinctive appearance. According to the subsidiarity principle[10], the vast bulk of these measures should be for individual Member States to decide upon in responding to their diverse national situations. However, the Union can and must play an important role by: firstly, providing

---

1 OJ C 168, 08.07.1980.
2 Resolution, OJ C 186, 21.07.1982, p. 1-2.
3 Resolution, OJ C 29, 04.02.1984, p. 1-3.
4 Resolution, OJ C 161, 21.06.1984 p. 4-6.
5 Resolution, OJ C 161, 21.06.1984 p. 1-3.
6 Resolution, OJ C 2, 01.01.1985, p. 3-5.
7 Resolution, OJ C 333, 28.12.1988, p. 1-2.
8 Resolution, OJ C 157, 27.06.1990, p. 4-6.
9 COM (95) 273, 13 June 1995.
10 Moussis (2004), section 3.2.

a forum where a common broad framework strategy can be agreed; and secondly, by underpinning national measures with complementary financial support through the European Social Fund.

The Amsterdam European Council, which approved the Amsterdam Treaty, adopted a **Resolution on Growth and Employment** in order to give a new impulse for keeping employment firmly at the top of the political agenda of the Union. The Resolution asserts inter alia that: social protection systems should be modernised; the coordination of the Member States' economic policies should focus on policies for employment; full attention should be given to training and education systems including life-long learning; taxation and social protection systems should be made more employment friendly.

The EU Treaty sets among the objectives of the Union, mentioned in Article 2 (TEU), that of promoting economic and social progress and a "high level of employment". The new **Title on Employment** of the EC Treaty urges the Member States and the Community to work towards developing a coordinated strategy for employment and particularly for promoting a skilled, trained and adaptable workforce and labour markets responsive to economic change (Art. 125 TEC) [see annex 2.1.]. To this end, Member States must regard promoting employment as a matter of common concern and must coordinate their action in this respect within the Council (Art. 126 TEC). The Community must encourage cooperation between the Member States, support and, if necessary, complement their action (Art. 127 TEC). The European Council should each year consider the employment situation of the Community and adopt conclusions thereon, on the basis of which the Council should draw up employment guidelines, consistent with the broad guidelines of economic policies[1], which the Member States should take into account in their employment policies (Art 128 TEC). The Council, under the co-decision procedure with the Parliament [see section 1.2.], may adopt incentive measures designed to encourage cooperation between Member States and to support their action in the field of employment through initiatives aimed at developing exchanges of information and best practices (Art 129 TEC). Indeed, a Council decision aims at: fostering cooperation in the field of employment as regards analysis, research and monitoring; identifying good practices and promoting exchanges and transfers of information and experience; and developing an active information policy[2].

An extraordinary European Council on employment took place in Luxembourg on 20 and 21 November 1997. It enacted the definition, as from 1998, of **guidelines for employment** and placed emphasis on harnessing systematically the common policies of the Community in support of employment. In adopting the 1999 employment guidelines, the Council set out the subsequent procedures for monitoring the application of the guidelines by the Member States[3]. These guidelines help the Member States to devise their own strategies, while preserving the four-pillar structure established in 1998[4]: improving employability, i.e. giving unemployed people and workers in general better opportunities to find work, with the emphasis on suitable training; developing entrepreneurship; encouraging adaptability; and strengthening equal opportunities policies for women and men. By mid-June, each Member State must submit to the Council and the Commission a report concerning the implementation of the previous national action plan and describing the adjustments made to this plan in the light of the changes introduced by the current employment guidelines. By the end of the year, the Council adopts guidelines for the Member States' employment policies for the next year and publishes a recommendation on the implementation of employment policies in the Member States[5]. The Commission monitors the employment strategy pursued by the Member States and publishes an annual report on employment rates considering how each Member State could help to achieve the goal of raising employment rates as an objective of economic policy. The Council has provided a legal basis for Commission activities form-

[1] Moussis (2004), section 7.3.1.
[2] Decision 98/171, OJ L 63, 04.03.1998.
[3] Resolution, OJ C 69, 12.03.1999, p. 2-8.
[4] Resolution, OJ C 30, 28.01.1998, p. 1-5.
[5] See, e.g. Decision 2003/578, OJ L 197, 05.08.2003.

ing part of the European employment strategy, concerning analysis, research, cooperation and action in the field of employment[1].

Going a step further in the coordination of employment policies, the Cologne European Council (3 and 4 June 1999) adopted a **European Employment Pact** aimed at a sustainable reduction of unemployment. The European Employment Pact embodies a comprehensive overall approach bringing together all the Union's employment policy measures, which support and mutually reinforce one another. In the broad economic policy guidelines, the Member States and the Community agree annually on the main elements of their economic policy[2]; in the employment guidelines the Member States and the Community agree annually on the main elements of the coordinated employment strategy; in the macroeconomic dialogue (within the framework of the ECOFIN Council), information and opinions of the relevant Community institutions and the social partners are exchanged in an appropriate manner concerning the question of how to design macroeconomic policy in order to increase and make full use of the potential for growth and employment.

The Lisbon European Council (23 and 24 March 2000) agreed to a **strategic goal** to be pursued over the first decade of the 21st century, with the aim of boosting employment, economic reform and social cohesion within the framework of a knowledge-based economy. The three key elements of this strategy are geared to: preparing the transition to a knowledge-based economy and society by means of policies tailored more to the needs of the information society and research and development, stepping up the process of structural reform to boost competitiveness and innovation, while completing the internal market; modernising the European social model, investing in people and combating social exclusion; and sustaining a healthy economic outlook and favourable growth prospects by applying an appropriate macroeconomic policy mix. Implementation of the Lisbon strategic goal involves: fixing guidelines for the Union combined with specific timetables for achieving the goals in the short, medium and long terms; translating these European guidelines into national and regional policies; and periodic monitoring, evaluation and peer review.

With the European Employment Strategy being seen as a key component of the Lisbon agenda, the Commission promotes a new generation of employment guidelines entailing three overall objectives (full employment, quality and productivity at work, cohesion and an inclusive labour market) focusing on the following priorities: active and preventive measures for the unemployed and the inactive; making work more worthwhile; fostering entrepreneurship to create more and better jobs; transforming undeclared work into regular employment; promoting active ageing; developing and reinforcing immigration policy; promoting adaptability in the labour market; investing in human capital and strategies for lifelong learning; fostering gender equality; supporting integration and combating discrimination in the labour market for people who are at a disadvantage; and addressing regional employment disparities[3]. Responding to the invitation of the European Council, the Commission made proposals for the application of the open coordination method [see section 2.1.] in the field of social protection in the framework of the Lisbon strategy[4].

6.3. The actions of the European Social Fund

According to Article 146 (TEC) the **European Social Fund (ESF)** aims to: (a) render the employment of workers easier and to increase their geographical and occupational mobility within the Community; and (b) facilitate their adaptation to industrial changes and to changes in

1 Decision 98/171, OJ L 63, 04.03.1998.
2 Moussis (2004), section 7.3.1.
3 COM (2003) 6, 14 January 2003.
4 COM (2003) 261, 27 May 2003.

production systems, in particular through vocational training and retraining [see annex 2.1.]. The ESF is administered by the Commission, which is assisted in this task by a Committee composed of representatives of the governments, trade unions and employers' organisations (Art. 147 TEC).

The framework and **political priorities** of the ESF for the period 2000-2006 are defined in Regulation 1784/99 on the European Social Fund[1] [see annex 6.1.]. This Regulation falls within the overall framework set up under Council Regulation 1260/99 laying down general provisions on the Structural Funds[2] [see annex 3.3.]. The latter contains specific provisions concerning the ESF inviting it to intervene on the whole territory of the EU in pursuit of Objectives 1, 2 and 3 fixed by the general regulation [see sections 3.3.3 and 3.3.4.]. According to its own Regulation No 1784/99, **the ESF's task** is to support measures which aim to prevent and combat unemployment, develop human resources and foster social integration in the labour market, so as to promote a high level of employment, equal opportunities for men and women, sustainable development and economic and social cohesion. In particular, it must assist the measures taken in line with the European strategy and guidelines on employment.

The Regulation on the European Social Fund assigns to it five **key policy areas**:

(a) development of active labour market policies to combat and prevent unemployment, to avoid long-term unemployment, to facilitate the reintegration of the long-term unemployed and to support integration into the labour market of young people and persons returning to work after a period of absence;

(b) promotion of equal opportunities for all in terms of access to the labour market, with particular attention to persons at risk of social exclusion;

(c) promotion and improvement of vocational training, education and counselling in the context of a lifelong learning policy;

(d) promotion of a skilled, well-trained and flexible workforce, innovative and adaptable forms of work organisation, and entrepreneurship;

(e) specific measures to improve access and active participation of women in the labour market (career prospects, access to new job opportunities, setting up businesses, etc.).

In general, **three forms of activities are eligible for ESF funding**: assistance for individuals, which should represent the main form of aid, covering areas such as vocational training or education and careers guidance, etc.; assistance for structures and systems to make support activities for individuals more effective (e.g. improving personal effectiveness); accompanying measures (provision of services and equipment for the care of dependent persons, promotion of social skills training, and public awareness and information campaigns).

The **Objective 3 of the Structural Funds**, which is the exclusive responsibility of the ESF, contributes to the adaptation and modernisation of national policies and systems of education, training and employment outside the regions covered by Objective 1 and provides a policy frame of reference for all measures promoting human resource development [see section 3.3.3.]. In addition, the ESF encompasses three horizontal issues: promotion of local employment initiatives (including territorial pacts for employment); the social dimension and employment in the information society; equal opportunities for men and women.

In accordance with the provisions laid down in the General Regulation governing the Structural Funds [see section 3.3.3 and annex 3.3.], the ESF helps to implement the Community initiative to combat all forms of discrimination and inequality in the labour market **(EQUAL)** [see sections 3.3.6 and 4.2.]. The Equal Initiative aims to develop cooperation between the Member States and the Commission with a view to promoting new ways of **combating all forms of exclusion, discrimination and inequalities** in the labour market, in the context of implementing the European employment strategy [see section 6.2.] and the National Action Plans.

---

1 Regulation 1784/99, OJ L 21, 13.08.1999
2 Regulation 1260/1999, OJ L 161, 26.06.1999.

The Community initiative **EQUAL,** against social exclusion, supports: partnerships of players (public and private partners and NGOs), by trying out new approaches, methods and practices of transnational cooperation; policy formulation in the Member States and the dissemination of best practices via networking of the national partners, by providing a window on innovation and best practices in other parts of the Union; the formulation of a European policy, by creating forums for political debate and development. Transnational cooperation boosts innovation by transferring skills, identifying new ways of breaking down local constraints and changing the way in which the public administrations address employment problems. Furthermore, transnational networking of groups interested in combating social exclusion promotes the multinational integration process.

COMMON EMPLOYMENT POLICY

Annex 6.1.

Regulation (EC) No 1784/1999 of the European Parliament and of the Council of 12 July 1999 on the **European Social Fund**
Official Journal L 213 , 13/08/1999 P. 0005 - 0008

MAIN PROVISIONS

Article 1
Tasks
Within the framework of the task entrusted to the European Social Fund (the "Fund") by Article 146 of the Treaty and of the tasks entrusted to the Structural Funds pursuant to Article 159 of the Treaty and in accordance with the provisions of Regulation (EC) No 1260/1999, the Fund shall support measures to prevent and combat unemployment and to develop human resources and social integration into the labour market in order to promote a high level of employment, equality between men and women, sustainable development, and economic and social cohesion. In particular, the Fund shall contribute to the actions undertaken in pursuance of the European Employment Strategy and the Annual Guidelines on Employment.

Article 2
Scope
1. The Fund shall support and complement the activities of Member States directed towards developing the labour market and human resources in the following policy fields, in particular in the context of their multiannual national action plans for employment:
(a) developing and promoting active labour market policies to combat and prevent unemployment, to prevent both women and men from moving into long-term unemployment, to facilitate the reintegration of the long-term unemployed into the labour market, and to support the occupational integration of young people and of persons returning to the labour market after a period of absence;
(b) promoting equal opportunities for all in accessing the labour market, with particular emphasis on those exposed to social exclusion;
(c) promoting and improving:
- training,
- education,
- counselling
as part of lifelong learning policy to:
- facilitate and improve access to, and integration into, the labour market,
- improve and maintain employability, and
- promote job mobility;
(d) promoting a skilled, trained and adaptable workforce, innovation and adaptability in work organisation, developing entrepreneurship and conditions facilitating job creation, and enhancing skills and boosting human potential in research, science and technology;
(e) specific measures to improve women's access to and participation in the labour market, including their career development, their access to new job opportunities and to starting up of businesses, and to reduce vertical and horizontal segregation on the basis of sex in the labour market.
2. Within the policy fields set out in paragraph 1 the Fund shall take account of:
(a) support for local initiatives concerning employment, in particular initiatives to support local employment and territorial employment pacts;
(b) the social and labour market dimensions of the information society, notably by developing policy and programmes designed to harness the employment potential of the information society and by ensuring equal access to its facilities and benefits;
(c) equal opportunities for women and men as part of the mainstreaming approach.

Article 3
Eligible activities
1. The financial support of the Fund shall mainly take the form of assistance to persons and be devoted to the following activities to develop human resources which may be part of a pathway approach to labour market integration:
(a) education and vocational training - including vocational training equivalent to compulsory schooling - apprenticeships, pre-training, in particular the provision and upgrading of basic skills, rehabilitation in employment, measures to promote employability on the labour market, guidance, counselling and continuing training;
(b) employment aids and aids for self-employment;
(c) in the fields of research, science and technology development, post-graduate training and the training of managers and technicians at research establishments and in enterprises;
(d) development of new sources of employment, including in the social economy (Third System).
2. In order to increase the effectiveness of the activities referred to in paragraph 1 assistance may also be given to:
(a) structures and systems:
(i) development and improvement of training, education and skills acquisition, including the training of teachers, trainers and staff, and improving the access of workers to training and qualifications;
(ii) modernisation and improved efficiency of employment services;
(iii) development of links between the worlds of work and education, training, and research establishments;
(iv) development, as far as possible, of systems for anticipating changes in employment and in qualification needs, particularly in relation to new patterns of work and new forms of work organisation, taking into account the need for reconciliation of family and working life and for enabling older workers to have a fulfilling occupation until retirement. This shall not, however, include the financing of early-retirement schemes;
(b) accompanying measures:
(i) assistance in the provision of services to beneficiaries, including the provision of care services and facilities for dependants;
(ii) promoting socio-educational development to facilitate the pathway approach to labour market integration;
(iii) awareness-raising, information and publicity.
3. The Fund may finance activities pursuant to the second subparagraph of Article 2(4) of Regulation (EC) No 1260/1999.

Article 4
Concentration of assistance
1. With due regard to national priorities as laid down in particular in the national action plans for employment as well as to the ex-ante evaluation, a strategy shall be set out taking account of all relevant policy fields and paying particular attention to the areas referred to in Article 2(1)(d) and (e). In order to maximise the efficiency of Fund support, its interventions within this strategy and taking into account the priority fields referred to in Article 2(1) shall be concentrated on a limited number of areas or themes and be directed towards the most important needs and the most effective operations.
In allocating appropriations to each intervention by the Fund a joint selection shall be made of the policy fields to be given priority. The measures provided for in Article 2(1) shall, in accordance with national priorities, be taken into account.
2. The programming of Fund interventions shall provide that a reasonable amount of the Fund appropriations made available for the intervention within Objectives 1 and 3 shall be available, in conformity with Article 27 of Regulation (EC) No 1260/1999, in the form of small grants, with special arrangements for access by non-governmental organisations and local partnerships. Member States may choose to implement this paragraph in accordance with financing arrangements set out in Article 29(6) of Regulation (EC) No 1260/1999.

Article 5
Community initiative
1. Pursuant to Article 20 of Regulation (EC) No 1260/1999, the Fund shall, in accordance with Article 21(2) of that Regulation, contribute to the implementation of the Community Initiative for combating discrimination and inequalities in connection with the labour market (EQUAL).
2. In accordance with Article 21(2) of Regulation (EC) No 1260/1999, the Decisions on the contribution of the Fund to the Community Initiative may extend the scope of eligible activities referred to in Article 3 of this Regulation to cover measures which can be funded by Regulations (EC) No 1783/1999(11), (EC) No 1257/1999(12) and (EC) No 1263/1999(13) so as to permit the implementation of all the measures provided for in the Initiative.

Article 6
Innovative measures and technical assistance
1. In accordance with Article 22(2) of Regulation (EC) No 1260/1999, the Commission may finance preparatory, monitoring and evaluation operations in Member States or at Community level which are necessary for the implementation of the operations referred to in this Regulation. They may include:
(a) operations of an innovatory nature and pilot projects concerning labour markets, employment, and vocational training;
(b) studies, technical assistance and the exchange of experience having a multiplier effect;
(c) technical assistance connected with the preparation, implementation, monitoring, and evaluation, as well as control of operations financed by the Fund;
(d) operations directed, within the framework of social dialogue, at staff from enterprises in two or more Member States and concerning the transfer of special knowledge relating to areas of intervention by the Fund;
(e) informing the various partners involved, the final beneficiaries of assistance from the Fund and the general public.
2. In accordance with Article 22(2) of Regulation (EC) No 1260/1999, the scope of the operations referred to in paragraph 1(a) of this Article shall be extended, by a Decision for Fund participation, to measures that may be financed under Regulations (EC) No 1783/1999, (EC) No 1257/1999 and (EC) No 1263/1999, so as to cover all the measures necessary for the implementation of the innovative actions in question.

Article 7
Applications for assistance
Applications for a contribution from the Fund shall be accompanied by a computerised form, drawn up jointly, listing the operations regarding each form of assistance so that it can be followed through from budgetary commitment to final payment.

Article 8
Implementing provisions
All detailed implementing rules for this Regulation shall be adopted by the Commission according to the procedure laid down in Article 49 of Regulation (EC) No 1260/1999.

Annexes - Chapter 6: Common Employment Policy

Chapter 7

EDUCATION, VOCATIONAL TRAINING AND YOUTH POLICIES

The problems of employment and vocational training are related, as very often the jobs offered require qualifications, which those seeking employment lack. That is why **employment and vocational training policies are also linked**. In fact, training is an instrument of active labour market policy. At the same time, measures promoting vocational training or retraining promote the employment or re-employment of workers in sectors where qualified labour is needed. Many workers cannot secure employment without becoming specialised, but they cannot acquire specialisation through experience until they have found a job. Breaking this vicious circle through vocational training is vital as workers should be able to change more frequently jobs throughout their working lives in the future.

Vocational training is not only a basic human right, enabling workers to realise their full potential, but also a **prerequisite for technological progress** and regional development. Indeed, a skilled, adaptable and mobile workforce is an essential component in the competitiveness, productivity and quality of companies, since it allows industries and regions to adapt rapidly to the requirements of technology and market trends and thus to become or remain competitive. Unemployment is in fact rife especially in the traditional industries in decline (steel, shipbuilding, textiles...), whilst the new industries (information technology, telecommunications, aerospace...) are badly in need of qualified labour. Tomorrow's trades will require the autonomy, the independence of spirit, the analytical ability and the capacity to make diagnoses, qualities which depend on knowledge. The new qualifications can help the European economy to effect the necessary structural changes in the information society and enable it better to face competition from the newly industrialised countries. The EU's education and training policies aim therefore to develop human resources throughout people's working lives, starting with basic education and working through initial training to continuing training.

7.1. The foundations of education and training policies

Underlying the common education policy is the collection and dissemination of information on the programmes and projects of the various higher education establishments in the Member States. An **Education Information Network** in the European Community, under the name of EURYDICE, is available to users with responsibilities in the field of education, such as the Community institutions, national authorities and officials responsible for higher education in the Member States[1]. The Eurydice network is the chief instrument for providing information on national and Community structures, systems and developments in the field of education. The net-

[1] Resolution, OJ C 329, 31.12.1990, p. 23-24 and Council Conclusions, OJ C 336, 19.12.1992, p. 7.

work consists of a European unit and units in the Member States. It is designed as a system permitting the mutual exchange of documentary information. In addition, it assists the drawing up of comparative analyses, reports and surveys on common priority topics determined inter alia in the Education Committee and at the regular meetings of senior officials.

An organ of the common policy on professional training is the **European Centre for the Development of Vocational Training (CEDEFOP)**, located in Thessaloniki[1] [see annex 7.1.]. Cedefop's programme of work focuses on two priority areas, namely qualifications and vocational training systems. The former is essentially concerned with the transparency of qualifications and new occupations at European level and the impact of new forms of work organisation and qualifications on training systems. The latter is concerned with strategies for the optimum combination of types and phases of training with a view to achieving a lifelong learning process and with improved teacher training.

The **European Training Foundation**, established in Turin, endeavours to play a part in developing vocational training systems in the countries of Central and Eastern Europe, the Independent States of the former Soviet Union, the Balkan countries and the Mediterranean non-member countries[2] [see annex 7.2.].

As agreed at the Lisbon European Council (23 and 24 March 2000)[3] [see section 6.2.], the ***e*Learning initiative** is designed to make good the shortcomings in Europe in the use of new information and communications technologies, thereby accelerating the pace of change in education and training systems and helping Europe to move towards a knowledge-based society[4]. The key objectives are focused on: improving infrastructure, notably equipping all schools in the Union; training the population at all levels by making schools, training centres and other places of learning accessible to all; development of high-quality multimedia services and content; and networking of schools (European Schoolnet). The Commission mobilises Community programmes and instruments to achieve these objectives.

A Council decision on the promotion of European pathways for work-linked training including apprenticeship established a **"Europass" document** recording, at Community level, periods of work-linked training, including apprenticeship undergone by an individual in a Member State other than that in which his/her training is based[5] [see annex 7.3.]. A Council Resolution invited the Commission to promote the **involvement of young people** in the development, execution and evaluation of Community youth activities and programmes[6].

Sporting activities are covered in a declaration to the final act of the Amsterdam Treaty, which contains two essential principles: that sport has a role in forging identity, which amounts to saying that national identities in this field should be respected; and that sports associations should be listened to by the bodies of the European Union when important questions affecting sport are at issue, which gives them a consultative function in these matters[7] [see section 5.1.1.]. A Council Resolution invited the Commission to devise, in cooperation with the Member States, a coherent approach with a view to exploiting the non-formal educational potential of sporting activities[8]. The year 2004 was designated "European Year of Education through Sport", in order to make educational institutions and sports organisations aware of the need for cooperation and to promote awareness of the positive contribution that voluntary activities make to non-formal education[9].

Amongst European actions in the university field one must include the Convention setting up the **European University Institute in Florence**[10]. The Institute specialises in research in four

[1] Regulation 337/75, OJ L 39, 13.02.1975 and Regulation 251/95, OJ L 30, 09.02.1995.
[2] Regulation 1360/90, OJ L 131, 23.05.1990 and Regulation 2666/2000, OJ L 306, 07.12.2000.
[3] Moussis (2004), section 13.3.2.
[4] COM (2000) 318, 24 May 2000.
[5] Decision 1999/51, OJ L 17, 22.01.1999.
[6] Resolution, OJ C 42, 17.02.1999, p. 1-2.
[7] Moussis (2004), section 6.4.1.
[8] Resolution 2000/C 8/03, JO C8, 12.01.2000.
[9] Decision 291/2003, OJ L 43, 18.02.2003.
[10] Convention, OJ C 29, 09.02.1976, p.1-10.

areas, viz.: history and civilisation, economics, law and political and social sciences. The task of the Institute is to contribute to the development of the cultural and scientific heritage of Europe, as a whole and in its constituent parts. The Institute runs interdisciplinary research programmes on the main issues European society has to address, especially those involving European integration. Its research work has to cover the great movements and institutions, which characterise the history and development of Europe. The Commission contributes financially towards the Institute's scientific and research activities, namely the research library and European library (Eurolib programme). In addition, the Commission covers the cost concerning the historical archives of the European Communities, which are managed by the Institute.

The Community has concluded agreements for cooperation in the fields of higher education and vocational training with the United States[1] and Canada[2]. These cooperation programmes seek to encourage, on the one hand, exchanges of knowledge, students and staff and, on the other, interaction between higher education establishments, training providers and undertakings in the EU, the USA and Canada.

A Council Resolution advocated that Community languages be taught at an early stage in order to **promote European multilingualism** while preserving cultural diversity[3]. A Council Recommendation urged the Member States to establish transparent systems of quality assessment and quality assurance in higher education by promoting cooperation between them and, if necessary, by supporting their action, with due regard for the autonomy and independence of the competent authorities[4].

With a view to promoting a European dimension in education and ensuring the quality of school education, the European Parliament and the Council recommend that the Member States support transparent evaluation systems, encourage the involvement of school stakeholders in the evaluation process and encourage cooperation between all competent authorities[5]. They also recommend to the Member States to encourage mobility within the Community for students, persons undergoing training, young volunteers, teachers and trainers participating in Community education and training programmes[6].

7.2. Education and training programmes

The Maastricht Treaty [see section 1.1.] has consecrated Community action in the fields of education, vocational training and youth. Article 149 (TEC) specifies that the Community contributes to the development of quality education by encouraging cooperation between Member States and, if necessary, by supporting and supplementing their action in the fields of: developing the European dimension in education, particularly through the teaching and dissemination of languages; mobility of students and teachers; cooperation between educational establishments; exchanges of information and experience; exchanges of young people and socio-educational instructors; and the development of distance education. Incentive measures, excluding any harmonisation of the laws and regulations of the Member States, are adopted by the Council acting in accordance with the procedure referred to in Article 251 (co-decision with the European Parliament). Community action must, however, fully respect the responsibility of the Member States for the content of teaching, the organisation of education systems and vocational training and their cultural and linguistic diversity. It is evident that the EU not only respects the cultural diversity of its Member States but also encourages it[7].

1 Decision 95/487 and Agreement, OJ L 279, 22.11.1995, p. 11-17 and Decision 2001/196, OJ L 71, 13.03.2001.
2 Decision 95/523 and Agreement, OJ L 300, 13.12.1995, p. 18-22 and Decision 2001/197, OJ L 71, 13.03.2001.
3 OJ C 1, 03.01.1998.
4 Recommendation 98/561, OJ L 270, 07.10.1998.
5 Recommendation 2001/166, OJ L 60, 01.03.2001.
6 Recommendation, OJ L 215, 09.08.2001, p.30.
7 Moussis (2004), section 10.3.

According to Article 150 of the EC Treaty, the Community implements a vocational training policy, which supports and supplements the action of the Member States and which aims to: facilitate adaptation to industrial changes, in particular through vocational training and retraining; improve initial and continuing vocational training in order to facilitate vocational integration and reintegration into the labour market; facilitate access to vocational training and encourage mobility of instructors and trainees; stimulate cooperation between educational or training establishments and firms; and develop exchanges of information and experience on issues common to the training systems of the Member States. This Article is the foundation of the common training policy.

The Union's new generation of education and training programmes is designed to develop a European dimension of education from the primary school to the university and to establish a genuine European market in skills and training. Indeed, the three five-year programmes (1 January 2000 to 31 December 2004) in the fields of education (Socrates) [see section 7.2.1.], vocational training (Leonardo da Vinci) [see section 7.2.2.] and youth [see section 7.2.3.] are interlinked by means of a common framework encompassing six broad elements: physical mobility for people; different forms of virtual mobility (use of new information and communications technologies); development of cooperation networks; promotion of linguistic and cultural skills; development of innovation through pilot projects based on transnational partnerships; and ongoing improvement of Community references (databases, exchanges of good practice) for the systems and policies relating to education, training and youth in the Member States. During the years 2000-2004, the three programmes will give the opportunity to 2.5 million young Europeans to participate in an exchange programme, a very important fact for multination integration[1].

Over the five years 2000-2004, the three programmes - Socrates, Leonardo, Youth - should enable 2.5 million Europeans to benefit from a mobility programme: 1.2 million students and 200 000 teachers under the Socrates programme, 400 000 young people undergoing training under the Leonardo programme and 660 000 young people under the youth-oriented programme.

7.2.1. The SOCRATES programme

The SOCRATES programme in the field of education pursues four primary objectives: to strengthen the European dimension in education at all levels; to promote improvement of knowledge of the languages of the Union; to promote mobility in the field of education and remove obstacles in this connection, in particular by improving the recognition of diplomas and periods of study; and to encourage innovation in the development of educational practices. It comprises measures and projects intended to promote transnational cooperation in the field of education, centred around three themes: cooperation in higher education through the promotion of student and teaching staff mobility, the establishment of university networks and the incorporation of the European dimension into all levels of study (Erasmus and Lingua strands); cooperation in secondary school education through the promotion of partnerships between schools in different Member States and networks of schools for the joint pursuit of educational projects, with special reference to languages, the new information technologies, cultural heritage and environmental protection (Comenius strand); and measures applicable to all levels of education, concerning the promotion of language skills, open and distance education, and exchange of information and experience[2] [see annex 7.4.]. The projects funded by Socrates include joint syllabus development, masters' programmes, European modules, an Internet-based European schools network, integrated language courses and the development of the European dimension in a given academic discipline.

The Socrates programme encompasses six main actions:

Action 1, "**COMENIUS**" on school education, seeks to enhance the quality and reinforce the

[1] Moussis (2004), section 9.4.
[2] Decision 253/2000, OJ L 28, 03.02.2000 and Decision 451/2003, OJ L 69, 13.03.2003.

European dimension of school education, in particular by encouraging transnational cooperation between schools and contributing to improved professional development of staff directly involved in the school education sector, and to promote the learning of languages and intercultural awareness.

Action 2, "**ERASMUS**" on higher education, seeks to enhance the quality and reinforce the European dimension of higher education, to encourage transnational cooperation between universities, to boost European mobility in the higher education sector and to improve transparency and academic recognition of studies and qualifications throughout the Community. Participating universities conclude "institutional contracts" with the Commission covering all the Erasmus activities approved. Such contracts will normally be of three years' duration and will be renewable.

Action 3, "**GRUNDTVIG**" on adult education and other educational pathways, seeks to encourage the European dimension of life-long learning, to contribute - through enhanced transnational cooperation - to innovation and improved availability, accessibility and quality of other educational pathways, and to promote the learning of languages.

Action 4, "**LINGUA**" on teaching and learning of languages aims to support transversal measures relating to the learning of languages, with a view to helping to promote and maintain linguistic diversity within the Community, to improve the quality of language teaching and learning and to facilitate access to life-long language learning opportunities tailored to individual requirements. Lingua both complements and enriches measures related to the promotion of language-learning under other actions of the Socrates programme, in particular Actions 1, 2 and 3.

Action 5: "**MINERVA**" on open and distance learning, information and communication technologies in the field of education, supports transversal measures relating to open and distance learning (ODL) and the use of information and communication technologies (ICT), including multimedia, in the field of education. In so doing, it complements and enriches the corresponding measures provided for within the other actions of the Socrates programme.

Action 6 on **observation and innovation**, contributes to improving the quality and transparency of education systems and furthering the process of educational innovation in Europe through the exchange of information and experience, the identification of good practice, the comparative analysis of systems and policies in this field, and the discussion and analysis of matters of common educational policy interest to be determined by the Council.

7.2.2. The LEONARDO programme

The LEONARDO da Vinci programme in the field of vocational training (2000-2004), which is endowed with EUR 1 150 million, aims at boosting quality, innovation and the European dimension in vocational systems and practices, through transnational cooperation[1] [see annex 7.5.]. The three objectives pursued by the action programme are social and occupational integration of young people, development of access to high-quality continuing training, and helping those in difficult circumstances to integrate better on the labour market. The Community measures implemented under the programme fall into five categories: mobility projects; pilot projects; linguistic competence; transnational networks; and reference material.

The Leonardo programme supports the following measures:

- **transnational mobility projects** for people undergoing vocational training, especially young people, and for trainers, notably: preparation and implementation of transnational placement projects for people undergoing initial vocational training, students, young workers and recent graduates; transnational projects of exchanges between undertakings, on the one hand, and vocational training organisations or universities, on the other; study visits for those responsible for vocational training;
- **transnational pilot projects** to develop and transfer innovation and quality in vocational

[1] Decision 1999/382, OJ L 146, 11.06.1999.

training, including actions aiming at the use of information and communication technologies (ICT) in vocational training;
- **projects to develop language competencies** in a vocational training context, notably projects on less widely used and taught languages;
- **vocational training networks**, bringing together in the Member States, at the regional or sectoral level, the public and private players concerned;
- **actions undertaken on a transnational basis** on priority themes of common interest, notably those establishing comparable data on vocational training systems and arrangements, practices and various approaches to qualifications and competencies in the Member States;
- **joint actions with other Community actions** promoting a Europe of knowledge, particularly the Community programmes in the fields of education and youth;
- **accompanying measures** such as: management, coordination, monitoring and evaluation activities by the Member States.

7.2.3. The YOUTH programme

The action programme in the youth field (2000-2004) incorporates the pre-existing "**Youth for Europe**" programme, which seeks to help young people in their education outside the formal school system and the new "European voluntary service for young people"[1] [see annex 7.6.]. Both strands of the programme for youth focus on four aspects: individual mobility within the framework of European voluntary service; group mobility entailing transnational exchanges; initiatives giving young people an opportunity to play an active role in society; and activities tying in with other areas of Community action. The programme aims to help young people acquire the knowledge and skills to help them in their future development. It seeks also to foster a spirit of initiative, enterprise and creativity, promote respect for human rights and combat racism and xenophobia.

The youth programme comprises five categories of action:

Action 1 "**Youth for Europe**", which has two facets: intra-Community exchanges for young people; and exchanges of young people (Community residents) with third countries;

Action 2 "**European voluntary service" (EVS)**, which supports transnational projects with various Member States or with third countries that involve young people, actively and personally, in activities designed to help meet the needs of society in a wide range of fields (social, sociocultural, environmental, cultural, etc.), activities constituting at the same time an experience of informal education with a view to acquiring social and cultural skills[2];

Action 3, "**Youth initiatives**", involving projects in which young people actively and directly participate in innovative and creative schemes and in schemes which focus on the social commitment of young people at local, regional, national or European level;

Action 4, "**Joint actions**" undertaken with other Community schemes relating to the Europe of knowledge, in particular Community programmes in the field of education and vocational training;

Action 5, "**Support measures**", notably: training and cooperation in relation to those involved in youth policy; information for young people and youth studies.

Responding to a Commission White Paper suggesting a new framework for European cooperation in youth matters[3], the Council called on the Member States and the Commission to ensure that those policies and initiatives affecting young people at national and European level take account of issues such as the needs, situation, living conditions and expectations of young people[4]. The Council supported the Commission proposal aiming to include the youth dimension in other

[1] Decision 1031/2000, OJ L 117, 18.05.2000.
[2] Decision 1686/98, OJ L 214, 31.07.1998.
[3] COM (2001) 681.
[4] Council resolution, 27 June 2002.

policies and programmes, at both national and European level.

7.2.4. The TEMPUS programme

The Trans-European Mobility programme for University Studies (**TEMPUS III**) (2000-2006) is designed to promote, in line with the general guidelines and objectives of the Phare and Tacis programmes[1], the development of higher education systems in the eligible countries (independent States of the former Soviet Union, non-associated countries of Central Europe, Mongolia and Mediterranean countries) through cooperation with partners in the EU Member States[2] [see annex 7.7.]. Joint European projects (JEPs), involving at least one Member State University, a partner in another Member State and a university in a beneficiary country, are the main instruments of the programme. In addition, Tempus III supports the provision of individual grants to teachers, trainers, university administrators, senior ministerial officials, education planners and other experts in the higher education field from the eligible countries or from the Community, with a view to promoting, through courses, seminars and visits, the development and restructuring of higher education systems in the eligible countries.

In association with the TEMPUS programme the European Community provides support for joint European projects (JEPs) associating at least one university in an eligible country, one university from a Member State and a partner establishment (university, company or institution) in another Member State. Support for JEPs can be provided for activities according to the specific needs of the establishments concerned and in line with the priorities established, including:

- **joint education and training actions**, particularly with a view to curriculum development and updating,
- **measures for the reform and development of higher education** and its capacity, particularly by restructuring the management of higher education establishments and systems;
- **the promotion of cooperation** between universities, industry and institutions;
- **the development of mobility** for teachers, administrative staff of universities and students;
- activities to ensure the success of a JEP involving two or more eligible countries.

1 Moussis (2004), sections 25.2. and 25.4.
2 Decision 1999/311, OJ L 120, 08.05.1999 and Decision 2002/601, OJ L 195, 24.07.2002.

Annex 7

EDUCATION, VOCATIONAL TRAINING AND YOUTH POLICIES

Annex 7.1.

Regulation (EEC) No 337/75 of the Council of 10 February 1975 establishing a **European Centre for the Development of Vocational Training**
Official Journal L 039 , 13/02/1975 P. 0001 - 0004.

MAIN PROVISIONS

Article 1
A European Centre for the Development of Vocational Training, hereinafter called "the centre", is hereby set up. In each of the Member States, the centre shall enjoy the most extensive legal capacity accorded to legal persons. The centre shall be non-profit making. It shall have its seat in Berlin (West).

Article 2
1. The aim of the centre shall be to assist the Commission in encouraging, at Community level, the promotion and development of vocational training and of in-service training.
To that end, within the framework of the guidelines laid down by the Community, it shall contribute, through its scientific and technical activities, to the implementation of a common vocational training policy.
It shall, in particular, encourage the exchange of information and the comparison of experience. (1)OJ No C 127, 18.10.1974, p. 20. (2)OJ No C 125, 16.10.1974, p. 41. (3)OJ No 63, 20.4.1963, p. 1338/63. (4)OJ No C 13, 12.2.1974, p. 1.
2. The main tasks of the centre shall be: - to compile selected documentation relating in particular to the present situation, the latest developments and research in the relevant fields, and to matters of vocational training structure;
- to contribute to the development and coordination of research in the above fields;
- to disseminate all useful documentation and information;
- to encourage and support any initiative likely to facilitate a concerted approach to vocational training problems. The centre's activity in this respect shall deal in particular with the problem of the approximation of standards of vocational training with a view to the mutual recognition of certificates and other documents attesting completion of vocational training;
- to provide a forum for all those concerned.

3. In its activities the centre shall take into account the links which exist between vocational training and the other branches of education.

Article 3
1. The centre shall take the measures necessary for the attainment of its objectives. It may in particular: - organize courses and seminars;
- conclude study contracts and Commission or, where necessary, carry out pilot projects or individual projects to assist the implementation of the centre's work programme;
- publish and distribute useful documentation, including a Community vocational training bulletin.

2. In carrying out its tasks, the centre shall establish appropriate contacts, particularly with specialized bodies, whether public or private, national or international, with public authorities and educational institutions and with workers "and employers" organizations.

Article 4
1. The centre shall be administered by a Management Board comprising 30 members of whom: (a) nine

members shall represent the Governments of the Member States;
(b) nine members shall represent the employers' professional organizations;
(c) nine members shall represent the employees' trade union organizations;
(d) three members shall represent the Commission.

The members referred to in (a), (b) and (c) shall be appointed by the Council on the basis of one member per Member State for each of those groups.
The Commission shall appoint the members who are to represent it.
2. The term of office of members shall be three years. It shall be renewable. Upon the expiry of their term of office or in the event of their resignation, members shall remain in office until their appointments are renewed or until they are replaced.
3. The Management Board shall elect its Chairman and three Vice-Chairmen from among its members, to serve for a period of one year.
4. The Chairman shall convene the Management Board at least twice a year or at the request of at least one-third of its members.
5. Decisions by the Management Board shall be taken by an absolute majority of its members.

Article 5
The Management Board shall adopt its rules of procedure, which shall enter into force when approved by the Council, acting on the Opinion of the Commission.
It shall decide whether to set up ad boc working parties on the basis of the requirements of the annual work programme. It shall regularly inform the Commission of the activities of the centre.

Article 6
1. The director of the centre shall be appointed by the Commission from a list of candidates submitted by the Management Board.
2. The term of office of the director shall be renewable every five years.

Article 7
1. The director shall carry out the decisions of the Management Board and shall be responsible for the day-to-day administration of the centre. He shall be the legal representative of the centre.
2. He shall prepare and organize the work of the Management Board and provide the Secretariat for their meetings.
3. He shall coordinate the activities of the working parties.
4. He shall be responsible for all staff matters and for engaging and dismissing staff.
5. He shall be accountable to the Management Board for his activities.

Article 8
1. On the basis of a draft submitted by the director, the Management Board shall adopt the annual work programme in agreement with the Commission. The programme shall take into account the priority needs indicated by the Community institutions.
2. The centre shall take into account the activities of other bodies working in the field of vocational training when planning its own work.

Article 9
The Management Board shall, by 31 March at the latest, adopt an annual general report on the activities and financial situation of the centre and shall submit it to the Commission.

Article 10
The Management Board shall draw up a statement of all revenue and expenditure, which shall be in balance, for each financial year, which shall be the same as the calendar year.

Article 11
1. The Management Board shall, by 31 March each year at the latest, send the Commission an estimate of revenue and expenditure. This estimate, which shall include an establishment plan, shall be forwarded by the Commission to the Council with the preliminary draft budget of the European Communities.
2. The budget of the European Communities shall each year, under a specific heading, include a subsidy for the centre.
The procedure in force for the transfer of appropriations from one chapter to another shall apply to the appropriation for this subsidy.

The budget authority shall draw up the establishment plan of the centre.
3. The Management Board shall adopt the estimate of revenue and expenditure before the beginning of the financial year, adjusting it to the subsidy granted by the budget authority. The estimate thus adopted shall be forwarded by the Commission to the budget authority.

Article 12
1. The financial provisions applying to the centre shall be adopted under Article 209 of the Treaty.
2. The Management Board shall, by 31 March at the latest, send the accounts of all the revenue and expenditure of the centre for the preceding financial year to the Commission and to the Audit Board. The latter shall examine them in accordance with the second paragraph of Article 206 of the Treaty.
3. The Commission shall submit the accounts and the report of the Audit Board, together with its own comments, to the Council and to the European Parliament by 31 October at the latest. The Council and the European Parliament shall give a discharge to the Management Board of the centre under the procedure laid down in the fourth paragraph of Article 206 of the Treaty.
4. The financial controller of the Commission shall be responsible for checking the commitment and payment of all expenditure and the recording and recovery of all revenue of the centre.

Article 13
The provisions governing the staff of the centre shall be adopted by the Council, acting on a proposal from the Commission.

Article 14
Members of the Management Board, the Director, the staff and all other persons participating in the activities of the centre shall be required, even after their duties have ceased, not to disclose information of the kind covered by the obligation of professional secrecy.

Article 15
The rules governing the languages of the European Communities shall apply to the centre.

Article 16
The Protocol on the privileges and immunities of the European Communities shall apply to the centre.

Article 17
1. The contractual liability of the centre shall be governed by the law applicable to the contract in question. The Court of Justice of the European Communities shall have jurisdiction to give judgment pursuant to any arbitration clause contained in a contract concluded by the centre.
2. In the case of non-contractual liability, the centre shall, in accordance with the general principles common to the laws of the Member States, make good any damage caused by the centre or its servants in the performance of their duties.
The Court of Justice shall have jurisdiction in disputes relating to compensation for any such damage.
3. The personal liability of servants towards the centre shall be governed by the relevant provisions applying to the staff of the centre.

Article 18
Member States, members of the Management Board and third parties directly and personally involved may refer to the Commission any act of the centre, whether express or implied, for the Commission to examine the legality of that act.
Referral shall be made to the Commission within 15 days of the day on which the party concerned first became aware of the act in question.
The Commission shall take a Decision within one month. If no Decision has been taken within this period, the case shall be deemed to have been dismissed.

Annex 7.2.

Council Regulation (EEC) No 1360/90 of 7 May 1990 establishing a **European Training Foundation**

Official Journal L 131 , 23/05/1990 P. 0001 - 0005

MAIN PROVISIONS

Article 1

Objectives

This Regulation hereby establishes the European Training Foundation (hereinafter referred to as the Foundation) whose objective shall be to contribute to the development of the vocational training systems of the countries of Central and Eastern Europe designated as eligible for economic aid by the Council in Regulation (EEC) No 3906/89 or in any subsequent relevant legal act. These countries shall be hereinafter referred to as 'the eligible countries'.

The Foundation shall in particular:

- seek to promote effective cooperation between the Community and the eligible countries in the field of vocational training,
- contribute to the coordination of assistance provided by the Community, its Member States and the third countries referred to in Article 16.

Article 2

Scope

The Foundation shall work in the training field, covering initial and continuing vocational training as well as retraining for young people and adults, including in particular management training.

Article 3

Functions

For the purpose of achieving the objectives set out in Article 1, the Foundation shall:

(a) provide assistance in the definition of training needs and priorities through the implementation of measures of technical assistance in the training field, and through cooperation with the appropriate designated bodies in the eligible countries;

(b) act as a clearing house to provide the Community, its Member States and the third countries referred to in Article 16, together with the eligible countries and all other interested parties, with information on current initiatives and future needs in the training field, and provide a framework through which offers of assistance can be channelled;

(c) on the basis of (a) and (b):

examine the scope for joint ventures of training assistance including pilot projects, for the setting up of specialized multinational teams for specific projects and for identifying operations which could be cofinanced, and fund the design and the preparation of such projects, the implementation of which may be financed by contributions from one or several countries, together with the Foundation, or, in exceptional cases, from the Foundation on its own;

(d) for activities and projects which are funded by the Foundation: arrange for the appropriate public and/or private bodies with a proven training record and the necessary expertise to design, prepare, implement and/or manage projects on a flexible, decentralized basis;

(e) for projects funded or cofinanced by the Foundation, tendering procedures shall be laid down by the governing board referred to in Article 5, taking full account of the procedures established in the context of Regulation (EEC) No 3906/89 and, in particular, Article 7 thereof; or in any subsequent relevant legal act;

(f) in collaboration with the Commission, assist in the monitoring and evaluation of the overall effectiveness of training assistance to the eligible countries;

(g) disseminate information and encourage exchanges of experience, through publications, meetings, and other appropriate means;

(h) within the general framework of this Regulation, undertake such other tasks as may be agreed between the governing board and the Commission.

Article 4

General provisions

1. The Foundation shall have legal personality. It shall enjoy in each of the Member States the most extensive legal capacity accorded to legal persons under their laws; it may, in particular, acquire or dispose of movable and immovable property and may be a party to legal proceedings. It shall be non-profit making.

The Foundation shall seek the cooperation of other Community bodies, in particular Cedefop.
2. Representatives of the social partners at European level which are already active in the work of the Community institutions, and international organizations active in the training field, may be associated with the work of the Foundation, notably as provided for in Articles 5 (8) and 6 (1) and (2).

Article 5
Governing board
1. The Foundation shall have a governing board consisting of one representative of each Member State and two representatives of the Commission.
An alternate member may represent or accompany each member of the governing board; when accompanying a member, the alternate member shall attend without having the right to vote.
2. The representatives of the Member States shall be appointed by the Member States concerned.
The Commission shall appoint the members who are to represent it.
3. The term of office of representatives shall be three years. It shall be renewable.
4. The governing board shall be chaired by one of the representatives of the Commission. The chairman shall not vote.
The governing board shall adopt its rules of procedure.
Each member of the governing board shall have one vote.
Decisions of the governing board shall require a two-thirds majority of the members of the board, except in the case referred to in paragraph 5.
5. The governing board shall determine, by a unanimous decision of its members, the rules governing the languages of the Foundation, taking into account the need to ensure access to, and participation in, the work of the Foundation by all interested parties.
6. The chairman shall convene the governing board at least twice a year and at the request of at least a simple majority of the members of the board.
The Chairman shall be responsible for informing the board of other Community activities relevant to their work and of the expectations from the Foundation in the forthcoming year.
7. On the basis of a draft submitted by the director of the Foundation, and within the framework of a three-year rolling perspective, the governing board shall adopt, by 30 November each year at the latest, the annual work programme of the Foundation for the following year in consultation with the Commission.
The projects in the annual work programme shall be accompanied by an estimate of the necessary expenditure.
8. The governing board shall approve, as necessary and on a case-by-case basis, the setting up of ad hoc sectoral working parties involving all the countries or organizations contributing to the finance of the different projects concerned as well as other interested parties, including where appropriate representatives of social partners.
9. The governing board shall, by 31 March each year at the latest, present a draft annual report on the activities of the Foundation for the previous year and their financing to the Commission.
The Commission shall approve the annual report and submit it to the European Parliament, the Council, the Economic and Social Committee and the Member States.
The Commission shall also forward this report, for information, to the eligible countries.

Article 6
Advisory forum
1. The Foundation shall have an advisory forum appointed by the governing board.
The members of the forum shall be selected from experts among training and other circles concerned in the work of the Foundation, taking into account the need to ensure the presence of representatives of the social partners, of those international organizations active in the provision of training assistance, and of the eligible countries.
There shall be appointed two experts from each of the Member States, from each of the eligible countries and from the social partners at European level.
2. The governing board shall seek nominations for appointment from:
- each of the Member States,
- each of the eligible countries,
- the social partners at European level which are already active in the work of the Community institutions, and
- relevant international organizations.
3. The term of office of the members of the advisory forum shall normally be for three years, subject to regular review by the governing board.
4. The task of the advisory forum shall be to deliver opinions to the governing board either at the request of the board or on its own initiative concerning the annual work programme of the Foundation referred to in Article 5 (7).
All opinions shall be communicated to the governing board.

5. The director of the Foundation shall be the chairman of the advisory forum.
The advisory forum shall draw up its rules of procedure, subject to the approval of the governing board.
6. The advisory forum shall be convened by its chairman once a year.

Article 7
The director
1. The director of the Foundation shall be appointed by the governing board, on a proposal from the Commission, for a term of office of five years, which shall be renewable.
The director shall be responsible:
- for the preparation and organization of the work of the governing board, of any ad hoc working parties convened by the governing board and, in particular, for the preparation of the draft annual work programme of the Foundation,
- for the day-to-day administration of the Foundation,
- for the preparation of the statement of revenue and expenditure and execution of the budget of the Foundation,
- for the preparation and publication of reports specified under this Regulation,
- for all staff matters,
- for undertaking the tasks referred to in Article 3.
2. The director shall be accountable to the governing board for his activities and shall attend its meetings.
3. The director shall be the legal representative of the Foundation.

Article 8
Links with other Community actions
The Commission, in cooperation with the governing board and, where appropriate, in accordance with the procedure set out in Article 9 of Regulation (EEC) No 3906/89, shall ensure consistency and, where necessary, complementarity between the work of the Foundation and other actions at Community level, both within the Community and in assistance to the eligible countries, with particular reference to actions under the Tempus scheme.

Article 9
Budget content
1. Estimates of all the revenue and expenditure of the Foundation shall be prepared for each financial year and shall be shown in the budget of the Foundation, which shall include an establishment plan, and each financial year shall correspond to the calendar year.
2. The revenue and expenditure shown in the budget of the Foundation shall be in balance.
3. The revenue of the Foundation shall comprise, without prejudice to other types of income, a subsidy from the general budget of the European Communities, payments made as remuneration for services performed as well as finance from other sources.
4. The budget shall also include details of any funds made available by the eligible countries themselves for projects benefiting from financial assistance from the Foundation.

Article 10
Budget procedure
1. The director shall establish each year a proposed draft budget for the Foundation covering running costs and the proposed operational programme for the following financial year and shall submit it to the governing board.
2. On this basis, the governing board shall, by 15 February at the latest, adopt a draft budget for the Foundation and submit it to the Commission.
3. The Commission shall assess the draft budget of the Foundation having regard to the vocational training priorities in the eligible countries and to the overall financial orientations on economic aid to these countries. It shall establish on this basis, and within the proposed limits of the overall amount to be made available for economic aid to the countries of Central and Eastern Europe, the annual contribution for the budget of the Foundation to be included in the preliminary draft of the general budget of the European Communities.
4. The governing board, after receiving the advice of the Commission, shall adopt the budget of the Foundation at the beginning of each financial year, adjusting it to the several contributions granted to the Foundation and to its other resources.

Article 11
Budget implementation and control
1. The director shall implement the budget of the Foundation.
2. The checking of the commitment and payment of all expenditure and the recording and recovery of all revenue of the Foundation will be undertaken by the financial controller appointed by the governing board on a

proposal from the Commission.
3. By 31 March each year at the latest, the director shall submit to the Commission, the governing board and the Court of Auditors the detailed accounts of all revenue and expenditure from the previous financial year.
The Court of Auditors will examine these accounts in accordance with Article 206a of the Treaty.
4. The governing board shall give a discharge to the director in respect of the implementation of the budget.

Article 12
Financial rules
The governing board shall set down, following consultation of the Commission and the Court of Auditors, detailed financial rules specifying in particular the procedure for the establishment and implementation of the budget of the Foundation.

Article 13
Privileges and immunities
The Protocol on the privileges and immunities of the European Communities shall apply to the Foundation
.

Article 14
Staff rules
The rules and regulations governing the statutory personnel of the Foundation, including the director, shall be analogous to those laid down in Council Regulation (ECSC, EEC, Euratom) No 1859/76 of 29 June 1976 laying down the conditions of employment of staff of the European Centre for the Development of Vocational Training (1), and shall be contained in a separate Regulation to be adopted by the Council on a proposal from the Commission.

Article 15
Legal liability
1. The contractual liability of the Foundation shall be governed by the law applicable to the contract in question.
2. In the case of non-contractual liability, the Foundation shall, in accordance with the general principles common to laws of the Member States, make good any damage caused by the Foundation or its servants in the performance of their duties.
The Court of Justice shall have jurisdiction in disputes relating to compensation for any such damage.
3. The personal liability of servants towards the Foundation shall be governed by the relevant provisions applying to the staff of the Foundation.

Article 16
Participation of third countries
1. The Foundation shall be open to the participation of countries which are not members of the European Community, and which share the commitment of the Community and the Member States to the provision of aid to Central and Eastern Europe in the training field, under arrangements to be laid down in agreements between the Community and themselves, following the procedure laid down in Article 228 of the Treaty.
The agreements shall, inter alia, specify the nature and extent of and the detailed rules for the participation by these countries in the work of the Foundation including provisions on financial contributions and staff.
2. Participation of such countries in the ad hoc working parties provided for in Article 5 (8) may be decided as necessary by the governing board without the need for an agreement.

Article 17
Monitoring and evaluation procedure
The Commission shall, in consultation with the governing board, establish a monitoring and evaluation procedure of the experience acquired in the work of the Foundation.
It shall present the first results of this procedure in a report to be submitted to the European Parliament, the Council and the Economic and Social Committee before 31 December 1992.

Article 18
Review
This Regulation shall be reviewed by the Council on a proposal from the Commission within five years of its entry into force.

Article 19
This Regulation shall enter into force on the day following that on which the competent authorities have decided on the seat of the Foundation (1).
This Regulation shall be binding in its entirety and directly applicable in all Member States.

Annex 7.3.

1999/51/EC: Council Decision of 21 December 1998 on the promotion of **European pathways in work-linked training,** including apprenticeship
Official Journal L 017 , 22/01/1999 P. 0045 - 0050

MAIN PROVISIONS

Article 1
Objectives
1. This Decision established a document known as the "EUROPASS Training" on the basis of the common principles defined in Article 3. It is intended as a record at Community level of the period or periods of training which a person undergoing work-linked training, including apprenticeship, has followed in a Member State other than that in which his/her training is based (known as "European pathway(s)").
2. The use of this record and participation in a 'European pathway` is voluntary and does not impose any obligations or confer any rights other than those defined below.

Article 2
Definitions
For the purposes of the Decision, and taking account of the differences in the systems and arrangements for work-linked training, including apprenticeship, in the Member States, the following definitions shall apply:
1. "European pathway" means, where it has been agreed to use the EUROPASS Training, any period of vocational training, which is completed by a person in a Member State (host Member State) other than the one (Member State of provenance) where his or her work-linked training is based, which forms part of that work-linked training;
2. "person in work-linked training" means any person, of whatever age, in vocational training, at any level including higher education. This training, recognised or certified by the competent authorities in the Member State of provenance according to its own legislation, procedures or practices, involves structured periods of training in an undertaking and, where appropriate, in a training establishment or centre, whatever the person's status (contract of employment, apprenticeship contract, pupil or student);
3. "mentor" means any person with a private or public employer or a training establishment or centre in the host Member State who has the task of assisting, informing, guiding and monitoring trainees during their 'European pathway`;
4. "EUROPASS Training" means a document establishing that the holder has completed one or more periods of work-linked training, including apprenticeship, in another Member State under the conditions defined in this Decision;
5. "host partner" means any body in the host Member State (inter alia private or public employer, training establishment or centre) with which a partnership with the body responsible for organising the training in the Member State of provenance has been established, for the completion of a European pathway.

Article 3
Content and common principles
The following conditions shall apply to the EUROPASS Training:
1. each European pathway shall form part of the training followed in the Member State of provenance, according to its own legislation, procedures or practices;
2. the body responsible for organising the training in the Member State of provenance and the host partner shall agree within the context of the partnership on the content, objectives, duration and the practicalities of the European pathway;
3. the European pathways shall be monitored and supervised by a mentor.

Article 4
EUROPASS Training
1. A Community information document known as the 'EUROPASS Training`, the contents and presentation of which are described in the Annex, shall be issued by the body responsible for organising the training in the Member State of provenance to all persons completing a European pathway.
2. The EUROPASS Training document shall:
(a) specify the vocational training followed in the course of which the European pathway was completed and the qualification, diploma, title or other certificate to which the training leads;
(b) specify that the European pathway forms part of the training followed in the Member State of provenance, according to its own legislation, procedures or practices;

(c) identify the content of the European pathway, providing relevant details of any work experience or training followed during the pathway and, where appropriate, the skills acquired and the method of evaluation used;
(d) indicate the duration of the European pathway organised by the host partner during the work experience or training;
(e) identify the host partner;
(f) identify the mentor's function;
(g) be issued by the body responsible for organising the training in the Member State of provenance. It shall contain, for each European pathway, a record which shall form an integral part of the EUROPASS Training, completed by the host partner and signed by him/her and by the holder.

Article 5
Consistency and complementarity
With due regard for the procedures and resources specific to Community programmes and initiatives in education and vocational training, the Commission, in cooperation with the Member States, shall ensure overall consistency between the implementation of this Decision and those programmes and initiatives.

Article 6
Support measures and accompanying measures
1. The Commission shall be responsible for the production and appropriate dissemination and monitoring of the EUROPASS Training in close cooperation with the Member States. To that end, each Member State shall designate one or more bodies responsible for ensuring implementation at national level, in close cooperation with the social partners and, where appropriate, with representative organisations for work-linked training.
2. To that end, each Member State shall take steps to:
(a) facilitate access to the EUROPASS Training by disseminating appropriate information;
(b) allow an evaluation of the actions implemented, and
(c) facilitate equal opportunities, in particular by raising awareness among all relevant actors.
3. In close cooperation with the Member States, the Commission shall set up a coordination and mutual information system.
4. In implementing the provisions of this Decision, the Commission and the Member States shall take account of the importance of SMEs and crafts and of their particular needs.

Annex 7.4.

Decision No 253/2000/EC of the European Parliament and of the Council of 24 January 2000 establishing the second phase of the Community **action programme in the field of education 'Socrates'**
Official Journal L 028 , 03/02/2000 P. 0001 - 0015.

MAIN PROVISIONS

Article 1
Establishment of the programme
1. This Decision establishes the second phase of the Community action programme in the field of education, "Socrates", hereinafter referred to as "this programme".
2. This programme shall be implemented over the period starting on 1 January 2000 and ending on 31 December 2006.
3. This programme shall contribute to the promotion of a Europe of knowledge through the development of the European dimension in education and training by promoting life-long learning, based on formal and informal education and training. It shall support the building up of the knowledge, skills and competences likely to foster active citizenship and employability.
4. This programme shall support and supplement action taken by and in the Member States, while fully respecting their responsibility for the content of education and the organisation of education and training systems, and their cultural and linguistic diversity.

Article 2
Objectives of the programme
In order to contribute to the development of quality education and encourage life-long learning, while fully respecting the responsibility of the Member States, the objectives of the programme shall be:
(a) to strengthen the European dimension in education at all levels and to facilitate wide transnational access to educational resources in Europe while promoting equal opportunities throughout all fields of education;
(b) to promote a quantitative and qualitative improvement of the knowledge of the languages of the European Union, in particular those languages which are less widely used and less widely taught, so as to lead to greater understanding and solidarity between the peoples of the European Union and promote the intercultural dimension of education;
(c) to promote cooperation and mobility in the field of education, in particular by:
- encouraging exchanges between educational institutions,
- promoting open and distance learning,
- encouraging improvements in the recognition of diplomas and periods of study,
- developing the exchange of information,
and to help remove the obstacles in this regard;
(d) to encourage innovation in the development of educational practices and materials including, where appropriate, the use of new technologies, and to explore matters of common policy interest in the field of education.

Article 3
Community actions
1. The objectives of this programme as set out in Article 2 shall be pursued by means of the following actions, the operational content and the application procedures of which are described in the Annex.
2. These actions shall be implemented through the following types of measures, in the form of transnational operations which may combine several of the measures:
(a) support for the transnational mobility of people in the field of education in Europe;
(b) support for the use of information and communication technologies (ICT) in education;
(c) support for the development of transnational cooperation networks facilitating the exchange of experience and good practice;
(d) promotion of language skills and understanding of different cultures;
(e) support for innovatory pilot projects based on transnational partnerships designed to develop innovation and quality in education;
(f) constant improvement of Community reference material through the
- observation and analysis of national education policies,
- observation and dissemination of good practice and innovation,

- comprehensive exchange of information.

Article 4
Access to the programme
1. Under the conditions and arrangements for implementation specified in the Annex, this programme is aimed in particular at:
(a) pupils, students or other learners;
(b) staff directly involved in education;
(c) all types of educational institutions specified by each Member State;
(d) the persons and bodies responsible for education systems and policies at local, regional and national level within the Member States.
2. Public or private bodies cooperating with educational institutions may also take part in appropriate actions under this programme, in particular:
- local and regional bodies and organisations,
- associations working in the field of education, including students', pupils', teachers' and parents' associations,
- companies and consortia, trade organisations and Chambers of Commerce and Industry,
- social partners and their organisations at all levels,
- research centres and bodies.

Article 5
Implementation of the programme and cooperation with the Member States
1. The Commission shall
- ensure the implementation of the Community actions covered by this programme in conformity with the Annex,
- consult the social partners and relevant associations in the field of education at European level and shall inform the Committee referred to in Article 8(1) of their opinions.
2. The Member States shall
- take the necessary steps to ensure the efficient running of the programme at Member State level involving all the parties concerned in education in accordance with national practice,
- establish an appropriate structure for the coordinated management of the implementation of the programme's actions at Member State level (Socrates national agencies),
- endeavour to adopt such measures as they deem appropriate to remove legal and administrative obstacles to access to this programme,
- take steps to ensure that potential synergies with other Community programmes are realised at Member State level.
3. The Commission, in cooperation with the Member States, shall ensure
- the transition between those actions carried out within the framework of the preceding programme in the field of education (Socrates, established by Decision No 819/95/EC) and those to be implemented under this programme,
- the dissemination of the results of the actions undertaken within the framework of the preceding programme in the field of education (Socrates) and of those to be implemented under this programme,
- appropriate information, publicity and follow-up with regard to actions supported by this programme.

Article 6
Joint Actions
As part of the process of building up a Europe of knowledge, the measures contained in this programme may be implemented in accordance with the procedures laid down in Article 8(2) as joint actions with related Community programmes and actions, particularly Leonardo da Vinci and Youth as well as Community programmes in the field of research and development and new technologies.

Article 7
Implementing measures
1. The measures necessary for the implementation of this Decision relating to the matters referred to below shall be adopted in accordance with the management procedure referred to in Article 8(2).
(a) the annual plan of work, including priorities, themes for joint actions and the selection criteria and procedures;
(b) the financial support to be supplied by the Community (amounts, duration and recipients) and the general guidelines for implementing the programme;
(c) the annual budget and the breakdown of funds among the different actions of the programme;
(d) the breakdown of funds among the Member States for the actions to be managed on a decentralised basis;

(e) the arrangements for monitoring and evaluating the programme and for the dissemination and transfer of results;
(f) Commission proposals for project selection, including those under action 7 (Joint actions).
2. The measures necessary for the implementation of this Decision relating to all other matters shall be adopted in accordance with the advisory procedure referred to in Article 8(3).

Article 8
Committee
1. The Commission shall be assisted by a Committee.
2. Where reference is made to this paragraph, Articles 4 and 7 of Decision 1999/468/EC shall apply, having regard to the provisions of Article 8 thereof.
The period laid down in Article 4(3) of Decision 1999/468/EC shall be set at two months.
3. Where reference is made to this paragraph, Articles 3 and 7 of Decision 1999/468/EC shall apply, having regard to the provisions of Article 8 thereof.
4. The Committee shall adopt its rules of procedure.

Article 9
Cooperation with other programme committees and information on other Community initiatives
1. The Committee shall establish regular and structured cooperation with the Committee set up within the framework of the Leonardo da Vinci action programme for the implementation of a Community vocational training policy as well as with the Committee set up within the framework of the Youth Community action programme.
2. To ensure the consistency of this programme with other measures referred to in Article 11, the Commission shall keep the Committee regularly informed about Community initiatives taken in the fields of education, training and youth, including cooperation with third countries and international organisations.

Article 10
Funding
1. The financial framework for the implementation of this programme for the period specified in Article 1 is hereby set at EUR 1850 million.
2. The annual appropriations shall be authorised by the budgetary authority within the limits of the financial perspective.

Article 11
Consistency and complementarity
1. The Commission shall, in cooperation with the Member States, ensure overall consistency and complementarity with other relevant Community policies, instruments and actions. The programme shall contribute to achieving the aims of Community policy in the areas of equality, equal opportunities for women and men and promotion of social inclusion.
The Commission shall ensure an efficient link-up between this programme and the programmes and actions in the area of education undertaken within the framework of the Community's cooperation with third countries and the competent international organisations.
2. In implementing the measures of this programme, the Commission and the Member States shall have regard to the priorities set out in the employment guidelines adopted by the Council, as part of a coordinated employment strategy.

Article 12
Participation of the EFTA/EEA countries, the associated central and eastern European countries (CEEC), Cyprus, Malta and Turkey
This programme shall be open to the participation of
- the EFTA/EEA countries in accordance with the conditions established in the EEA agreement,
- the associated central and eastern European countries (CEEC) in accordance with the conditions established in the Europe agreements, in their additional protocols and in the decisions of the respective Association Councils,
- Cyprus, funded by additional appropriations in accordance with procedures to be agreed with that country,
- Malta and Turkey, funded by additional appropriations in accordance with the provisions of the Treaty.

Article 13
International cooperation
Under this programme, and in accordance with the procedure laid down in Article 8(2), the Commission may cooperate with third countries and with the competent international organisations, in particular the Council of

Europe.

Article 14
Monitoring and evaluation
1. The Commission shall regularly monitor this programme in cooperation with the Member States. The results of the monitoring and evaluation process should be utilised when implementing the programme.
This monitoring shall include the reports referred to in paragraph 3 and specific activities.
2. This programme shall be evaluated regularly by the Commission in cooperation with the Member States. This evaluation is intended to assess the relevance, effectiveness and impact of actions implemented with regard to the objectives referred to in Article 2. It will also look at the impact of the programme as a whole.
This evaluation will also examine the complementarity between action under this programme and that pursued under other relevant Community policies, instruments and actions.
In accordance with criteria established using the procedure described in Article 8(2), there will be regular independent external evaluations of this programme.
3. Member States shall submit to the Commission by 31 December 2003 and 30 June 2007, respectively, reports on the implementation and the impact of this programme.
4. The Commission shall submit to the European Parliament, the Council, the Economic and Social Committee and the Committee of the Regions:
- on the accession of new Member States, a report on the financial consequences of these accessions on the programme, followed, if appropriate, by financial proposals to deal with the financial consequences of these accessions on the programme, in accordance with the provisions of the interinstitutional Agreement of 6 May 1999 between the European Parliament, the Council and the Commission on budgetary discipline and improvement of the budgetary procedure and with the conclusions of the Berlin European Council of March 1999. The European Parliament and the Council will take a decision on such proposals as soon as possible,
- an interim evaluation report on the results achieved and on the qualitative and quantitative aspects of the implementation of this programme by 30 June 2004,
- a communication on the continuation of this programme by 31 December 2006,
- an ex post evaluation report by 31 December 2007.

Article 15
Entry into force
This Decision shall enter into force on the date of its publication in the Official Journal of the European Communities.

Done at Brussels, 24 January 2000.

For the European Parliament
The President
N. FONTAINE

For the Council
The President
J. GAMA

(1) OJ C 314, 13.10.1998, p. 5.
(2) OJ C 410, 30.12.1998, p. 2.
(3) OJ C 51, 22.2.1999, p. 77.
(4) Opinion of the European Parliament of 5 November 1998 (OJ C 359, 23.11.1998, p. 60), Council common position of 21 December 1998 (OJ C 49, 22.2.1999, p. 42), Decision of the European Parliament of 25 February 1999 (OJ C 153, 1.6.1999, p. 24) and Decision of the European Parliament of 15 December 1999 (not yet published in the Official Journal). Council Decision of 17 December 1999.
(5) OJ L 87, 20.4.1995, p. 10. Decision as amended by Decision No 576/98/EC (OJ L 77, 14.3.1998, p. 1).
(6) OJ L 146, 11.6.1999, p. 33.
(7) OJ C 172, 18.6.1999, p. 1.
(8) OJ L 184, 17.7.1999, p. 23.

ANNEX

I. INTRODUCTION AND GENERAL PROVISIONS

1. The objectives laid down in Article 2 are to be implemented by means of the actions set out in this Annex on the basis of the Community measures described in Article 3.
2. The provisions relating to the timetable, the conditions for the submission of applications and the eligibility and selection criteria are to be determined in accordance with Article 8(2) and published regularly by the Commission in the "Socrates Guidelines for Applicants". In addition calls for proposals will be published, specifying all deadlines for the submission of proposals.
3. In the context of activities involving the mobility of persons, adequate linguistic preparation should be provided in order to ensure that the beneficiaries possess the necessary competence in the language(s) of instruction in the host establishment. Appropriate organisational arrangements should be made at the home and host establishments in order to ensure that maximum benefit is derived from the mobility activity in question.
4. The projects coordinated by universities under the various actions of the programme should form part of the "institutional contract" of the institutions concerned provided for in Action 2.
5. Supporting measures may be taken to promote access and participation by persons with special educational needs. Where appropriate, positive actions may be taken in order to promote equal opportunities for women and men. Activities giving special emphasis to intercultural aspects or to promoting competence in other languages, in particular the less widely used and less taught languages of the Community, are to be particularly encouraged. The promotion of all types of open and distance learning, as well as the appropriate use of information and communication technology, is to be encouraged across all actions of the programme. Under all actions of the programme, particular attention will be paid to the dissemination of results.

II. COMMUNITY ACTIONS

This Annex contains two main types of actions:

- the first type, Actions 1 to 3, is aimed at the three basic stages of life-long education (school, university, other);
- the second type, Actions 4 to 8, concerns transversal measures in fields such as languages, information and communication technology (ICT) for educational purposes, including in particular educational multimedia and the exchange of information, as well as matters of horizontal interest such as innovation, the dissemination of results, joint actions and the evaluation of the programme.

ACTION 1: "COMENIUS": SCHOOL EDUCATION

Comenius seeks to enhance the quality and reinforce the European dimension of school education, in particular by encouraging transnational cooperation between schools and contributing to improved professional development of staff directly involved in the school education sector, and to promote the learning of languages and intercultural awareness.

Action 1.1: School partnerships

1. The Community encourages the creation of multilateral partnerships between schools. Such partnerships may also involve other appropriate bodies, such as teacher training establishments, local institutions and authorities, businesses or cultural establishments as well as parents', pupils' and other relevant organisations.
2. Community financial assistance may be awarded for the following:

(a) projects which focus on one or more topics of common interest to the participating schools, involving:

- the participation of pupils in project preparation and project activities, including project-related mobility where appropriate,
- the mobility of teachers to prepare and monitor a project or to teach in another Member State, including in-company placements,
- the development of teaching material and the exchange of good practice;

(b) projects aimed specifically at teaching and learning the official languages of the Community, together with Irish (one of the languages in which the Treaties establishing the European Communities are drawn up) and Lëtzeburgesch (a language spoken throughout the territory of Luxembourg), including in frontier regions of the Member States, the official languages of the Community in neighbouring regions of other Member States. The projects may be bilateral, especially where they target one of the less widely used or less widely taught of these languages and should include exchanges of pupils in addition to the activities referred to in point (a);

(c) projects aimed at promoting intercultural awareness and in particular those designed to help combat racism and xenophobia or to address the specific needs of the children of migrant workers, gypsies and travellers and occupational travellers;

(d) projects addressing issues related to pupils with special educational needs, with particular attention to the integration of such pupils into mainstream schooling.

3. Schools wishing to take part in this action shall submit a brief outline description of the activities which they plan to carry out during the coming school year within the framework of this programme ("Comenius Plan"). The Comenius Plan shall enable the Socrates national agencies to take into account the overall development of European activities of the respective school when carrying out the selection under this action.
Action 1.2: Initial and in-service training of staff involved in school education
1. The Community is to support multilateral projects undertaken by establishments and bodies active in the initial or in-service training of staff directly involved in school education. The participation of schools and other players involved in the field of education described in Article 4 of the Decision is to be encouraged, as is the involvement of supervisory bodies at regional and local level, where appropriate.
2. Community financial assistance may be awarded for the following:
Mobility actions:
(a) mobility undertaken for the purpose of initial training, including practical training periods, language assistantships and in-company placements;
(b) mobility undertaken for the purpose of in-service training and updating the skills of trained school education staff;
(c) mobility of limited duration, including immersion courses, for language teachers, staff retraining as language teachers, qualified teachers intending soon to return to employment as language teachers, and teaching staff of other disciplines required or wishing to teach in a foreign language;
Multilateral cooperation projects concerning:
(d) contributions to the development of curricula, courses, modules or teaching material in the context of reinforcing the European dimension of school education;
(e) training activities and information exchange concerning school management and related services such as guidance and counselling;
(f) education and training activities and information exchange designed to enhance intercultural awareness in school education or to promote the integration and improved educational achievement of children of migrant workers, gypsies and travellers and occupational travellers;
(g) activities concerning the training and development of staff involved in the education of pupils at risk and of pupils with special educational needs.
Action 1.3: Networks related to school partnerships and the training of staff involved in school education
The Community is to promote the networking of school partnerships and of projects concerned with the training of staff involved in school education, supported within Actions 1.1 and 1.2 respectively, to enable cooperation to take place on subjects of mutual interest, the dissemination of results and good practice and discussion of qualitative and innovatory aspects of school education. The staff training networks are to be developed, where appropriate, in close cooperation with the university "thematic networks" provided for in the Erasmus action.

ACTION 2: "ERASMUS": HIGHER EDUCATION

Erasmus seeks to enhance the quality and reinforce the European dimension of higher education, to encourage transnational cooperation between universities, to boost European mobility in the higher education sector and to improve transparency and academic recognition of studies and qualifications throughout the Community. Participating universities conclude "institutional contracts" with the Commission covering all the Erasmus activities approved. Such contracts will normally be of three years' duration and will be renewable.

Action 2.1: European interuniversity cooperation
1. The Community supports interuniversity cooperation activities including the development of innovative projects, carried out by universities in conjunction with partners in other Member States, with the participation, where appropriate, of other players involved in education, as described in Article 4 of the Decision.
2. Community financial assistance may be awarded for the following:
(a) the organisation of mobility of students and university teachers;
(b) joint development and implementation of curricula, modules, intensive courses or other educational activities, including multidisciplinary activities and the teaching of subjects in other languages;
(c) consolidation, extension and further development of the European credit transfer system (ECTS), which is designed to facilitate academic recognition in other Member States.

Action 2.2: Mobility of students and university teachers
1. The Community supports transnational mobility activities concerning:
(a) students, in accordance with point 2;
(b) university teachers, for the purpose of carrying out teaching assignments likely to enhance the European dimension or extend the range of courses offered by the universities concerned.
2. Students who, after completing at least their first year of studies, spend three to 12 months in another Member

State within the framework of this Action, will be considered "Erasmus students", regardless whether they have been awarded financial support in accordance with point 3. Such periods are fully recognised under the interuniversity agreements forming part of the institutional contracts and may include integrated in-company placements where appropriate. The host universities will not charge tuition fees to Erasmus students. Students with special needs will be given particular attention.
3. Community financial assistance may be awarded for:
- the mobility of students. The Member States may, in awarding Community grants, take appropriate account of the economic situation of applicants. As the Community's contribution covers only part of the cost of students' mobility, Member States are invited to help provide the necessary funds. In this connection, grants or loans available to students in the Member State of origin shall continue to be paid during the period of study in a host Member State;
- the mobility of university teachers;
- preparatory measures, in accordance with Section IV B, point 4.

Action 2.3: Thematic networks
The Community promotes the development and consolidation of thematic networks, each enabling a large grouping of universities to cooperate on topics relating to one or more disciplines or on other matters of mutual interest in order to disseminate innovation, facilitate the spread of good practice, encourage discussion of qualitative and innovative aspects of higher education, improve teaching methods and stimulate the development of joint programmes and specialised courses. The involvement of representatives of learned societies, professional associations and socioeconomic circles is to be encouraged. Special attention will be paid to the dissemination of results.

ACTION 3: "GRUNDTVIG": ADULT EDUCATION AND OTHER EDUCATIONAL PATHWAYS

1. As a complement to Action 1 (school education) and Action 2 (higher education), Grundtvig seeks to encourage the European dimension of life-long learning, to contribute - through enhanced transnational cooperation - to innovation and improved availability, accessibility and quality of other educational pathways, and to promote the learning of languages. The action is thus addressed to people who, at whatever stage of their life, seek access to knowledge and competences within the framework of formal or non-formal education or by means of autonomous learning, thereby increasing their intercultural awareness and employability and enhancing their capacity to progress in education and play a full and active role in society.
2. Community financial assistance may be awarded for transnational projects and initiatives seeking to promote:
(a) adults' individual demand for and their participation in life-long learning activities;
(b) acquisition or updating of competences for persons lacking basic education and qualifications;
(c) the development, exchange and dissemination of innovative educational approaches and good practice, including the development and dissemination of modules and appropriate teaching material;
(d) the development of information and support services for adult learners and for providers of adult education, including services related to guidance and counselling;
(e) the development of tools and methods for the assessment, validation or certification of the knowledge, skills and competences acquired by adult learners, including by means of experiential or autonomous learning or through non-formal education;
(f) improved competence in other Community languages or enhanced international awareness among adult learners and those involved in the provision of adult education;
(g) the development of initial or in-service training for educational staff working in this sector;
(h) visits and exchanges, for persons including those providing adult education or the training of adult educators;
(i) projects addressing adult learners with special educational needs.
3. The Community encourages the creation of European networks to strengthen the links between the various parties involved in this area to enable them to cooperate on a more stable basis on matters of common interest, and to enhance their awareness of the European dimension of education.

ACTION 4: "LINGUA": TEACHING AND LEARNING OF LANGUAGES

1. The aim of the Lingua action is to support transversal measures relating to the learning of languages, with a view to helping to promote and maintain linguistic diversity within the Community, to improve the quality of language teaching and learning and to facilitate access to life-long language learning opportunities tailored to individual requirements. Particular attention is to be given to intensifying transnational contacts in the language teaching profession and among those responsible for language teaching policies throughout the Community in all educational sectors. In this way, Lingua both complements and enriches measures related to the promotion of language-learning under other actions of this programme, in particular Actions 1, 2 and 3.

2. In this context, language teaching covers the teaching and learning as foreign languages of all the official languages of the Community, together with Irish (one of the languages in which the Treaties establishing the European Communities are drawn up) and Lëtzeburgesch (a language spoken throughout the territory of Luxembourg). Special attention shall be paid throughout the programme to promoting the less widely used and less widely taught of these languages.
3. Community financial assistance may be awarded to the following transnational language-learning projects and activities:
(a) awareness-raising activities designed to draw attention to the importance of language-learning and the availability of language-learning opportunities;
(b) activities seeking to promote and/or spread innovations and good practice, such as the early learning of languages or multilingual comprehension;
(c) the development and exchange of curricula, production of new teaching material and improvement of methods and tools for the recognition of language competence;
(d) exchange of information and transnational networking of resource centres;
(e) the development of measures to promote competence in foreign languages as required in specific situations and contexts, and insofar as these are not related to specific professions;
(f) addressing issues related to the teaching and learning of languages arising from further enlargement of the Community.

ACTION 5: "MINERVA" OPEN AND DISTANCE LEARNING, INFORMATION AND COMMUNICATION TECHNOLOGIES IN THE FIELD OF EDUCATION

1. The aim of this action is to support transversal measures relating to open and distance learning (ODL) and the use of information and communication technologies (ICT), including multimedia, in the field of education. In so doing, it complements and enriches the corresponding measures provided for within the other actions of this programme.
These measures serve a triple purpose:
- to promote improved understanding among teachers, learners, educational decision-makers and the public at large of the implications of ODL and, in particular ICT for education, and the critical, responsible use of tools and methods which utilise such technologies for educational purposes,
- to support awareness of the need to ensure that pedagogical considerations are given proper weight in the development of ICT-based educational products, notably multimedia, and
- to promote access to improved methods and educational resources and to results achieved, in particular through transnational exchange of information, experience and good practice.
2. Community financial assistance may be awarded for the following:
(a) projects and studies aimed at helping those involved in education to understand and exploit the innovative processes under way, in particular those relating to the use of ICT in teaching and learning, the development of innovative instruments and approaches, and methods for establishing criteria for quality assessment of ICT-based educational products and services;
(b) projects to develop and test new methods, modules and resources for ODL and ICT;
(c) projects for the development and interconnection of services and systems providing information for teachers, decision-makers and other actors involved in education on educational methods and resources which utilise ODL and ICT;
(d) activities to support the exchange of ideas and experience relating to ODL and the use of ICT in education, in particular the networking of resource centres, teacher training institutions, experts, decision-makers and project coordinators on subjects of common interest.

ACTION 6: OBSERVATION AND INNOVATION

This action contributes to improving the quality and transparency of education systems and furthering the process of educational innovation in Europe through the exchange of information and experience, the identification of good practice, the comparative analysis of systems and policies in this field, and the discussion and analysis of matters of common educational policy interest to be determined by the Council.

Action 6.1: Observation of education systems, policies and innovation
1. Making optimal use of existing structures wherever possible, this action consists of the following:
(a) collection of descriptive and statistical data, and comparative analysis of educational systems and policies in the Member States;
(b) development of methods for evaluating the quality of education, including the development of appropriate criteria and indicators;

(c) development and updating of databases and other information resources on innovatory experiments;
(d) dissemination of experience resulting from relevant activities supported at Community and Member State level;
(e) facilitation of the recognition of diplomas, qualifications and periods of learning at all educational levels in other Member States.
2. To this end, Community financial assistance may be awarded for:
(a) the information network on education in Europe, "Eurydice", comprising the European Unit set up by the Commission and units set up by the Member States to enable it to make a full contribution to the implementation of this action. The network will in particular be called upon to collect and exchange information on education systems and policies, to develop data bases, to produce comparative studies and to draw up indicators. Eurydice will seek, when necessary, relevant support from external experts;
(b) the organisation of and participation in "Arion" multilateral study visits for decision-makers and senior managers of educational institutions in any sector of education, designed to facilitate exchanges of information and experience on subjects of mutual interest to the Member States. The Commission and Member States will ensure appropriate dissemination of the results of the visits and promote their interactivity with other actions within this programme;
(c) networking of institutes and other appropriately qualified bodies engaged in analysing educational systems and policies, as well as of the bodies involved in the evaluation of educational quality;
(d) studies, analyses, pilot projects, seminars, exchanges of experts and other appropriate actions relating to matters of common educational policy interest bringing together decision-makers on the priority themes to be determined by the Council. The Commission may call upon the services of a group of experts to assist it in ensuring the reliability of the analytical work carried out within the framework of these activities. The arrangements for establishing the group will be determined in accordance with Article 8(2) of the Decision;
(e) activities designed to promote the recognition of diplomas, qualifications and periods of learning, notably studies, analyses, pilot projects and the exchange of information and experience. The Community network of national academic recognition information centres (NARIC) will make a full contribution in this regard. In particular, it will collect and disseminate authenticated information which is necessary for the purpose of academic recognition, also bearing in mind synergies with the professional recognition of diplomas.
3. In implementing this action, close cooperation will be ensured in particular with the Statistical Office of the European Communities (Eurostat), the European Centre for the Development of Vocational Training (Cedefop), the European Training Foundation (ETF) and appropriate international organisations, notably the Council of Europe, the Organisation for Economic Cooperation and Development (OECD) and the United Nations Educational, Scientific and Cultural Organisation (UNESCO).

Action 6.2: Innovatory initiatives responding to emerging needs
In addition to the cooperation activities provided for in the other actions of the present programme, the Community may support transnational projects and studies aimed at helping to develop innovations in one or more specific sectors of education. The subjects to be given priority are to be determined by the Council and reviewed regularly to enable adaptation to the new requirements which emerge during the period covered by this programme.

ACTION 7: JOINT ACTIONS
1. In accordance with Article 6 of the Decision, Community support may be provided within the framework of this programme for Joint Actions with other Community programmes and actions promoting a Europe of knowledge, in particular the Leonardo da Vinci and Youth programmes.
2. Such joint actions may be carried out by common calls for proposals on selected themes of common interest which are not exclusively covered by any single programme concerned, to be determined in accordance with Article 8(2), of the Decision and agreed with the committees of the other programmes and actions involved.
3. Appropriate steps will be taken to promote regional and local contact and interaction between the players taking part in this programme and in the Leonardo da Vinci and Youth programmes.

ACTION 8: ACCOMPANYING MEASURES
1. Community financial assistance may be awarded to the following initiatives aimed at promoting the objectives of this programme, provided that such initiatives are not eligible for assistance under other actions of the programme:
(a) awareness-raising activities to promote cooperation in the field of education, including support for appropriate competitions and other events designed to enhance the European dimension of education;
(b) transnational activities carried out by associations and other non-governmental bodies active in the field of education, as well as bodies concerned with educational guidance and counselling;
(c) conferences and symposia on innovations in the sectors targeted by the programme;

(d) activities aimed at training persons involved in the management of European cooperation projects in the field of education;
(e) measures to optimise and disseminate the results of projects and activities carried out with the support of this programme or its previous phase;
(f) activities involving cooperation with third countries and with the competent international organisations, in particular the Council of Europe, in accordance with Article 13 of the Decision.
2. Community financial assistance will be provided to support the activities of the Socrates national agencies set up by the Member States in accordance with Article 5 of the Decision, and to ensure the effective monitoring and evaluation of this programme.
3. In carrying out the programme, the Commission may have recourse to experts and to technical assistance organisations, the financing of which may be provided for within the overall financial framework for the programme. Furthermore, the Commission may organise such seminars, colloquia or other meetings of experts as are likely to facilitate the implementation of the programme, and undertake appropriate information, publication and dissemination actions.

III. SELECTION PROCEDURES

Procedures for the proposal and selection of the activities referred to in this Annex are as follows:

1. Decentralised actions
The following actions, under which the selection decisions are taken by the Member States, are to be considered "decentralised":
(a) - Action 1.1 (School partnerships)
- Action 1.2, point 2(a), (b), (c) (Mobility actions within training partnerships for school educational staff)
- Action 3, point 2(h) (Visits and exchanges in adult education)
- Action 6.1, point 2(b) (Arion study visits)
- preparatory visits under all actions.
Requests for financial assistance submitted under these actions are to be submitted to the Socrates national agencies designated by the Member States in accordance with Article 5 of the Decision. The Member States, with the assistance of the Socrates national agencies, will carry out the selection and allocate financial assistance to the applicants selected in accordance with general guidelines to be established under Article 8(2) of the Decision.

(b) Action 2.2, point 3 (Mobility of students and university teachers)
The awarding of the financial assistance to students and university teachers for mobility assignments within the institutional contracts mentioned in Action 2.1 and for the organisation of the mobility of students and university teachers will be carried out by Member States with the assistance of the Socrates national agencies designated pursuant to Article 5 of the Decision, taking into account the past performance of the universities concerned, in accordance with general guidelines to be established under Article 8(2) of the Decision.

2. Centralised actions
The following actions, under which the selection decisions are taken by the Commission, are to be considered "centralised":
(a) - Action 1.2, point 2(d), (e), (f), (g) (Multilateral cooperation activities)
- Action 3, point 2(a) to (g) and (i) (Multilateral cooperation activities)
- Action 4 (Lingua)
- Action 5 (Minerva)
- Action 6.2 (Innovatory initiatives).
For the selection of projects under these actions, the following procedure will apply:
(i) project coordinators will submit a project proposal to the Commission and send a copy to the Socrates national agency designated by the respective Member State;
(ii) the Commission, with the assistance of independent experts will assess the project proposals. National agencies may provide the Commission with their assessment of these proposals;
(iii) in cases where the Commission's assessment is at variance with the assessment received from the national agency in the coordinating country concerning the quality or appropriateness of the project, the Commission shall, upon request of the Member State, consult with the Member State concerned. The duration of this consultation process shall not exceed two weeks;
(iv) the Commission will submit to the committee a proposal on the final selection (projects to be supported and amounts to be awarded) in accordance with the procedure set out in Article 8(2) of the Decision;
(v) after receiving the opinion of the committee, the Commission will establish the list of selected projects and

allocate the amounts to be awarded.
In certain cases, owing in particular to the scale and nature of the activities in question, a two-phase procedure may be adopted. In such cases, the procedure set out above is preceded by the submission and selection of pre-proposals. The decision in this regard and the arrangements for the pre-selection will be determined in accordance with Article 8(2) of the Decision.

(b) - Action 1.3 (Networks related to school partnerships and the training of staff involved in school education)
- Action 2.1 (European inter-university cooperation)
- Action 2.3 (Erasmus thematic networks)
- Action 3.3 (Networks in adult education)
- Action 6.1, points 2(a), (c), (d), (e) (Observation)
- Action 8 (Accompanying Measures)

Project proposals under these actions will be submitted to the Commission. The Commission, in the case of Actions 1.3, 2.3 and 3.3 with the assistance of independent experts, will assess the project proposals. Decisions on the project proposals will be taken by the Commission after receiving the opinion of the committee in accordance with Article 8(2) of the Decision.
The two-phase procedure referred to in the final paragraph of Section III.2(a) will apply to Actions 1.3, 2.3 and 3.3 under the same conditions as set out in that paragraph.

3. Joint actions
Procedures for selection under Action 7 of the programme (Joint Actions) will be determined in accordance with Article 8(2) of the Decision. Where appropriate, the procedures set out above may be adapted in order to meet the special requirements of the Joint Actions in question. The Commission will make every effort to ensure optimal coordination between these procedures and those adopted within the other Community programmes or actions with which the Joint Actions in question are implemented.
4. The Commission, assisted by the Member States, will endeavour to ensure that the selection decisions are made known to applicants at the latest five months after the closing date for submission of applications under the action in question. For projects selected in accordance with the two-phase procedure provided for under point 2(a) and (b), this will only refer to the second stage of the selection (full project proposal).
5. The Commission and, in the case of decentralised actions, the Member States will seek to ensure optimal coordination between the procedures and deadlines for submitting and selecting applications for support within this programme and the Community programmes in the fields of vocational training and youth respectively.

IV. FINANCIAL PROVISIONS

A. Decentralised actions
1. The Community funds intended to provide financial support under the actions identified as decentralised in Section III, point l, are to be allocated among the Member States in accordance with the following formulae:
(a) a minimum amount to be determined in accordance with budgetary availability for the action concerned will be allocated to each Member State;
(b) the remainder will be allocated to the various Member States on the basis of:
(i) the difference in the cost of living between the Member State of origin and the host Member State;
(ii) the distance and cost of travel between the Member State of origin and the host Member State to be calculated taking into account the lowest travel price for the journey concerned;
(iii) the country's total number of:
- pupils and teachers in school education for Action 1.1 (School partnerships) and Action 1.2 point 2(a), (b), (c) (Mobility actions within training partnerships for school education staff);
- students in higher education for Action 2.2, point 3 (Mobility of students). The number of graduates should be limited in its scope as a subsidiary and complementary factor to be determined in accordance with Article 8(2) of the Decision to qualify, where appropriate, the allocation to the Member States;
- university teachers for Action 2.2 point 3 (Mobility of university teachers).
2. The Community funds thus distributed are to be administered by the Member States with the assistance of the Socrates national agencies provided for in Article 5 of the Decision.
3. The Commission, acting in cooperation with the Member States, will take the necessary measures to encourage balanced participation at Community, national and, where appropriate, regional level, and, in the case of higher education, across the various fields of study. The proportion allocated to these measures must not exceed 5 % of the annual budget for financing each of the Actions in question.
4. The arrangements for the allocation of funds to each Member State for the mobility activities provided for in Action 3, point 2(h) (Adult education visits and exchanges) and 6.1, point 2, second indent (Arion), for the organisation of the mobility of students and university teachers in accordance with Section III. l.(b), for the

support of preparatory visits and for the preparatory measures referred to in Section IV, point B.4 will be decided upon by the Commission after receiving the opinion of the committee in accordance with Article 8(2) of the Decision.

B. Other provisions
1. Having due regard to the quality and quantity of applications for financial support, the following guidelines will be taken into account when allocating resources in accordance with Article 8(2) of the Decision:
(a) the resources to be committed under Action 1 (Comenius) will not be less than 27 % of the total budget available for this programme;
(b) the resources to be committed under Action 2 (Erasmus) will not be less than 51 % of the total budget available for this programme;
(c) the resources to be committed under Action 3 (Grundtvig) will not be less than 7 % of the total budget available for this programme;
(d) the resources to be committed for financial assistance for the Socrates national agencies under Action 8.2 and for technical assistance under Action 8.3 will not exceed 4,5 % of the total annual budget available for this programme.
The above percentages are indicative and may be adapted in accordance with Article 8(2) of the Decision.
2. As a general rule, Community financial assistance granted for projects under this programme is intended partially to offset the estimated cost necessary to carry out the activities concerned and may cover a maximum period of three years, subject to a periodic review of progress achieved. The Community contribution will not normally exceed 75 % of the total cost of any specific project, except in the case of accompanying measures. Assistance may be granted in advance to enable preparatory visits to take place in respect of the projects in question.
The amount to be made available in the annual budget of the programme for activities under Action 8.1 (f) shall not exceed EUR 250000.
3. The specific situation of persons with special needs will be taken into account when determining the amount of Community financial assistance to be awarded.
4. With regard to activities involving the mobility of persons, Community financial assistance may be awarded to help ensure adequate preparation for the period to be spent in another Member State. Such preparatory measures may include in particular language courses, information on social and cultural aspects of the host Member State, etc.

V. DEFINITIONS

For the purposes of this Decision:
1. "company" means all companies in the public or private sector whatever their size, legal status or the economic sector in which they operate, and all types of economic activities, including the social economy;
2. "decision-makers" means any category of staff with managerial, assessment, training, guidance and inspection duties in the field of education and persons responsible for this area at local, regional and national level and within ministries;
3. "guidance and counselling" means a range of activities such as information, assessment, orientation and advice to assist learners to make choices relating to education and training programmes or employment opportunities;
4. "life-long learning" means the education and training opportunities offered to individuals throughout their lives to enable them continually to acquire, update and adapt their knowledge, skills and competences;
5. "open and distance learning" means any form of flexible education, whether or not involving the use of information and communication technologies;
6. "project" means transnational cooperation activity developed jointly by a formal or informal grouping of organisations or institutions;
7. "pupil" means persons enrolled in that capacity at a "school" as defined in this Annex;
8. "resource centre" means a body engaged in the production, collection or dissemination of documentation, materials or methodologies relating to a sector of activity addressed by this programme, such as languages or information and communication technologies related to education;
9. "school" means all types of institutions providing general (nursery, primary or secondary), vocational or technical education and, exceptionally, in the case of measures to promote language learning, non-school institutions providing apprenticeship training;
10. "social partners" means, at national level, employers' and workers' organisations in conformity with national laws and/or practices and, at Community level, employers' and workers' organisations taking part in the social dialogue at Community level;
11. "student" means persons registered in "universities" as defined by this Annex, whatever their field of study,

in order to follow higher education studies leading to a degree or diploma, up to and including the level of doctorate;

12. "teacher/educational staff" means persons who, through their duties, are involved directly in the educational process in the Member States, in accordance with the organisation of their respective education system;

13. "university" means any type of higher education institution, according to national legislation or practice, which offers qualifications or diplomas at that level, whatever such establishments may be called in the Member States;

14. "university teacher" means any category of personnel employed in that capacity at a "university" as defined in this Annex.

Annex 7.5.

1999/382/EC: Council Decision of 26 April 1999 establishing the second phase of the **Community vocational training action programme 'Leonardo da Vinci'**
Official Journal L 146 , 11/06/1999 P. 0033 - 0047.

MAIN PROVISIONS

Article 1
Establishment of the programme
1. This Decision establishes the second phase of the action programme for the implementation of a Community vocational training policy "Leonardo da Vinci", hereinafter referred to as "this programme".
2. This programme shall be implemented over the period starting on 1 January 2000 and ending on 31 December 2006.
3. This programme shall contribute to the promotion of a Europe of knowledge by developing a European area of cooperation in the field of education and vocational training. It shall support Member States' policies on life-long learning and the building up of the knowledge and skills and competences likely to foster active citizenship and employability.
4. This programme shall support and supplement action taken by, and in, the Member States while fully respecting their responsibility for the content and organisation of vocational training, and of their cultural and linguistic diversity.

Article 2
Objectives of the programme
1. Within the framework of the objectives set out in Article 127 of the Treaty, this programme aims at developing the quality, innovation and European dimension in vocational training systems and practices, through transnational cooperation. The objectives of the programme shall be to:
(a) improve the skills and competences of people, especially young people, in initial vocational training at all levels; this may be achieved inter alia through work-linked vocational training and apprenticeship with a view to promoting employability and facilitating vocational integration and reintegration;
(b) improve the quality of, and access to, continuing vocational training and the life-long acquisition of skills and competences with a view to increasing and developing adaptability, particularly in order to consolidate technological and organisational change;
innovative counselling and guidance approaches are of particular importance for the fulfilment of the objectives set out in (a) and (b) and shall be given support;
(c) promote and reinforce the contribution of vocational training to the process of innovation, with a view to improving competitiveness and entrepreneurship, also in view of new employment possibilities; special attention shall be paid in this respect to fostering cooperation between vocational training institutions, including universities, and undertakings, particularly SMEs.
2. In implementing the objectives set out in paragraph 1, particular attention shall be paid to people at a disadvantage in the labour market, including disabled people, to practices facilitating their access to training, to the promotion of equality, to equal opportunities for women and men and to the fight against discrimination.

Article 3
Community measures
1. The objectives of this programme shall be pursued by means of the following measures, the operational content and application procedures thereof which are described in the Annexes and which may be combined:
(a) support for the transnational mobility of people undergoing vocational training, especially young people, and for those responsible for training ("Mobility");
(b) support for pilot projects based on transnational partnerships designed to develop innovation and quality in vocational training ("pilot projects");
(c) promotion of language competences, including for less widely used and taught languages, and understanding of different cultures in the context of vocational training ("language competences");
(d) support for the development of transnational cooperation networks facilitating the exchange of experience and good practice ("transnational networks");
(e) the development and updating of reference material through support for surveys and analyses, the establishement and updating of comparable data, the observation and dissemination of good practices and the comprehensive exchange of information ("reference material").
2. In carrying out the measures referred to in paragraph 1, specific support for transnational actions shall be available for the promotion and use of information and communication technologies (ICT) in vocational

training.

Article 4
Access to the programme
Under the conditions and arrangements for implementation specified in the Annexes, access to this programme shall be open to all public and/or private bodies and institutions involved in vocational training and, in particular:
(a) vocational training establishments, centres and bodies at all levels, including universities;
(b) research centres and bodies;
(c) undertakings, particularly SMEs and the craft industry, or public or private sector establishments, including those involved in vocational training;
(d) trade organisations, including chambers of commerce, etc.;
(e) social partners;
(f) local and regional bodies and organisations;
(g) non profit making organisations, voluntary bodies and NGOs.

Article 5
Implementation of the programme and cooperation with the Member States
1. The Commission shall ensure the implementation of the Community actions covered by this programme.
2. Member States shall:
- take the necessary steps to secure, by means of appropriate structures, the coordination, an integrated management and the follow-up for the attainment of the objectives of this programme, involving all the parties concerned by vocational training, in accordance with national practice,
- ensure that relevant information and publicity is provided in respect of the actions of this programme,
- take the necessary steps to ensure the efficient running of this programme,
- endeavour, as far as possible, to adopt such measures as they deem necessary and desirable to remove obstacles to access to this programme.
3. In cooperation with Member States, the Commission shall:
- take the steps described in the Annexes to build upon the achievements of the first phase of this programme and the Community initiatives in the area of vocational training,
- ensure the smooth transition between those actions developed in the framework of the first phase of this programme and those to be implemented under the second phase.

Article 6
Joint actions
As part of the process of building up a Europe of knowledge, the measures contained in this programme may be implemented, in conformity with the procedure laid down in Article 7, as joint actions with related Community programmes and actions, particularly those in the fields of education and youth.

Article 7
Committee
1. The Commission shall be assisted by a committee composed of two representatives from each Member State and chaired by the representative of the Commission.
2. The Committee shall deliver opinions on the following points:
(a) the general guidelines for the implementation of this programme and the financial support to be supplied by the Community;
(b) the annual plan of work for the implementation of this programme's actions, including priorities, the themes for the thematic actions and the joint actions and the Commission proposals for project selection, including those under the joint actions;
(c) the annual budgets and distribution of funding between measures, as well as joint actions, accompanying measures and projects of European organisations;
(d) the criteria applicable for establishing the indicative breakdown of funds among the Member States for the purpose of the actions to be managed according to selection procedure A (Annex I, Section III);
(e) the arrangements for monitoring and evaluating the programme and for the dissemination and transfer of results.
3. As regards the points referred to in paragraph 2, the representative of the Commission shall submit to the Committee a draft of the measures to be taken. The Committee shall deliver its opinion on the draft within a time limit which the Chairman may lay down according to the urgency of the matter. The opinion shall be delivered by the majority laid down in Article 148(2) of the Treaty in the case of decisions which the Council is required to adopt on a proposal from the Commission. The votes of the representatives of the Member States

within the Committee shall be weighted in the manner set out in that Article. The Chairman shall not vote.
4. (a) The Commission shall adopt measures which apply immediately.
(b) However, if these measures are not in accordance with the opinion of the Committee, they shall be communicated by the Commission to the Council forthwith. In that event,
- the Commission shall defer application of the measures which it has decided for a period of up to two months from the date of the communication,
- the Council, acting by a qualified majority, may take a different decision within the time limit referred to in the preceding indent.
5. The representative of the Commission shall consult the Committee on other appropriate matters concerning implementation of this programme. In that event, the representative of the Commission shall submit to the Committee a draft of the measures to be taken. The Committee shall deliver its opinion on the draft within a time limit which the Chairman may lay down according to the urgency of the matter, if necessary by taking a vote.
The opinion shall be recorded in the minutes; in addition, each Member State shall have the right to ask to have its position recorded in the minutes.
The Commission shall take the utmost account of the opinion delivered by the Committee. It shall inform the Committee of the manner in which its opinion has been taken into account.
6. The Committee shall draw up its rules of procedure.
7. The Commission, in cooperation with the Committee, shall establish regular and structured cooperation with the Committees established for the implementation of the European Community educational and youth programmes.
8. To ensure the consistency of this programme with other measures referred to in Article 9, the Commission shall keep the Committee regularly informed about Community initiatives taken in the fields of education, vocational training and youth, including cooperation with third countries and international organisations.

Article 8
Social partners
Without prejudice to the procedures described in Article 7(3), (4) and (5), the Commission may consult the Committee on any matter concerning the application of this Decision.
Whenever such consultation takes place, a number, equal to that of the representatives of the Member States, of representatives of the social partners, appointed by the Commission on the basis of proposals from the social partners at Community level, shall participate in the work of the Committee as observers.
They shall have the right to request that their position be recorded in the minutes of Committee meetings.

Article 9
Consistency and complementarity
1. The Commission shall, in cooperation with the Member States, ensure the overall consistency and complementarity with other relevant Community policies, instruments and actions, in particular the European Social Fund, in particular those contributing to a Europe of knowledge, in particular in the fields of education, vocational training, youth, research and technological development, and innovation.
2. In implementing the measures of this programme, the Commission and the Member States shall have regard to the priorities set out in the employment guidelines adopted by the Council, as part of a coordinated employment strategy.
3. In partnership with Community social partners, the Commission shall endeavour to develop the coordination between this programme and the social dialogue at Community level, including at sectoral levels.
4. The Commission shall secure the assistance of the European Centre for the Development of Vocational Training (Cedefop) in implementing this programme, in accordance with the arrangements set out in Regulation (EEC) No 337/75(6) establishing the Cedefop. Subject to the same conditions and in the areas which lend themselves to it, coordination shall be established under the auspices of the Commission with the European Training Foundation as specified by Regulation (EEC) No 1360/90(7).
5. The Commission shall keep the Advisory Committee on Vocational Training regularly informed of the progress of this programme.

Article 10
Participation of the EFTA/EEA countries, the associated central and eastern European countries (CEEC), Cyprus, Malta and Turkey
This programme shall be open to the participation of:
- the EFTA/EEA countries in accordance with the conditions established in the EEA agreement,
- the associated central and eastern European countries (CEEC) in accordance with the conditions established in the Europe agreements, in their additional protocols and in the decisions of the respective Association Councils,

- Cyprus, under the same conditions as those applied to the EFTA/EEA countries, funded by additional appropriations in accordance with the procedures to be agreed with that country,
- Malta and Turkey, funded by additional appropriations, in accordance with the provisions of the Treaty.

Article 11
International cooperation
Under this programme, and in accordance with the procedure laid down in Article 7(2), (3) and (4), the Commission shall strengthen its cooperation with third countries and with the competent international organisations.

Article 12
Funding
1. The financial reference amount for the implementation of this programme for the period 2000 to 2006 shall be EUR 1150 million.
2. The annual appropriations shall be authorised by the budgetary authority within the limits of the financial perspective.

Article 13
Monitoring and evaluation
1. The Commission shall regularly monitor this programme in cooperation with the Member States.
This monitoring shall include the reports referred to in paragraph 4 and specific activities.
2. The Commission shall regularly evaluate the implementation of this programme in cooperation with the Member States, in accordance with the procedure laid down in Article 7(2), (3) and (4) and on the basis of criteria devised in cooperation with the Member States. The main objective shall be the evaluation of the effectiveness and the impact of actions implemented in comparison with the objectives aimed at in Article 2. The evaluation shall also look at the dissemination of the results of actions under this programme, of good practiced and the impact of this programme as a whole in terms of its objectives.
This evaluation shall also examine the complementarity between actions under this programme and those pursued under other relevant Community policies, instruments and actions.
In accordance with criteria established using the procedure described in Article 7(2), (3) and (4), there shall be regular independent external evaluations of the results of the Community actions.
3. The findings of the monitoring and evaluation should be taken into account when implementing this programme.
4. Member States shall submit to the Commission by 31 December 2003 and 30 June 2007 respectively reports on the implementation and effectiveness of this programme and its impact on the vocational training systems and arrangements which exist in the Member States. The reports shall also take into account the promotion of equality, and of equal opportunities, between women and men.
5. The Commission shall submit to the European Parliament, the Council and the Economic and Social Committee:
- a first interim report on the initial operational implementation of this programme by 30 June 2002,
- a second interim report on the implementation of this programme by 30 June 2004,
- a communication on the continuation of this programme by 31 December 2004; where appropriate, that communication shall contain a suitable proposal,
- a final report on the implementation of this programme by 31 December 2007.

Article 14
Entry into force
This Decision shall enter into force on the date of its publication in the Official Journal of the European Communities.

Done at Luxembourg, 26 April 1999.

For the Council
The President
J. FISCHER

(1) OJ C 309, 9.10.1998, p. 9.
(2) OJ C 410, 30.12.1998, p. 6.
(3) Opinion, of the European Parliament of 5 November 1998 (OJ 359, 23.11.1998, p. 59), Council Common Position of 21 December 1998 (OJ C 49, 22.2.1999, p 65) and Decision of the European Parliament of 23 March

1999 (not yet published in the Official Journal).
(4) OJ L 340, 29.12.1994, p. 8.
(5) OJ C 102, 4.4.1996, p. 4.
(6) OJ L 39, 13.2.1975, p. 1. Regulation as last amended by Regulation (EC) No 354/95 (OJ L 41, 23.2.1995, p. 1).
(7) OJ L 131, 23.4.1990, p. 1. Regulation as last amended by Regulation (EC) No 1572/98 (OJ L 206, 23.7.1998, p. 1).

ANNEX I - COMMUNITY ACTIONS AND MEASURES

SECTION I: GENERAL PRINCIPLES

1. The objectives set out in Article 2 of the Decision will be implemented by means of transnational partnerships which submit proposals for action on the basis of the Community measures described in Article 3.
2. Each proposal submitted by a transnational partnership will pursue one or more of the objectives of the programme, and will indicate the measure(s) it intends to implement in order to achieve its aims. Proposals can be submitted for activities integrating various measures according to Article 3(1) and in a manner to be determined by the Committee referred to in Article 7 of the Decision. With the exception of measures 1 (Mobility) and 3 (Language competences) as described in Section II, each proposal must involve partners from at least three participating countries, of which at least one must be a Member State of the European Union. In the case of project proposals under Measures 1 and 3, each proposal must involve partners from at least two participating countries, of which at least one must be a Member State of the European Union.
3. Community calls for proposals will define the priorities for the objectives, the timetable, the conditions of submission, the common eligibility criteria, particularly in terms of transnationality, project evaluation and selection procedures. The indicative timetable will include Community annual deadlines for submission, selection and approval of project applications.
A first call for proposals will remain valid for three years. A second call for proposals, will be drawn up in 2002 valid for two years, a third in 2004 valid for two years on, the basis of the interim reports referred to in Article 13(5) of the Decision.
The Community calls for proposals will be published by the Commission after having sought the opinion of the Committee referred to in Article 7 of the Decision.
4. The proposals for action must set out clearly the aims established, the methods of implementation, the results anticipated, the mechanisms for evaluating the actual results, the plans for dissemination, the beneficiaries and the partners associated, as well as the nature and level of participation of these partners, including their financial contribution and the timetable of work.
5. The proposals can be sent in during the periods specified for each year by the call for proposals. Proposal selections will take place at least once yearly in accordance with the procedures defined in Section III.
6. Member States will take appropriate steps to promote interaction between the players taking part in this programme and in education and youth-related programmes.
7. Under no circumstances may the project partners' own resources derive from other Community funding.

SECTION II: MEASURES

1. Mobility
Support for transnational mobility projects for people undergoing vocational training, especially young people, and for trainers.
Community support will be provided for the following actions:
(a) preparation and implementation of transnational placement projects for:
- people undergoing initial vocational training (placements of normally three weeks to nine months in vocational training institutions and undertakings; these placements form an integral part of the vocational training programme for the people concerned),
- students (placements of three to twelve months in undertakings),
- young workers and recent graduates (placements of two to twelve months in vocational training institutions and undertakings);
Whenever possible, these placements should involve the validation of skills and competences acquired during the placement, according to the practices of the country of origin.
These placements may also include projects which are part of "European pathways for work-linked vocational training and apprenticeship" within the meaning of Decision 1999/51/EC(1).
The transnational placement projects for people undergoing vocational training which involve SMEs and craft industry as host bodies will receive special financial support under the conditions described below.

(b) The organisation of transnational projects of exchanges
- between undertakings, on the one hand, and vocational training organisations or universities, on the other, targeting human resources managers in the business sector, and vocational training programme planners and managers, particularly trainers, and occupational guidance specialists,
- for trainers and mentors in the area of language competences (between the business sector, on the one hand, and the specialised language vocational training establishments, including universities, or vocational training bodies on the other).
Exchanges for these target groups will last between one week and a maximum of six weeks.
(c) Study visits for those responsible for vocational training on the themes proposed by the Commission can be provided by the cedefop.
The transnational placement and exchange projects may last up to two years. For the implementation of placement and exchange projects, measures for specific help for disabled participants are to be elaborated by the Committee referred to in Article 7 of the Decision.
Funding
The Community's financial contribution to the transnational placement and exchange projects defined under this measure may not exceed EUR 5000 per beneficiary for a placement or an exchange - the maximum amount of this contribution corresponding to the maximum duration indicated in (a) and (b). This maximum amount may be exceeded in the case of participants with a disability.
For this measure, the Commission will allocate to each Member State an annual global grant the amount of which will be defined in accordance with the procedures described in Annex II.
Up to 10 % of this allocation will be set aside, in accordance with procedures agreed upon with the management structure concerned to help:
- SME promoters submitting their first application to the programme. The sum may not exceed EUR 500 per promoter,
- all promoters preparing the target group mentioned under (a). The sum allowed for the pedagogic, cultural and linguistic preparation of that target group, may not exceed EUR 200 per placement of less than three months duration or EUR 500 per placement of more than three months duration, with a ceiling of EUR 25000 per promoter.
This amount is on top of that set aside for the sending organisation for the management and monitoring of transnational placement projects.
Any unused part of this allocation may be redeployed by the management structure elsewhere within this measure. The reasons for the redeployment must be communicated to the Commission.

2. Pilot projects
Support for transnational pilot projects to develop and transfer innovation and quality in vocational training, including actions aiming at the use of information and communication technologies (ICT) in vocational training.
Community support is available for the design, development, testing and assessment of transnational pilot projects to develop and/or disseminate innovation in vocational training.
Such transnational pilot projects may relate to the development of quality in vocational training, to the development of new methods of vocational training and to vocational guidance in the context of lifelong learning.
Transnational pilot projects may also aim at:
- developing the use of ICT in vocational training actions and products,
- promoting access for people undergoing vocational training to new tools, services and vocational training products which use ICT,
- supporting the development of transnational open and distance vocational training networks through the use of ICT (multimedia products, WEB sites, network transmission, etc.),
- designing, testing and validating new vocational training approaches arising from new work situations (e.g. teleworking).
Community support for projects under this measure may be available for up to three years.
Thematic actions
Special support will be given to a small number of projects on themes of particular interest at Community level, for example:
- the development of new methods of promoting transparency with an emphasis on new forms of certification or accreditation of skills and expertise learned on the job,
- actions in support of Member States' policies and initiatives to equip with appropriate skills those at a disadvantage in the labour market, particularly those young people who have no qualifications or people whose qualifications need updating,
- developing European arrangements for vocational guidance, counselling and vocational training in business-related services.

Funding
The Community may contribute up to 75 % of eligible expenditure for the transnational pilot projects, with a ceiling of EUR 200000 per year and per project. For the thematic actions, the ceiling may be raised to EUR 300000 per year and per project, if justified by the scope of the project concerned.

3. Language competences
Support for projects to promote language and cultural competences in vocational training
Community support is available for transnational pilot projects to develop language competences in a vocational training context. Special attention will be paid to projects on less widely used and taught languages.
The point of these projects is to design, test and validate, assess and disseminate teaching material as well as innovative pedagogical methods tailored to the specific needs of each occupational area and economic sector, including through the use of language audits, and also innovatory pedagogical approaches based on language self-tuition and the dissemination of their results.
Proposals for linguistic and cultural support may also be submitted under other actions and measures, particularly in order to improve language and cultural competences amongst the trainers and mentors responsible for the pedagogic supervision of people taking part in transnational mobility programmes.
Community support is also available for transnational programmes between the business sector on the one hand and the specialised language vocational training establishments or vocational training bodies on the other.
Community support for projects under this meaure may be available for up to three years.
Funding
The Community may contribute up to 75 % of eligible expenditure, with a ceiling of EUR 200000 per project and per year.

4. Transnational networks
Support for transnational networks of European expertise and dissemination
Community support is available for the activities of multi-player vocational training networks, bringing together in the Member States, at the regional or sectoral level, the public and private players concerned. Those players include the local authorities, local chambers of commerce, trade organisations for employers and employees, undertakings and research and vocational training centres - including universities - as providers of services, advice and information on access to validated vocational training methods and products. These activities aim at:
(i) assembling, distilling and building on European expertise and innovatory approaches,
(ii) improving the analysis and anticipation of skills requirements,
(iii) disseminating the network outputs and project results throughout the Union in the appropriate circles.
Community support for transnational networks may be available for up to three years.
Funding
The Community may contribute up to 50 % of eligible expenditure for the activities of transnational networks, with a ceiling of EUR 150000 per year and per network.

5. Reference material
Support for actions to establish, update and disseminate reference material
Community support is available for actions undertaken on a transnational basis on priority themes of common interest. Such actions shall make a contribution to:
- establishing comparable data on vocational training systems and arrangements, practices and various approaches to qualifications and competences in the Member States, or
- producing quantitative and/or qualitative information, analyses and observing best practices in support of policies and vocational training practices for lifelong learning that cannot be made available by Eurostat or Cedefop. Eurostat and Cedefop are closely associated with the production of statistical instruments within the procedures currently in place notably those defined by Council Regulation (EC) No 322/97 of 17 February 1997 on Community Statistics(2), taking into account Council Decision 99/126/EC of 22 December 1998 on the Community statistical programme 1998 to 2002(3).
Community support for projects under this measure may be available for up to three years.
The Commission and the Member States will ensure that such reference material is disseminated as widely as possible, particularly in order to make it available to public and private decision-makers in vocational training.
Funding
The Community's financial contribution will be between 50 % and 100 % of eligible expenditure, with a ceiling of EUR 200000 per year and per project. If justified by the scope of the project proposed, this ceiling could be raised to EUR 300000.
6. Joint actions
1. For the joint actions described in Article 6 of the Decision, Community support may be provided for joint actions with other Community actions promoting a Europe of knowledge, particularly the Community

programmes in the fields of education and youth.
2. Such joint actions may be carried out by common calls for proposals for selected themes of interest in fields of activity which are not exclusively covered by one single programme. The themes for joint actions will be agreed by the committees concerned, in accordance with the procedure laid down in Article 7(2), (3) and (4) of the Decision.
The common calls for proposals may also respond to new demands originating during the running of the programmes concerned.
Community support for projects under this measure may be available for up to three years.
Funding
The Community may contribute up to 75 % of eligible expenditure.

7. Accompanying measures
1. To attain the objectives set out in Article 2 of the Decision, Community support is available for:
- management, coordination, monitoring and evaluation activities by the Member States as described in Articles 5 and 13 and of the Decision and in Section 1(6) of this Annex,
- information, monitoring, assessment and dissemination activities by the Member States and the Commission to facilitate access to the programme and consolidate the transfer of methods, products and tools designed, and of the results obtained by this programme, among others through data banks accessible to a wide public,
- the transnational network of national resource centres for vocational guidance,
- cooperation activities with third countries and with relevant international organisations according to Article 11 of the Decision.
2. Community financial assistance shall be provided to support the activities of the appropriate structures set up by the Member States in accordance with Article 5 of the Decision.
3. In carrying out the programme, the Commission can have recourse to technical assistance organisations the financing of which shall be provided for within the overall envelope for the programme. It can, under the same conditions, have recourse to experts. Furthermore, the Commission will be able to organise seminars, colloquia or other meetings of experts, likely to facilitate the implementation of the programme and take forward information, publication and dissemination actions.
4. The respective roles and operational tasks of the technical assistance organisation(s) and the national management structures must be clearly defined, in accordance with Article 5.

SECTION III: SELECTION PROCEDURES

The proposals submitted by promoters under the calls for proposals shall be selected according to one of the following procedures:
1. Procedure A applicable to mobility actions (measure 1);
2. Procedure B applicable to:
- pilot projects (measure 2) except for thematic actions,
- language competences (measure 3),
- transnational networks (measure 4);
3. Procedure C applicable to:
- reference material (measure 5),
- thematic actions (within measure 2),
- joint actions (measure 6),
- projects of European organisations (under all measures).

1. Procedure A
This selection procedure consists of the following stages:
(i) The Commission will allocate a global grant to each participating country according to the procedure defined in Annex II, after having sought the opinion of the Committee referred to in Article 7 of the Decision.
(ii) Under the rules defined in the calls for proposals, proposals are to be submitted by the promoters to the management structure designated by the Member State.
(iii) The management structure will assess the proposals on the basis of specifications established at Community level. The management structure will establish a list of the mobility programmes selected and circulate this list, for information, to the Commission and the management structures in the other Member States.
(iv) The Member States, with the assistance of the respective management structures, shall be responsible for contracting and allocating the global grant to the individual promoters.
(v) The Member States will submit to the Commission an annual report on the results of the mobility programmes. The report includes information inter alia on the following topics:
- the target publics of the programme,

- the contents and objectives in terms of skills and/or qualifications,
- the duration of training and/or work learning experience in a training establishment and/or company,
- the partners associated in the other Member State or States.

2. Procedure B
This selection procedure consists of a two-step selection process:
- selection of pre-proposals;
- selection of full proposals.

(i) Under the rules defined in the call for proposals, pre-proposals are to be submitted by the promoters to the management structure designated by the Member State.
(ii) Member States will evaluate and select the pre-proposals. The promoters will be informed of the outcome of this selection. Only promoters of successful pre-proposals will be invited to submit a full proposal to the management structure in the respective Member State. The promoters will also send a copy of their full proposals to the Commission.
(iii) Member States will evaluate and rank the full proposals and submit a report to the Commission, presenting the outcome of this pre-selection by objective and by measure, the assessment procedure, the parties involved in this procedure as well as a descriptive and reasoned list of proposals likely to be retained in order of priority. This report will also present the information and publicity measures taken to facilitate participation in the programme.
(iv) The Commission, with the assistance of independent experts, will evaluate the proposals, with a view to assessing and ensuring their transnational and innovative nature. These independent experts will be appointed by the Commission, taking full account of the views of the Member States and the social partners. The Commission will examine the national reports and consult accordingly with each Member State.
(v) The Commission will submit to the Committee a proposal on the allocation of the budgetary resources by measure and by Member State and will obtain its opinion in accordance with the procedure set out in Article 7 of the Decision.
(vi) After receiving the opinion of the Committee, the Commission will establish the list of selected projects per Member State and allocate the funds for the implementation of the selected projects to each Member State.
(vii) Member States, with the assistance of the respective management structures, will be responsible for contracting and allocating funds to the individual promoters.
(viii) The selection of pre-proposals has to be carried out within two months after the end of the period for submission of proposals as specified in the call for proposals; the process on stages (iii) to (vi) should not take more than five months.

3. Procedure C
This procedure consists of a two-step selection process:
- selection of pre-proposals;
- selection of full proposals.

(i) Under the rules defined in the call for proposals, pre-proposals are to be submitted by the promoters to the Commission. The promoters will also send a copy of their pre-proposals to the management structure in their Member States.
(ii) The Commission will evaluate all the pre-proposals and, having sought the opinion of the programme Committee, make a selection. The promoters will be informed of the outcome of this selection.
(iii) Only promoters of successful pre-proposals will be invited to submit a full proposal to the Commission. The promoters will also send a copy of their full proposals to the management structure of their Member States.
(iv) The Commission, with the assistance of independent experts, will undertake a transnational appraisal of the proposals received and establish a short list of projects. These independent experts will be appointed by the Commission, taking full account of the views of the Member States and the social partners.
(v) In accordance with the procedure set out in Article 7 of the Decision, the Commission shall seek the opinion of the Committee on this short-list.
(vi) The Commission will establish the final list of proposals selected and inform the Committee. It will set out the conditions for monitoring these projects in conjunction with the management structures in the Member States.
(vii) The Commission, with the appropriate technical assistance, will be responsible for contracting and allocating funds to the individual promoters.
(viii) The selection of pre-proposals has to be carried out within three months after the end of the period for submission of proposals as specified in the call for proposals; the process on stages (iii) to (vi) should not take more than five months.

(1) OJ L 17, 22.1.1999, p. 45.

(2) OJ L 52, 22.2.1997, p. 1.
(3) OJ L 42, 16.2.1999, p. 1.

ANNEX II

SECTION I: OVERALL BUDGET BREAKDOWN
1. At the beginning of the operation, and no later than 1 March every year, the Commission will submit to the Committee an ex ante breakdown of budget resources by type of measure, by procedure and taking into account, to this end, the objectives set out in Article 2 of the Decision and will seek its opinion. The Commission will on this basis define an indicative budget for each Member State for the implementation of the actions covered by selection procedure A referred to in Annex I.

2. The funds available will be broken down internally subject to the following restrictions:
(a) The funds allocated to mobility programmes may not be less than 39 % of the annual budget for the programme.
(b) The funds allocated in support of devising, developing and testing transnational pilot projects may not be less than 36 % of the annual budget for the programme. Within this allocation the funds allocated in support of Thematic Action projects may not be more than 5 %.
(c) The funds allocated in support of devising, developing and testing Language Competence projects may not be less than 5 % of the annual budget for the programme.
(d) The remaining expenditure may not be less than 15 %. Within this expenditure, the funds allocated for the accompanying measures is not to exceed 9 %. The funds allocated for activities under Article 11 of the Decision is not to exceed 0,2 % of the annual budget of the programme.

3. All the percentages given above are indicative and can be adapted by the Committee according to the procedure laid down in Article 7(2), (3) and (4) of the Decision.

SECTION II: SPECIFIC REGULATIONS FOR MOBILITY GLOBAL GRANTS

1. Before the start of the transnational exchange and placement programmes, the Commission will allocate a global grant established on the basis of calculation criteria defined within the procedures described in Article 7 of the Decision, taking into account:
- the population,
- the difference in the cost of living between the Member State of origin of the sending organisation and the host Member State,
- the geographical distance and the costs of transport,
- the weight of the target public concerned in relation to the overall population, depending on the availability of data for all Member States.
In any event, the application of these criteria cannot result in the exclusion of any Member State from funding of the transnational placement and exchange programmes described in Annex I.
2. The overall grant is allocated to each Member State on the basis of an operational plan which must set out clearly:
- the arrangements for managing financial support,
- the steps to be taken to assist placement and exchange organisers to identify potential partners,
- appropriate measures to be taken in the interests of sound preparation, organisation and follow-up of placements and exchanges, also regarding the promotion of equal opportunities.
3. For the first year of programme implementation, Member States will submit this operational plan to the Commission no later than 31 March 2000. The Commission will on this basis allocate to each Member State an amount on the basis of which it can go ahead with transnational programmes. The amounts not used up within this allocation at 1 October 2000 will be incorporated in the final amount of the global grant.

ANNEX III

DEFINITIONS
For the purposes of this Decision and taking account of the differences which exist between the systems and arrangements in the Member States:
(a) initial vocational training means any form of initial vocational training, including technical and vocational teaching, apprenticeship and vocationally oriented education, which contributes to the achievement of a vocational qualification recognised by the competent authorities in the Member State in which it is obtained,

(b) work-linked training means vocational training, at any level including higher education. This vocational training, recognised or certified by the competent authorities of the Member State of provenance according to its own legislation, procedures or practices, involves structured periods of training in an undertaking and, where appropriate, in a vocational training establishment or centre,
(c) continuing vocational training means any vocational training undertaken by a worker in the Community during his or her working life,
(d) life-long learning means the education and vocational training opportunities offered to individuals throughout their lives to enable them continually to acquire, update and adapt their knowledge, skills and competences,
(e) open and distance vocational training means any form of flexible vocational training involving:
- the use of ICT techniques and services in traditional or modern form, and
- support in the form of individualised advice and mentoring,
(f) European pathways for work-linked vocational training and apprenticeship means any period which is completed by a person in a Member State other than the one where his or her work-linked vocational training is based, which forms part of the work-linked vocational training,
(g) vocational guidance means a range of activities such as counselling, information, assessment and advice, to assist people to make choices relating to initial and continuing vocational education and vocational training programmes, and to employment opportunities,
(h) undertaking means all undertakings in the public or private sector whatever their size, legal status or the economic sector in which they operate, and all types of economic activities, including the social economy,
(i) workers means all persons available on the labour market in accordance with national laws and practices, including the self-employed,
(j) vocational training bodies means any type of public, semi-public or private establishment which, in accordance with national laws and/or practices design or undertake vocational training, further vocational training, refresher vocational training or retraining, irrespective of the designation given to it in the Member States,
(k) university means any type of higher education institution, according to national legislation or practice, which offers qualifications or diplomas at that level, whatever such establishments may be called in the Member States,
(l) students means persons registered in universities as defined in this Annex, whatever their field of study, in order to follow higher education studies leading to a degree or diploma, up to and including the level of doctorate,
(m) social partners means, at national level, employers' and workers' organisations in conformity with national laws and/or practices and, at Community level, employers' and workers' organisations taking part in the social dialogue at Community level,
(n) local and regional partners means any player in regional and local life - local authority, association, local chambers of commerce and associations, consortia, advisory bodies, the media - participating in local or regional cooperation activities which include vocational training,
(o) European organisations means social partners at Community level, European employers' and trade union federations in specific sectors, and bodies and organisations with a European status or scope,
(p) reference material means all the analyses, studies, surveys and identification of good practice which make it possible to locate, at Community level, the relative position of the various Member States and the progress made on a given subject or in a given area.

Annex 7.6.

Decision No 1031/2000/EC of the European Parliament and of the Council of 13 April 2000 establishing **the 'Youth' Community action programme**
Official Journal L 117 , 18/05/2000 P. 0001 - 0010.

MAIN PROVISIONS

Article 1
Establishment of the programme
1. This decision establishes the "Youth" Community action programme, hereinafter referred to as "this programme", concerning cooperation policy in the youth field, including European voluntary service and youth exchanges both within the Community and with third countries.
2. This programme shall be implemented over the period starting on 1 January 2000 and ending on 31 December 2006.
3. This programme shall contribute to the promotion of a Europe of knowledge by developing a European area of cooperation in the field of youth policy, based on informal education and training. It shall promote lifelong learning and the building up of the knowledge and skills and competences likely to foster active citizenship and employability.
4. This programme shall support and supplement action taken by and in the Member States while fully respecting their cultural and linguistic diversity.

Article 2
Objectives of the programme
1. In order to allow young people to acquire knowledge, skills and competences which may be one of the foundations of their future development, and to exercise responsible citizenship so as to become an active part of society and bearing in mind the importance of promoting equal opportunities, the objectives of this programme are as follows:
(a) to promote an active contribution by young people to the building of Europe through their participation in transnational exchanges within the Community or with third countries so as to develop understanding of the cultural diversity of Europe and its fundamental common values, thus helping to promote respect for human rights and to combat racism, anti-Semitism and xenophobia;
(b) to strengthen their sense of solidarity through more extensive participation by young people in transnational community-service activities within the Community or with third countries, in particular those with which the Community has concluded cooperation agreements;
(c) to encourage young people's initiative, enterprise and creativity so that they may take an active role in society and, at the same time, to stimulate recognition of the value of informal education acquired within a European context;
(d) reinforce cooperation in the field of youth by fostering the exchange of good practice, the training of youth workers/leaders and the development of innovative actions at Community level.
2. This programme shall also contribute to attaining the objectives of other relevant areas of Community policy.

Article 3
Community actions
1. The objectives of this programme as set out in Article 2 shall be pursued by means of the following actions, the operational content and the application procedures of which are described in the Annex:
- Youth for Europe,
- European voluntary service,
- youth initiatives,
- joint actions,
- support measures.
2. These actions shall be implemented through the following types of measures, which may, where appropriate, be combined:
(a) support for the transnational mobility of young people;
(b) support for the use of information and communication technologies (ICT) in the youth field;
(c) support for the development of cooperation networks at the European level permitting mutual exchange of experience and good practice;
(d) support for transnational projects to promote citizenship of the Union and the commitment of young people to the development of the Union;
(e) promotion of language skills and understanding of different cultures;

(f) support for pilot projects based on transnational partnerships designed to develop innovation and quality in the youth field;
(g) development, at a European level, of methods of analysis and follow-up of youth policies and their evolution (e.g. databases, key figures, mutual knowledge of "systems") and of methods of disseminating good practice.

Article 4
Access to the programme
1. This programme is aimed at young people, in principle between the ages of 15 and 25, as well as those involved in youth work, who are legal residents of a Member State. The age limits may be slightly adjusted, where justified by the specific circumstances of certain projects.
Within the framework of actions 1.2, 2.2 and 5 set out in the Annex, this programme may also be aimed at young people, in principle aged from 15 to 25, and those involved in youth work who reside in third countries, without prejudice to the competences of the Member States.
2. Particular attention should be paid to ensuring that all young people, without discrimination, have access to the activities of this programme.
3. The Commission and the Member States shall ensure that special efforts are made to assist young people who, for cultural, social, physical, mental, economic or geographical reasons, find it more difficult to participate in relevant action programmes at Community, national, regional or local level, as well as to assist small local groups. The Commission shall accordingly take account of the difficulties faced by these target groups, thus contributing to combating exclusion.
4. The Member States shall endeavour to take appropriate measures so that participants in the programme can have access to health care in accordance with the provisions of Community law. The Member State of origin shall endeavour to take appropriate measures so that participants in the European voluntary service can retain their social protection.

Article 5
Implementation of the programme and cooperation with the Member States
1. The Commission shall ensure the implementation of the Community actions covered by this programme in accordance with the Annex.
2. The Commission, in cooperation with the Member States, shall take the steps described in the Annex (action 5) in order to make the best use of what has been achieved through Community cooperative action in the youth field.
3. The Commission and Member States shall take appropriate action to develop structures established at Community and national level to achieve the objectives of the programme, in a user-friendly way, so as to facilitate access to the programme for young people and other partners at local level, to evaluate and monitor actions called for under the programme and to apply transparent consultation and selection arrangements.
The Commission and the Member States shall ensure that they take measures to facilitate young people's access to transnational mobility through measures designed adequately to inform them and raise their awareness of this subject. The Commission and the Member States shall ensure that appropriate information and publicity is provided about actions supported by the programme.
4. The Member States shall take the necessary steps to ensure the efficient running of the programme; they shall also endeavour, as far as possible, to adopt such measures as they deem necessary and desirable to remove legal and administrative obstacles to access to this programme.
5. The Commission, in cooperation with the Member States, shall ensure the transition between those actions carried out within the framework of the previous Community programmes in the youth field (Youth for Europe III and European voluntary service) and the actions to be implemented under this programme.

Article 6
Joint actions
As part of the process of building up a Europe of knowledge, the measures of this programme may be implemented in accordance with the procedures laid down in Article 8 as joint actions with related Community programmes and actions in the areas of youth, education and vocational training.

Article 7
Implementing measures
1. The measures necessary for the implementation of this Decision relating to the matters referred to below shall be adopted in accordance with the management procedure referred to in Article 8(2):
(a) the arrangements for implementing this programme, including the annual plan of work for the implementation of the programme's actions;
(b) the general balance between the different actions of the programme;

(c) the criteria applicable for establishing the indicative breakdown of funds among the Member States for the purpose of the actions to be managed on a decentralised basis;
(d) the arrangements for implementing the joint actions;
(e) the arrangements for evaluating the programme;
(f) the arrangements for attesting to participation of young volunteers.
2. The measures necessary for the implementation of this Decision relating to all other matters shall be adopted in accordance with the advisory procedure referred to in Article 8(3).

Article 8
Committee
1. The Commission shall be assisted by a committee.
2. Where reference is made to this paragraph, Articles 4 and 7 of Decision 1999/468/EC shall apply, having regard to the provisions of Article 8 thereof.
The period laid down in Article 4(3) of Decision 1999/468/EC shall be set at two months.
3. Where reference is made to this paragraph, Articles 3 and 7 of Decision 1999/468/EC shall apply, having regard to the provisions of Article 8 thereof.
4. The committee shall adopt its rules of procedure.

Article 9
Funding
1. The financial framework for the implementation of this programme for the period specified in Article 1 is hereby set at EUR 520 million.
2. The annual appropriations shall be authorised by the budgetary authority within the limits of the financial perspective.

Article 10
Consistency and complementarity
1. The Commission, in cooperation with the Member States and without prejudice to the individual character and specificity of each programme, shall ensure overall consistency and complementarity with other relevant Community policies, instruments and actions. Particular attention shall be paid to the promotion of equality and to equal opportunities for women and men.
2. The Commission, in cooperation with the Member States, shall ensure consistency between the implementation of this programme and the other Community activities relating to youth, in particular in the area of culture and the audiovisual sector, the completion of the internal market, the information society, environment, consumer protection, SMEs, social policy, employment, and public health.
3. The Commission and the Member States shall ensure that the measures of this programme have regard to the employment guidelines adopted by the Council as part of a coordinated strategy for employment.
4. The Commission shall ensure an efficient link-up between this programme and the programmes and actions in the youth field undertaken as part of the Community's external relations.

Article 11
Participation of the EFTA/EEA countries, the associated central and east European countries (CEEC), Cyprus, Malta and Turkey
This programme shall be open to the participation of:
- the EFTA/EEA countries in accordance with the conditions established in the EEA Agreement,
- the associated central and east European countries (CEEC) in accordance with the conditions established in the Europe Agreements, in their additional protocols and in the decisions of the respective Association Councils,
- Cyprus, funded by additional appropriations in accordance with the procedures to be agreed with that country,
- Malta and Turkey, funded by additional appropriations in accordance with the provisions of the Treaty.

Article 12
International cooperation
Under this programme, the Commission, acting in accordance with the procedures laid down in Article 7, shall strengthen its cooperation with non-Community countries and relevant international organisations, in particular the Council of Europe.

Article 13
Monitoring and evaluation
1. The Commission shall regularly monitor this programme in cooperation with the Member States.
This monitoring shall include the reports referred to in paragraph 3 and specific activities.

2. This programme shall be evaluated regularly by the Commission in cooperation with the Member States. This evaluation is intended to increase the effectiveness of actions implemented with regard to the objectives referred to in Article 2 and to ensure that equality of access to the programme as laid down in Article 4(2) and (3) is guaranteed.
This evaluation will also examine the complementarity between actions under this programme and those pursued under other relevant Community policies, instruments and actions.
In accordance with criteria established using the procedure described in Article 8(2), there will be regular external evaluations of the results of the Community actions.
3. Member States shall submit to the Commission by 31 December 2004 and 30 June 2007, respectively, reports on the implementation and the impact of this programme.
4. The Commission shall submit to the European Parliament, the Council, the Economic and Social Committee and the Committee of the Regions:
- on the accession of new Member States, a report on the financial consequences of these accessions on the programme, followed, if appropriate, by financial proposals to deal with the financial consequences of these accessions on the programme, in accordance with the provisions of the Interinstitutional Agreement of 6 May 1999 between the European Parliament, the Council and the Commission on budgetary discipline and improvement of the budgetary procedure and with the conclusions of the Berlin European Council of March 1999. The European Parliament and the Council will take a decision on such proposals as soon as possible,
- an interim evaluation report on the qualitative and quantitative aspects of the implementation of this programme by 30 June 2005,
- a final report on the implementation of this programme by 31 December 2007.

Article 14
Entry into force
This Decision shall enter into force on the date of its publication in the Official Journal of the European Communities.

Done at Luxembourg, 13 April 2000.

For the European Parliament
The President
N. Fontaine

For the Council
The President
A. Vara

(1) OJ C 311, 10.10.1998, p. 6.
(2) OJ C 410, 30.12.1998, p. 11.
(3) OJ C 51, 22.2.1999, p. 77.
(4) Opinion of the European Parliament of 5 November 1998 (OJ C 359, 23.11.1998, p. 75), Council common position of 28 June 1999 (OJ C 210, 22.7.1999, p. 1) and Decision of the European Parliament of 28 October 1999 (not yet published in the Official Journal). Decision of the Council of 10 April 2000 and Decision of the European Parliament of 12 April 2000 (not yet published in the Official Journal).
(5) OJ L 87, 20.4.1995, p. 1.
(6) OJ C 30, 28.1.1998, p. 1.
(7) OJ C 167, 1.6.1998, p. 230.
(8) OJ L 214, 31.7.1998, p. 1.
(9) OJ C 226, 20.7.1998, p. 66.
(10) OJ C 172, 18.6.1999, p. 1.
(11) OJ L 184, 17.7.1999, p. 23.

ANNEX

Funding approved under the programme is to observe the principles of co-financing and additionality. In accordance with Article 4(3) of the Decision, efforts must be made to facilitate access to the programme for young people who face difficulties of a cultural, social, physical, mental, economic or geographical nature, as well as for small local groups. The committee referred to in Article 8 of the Decision is to lay down the specific form these efforts should take. Community funding is to be distributed in such a way as to take account of the need to ensure balance between the mobility actions undertaken and an equal opportunity of participation for the

young people of every Member State; that is to say, Article 4(3) is to be taken into account.
Initiatives designed to encourage tolerance and the acceptance of differences, as well as measures combating all forms of exclusion, should be given specific encouragement and stimulation. The Community will be receptive to activities giving a prominent position to culture and sport in the context of informal education for young people.
In order to achieve the objectives of the programme, five categories of action are to be implemented on the basis of the measures described in Article 3 of the Decision:
- Youth for Europe
- European voluntary service
- Youth initiatives
- Joint actions
- Support measures.

ACTION 1 - YOUTH FOR EUROPE

Action 1.1: Intra-Community exchanges for young people
The Community will support mobility activities for young people provided that the activities in question last at least one week, are carried out on the basis of joint projects within the Community and involve groups of young people aged in principle between 15 and 25 years and legally resident in a Member State. The age limits may be slightly adjusted where justified by the specific circumstances of certain projects.
Those activities, based on transnational partnerships between groups of young people, are to involve their active participation and be designed to make it possible for them to discover and become aware of different social and cultural realities and to encourage them to participate in, or initiate, other activities at European level. Particular attention is to be paid to participation by young people for whom it is their first European activity and to small-scale or local groups without experience at European level.
In order to move towards a better balance between bilateral and multilateral activities, Community support will be progressively focused on multilateral group-mobility activities. Bilateral group mobility will receive funding if this is justified in terms of the target groups or a specific pedagogical approach.
Activities designed to strengthen the active involvement of young people in group mobility projects may receive funding under this action, particularly in the form of activities to provide the young people in question with linguistic and intercultural preparation.

Action 1.2: Exchanges of young people with third countries
The Community will support mobility activities for young people provided that the activities in question last at least one week, are carried out on the basis of joint projects and involve groups of young people aged in principle between 15 and 25 years and legally resident in a Member State or in a third country. These mobility activities are to involve at least two Member States.
Those activities, based on transnational partnerships between groups of young people are to involve their active participation and be designed to make it possible for them to discover and become aware of different social and cultural realities and to encourage them to participate in, or initiate, other activities at European level. Moreover, these projects are to make it possible for partners in the third countries to gain experience of this kind of activity in the field of informal education and to contribute to the development of youth work and associations in those countries.
Activities designed to strengthen the active involvement of young people in group mobility projects may receive funding, particularly in the form of activities to provide the young people in question with linguistic and intercultural preparation before their departure.

ACTION 2 - EUROPEAN VOLUNTARY SERVICE

For the purposes of this programme, "young volunteer" is taken to be a person aged in principle between 18 and 25 years and legally resident in a Member State.
Young volunteers will undertake, as active citizens, to carry out an activity which gives tangible form to solidarity, with the view to acquiring social and personal abilities and skills thus laying the foundations for their future development, while at the same time contributing to society. To this end, young volunteers will participate, in a Member State other than the one in which they reside, or in a third country, in a non-profit-making and unpaid activity of importance to the community and of a limited duration (12 months maximum) in the context of a project recognised by the Member State and the Community, in compliance with the aims of this programme set out in Article 2. In particular it should not result in job substitution. Full board and lodging as well as mentoring will be provided. The voluntary service project will ensure that young volunteers are covered by health and appropriate insurance. Young volunteers will receive an allowance/pocket money.

European voluntary service is based on a partnership and shared responsibilities between the young volunteers, the sending organisation and the host organisation.
In accordance with the provisions relating to the programme committee referred to in Article 8, a document, issued by the Commission, will attest to the participation of the young volunteers in European voluntary service and to the experience and skills that they have acquired during the relevant period.
Action 2.1: Intra-Community European voluntary service
The Community will support transnational projects (for a limited period ranging in principle from three weeks to one year) which involve young people, actively and personally, in activities designed to help meet the needs of society in a wide range of fields (social, sociocultural, environmental, cultural, etc.) which constitute at the same time an experience of informal education with a view to acquiring social and cultural skills. These projects are designed to bring young people into contact with other cultures and other languages and to experience new ideas and projects in a multicultural civil society.
The Community may support schemes, particularly those with a linguistic or intercultural element, which aim at preparing young volunteers for their departure and easing their social integration during those activities as well as when they have completed their period of European voluntary service. Particular attention is to be paid to pedagogical support and mentoring.

Action 2.2: European voluntary service with third countries
The Community will support transnational projects with third countries (for a limited period ranging in principle from three weeks to one year) which involve young people, actively and personally, in activities designed to help meet the needs of society in a wide range of fields (social, sociocultural, environmental, cultural, etc.) which constitute at the same time an experience of informal education with a view to acquiring social and cultural skills. These projects are designed to bring young people into contact with other cultures and other languages and to experience new ideas and projects in a multicultural civil society.
Support may be given to action laying or consolidating the necessary foundations for developing transnational European voluntary service projects with third countries.
The Community may support schemes, particularly those with a linguistic or intercultural element, which aim at preparing young volunteers for their departure and easing their social integration during those activities as well as when they have completed their period of European voluntary service. Particular attention is to be paid to pedagogical support and mentoring.

ACTION 3 - YOUTH INITIATIVES

In order to encourage initiative and creativity among young people, the Community will support projects in which young people actively and directly participate in innovative and creative schemes and in schemes which focus on the social commitment of young people at local, regional, national or European level. These projects will allow young people to develop their initiative and to put into practice activities of their own devising in which they play the key roles.
The Community will support initiatives designed to help young volunteers to make the best possible use of the experience they have gained during their period of voluntary service and to encourage their active integration into society. Those initiatives taken by young people after completing their European voluntary service will allow them to launch and promote activities of a social, cultural, sociocultural and economic nature and/or aim at their personal development. Priority access will be given to those young people most in need.
Support will aim at encouraging extension of these projects to include similar initiatives conducted in other Member States in order to strengthen their transnational nature and greatly expand exchanges of experience and cooperation between young people. This aid may include organising meetings of young promoters of Europe-wide initiatives. Financial aid may be granted towards the effective establishment of stable, transnational partnerships between such projects

ACTION 4 - JOINT ACTIONS

Having regard to the need for a flexible and creative approach as a precondition for cooperation between sectors, Community aid may be granted for the actions referred to in Article 6 of the Decision and for activities to be undertaken jointly with other Community schemes relating to the Europe of knowledge, in particular Community programmes in the field of education and vocational training.
The Commission, in cooperation with the Member States, will aim at developing a common system of information, observation and dissemination concerning good practice in the field of knowledge and lifelong learning, alongside joint actions with regard to multimedia for educational and training purposes. Those projects will cover a range of schemes from a number of different sectors including youth. They may be funded in a complementary manner by a number of different Community programmes, and may be implemented by means

of calls for joint projects.
Appropriate measures may be adopted to promote, at regional and local level, contact and interaction between those participating in this programme and in programmes dealing with vocational training and education. In this context, activities increasing awareness of the opportunities provided by the Community to young people may be supported.

ACTION 5 - SUPPORT MEASURES

Action 5.1: Training and cooperation in relation to those involved in youth policy
Funding shall be granted to:
1. Activities designed to give further training to persons involved in youth work, particularly European voluntary service instructors, youth workers/leaders, those running European projects and youth initiative counsellors, who take part in schemes directly involving young people, of the kind described in actions 1, 2 and 3 of the programme, the aim being to ensure that such schemes are of an appropriately high quality. Particular attention is to be paid to activities seeking to encourage the participation of those young people who find it most difficult to participate in Community actions.
2. Activities designed to develop European modules fulfilling the requirements for transnational cooperation.
3. Activities, such as study visits, feasibility studies, seminars, work-experience, which focus particularly on exchanges of experience and good practice in relation to joint actions or issues of common interest or which are designed to facilitate and promote the establishment of sustainable transnational partnerships and/or multilateral networks between those active in the field of youth work.
4. Experimental activities which comprise a source of innovation and enrichment of youth policy through the implementation of new approaches and new forms of cooperation, as well as through the shared efforts of participants from differing backgrounds.
5. Community support may also be given to conferences and seminars which seek to promote cooperation and the exchange of good practice in the field of youth, as well as to other promotion and dissemination measures regarding the results of the projects and activities supported within the framework of Community actions related to youth.
Activities associated with these measures may be solely intra-Community in nature or involve non-member countries. Particular attention is to be paid to those who work with youth at a regional or local level and who have no or little experience of, or scope for, contacts at European level, as well as to activities in which young people play the key roles.

Action 5.2: Information for young people and youth studies
1. In line with the objectives of the programme and in particular to improve access for all young people and to enhance their initiative and active participation in society, the Commission will encourage those active in the field of youth work to become involved in informing young people at European level, as well as boosting cooperation between the information and communication systems for young people established in the Member States and at Community level. In this context, particular stress is to be laid on broadening cooperation to include the fields of education and training, as well as on the dialogue both between and with young people.
2. Accordingly, funding is to be provided for initiatives involving:
- the acquisition of the necessary experience and skills to carry out youth information projects based on transnational cooperation and projects which provide information and, in particular, advisory services for young people,
- cooperative projects focusing on information dissemination, enhancing the awareness among young people of the field covered by the programme and giving young people access to all necessary information to achieve the objectives of the programme,
- the implementation, as part of transnational cooperation projects, of mechanisms permitting dialogue both between and with young people, particularly through the use of youth-oriented media and new technologies.
3. With regard to the youth studies associated with the programme objectives, the Commission will support studies focusing, among other subjects, on the impact of measures taken on behalf of young people and, in particular, measures that seek to promote cooperation in this field. Such studies shall analyse the impact of other policies on the world of youth and shall seek to provide a clearer and more comprehensive picture of young people's needs and of the circumstances in which they live.
Priority shall be given to studies concerning the paths taken by less-favoured and marginalised young people; they shall analyse, in particular, the factors which have promoted or hampered the social integration of young people, and shall bring to the fore input from the informal education sector and from the third sector in general.
Priority shall also be given to comparative studies of measures designed to promote the spirit of initiative, including their impact on local development, particularly through the creation of activities (creation of jobs,

creation of cultural or social enterprises, etc.). This research may take the form of case studies, the most relevant of which shall be made public.

Action 5.3: Information and visibility of measures
The Commission shall take all necessary measures to, inter alia, collect information on measures in the youth field from a range of sources, draw benefits from EU youth projects and increase the visibility of the actions aimed at young people at Community level by developing appropriate means of dialogue with them, including through the Internet.

Action 5.4: Support measures
1. National agencies
Community assistance may be provided to support the activities of the structures set up by Member States, in accordance with Article 5 of the Decision.
2. Technical assistance and operational support
In carrying out the programme, the Commission may have recourse to technical-assistance organisations the financing of which may be provided for within the overall financial framework for the programme. It may have recourse to experts under the same conditions. Furthermore, the Commission will be able to undertake evaluation studies and organise such seminars, colloquia or other meetings of experts as are likely to facilitate the implementation of the programme, including application of Article 12 of the Decision. The Commission may also undertake information, publication and dissemination actions.

Annex 7.7.

1999/311/EC: Council Decision of 29 April 1999 adopting the third phase of the **trans-European cooperation scheme for higher education (Tempus III)** (2000-2006)
Official Journal L 120 , 08/05/1999 P. 0030 - 0036.

MAIN PROVISIONS

Article 1
Duration of Tempus III
The third phase of the trans-European cooperation scheme for higher education (hereinafter referred to as "Tempus III") is hereby adopted for a period of six years as from 1 July 2000.

Article 2
Eligible countries
Tempus III shall concern the non-associated countries of central and eastern Europe eligible for economic aid by virtue of Regulation (EEC) No 3906/89 (PHARE programme)(9), and the new independent States of the former Soviet Union and Mongolia mentioned in Regulation (Euratom, EC) No 1279/96 (TACIS programme), subject to these assistance programmes being prolonged for the period referred to. These countries are hereinafter referred to as "eligible countries".
On the basis of an evaluation of the specific situation of each country the Commission, in accordance with the procedures set out in the said Regulations, shall agree with the eligible countries concerned whether they should participate in Tempus III, and the nature and conditions of their participation in the national planning of Community assistance for social and economic reform.

Article 3
Involvement of associated countries
Actions under Tempus III are also open to the associated countries of central and eastern Europe so that what has been achieved through Tempus can be shared with the neighbouring countries and in order to develop regional and cross-border cooperation. Taking into account the respective financial rules and regulations, cooperation between Tempus and Erasmus projects should be encouraged.

Article 4
Definitions
For the purposes of Tempus III:
(a) the term "university" shall be used to cover all types of post-secondary educational and vocational training establishments which offer, within the framework of advanced education and training, qualifications or diplomas of that level, whatever such establishments may be called;
(b) the terms "industry" and "company" shall be used to cover all types of economic activity, irrespective of legal status, autonomous business organisations, chambers of commerce and industry and/or their equivalents, professional associations, and the training bodies of the institutions and organisations mentioned above;
(c) the term "institution" shall be used to cover local and public authorities, and the social partners' and their training bodies.
Each Member State or eligible country may determine what types of establishment referred to in point (a) can participate in Tempus III.

Article 5
Aims
The aim of Tempus III is to promote, in line with the guidelines and general objectives of the PHARE and TACIS programmes for economic and social reform, the development of the higher education systems in the eligible countries through the most balanced cooperation possible with the partners from all the Member States of the Community.
More specifically, Tempus III is intended to facilitate the adaptation of higher education to the new socio-economic and cultural needs of the eligible countries by addressing:
(a) issues relating to the development and reshaping of curricula in the priority areas;
(b) reform of higher education structures and establishments and their management;
(c) the development of training leading to qualifications, with a view to making good the shortage of high-level skills needed in the context of economic reform, particularly by improving and increasing links with industry;
(d) the contribution of higher education and training to citizenship and the strengthening of democracy.
The Commission will, when pursuing the objectives of Tempus III, endeavour to adhere to the Community's

general policy on equal opportunities for men and women. The Commission will also endeavour to ensure that no group of citizens is excluded or disadvantaged.

Article 6
Dialogue with the eligible countries
In agreement with the competent authorities in each country, the Commission will define the detailed priorities and objectives for the role of Tempus III in the national strategy for economic and social reform, on the basis of the programme's objectives and the provisions set out in the Annex, and in conformity in particular with:
(a) (i) the general objectives of the PHARE programme;
(ii) the general objectives of the TACIS programme, with particular reference to its sectoral aspects;
(b) the policy of each eligible country on economic, social and educational reforms;
(c) the need to strike an appropriate balance between the priority areas selected and the resources allocated to Tempus III.

Article 7
Committee
1. The Commission shall implement the Tempus III programme in accordance with the provisions of the Annex, on the basis of detailed guidelines to be adopted annually and following the detailed objectives and priorities agreed with the competent authorities in each eligible country, as provided for in Article 6.
2. In the performance of that task, the Commission shall be assisted by a committee composed of two representatives appointed by each Member State and chaired by the Commission representative. The members of the committee may be assisted by experts and advisers.
The committee shall, in particular, assist the Commission in the implementation of the scheme having regard to the objectives set out in Article 5 and shall coordinate its work with that of other programme committees established in the field of education (Socrates) and training (Leonardo).
3. The Commission representative shall submit to the Committee drafts for measures concerning:
(a) the general guidelines governing Tempus III;
(b) the selection procedures and general guidelines for the Community's financial assistance (amounts, duration and beneficiaries);
(c) questions relating to the overall balance of Tempus III, including the breakdown between the various actions;
(d) the detailed priorities and objectives to be agreed with the competent authorities in each eligible country;
(e) the arrangements for monitoring and evaluating Tempus III.
4. The committee shall deliver its opinion on these draft measures within a time limit which the chairman may lay down according to the urgency of the matter. The opinion shall be delivered by the majority laid down in Article 148(2) of the Treaty in the case of decisions which the Council is required to adopt on a proposal from the Commission. The votes of the representatives of the Member States within the committee shall be weighted in the manner set out in that Article. The chairman shall not vote.
The Commission shall adopt measures which shall apply immediately. However, if these measures are not in accordance with the opinion of the committee, they shall be communicated by the Commission to the Council forthwith.
In that event the Commission may defer application of the measures which it has decided upon for a period of one month.
The Council, acting by a qualified majority, may take a different decision within the time limit referred to in the previous subparagraph.
5. In addition, the Commission may consult the committee on any other matter concerning the implementation of Tempus III, including the annual report.
The representative of the Commission shall submit to the committee a draft of the measures to be taken. The committee shall deliver its opinion on this draft, within a time limit which the chairman may lay down according to the urgency of the matter, if necessary by taking a vote.
The opinion shall be recorded in the minutes; in addition, each Member State shall have the right to ask to have its position recorded in the minutes.
The Commission shall take the utmost account of the opinion delivered by the committee. It shall inform the committee on the manner in which its opinion has been taken into account.

Article 8
Cooperation with the competent bodies
1. The Commission shall cooperate with the agencies of each of the eligible countries designated and set up to coordinate the relations and structures needed to implement Tempus III, including the allocation of funds earmarked by the eligible countries themselves.
2. In addition, for the implementation of Tempus III, the Commission shall cooperate closely with the competent

national structures designated by the Member States. It shall take due account whenever possible of bilateral measures taken in this context by the Member States.

Article 9
Links with other Community actions
In line with the procedure set out in Article 7(3) of this Decision and, if applicable, the procedure defined in Article 9 of Regulation (EEC) No 3906/89 and in Article 8 of Regulation (Euratom, EC) No 1279/96, within the limits established by the annual budgetary decisions, the Commission shall ensure consistency and, where necessary, complementarity between Tempus III and other Community actions undertaken both in the Community and as part of assistance provided to eligible countries, particularly with regard to the activities of the European Training Foundation.

Article 10
Coordination with action taken in non-Community countries
1. The Commission shall organise appropriate coordination with actions undertaken by countries not members of the Community(10) or by universities and the business sector in these countries in the same field as Tempus III, including, where applicable, participation in Tempus III projects.
2. This participation may take a variety of forms, including one or more of the following:
- participation in Tempus III projects on a co-financing basis,
- using the opportunities available under Tempus III to channel exchange actions receiving bilateral funding,
- coordination between Tempus III and national initiatives which have the same aims but which are funded and managed separately,
- mutual exchange of information on all relevant initiatives in this field.

Article 11
Annual report
An annual report on the operation of Tempus III shall be forwarded by the Commission to the European Parliament, the Council, the Economic and Social Committee and the Committee of the Regions. This report shall also be forwarded to the eligible countries for information.

Article 12
Monitoring and evaluation - reports
In accordance with the procedure set out in Article 7(3), the Commission shall supervise the arrangements for regular monitoring and external evaluation of experience gained with Tempus III, taking due account of the specific objectives in Article 5 and the national objectives defined in accordance with Article 6.
It shall submit by 30 April 2004 an interim report on the findings of the evaluation, together with any proposals for extending or adjusting Tempus for the period commencing on 1 July 2006.
The Commission shall submit a final report no later than 30 June 2009.

Done at Luxembourg, 29 April 1999.

For the Council
The President
W. MÜLLER

(1) OJ C 270, 29.8.1998, p. 9, and OJ C 87, 29.3.1999, p. 102.
(2) OJ C 98, 9.4.1999.
(3) OJ C 40, 15.2.1999, p. 23.
(4) OJ C 51, 22.2.1999, p. 86.
(5) OJ L 375, 23.12.1989, p. 11. Regulation as last amended by Regulation (EC) No 753/96 (OJ L 103, 26.4.1996, p. 5).
(6) OJ L 165, 4.7.1996, p. 1.
(7) OJ L 112, 6.5.1993, p. 34.
(8) OJ L 306, 28.11.1996, p. 36.
(9) At present Albania, Bosnia-Herzegovina and the former Yugoslav Republic of Macedonia.
(10) These countries are the members of the Group of 24, other than the Member States of the Community, the Republic of Cyprus and Malta, and the associated countries of central and eastern Europe, and participation relates to projects with the non-associated countries of central and eastern Europe eligible under the PHARE programme.

ANNEX

Joint European projects

1. The European Community will provide support for joint European projects (JEPs) of a maximum of three years' duration.
The JEPs will associate at least one university in an eligible country, one university from a Member State and a partner establishment (university, company or institution as defined in Article 4) in another Member State.
2. Support for JEPs can be provided for activities according to the specific needs of the establishments concerned and in line with the priorities established, including:
(i) joint education and training actions, particularly with a view to curriculum development and updating, boosting university capacity to provide continuing education and retraining, development of short intensive courses, and development of open and distance learning systems including information and communication technology;
(ii) measures for the reform and development of higher education and its capacity, particularly by restructuring the management of higher education establishments and systems, by modernising existing infrastructures, by acquiring the equipment needed to implement a JEP and, where applicable, by providing technical and financial assistance to the authorities responsible;
(iii) the promotion of cooperation between universities, industry and institutions as defined in Article 4 through JEPs;
(iv) the development of mobility for teachers, administrative staff of universities and students under JEPs:
(a) grants will be provided for teaching/administrative staff of universities or to trainers in companies in the Member States to carry out teaching/training assignments for periods lasting up to one year in eligible countries and vice versa;
(b) grants will be awarded to teaching/administrative staff of universities in the eligible countries to undertake periods of retraining and updating in the European Community;
(c) grants will be available for students up to and including postgraduate at doctoral level, targeting both students in the eligible countries undertaking a period of study in the European Community and European Community students undertaking a period of study in the eligible countries. These grants will normally be granted for a period of three months to one year;
(d) grants will be available for students taking part in JEPs with the specific aim of promoting mobility, priority will go to students taking part in projects for which their university of origin will give full academic recognition to the period of study spent abroad;
(e) support will be provided for practical or in-company training periods of one month to one year for teachers, trainers, students and graduates of the eligible countries between the end of their studies and their first job, so that they can undertake a period of practical training in companies in the Community and vice versa;
(v) activities to ensure the success of a JEP involving two or more eligible countries.
Structural and/or complementary measures
Financial support will be provided for certain structural and/or complementary measures (particularly technical assistance, seminars, studies, publications, information activities) to support the objectives of the programme, particularly the development and restructuring of higher education systems in the eligible countries. Under the structural measures, financial aid will be granted to assist the eligible countries inter alia to:
- develop and strengthen the capacity for strategic planning and institutional development of higher education establishments at university or faculty level,
- establish a development plan for universities to help them build up international relations,
- support the spread of durable cooperation actions targeting the Tempus objectives,
- prepare a national strategy in a given eligible country to develop a specific aspect of higher education.

Individual grants

In addition to the JEPs and the structural and/or complementary measures, the European Community will also support the provision of individual grants to teachers, trainers, university administrators, senior ministerial officials, education planners and other experts in training from eligible countries or from the Community, for visits to promote the quality, development and restructuring of higher education and training in the eligible countries.
These visits could inter alia cover the following areas:
- the development of courses and teaching material,
- the development of staff, particularly through periods of refresher training and in-company placements,
- teaching and training assignments,
- activities to support the development of higher education,

- participation in the activities of European associations, in particular university associations.

Support actions

1. The Commission will receive the technical assistance needed to underpin the action taken pursuant to this Decision and to monitor programme implementation.

2. Support will be provided for appropriate external evaluation of Tempus III. Support will also be provided for dissemination in relation to JEPs, structural and/or complementary measures and individual mobility and for dissemination of successful outcomes from specific projects in earlier stages of the Tempus programme.

Chapter 8

LIVING AND WORKING CONDITIONS

The concern of the European Union for the living and working conditions of its citizens is not new, but its commitment in this respect has grown apace with economic integration. In article 117 of the EEC Treaty the States of the Community agreed on "the need to **promote improved working conditions and an improved standard of living for workers**, so as to make possible their harmonisation while the improvement is being maintained". They expected such a development to ensue, in the first place, from the functioning of the common market, which would favour the harmonisation of social systems and, to the extent necessary, from the approximation of provisions laid down by law, regulation or administrative action.

In Article 136 of the EC Treaty the Member States declare having as their **objectives** the promotion of employment, improved living and working conditions, proper social protection, dialogue between management and labour, the development of human resources with a view to lasting employment and the combating of social exclusion [see annex 2.1.]. Under Article 137 of the EC Treaty, the Community supports and complements the activities of the Member States tending to improve, in particular: the working environment so as to protect workers health and safety, the working conditions, the information and consultation of workers, the integration of persons excluded from the labour market and the equality of opportunities between men and women. The Council and the Parliament adopt, by means of Directives, minimal requirements for the gradual implementation of these objectives. These subjects are examined below.

The determination of wages is the sole responsibility of the Member States. Wages are, in fact, usually determined within the framework of collective bargaining or by reference to such bargaining by various practices in the Member States. The notion of a **guaranteed minimum wage** depends on different criteria in the Member States of the EU and its definition is left to them. However, the Social Charter of 1989 called on the Member States to ensure that workers secure an **equitable remuneration** (which is a different notion from the minimum wage), meaning a reward for work done which is fair and sufficient to enable them to have a decent standard of living[1].

The **European Foundation for the Improvement of Living and Working Conditions**, which is located in Dublin, has the task to develop and to pursue ideas on the medium and long-term improvement of living and working conditions in the light of practical experience and to identify factors leading to change[2].

[1] Commission opinion, OJ C 248, 11.09.1993.
[2] Regulation 1365/75, OJ L 139, 30.05.1975 and Regulation 354/95, OJ L 41, 23.02.1995.

8.1. The social dialogue in the EU

The legal process has difficulty in keeping pace with progress in European integration, technological change and the organisation of work. These changes require new mechanisms of social organisation parallel to legislation and State regulation. The social and cultural traditions of the Member States make it possible to build a European model of consensus, reconciling economic effectiveness and social solidarity. The **social partners** can play a crucial role in this process, both through cooperation between the state, employers and the trade unions on economic and social policies, and through the establishment of relations based on agreement between employers and the trade unions. The **Economic and Social Committee**, which is composed of employers' representatives, workers' representatives and other interest groups, is the oldest and most institutional provider of the opinions of the social partners to the decision-making bodies [see section 1.2.].

The social dialogue which was under way from the beginning of the Community, was consecrated first by the Single European Act and then by the Treaty on European Union [see section 1.1.], which commits the Commission to develop the **dialogue between management and labour at European level** by submitting to them its guidelines for proposals in the social field (Art. 138 TEC) [see annex 2.1.]. Social dialogue at European level covers the negotiations between European social partners themselves and between them and the organs of the European Union. This dialogue contributes to the improvement of mutual understanding between the social partners and to the stimulation and/or acceptance of economic and social policies implemented at European level.

At general European level the social partners are represented by the European Trade Union Confederation (ETUC), the Union of Industries of the European Community (UNICE) and the European Centre of Public Enterprises (CEEP). The **Tripartite Social Summit for Growth and Employment** is intended to ensure that there is continuous consultation between the Council, the Commission and the social partners on economic, social and employment matters[1]. The summit consists of representatives, at the highest level, of the Council Presidency, the two subsequent Presidencies, the Commission and the social partners.

At sectoral level, the social dialogue is promoted through the Sectoral Dialogue Committees, which are established in those sectors where the social partners make a joint request to take part in a dialogue at European level, and where the organisations representing both sides of industry fulfil certain criteria[2] [see annex 8.1.]. Since 1995, the Commission and the social partners have set up, in Florence, the European Centre for Industrial Relations (ECIR)[3].

The dialogue between social partners may lead to common opinions and/or, should the partners so desire, to **contractual relations, including agreements**. Such agreements may be implemented either in accordance with the procedures and practices specific to management and labour in each Member State or, in matters concerning working conditions, at the joint request of the signatory parties, by a Council decision on a proposal from the Commission (Art. 139 TEC). Thus, the social partners negotiated and signed, on 14 December 1995, a collective agreement, that entitles both male and female workers to unpaid **parental leave** of at least three months' duration and to time off work in the event of an unforeseen family emergency. At the request of the social partners, a 1996 Directive, which originally excluded the United Kingdom but in 1998 was extended to it, lays down minimum requirements concerning parental leave and absence by dint of "force majeure"[4] [see annex 8.2.].

---

1 Decision 2003/174, OJ L 70, 14.03.2003.
2 Decision 98/500, OJ L 225, 12.08.1998, p. 27-28.
3 COM (95) 445, 25 December 1995.
4 Directive 96/34, OJ L 145, 19.06.1996 and Directive 97/75, OJ L 10, 16.01.1998.

8.2. Worker information, consultation and participation

In addition to the social dialogue, the 1989 Social Charter, now incorporated in the EC Treaty (Art. 136 and 137), stipulates that information, consultation and participation for workers must be **developed along appropriate lines**, taking account of the practices in the various Member States [see annex 2.1.]. Such information, consultation and participation must be implemented in due time, particularly in the following cases:

- when technological changes which, from the point of view of working conditions and work organisation, have major implications for the work-force, are introduced into undertakings;
- in connection with restructuring operations in undertakings or in cases of mergers having an impact on the employment of workers;
- in cases of collective redundancy procedures; and
- when workers, especially transboundary ones, are affected by the employment policies of the company where they are employed.

A general framework for minimum requirements relating to the right of employees to be informed and consulted is applicable to undertakings and establishments operating **within a single Member State** and with at least 50 or 20 employees respectively[1] [see annex 8.3.]. The emphasis is on fostering social dialogue and ways of ensuring information for employees and effective consultation of their representatives at the earliest possible stage of the company decision-making process. Employers must inform employees about: the recent and foreseeable development of the company's activities and its economic and financial situation; the situation, structure and reasonably foreseeable developments of employment within the company; decisions which may lead to substantial changes in work organisation or in contractual relations (consultation between the employer and employees entails dialogue and exchange of views, including efforts to reach prior agreement on the decision in question).

The information and consultation of workers **in multinational companies** is pursued by Directive 94/45 - extended in 1998 to the United Kingdom - providing for the establishment of a **European Works Council** or a procedure for the purposes of informing and consulting employees in European-scale undertakings[2] [see annex 8.4.]. The companies or groups of companies concerned are those with more than 1000 employees in total in the Community and with at least two establishments in different Member States, each employing at least 150 people. The Directive also covers undertakings or groups of undertakings with headquarters outside the territory of the Member States, in so far as they meet the above criteria. The Directive provides for the establishment, at the initiative of the company or group management or at the written request of at least 100 employees or their representatives in at least two Member States, of a "special negotiating body" with the task of concluding an agreement between the management and the employees' representatives, on the scope, composition, powers and term of office of the European committee to be set up in the undertaking or group, or the practical arrangements for an alternative procedure for the information and consultation of employees.

In parallel with the regulation on the statute for a European company, with the Latin designation ***Societas Europaea* (SE)**[3], the Council adopted a directive supplementing this statute with regard to the involvement of employees[4] [see annex 8.5.]. The rules relating to **employee involvement in the SE** seek to ensure that the creation of an SE does not entail the disappearance or reduction of practices of employee involvement existing within the companies participating in the establishment of an SE. Therefore, when the management or administrative organs of the participating companies draw up a plan for the establishment of an SE, they must as soon as possible after publishing the draft terms of merger or creating a holding company or after agreeing a plan

---

1 Directive 2002/14, OJ L 80, 23.03.2002.
2 Directive 94/45, OJ L 254, 30.09.1994 and Directive 97/74, OJ L 10, 16.01.1998.
3 Moussis (2004), section 17.2.1.
4 Regulation 2157/2001 and directive 2001/86, OJ L 294, 10.11.2001.

to form a subsidiary or to transform into an SE, take the necessary steps (including providing information about the identity of the participating companies, concerned subsidiaries or establishments, and the number of their employees) to start negotiations with the representatives of the companies' employees on arrangements for the involvement of employees in the SE. For this purpose, a **special negotiating body** representative of the employees of the participating companies and concerned subsidiaries or establishments must be created in accordance with the provisions laid down in the directive. The special negotiating body and the competent organs of the participating companies must determine, by written agreement, arrangements for the involvement of employees within the SE. Member States must lay down standard rules on employee involvement which must satisfy the provisions of the directive.

The directives above concern the information of workers in European-size companies. The Directives discussed below concerning **large-scale redundancies** and the maintenance of workers' rights in the event of **company take-overs** stipulate that the workers must be informed and consulted in good time, so that they can make constructive proposals [see section 8.3.]. By the same token, the 1989 Directive on the improvement of the health and safety of workers in the workplace, also makes worker participation compulsory [see section 9.1.].

Another issue is **worker participation in the company's capital and profits**. Some see this as relinquishing management control, diminishing the shareholders' authority and "forfeiting dividend income". Others believe that allowing employees to share in the profits makes for greater flexibility in their earned income, has a stabilising effect in macro economic terms and is a motivating force resulting in greater productivity and consequently in an improved financial performance. Siding with the latter point of view, the Council has adopted a Recommendation concerning the promotion of employee participation in a company's capital and profits[1]. The Recommendation, which has not a binding character, encourages the Member States to: ensure that they have the appropriate legal structures for implementing various forms of financial participation effectively; consider the possibility of offering tax or other incentives for doing this; encourage the distribution of information about participation and about the experiences of other countries in the Community; and make sure that the social partners have a wide enough range of formulae to choose from based on consultations between employers and employees or their representatives. In any event, companies and employees alike must be able to decide freely whether or not to participate. From a Commission report on the implementation of the Council Recommendation by the Member States, it emerges that participation in profits goes hand in hand with better productivity, and that participation schemes have positive effects on wage flexibility, employment and worker involvement[2]. The Commission provided guidance for the development of employee financial participation in Europe by outlining the transnational obstacles hampering the introduction of Europe-wide financial participation schemes and by proposing concrete measures to overcome them[3].

8.3. Social protection

The **European Social Protection Committee (ESPC)**, composed of two representatives from each Member State and two representatives of the Commission, is an advisory body responsible for assisting the Council and the Commission[4]. Its main tasks are to monitor social protection policies in the Member States and the Community, to foster exchanges of information, experience and good practice between the Member States and with the Commission, and to prepare an annual report. In 1990, the Commission set up a system for mutual information on social pro-

[1] Recommendation 92/443, OJ L 245, 26.08.1992.
[2] COM (96) 697, 8 January 1997.
[3] COM (2002) 364, 5 July 2002.
[4] Decision, OJ L 172, 12.07.2000.

tection (the MISSOC programme), which is run by a network of national correspondents and coordinated by the European Social Security Institute.

As part of the implementation of the Charter of workers' fundamental social rights, the Council adopted, in 1992, two important Recommendations. The first is aimed at helping the most disadvantaged by inviting the Member States to recognise **a general right to guaranteed resources** and benefits for anyone living in a Member State who has insufficient means[1]. The second is aimed at promoting **a harmonisation of social protection objectives and policies**, so that the free movement of people is not impeded by the different levels of social protection in the Member States and social protection is not adversely affected by competition between the various national systems[2]. This last Recommendation is particularly important because the Member States acknowledge in it that comparable trends lead to common problems and challenges (unemployment, ageing, changing family structures) and that a single market can be created while maintaining the diversity of social protection systems in the Member States, mainly as regards the arrangements for financing and organising them, but that the long-term objective of the Union is the convergence of social protection systems. In view of this objective and the changes made necessary by the deteriorating relationship between the size of the labour force and the number of pensioners, the Commission launched a debate on the future of social protection, particularly concerning its financing and the way to make it more employment-friendly[3].

Article 136 (TEC) names proper social protection and improved living and working conditions among the objectives of the Community and the Member States. **Social protection in the strict sense** usually means social security, while **social protection in a broad sense** includes social security among other social rights of the citizens. In fact, under the heading "solidarity", the Charter of Fundamental Rights of the European Union[4] [see section 4.2.] mentions several rights, such as: the workers' right to information and consultation within the undertaking; the protection in the event of unjustified dismissal; fair and just working conditions; protection of young people at work; and, of course, social security and social assistance.

Concerning this last subject, namely social protection in the strict sense, the Charter of Fundamental Rights declares that the Union recognises and respects the entitlement to social security benefits and social services providing protection in cases such as maternity, illness, industrial accidents, dependency or old age, and in the case of loss of employment, in accordance with the rules laid down by Community law and national laws and practices. The Charter acknowledges that everyone residing and moving legally within the European Union is entitled to social security benefits and social advantages in accordance with Community law and national laws and practices. According to the subsidiarity principle[5], however, the Member States must apply Community law if and where it exists. Concerning social security, Community provisions concern only the implementation of the principle of equal treatment for certain categories of workers, i.e. immigrants [see section 5.1.2.] and women [see section 8.5.]. For the rest, social security is covered by the national law of each Member State.

In fact, the Member States have preferred coordination rather than harmonisation of social protection and particularly social security legislation. On these subjects the Council decides alone (without the Parliament) and by unanimity, which means that any Member State may veto the adoption of Community legislation (Art 137 TEC). It is true that as systems of social protection reflect the traditions and existing social benefits of each individual State, it is not easy to change them. However, in an internal market and even more in an economic and monetary union, differences between the various social security systems can constitute distortions of competition, hinder the free movement of labour and exacerbate regional imbalances. Therefore, without chang-

[1] Recommendation 92/441, OJ L 245, 26.08.1992, p. 46-48.
[2] Recommendation 92/442, OJ L 245, 26.08.1992, p. 49-52.
[3] COM (95) 466, 31 October 1995.
[4] Solemn declaration, OJ C 364, 18.12.2000.
[5] Moussis (2004), section 3.2.

ing the actual social security systems, there needs to be a strategy whereby their objectives are brought into alignment.

The Community has already made headway when the term "social protection" is taken in its broadest sense to cover social security and the right to work. An important Community measure for the social protection of employees, particularly those of multinational companies, is the Directive on the approximation of the laws of the Member States relating to **collective redundancies**[1] [see annex 8.6.]. Employers who envisage such redundancies have to hold consultations with workers' representatives on the possibilities of avoiding or reducing such redundancies. Moreover, the employer has to notify any proposed collective redundancy to the competent official authority and may not implement it before the expiry of a period of 30 days which the authority uses to try to find solutions to the problems that have arisen and/or to lessen the impact of the redundancies. This Directive is particularly important for workers employed by multinational companies which operate in one or more EU countries, as, by laying down provisions common to all Member States it prevents multinational companies from taking advantage of differences between national laws.

In the same vein, a Directive on the approximation of the laws of the Member States aims at safeguarding employees' rights in the event of **transfers of undertakings**, businesses or parts of businesses[2] [see annex 8.7.]. Before any such amalgamation, the workers' representatives have to be informed of the reasons for it and of its consequences for the employees and of the measures envisaged in their favour. In principle, the workers' rights and obligations are transferred to the new employer for at least a year and agreement on the conditions of the take-over has to be reached in consultation with the work force. Failing agreement between the employer or employers and the workers, an arbitration body gives a final ruling on the steps to be taken in favour of the workers. A representation scheme not dependent on the employer's will is necessary for compliance with the Directive[3].

But the workers' interests also need to be protected **in the event of the insolvency** of their employer, especially where assets are not sufficient to cover outstanding claims resulting from contracts of employment or employment relationships, even where the latter are privileged. To prevent such situations, a Council Directive obliges Member States to set up guarantee institutions independent of the employers' operating capital so that their assets are inaccessible to proceedings for insolvency[4] [see annex 8.8.]. In such an eventuality, those institutions must settle the claims of employees arising prior to the insolvency of the employer, including contributions under social security schemes.

A Directive on the **protection of young people at work** prohibits work by children (less than 15 years of age or still subject to compulsory full-time schooling), with the exception of certain cultural, artistic or sporting activities. Children of at least 14 years of age may take up combined work/ training schemes, in-plant work-experience schemes and certain light work[5] [see annex 8.9.]. The Directive asks Member States to strictly regulate work done by adolescents of more than 18 years of age, by imposing specific rules in respect of working time, daily rest periods, weekly rest periods and night work, and laying down technical, health and safety standards.

A clear link exists nowadays between social protection systems and the European employment strategy[6] [see section 6.2.]. Noting with satisfaction the views expressed by the Commission in its communication on a concerted **strategy for modernising social protection**[7], the Council, on 29 November 1999, underlined the need for cooperation between the Member States and at European level, entailing a structured and ongoing dialogue, follow-up and exchange of informa-

1 Directive 98/59, OJ L 225, 12.08.1998.
2 Directive 2001/23, OJ L 82, 28.03.2001.
3 Judgments given on 8 June 1994, Cases C-382/92 and C-383/92, Commission v United Kingdom, ECR 1994, p. I-2435.
4 Directive 80/987, OJ L 283, 20.10.1980 and Directive 2002/74, OJ L 270, 08.10.2002.
5 Directive 94/33, OJ L 216, 20.08.1994.
6 COM (1998) 243, 23 April 1998.
7 COM (1999) 347, 14 July 1999.

tion, experience and good practice. It endorsed the four key objectives identified by the Commission for modernising social protection (creating more incentives to work and provide a secure income, safeguarding pensions with sustainable pension schemes, promoting social inclusion and ensuring high-quality, sustainable health protection), adding that the principle of equality between women and men should be duly taken into account in pursuing these objectives.

With the progressive ageing of Europe's population, the problems of retirement and post-retirement become increasingly acute and require cooperation between Member States. In a Resolution on **flexible retirement arrangements** the Council wants older people to continue to play an active part in society and maintain a link with the labour market[1]. It emphasises that a flexible retirement policy could constitute a rational response to changing demographic patterns and to labour-market changes, but that flexible retirement arrangements are a matter for each Member State, bearing in mind the principle of subsidiarity[2]. However, it calls on the Commission to promote exchanges of information and to examine whether measures taken by the Member States need to be completed.

In a communication entitled "The future evolution of social protection from a long-term point of view: safe and sustainable pensions", the Commission proposed formalising and strengthening cooperation between the Member States by using the "**open method of coordination**"[3]. This involves setting common objectives, translating these objectives into national policy strategies and, finally, as part of a mutual learning process, periodic monitoring on the basis, *inter alia*, of commonly agreed and defined indicators. The overall strategy proposed by the Commission covers the three pillars of the pension systems, i.e. statutory social security schemes, occupational schemes and personal pension schemes. On the basis of the national strategy reports submitted in September 2002, the Commission noted that all the Member States had, to varying degrees, launched reforms aimed at safeguarding the adequacy of pensions in the future without undermining public finances or overburdening future generations. However, it concluded that most of the Member States would have to make further reforms to guarantee adequate and sustainable pensions in an ageing society. Extending working life was one possible solution proposed, with older workers being encouraged to stay longer in the labour market and given incentives through pension schemes[4].

8.4. The organisation of work

Social protection in the EU covers also **atypical work**, i.e. other forms of work than that for an indefinite period, such as work for a specific duration, interim work, temporary work and seasonal work. These different forms of work enable companies to organise their work and their production in such a way as to improve productivity and thus become more competitive. Similarly, they enable workers to adapt the hours they work to suit their personal and family circumstances. But in a single market, certain essential conditions must be determined both to avoid distortions of competition and to protect the workers who opt for or accept (for want of something better) these new forms of work. These two objectives are contained in the Directives on atypical work. Thus a Directive guarantees satisfactory health and safety conditions of workers with a fixed-duration employment relationship (whose duration is fixed by objective criteria) or a temporary employment relationship (between the employer - a temporary employment agency - and the employee)[5] [see annex 8.10.]. Another Directive, based on a framework agreement on fixed-term

[1] OJ C 188, 10.07.1993, p. 1-2.
[2] Moussis (2004), section 3.2.
[3] COM (2001) 362, 3 July 2001.
[4] COM (2002) 737, 17 December 2002.
[5] Directive 91/383, OJ L 206, 29.07.1991.

work concluded between the social partners, ensures compliance with the principle of non-discrimination *vis-à-vis* employment of indefinite duration[1] [see annex 8.11.].

Contract duration is but one of the areas where there have been changes in the organisation of work in Europe. Alongside traditional work practices of indefinite time, recent years have seen the growth of **new forms of work**: homeworking (out-workers), part-time work, job sharing, job splitting, being "on call", distance working, etc. These new work forms have arisen as a result of new technologies, to accommodate companies' needs for flexibility and to meet the personal and family demands of many workers. However, they can obscure the situation of these workers if there is no written proof of the essential points of the employment relationship. Therefore, a Directive provides for the drawing up of a written declaration **regarding an employment relationship**[2] [see annex 8.12.]. It stipulates that an employer shall notify an employee of the essential aspects of the contract or employment relationship by written declaration not later than two months after the commencement of employment. Essential aspects are considered to be: the place of work, the nature of the work and the category of employment, the duration of the employment relationship, the number of hours worked and paid holidays, pay and social rights. The Commission meanwhile recommended that the Member States ratify the International Labour Organisation's Convention on home work[3].

A Directive concerning certain aspects of the **organisation of working time** lays down a basic set of minimum provisions covering more particularly: the maximum weekly working time (48 hours), the minimum daily rest period (11 uninterrupted hours), the minimum period of paid leave (4 weeks), conditions relating to night work and the maximum period of such work (8 hours), and breaks in the event of prolonged periods of work[4] [see annex 8.13.]. Although, in theory, most workers in the European Union enjoy better organisation of working time than is embodied in the European Directive, this is intended to exercise a pressure on the Governments of the Member States to better enforce the relative legislations. Another Directive aims to prevent part-time workers from being treated less favourably than full-time workers, concerning particularly employment conditions and continuing training[5] [see annex 8.14.].

A special directive aims at the enforcement of seafarers' hours of work on board ships using Community ports[6]. Special directives concern also the organisation of working time and hence the improvement of health and safety protection regarding: **mobile workers** (flying personnel) in civil aviation[7]; those performing road transport activities and self-employed drivers[8].

8.5. Equal treatment for men and women

Article 141 of the EC Treaty (ex-Art. 119 EEC) stipulates that each Member State shall ensure the application of the principle that men and women should receive **equal pay for equal work.** This principle means: (a) that pay for the same work at piece rates shall be calculated on the basis of the same unit of measurement; and (b) that pay for work at time rates shall be the same for the same job. The original Community's concern for equality of the sexes - compared to its non-commitment in other important issues - stemmed from the fact that competition between Community countries could be distorted by the employment in some of them of women who were paid less than men for the same job. Moreover, unequal conditions of employment and remuneration between the sexes could be eliminated only through Community action, as no country could go it alone with a reform, which would be likely to alter conditions of competition to its detri-

[1] Directive 1999/70, OJ L 175, 10.07.1999.
[2] Directive, 91/533, OJ L 288, 18.10.1991.
[3] Recommendation 98/370, OJ L 165, 10.06.1998, p. 32.
[4] Directive 93/104, OJ L 307, 13.12.1993 and Directive 2000/34, OJ L 195, 01.08.2000.
[5] Directive 97/81, OJ L 14, 20.01.1998 and Directive 98/23, OJ L 131, 05.05.1998.
[6] Directive 1999/95, OJ L 14, 20.01.2000.
[7] Directive 2000/79, OJ L 302, 01.12.2000.
[8] Directive 2002/15, OJ L 80, 23.03.2002.

ment, in particular in industries employing large numbers of women. In any case, the EC Treaty places the achievement of equal treatment between men and women among the tasks of the Community (Art. 2 TEC).

The original Member States did not hasten to take the legislative and administrative measures necessary in order to implement the principle of non-discrimination based on the sex, as they were invited to do by Article 119 (EEC). However, the Court of Justice in three famous judgments bearing the name of Gabrielle Defrenne, air hostess of Sabena, established that, although Article 119 had a horizontal direct effect and could be evoked in national courts, it needed **interpretation by the Community legislative authority**, particularly concerning indirect or disguised discriminations and equal working conditions other than payment[1].

The opinion of the Court was followed by the Commission in its proposals and finally by the Council, which adopted a Directive on the approximation of the laws of the Member States relating to the **application of the principle of equal pay** for men and women[2] [see annex 8.15.]. The purpose of that Directive was to eliminate any discrimination on grounds of sex as regards all aspects and conditions of pay. It called on the Member States to "cleanse" their legal provisions of all discriminatory aspects and to repeal all collective or contractual provisions that were at variance with the principle of equal pay. Thus, for instance, the Court of Justice has established that the employers' contributions in favour of a pension scheme should be considered as part of gross payment and that, in this context, the burden of proof of non-discrimination based on sex should be borne by the employer[3]. A Commission code of practice on the implementation of equal pay for work of equal value for women and men, drawn up in close collaboration with the social partners, aims to provide concrete advice for employers and collective bargaining partners at business level to ensure that the principle of equality is applied to all aspects of pay[4].

Equal pay was only one battle won in the war against discrimination against women, which was based on historical and cultural causes and was reinforced in practice by the education system, inadequate vocational guidance and the demanding role imposed on women as wives and mothers. Therefore, the Council adopted, in 1976, a Directive on the implementation of the principle of equal treatment for men and women as regards **access to employment, vocational training and promotion**, and working conditions[5] [see annex 8.16.]. That Directive prohibits any indirect discrimination, i.e. the ways in which women are disadvantaged in relation to men in spite of apparently equal treatment, viz.: individual or collective contracts concerning employment and working conditions. For example, according to the ECJ, a discriminatory recruitment system is contrary to Directive 76/207[6], as is a general exclusion of women from military posts involving the use of arms[7]. A specific Directive provides for the equal treatment between men and women engaged in an activity, including agriculture, in a self-employed capacity, and on the protection of self-employed women during pregnancy and motherhood[8].

The principle of equal opportunity means, among other things, that there should be no discrimination based on sex especially as regards: the scope and the conditions governing the right to any work regime; the calculation of contributions; the calculation of benefits and the conditions governing the duration and preservation of pension rights. Two Directives concern, indeed, the implementation of the principle of equal treatment for men and women in matters of social security[9] [see annex 8.17.] and in occupational social security schemes[10]. According to the ECJ, the

[1] Judgments of: 25 May 1971, ECR 1971, p. 445; 8 April 1976, ECR 1976, p. 455; and 15 June 1978, ECR 1978, p. 1365.
[2] Directive 75/117, OJ L 45, 19.02.1975 and Agreement on the European Economic Area, OJ L 1, 03.01.1994.
[3] Judgment of 11 March 1981, Worringham, ECR 1981, p. 767 and judgment of 17 October 1989, ECR 1989, p. 3199.
[4] COM (96) 336, 17 July 1996.
[5] Directive 76/207, OJ L 39, 14.02.1976 and Directive 2002/73, OJ L 269, 05.10.2002.
[6] Judgment of 30 June 1988, ECR 1988, p. 3559.
[7] Judgment of 11 January 2000, Case C-295/98 Kreil v Germany, OJ C 63, 04.03.2000.
[8] Directive 86/613, OJ L 359, 19.12.1986.
[9] Directive 79/7, OJ L 6, 10.01.1979.
[10] Directive 86/378, OJ L 225, OJ L 225, 12.08.1986 and Directive 96/97, OJ L 46, 17.02.1997.

provisions concerning social security do not apply to women who have never been employed, those who do not look for a job and those who have voluntarily stopped working[1].

On the contrary, again according to the Court, the principle of non-discrimination applies indifferently to both men and women. Indeed, in its "Barber" judgment the Court of Justice held that any sex discrimination in the granting or calculation of an occupational pension, notably the differentiation of the age of pension according to the sex, is prohibited by Article 119 (EEC)[2]. As the Barber judgment had important financial implications for the professional schemes of social security, the Council amended the 1986 Directive in order to bring it into line with Article 119 of the EEC Treaty as interpreted by the Court in this judgment[3] [see annex 8.18.]. According to the Court, however, different treatment of **stable relationships between two persons of the same sex** and marriages or stable relationships outside marriage between persons of opposite sex in matters of social security, does not constitute discrimination directly based on sex[4].

Measures must be taken in all Member States to improve the **health and safety protection of women workers** who are pregnant, have just given birth or are breast-feeding[5] [see annex 8.19 and section 9.1.]. These measures on the one hand prohibit the dismissing of the women workers in question and their exposure to specific agents or working conditions which could endanger their health and safety, and on the other ensure the preservation of the rights derived from the employment contract and of maternity leave of at least fourteen consecutive weeks. In addition, according to the ECJ, the non-recruitment of pregnant women or the laying off of women who have a bad health condition after having given birth are discriminatory and cannot be tolerated[6]. The dismissal would be illegal even if the worker was recruited for a fixed period and because of her pregnancy was unable to work during a substantial part of the term of the contract[7]. A Declaration to the Final Act of the Amsterdam European Council of June 1997 urges the Member States, when adopting measures referred to in Article 141 (TEC) to aim at improving the situation of women in working life.

Under the Community legislation and the case law of the Court of Justice, any woman who feels that she is the subject of discrimination on grounds of sex or her matrimonial or family situation **may bring proceedings before the national courts** and enjoy, in so doing, legal protection against any attempt at reprisals on the part of her employer. She can directly, or through the Commission, bring the matter before the Court of Justice of the European Communities. According to the case-law of the Court of Justice, national courts must be consistent in ensuring the full effect of Community rules, where necessary disregarding any national provisions to the contrary[8]. Following the "Bilka" judgment, the national court must determine if a discriminatory practice is objectively justifiable on reasons other than the sex and if it is proportionate[9]. Consolidating the relevant case law of the Court of Justice, notably the Worringham case mentioned above, a Directive places the burden of proof in cases of discrimination based on sex on the defendant (employer) rather than on the plaintiff (employee)[10] [see annex 8.20].

However, in the "Kalanke" case the Court held that national rules giving absolute and unconditional priority to women holding the same qualifications as their male counterparts would also entail sex-based discrimination[11]. In this case, the Court has not condemned the implementation of positive action measures in general, but only a rigid quota system under which there is no possibility of taking particular individual circumstances into account. Thus, in another case the Court has held that a candidate belonging to the under-represented sex may be granted preference over a

---

1 Judgment of 27 June 1989, ECR 1989, p. 1963.
2 Judgment given on 17 May 1990, Case C-262/89, Barber v Guardian Royal Exchange, ECR 1990, p.1889.
3 Commission proposal, OJ C 379, 14.12.1996.
4 Judgment of 17 February 1998, Case C-249/96, ECR 1998 I-621.
5 Directive 92/85, OJ L 348, 28.11.1992.
6 Judgments of 8 November 1990, ECR 1990, I-3941 and I-3979.
7 Judgment of 4 October 2001, Case C-109/2000, ECR 2001, p. I-06993.
8 Judgment given on 25 July 1991, Case C-345/89, Stoeckel, ECR 1991, I-4047.
9 Judgment of 13 May 1986, Bilka-Kaufhaus, ECR 1986, p. 1607.
10 Directive 97/80, OJ L 14, 20.01.1998 and Directive 98/52, OJ L 205, 22.07.1998.
11 Judgment of 17 October 1995, case C-450/93, Kalanke, ECR 1995, p. I-3051.

competitor of the opposite sex, provided that the candidates possess equivalent or substantially equivalent merits[1].

But equal treatment for men and women would lead to a high level of female unemployment as long as the **occupational qualifications** of the sexes were not the same. For that reason, the equal opportunities dimension is increasingly taken into consideration in other common policies, notably on employment and on vocational training [see sections 6.2 and 7.2.]. The common employment strategy provides a good example of the positive consequences of incorporating the gender dimension into a broadly coordinated economic process.

The gender balance of sexes in economic activities is affected by **structural economic change**, in particular the growing role of services, the new technologies and the new flexibilities of work contracts that public and private enterprises are seeking. This is especially relevant to homeworking and teleworking, which offer significant opportunities for women, but under certain conditions. Positive and sustained action is needed to maximise the opportunities and reduce the dangers. A Resolution of the Council and of the representatives of the Member States on equal participation by women in an employment-intensive economic growth strategy aims at improving the flexibility of working hours, promoting a high level of skills among women and encouraging self-employment and the creation of businesses by women[2]. A Council Recommendation aims to promote the balanced participation of women and men at all levels of the decision-making process in the political, economic, social and cultural life[3]. A Community programme coordinates, supports and finances the implementation of horizontal activities in the fields covered by the Community framework strategy on gender equality, whilst also complementing the Community action programme on combating discrimination in general[4] [see section 4.2.].

Responding to a Council Resolution, the Commission adopted, on November 27, 1991, a Recommendation combined with a Code of Good Practice on the protection of the dignity of women and men at work in which it invites the Member States to take steps with a view to improving the prevention of and fight against all forms of **sexual harassment**[5]. A Resolution of the Council and the representatives of the governments of the Member States calls on the latter to take action aimed at promoting and disseminating a diversified and realistic image of men and women in advertising and the media[6].

8.6. Action to combat social exclusion

Social exclusion represents one of the major challenges facing the European Union. The challenge cannot be addressed merely by offering better assistance to those who are excluded or at risk of exclusion from work, but also requires active measures to tackle the obstacles to social inclusion. Article 137 (TEC) gives the Community a specific role in **supporting and complementing the activities of the Member States** as regards the integration of persons excluded from the labour market. In compliance with the principle of subsidiarity however, initiatives to combat poverty and social exclusion are primarily the preserve of the Member States' local, regional and national authorities. The European Union can only complete and stimulate the work of the Member States in these fields by promoting the exchange of information, the comparison of experiences, the transfer of know-how and the demonstration of the validity of the projects based on partnerships. Thus, the Community action against social exclusion is mainly centred on vocational training [see section 7.2.2.].

---

1 Case C-407/98, Abrahamsson and Anderson, ECR 2000, p. I-5539.
2 OJ C 368, 23.12.1994, p. 3-6.
3 Recommendation 96/694, OJ L 319, 10.12.1996.
4 Decision 2001/51, OJ L 17, 19.01.2001 and COM (2001) 773, 17 December 2001.
5 Resolution, OJ C 157, 27.06.1990, p. 3-4 and Recommendation 92/131, OJ L 49, 24.02.1992.
6 OJ C 296, 10.11.1995, p. 15-16.

A Community action programme, covering the period from 1 January 2002 to 31 December 2006, encourages cooperation between Member States to combat poverty and social exclusion[1] [see annex 8.21.]. The objectives of the **social exclusion action programme** are, in particular, to improve understanding of social exclusion and poverty, to organise discussions on policies pursued and mutual lessons, and to develop the capacity of actors to address social exclusion and poverty effectively, by promoting innovative approaches and supporting networks of all those involved at EU, national and regional levels. The URBAN initiative, on its part, can help in a number of inner-city neighbourhoods where an accumulation of exclusion factors exists [see section 3.3.6.].

Various initiatives of the Community help combat poverty and social exclusion. Food surpluses from the common agricultural policy are distributed in the framework of winter aid campaigns for the most needy organised by non-governmental organisations (NGOs). The Commission supports the work of the European Anti-Poverty Network and has established a permanent dialogue with this group.

The **European Year of People with Disabilities 2003** aimed at raising public awareness on the rights of people with disabilities and the positive contribution they can make to society, as well as consideration of the problems they face as a result of their disability and the many forms of discrimination to which they are exposed[2]. In fact, the Council adopted resolutions inviting the Member States to promote employment and social integration, the accessibility of cultural infrastructure and cultural activities for people with disabilities as well as their integration into society through education and training systems adapted to their needs[3].

Concerning the improvement of **access for people with disabilities**, particular emphasis is placed on interlinking of related issues in the fields of employment, education and vocational training, transport, the internal market, the information society, the new technologies and consumer policy[4]. Lack of mobility is a factor restricting the participatory rights of people with disabilities, to the detriment of all. Advances must be made consistently on all fronts, in order to get the best results out of enhanced access for people with disabilities[5]

In a resolution on an **information society for all**, the Council affirmed that the information society should not be the source of new exclusions[6]. It called upon the Member States to tap the potential of "e-inclusion" for disadvantaged people (the unemployed and inactive people, and people at risk of exclusion such as older workers and disabled persons), to remove the barriers which exist in the information society, and to encourage partnerships of all stakeholders, with an emphasis on regional and local dimensions.

---

1 OJ C Decision 50/2002, OJ L 10, 12.01.2002.
2 Decision 2001/903, OJ L 335, 19.12.2001.
3 Council resolution, OJ C 134, 07.06.2003.
4 Resolution, OJ C 186, 02.07.1999.
5 COM(2000) 284, 12 May 2000.
6 Council resolution, OJ C 292, 18.10.2001.

LIVING AND WORKING CONDITIONS

Annex 8.1.

98/500/EC: Commission Decision of 20 May 1998 on the **establishment of Sectoral Dialogue Committees** promoting the Dialogue between the social partners at European level (notified under document number C(1998) 2334) (Text with EEA relevance)
Official Journal L 225 , 12/08/1998 P. 0027 - 0028

MAIN PROVISIONS

Article 1
Sectoral Dialogue Committees (hereinafter referred to as 'the Committees`) are hereby established in those sectors where the social partners make a joint request to take part in a dialogue at European level, and where the organisations representing both sides of industry fulfil the following criteria:
(a) they shall relate to specific sectors or categories and be organised at European level;
(b) they shall consist of organisations which are themselves an integral and recognized part of Member States' social partner structures and have the capacity to negotiate agreements, and which are representative of several Member States;
(c) they shall have adequate structures to ensure their effective participation in the work of the Committees.

Article 2
Each Committee shall, for the sector of activity for which it is established,
(a) be consulted on developments at Community level having social implications, and
(b) develop and promote the social dialogue at sectoral level.

Article 3
The representatives of the two sides of industry taking part in the meetings of each Committee shall number a maximum of 40 in all, with an equal number of representatives of the employers' and workers' delegations.

Article 4
The Commission shall invite the representatives to participate in the meetings of the Committees on a proposal from the social partner organisations which have made the request set out in Article 1.

Article 5
1. Each Committee shall, together with the Commission, establish its own rules of procedure.
2. The Committees shall be chaired by a representative of the employers' or employees' delegations or, at their joint request, by a representative of the Commission.
3. The Committees shall meet at least once a year. A maximum of 30 representatives drawn from the two sides of industry taking part in a meeting of a Committee shall receive subsistence allowance and travelling expenses.
4. The Commission shall regularly review, in consultation with the social partners, the functioning of the Sectoral Committee and the pursuit of their activities in the different sectors.

Article 6
If the Commission has informed a Committee that a subject discussed relates to a matter of a confidential nature, members of the Committee shall be bound, without prejudice to the provisions of Article 214 of the Treaty, not to disclose any information acquired at the meetings of the Committee or its secretariat.

Article 7
1. The Sectoral Dialogue Committees shall replace the existing Joint Committees, namely:

(a) Joint Committee on Maritime Transport established by Commission Decision 87/467/EEC (4);
(b) Joint Committee on Civil Aviation established by Commission Decision 90/449/EEC (5);
(c) Joint Committee on Inland Navigation established by Commission Decision 80/991/EEC (6);
(d) Joint Committee on Road Transport established by Commission Decision 85/516/EEC (7);
(e) Joint Committee on Railways established by Commission Decision 85/13/EEC (8);
(f) Joint Committee on Telecommunications Services established by Commission Decision 90/450/EEC (9);
(g) Joint Committee on Social Problems of Agricultural Workers established by Commission Decision 74/442/EEC (10);
(h) Joint Committee on Social Problems in Sea Fishing established by Commission Decision 74/441/EEC (11);
(i) Joint Committee on Postal Services established by Commission Decision 94/595/EC (12).

However, the Committees established by those decisions shall remain in office until the Sectoral Committees established by this Decision take office, but in any event no later than 31 December 1998.

2. Subject to Article 1, the Sectoral Dialogue Committee shall also replace other informal working groups through which the Commission has heretofore promoted the social dialogue in certain sectors not covered by a Commission decision establishing a Joint Committee.

Annex 8.2.

Council Directive 96/34/EC of 3 June 1996 on the framework agreement on **parental leave** concluded by UNICE, CEEP and the ETUC
Official Journal L 145 , 19/06/1996 P. 0004 - 0009

MAIN PROVISIONS

Article 1
Implementation of the framework agreement
The purpose of this Directive is to put into effect the annexed framework agreement on parental leave concluded on 14 December 1995 between the general cross-industry organizations (Unice, CEEP and the ETUC).

Article 2
Final provisions
1. The Member States shall bring into force the laws, regulations and administrative provisions necessary to comply with this Directive by 3 June 1998 at the latest or shall ensure by that date at the latest that management and labour have introduced the necessary measures by agreement, the Member States being required to take any necessary measure enabling them at any time to be in a position to guarantee the results imposed by this Directive. They shall forthwith inform the Commission thereof.
2. The Member States may have a maximum additional period of one year, if this is necessary to take account of special difficulties or implementation by a collective agreement.
They must forthwith inform the Commission of such circumstances.
3. When Member States adopt the measures referred to in paragraph 1, they shall contain a reference to this Directive or be accompanied by such reference on the occasion of their official publication. The methods of making such reference shall be laid down by Member States.

Article 3
This Directive is addressed to the Member States.

ANNEX: FRAMEWORK AGREEMENT ON PARENTAL LEAVE

THE SIGNATORY PARTIES HAVE AGREED THE FOLLOWING:

II. CONTENT

Clause 1: Purpose and scope
1. This agreement lays down minimum requirements designed to facilitate the reconciliation of parental and professional responsibilities for working parents.
2. This agreement applies to all workers, men and women, who have an employment contract or employment relationship as defined by the law, collective agreements or practices in force in each Member State.

Clause 2: Parental leave
1. This agreement grants, subject to clause 2.2, men and women workers an individual right to parental leave on the grounds of the birth or adoption of a child to enable them to take care of that child, for at least three months, until a given age up to 8 years to be defined by Member States and/or management and labour.
2. To promote equal opportunities and equal treatment between men and women, the parties to this agreement consider that the right to parental leave provided for under clause 2.1 should, in principle, be granted on a non-transferable basis.
3. The conditions of access and detailed rules for applying parental leave shall be defined by law and/or collective agreement in the Member States, as long as the minimum requirements of this agreement are respected. Member States and/or management and labour may, in particular:
(a) decide whether parental leave is granted on a full-time or part-time basis, in a piecemeal way or in the form of a time-credit system;
(b) make entitlement to parental leave subject to a period of work qualification and/or a length of service qualification which shall not exceed one year;
(c) adjust conditions of access and detailed rules for applying parental leave to the special circumstances of adoption;
(d) establish notice periods to be given by the worker to the employer when exercising the right to parental leave, specifying the beginning and the end of the period of leave;

(e) define the circumstances in which an employer, following consultation in accordance with national law, collective agreements and practices, is allowed to postpone the granting of parental leave for justifiable reasons related to the operation of the undertaking (e.g. where work is of a seasonal nature, where a replacement cannot be found within the notice period, where a significant proportion of the workforce applies for parental leave at the same time, where a specific function is of strategic importance). Any problem arising from the application of this provision should be dealt with in accordance with national law, collective agreements and practices;
(f) in addition to (e), authorize special arrangements to meet the operational and organizational requirements of small undertakings.
4. In order to ensure that workers can exercise their right to parental leave, Member States and/or management and labour shall take the necessary measures to protect workers against dismissal on the grounds of an application for, or the taking of, parental leave in accordance with national law, collective agreements or practices.
5. At the end of parental leave, workers shall have the right to return to the same job or, if that is not possible, to an equivalent or similar job consistent with their employment contract or employment relationship.
6. Rights acquired or in the process of being acquired by the worker on the date on which parental leave starts shall be maintained as they stand until the end of parental leave. At the end of parental leave, these rights, including any changes arising from national law, collective agreements or practice, shall apply.
7. Member States and/or management and labour shall define the status of the employment contract or employment relationship for the period of parental leave.
8. All matters relating to social security in relation to this agreement are for consideration and determination by Member States according to national law, taking into account the importance of the continuity of the entitlements to social security cover under the different schemes, in particular health care.

Clause 3: Time off from work on grounds of force majeure
1. Member States and/or management and labour shall take the necessary measures to entitle workers to time off from work, in accordance with national legislation, collective agreements and/or practice, on grounds of force majeure for urgent family reasons in cases of sickness or accident making the immediate presence of the worker indispensable.
2. Member States and/or management and labour may specify the conditions of access and detailed rules for applying clause 3.1 and limit this entitlement to a certain amount of time per year and/or per case.

Clause 4: Final provisions
1. Member States may apply or introduce more favourable provisions that those set out in this agreement.
2. Implementation of the provisions of this agreement shall not constitute valid grounds for reducing the general level of protection afforded to workers in the field covered by this agreement. This shall not prejudice the right of Member States and/or management and labour to develop different legislative, regulatory or contractual provisions, in the light of changing circumstances (including the introduction of non-transferability), as long as the minimum requirements provided for in the present agreement are complied with.
3. The present agreement shall not prejudice the right of management and labour to conclude, at the appropriate level including European level, agreements adapting and/or complementing the provisions of this agreement in order to take into account particular circumstances.
4. Member States shall adopt the laws, regulations and administrative provisions necessary to comply with the Council decision within a period of two years from its adoption or shall ensure that management and labour (1) introduce the necessary measures by way of agreement by the end of this period. Member States may, if necessary to take account of particular difficulties or implementation by collective agreement, have up to a maximum of one additional year to comply with this decision.
5. The prevention and settlement of disputes and grievances arising from the application of this agreement shall be dealt with in accordance with national law, collective agreements and practices.
6. Without prejudice to the respective role of the Commission, national courts and the Court of Justice, any matter relating to the interpretation of this agreement at European level should, in the first instance, be referred by the Commission to the signatory parties who will give an opinion.
7. The signatory parties shall review the application of this agreement five years after the date of the Council decision if requested by one of the parties to this agreement.

Annex 8.3.

Directive 2002/14/EC of the European Parliament and of the Council of 11 March 2002 establishing a **general framework for informing and consulting employees** in the European Community - Joint declaration of the European Parliament, the Council and the Commission on employee representation
Official Journal L 080 , 23/03/2002 P. 0029 - 0034.

MAIN PROVISIONS

Article 1
Object and principles
1. The purpose of this Directive is to establish a general framework setting out minimum requirements for the right to information and consultation of employees in undertakings or establishments within the Community.
2. The practical arrangements for information and consultation shall be defined and implemented in accordance with national law and industrial relations practices in individual Member States in such a way as to ensure their effectiveness.
3. When defining or implementing practical arrangements for information and consultation, the employer and the employees' representatives shall work in a spirit of cooperation and with due regard for their reciprocal rights and obligations, taking into account the interests both of the undertaking or establishment and of the employees.

Article 2
Definitions
For the purposes of this Directive:
(a) "undertaking" means a public or private undertaking carrying out an economic activity, whether or not operating for gain, which is located within the territory of the Member States;
(b) "establishment" means a unit of business defined in accordance with national law and practice, and located within the territory of a Member State, where an economic activity is carried out on an ongoing basis with human and material resources;
(c) "employer" means the natural or legal person party to employment contracts or employment relationships with employees, in accordance with national law and practice;
(d) "employee" means any person who, in the Member State concerned, is protected as an employee under national employment law and in accordance with national practice;
(e) "employees' representatives" means the employees' representatives provided for by national laws and/or practices;
(f) "information" means transmission by the employer to the employees' representatives of data in order to enable them to acquaint themselves with the subject matter and to examine it;
(g) "consultation" means the exchange of views and establishment of dialogue between the employees' representatives and the employer.

Article 3
Scope
1. This Directive shall apply, according to the choice made by Member States, to:
(a) undertakings employing at least 50 employees in any one Member State, or
(b) establishments employing at least 20 employees in any one Member State.
Member States shall determine the method for calculating the thresholds of employees employed.
2. In conformity with the principles and objectives of this Directive, Member States may lay down particular provisions applicable to undertakings or establishments which pursue directly and essentially political, professional organisational, religious, charitable, educational, scientific or artistic aims, as well as aims involving information and the expression of opinions, on condition that, at the date of entry into force of this Directive, provisions of that nature already exist in national legislation.
3. Member States may derogate from this Directive through particular provisions applicable to the crews of vessels plying the high seas.

Article 4
Practical arrangements for information and consultation
1. In accordance with the principles set out in Article 1 and without prejudice to any provisions and/or practices in force more favourable to employees, the Member States shall determine the practical arrangements for

exercising the right to information and consultation at the appropriate level in accordance with this Article.
2. Information and consultation shall cover:
(a) information on the recent and probable development of the undertaking's or the establishment's activities and economic situation;
(b) information and consultation on the situation, structure and probable development of employment within the undertaking or establishment and on any anticipatory measures envisaged, in particular where there is a threat to employment;
(c) information and consultation on decisions likely to lead to substantial changes in work organisation or in contractual relations, including those covered by the Community provisions referred to in Article 9(1).
3. Information shall be given at such time, in such fashion and with such content as are appropriate to enable, in particular, employees' representatives to conduct an adequate study and, where necessary, prepare for consultation.
4. Consultation shall take place:
(a) while ensuring that the timing, method and content thereof are appropriate;
(b) at the relevant level of management and representation, depending on the subject under discussion;
(c) on the basis of information supplied by the employer in accordance with Article 2(f) and of the opinion which the employees' representatives are entitled to formulate;
(d) in such a way as to enable employees' representatives to meet the employer and obtain a response, and the reasons for that response, to any opinion they might formulate;
(e) with a view to reaching an agreement on decisions within the scope of the employer's powers referred to in paragraph 2(c).

Article 5
Information and consultation deriving from an agreement
Member States may entrust management and labour at the appropriate level, including at undertaking or establishment level, with defining freely and at any time through negotiated agreement the practical arrangements for informing and consulting employees. These agreements, and agreements existing on the date laid down in Article 11, as well as any subsequent renewals of such agreements, may establish, while respecting the principles set out in Article 1 and subject to conditions and limitations laid down by the Member States, provisions which are different from those referred to in Article 4.

Article 6
Confidential information
1. Member States shall provide that, within the conditions and limits laid down by national legislation, the employees' representatives, and any experts who assist them, are not authorised to reveal to employees or to third parties, any information which, in the legitimate interest of the undertaking or establishment, has expressly been provided to them in confidence. This obligation shall continue to apply, wherever the said representatives or experts are, even after expiry of their terms of office. However, a Member State may authorise the employees' representatives and anyone assisting them to pass on confidential information to employees and to third parties bound by an obligation of confidentiality.
2. Member States shall provide, in specific cases and within the conditions and limits laid down by national legislation, that the employer is not obliged to communicate information or undertake consultation when the nature of that information or consultation is such that, according to objective criteria, it would seriously harm the functioning of the undertaking or establishment or would be prejudicial to it.
3. Without prejudice to existing national procedures, Member States shall provide for administrative or judicial review procedures for the case where the employer requires confidentiality or does not provide the information in accordance with paragraphs 1 and 2. They may also provide for procedures intended to safeguard the confidentiality of the information in question.

Article 7
Protection of employees' representatives
Member States shall ensure that employees' representatives, when carrying out their functions, enjoy adequate protection and guarantees to enable them to perform properly the duties which have been assigned to them.

Article 8
Protection of rights
1. Member States shall provide for appropriate measures in the event of non-compliance with this Directive by the employer or the employees' representatives. In particular, they shall ensure that adequate administrative or judicial procedures are available to enable the obligations deriving from this Directive to be enforced.
2. Member States shall provide for adequate sanctions to be applicable in the event of infringement of this

Directive by the employer or the employees' representatives. These sanctions must be effective, proportionate and dissuasive.

Article 9
Link between this Directive and other Community and national provisions
1. This Directive shall be without prejudice to the specific information and consultation procedures set out in Article 2 of Directive 98/59/EC and Article 7 of Directive 2001/23/EC.
2. This Directive shall be without prejudice to provisions adopted in accordance with Directives 94/45/EC and 97/74/EC.
3. This Directive shall be without prejudice to other rights to information, consultation and participation under national law.
4. Implementation of this Directive shall not be sufficient grounds for any regression in relation to the situation which already prevails in each Member State and in relation to the general level of protection of workers in the areas to which it applies.

Article 10
Transitional provisions
Notwithstanding Article 3, a Member State in which there is, at the date of entry into force of this Directive, no general, permanent and statutory system of information and consultation of employees, nor a general, permanent and statutory system of employee representation at the workplace allowing employees to be represented for that purpose, may limit the application of the national provisions implementing this Directive to:
(a) undertakings employing at least 150 employees or establishments employing at least 100 employees until 23 March 2007, and
(b) undertakings employing at least 100 employees or establishments employing at least 50 employees during the year following the date in point (a).

Article 11
Transposition
1. Member States shall adopt the laws, regulations and administrative provisions necessary to comply with this Directive not later than 23 March 2005 or shall ensure that management and labour introduce by that date the required provisions by way of agreement, the Member States being obliged to take all necessary steps enabling them to guarantee the results imposed by this Directive at all times. They shall forthwith inform the Commission thereof.
2. Where Member States adopt these measures, they shall contain a reference to this Directive or shall be accompanied by such reference on the occasion of their official publication. The methods of making such reference shall be laid down by the Member States.

Annex 8.4.

Council Directive 94/45/EC of 22 September 1994 on the establishment of a **European Works Council** or a procedure in Community-scale undertakings and Community-scale groups of undertakings for the purposes of informing and consulting employees
Official Journal L 254 , 30/09/1994 P. 0064 - 0072.

MAIN PROVISIONS

Article 1
Objective

1. The purpose of this Directive is to improve the right to information and to consultation of employees in Community-scale undertakings and Community-scale groups of undertakings.
2. To that end, a European Works Council or a procedure for informing and consulting employees shall be established in every Community-scale undertaking and every Community-scale group of undertakings, where requested in the manner laid down in Article 5 (1), with the purpose of informing and consulting employees under the terms, in the manner and with the effects laid down in this Directive.
3. Notwithstanding paragraph 2, where a Community-scale group of undertakings within the meaning of Article 2 (1) (c) comprises one or more undertakings or groups of undertakings which are Community-scale undertakings or Community-scale groups of undertakings within the meaning of Article 2 (1) (a) or (c), a European Works Council shall be established at the level of the group unless the agreements referred to in Article 6 provide otherwise.
4. Unless a wider scope is provided for in the agreements referred to in Article 6, the powers and competence of European Works Councils and the scope of information and consulation procedures established to achieve the purpose specified in paragraph 1 shall, in the case of a Community-scale undertaking, cover all the establishments located within the Member States and, in the case of a Community-scale group of undertakings, all group undertakings located within the Member States.
5. Member States may provide that this Directive shall not apply to merchant navy crews.

Article 2
Definitions

1. For the purposes of this Directive:
(a) 'Community-scale undertaking' means any undertaking with at least 1 000 employees within the Member States and at least 150 employees in each of at least two Member States;
(b) 'group of undertakings' means a controlling undertaking and its controlled undertakings;
(c) 'Community-scale group of undertakings' means a group of undertakings with the following characteristics:
- at least 1 000 employees within the Member States,
- at least two group undertakings in different Member States, and
- at least one group undertaking with at least 150 employees in one Member State and at least one other group undertaking with at least 150 employees in another Member State;
(d) 'employees' representatives' means the employees' representatives provided for by national law and/or practice;
(e) 'central management' means the central management of the Community-scale undertaking or, in the case of a Community-scale group of undertakings, of the controlling undertaking;
(f) 'consultation' means the exchange of views and establishment of dialogue between employees' representatives and central management or any more appropriate level of management;
(g) 'European Works Council' means the council established in accordance with Article 1 (2) or the provisions of the Annex, with the purpose of informing and consulting employees;
(h) 'special negotiating body' means the body established in accordance with Article 5 (2) to negotiate with the central management regarding the establishment of a European Works Council or a procedure for informing and consulting employees in accordance with Article 1 (2).

2. For the purposes of this Directive, the prescribed thresholds for the size of the workforce shall be based on the average number of employees, including part-time employees, employed during the previous two years calculated according to national legislation and/or practice.

Article 3
Definition of 'controlling undertaking'

1. For the purposes of this Directive, 'controlling undertaking' means an undertaking which can exercise a dominant influence over another undertaking ('the controlled undertaking') by virtue, for example, of ownership, financial participation or the rules which govern it.
2. The ability to exercise a dominant influence shall be presumed, without prejudice to proof to the contrary, when, in relation to another undertaking directly or indirectly:
(a) holds a majority of that undertaking's subscribed capital; or
(b) controls a majority of the votes attached to that undertaking's issued share capital; or
(c) can appoint more than half of the members of that undertaking's administrative, management or supervisory body.
3. For the purposes of paragraph 2, a controlling undertaking's rights as regards voting and appointment shall include the rights of any other controlled undertaking and those of any person or body acting in his or its own name but on behalf of the controlling undertaking or of any other controlled undertaking.
4. Notwithstanding paragraphs 1 and 2, an undertaking shall not be deemed to be a 'controlling undertaking' with respect to another undertaking in which it has holdings where the former undertaking is a company referred to in Article 3 (5) (a) or (c) of Council Regulation (EEC) No 4064/89 of 21 December 1989 on the control of concentrations between undertakings (6).
5. A dominant influence shall not be presumed to be exercised solely by virtue of the fact that an office holder is exercising his functions, according to the law of a Member State relating to liquidation, winding up, insolvency, cessation of payments, compositions or analogous proceedings.
6. The law applicable in order to determine whether an undertaking is a 'controlling undertaking' shall be the law of the Member State which governs that undertaking.
Where the law governing that undertaking is not that of a Member State, the law applicable shall be the law of the Member State within whose territory the representative of the undertaking or, in the absence of such a representative, the central management of the group undertaking which employs the greatest number of employees is situated.
7. Where, in the case of a conflict of laws in the application of paragraph 2, two or more undertakings from a group satisfy one or more of the criteria laid down in that paragraph, the undertaking which satisfies the criterion laid down in point (c) thereof shall be regarded as the controlling undertaking, without prejudice to proof that another undertaking is able to exercise a dominant influence.

SECTION II ESTABLISHMENT OF A EUROPEAN WORKS COUNCIL OR AN EMPLOYEE INFORMATION AND CONSULTATION PROCEDURE

Article 4
Responsibility for the establishment of a European Works Council or an employee information and consultation procedure

1. The central management shall be responsible for creating the conditions and means necessary for the setting up of a European Works Council or an information and consultation procedure, as provided for in Article 1 (2), in a Community-scale undertaking and a Communuty-scale group of undertakings.
2. Where the central management is not situated in a Member State, the central management's representative agent in a Member State, to be designated if necessary, shall take on the responsibility referred to in paragraph 1.
In the absence of such a representative, the management of the establishment or group undertaking employing the greatest number of employees in any one Member State shall take on the responsiiblity referred to in paragraph 1.
3. For the purposes of this Directive, the representative or representatives or, in the absence of any such representatives, the management referred to in the second subparagraph of paragraph 2, shall be regarded as the central management.

Article 5
Special negotiating body

1. In order to achieve the objective in Article 1 (1), the central management shall initiate negotiations for the establishment of a European Works Council or an information and consultation procedure on its own initiative or at the written request of at least 100 employees or their representatives in at least two undertakings or establishments in at least two different Member States.

2. For this purpose, a special negotiating body shall be established in accordance with the following guidelines:
(a) The Member States shall determine the method to be used for the election or appointment of the members of the special negotiating body who are to be elected or appointed in their territories.
Member States shall provide that employees in undertakings and/or establishments in which there are no employees' representatives throguh no fault of their own, have the right to elect or appoint members of the special negotiating body.
The second subparagraph shall be without prejudice to national legislation and/or practice laying down thresholds for the establishment of employee representation bodies.
(b) The special negotiating body shall have a minimum of three and a maximum of 17 members.
(c) In these elections or appointments, it must be ensured:
- firstly, that each Member State in which the Community-scale undertaking has one or more establishbments or in which the Community-scale group of undertakings has the controlling undertaking or one or more controlled undertakings is represented by one member,
- secondly, that there are supplementary members in proportion to the number of employees working in the establishments, the controlling undertaking or the controlled undertakings as laid down by the legislation of the Member State within the territory of which the central management is situated.
(d) The central management and local management shall be informed of the composition of the special negotiating body.
3. The special negotiating body shall have the task of determining, with the central management, by written agreement, the scope, composition, functions, and term of office of the European Works Council(s) or the arrangements for implementing a procedure for the information and consultation of employees.
4. With a view to the conclusion of an agreement in accordance with Article 6, the central management shall convene a meeting with the special negotiating body. It shall inform the local managements accordingly.
For the purpose of the negotiations, the special negotiating body may be assisted by experts of its choice.
5. The special negotiating body may decide, by at least two-thirds of the votes, not to open negotiations in accordance with paragraph 4, or to terminate the negotiations already opened.
Such a decision shall stop the procedure to conclude the agreement referred to in Article 6. Where such a decision has been taken, the provisions in the Annex shall not apply.
A new request to convene the special negotiating body may be made at the earliest two years after the abovementioned decision unless the parties concerned lay down a shorter period.
6. Any expenses relating to the negotiations referred to in paragraphs 3 and 4 shall be borne by the central management so as to enable the special negotiating body to carry out its task in an appropriate manner.
In compliance with this principle, Member States may lay down budgetary rules regarding the operation of the special negotiating body. They may in particular limit the funding to cover one expert only.

Article 6
Content of the agreement

1. The central management and the special negotiating body must negotiate in a spirit of cooperation with a view to reaching an agreement on the detailed arrangements for implementing the information and consultation of employees provided for in Article 1 (1).
2. Without prejudice to the autonomy of the parties, the agreement referred to in paragraph 1 between the central management and the special negotiating body shall determine:
(a) the undertakings of the Community-scale group of undertakings or the establishments of the Community-scale undertaking which are covered by the agreement;
(b) the composition of the European Works Council, the number of members, the allocation of seats and the term of office;
(c) the functions and the procedure for information and consultation of the European Works Council;
(d) the venue, frequency and duration of meetings of the European Works Council;
(e) the financial and material resources to be allocated to the European Works Council;
(f) the duration of the agreement and the procedure for its renegotiation.
3. The central management and the special negotiating body may decide, in writing, to establish one or more information and consultation procedures instead of a European Works Council.
The agreement must stipulate by what method the employees' representatives shall have the right to meet to discuss the information conveyed to them.
This information shall relate in particular to transnational questions which significantly affect workers' interests.
4. The agreements referred to in paragraphs 2 and 3 shall not, unless provision is made otherwise therein, be subject to the subsidiary requirements of the Annex.
5. For the purposes of concluding the agreements referred to in paragraphs 2 and 3, the special negotiating body shall act by a majority of its members.

Article 7
Subsidiary requirements

1. In order to achieve the objective in Article 1 (1), the subsidiary requirements laid down by the legislation of the Member State in which the central management is situated shall apply:
- where the central management and the special negotiating body so decide, or
- where the central management refuses to commence negotiations within six months of the request referred to in Article 5 (1), or
- where, after three years from the date of this request, they are unable to conclude an agreement as laid down in Article 6 and the special negotiating body has not taken the decision provided for in Article 5 (5).
2. The subsidiary requirements referred to in paragraph 1 as adopted in the legislation of the Member States must satisfy the provisions set out in the Annex.

SECTION III MISCELLANEOUS PROVISIONS

Article 8
Confidential information

1. Member States shall provide that members of special negotiating bodies or of European Works Councils and any experts who assist them are not authorized to reveal any information which has expressly been provided to them in confidence. The same shall apply to employees' representatives in the framework of an information and consultation procedure. This obligation shall continue to apply, wherever the persons referred to in the first and second subparagraphs are, even after the expiry of their terms of office.
2. Each Member State shall provide, in specific cases and under the conditions and limits laid down by national legislation, that the central management situated in its territory is not obliged to transmit information when its nature is such that, according to objective criteria, it would seriously harm the functioning of the undertakings concerned or would be prejudicial to them. A Member State may make such dispensation subject to prior administrative or judicial authorization.
3. Each Member State may lay down particular provisions for the central management of undertakings in its territory which pursue directly and essentially the aim of ideological guidance with respect to information and the expression of opinions, on condition that, at the date of adoption of this Directive such particular provisions already exist in the national legislation.

Article 9
Operation of European Works Council and information and consultation procedure for workers The central management and the European Works Council shall work in a spirit of cooperation with due regard to their reciprocal rights and obligations. The same shall apply to cooperation between the central management and employees' representatives in the framework of an information and consultation procedure for workers.

Article 10
Protection of employees' representatives Members of special negotiating bodies, members of European Works Councils and employees' representatives exercising their functions under the procedure referred to in Article 6 (3) shall, in the exercise of their functions, enjoy the same protection and guarantees provided for employees' representatives by the national legislation and/or practice in force in their country of employment.
This shall apply in particular to attendance at meetings of special negotiating bodies or European Works Councils or any other meetings within the framework of the agreement referred to in Article 6 (3), and the payment of wages for members who are on the staff of the Community-scale undertaking or the Community-scale group of undertakings for the period of absence necessary for the performance of their duties.

Article 11
Compliance with this Directive

1. Each Member State shall ensure that the management of establishments of a Community-scale undertaking and the management of undertakings which form part of a Community-scale group of undertakings which are situated within its territory and their employees' representatives or, as the case may be, employees abide by the obligations laid down by this Directive, regardless of whether or not the central management is situated within its territory.
2. Member States shall ensure that the information on the number of employees referred to in Article 2 (1) (a) and (c) is made available by undertakings at the request of the parties concerned by the application of this Directive.

3. Member States shall provide for appropriate measures in the event of failure to comply with this Directive; in particular, they shall ensure that adequate administrative or judicial procedures are available to enable the obligations deriving from this Directive to be enforced.
4. Where Member States apply Article 8, they shall make provision for administrative or judicial appeal procedures which the employees' representatives may initiate when the central management requires confidentiality or does not give information in accordance with that Article.
Such procedures may include procedures designed to protect the confidentiality of the information in question.

Article 12
Link between this Directive and other provisions

1. This Directive shall apply without prejudice to measures taken pursuant to Council Directive 75/129/EEC of 17 February 1975 on the approximation of the laws of the Member States relating to collective redundancies (7), and to Council Directive 77/187/EEC of 14 February 1977 on the approximation of the laws of the Member States relating to the safeguarding of employees' rights in the event of transfers of undertakings, businesses or parts of businesses (8).
2. This Directive shall be without prejudice to employees' existing rights to information and consultation under national law.

Article 13
Agreements in force

1. Without prejudice to paragraph 2, the obligations arising from this Directive shall not apply to Community-scale undertakings or Community-scale groups of undertakings in which, on the date laid down in Article 14 (1) for the implementation of this Directive or the date of its transposition in the Member State in question, where this is earlier than the abovementioned date, there is already an agreement, covering the entire workforce, providing for the transnational information and consultation of employees.
2. When the agreements referred to in paragraph 1 expire, the parties to those agreements may decide jointly to renew them.
Where this is not the case, the provisions of this Directive shall apply.

Article 14
Final provisions

1. Member States shall bring into force the laws, regulations and administrative provisions necessary to comply with this Directive no later than 22 September 1996 or shall ensure by that date at the latest that management and labour introduce the required provisions by way of agreement, the Member States being obliged to take all necessary steps enabling them at all times to guarantee the results imposed by this Directive. They shall forthwith inform the Commission thereof.
2. When Member States adopt these measures, they shall contain a reference to this Directive or shall be accompanied by such reference on the occasion of their official publication. The methods of making such reference shall be laid down by Member States.

Article 15
Review by the Commission not later than 22 September 1999, the Commission shall, in consultation with the Member States and with management and labour at European level, review its operation and, in particular examine whether the workforce size thresholds are appropriate with a view to proposing suitable amendments to the Council, where necessary.

Article 16
This Directive is addressed to the Member States.

Done at Brussels, 22 September 1994.
For the Council
The President
N. BLUEM

(1) OJ No C 135, 18. 5. 1994, p. 8 and OJ No C 199, 21. 7. 1994, p. 10.
(2) Opinion delivered on 1 June 1994 (not yet published in the Official Journal).
(3) Opinion of the European Parliament of 4 May 1994 (OJ No C 205, 25. 7. 1994) and Council common

position of 18 July 1994 (OJ No C 244, 31. 8. 1994, p. 37).
(4) OJ No C 39, 15. 2. 1991, p. 10.
(5) OJ No C 336, 31. 12. 1991, p. 11.
(6) OJ No L 395, 30. 12. 1989, p. 1.
(7) OJ No L 48, 22. 2. 1975, p. 29. Regulation as last amended by Directive 92/56/EEC (OJ No L 245, 26. 8. 1992, p. 3).
(8) OJ No L 61, 5. 3. 1977, p. 26.

ANNEX
SUBSIDIARY REQUIREMENTS referred to in Article 7 of the Directive

1. In order to achieve the objective in Article 1 (1) of the Directive and in the cases provided for in Article 7 (1) of the Directive, the establishment, composition and competence of a European Works Council shall be governed by the following rules:
(a) The competence of the European Works Council shall be limited to information and consultation on the matters which concern the Community-scale undertaking or Community-scale group of undertakings as a whole or at least two of its establishments or group undertakings situated in different Member States.
In the case of undertakings or groups of undertakings referred to in Article 4 (2), the competence of the European Works Council shall be limited to those matters concerning all their establishments or group undertakings situated within the Member States or concerning at least two of their establishments or group undertakings situated in different Member States.
(b) The European Works Council shall be composed of employees of the Community-scale undertaking or Community-scale group of undertakings elected or appointed from their number by the employees' representatives or, in the absence thereof, by the entire body of employees.
The election or appointment of members of the European Works Council shall be carried out in accordance with national legislation and/or practice.
(c) The European Works Council shall have a minimum of three members and a maximum of 30.
Where its size so warrants, it shall elect a select committee from among its members, comprising at most three members. It shall adopt its own rules of procedure.
(d) In the election or appointment of members of the European Works Council, it must be ensured:
- firstly, that each Member State in which the Community-scale undertaking has one or more establishments or in which the Community-scale group of undertakings has the controlling undertaking or one or more controlled undertakings is represented by one member,
- secondly, that there are supplementary members in proportion to the number of employees working in the establishments, the controlling undertaking or the controlled undertakings as laid down by the legislation of the Member State within the territory of which the central management is situated.
(e) The central management and any other more appropriate level of management shall be informed of the composition of the European Works Council.
(f) Four years after the European Works Council is established it shall examine whether to open negotiations for the conclusion of the agreement referred to in Article 6 of the Directive or to continue to apply the subsidiary requirements adopted in accordance with this Annex.

Articles 6 and 7 of the Directive shall apply, mutatis mutandis, if a decision has been taken to negotiate an agreement according to Article 6 of the Directive, in which case 'special negotiating body' shall be replaced by 'European Works Council'.
2. The European Works Council shall have the right to meet with the central management once a year, to be informed and consulted, on the basis of a report drawn up by the central management, on the progress of the business of the Community-scale undertaking or Community-scale group of undertakings and its prospects. The local managements shall be informed accordingly.
The meeting shall relate in particular to the structure, economic and financial situation, the probable development of the business and of production and sales, the situation and probable trend of employment, investments, and substantial changes concerning organization, introduction of new working methods or production processes, transfers of production, mergers, cut-backs or closures of undertakings, establishments or important parts thereof, and collective redundancies.
3. Where there are exceptional circumstances affecting the employees' interests to a considerable extent, particularly in the event of relocations, the closure of establishments or undertakings or collective redundancies, the select committee or, where no such committee exists, the European Works Council shall have the right to be informed. It shall have the right to meet, at its request, the central management, or any other more appropriate level of management within the Community-scale undertaking or group of undertakings having its own powers

of decision, so as to be informed and consulted on measures significantly affecting employees' interests.
Those members of the European Works Council who have been elected or appointed by the establishments and/or undertakings which are directly concerned by the measures in question shall also have the right to participate in the meeting organized with the select committee.
This information and consultation meeting shall take place as soon as possible on the basis of a report drawn up by the central management or any other appropriate level of management of the Communityscale undertaking or group of undertakings, on which an opinion may be delivered at the end of the meeting or within a reasonable time.
This meeting shall not affect the prerogatives of the central management.
4. The Member States may lay down rules on the chairing of information and consultation meetings.
Before any meeting with the central management, the European Works Council or the select committee, where necessary enlarged in accordance with the second paragraph of point 3, shall be entitled to meet without the management concerned being present.
5. Without prejudice to Article 8 of the Directive, the members of the European Works Council shall inform the representatives of the employees of the establishments or of the undertakings of a Communityscale group of undertakings or, in the absence of representatives, the workforce as a whole, of the content and outcome of the information and consultation procedure carried out in accordance with this Annex.
6. The European Works Council or the select committee may be assisted by experts of its choice, in so far as this is necessary for it to carry out its tasks.
7. The operating expenses of the European Works Council shall be borne by the central management.
The central management concerned shall provide the members of the European Works Council with such financial and material resources as enable them to perform their duties in an appropriate manner.
In particular, the cost of organizing meetings and arranging for interpretation facilities and the accomodation and travelling expenses of members of the European Works Council and its select committee shall be met by the central management unless otherwise agreed.
In compliance with these principles, the Member States may lay down budgetary rules regarding the operation of the European Works Council. They may in particular limit funding to cover one expert only.

Annex 8.5.

Council Directive 2001/86/EC of 8 October 2001 supplementing the Statute for a European company with regard to **the involvement of employees**
Official Journal L 294, 10/11/2001 P. 0022 - 0032.

MAIN PROVISIONS

Article 1
Objective
1. This Directive governs the involvement of employees in the affairs of European public limited-liability companies (Societas Europaea, hereinafter referred to as "SE"), as referred to in Regulation (EC) No 2157/2001.
2. To this end, arrangements for the involvement of employees shall be established in every SE in accordance with the negotiating procedure referred to in Articles 3 to 6 or, under the circumstances specified in Article 7, in accordance with the Annex.

Article 2
Definitions
For the purposes of this Directive:
(a) "SE" means any company established in accordance with Regulation (EC) No 2157/2001;
(b) "participating companies" means the companies directly participating in the establishing of an SE;
(c) "subsidiary" of a company means an undertaking over which that company exercises a dominant influence defined in accordance with Article 3(2) to (7) of Directive 94/45/EC;
(d) "concerned subsidiary or establishment" means a subsidiary or establishment of a participating company which is proposed to become a subsidiary or establishment of the SE upon its formation;
(e) "employees' representatives" means the employees' representatives provided for by national law and/or practice;
(f) "representative body" means the body representative of the employees set up by the agreements referred to in Article 4 or in accordance with the provisions of the Annex, with the purpose of informing and consulting the employees of an SE and its subsidiaries and establishments situated in the Community and, where applicable, of exercising participation rights in relation to the SE;
(g) "special negotiating body" means the body established in accordance with Article 3 to negotiate with the competent body of the participating companies regarding the establishment of arrangements for the involvement of employees within the SE;
(h) "involvement of employees" means any mechanism, including information, consultation and participation, through which employees' representatives may exercise an influence on decisions to be taken within the company;
(i) "information" means the informing of the body representative of the employees and/or employees' representatives by the competent organ of the SE on questions which concern the SE itself and any of its subsidiaries or establishments situated in another Member State or which exceed the powers of the decision-making organs in a single Member State at a time, in a manner and with a content which allows the employees' representatives to undertake an in-depth assessment of the possible impact and, where appropriate, prepare consultations with the competent organ of the SE;
(j) "consultation" means the establishment of dialogue and exchange of views between the body representative of the employees and/or the employees' representatives and the competent organ of the SE, at a time, in a manner and with a content which allows the employees' representatives, on the basis of information provided, to express an opinion on measures envisaged by the competent organ which may be taken into account in the decision-making process within the SE;
(k) "participation" means the influence of the body representative of the employees and/or the employees' representatives in the affairs of a company by way of:
- the right to elect or appoint some of the members of the company's supervisory or administrative organ, or
- the right to recommend and/or oppose the appointment of some or all of the members of the company's supervisory or administrative organ.

SECTION II
NEGOTIATING PROCEDURE

Article 3
Creation of a special negotiating body
1. Where the management or administrative organs of the participating companies draw up a plan for the

establishment of an SE, they shall as soon as possible after publishing the draft terms of merger or creating a holding company or after agreeing a plan to form a subsidiary or to transform into an SE, take the necessary steps, including providing information about the identity of the participating companies, concerned subsidiaries or establishments, and the number of their employees, to start negotiations with the representatives of the companies' employees on arrangements for the involvement of employees in the SE.

2. For this purpose, a special negotiating body representative of the employees of the participating companies and concerned subsidiaries or establishments shall be created in accordance with the following provisions:
(a) in electing or appointing members of the special negotiating body, it must be ensured:

(i) that these members are elected or appointed in proportion to the number of employees employed in each Member State by the participating companies and concerned subsidiaries or establishments, by allocating in respect of a Member State one seat per portion of employees employed in that Member State which equals 10 %, or a fraction thereof, of the number of employees employed by the participating companies and concerned subsidiaries or establishments in all the Member States taken together;
(ii) that in the case of an SE formed by way of merger, there are such further additional members from each Member State as may be necessary in order to ensure that the special negotiating body includes at least one member representing each participating company which is registered and has employees in that Member State and which it is proposed will cease to exist as a separate legal entity following the registration of the SE, in so far as:
- the number of such additional members does not exceed 20 % of the number of members designated by virtue of point (i), and
- the composition of the special negotiating body does not entail a double representation of the employees concerned.
If the number of such companies is higher than the number of additional seats available pursuant to the first subparagraph, these additional seats shall be allocated to companies in different Member States by decreasing order of the number of employees they employ;

(b) Member States shall determine the method to be used for the election or appointment of the members of the special negotiating body who are to be elected or appointed in their territories. They shall take the necessary measures to ensure that, as far as possible, such members shall include at least one member representing each participating company which has employees in the Member State concerned. Such measures must not increase the overall number of members.
Member States may provide that such members may include representatives of trade unions whether or not they are employees of a participating company or concerned subsidiary or establishment.
Without prejudice to national legislation and/or practice laying down thresholds for the establishing of a representative body, Member States shall provide that employees in undertakings or establishments in which there are no employees' representatives through no fault of their own have the right to elect or appoint members of the special negotiating body.

3. The special negotiating body and the competent organs of the participating companies shall determine, by written agreement, arrangements for the involvement of employees within the SE.
To this end, the competent organs of the participating companies shall inform the special negotiating body of the plan and the actual process of establishing the SE, up to its registration.

4. Subject to paragraph 6, the special negotiating body shall take decisions by an absolute majority of its members, provided that such a majority also represents an absolute majority of the employees. Each member shall have one vote. However, should the result of the negotiations lead to a reduction of participation rights, the majority required for a decision to approve such an agreement shall be the votes of two thirds of the members of the special negotiating body representing at least two thirds of the employees, including the votes of members representing employees employed in at least two Member States,
- in the case of an SE to be established by way of merger, if participation covers at least 25 % of the overall number of employees of the participating companies, or
- in the case of an SE to be established by way of creating a holding company or forming a subsidiary, if participation covers at least 50 % of the overall number of employees of the participating companies.
Reduction of participation rights means a proportion of members of the organs of the SE within the meaning of Article 2(k), which is lower than the highest proportion existing within the participating companies.

5. For the purpose of the negotiations, the special negotiating body may request experts of its choice, for example representatives of appropriate Community level trade union organisations, to assist it with its work.

Such experts may be present at negotiation meetings in an advisory capacity at the request of the special negotiating body, where appropriate to promote coherence and consistency at Community level. The special negotiating body may decide to inform the representatives of appropriate external organisations, including trade unions, of the start of the negotiations.

6. The special negotiating body may decide by the majority set out below not to open negotiations or to terminate negotiations already opened, and to rely on the rules on information and consultation of employees in force in the Member States where the SE has employees. Such a decision shall stop the procedure to conclude the agreement referred to in Article 4. Where such a decision has been taken, none of the provisions of the Annex shall apply.
The majority required to decide not to open or to terminate negotiations shall be the votes of two thirds of the members representing at least two thirds of the employees, including the votes of members representing employees employed in at least two Member States.
In the case of an SE established by way of transformation, this paragraph shall not apply if there is participation in the company to be transformed.
The special negotiating body shall be reconvened on the written request of at least 10 % of the employees of the SE, its subsidiaries and establishments, or their representatives, at the earliest two years after the abovementioned decision, unless the parties agree to negotiations being reopened sooner. If the special negotiating body decides to reopen negotiations with the management but no agreement is reached as a result of those negotiations, none of the provisions of the Annex shall apply.

7. Any expenses relating to the functioning of the special negotiating body and, in general, to negotiations shall be borne by the participating companies so as to enable the special negotiating body to carry out its task in an appropriate manner.
In compliance with this principle, Member States may lay down budgetary rules regarding the operation of the special negotiating body. They may in particular limit the funding to cover one expert only.

Article 4
Content of the agreement

1. The competent organs of the participating companies and the special negotiating body shall negotiate in a spirit of cooperation with a view to reaching an agreement on arrangements for the involvement of the employees within the SE.
2. Without prejudice to the autonomy of the parties, and subject to paragraph 4, the agreement referred to in paragraph 1 between the competent organs of the participating companies and the special negotiating body shall specify:
(a) the scope of the agreement;
(b) the composition, number of members and allocation of seats on the representative body which will be the discussion partner of the competent organ of the SE in connection with arrangements for the information and consultation of the employees of the SE and its subsidiaries and establishments;
(c) the functions and the procedure for the information and consultation of the representative body;
(d) the frequency of meetings of the representative body;
(e) the financial and material resources to be allocated to the representative body;
(f) if, during negotiations, the parties decide to establish one or more information and consultation procedures instead of a representative body, the arrangements for implementing those procedures;
(g) if, during negotiations, the parties decide to establish arrangements for participation, the substance of those arrangements including (if applicable) the number of members in the SE's administrative or supervisory body which the employees will be entitled to elect, appoint, recommend or oppose, the procedures as to how these members may be elected, appointed, recommended or opposed by the employees, and their rights;
(h) the date of entry into force of the agreement and its duration, cases where the agreement should be renegotiated and the procedure for its renegotiation.
3. The agreement shall not, unless provision is made otherwise therein, be subject to the standard rules referred to in the Annex.
4. Without prejudice to Article 13(3)(a), in the case of an SE established by means of transformation, the agreement shall provide for at least the same level of all elements of employee involvement as the ones existing within the company to be transformed into an SE.

Article 5
Duration of negotiations
1. Negotiations shall commence as soon as the special negotiating body is established and may continue for six

months thereafter.
2. The parties may decide, by joint agreement, to extend negotiations beyond the period referred to in paragraph 1, up to a total of one year from the establishment of the special negotiating body.

Article 6
Legislation applicable to the negotiation procedure
Except where otherwise provided in this Directive, the legislation applicable to the negotiation procedure provided for in Articles 3 to 5 shall be the legislation of the Member State in which the registered office of the SE is to be situated.

Article 7
Standard rules
1. In order to achieve the objective described in Article 1, Member States shall, without prejudice to paragraph 3 below, lay down standard rules on employee involvement which must satisfy the provisions set out in the Annex.
The standard rules as laid down by the legislation of the Member State in which the registered office of the SE is to be situated shall apply from the date of the registration of the SE where either:
(a) the parties so agree; or
(b) by the deadline laid down in Article 5, no agreement has been concluded, and:
- the competent organ of each of the participating companies decides to accept the application of the standard rules in relation to the SE and so to continue with its registration of the SE, and
- the special negotiating body has not taken the decision provided in Article 3(6).

2. Moreover, the standard rules fixed by the national legislation of the Member State of registration in accordance with part 3 of the Annex shall apply only:
(a) in the case of an SE established by transformation, if the rules of a Member State relating to employee participation in the administrative or supervisory body applied to a company transformed into an SE;
(b) in the case of an SE established by merger:
- if, before registration of the SE, one or more forms of participation applied in one or more of the participating companies covering at least 25 % of the total number of employees in all the participating companies, or
- if, before registration of the SE, one or more forms of participation applied in one or more of the participating companies covering less than 25 % of the total number of employees in all the participating companies and if the special negotiating body so decides,
(c) in the case of an SE established by setting up a holding company or establishing a subsidiary:
- if, before registration of the SE, one or more forms of participation applied in one or more of the participating companies covering at least 50 % of the total number of employees in all the participating companies; or
- if, before registration of the SE, one or more forms of participation applied in one or more of the participating companies covering less than 50 % of the total number of employees in all the participating companies and if the special negotiating body so decides.
If there was more than one form of participation within the various participating companies, the special negotiating body shall decide which of those forms must be established in the SE. Member States may fix the rules which are applicable in the absence of any decision on the matter for an SE registered in their territory. The special negotiating body shall inform the competent organs of the participating companies of any decisions taken pursuant to this paragraph.

3. Member States may provide that the reference provisions in part 3 of the Annex shall not apply in the case provided for in point (b) of paragraph 2.

SECTION III
MISCELLANEOUS PROVISIONS

Article 8
Reservation and confidentiality
1. Member States shall provide that members of the special negotiating body or the representative body, and experts who assist them, are not authorised to reveal any information which has been given to them in confidence.
The same shall apply to employees' representatives in the context of an information and consultation procedure. This obligation shall continue to apply, wherever the persons referred to may be, even after the expiry of their terms of office.

2. Each Member State shall provide, in specific cases and under the conditions and limits laid down by national legislation, that the supervisory or administrative organ of an SE or of a participating company established in its territory is not obliged to transmit information where its nature is such that, according to objective criteria, to do so would seriously harm the functioning of the SE (or, as the case may be, the participating company) or its subsidiaries and establishments or would be prejudicial to them. A Member State may make such dispensation subject to prior administrative or judicial authorisation.
3. Each Member State may lay down particular provisions for SEs in its territory which pursue directly and essentially the aim of ideological guidance with respect to information and the expression of opinions, on condition that, on the date of adoption of this Directive, such provisions already exist in the national legislation.
4. In applying paragraphs 1, 2 and 3, Member States shall make provision for administrative or judicial appeal procedures which the employees' representatives may initiate when the supervisory or administrative organ of an SE or participating company demands confidentiality or does not give information.
Such procedures may include arrangements designed to protect the confidentiality of the information in question.

Article 9
Operation of the representative body and procedure for the information and consultation of employees
The competent organ of the SE and the representative body shall work together in a spirit of cooperation with due regard for their reciprocal rights and obligations.
The same shall apply to cooperation between the supervisory or administrative organ of the SE and the employees' representatives in conjunction with a procedure for the information and consultation of employees.

Article 10
Protection of employees' representatives
The members of the special negotiating body, the members of the representative body, any employees' representatives exercising functions under the information and consultation procedure and any employees' representatives in the supervisory or administrative organ of an SE who are employees of the SE, its subsidiaries or establishments or of a participating company shall, in the exercise of their functions, enjoy the same protection and guarantees provided for employees' representatives by the national legislation and/or practice in force in their country of employment.
This shall apply in particular to attendance at meetings of the special negotiating body or representative body, any other meeting under the agreement referred to in Article 4(2)(f) or any meeting of the administrative or supervisory organ, and to the payment of wages for members employed by a participating company or the SE or its subsidiaries or establishments during a period of absence necessary for the performance of their duties.

Article 11
Misuse of procedures
Member States shall take appropriate measures in conformity with Community law with a view to preventing the misuse of an SE for the purpose of depriving employees of rights to employee involvement or withholding such rights.

Article 12
Compliance with this Directive
1. Each Member State shall ensure that the management of establishments of an SE and the supervisory or administrative organs of subsidiaries and of participating companies which are situated within its territory and the employees' representatives or, as the case may be, the employees themselves abide by the obligations laid down by this Directive, regardless of whether or not the SE has its registered office within its territory.
2. Member States shall provide for appropriate measures in the event of failure to comply with this Directive; in particular they shall ensure that administrative or legal procedures are available to enable the obligations deriving from this Directive to be enforced.

Article 13
Link between this Directive and other provisions
1. Where an SE is a Community-scale undertaking or a controlling undertaking of a Community-scale group of undertakings within the meaning of Directive 94/45/EC or of Directive 97/74/EC(6) extending the said Directive to the United Kingdom, the provisions of these Directives and the provisions transposing them into national legislation shall not apply to them or to their subsidiaries.
However, where the special negotiating body decides in accordance with Article 3(6) not to open negotiations or to terminate negotiations already opened, Directive 94/45/EC or Directive 97/74/EC and the provisions transposing them into national legislation shall apply.

2. Provisions on the participation of employees in company bodies provided for by national legislation and/or practice, other than those implementing this Directive, shall not apply to companies established in accordance with Regulation (EC) No 2157/2001 and covered by this Directive.
3. This Directive shall not prejudice:
(a) the existing rights to involvement of employees provided for by national legislation and/or practice in the Member States as enjoyed by employees of the SE and its subsidiaries and establishments, other than participation in the bodies of the SE;
(b) the provisions on participation in the bodies laid down by national legislation and/or practice applicable to the subsidiaries of the SE.
4. In order to preserve the rights referred to in paragraph 3, Member States may take the necessary measures to guarantee that the structures of employee representation in participating companies which will cease to exist as separate legal entities are maintained after the registration of the SE.

Article 14
Final provisions
1. Member States shall adopt the laws, regulations and administrative provisions necessary to comply with this Directive no later than 8 October 2004, or shall ensure by that date at the latest that management and labour introduce the required provisions by way of agreement, the Member States being obliged to take all necessary steps enabling them at all times to guarantee the results imposed by this Directive. They shall forthwith inform the Commission thereof.
2. When Member States adopt these measures, they shall contain a reference to this Directive or shall be accompanied by such reference on the occasion of their official publication. The methods of making such reference shall be laid down by the Member States.

Article 15
Review by the Commission
No later than 8 October 2007, the Commission shall, in consultation with the Member States and with management and labour at Community level, review the procedures for applying this Directive, with a view to proposing suitable amendments to the Council where necessary.

Article 16
Entry into force
This Directive shall enter into force on the day of its publication in the Official Journal of the European Communities.

Article 17
Addressees
This Directive is addressed to the Member States.

ANNEX

STANDARD RULES
(referred to in Article 7)

Part 1: Composition of the body representative of the employees
In order to achieve the objective described in Article 1, and in the cases referred to in Article 7, a representative body shall be set up in accordance with the following rules.
(a) The representative body shall be composed of employees of the SE and its subsidiaries and establishments elected or appointed from their number by the employees' representatives or, in the absence thereof, by the entire body of employees.
(b) The election or appointment of members of the representative body shall be carried out in accordance with national legislation and/or practice.
Member States shall lay down rules to ensure that the number of members of, and allocation of seats on, the representative body shall be adapted to take account of changes occurring within the SE and its subsidiaries and establishments.
(c) Where its size so warrants, the representative body shall elect a select committee from among its members, comprising at most three members.
(d) The representative body shall adopt its rules of procedure.
(e) The members of the representative body are elected or appointed in proportion to the number of employees

employed in each Member State by the participating companies and concerned subsidiaries or establishments, by allocating in respect of a Member State one seat per portion of employees employed in that Member State which equals 10 %, or a fraction thereof, of the number of employees employed by the participating companies and concerned subsidiaries or establishments in all the Member States taken together.
(f) The competent organ of the SE shall be informed of the composition of the representative body.
(g) Four years after the representative body is established, it shall examine whether to open negotiations for the conclusion of the agreement referred to in Articles 4 and 7 or to continue to apply the standard rules adopted in accordance with this Annex.
Articles 3(4) to (7) and 4 to 6 shall apply, mutatis mutandis, if a decision has been taken to negotiate an agreement according to Article 4, in which case the term "special negotiating body" shall be replaced by "representative body". Where, by the deadline by which the negotiations come to an end, no agreement has been concluded, the arrangements initially adopted in accordance with the standard rules shall continue to apply.

Part 2: Standard rules for information and consultation

The competence and powers of the representative body set up in an SE shall be governed by the following rules.
(a) The competence of the representative body shall be limited to questions which concern the SE itself and any of its subsidiaries or establishments situated in another Member State or which exceed the powers of the decision-making organs in a single Member State.
(b) Without prejudice to meetings held pursuant to point (c), the representative body shall have the right to be informed and consulted and, for that purpose, to meet with the competent organ of the SE at least once a year, on the basis of regular reports drawn up by the competent organ, on the progress of the business of the SE and its prospects. The local managements shall be informed accordingly.
The competent organ of the SE shall provide the representative body with the agenda for meetings of the administrative, or, where appropriate, the management and supervisory organ, and with copies of all documents submitted to the general meeting of its shareholders.
The meeting shall relate in particular to the structure, economic and financial situation, the probable development of the business and of production and sales, the situation and probable trend of employment, investments, and substantial changes concerning organisation, introduction of new working methods or production processes, transfers of production, mergers, cut-backs or closures of undertakings, establishments or important parts thereof, and collective redundancies.
(c) Where there are exceptional circumstances affecting the employees' interests to a considerable extent, particularly in the event of relocations, transfers, the closure of establishments or undertakings or collective redundancies, the representative body shall have the right to be informed. The representative body or, where it so decides, in particular for reasons of urgency, the select committee, shall have the right to meet at its request the competent organ of the SE or any more appropriate level of management within the SE having its own powers of decision, so as to be informed and consulted on measures significantly affecting employees' interests.
Where the competent organ decides not to act in accordance with the opinion expressed by the representative body, this body shall have the right to a further meeting with the competent organ of the SE with a view to seeking agreement.
In the case of a meeting organised with the select committee, those members of the representative body who represent employees who are directly concerned by the measures in question shall also have the right to participate.
The meetings referred to above shall not affect the prerogatives of the competent organ.
(d) Member States may lay down rules on the chairing of information and consultation meetings.
Before any meeting with the competent organ of the SE, the representative body or the select committee, where necessary enlarged in accordance with the third subparagraph of paragraph (c), shall be entitled to meet without the representatives of the competent organ being present.
(e) Without prejudice to Article 8, the members of the representative body shall inform the representatives of the employees of the SE and of its subsidiaries and establishments of the content and outcome of the information and consultation procedures.
(f) The representative body or the select committee may be assisted by experts of its choice.
(g) In so far as this is necessary for the fulfilment of their tasks, the members of the representative body shall be entitled to time off for training without loss of wages.
(h) The costs of the representative body shall be borne by the SE, which shall provide the body's members with the financial and material resources needed to enable them to perform their duties in an appropriate manner.
In particular, the SE shall, unless otherwise agreed, bear the cost of organising meetings and providing interpretation facilities and the accommodation and travelling expenses of members of the representative body and the select committee.

In compliance with these principles, the Member States may lay down budgetary rules regarding the operation of the representative body. They may in particular limit funding to cover one expert only.

Part 3: Standard rules for participation

Employee participation in an SE shall be governed by the following provisions
(a) In the case of an SE established by transformation, if the rules of a Member State relating to employee participation in the administrative or supervisory body applied before registration, all aspects of employee participation shall continue to apply to the SE. Point (b) shall apply mutatis mutandis to that end.
(b) In other cases of the establishing of an SE, the employees of the SE, its subsidiaries and establishments and/or their representative body shall have the right to elect, appoint, recommend or oppose the appointment of a number of members of the administrative or supervisory body of the SE equal to the highest proportion in force in the participating companies concerned before registration of the SE.
If none of the participating companies was governed by participation rules before registration of the SE, the latter shall not be required to establish provisions for employee participation.
The representative body shall decide on the allocation of seats within the administrative or supervisory body among the members representing the employees from the various Member States or on the way in which the SE's employees may recommend or oppose the appointment of the members of these bodies according to the proportion of the SE's employees in each Member State. If the employees of one or more Member States are not covered by this proportional criterion, the representative body shall appoint a member from one of those Member States, in particular the Member State of the SE's registered office where that is appropriate. Each Member State may determine the allocation of the seats it is given within the administrative or supervisory body.
Every member of the administrative body or, where appropriate, the supervisory body of the SE who has been elected, appointed or recommended by the representative body or, depending on the circumstances, by the employees shall be a full member with the same rights and obligations as the members representing the shareholders, including the right to vote.

Annex 8.6.

Council Directive 98/59/EC of 20 July 1998 on the approximation of the laws of the Member States relating to **collective redundancies**
Official Journal L 225 , 12/08/1998 P. 0016 - 0021.

MAIN PROVISIONS

Definitions and scope

Article 1
1. For the purposes of this Directive:
(a) "collective redundancies" means dismissals effected by an employer for one or more reasons not related to the individual workers concerned where, according to the choice of the Member States, the number of redundancies is:
(i) either, over a period of 30 days:
- at least 10 in establishments normally employing more than 20 and less than 100 workers,
- at least 10 % of the number of workers in establishments normally employing at least 100 but less than 300 workers,
- at least 30 in establishments normally employing 300 workers or more,
(ii) or, over a period of 90 days, at least 20, whatever the number of workers normally employed in the establishments in question;
(b) "workers' representatives" means the workers' representatives provided for by the laws or practices of the Member States.
For the purpose of calculating the number of redundancies provided for in the first subparagraph of point (a), terminations of an employment contract which occur on the employer's initiative for one or more reasons not related to the individual workers concerned shall be assimilated to redundancies, provided that there are at least five redundancies.

2. This Directive shall not apply to:
(a) collective redundancies effected under contracts of employment concluded for limited periods of time or for specific tasks except where such redundancies take place prior to the date of expiry or the completion of such contracts;
(b) workers employed by public administrative bodies or by establishments governed by public law (or, in Member States where this concept is unknown, by equivalent bodies);
(c) the crews of seagoing vessels.

SECTION II
Information and consultation

Article 2
1. Where an employer is contemplating collective redundancies, he shall begin consultations with the workers' representatives in good time with a view to reaching an agreement.
2. These consultations shall, at least, cover ways and means of avoiding collective redundancies or reducing the number of workers affected, and of mitigating the consequences by recourse to accompanying social measures aimed, inter alia, at aid for redeploying or retraining workers made redundant.
Member States may provide that the workers' representatives may call on the services of experts in accordance with national legislation and/or practice.
3. To enable workers' representatives to make constructive proposals, the employers shall in good time during the course of the consultations:
(a) supply them with all relevant information and
(b) in any event notify them in writing of:
(i) the reasons for the projected redundancies;
(ii) the number of categories of workers to be made redundant;
(iii) the number and categories of workers normally employed;
(iv) the period over which the projected redundancies are to be effected;
(v) the criteria proposed for the selection of the workers to be made redundant in so far as national legislation and/or practice confers the power therefore upon the employer;
(vi) the method for calculating any redundancy payments other than those arising out of national legislation and/or practice.

The employer shall forward to the competent public authority a copy of, at least, the elements of the written communication which are provided for in the first subparagraph, point (b), subpoints (i) to (v).
4. The obligations laid down in paragraphs 1, 2 and 3 shall apply irrespective of whether the decision regarding collective redundancies is being taken by the employer or by an undertaking controlling the employer.
In considering alleged breaches of the information, consultation and notification requirements laid down by this Directive, account shall not be taken of any defence on the part of the employer on the ground that the necessary information has not been provided to the employer by the undertaking which took the decision leading to collective redundancies.

SECTION III
Procedure for collective redundancies

Article 3
1. Employers shall notify the competent public authority in writing of any projected collective redundancies.
However, Member States may provide that in the case of planned collective redundancies arising from termination of the establishment's activities as a result of a judicial decision, the employer shall be obliged to notify the competent public authority in writing only if the latter so requests.
This notification shall contain all relevant information concerning the projected collective redundancies and the consultations with workers' representatives provided for in Article 2, and particularly the reasons for the redundancies, the number of workers to be made redundant, the number of workers normally employed and the period over which the redundancies are to be effected.
2. Employers shall forward to the workers' representatives a copy of the notification provided for in paragraph 1.
The workers' representatives may send any comments they may have to the competent public authority.

Article 4
1. Projected collective redundancies notified to the competent public authority shall take effect not earlier than 30 days after the notification referred to in Article 3(1) without prejudice to any provisions governing individual rights with regard to notice of dismissal.
Member States may grant the competent public authority the power to reduce the period provided for in the preceding subparagraph.
2. The period provided for in paragraph 1 shall be used by the competent public authority to seek solutions to the problems raised by the projected collective redundancies.
3. Where the initial period provided for in paragraph 1 is shorter than 60 days, Member States may grant the competent public authority the power to extend the initial period to 60 days following notification where the problems raised by the projected collective redundancies are not likely to be solved within the initial period.
Member States may grant the competent public authority wider powers of extension.
The employer must be informed of the extension and the grounds for it before expiry of the initial period provided for in paragraph 1.
4. Member States need not apply this Article to collective redundancies arising from termination of the establishment's activities where this is the result of a judicial decision.

SECTION IV
Final provisions

Article 5
This Directive shall not affect the right of Member States to apply or to introduce laws, regulations or administrative provisions which are more favourable to workers or to promote or to allow the application of collective agreements more favourable to workers.

Article 6
Member States shall ensure that judicial and/or administrative procedures for the enforcement of obligations under this Directive are available to the workers' representatives and/or workers.

Article 7
Member States shall forward to the Commission the text of any fundamental provisions of national law already adopted or being adopted in the area governed by this Directive.

Article 8
1. The Directives listed in Annex I, Part A, are hereby repealed without prejudice to the obligations of the Member States concerning the deadlines for transposition of the said Directive set out in Annex I, Part B.

2. References to the repealed Directives shall be construed as references to this Directive and shall be read in accordance with the correlation table in Annex II.

Annex 8.7.

Council Directive 2001/23/EC of 12 March 2001 on the approximation of the laws of the Member States relating to the safeguarding of employees' rights in the event of **transfers of undertakings, businesses or parts of undertakings or businesses**
Official Journal L 082 , 22/03/2001 P. 0016 - 0020.

MAIN PROVISIONS

CHAPTER I
Scope and definitions

Article 1
1. (a) This Directive shall apply to any transfer of an undertaking, business, or part of an undertaking or business to another employer as a result of a legal transfer or merger.
(b) Subject to subparagraph (a) and the following provisions of this Article, there is a transfer within the meaning of this Directive where there is a transfer of an economic entity which retains its identity, meaning an organised grouping of resources which has the objective of pursuing an economic activity, whether or not that activity is central or ancillary.
(c) This Directive shall apply to public and private undertakings engaged in economic activities whether or not they are operating for gain. An administrative reorganisation of public administrative authorities, or the transfer of administrative functions between public administrative authorities, is not a transfer within the meaning of this Directive.
2. This Directive shall apply where and in so far as the undertaking, business or part of the undertaking or business to be transferred is situated within the territorial scope of the Treaty.
3. This Directive shall not apply to seagoing vessels.

Article 2
1. For the purposes of this Directive:
(a) "transferor" shall mean any natural or legal person who, by reason of a transfer within the meaning of Article 1(1), ceases to be the employer in respect of the undertaking, business or part of the undertaking or business;
(b) "transferee" shall mean any natural or legal person who, by reason of a transfer within the meaning of Article 1(1), becomes the employer in respect of the undertaking, business or part of the undertaking or business;
(c) "representatives of employees" and related expressions shall mean the representatives of the employees provided for by the laws or practices of the Member States;
(d) "employee" shall mean any person who, in the Member State concerned, is protected as an employee under national employment law.
2. This Directive shall be without prejudice to national law as regards the definition of contract of employment or employment relationship.
However, Member States shall not exclude from the scope of this Directive contracts of employment or employment relationships solely because:
(a) of the number of working hours performed or to be performed,
(b) they are employment relationships governed by a fixed-duration contract of employment within the meaning of Article 1(1) of Council Directive 91/383/EEC of 25 June 1991 supplementing the measures to encourage improvements in the safety and health at work of workers with a fixed-duration employment relationship or a tempory employment relationship(6), or
(c) they are temporary employment relationships within the meaning of Article 1(2) of Directive 91/383/EEC, and the undertaking, business or part of the undertaking or business transferred is, or is part of, the temporary employment business which is the employer.

CHAPTER II
Safeguarding of employees' rights

Article 3
1. The transferor's rights and obligations arising from a contract of employment or from an employment relationship existing on the date of a transfer shall, by reason of such transfer, be transferred to the transferee.
Member States may provide that, after the date of transfer, the transferor and the transferee shall be jointly and severally liable in respect of obligations which arose before the date of transfer from a contract of employment or an employment relationship existing on the date of the transfer.
2. Member States may adopt appropriate measures to ensure that the transferor notifies the transferee of all the

rights and obligations which will be transferred to the transferee under this Article, so far as those rights and obligations are or ought to have been known to the transferor at the time of the transfer. A failure by the transferor to notify the transferee of any such right or obligation shall not affect the transfer of that right or obligation and the rights of any employees against the transferee and/or transferor in respect of that right or obligation.
3. Following the transfer, the transferee shall continue to observe the terms and conditions agreed in any collective agreement on the same terms applicable to the transferor under that agreement, until the date of termination or expiry of the collective agreement or the entry into force or application of another collective agreement.
Member States may limit the period for observing such terms and conditions with the proviso that it shall not be less than one year.
4. (a) Unless Member States provide otherwise, paragraphs 1 and 3 shall not apply in relation to employees' rights to old-age, invalidity or survivors' benefits under supplementary company or intercompany pension schemes outside the statutory social security schemes in Member States.
(b) Even where they do not provide in accordance with subparagraph (a) that paragraphs 1 and 3 apply in relation to such rights, Member States shall adopt the measures necessary to protect the interests of employees and of persons no longer employed in the transferor's business at the time of the transfer in respect of rights conferring on them immediate or prospective entitlement to old age benefits, including survivors' benefits, under supplementary schemes referred to in subparagraph (a).

Article 4
1. The transfer of the undertaking, business or part of the undertaking or business shall not in itself constitute grounds for dismissal by the transferor or the transferee. This provision shall not stand in the way of dismissals that may take place for economic, technical or organisational reasons entailing changes in the workforce.
Member States may provide that the first subparagraph shall not apply to certain specific categories of employees who are not covered by the laws or practice of the Member States in respect of protection against dismissal.
2. If the contract of employment or the employment relationship is terminated because the transfer involves a substantial change in working conditions to the detriment of the employee, the employer shall be regarded as having been responsible for termination of the contract of employment or of the employment relationship.

Article 5
1. Unless Member States provide otherwise, Articles 3 and 4 shall not apply to any transfer of an undertaking, business or part of an undertaking or business where the transferor is the subject of bankruptcy proceedings or any analogous insolvency proceedings which have been instituted with a view to the liquidation of the assets of the transferor and are under the supervision of a competent public authority (which may be an insolvency practioner authorised by a competent public authority).
2. Where Articles 3 and 4 apply to a transfer during insolvency proceedings which have been opened in relation to a transferor (whether or not those proceedings have been instituted with a view to the liquidation of the assets of the transferor) and provided that such proceedings are under the supervision of a competent public authority (which may be an insolvency practioner determined by national law) a Member State may provide that:
(a) notwithstanding Article 3(1), the transferor's debts arising from any contracts of employment or employment relationships and payable before the transfer or before the opening of the insolvency proceedings shall not be transferred to the transferee, provided that such proceedings give rise, under the law of that Member State, to protection at least equivalent to that provided for in situations covered by Council Directive 80/987/EEC of 20 October 1980 on the approximation of the laws of the Member States relating to the protection of employees in the event of the insolvency of their employer(7), and, or alternatively, that,
(b) the transferee, transferor or person or persons exercising the transferor's functions, on the one hand, and the representatives of the employees on the other hand may agree alterations, in so far as current law or practice permits, to the employees' terms and conditions of employment designed to safeguard employment opportunities by ensuring the survival of the undertaking, business or part of the undertaking or business.
3. A Member State may apply paragraph 20(b) to any transfers where the transferor is in a situation of serious economic crisis, as defined by national law, provided that the situation is declared by a competent public authority and open to judicial supervision, on condition that such provisions already existed in national law on 17 July 1998.
The Commission shall present a report on the effects of this provision before 17 July 2003 and shall submit any appropriate proposals to the Council.
4. Member States shall take appropriate measures with a view to preventing misuse of insolvency proceedings in such a way as to deprive employees of the rights provided for in this Directive.

Article 6

1. If the undertaking, business or part of an undertaking or business preserves its autonomy, the status and function of the representatives or of the representation of the employees affected by the transfer shall be preserved on the same terms and subject to the same conditions as existed before the date of the transfer by virtue of law, regulation, administrative provision or agreement, provided that the conditions necessary for the constitution of the employee's representation are fulfilled.

The first subparagraph shall not supply if, under the laws, regulations, administrative provisions or practice in the Member States, or by agreement with the representatives of the employees, the conditions necessary for the reappointment of the representatives of the employees or for the reconstitution of the representation of the employees are fulfilled.

Where the transferor is the subject of bankruptcy proceedings or any analoguous insolvency proceedings which have been instituted with a view to the liquidation of the assets of the transferor and are under the supervision of a competent public authority (which may be an insolvency practitioner authorised by a competent public authority), Member States may take the necessary measures to ensure that the transferred employees are properly represented until the new election or designation of representatives of the employees.

If the undertaking, business or part of an undertaking or business does not preserve its autonomy, the Member States shall take the necessary measures to ensure that the employees transferred who were represented before the transfer continue to be properly represented during the period necessary for the reconstitution or reappointment of the representation of employees in accordance with national law or practice.

2. If the term of office of the representatives of the employees affected by the transfer expires as a result of the transfer, the representatives shall continue to enjoy the protection provided by the laws, regulations, administrative provisions or practice of the Member States.

CHAPTER III

Information and consultation

Article 7

1. The transferor and transferee shall be required to inform the representatives of their respective employees affected by the transfer of the following:

- the date or proposed date of the transfer,
- the reasons for the transfer,
- the legal, economic and social implications of the transfer for the employees,
- any measures envisaged in relation to the employees.

The transferor must give such information to the representatives of his employees in good time, before the transfer is carried out.

The transferee must give such information to the representatives of his employees in good time, and in any event before his employees are directly affected by the transfer as regards their conditions of work and employment.

2. Where the transferor or the transferee envisages measures in relation to his employees, he shall consult the representatives of this employees in good time on such measures with a view to reaching an agreement.

3. Member States whose laws, regulations or administrative provisions provide that represenatives of the employees may have recourse to an arbitration board to obtain a decision on the measures to be taken in relation to employees may limit the obligations laid down in paragraphs 1 and 2 to cases where the transfer carried out gives rise to a change in the business likely to entail serious disadvantages for a considerable number of the employees.

The information and consultations shall cover at least the measures envisaged in relation to the employees.

The information must be provided and consultations take place in good time before the change in the business as referred to in the first subparagraph is effected.

4. The obligations laid down in this Article shall apply irrespective of whether the decision resulting in the transfer is taken by the employer or an undertaking controlling the employer.

In considering alleged breaches of the information and consultation requirements laid down by this Directive, the argument that such a breach occurred because the information was not provided by an undertaking controlling the employer shall not be accepted as an excuse.

5. Member States may limit the obligations laid down in paragraphs 1, 2 and 3 to undertakings or businesses which, in terms of the number of employees, meet the conditions for the election or nomination of a collegiate body representing the employees.

6. Member States shall provide that, where there are no representatives of the employees in an undertaking or business through no fault of their own, the employees concerned must be informed in advance of:

- the date or proposed date of the transfer,
- the reason for the transfer,
- the legal, economic and social implications of the transfer for the employees,

- any measures envisaged in relation to the employees.

CHAPTER IV
Final provisions

Article 8
This Directive shall not affect the right of Member States to apply or introduce laws, regulations or administrative provisions which are more favourable to employees or to promote or permit collective agreements or agreements between social partners more favourable to employees.

Article 9
Member States shall introduce into their national legal systems such measures as are necessary to enable all employees and representatives of employees who consider themselves wronged by failure to comply with the obligations arising from this Directive to pursue their claims by judicial process after possible recourse to other competent authorities.

Article 10
The Commission shall submit to the Council an analysis of the effect of the provisions of this Directive before 17 July 2006. It shall propose any amendment which may seem necessary.

Article 11
Member States shall communicate to the Commission the texts of the laws, regulations and administrative provisions which they adopt in the field covered by this Directive.

Article 12
Directive 77/187/EEC, as amended by the Directive referred to in Annex I, Part A, is repealed, without prejudice to the obligations of the Member States concerning the time limits for implementation set out in Annex I, Part B.
References to the repealed Directive shall be construed as references to this Directive and shall be read in accordance with the correlation table in Annex II.

Annex 8.8.

Council Directive 80/987/EEC of 20 October 1980 on the approximation of the laws of the Member States relating to the protection of employees in the event of the **insolvency of their employer**
Official Journal L 283 , 28/10/1980 P. 0023 - 0027.

MAIN PROVISIONS

Article 1
1. This Directive shall apply to employees' claims arising from contracts of employment or employment relationships and existing against employers who are in a state of insolvency within the meaning of Article 2 (1).
2. Member States may, by way of exception, exclude claims by certain categories of employee from the scope of this Directive, by virtue of the special nature of the employee's contract of employment or employment relationship or of the existence of other forms of guarantee offering the employee protection equivalent to that resulting from this Directive.
The categories of employee referred to in the first subparagraph are listed in the Annex.
3. This Directive shall not apply to Greenland. This exception shall be re-examined in the event of any development in the job structures in that region.

Article 2
1. For the purposes of this Directive, an employer shall be deemed to be in a state of insolvency: (a) where a request has been made for the opening of proceedings involving the employer's assets, as provided for under the laws, regulations and administrative provisions of the Member State concerned, to satisfy collectively the claims of creditors and which make it possible to take into consideration the claims referred to in Article 1 (1), and
(b) where the authority which is competent pursuant to the said laws, regulations and administrative provisions has: - either decided to open the proceedings,
- or established that the employer's undertaking or business has been definitively closed down and that the available assets are insufficient to warrant the opening of the proceedings. (1)OJ No C 135, 9.6.1978, p. 2. (2)OJ No C 39, 12.2.1979, p. 26. (3)OJ No C 105, 26.4.1979, p. 15.

2. This Directive is without prejudice to national law as regards the definition of the terms "employee", "employer", "pay", "right conferring immediate entitlement" and "right conferring prospective entitlement".

SECTION II Provisions concerning guarantee institutions

Article 3
1. Member States shall take the measures necessary to ensure that guarantee institutions guarantee, subject to Article 4, payment of employees' outstanding claims resulting from contracts of employment or employment relationships and relating to pay for the period prior to a given date.
2. At the choice of the Member States, the date referred to in paragraph 1 shall be: - either that of the onset of the employer's insolvency;
- or that of the notice of dismissal issued to the employee concerned on account of the employer's insolvency;
- or that of the onset of the employer's insolvency or that on which the contract of employment or the employment relationship with the employee concerned was discontinued on account of the employer's insolvency.

Article 4
1. Member States shall have the option to limit the liability of guarantee institutions, referred to in Article 3.
2. When Member States exercise the option referred to in paragraph 1, they shall: - in the case referred to in Article 3 (2), first indent, ensure the payment of outstanding claims relating to pay for the last three months of the contract of employment or employment relationship occurring within a period of six months preceding the date of the onset of the employer's insolvency;
- in the case referred to in Article 3 (2), second indent, ensure the payment of outstanding claims relating to pay for the last three months of the contract of employment or employment relationship preceding the date of the notice of dismissal issued to the employee on account of the employer's insolvency;
- in the case referred to in Article 3 (2), third indent, ensure the payment of outstanding claims relating to pay for the last 18 months of the contract of employment or employment relationship preceding the date of the onset of the employer's insolvency or the date on which the contract of employment or the employment relationship with the employee was discontinued on account of the employer's insolvency. In this case, Member States may

limit the liability to make payment to pay corresponding to a period of eight weeks or to several shorter periods totalling eight weeks.

3. However, in order to avoid the payment of sums going beyond the social objective of this Directive, Member States may set a ceiling to the liability for employees' outstanding claims.
When Member States exercise this option, they shall inform the Commission of the methods used to set the ceiling.

Article 5
Member States shall lay down detailed rules for the organization, financing and operation of the guarantee institutions, complying with the following principles in particular:
(a) the assets of the institutions shall be independent of the employers' operating capital and be inaccessible to proceedings for insolvency;
(b) employers shall contribute to financing, unless it is fully covered by the public authorities;
(c) the institutions' liabilities shall not depend on whether or not obligations to contribute to financing have been fulfilled.

SECTION III Provisions concerning social security

Article 6
Member States may stipulate that Articles 3, 4 and 5 shall not apply to contributions due under national statutory social security schemes or under supplementary company or inter-company pension schemes outside the national statutory social security schemes.

Article 7
Member States shall take the measures necessary to ensure that non-payment of compulsory contributions due from the employer, before the onset of his insolvency, to their insurance institutions under national statutory social security schemes does not adversely affect employees' benefit entitlement in respect of these insurance institutions inasmuch as the employees' contributions were deducted at source from the remuneration paid.

Article 8
Member States shall ensure that the necessary measures are taken to protect the interests of employees and of persons having already left the employer's undertaking or business at the date of the onset of the employer's insolvency in respect of rights conferring on them immediate or prospective entitlement to old-age benefits, including survivors' benefits, under supplementary company or inter-company pension schemes outside the national statutory social security schemes.

SECTION IV General and final provisions

Article 9
This Directive shall not affect the option of Member States to apply or introduce laws, regulations or administrative provisions which are more favourable to employees.

Article 10
This Directive shall not affect the option of Member States:
(a) to take the measures necessary to avoid abuses;
(b) to refuse or reduce the liability referred to in Article 3 or the guarantee obligation referred to in Article 7 if it appears that fulfilment of the obligation is unjustifiable because of the existence of special links between the employee and the employer and of common interests resulting in collusion between them.

Annex 8.9.

Council Directive 94/33/EC of 22 June 1994 on the **protection of young people at work**
Official Journal L 216 , 20/08/1994 P. 0012 - 0020.

MAIN PROVISIONS

Article 1
Purpose
1. Member States shall take the necessary measures to prohibit work by children.
They shall ensure, under the conditions laid down by this Directive, that the minimum working or employment age is not lower than the minimum age at which compulsory full-time schooling as imposed by national law ends or 15 years in any event.
2. Member States ensure that work by adolescents is strictly regulated and protected under the conditions laid down in this Directive.
3. Member States shall ensure in general that employers guarantee that young people have working conditions which suit their age.
They shall ensure that young people are protected against economic exploitation and against any work likely to harm their safety, health or physical, mental, moral or social development or to jeopardize their education.

Article 2
Scope
1. This Directive shall apply to any person under 18 years of age having an employment contract or an employment relationship defined by the law in force in a Member State and/or governed by the law in force in a Member State.
2. Member States may make legislative or regulatory provision for this Directive not to apply, within the limits and under the conditions which they set by legislative or regulatory provision, to occasional work or short-term work involving:
(a) domestic service in a privat household, or
(b) work regarded as not being harmful, damaging or dangerous to young people in a family undertaking.

Article 3
Definitons
For the purposes of this Directive:
(a) 'young person' shall mean any person under 18 years of age referred to in Article 2 (1);
(b) 'child' shall mean any young person of less than 15 years of age or who is still subject to compulsory full-time schooling under national law;
(c) 'adolescent' shall mean any young person of at least 15 years of age but less than 18 years of age who is no longer subject to compulsory full-time schooling under national law;
(d) 'light work' shall mean all work which, on account of the inherent nature of the tasks which it involves and the particular conditions under which they are performed:
(i) is not likely to be harmful to the safety, health or development of children, and
(ii) is not such as to be harmful to their attendance at school, their participation in vocational guidance or training programmes approved by the competent authority or their capacity to benefit from the instruction received;
(e) 'working time' shall mean any period during which the young person is at work, at the employer's disposal and carrying out his activity or duties in accordance with national legislation and/or practice;
(f) 'rest period' shall mean any period which is not working time.

Article 4
Prohibition of work by children
1. Member States shall adopt the measures necessary to prohibit work by children.
2. Taking into account the objectives set out in Article 1, Member States may make legislative or regulatory provision for the prohibition of work by children not to apply to:
(a) children pursuing the activities set out in Article 5;
(b) children of at least 14 years of age working under a combined work/training scheme or an in-plant work-experience scheme, provided that such work is done in accordance with the conditions laid down by the competent authority;
(c) children of at least 14 years of age performing light work other than that covered by Article 5; light work

other than that covered by Article 5 may, however, be performed by children of 13 years of age for a limited number of hours per week in the case of categories of work determined by national legislation.
3. Member States that make use of the opinion referred to in paragraph 2 (c) shall determine, subject to the provisions of this Directive, the working conditions relating to the light work in question.

Article 5
Cultural or similar activities
1. The employment of children for the purposes of performance in cultural, artistic, sports or advertising activities shall be subject to prior authorization to be given by the competent authority in individual cases.
2. Member States shall by legislative or regulatory provision lay down the working conditions for children in the cases referred to in paragraph 1 and the details of the prior authorization procedure, on condition that the activities:
(i) are not likely to be harmful to the safety, health or development of children, and
(ii) are not such as to be harmful to their attendance at school, their participation in vocational guidance or training programmes approved by the competent authority or their capacity to benefit from the instruction received.
3. By way of derogation from the procedure laid down in paragraph 1, in the case of children of at least 13 years of age, Member States may authorize, by legislative or regulatory provision, in accordance with conditions which they shall determine, the employment of children for the purposes of performance in cultural, artistic, sports or advertising activities.
4. The Member States which have a specific authorization system for modelling agencies with regard to the activities of children may retain that system.

SECTION II

Article 6
General obligations on employers
1. Without prejudice to Article 4 (1), the employer shall adopt the measures necessary to protect the safety and health of young people, taking particular account of the specific risks referred to in Article 7 (1).
2. The employer shall implement the measures provided for in paragraph 1 on the basis of an assessment of the hazards to young people in connection with their work.
The assessment must be made before young people begin work and when there is any major change in working conditions and must pay particular attention to the following points:
(a) the fitting-out and layout of the workplace and the workstation;
(b) the nature, degree and duration of exposure to physical, biological and chemical agents;
(c) the form, range and use of work equipment, in particular agents, machines, apparatus and devices, and the way in which they are handled;
(d) the arrangement of work processes and operations and the way in which these are combined (organization of work);
(e) the level of training and instruction given to young people.
Where this assessment shows that there is a risk to the safety, the physical or mental health or development of young people, an appropriate free assessment and monitoring of their health shall be provided at regular intervals without prejudice to Directive 89/391/EEC.
The free health assessment and monitoring may form part of a national health system.
3. The employer shall inform young people of possible risks and of all measures adopted concerning their safety and health.
Furthermore, he shall inform the legal representatives of children of possible risks and of all measures adopted concerning children's safety and health.
4. The employer shall involve the protective and preventive services referred to in Article 7 of Directive 89/391/EEC in the planning, implementation and monitoring of the safety and health conditions applicable to young people.

Article 7
Vulnerability of young people - Prohibition of work
1. Member States shall ensure that young people are protected from any specific risks to their safety, health and development which are a consequence of their lack of experience, of absence of awareness of existing or potential risks or of the fact that young people have not yet fully matured.
2. Without prejudice to Article 4 (1), Member States shall to this end prohibit the employment of young people for:
(a) work which is objectively beyond their phyiscal or psychological capacity;

(b) work involving harmful exposure to agents which are toxic, carcinogenic, cause heritable genetic damage, or harm to the unborn child or which in any other way chronically affect human health;
(c) work involving harmful exposure to radiation;
(d) work involving the risk of accidents which it may be assumed cannot be recognized or avoided by young persons owing to their insufficient attention to safety or lack of experience or training; or
(e) work in which there is a risk to health from extreme cold or heat, or from noise or vibration.
Work which is likely to entail specific risks for young people within the meaning of paragraph 1 includes:
- work involving harmful exposure to the physical, biological and chemical agents referred to in point I of the Annex, and
- processes and work referred to in point II of the Annex.
3. Member States may, by legislative or regulatory provision, authorize derogations from paragraph 2 in the case of adolescents where such derogations are indispensable for their vocational training, provided that protection of their safety and health is ensured by the fact that the work is performed under the supervision of a competent person within the meaning of Article 7 of Directive 89/391/EEC and provided that the protection afforded by that Directive is guaranteed.

SECTION III

Article 8
Working time
1. Member States which make use of the option in Article 4 (2) (b) or (c) shall adopt the measures necessary to limit the working time of children to:
(a) eight hours a day and 40 hours a week for work performed under a combined work/training scheme or an in-plant work-experience scheme;
(b) two hours on a school day and 12 hours a week for work performed in term-time outside the hours fixed for school attendance, provided that this is not prohibited by national legislation and/or practice;
in no circumstances may the daily working time exceed seven hours; this limit may be raised to eight hours in the case of children who have reached the age of 15;
(c) seven hours a day and 35 hours a week for work performed during a period of at least a week when school is not operating; these limits may be raised to eight hours a day and 40 hours a week in the case of chidren who have reached the age of 15;
(d) seven hours a day and 35 hours a week for light work performed by children no longer subject to compulsory full-time schooling under national law.
2. Member States shall adopt the measures necessary to limit the working time of adolescents to eight hours a day and 40 hours a week.
3. The time spent on training by a young person working under a theoretical and/or practical combined work/training scheme or an in-plant work-experience scheme shall be counted as working time.
4. Where a young person is employed by more than one employer, working days and working time shall be cumulative.
5. Member States may, by legislative or regulatory provision, authorize derogations from paragraph 1 (a) and paragraph 2 either by way of exception or where there are objective grounds for so doing.
Member States shall, by legislative or regulatory provision, determine the conditions, limits and procedure for implementing such derogations.

Article 9
Night work
1. (a) Member States which make use of the option in Article 4 (2) (b) or (c) shall adopt the measures necessary to prohibit work by children between 8 p.m. and 6 a.m.
(b) Member States shall adopt the measures necessary to prohibit work by adolescents either between 10 p.m. and 6 a.m. or between 11 p.m. and 7 a.m.
2. (a) Member States may, by legislative or regulatory provision, authorize work by adolescents in specific areas of activity during the period in which night work is prohibited as referred to in paragraph 1 (b).
In that event, Member States shall take appropriate measures to ensure that the adolescent is supervised by an adult where such supervision is necessary for the adolescent's protection.
(b) If point (a) is applied, work shall continue to be prohibited between midnight and 4 a.m.
However, Member States may, by legislative or regulatory provision, authorize work by adolescents during the period in which night work is prohibited in the following cases, where there are objective grounds for so doing and provided that adolescents are allowed suitable compensatory rest time and that the objectives set out in Article 1 are not called into question:
- work performed in the shipping or fisheries sectors;

- work performed in the context of the armed forces or the police;
- work performed in hospitals or similar establishments;
- cultural, artistic, sports or advertising activities.

3. Prior to any assignment to night work and at regular intervals thereafter, adolescents shall be entitled to a free assessment of their health and capacities, unless the work they do during the period during which work is prohibited is of an exceptional nature.

Article 10
Rest period

1. (a) Member States which make use of the option in Article 4 (2) (b) or (c) shall adopt the measures necessary to ensure that, for each 24-hour period, children are entitled to a minimum rest period of 14 consecutive hours.
(b) Member States shall adopt the measures necessary to ensure that, for each 24-hour period, adolescents are entitled to a minimum rest period of 12 consecutive hours.
2. Member States shall adopt the measures necessary to ensure that, for each seven-day period:
- children in respect of whom they have made use of the option in Article 4 (2) (b) or (c), and
- adolescents

are entitled to a minimum rest period of two days, which shall be consecutive if possible.
Where justified by technical or organization reasons, the minimum rest period may be reduced, but may in no circumstances be less than 36 consecutive hours.
The minimum rest period referred to in the first and second subparagraphs shall in principle include Sunday.
3. Member States may, by legislative or regulatory provision, provide for the minimum rest periods referred to in paragraphs 1 and 2 to be interrupted in the case of activities involving periods of work that are split up over the day or are of short duration.
4. Member States may make legislative or regulatory provision for derogations from paragraph 1 (b) and paragraph 2 in respect of adolescents in the following cases, where there are objective grounds for so doing and provided that they are granted appropriate compensatory rest time and that the objectives set out in Article 1 are not called into question:
(a) work performed in the shipping or fisheries sectors;
(b) work performed in the context of the armed forces or the police;
(c) work performed in hospitals or similar establishments;
(d) work performed in agriculture;
(e) work performed in the tourism industry or in the hotel, restaurant and café sector;
(f) activities involving periods of work split up over the day.

Article 11
Annual rest

Member States which make use of the option referred to in Article 4 (2) (b) or (c) shall see to it that a period free of any work is included, as far as possible, in the school holidays of children subject to compulsory full-time schooling under national law.

Article 12
Breaks

Member States shall adopt the measures necessary to ensure that, where daily working time is more than four and a half hours, young people are entitled to a break of at least 30 minutes, which shall be consecutive if possible.

Article 13
Work by adolescents in the event of force majeure

Member States may, by legislative or regulatory provision, authorize derogations from Article 8 (2), Article 9 (1) (b), Article 10 (1) (b) and, in the case of adolescents, Article 12, for work in the circumstances referred to in Article 5 (4) of Directive 89/391/EEC, provided that such work is of a temporary nature and must be performed immediately, that adult workers are not available and that the adolescents are allowed equivalent compensatory rest time within the following three weeks.

SECTION IV

Article 14
Measures

Each Member State shall lay down any necessary measures to be applied in the event of failure to comply with the provisions adopted in order to implement this Directive; such measures must be effective and proportionate.

Article 15
Adaptation of the Annex
Adaptations of a strictly technical nature to the Annex in the light of technical progress, changes in international rules or specifications and advances in knowledge in the field covered by this Directive shall be adopted in accordance with the procedure provided for in Article 17 of Directive 89/391/EEC.

Article 16
Non-reducing clause
Without prejudice to the right of Member States to develop, in the light of changing circumstances, different provisions on the protection of young people, as long as the minimum requirements provided for by this Directive are complied with, the implementation of this Directive shall not constitute valid grounds for reducing the general level of protection afforded to young people.

Article 17
Final provisions
1. (a) Member States shall bring into force the laws, regulations and administrative provisions necessary to comply with this Directive not later than 22 June 1996 or ensure, by that date at the latest, that the two sides of industry introduce the requisite provisions by means of collective agreements, with Member States being required to make all the necessary provisions to enable them at all times to guarantee the results laid down by this Directive.
(b) The United Kingdom may refrain from implementing the first subparagraph of Article 8 (1) (b) with regard to the provision relating to the maximum weekly working time, and also Article 8(2) and Article 9 (1) (b) and (2) for a period of four years from the date specified in subparagraph (a).
The Commission shall submit a report on the effects of this provision.
The Council, acting in accordance with the conditions laid down by the Treaty, shall decide whether this period should be extended.
(c) Member States shall forthwith inform the Commission thereof.
2. When Member States adopt the measures referred to in paragraph 1, such measures shall contain a reference to this Directive or shall be accompanied by such reference on the occasion of their official publication. The methods of making such reference shall be laid down by Member States.
3. Member States shall communicate to the Commission the texts of the main provisions of national law which they have already adopted or adopt in the field governed by this Directive.
4. Member States shall report to the Commission every five years on the practical implementation of the provisions of this Directive, indicating the viewpoints of the two sides of industry.
The Commission shall inform the European Parliament, the Council and the Economic and Social Committee thereof.
5. The Commission shall periodically submit to the European Parliament, the Council and the Economic and Social Committee a report on the application of this Directive taking into account pargraphs 1, 2, 3 and 4.

Annex 8.10.

Council Directive 91/383/EEC of 25 June 1991 supplementing the measures to encourage improvements in the **safety and health at work of workers with a fixed-duration employment relationship** or a temporary employment relationship
Official Journal L 206 , 29/07/1991 P. 0019 - 0021.

MAIN PROVISIONS

Article 1
Scope
This Directive shall apply to:
1.employment relationships governed by a fixed-duration contract of employment concluded directly between the employer and the worker, where the end of the contract is established by objective conditions such as: reaching a specific date, completing a specific task or the occurence of a specific event;
2.temporary employment relationships between a temporary employment business which is the employer and the worker, where the latter is assigned to work for and under the control of an undertaking and/or establishment making use of his services.

Article 2
Object
1. The purpose of this Directive is to ensure that workers with an employment relationship as referred to in Article 1 are afforded, as regards safety and health at work, the same level of protection as that of other workers in the user undertaking and/or establishment.
2. The existence of an employment relationship as referred to in Article 1 shall not justify different treatment with respect to working conditions inasmuch as the protection of safety and health at work are involved, especially as regards access to personal protective equipment.
3. Directive 89/391/EEC and the individual Directives within the meaning of Article 16 (1) thereof shall apply in full to workers with an employment relationship as referred to in Article 1, without prejudice to more binding and/or more specific provisions set out in this Directive.

SECTION II GENERAL PROVISIONS

Article 3
Provision of information to workers
Without prejudice to Article 10 of Directive 89/391/EEC, Member States shall take the necessary steps to ensure that:
1.before a worker with an employment relationship as referred to in Article 1 takes up any activity, he is informed by the undertaking and/or establishment making use of his services of the risks which he faces;
2.such information:
-covers, in particular, any special occupational qualifications or skills or special medical surveillance required, as defined in national legislation, and
-states clearly any increased specific risks, as defined in national legislation, that the job may entail.

Article 4
Workers' training
Without prejudice to Article 12 of Directive 89/391/EEC, Member States shall take the necessary measures to ensure that, in the cases referred to in Article 3, each worker receives sufficient training appropriate to the particular characteristics of the job, account being taken of his qualifications and experience.

Article 5
Use of workers' services and medical surveillance of workers
1. Member States shall have the option of prohibiting workers with an employment relationship as referred to in Article 1 from being used for certain work as defined in national legislation, which would be particularly dangerous to their safety or health, and in particular for certain work which requires special medical surveillance, as defined in national legislation.
2. Where Member States do not avail themselves of the option referred to in paragraph 1, they shall, without prejudice to Article 14 of Directive 89/391/EEC, take the necessary measures to ensure that workers with an employment relationship as referred to in Article 1 who are used for work which requires special medical

surveillance, as defined in national legislation, are provided with appropriate special medical surveillance.
3. It shall be open to Member States to provide that the appropriate special medical surveillance referred to in paragraph 2 shall extend beyond the end of the employment relationship of the worker concerned.

Article 6
Protection and prevention services
Member States shall take the necessary measures to ensure that workers, services or persons designated, in accordance with Article 7 of Directive 89/391/EEC, to carry out activities related to protection from and prevention of occupational risks are informed of the assignment of workers with an employment relationship as referred to in Article 1, to the extent necessary for the workers, services or persons designated to be able to carry out adequately their protection and prevention activities for all the workers in the undertaking and/or establishment.

SECTION III SPECIAL PROVISIONS

Article 7
Temporary employment relationships: information
Without prejudice to Article 3, Member States shall take the necessary steps to ensure that:
1.before workers with an employment relationship as referred to in Article 1 (2) are supplied, a user undertaking and/or establishment shall specify to the temporary employment business, inter alia, the occupational qualifications required and the specific features of the job to be filled;
2.the temporary employment business shall bring all these facts to the attention of the workers concerned.
Member States may provide that the details to be given by the user undertaking and/or establishment to the temporary employment business in accordance with point 1 of the first subparagraph shall appear in a contract of assignment.

Article 8
Temporary employment relationships: responsibility
Member States shall take the necessary steps to ensure that:
1.without prejudice to the responsibility of the temporary employment business as laid down in national legislation, the user undertaking and/or establishment is/are responsible, for the duration of the assignment, for the conditions governing performance of the work;
2.for the application of point 1, the conditions governing the performance of the work shall be limited to those connected with safety, hygiene and health at work.

SECTION IV MISCELLANEOUS PROVISIONS

Article 9
More favourable provisions
This Directive shall be without prejudice to existing or future national or Community provisions which are more favourable to the safety and health protection of workers with an employment relationship as referred to in Article 1.

Article 10
Final provisions
1. Member States shall bring into force the laws, regulations and administrative provisions necessary to comply with this Directive by 31 December 1992 at the latest. They shall forthwith inform the Commission thereof.
When Member States adopt these measures, the latter shall contain a reference to this Directive or shall be accompanied by such reference on the occasion of their official publication. The methods of making such a reference shall be laid down by the Member States.
2. Member States shall forward to the Commission the texts of the provisions of national law which they have already adopted or adopt in the field covered by this Directive.
3. Member States shall report to the Commission every five years on the practical implementation of this Directive, setting out the points of view of workers and employers.
The Commission shall bring the report to the attention of the European Parliament, the Council, the Economic and Social Committee and the Advisory Committee on Safety, Hygiene and Health Protection at Work.
4. The Commission shall submit to the European Parliament, the Council and the Economic and Social Committee a regular report on the implementation of this Directive, due account being taken of paragraphs 1, 2 and 3.

Annex 8.11.

Council Directive 1999/70/EC of 28 June 1999 concerning the **framework agreement on fixed-term work** concluded by ETUC, UNICE and CEEP
Official Journal L 175 , 10/07/1999 P. 0043 - 0048.

MAIN PROVISIONS

THE SIGNATORY PARTIES HAVE AGREED THE FOLLOWING
Purpose (clause 1)
The purpose of this framework agreement is to:
(a) improve the quality of fixed-term work by ensuring the application of the principle of non-discrimination;
(b) establish a framework to prevent abuse arising from the use of successive fixed-term employment contracts or relationships

Scope (clause 2)
1. This agreement applies to fixed-term workers who have an employment contract or employment relationship as defined in law, collective agreements or practice in each Member State.
2. Member States after consultation with the social partners and/or the social partners may provide that this agreement does not apply to:
(a) initial vocational training relationships and apprenticeship schemes;
(b) employment contracts and relationships which have been concluded within the framework of a specific public or publicly-supported training, integration and vocational retraining programme.

Definitions (clause 3)
1. For the purpose of this agreement the term "fixed-term worker" means a person having an employment contract or relationship entered into directly between an employer and a worker where the end of the employment contract or relationship is determined by objective conditions such as reaching a specific date, completing a specific task, or the occurrence of a specific event.
2. For the purpose of this agreement, the term "comparable permanent worker" means a worker with an employment contract or relationship of indefinite duration, in the same establishment, engaged in the same or similar work/occupation, due regard being given to qualifications/skills.
Where there is no comparable permanent worker in the same establishment, the comparison shall be made by reference to the applicable collective agreement, or where there is no applicable collective agreement, in accordance with national law, collective agreements or practice.

Principle of non-discrimination (clause 4)
1. In respect of employment conditions, fixed-term workers shall not be treated in a less favourable manner than comparable permanent workers solely because they have a fixed-term contract or relation unless different treatment is justified on objective grounds.
2. Where appropriate, the principle of pro rata temporis shall apply.
3. The arrangements for the application of this clause shall be defined by the Member States after consultation with the social partners and/or the social partners, having regard to Community law and national law, collective agreements and practice.
4. Period-of service qualifications relating to particular conditions of employment shall be the same for fixed-term workers as for permanent workers except where different length-of service qualifications are justified on objective grounds.

Measures to prevent abuse (clause 5)
1. To prevent abuse arising from the use of successive fixed-term employment contracts or relationships, Member States, after consultation with social partners in accordance with national law, collective agreements or practice, and/or the social partners, shall, where there are no equivalent legal measures to prevent abuse, introduce in a manner which takes account of the needs of specific sectors and/or categories of workers, one or more of the following measures:
(a) objective reasons justifying the renewal of such contracts or relationships;
(b) the maximum total duration of successive fixed-term employment contracts or relationships;
(c) the number of renewals of such contracts or relationships.
2. Member States after consultation with the social partners and/or the social partners shall, where appropriate, determine under what conditions fixed-term employment contracts or relationships:

(a) shall be regarded as "successive"
(b) shall be deemed to be contracts or relationships of indefinite duration.

Information and employment opportunities (clause 6)
1. Employers shall inform fixed-term workers about vacancies which become available in the undertaking or establishment to ensure that they have the same opportunity to secure permanent positions as other workers. Such information may be provided by way of a general announcement at a suitable place in the undertaking or establishment.
2. As far as possible, employers should facilitate access by fixed-term workers to appropriate training opportunities to enhance their skills, career development and occupational mobility.

Information and consultation (clause 7)
1. Fixed-term workers shall be taken into consideration in calculating the threshold above which workers' representative bodies provided for in national and Community law may be constituted in the undertaking as required by national provisions.
2. The arrangements for the application of clause 7.1 shall be defined by Member States after consultation with the social partners and/or the social partners in accordance with national law, collective agreements or practice and having regard to clause 4.1.
3. As far as possible, employers should give consideration to the provision of appropriate information to existing workers' representative bodies about fixed-term work in the undertaking.

Provisions on implementation (clause 8)
1. Member States and/or the social partners can maintain or introduce more favourable provisions for workers than set out in this agreement.
2. This agreement shall be without prejudice to any more specific Community provisions, and in particular Community provisions concerning equal treatment or opportunities for men and women.
3. Implementation of this agreement shall not constitute valid grounds for reducing the general level of protection afforded to workers in the field of the agreement.
4. The present agreement does not prejudice the right of the social partners to conclude at the appropriate level, including European level, agreements adapting and/or complementing the provisions of this agreement in a manner which will take note of the specific needs of the social partners concerned.
5. The prevention and settlement of disputes and grievances arising from the application of this agreement shall be dealt with in accordance with national law, collective agreements and practice.
6. The signatory parties shall review the application of this agreement five years after the date of the Council decision if requested by one of the parties to this agreement.

Annex 8.12.

Council Directive 91/533/EEC of 14 October 1991 on an employer's obligation to inform employees of the **conditions applicable to the contract or employment relationship**
Official Journal L 288 , 18/10/1991 P. 0032 - 0035.

MAIN PROVISIONS

Article 1
Scope
1. This Directive shall apply to every paid employee having a contract or employment relationship defined by the law in force in a Member State and/or governed by the law in force in a Member State.
2. Member States may provide that this Directive shall not apply to employees having a contract or employment relationship:
(a) - with a total duration not exceeding one month, and/or
- with a working week not exceeding eight hours; or
(b) of a casual and/or specific nature provided, in these cases, that its non-application is justified by objective considerations.

Article 2
Obligation to provide information
1. An employer shall be obliged to notify an employee to whom this Directive applies, hereinafter referred to as 'the employee', of the essential aspects of the contract or employment relationship.
2. The information referred to in paragraph 1 shall cover at least the following:
(a) the identities of the parties;
(b) the place of work; where there is no fixed or main place of work, the principle that the employee is employed at various places and the registered place of business or, where appropriate, the domicile of the employer;
(c) (i) the title, grade, nature or category of the work for which the employee is employed; or
(ii) a brief specification or description of the work;
(d) the date of commencement of the contract or employment relationship;
(e) in the case of a temporary contract or employment relationship, the expected duration thereof;
(f) the amount of paid leave to which the employee is entitled or, where this cannot be indicated when the information is given, the procedures for allocating and determining such leave;
(g) the length of the periods of notice to be observed by the employer and the employee should their contract or employment relationship be terminated or, where this cannot be indicated when the information is given, the method for determining such periods of notice;
(h) the initial basic amount, the other component elements and the frequency of payment of the remuneration to which the employee is entitled;
(i) the length of the employee's normal working day or week;
(j) where appropriate;
(i) the collective agreements governing the employee's conditions of work;
or
(ii) in the case of collective agreements concluded outside the business by special joint bodies or institutions, the name of the competent body or joint institution within which the agreements were concluded.
3. The information referred to in paragraph 2 (f), (g), (h) and (i) may, where appropriate, be given in the form of a reference to the laws, regulations and administrative or statutory provisions or collective agreements governing those particular points.

Article 3
Means of information
1. The information referred to in Article 2 (2) may be given to the employee, not later than two months after the commencement of employment, in the form of:
(a) a written contract of employment; and/or
(b) a letter of engagement; and/or
(c) one or more other written documents, where one of these documents contains at least all the information referred to in Article 2 (2) (a), (b), (c), (d), (h) and (i).
2. Where none of the documents referred to in paragraph 1 is handed over to the employee within the prescribed

period, the employer shall be obliged to give the employee, not later than two months after the commencement of employment, a written declaration signed by the employer and containing at least the information referred to in Article 2 (2).
Where the document(s) referred to in paragraph 1 contain only part of the information required, the written declaration provided for in the first subparagraph of this paragraph shall cover the remaining information.
3. Where the contract or employment relationship comes to an end before expiry of a period of two months as from the date of the start of work, the information provided for in Article 2 and in this Article must be made available to the employee by the end of this period at the latest.

Article 4
Expatriate employees
1. Where an employee is required to work in a country or countries other than the Member State whose law and/or practice governs the contract or employment relationship, the document(s) referred to in Article 3 must be in his/her possession before his/her departure and must include at least the following additional information:
(a) the duration of the employment abroad;
(b) the currency to be used for the payment of remuneration;
(c) where appropriate, the benefits in cash or kind attendant on the employment abroad;
(d) where appropriate, the conditions governing the employee's repatriation.
2. The information referred to in paragraph 1 (b) and (c) may, where appropriate, be given in the form of a reference to the laws, regulations and administrative or statutory provisions or collective agreements governing those particular points.
3. Paragraphs 1 and 2 shall not apply if the duration of the employment outside the country whose law and/or practice governs the contract or employment relationship is one month or less.

Article 5
Modification of aspects of the contract or employment relationship
1. Any change in the details referred to in Articles 2 (2) and 4 (1) must be the subject of a written document to be given by the employer to the employee at the earliest opportunity and not later than one month after the date of entry into effect of the change in question.
2. The written document referred to in paragraph 1 shall not be compulsory in the event of a change in the laws, regulations and administrative or statutory provisions or collective agreements cited in the documents referred to in Article 3, supplemented, where appropriate, pursuant to Article 4 (1).

Article 6
Form and proof of the existence of a contract or employment relationship and procedural rules
This Directive shall be without prejudice to national law and practice concerning:
- the form of the contract or employment relationship,
- proof as regards the existence and content of a contract or employment relationship,
- the relevant procedural rules.

Article 7
More favourable provisions This Directive shall not affect Member States' prerogative to apply or to introduce laws, regulations or administrative provisions which are more favourable to employees or to encourage or permit the application of agreements which are more favourable to employees.

Article 8
Defence of rights
1. Member States shall introduce into their national legal systems such measures as are necessary to enable all employees who consider themselves wronged by failure to comply with the obligations arising from this Directive to pursue their claims by judicial process after possible recourse to other competent authorities.
2. Member States may provide that access to the means of redress referred to in paragraph 1 are subject to the notification of the employer by the employee and the failure by the employer to reply within 15 days of notification.
However, the formality of prior notification may in no case be required in the cases referred to in Article 4, neither for workers with a temporary contract or employment relationship, nor for employees not covered by a collective agreement or by collective agreements relating to the employment relationship.

Article 9
Final provisions
1. Member States shall adopt the laws, regulations and administrative provisions necessary to comply with this Directive no later than 30 June 1993 or shall ensure by that date that the employers' and workers' representatives introduce the required provisions by way of agreement, the Member States being obliged to take the necessary steps enabling them at all times to guarantee the results imposed by this Directive.
They shall forthwith inform the Commission thereof.
2. Member States shall take the necessary measures to ensure that, in the case of employment relationships in existence upon entry into force of the provisions that they adopt, the employer gives the employee, on request, within two months of receiving that request; any of the documents referred to in Article 3, supplemented, where appropriate, pursuant to Article 4 (1).
3. When Member States adopt the measures referred to in paragraph 1, such measures shall contain a reference to this Directive or shall be accompanied by such reference on the occasion of their official publication. The methods of making such a reference shall be laid down by the Member States.
4. Member States shall forthwith inform the Commission of the measures they take to implement this Directive.

Annex 8.13.

Council Directive 93/104/EC of 23 November 1993 concerning certain aspects of the **organization of working time**
Official Journal L 307 , 13/12/1993 P. 0018 - 0024.

MAIN PROVISIONS

Article 1
Purpose and scope
1. This Directive lays down minimum safety and health requirements for the organization of working time.
2. This Directive applies to:
(a) minimum periods of daily rest, weekly rest and annual leave, to breaks and maximum weekly working time; and
(b) certain aspects of night work, shift work and patterns of work.
3. This Directive shall apply to all sectors of activity, both public and private, within the meaning of Article 2 of Directive 89/391/EEC, without prejudice to Article 17 of this Directive, with the exception of air, rail, road, sea, inland waterway and lake transport, sea fishing, other work at sea and the activities of doctors in training;
4. The provisions of Directive 89/391/EEC are fully applicable to the matters referred to in paragraph 2, without prejudice to more stringent and/or specific provisions contained in this Directive.

Article 2
Definitions
For the purposes of this Directive, the following definitions shall apply:
1. working time shall mean any period during which the worker is working, at the employer's disposal and carrying out his activity or duties, in accordance with national laws and/or practice;
2. rest period shall mean any period which is not working time;
3. night time shall mean any period of not less than seven hours, as defined by national law, and which must include in any case the period between midnight and 5 a. m.;
4. night worker shall mean:
(a) on the one hand, any worker, who, during night time, works at least three hours of his daily working time as a normal course; and
(b) on the other hand, any worker who is likely during night time to work a certain proportion of his annual working time, as defined at the choice of the Member State concerned:
(i) by national legislation, following consultation with the two sides of industry; or
(ii) by collective agreements or agreements concluded between the two sides of industry at national or regional level;
5. shift work shall mean any method of organizing work in shifts whereby workers succeed each other at the same work stations according to a certain pattern, including a rotating pattern, and which may be continuous or discontinuous, entailing the need for workers to work at different times over a given period of days or weeks;
6. shift worker shall mean any worker whose work schedule is part of shift work.

SECTION II MINIMUM REST PERIODS - OTHER ASPECTS OF THE ORGANIZATION OF WORKING TIME

Article 3
Daily rest
Member States shall take the measures necessary to ensure that every worker is entitled to a minimum daily rest period of 11 consecutive hours per 24-hour period.

Article 4
Breaks
Member States shall take the measures necessary to ensure that, where the working day is longer than six hours, every worker is entitled to a rest break, the details of which, including duration and the terms on which it is granted, shall be laid down in collective agreements or agreements between the two sides of industry or, failing that, by national legislation.

Article 5
Weekly rest period
Member States shall take the measures necessary to ensure that, per each seven-day period, every worker is entitled to a minimum uninterrupted rest period of 24 hours plus the 11 hours' daily rest referred to in Article 3.
The minimum rest period referred to in the first subparagraph shall in principle include Sunday.
If objective, technical or work organization conditions so justify, a minimum rest period of 24 hours may be applied.

Article 6
Maximum weekly working time
Member States shall take the measures necessary to ensure that, in keeping with the need to protect the safety and health of workers:
1. the period of weekly working time is limited by means of laws, regulations or administrative provisions or by collective agreements or agreements between the two sides of industry;
2. the average working time for each seven-day period, including overtime, does not exceed 48 hours.

Article 7
Annual leave
1. Member States shall take the measures necessary to ensure that every worker is entitled to paid annual leave of at least four weeks in accordance with the conditions for entitlement to, and granting of, such leave laid down by national legislation and/or practice.
2. The minimum period of paid annual leave may not be replaced by an allowance in lieu, except where the employment relationship is terminated.

SECTION III NIGHT WORK - SHIFT WORK - PATTERNS OF WORK

Article 8
Length of night work
Member States shall take the measures necessary to ensure that:
1. normal hours of work for night workers do not exceed an average of eight hours in any 24-hour period;
2. night workers whose work involves special hazards or heavy physical or mental strain do not work more than eight hours in any period of 24 hours during which they perform night work.
For the purposes of the aforementioned, work involving special hazards or heavy physical or mental strain shall be defined by national legislation and/or practice or by collective agreements or agreements concluded between the two sides of industry, taking account of the specific effects and hazards of night work.

Article 9
Health assessment and transfer of night workers to day work
1. Member States shall take the measures necessary to ensure that:
(a) night workers are entitled to a free health assessment before their assignment and thereafter at regular intervals;
(b) night workers suffering from health problems recognized as being connected with the fact that they perform night work are transferred whenever possible to day work to which they are suited.
2. The free health assessment referred to in paragraph 1 (a) must comply with medical confidentiality.
3. The free health assessment referred to in paragraph 1 (a) may be conducted within the national health system.

Article 10
Guarantees for night-time working
Member States may make the work of certain categories of night workers subject to certain guarantees, under conditions laid down by national legislation and/or practice, in the case of workers who incur risks to their safety or health linked to night-time working.

Article 11
Notification of regular use of night workers
Member States shall take the measures necessary to ensure that an employer who regularly uses night workers brings this information to the attention of the competent authorities if they so request.

Article 12
Safety and health protection
Member States shall take the measures necessary to ensure that:

1. night workers and shift workers have safety and health protection appropriate to the nature of their work;
2. appropriate protection and prevention services or facilities with regard to the safety and health of night workers and shift workers are equivalent to those applicable to other workers and are available at all times.

Article 13
Pattern of work
Member States shall take the measures necessary to ensure that an employer who intends to organize work according to a certain pattern takes account of the general principle of adapting work to the worker, with a view, in particular, to alleviating monotonous work and work at a predetermined work-rate, depending on the type of activity, and of safety and health requirements, especially as regards breaks during working time.

SECTION IV MISCELLANEOUS PROVISIONS

Article 14
More specific Community provisions
The provisions of this Directive shall not apply where other Community instruments contain more specific requirements concerning certain occupations or occupational activities.

Article 15
More favourable provisions
This Directive shall not affect Member States' right to apply or introduce laws, regulations or administrative provisions more favourable to the protection of the safety and health of workers or to facilitate or permit the application of collective agreements or agreements concluded between the two sides of industry which are more favourable to the protection of the safety and health of workers.

Article 16
Reference periods
Member States may lay down:
1. for the application of Article 5 (weekly rest period), a reference period not exceeding 14 days;
2. for the application of Article 6 (maximum weekly working time), a reference period not exceeding four months.
The periods of paid annual leave, granted in accordance with Article 7, and the periods of sick leave shall not be included or shall be neutral in the calculation of the average;
3. for the application of Article 8 (length of night work), a reference period defined after consultation of the two sides of industry or by collective agreements or agreements concluded between the two sides of industry at national or regional level.
If the minimum weekly rest period of 24 hours required by Article 5 falls within that reference period, it shall not be included in the calculation of the average.

Article 17
Derogations
1. With due regard for the general principles of the protection of the safety and health of workers, Member States may derogate from Article 3, 4, 5, 6, 8 or 16 when, on account of the specific characteristics of the activity concerned, the duration of the working time is not measured and/or predetermined or can be determined by the workers themselves, and particularly in the case of:
(a) managing executives or other persons with autonomous decision-taking powers;
(b) family workers; or
(c) workers officiating at religious ceremonies in churches and religious communities.
2. Derogations may be adopted by means of laws, regulations or administrative provisions or by means of collective agreements or agreements between the two sides of industry provided that the workers concerned are afforded equivalent periods of compensatory rest or that, in exceptional cases in which it is not possible, for objective reasons, to grant such equivalent periods of compensatory rest, the workers concerned are afforded appropriate protection:
2.1. from Articles 3, 4, 5, 8 and 16:
(a) in the case of activities where the worker's place of work and his place of residence are distant from one another or where the worker's different places of work are distant from one another;
(b) in the case of security and surveillance activities requiring a permanent presence in order to protect property and persons, particularly security guards and caretakers or security firms;
(c) in the case of activities involving the need for continuity of service or production, particularly:
(i) services relating to the reception, treatment and/or care provided by hospitals or similar establishments,

residential institutions and prisons;
(ii) dock or airport workers;
(iii) press, radio, television, cinematographic production, postal and telecommunications services, ambulance, fire and civil protection services;
(iv) gas, water and electricity production, transmission and distribution, household refuse collection and incineration plants;
(v) industries in which work cannot be interrupted on technical grounds;
(vi) research and development activities;
(vii) agriculture;
(d) where there is a foreseeable surge of activity, particularly in:
(i) agriculture;
(ii) tourism;
(iii) postal services;
2.2. from Articles 3, 4, 5, 8 and 16:
(a) in the circumstances described in Article 5 (4) of Directive 89/391/EEC;
(b) in cases of accident or imminent risk of accident;
2.3. from Articles 3 and 5:
(a) in the case of shift work activities, each time the worker changes shift and cannot take daily and/or weekly rest periods between the end of one shift and the start of the next one;
(b) in the case of activities involving periods of work split up over the day, particularly those of cleaning staff.
3. Derogations may be made from Articles 3, 4, 5, 8 and 16 by means of collective agreements or agreements concluded between the two sides of industry at national or regional level or, in conformity with the rules laid down by them, by means of collective agreements or agreements concluded between the two sides of industry at a lower level.
Member States in which there is no statutory system ensuring the conclusion of collective agreements or agreements concluded between the two sides of industry at national or regional level, on the matters covered by this Directive, or those Member States in which there is a specific legislative framework for this purpose and within the limits thereof, may, in accordance with national legislation and/or practice, allow derogations from Articles 3, 4, 5, 8 and 16 by way of collective agreements or agreements concluded between the two sides of industry at the appropriate collective level.
The derogations provided for in the first and second subparagraphs shall be allowed on condition that equivalent compensating rest periods are granted to the workers concerned or, in exceptional cases where it is not possible for objective reasons to grant such periods, the workers concerned are afforded appropriate protection.
Member States may lay down rules:
- for the application of this paragraph by the two sides of industry, and
- for the extension of the provisions of collective agreements or agreements concluded in conformity with this paragraph to other workers in accordance with national legislation and/or practice.
4. The option to derogate from point 2 of Article 16, provided in paragraph 2, points 2.1. and 2.2. and in paragraph 3 of this Article, may not result in the establishment of a reference period exceeding six months. However, Member States shall have the option, subject to compliance with the general principles relating to the protection of the safety and health of workers, of allowing, for objective or technical reasons or reasons concerning the organization of work, collective agreements or agreements concluded between the two sides of industry to set reference periods in no event exceeding 12 months.
Before the expiry of a period of seven years from the date referred to in Article 18 (1) (a), the Council shall, on the basis of a Commission proposal accompanied by an appraisal report, re-examine the provisions of this paragraph and decide what action to take.

Article 18
Final provisions
1. (a) Member States shall adopt the laws, regulations and administrative provisions necessary to comply with this Directive by 23 November 1996, or shall ensure by that date that the two sides of industry establish the necessary measures by agreement, with Member States being obliged to take any necessary steps to enable them to guarantee at all times that the provisions laid down by this Directive are fulfilled.
(b) (i) However, a Member State shall have the option not to apply Article 6, while respecting the general principles of the protection of the safety and health of workers, and provided it takes the necessary measures to ensure that:
- no employer requires a worker to work more than 48 hours over a seven-day period, calculated as an average for the reference period referred to in point 2 of Article 16, unless he has first obtained the worker's agreement to perform such work,
- no worker is subjected to any detriment by his employer because he is not willing to give his agreement to

perform such work,
- the employer keeps up-to-date records of all workers who carry out such work,
- the records are placed at the disposal of the competent authorities, which may, for reasons connected with the safety and/or health of workers, prohibit or restrict the possibility of exceeding the maximum weekly working hours,
- the employer provides the competent authorities at their request with information on cases in which agreement has been given by workers to perform work exceeding 48 hours over a period of seven days, calculated as an average for the reference period referred to in point 2 of Article 16.

Before the expiry of a period of seven years from the date referred to in (a), the Council shall, on the basis of a Commission proposal accompanied by an appraisal report, re-examine the provisions of this point (i) and decide on what action to take.

(ii) Similarly, Member States shall have the option, as regards the application of Article 7, of making use of a transitional period of not more than three years from the date referred to in (a), provided that during that transitional period:
- every worker receives three weeks' paid annual leave in accordance with the conditions for the entitlement to, and granting of, such leave laid down by national legislation and/or practice, and
- the three-week period of paid annual leave may not be replaced by an allowance in lieu, except where the employment relationship is terminated.

(c) Member states shall forthwith inform the Commission thereof.

2. When Member States adopt the measures referred to in paragraph 1, they shall contain a reference to this Directive or shall be accompanied by such reference on the occasion of their official publication. The methods of making such a reference shall be laid down by the Member states.

3. Without prejudice to the right of Member States to develop, in the light of changing circumstances, different legislative, regulatory or contractual provisions in the field of working time, as long as the minimum requirements provided for in this Directive are complied with, implementation of this Directive shall not constitute valid grounds for reducing the general level of protection afforded to workers.

4. Member States shall communicate to the Commission the texts of the provisions of national law already adopted or being adopted in the field governed by this Directive.

5. Member States shall report to the Commission every five years on the practical implementation of the provisions of this Directive, indicating the viewpoints of the two sides of industry.

The Commission shall inform the European Parliament, the Council, the Economic and Social Committee and the Advisory Committee on Safety, Hygiene and Health Protection at Work thereof.

Annex 8.14.

Council Directive 97/81/EC of 15 December 1997 concerning the Framework Agreement on **part-time work** concluded by UNICE, CEEP and the ETUC - Annex : Framework agreement on part-time work
Official Journal L 014 , 20/01/1998 P. 0009 - 0014

MAIN PROVISIONS

Article 1
The purpose of this Directive is to implement the Framework Agreement on part-time work concluded on 6 June 1997 between the general cross-industry organizations (UNICE, CEEP and the ETUC) annexed hereto.

Article 2
1. Member States shall bring into force the laws, regulations and administrative provisions necessary to comply with this Directive not later than 20 January 2000, or shall ensure that, by that date at the latest, the social partners have introduced the necessary measures by agreement, the Member States being required to take any necessary measures to enable them at any time to be in a position to guarantee the results imposed by this Directive. They shall forthwith inform the Commission thereof.
Member States may have a maximum of one more year, if necessary, to take account of special difficulties or implementation by a collective agreement.
They shall inform the Commission forthwith in such circumstances.
When Member States adopt the measures referred to in the first subparagraph, they shall contain a reference to this Directive or shall be accompanied by such reference on the occasion of their official publication. The methods of making such a reference shall be laid down by the Member States.
2. Member States shall communicate to the Commission the text of the main provisions of domestic law which they have adopted or which they adopt in the field governed by this Directive.

ANNEX

UNION OF INDUSTRIAL AND EMPLOYERS' CONFEDERATIONS OF EUROPE EUROPEAN TRADE UNION CONFEDERATION EUROPEAN CENTRE OF ENTERPRISES WITH PUBLIC PARTICIPATION

FRAMEWORK AGREEMENT ON PART-TIME WORK

THE SIGNATORY PARTIES HAVE AGREED THE FOLLOWING:

Clause 1: Purpose
The purpose of this Framework Agreement is:
(a) to provide for the removal of discrimination against part-time workers and to improve the quality of part-time work;
(b) to facilitate the development of part-time work on a voluntary basis and to contribute to the flexible organization of working time in a manner which takes into account the needs of employers and workers.

Clause 2: Scope
1. This Agreement applies to part-time workers who have an employment contract or employment relationship as defined by the law, collective agreement or practice in force in each Member State.
2. Member States, after consultation with the social partners in accordance with national law, collective agreements or practice, and/or the social partners at the appropriate level in conformity with national industrial relations practice may, for objective reasons, exclude wholly or partly from the terms of this Agreement part-time workers who work on a casual basis. Such exclusions should be reviewed periodically to establish if the objective reasons for making them remain valid.

Clause 3: Definitions
For the purpose of this agreement:
1. The term 'part-time worker` refers to an employee whose normal hours of work, calculated on a weekly basis or on average over a period of employment of up to one year, are less than the normal hours of work of a comparable full-time worker.
2. The term 'comparable full-time worker` means a full-time worker in the same establishment having the same

type of employment contract or relationship, who is engaged in the same or a similar work/occupation, due regard being given to other considerations which may include seniority and qualification/skills.
Where there is no comparable full-time worker in the same establishment, the comparison shall be made by reference to the applicable collective agreement or, where there is no applicable collective agreement, in accordance with national law, collective agreements or practice.

Clause 4: Principle of non-discrimination
1. In respect of employment conditions, part-time workers shall not be treated in a less favourable manner than comparable full-time workers solely because they work part time unless different treatment is justified on objective grounds.
2. Where appropriate, the principle of pro rata temporis shall apply.
3. The arrangements for the application of this clause shall be defined by the Member States and/or social partners, having regard to European legislation, national law, collective agreements and practice.
4. Where justified by objective reasons, Member States after consultation of the social partners in accordance with national law, collective agreements or practice and/or social partners may, where appropriate, make access to particular conditions of employment subject to a period of service, time worked or earnings qualification. Qualifications relating to access by part-time workers to particular conditions of employment should be reviewed periodically having regard to the principle of non-discrimination as expressed in Clause 4.1.

Clause 5: Opportunities for part-time work
1. In the context of Clause 1 of this Agreement and of the principle of non-discrimination between part-time and full-time workers:
(a) Member States, following consultations with the social partners in accordance with national law or practice, should identify and review obstacles of a legal or administrative nature which may limit the opportunities for part-time work and, where appropriate, eliminate them;
(b) the social partners, acting within their sphere of competence and through the procedures set out in collective agreements, should identify and review obstacles which may limit opportunities for part-time work and, where appropriate, eliminate them.
2. A worker's refusal to transfer from full-time to part-time work or vice-versa should not in itself constitute a valid reason for termination of employment, without prejudice to termination in accordance with national law, collective agreements and practice, for other reasons such as may arise from the operational requirements of the establishment concerned.
3. As far as possible, employers should give consideration to:
(a) requests by workers to transfer from full-time to part-time work that becomes available in the establishment;
(b) requests by workers to transfer from part-time to full-time work or to increase their working time should the opportunity arise;
(c) the provision of timely information on the availability of part-time and full-time positions in the establishment in order to facilitate transfers from full-time to part-time or vice versa;
(d) measures to facilitate access to part-time work at all levels of the enterprise, including skilled and managerial positions, and where appropriate, to facilitate access by part-time workers to vocational training to enhance career opportunities and occupational mobility;
(e) the provision of appropriate information to existing bodies representing workers about part-time working in the enterprise.

Clause 6: Provisions on implementation
1. Member States and/or social partners may maintain or introduce more favourable provisions than set out in this agreement.
2. Implementation of the provisions of this Agreement shall not constitute valid grounds for reducing the general level of protection afforded to workers in the field of this agreement. This does not prejudice the right of Member States and/or social partners to develop different legislative, regulatory or contractual provisions, in the light of changing circumstances, and does not prejudice the application of Clause 5.1 as long as the principle of non-discrimination as expressed in Clause 4.1 is complied with.
3. This Agreement does not prejudice the right of the social partners to conclude, at the appropriate level, including European level, agreements adapting and/or complementing the provisions of this Agreement in a manner which will take account of the specific needs of the social partners concerned.
4. This Agreement shall be without prejudice to any more specific Community provisions, and in particular Community provisions concerning equal treatment or opportunities for men and women.
5. The prevention and settlement of disputes and grievances arising from the application of this Agreement shall be dealt with in accordance with national law, collective agreements and practice.
6. The signatory parties shall review this Agreement, five years after the date of the Council decision, if requested by one of the parties to this Agreement.

(1) Within the meaning of Article 2(4) of the Agreement on social policy of the Treaty establishing the European Community.

Annex 8.15.

Council Directive 75/117/EEC of 10 February 1975 on the approximation of the laws of the Member States relating to the application of **the principle of equal pay for men and women**
Official Journal L 045 , 19/02/1975 P. 0019 - 0020.

MAIN PROVISIONS

Article 1
The principle of equal pay for men and women outlined in Article 119 of the Treaty, hereinafter called "principle of equal pay", means, for the same work or for work to which equal value is attributed, the elimination of all discrimination on grounds of sex with regard to all aspects and conditions of remuneration.
In particular, where a job classification system is used for determining pay, it must be based on the same criteria for both men and women and so drawn up as to exclude any discrimination on grounds of sex.

Article 2
Member States shall introduce into their national legal systems such measures as are necessary to enable all employees who consider themselves wronged by failure to apply the principle of equal pay to pursue their claims by judicial process after possible recourse to other competent authorities.

Article 3
Member States shall abolish all discrimination between men and women arising from laws, regulations or administrative provisions which is contrary to the principle of equal pay.

Article 4
Member States shall take the necessary measures to ensure that provisions appearing in collective agreements, wage scales, wage agreements or individual contracts of employment which are contrary to the principle of equal pay shall be, or may be declared, null and void or may be amended.

Article 5
Member States shall take the necessary measures to protect employees against dismissal by the employer as a reaction to a complaint within the undertaking or to any legal proceedings aimed at enforcing compliance with the principle of equal pay.

Article 6
Member States shall, in accordance with their national circumstances and legal systems, take the measures necessary to ensure that the priciple of equal pay is applied. They shall see that effective means are available to take care that this principle is observed.

Article 7
Member States shall take care that the provisions adopted pursuant to this Directive, together with the relevant provisions already in force, are brought to the attention of employees by all appropriate means, for example at their place of employment.

Article 8
1. Member States shall put into force the laws, regulations and administrative provisions necessary in order to comply with this Directive within one year of its notification and shall immediately inform the Commission thereof.
2. Member States shall communicate to the Commission the texts of the laws, regulations and administrative provisions which they adopt in the field covered by this Directive.

Article 9
Within two years of the expiry of the one-year period referred to in Article 8, Member States shall forward all necessary information to the Commission to enable it to draw up a report on the application of this Directive for submission to the Council.

Annex 8.16.

Council Directive 76/207/EEC of 9 February 1976 on the implementation of the principle of **equal treatment for men and women as regards access to employment, vocational training and promotion, and working conditions**
Official Journal L 039 , 14/02/1976 P. 0040 - 0042.

MAIN PROVISIONS

Article 1
1. The purpose of this Directive is to put into effect in the Member States the principle of equal treatment for men and women as regards access to employment, including promotion, and to vocational training and as regards working conditions and, on the conditions referred to in paragraph 2, social security. This principle is herinafter referred to as "the principle of equal treatment."
2. With a view to ensuring the progressive implementation of the principle of equal treatment in matters of social security, the Council, acting on a proposal from the Commission, will adopt provisions defining its substance, its scope and the arrangements for its application.

Article 2
1. For the purposes of the following provisions, the principle of equal treatment shall mean that there shall be no discrimination whatsover on grounds of sex either directly or indirectly by reference in particular to marital or family status.
2. This Directive shall be without prejudice to the right of Member States to exclude from its field of application those occupational activities and, where appropriate, the training leading thereto, for which, by reason of their nature or the context in which they are carried out, the sex of the worker constitutes a determining factor.
3. This Directive shall be without prejudice to provisions concerning the protection of women, particularly as regards pregnancy and maternity.
4. This Directive shall be without prejudice to measures to promote equal opportunity for men and women, in particular by removing existing inequalities which affect women's opportunities in the areas referred to in Article 1 (1). (1)OJ No C 111, 20.5.1975, p. 14. (2)OJ No C 286, 15.12.1975, p. 8. (3)OJ No C 13, 12.2.1974, p. 1. (4)OJ No L 45, 19.2.1975, p. 19.

Article 3
1. Application of the principle of equal treatment means that there shall be no discrimination whatsover on grounds of sex in the conditions, including selection criteria, for access to all jobs or posts, whatever the sector or branch of activity, and to all levels of the occupational hierarchy.
2. To this end, Member States shall take the measures necessary to ensure that:
(a) any laws, regulations and administrative provisions contrary to the principle of equal treatment shall be abolished;
(b) any provisions contrary to the principle of equal treatment which are included in collective agreements, individual contracts of employment, internal rules of undertakings or in rules governing the independent occupations and professions shall be, or may be declared, null and void or may be amended;
(c) those laws, regulations and administrative provisions contrary to the principle of equal treatment when the concern for protection which originally inspired them is no longer well founded shall be revised ; and that where similar provisions are included in collective agreements labour and management shall be requested to undertake the desired revision.

Article 4
Application of the principle of equal treatment with regard to access to all types and to all levels, of vocational guidance, vocational training, advanced vocational training and retraining, means that Member States shall take all necessary measures to ensure that:
(a) any laws, regulations and administrative provisions contrary to the principle of equal treatment shall be abolished;
(b) any provisions contrary to the principle of equal treatment which are included in collective agreements, individual contracts of employment, internal rules of undertakings or in rules governing the independent occupations and professions shall be, or may be declared, null and void or may be amended;
(c) without prejudice to the freedom granted in certain Member States to certain private training establishments, vocational guidance, vocational training, advanced vocational training and retraining shall be accessible on the

basis of the same criteria and at the same levels without any discrimination on grounds of sex.

Article 5
1. Application of the principle of equal treatment with regard to working conditions, including the conditions governing dismissal, means that men and women shall be guaranteed the same conditions without discrimination on grounds of sex.
2. To this end, Member States shall take the measures necessary to ensure that: (a) any laws, regulations and administrative provisions contrary to the principle of equal treatment shall be abolished;
(b) any provisions contrary to the principle of equal treatment which are included in collective agreements, individual contracts of employment, internal rules of undertakings or in rules governing the independent occupations and professions shall be, or may be declared, null and void or may be amended;
(c) those laws, regulations and administrative provisions contrary to the principle of equal treatment when the concern for protection which originally inspired them is no longer well founded shall be revised ; and that where similar provisions are included in collective agreements labour and management shall be requested to undertake the desired revision.

Article 6
Member States shall introduce into their national legal systems such measures as are necessary to enable all persons who consider themselves wronged by failure to apply to them the principle of equal treatment within the meaning of Articles 3, 4 and 5 to pursue their claims by judicial process after possible recourse to other competent authorities.

Article 7
Member States shall take the necessary measures to protect employees against dismissal by the employer as a reaction to a complaint within the undertaking or to any legal proceedings aimed at enforcing compliance with the principle of equal treatment.

Article 8
Member States shall take care that the provisions adopted pursuant to this Directive, together with the relevant provisions already in force, are brought to the attention of employees by all appropriate means, for example at their place of employment.

Article 9
1. Member States shall put into force the laws, regulations and administrative provisions necessary in order to comply with this Directive within 30 months of its notification and shall immediately inform the Commission thereof.
However, as regards the first part of Article 3 (2) (c) and the first part of Article 5 (2) (c), Member States shall carry out a first examination and if necessary a first revision of the laws, regulations and administrative provisions referred to therein within four years of notification of this Directive.
2. Member States shall periodically assess the occupational activities referred to in Article 2 (2) in order to decide, in the light of social developments, whether there is justification for maintaining the exclusions concerned. They shall notify the Commission of the results of this assessment.
3. Member States shall also communicate to the Commission the texts of laws, regulations and administrative provisions which they adopt in the field covered by this Directive.

Annex 8.17.

Council Directive 79/7/EEC of 19 December 1978 on the progressive **implementation of the principle of equal treatment for men and women in matters of social security**
Official Journal L 006 , 10/01/1979 P. 0024 - 0025.

MAIN PROVISIONS

Article 1
The purpose of this Directive is the progressive implementation, in the field of social security and other elements of social protection provided for in Article 3, of the principle of equal treatment for men and women in matters of social security, hereinafter referred to as "the principle of equal treatment".

Article 2
This Directive shall apply to the working population - including self-employed persons, workers and self-employed persons whose activity is interrupted by illness, accident or involuntary unemployment and persons seeking employment - and to retired or invalided workers and self-employed persons.

Article 3
1. This Directive shall apply to:
(a) statutory schemes which provide protection against the following risks:
- sickness,
- invalidity,
- old age,
- accidents at work and occupational diseases,
- unemployment;
(b) social assistance, in so far as it is intended to supplement or replace the schemes referred to in (a).
2. This Directive shall not apply to the provisions concerning survivors' benefits nor to those concerning family benefits, except in the case of family benefits granted by way of increases of benefits due in respect of the risks referred to in paragraph 1 (a).
3. With a view to ensuring implementation of the principle of equal treatment in occupational schemes, the Council, acting on a proposal from the Commission, will adopt provisions defining its substance, its scope and the arrangements for its application. (1)OJ No C 34, 11.2.1977, p. 3. (2)OJ No C 299, 12.12.1977, p. 13. (3)OJ No C 180, 28.7.1977, p. 36. (4)OJ No L 39, 14.2.1976, p. 40.

Article 4
1. The principle of equal treatment means that there shall be no discrimination whatsoever on ground of sex either directly, or indirectly by reference in particular to marital or family status, in particular as concerns: - the scope of the schemes and the conditions of access thereto,
- the obligation to contribute and the calculation of contributions,
- the calculation of benefits including increases due in respect of a spouse and for dependants and the conditions governing the duration and retention of entitlement to benefits.
2. The principle of equal treatment shall be without prejudice to the provisions relating to the protection of women on the grounds of maternity.

Article 5
Member States shall take the measures necessary to ensure that any laws, regulations and administrative provisions contrary to the principle of equal treatment are abolished.

Article 6
Member States shall introduce into their national legal systems such measures as art necessary to enable all persons who consider themselves wronged by failure to apply the principle of equal treatment to pursue their claims by judicial process, possibly after recourse to other competent authorities.

Article 7
1. This Directive shall be without prejudice to the right of Member States to exclude from its scope: (a) the determination of personable age for the purposes of granting old-age and retirement pensions and the possible consequences thereof for other benefits;

(b) advantages in respect of old-age pension schemes granted to persons who have brought up children ; the acquisition of benefit entitlements following periods of interruption of employment due to the bringing up of children;
(c) the granting of old-age or invalidity benefit entitlements by virtue of the derived entitlements of a wife;
(d) the granting of increases of long-term invalidity, old-age, accidents at work and occupational disease benefits for a dependent wife;
(e) the consequences of the exercise, before the adoption of this Directive, of a right of option not to acquire rights or incur obligations under a statutory scheme.

2. Member States shall periodically examine matters excluded under paragraph 1 in order to ascertain, in the light of social developments in the matter concerned, whether there is justification for maintaining the exclusions concerned.

Article 8
1. Member States shall bring into force the laws, regulations and administrative provisions necessary to comply with this Directive within six years of its notification. They shall immediately inform the Commission thereof.
2. Member States shall communicate to the Commission the text of laws, regulations and administrative provisions which they adopt in the field covered by this Directive, including measures adopted pursuant to Article 7 (2).
They shall inform the Commission of their reasons for maintaining any existing provisions on the matters referred to in Article 7 (1) and of the possibilities for reviewing them at a later date.

Annex 8.18.

Council Directive 96/97/EC of 20 December 1996 amending Directive 86/378/EEC on the **implementation of the principle of equal treatment for men and women in occupational social security schemes**
Official Journal L 046 , 17/02/1997 P. 0020 - 0024

MAIN PROVISIONS

Article 1
Directive 86/378/EEG shall be amended as follows:
1. Article 2 shall be replaced by the following:
Article 2
1. "Occupational social security schemes" means schemes not governed by Directive 79/7/EEC whose purpose is to provide workers, whether employees or self-employed, in an undertaking or group of undertakings, area of economic activity, occupational sector or group of sectors with benefits intended to supplement the benefits provided by statutory social security schemes or to replace them, whether membership of such schemes is compulsory or optional.
2. This Directive does not apply to:
(a) individual contracts for self-employed workers;
(b) schemes for self-employed workers having only one member;
(c) insurance contracts to which the employer is not a party, in the case of salaried workers;
(d) optional provisions of occupational schemes offered to participants individually to guarantee them:
- either additional benefits, or
- a choice of date on which the normal benefits for self-employed workers will start, or a choice between several benefits;
(e) occupational schemes in so far as benefits are financed by contributions paid by workers on a voluntary basis.
3. This Directive does not preclude an employer granting to persons who have already reached the retirement age for the purposes of granting a pension by virtue of an occupational scheme, but who have not yet reached the retirement age for the purposes of granting a statutory retirement pension, a pension supplement, the aim of which is to make equal or more nearly equal the overall amount of benefit paid to these persons in relation to the amount paid to persons of the other sex in the same situation who have already reached the statutory retirement age, until the persons benefiting from the supplement reach the statutory retirement age.

2. Article 3 shall be replaced by the following:
Article 3
This Directive shall apply to members of the working population, including self-employed persons, persons whose activity is interrupted by illness, maternity, accident or involuntary unemployment and persons seeking employment, to retired and disabled workers and to those claiming under them, in accordance with national law and/or practice.`

3. Article 6 shall be replaced by the following:
Article 6
1. Provisions contrary to the principle of equal treatment shall include those based on sex, either directly or indirectly, in particular by reference to marital or family status, for:
(a) determining the persons who may participate in an occupational scheme;
(b) fixing the compulsory or optional nature of participation in an occupational scheme;
(c) laying down different rules as regards the age of entry into the scheme or the minimum period of employment or membership of the scheme required to obtain the benefits thereof;
(d) laying down different rules, except as provided for in points (h) and (i), for the reimbursement of contributions when a worker leaves a scheme without having fulfilled the conditions guaranteeing a deferred right to long-term benefits;
(e) setting different conditions for the granting of benefits or restricting such benefits to workers of one or other of the sexes;
(f) fixing different retirement ages;
(g) suspending the retention or acquisition of rights during periods of maternity leave or leave for family reasons which are granted by law or agreement and are paid by the employer;
(h) setting different levels of benefit, except in so far as may be necessary to take account of actuarial

calculation factors which differ according to sex in the case of defined-contribution schemes.
In the case of funded defined-benefit schemes, certain elements (examples of which are annexed) may be unequal where the inequality of the amounts results from the effects of the use of actuarial factors differing according to sex at the time when the scheme's funding is implemented;
(i) setting different levels for workers' contributions;
setting different levels for employers' contributions, except:
- in the case of defined-contribution schemes if the aim is to equalize the amount of the final benefits or to make them more nearly equal for both sexes,
- in the case of funded defined-benefit schemes where the employer's contributions are intended to ensure the adequacy of the funds necessary to cover the cost of the benefits defined,
(j) laying down different standards or standards applicable only to workers of a specified sex, except as provided for in points (h) and (i), as regards the guarantee or retention of entitlement to deferred benefits when a worker leaves a scheme.
2. Where the granting of benefits within the scope of this Directive is left to the discretion of the scheme's management bodies, the latter must comply with the principle of equal treatment.`

4. Article 8 shall be replaced by the following:
Article 8
1. Member States shall take the necessary steps to ensure that the provisions of occupational schemes for self-employed workers contrary to the principle of equal treatment are revised with effect from 1 January 1993 at the latest.
2. This Directive shall not preclude rights and obligations relating to a period of membership of an occupational scheme for self-employed workers prior to revision of that scheme from remaining subject to the provisions of the scheme in force during that period.`

5. Article 9 shall be replaced by the following:
Article 9
As regards schemes for self-employed workers, Member States may defer compulsory application of the principle of equal treatment with regard to:
(a) determination of pensionable age for the granting of old-age or retirement pensions, and the possible implications for other benefits:
- either until the date on which such equality is achieved in statutory schemes,
- or, at the latest, until such equality is prescribed by a directive;
(b) survivors' pensions until Community law establishes the principle of equal treatment in statutory social security schemes in that regard;
(c) the application of the first subparagraph of point (i) of Article 6 (1) to take account of the different actuarial calculation factors, at the latest until 1 January 1999.
`

6. The following Article shall be inserted:
Article 9a
Where men and women may claim a flexible pensionable age under the same conditions, this shall not be deemed to be incompatible with this Directive.
`

7. The following Annex shall be added:
ANNEX
Examples of elements which may be unequal, in respect of funded defined-benefit schemes, as referred to in Article 6 (h):
- conversion into a capital sum of part of a periodic pension,
- transfer of pension rights,
- a reversionary pension payable to a dependant in return for the surrender of part of a pension,
- a reduced pension where the worker opts to take early retirement.`

Article 2
1. Any measure implementing this Directive, as regards paid workers, must cover all benefits derived from periods of employment subsequent to 17 May 1990 and shall apply retroactively to that date, without prejudice to workers or those claiming under them who have, before that date, initiated legal proceedings or raised an equivalent claim under national law. In that event, the implementation measures must apply retroactively to 8 April 1976 and must cover all the benefits derived from periods of employment after that date. For Member States which acceded to the Community after 8 April 1976, that date shall be replaced by the date on which Article 119 of the Treaty became applicable on their territory.

2. The second sentence of paragraph 1 shall not prevent national rules relating to time limits for bringing actions under national law from being relied on against workers or those claiming under them who initiated legal proceedings or raise an equivalent claim under national law before 17 May 1990, provided that they are not less favourable for that type of action than for similar actions of a domestic nature and that they do not render the exercise of Community law impossible in practice.
3. For Member States whose accession took place after 17 May 1990 and who were on 1 January 1994 Contracting Parties to the Agreement on the European Economic Area, the date of 17 May 1990 in paragraph 1 and 2 of this Directive is replaced by 1 January 1994.

Article 3
1. Member States shall bring into force the laws, regulations and administrative provisions necessary to comply with this Directive by 1 July 1997. They shall forthwith inform the Commission thereof.
When Member States adopt these provisions, they shall contain a reference to this Directive or be accompanied by such reference on the occasion of their official publication. The methods of making such a reference shall be laid down by the Member States.
2. Member States shall communicate to the Commission, at the latest two years after the entry into force of this Directive, all information necessary to enable the Commission to draw up a report on the application of this Directive.

Annex 8.19.

Council Directive 92/85/EEC of 19 October 1992 on the introduction of measures to encourage improvements in the **safety and health at work of pregnant workers and workers who have recently given birth or are breastfeeding** (tenth individual Directive within the meaning of Article 16 (1) of Directive 89/391/EEC)
Official Journal L 348 , 28/11/1992 P. 0001 - 0008

MAIN PROVISIONS

SECTION I
PURPOSE AND DEFINITIONS

Article 1
Purpose
1. The purpose of this Directive, which is the tenth individual Directive within the meaning of Article 16 (1) of Directive 89/391/EEC, is to implement measures to encourage improvements in the safety and health at work of pregnant workers and workers who have recently given birth or who are breastfeeding.
2. The provisions of Directive 89/391/EEC, except for Article 2 (2) thereof, shall apply in full to the whole area covered by paragraph 1, without prejudice to any more stringent and/or specific provisions contained in this Directive.
3. This Directive may not have the effect of reducing the level of protection afforded to pregnant workers, workers who have recently given birth or who are breastfeeding as compared with the situation which exists in each Member State on the date on which this Directive is adopted.

Article 2
Definitions
For the purposes of this Directive:
(a) pregnant worker shall mean a pregnant worker who informs her employer of her condition, in accordance with national legislation and/or national practice;
(b) worker who has recently given birth shall mean a worker who has recently given birth within the meaning of national legislation and/or national practice and who informs her employer of her condition, in accordance with that legislation and/or practice;
(c) worker who is breastfeeding shall mean a worker who is breastfeeding within the meaning of national legislation and/or national practice and who informs her employer of her condition, in accordance with that legislation and/or practice.

SECTION II
GENERAL PROVISIONS

Article 3
Guidelines
1. In consultation with the Member States and assisted by the Advisory Committee on Safety, Hygiene and Health Protection at Work, the Commission shall draw up guidelines on the assessment of the chemical, physical and biological agents and industrial processes considered hazardous for the safety or health of workers within the meaning of Article 2.
The guidelines referred to in the first subparagraph shall also cover movements and postures, mental and physical fatigue and other types of physical and mental stress connected with the work done by workers within the meaning of Article 2.
2. The purpose of the guidelines referred to in paragraph 1 is to serve as a basis for the assessment referred to in Article 4 (1).
To this end, Member States shall bring these guidelines to the attention of all employers and all female workers and/or their representatives in the respective Member State.

Article 4
Assessment and information
1. For all activities liable to involve a specific risk of exposure to the agents, processes or working conditions of which a non-exhaustive list is given in Annex I, the employer shall assess the nature, degree and duration of exposure, in the undertaking and/or establishment concerned, of workers within the meaning of Article 2, either

directly or by way of the protective and preventive services referred to in Article 7 of Directive 89/391/EEC, in order to:
- assess any risks to the safety or health and any possible effect on the pregnancys or breastfeeding of workers within the meaning of Article 2,
- decide what measures should be taken.
2. Without prejudice to Article 10 of Directive 89/391/EEC, workers within the meaning of Article 2 and workers likely to be in one of the situations referred to in Article 2 in the undertaking and/or establishment concerned and/or their representatives shall be informed of the results of the assessment referred to in paragraph 1 and of all measures to be taken concerning health and safety at work.

Article 5
Action further to the results of the assessment
1. Without prejudice to Article 6 of Directive 89/391/EEC, if the results of the assessment referred to in Article 4 (1) reveal a risk to the safety or health or an effect on the pregnancy or breastfeeding of a worker within the meaning of Article 2, the employer shall take the necessary measures to ensure that, by temporarily adjusting the working conditions and/or the working hours of the worker concerned, the exposure of that worker to such risks is avoided.
2. If the adjustment of her working conditions and/or working hours is not technically and/or objectively feasible, or cannot reasonably be required on duly substantiated grounds, the employer shall take the necessary measures to move the worker concerned to another job.
3. If moving her to another job is not technically and/or objectively feasible or cannot reasonably be required on duly substantiated grounds, the worker concerned shall be granted leave in accordance with national legislation and/or national practice for the whole of the period necessary to protect her safety or health.
4. The provisions of this Article shall apply mutatis mutandis to the case where a worker pursuing an activity which is forbidden pursuant to Article 6 becomes pregnant or starts breastfeeding and informs her employer thereof.

Article 6
Cases in which exposure is prohibited
In addition to the general provisions concerning the protection of workers, in particular those relating to the limit values for occupational exposure:
1. pregnant workers within the meaning of Article 2 (a) may under no circumstances be obliged to perform duties for which the assessment has revealed a risk of exposure, which would jeopardize safety or health, to the agents and working conditions listed in Annex II, Section A;
2. workers who are breastfeeding, within the meaning of Article 2 (c), may under no circumstances be obliged to perform duties for which the assessment has revealed a risk of exposure, which would jeopardize safety or health, to the agents and working conditions listed in Annex II, Section B.

Article 7
Night work
1. Member States shall take the necessary measures to ensure that workers referred to in Article 2 are not obliged to perform night work during their pregnancy and for a period following childbirth which shall be determined by the national authority competent for safety and health, subject to submission, in accordance with the procedures laid down by the Member States, of a medical certificate stating that this is necessary for the safety or health of the worker concerned.
2. The measures referred to in paragraph 1 must entail the possibility, in accordance with national legislation and/or national practice, of:
(a) transfer to daytime work; or
(b) leave from work or extension of maternity leave where such a transfer is not technically and/or objectively feasible or cannot reasonably by required on duly substantiated grounds.

Article 8
Maternity leave
1. Member States shall take the necessary measures to ensure that workers within the meaning of Article 2 are entitled to a continuous period of maternity leave of a least 14 weeks allocated before and/or after confinement in accordance with national legislation and/or practice.
2. The maternity leave stipulated in paragraph 1 must include compulsory maternity leave of at least two weeks allocated before and/or after confinement in accordance with national legislation and/or practice.

Article 9
Time off for ante-natal examinations
Member States shall take the necessary measures to ensure that pregnant workers within the meaning of Article 2 (a) are entitled to, in accordance with national legislation and/or practice, time off, without loss of pay, in order to attend ante-natal examinations, if such examinations have to take place during working hours.

Article 10
Prohibition of dismissal
In order to guarantee workers, within the meaning of Article 2, the exercise of their health and safety protection rights as recognized under this Article, it shall be provided that:
1. Member States shall take the necessary measures to prohibit the dismissal of workers, within the meaning of Article 2, during the period from the beginning of their pregnancy to the end of the maternity leave referred to in Article 8 (1), save in exceptional cases not connected with their condition which are permitted under national legislation and/or practice and, where applicable, provided that the competent authority has given its consent;
2. if a worker, within the meaning of Article 2, is dismissed during the period referred to in point 1, the employer must cite duly substantiated grounds for her dismissal in writing;
3. Member States shall take the necessary measures to protect workers, within the meaning of Article 2, from consequences of dismissal which is unlawful by virtue of point 1.

Article 11
Employment rights
In order to guarantee workers within the meaning of Article 2 the exercise of their health and safety protection rights as recognized in this Article, it shall be provided that:
1. in the cases referred to in Articles 5, 6 and 7, the employment rights relating to the employment contract, including the maintenance of a payment to, and/or entitlement to an adequate allowance for, workers within the meaning of Article 2, must be ensured in accordance with national legislation and/or national practice;
2. in the case referred to in Article 8, the following must be ensured:
(a) the rights connected with the employment contract of workers within the meaning of Article 2, other than those referred to in point (b) below;
(b) maintenance of a payment to, and/or entitlement to an adequate allowance for, workers within the meaning of Article 2;
3. the allowance referred to in point 2 (b) shall be deemed adequate if it guarantees income at least equivalent to that which the worker concerned would receive in the event of a break in her activities on grounds connected with her state of health, subject to any ceiling laid down under national legislation;
4. Member States may make entitlement to pay or the allowance referred to in points 1 and 2 (b) conditional upon the worker concerned fulfilling the conditions of eligibilty for such benefits laid down under national legislation.
These conditions may under no circumstances provide for periods of previous employment in excess of 12 months immediately prior to the presumed date of confinement.

Article 12
Defence of rights
Member States shall introduce into their national legal systems such measures as are necessary to enable all workers who should themselves wronged by failure to comply with the obligations arising from this Directive to pursue their claims by judicial process (and/or, in accordance with national laws and/or practices) by recourse to other competent authorities.

Article 13
Amendments to the Annexes
1. Strictly technical adjustments to Annex I as a result of technical progress, changes in international regulations or specifications and new findings in the area covered by this Directive shall be adopted in accordance with the procedure laid down in Article 17 of Directive 89/391/EEC.
2. Annex II may be amended only in accordance with the procedure laid down in Article 118a of the Treaty.

Article 14
Final provisions
1. Member States shall bring into force the laws, regulations and administrative provisions necessary to comply with this Directive not later than two years after the adoption thereof or ensure, at the latest two years after adoption of this Directive, that the two sides of industry introduce the requisite privisions by means of collective agreements, with Member States being required to make all the necessary provisions to enable them at all times

to guarantee the results laid down by this Directive. They shall forthwith inform the Commission thereof.
2. When Member States adopt the measures referred to in paragraph 1, they shall contain a reference of this Directive or shall be accompanied by such reference on the occasion of their official publication. The methods of making such a reference shall be laid down by the Member States.
3. Member States shall communicate to the Commission the texts of the essential provisions of national law which they have already adopted or adopt in the field governed by this Directive.
4. Member States shall report to the Commission every five years on the practical implementation of the provisions of this Directive, indicating the points of view of the two sides of industry.
However, Member States shall report for the first time to the Commission on the practical implementation of the provisions of this Directive, indicating the points of view of the two sides of industry, four years after its adoption.
The Commission shall inform the European Parliament, the Council, the Economic and Social Committee and the Advisory Committee on Safety, Hygiene and Health Protection at Work.
5. The Commission shall periodically submit to the European Parliament, the Council and the Economic and Social Committee a report on the implementation of this Directive, taking into account paragraphs 1, 2 and 3.
6. The Council will re-examine this Directive, on the basis of an assessment carried out on the basis of the reports referred to in the second subparagraph of paragraph 4 and, should the need arise, of a proposal, to be submitted by the Commission at the latest five years after adoption of the Directive.

Article 15
This Directive is addressed to the Member States.

Done at Luxembourg, 19 October 1992.
For the Council
The President
D. CURRY

(1) OJ N° C 281, 9. 11. 190, p. 3; and OJ N° C 25, 1. 2. 1991, p. 9.
(2) OJ N° C 19, 28. 1. 1991, p. 177; and OJ N° C 150, 15. 6. 1992, p. 99.
(3) OJ N° C 41, 18. 2. 1991, p. 29.
(4) OJ N° L 185, 9. 7 .1974, p. 15.
(5) OJ N° L 183, 29. 6. 1989, p. 1.

ANNEX I

NON-EXHAUSTIVE LIST OF AGENTS, PROCESSES AND WORKING CONDITIONS
referred to in Article 4 (1)

A. Agents
1. Physical agents where these are regarded as agents causing foetal lesions and/or likely to disrupt placental attachment, and in particular:
(a) shocks, vibration or movement;
(b) handling of loads entailing risks, particularly of a dorsolumbar nature;
(c) noise;
(d) ionizing radiation (*);
(e) non-ionizing radiation;
(f) extremes of cold or heat;
(g) movements and postures, travelling - either inside or outside the establishment - mental and physical fatigue and other physical burdens connected with the activity of the worker within the meaning of Article 2 of the Directive.

2. Biological agents
Biological agents of risk groups 2, 3 and 3 within the meaning of Article 2 (d) numbers 2, 3 and 4 of Directive 90/679/EEC (H), in so far as it is known that these agents or the therapeutic measures necessitated by such agents endanger the health of pregnant women and the unborn child and in so far as they do not yet appear in Annex II.

3. Chemical agents
The following chemical agents in so far as it is known that they endanger the health of pregnant women and the unborn child and in so far as they do not yet appear in Annex II:

(a) substances labelled R 40, R 45, R 46, and R 47 under Directive 67/548/EEC (²) in so far as they do not yet appear in Annex II;
(b) chemical agents in Annex I to Directive 90/394/EEC (³);
(c) mercury and mercury derivatives;
(d) antimitotic drugs;
(e) carbon monoxide;
(f) chemical agents of known and dangerous percutaneous absorption

B. Processes
Industrial processes listed in Annex I to Directive 90/394/EEC.

C. Working conditions
Underground mining work.
(*) See Directive 80/836/Euratom (OJ N° L 246, 17. 9. 1980, p. 1).
(H) OJ N° L 374, 31. 12. 1990, p. 1.
(²) OJ N° L 196, 16. 8. 1967, p. 1. Directive as last amended by Directive 90/517/EEC (OJ N° L 287, 19. 10. 1990, p. 37).
(³) OJ N° L 196, 26. 7. 1990, p. 1.

ANNEX II

NON-EXHAUSTIVE LIST OF AGENTS AND WORKING CONDITIONS
referred to in Article 6

A. Pregnant workers within the meaning of Article 2 (a)
1. Agents
(a) Physical agents
Work in hyperbaric atmosphere, e.g. pressurized enclosures and underwater diving.
(b) Biological agents
The following biological agents:
- toxoplasma,
- rubella virus,
unless the pregnant workers are proved to be adequately protected against such agents by immunization.
(c) Chemical agents
Lead and lead derivatives in so far as these agents are capable of being absorbed by the human organism.
2. Working conditions
Underground mining work.

B. Workers who are breastfeeding within the meaning of Article 2 (c)
1. Agents
(a) Chemical agents
Lead and lead derivatives in so far as these agents are capable of being absorbed by the human organism.
2. Working conditions
Underground mining work.

Statement of the Council and the Commission concerning Article 11 (3) of Directive 92/ 85/EEC, entered in the minutes of the 1608th meeting of the Council (Luxembourg, 19 October 1992)

THE COUNCIL AND THE COMMISSION stated that:
'In determining the level of the allowances referred to in Article 11 (2) (b) and (3), reference shall be made, for purely technical reasons, to the allowance which a worker would receive in the event of a break in her activities on grounds connected with her state of health. Such a reference is not intended in any way to imply that pregnancy and childbirth be equated with sickness. The national social security legislation of all Member States provides for an allowance to be paid during an absence from work due to sickness. The link with such allowance in the chosen formulation is simply intended to serve as a concrete, fixed reference amount in all Member States for the determination of the minimum amount of maternity allowance payable. In so far as allowances are paid in individual Member States which exceed those provided for in the Directive, such allowances are, of course, retained. This is clear from Article 1 (3) of the Directive.

Annex 8.20.

Council Directive 97/80/EC of 15 December 1997 on the **burden of proof in cases of discrimination based on sex**
Official Journal L 014 , 20/01/1998 P. 0006 - 0008.

MAIN PROVISIONS

Article 1
Aim
The aim of this Directive shall be to ensure that the measures taken by the Member States to implement the principle of equal treatment are made more effective, in order to enable all persons who consider themselves wronged because the principle of equal treatment has not been applied to them to have their rights asserted by judicial process after possible recourse to other competent bodies.

Article 2
Definitions
1. For the purposes of this Directive, the principle of equal treatment shall mean that there shall be no discrimination whatsoever based on sex, either directly or indirectly.
2. For purposes of the principle of equal treatment referred to in paragraph 1, indirect discrimination shall exist where an apparently neutral provision, criterion or practice disadvantages a substantially higher proportion of the members of one sex unless that provision, criterion or practice is appropriate and necessary and can be justified by objective factors unrelated to sex.

Article 3
Scope
1. This Directive shall apply to:
(a) the situations covered by Article 119 of the Treaty and by Directives 75/117/EEC, 76/207/EEC and, insofar as discrimination based on sex is concerned, 92/85/EEC and 96/34/EC;
(b) any civil or administrative procedure concerning the public or private sector which provides for means of redress under national law pursuant to the measures referred to in (a) with the exception of out-of-court procedures of a voluntary nature or provided for in national law.
2. This Directive shall not apply to criminal procedures, unless otherwise provided by the Member States.

Article 4
Burden of proof
1. Member States shall take such measures as are necessary, in accordance with their national judicial systems, to ensure that, when persons who consider themselves wronged because the principle of equal treatment has not been applied to them establish, before a court or other competent authority, facts from which it may be presumed that there has been direct or indirect discrimination, it shall be for the respondent to prove that there has been no breach of the principle of equal treatment.
2. This Directive shall not prevent Member States from introducing rules of evidence which are more favourable to plaintiffs.
3. Member States need not apply paragraph 1 to proceedings in which it is for the court or competent body to investigate the facts of the case.

Article 5
Information
Member States shall ensure that measures taken pursuant to this Directive, together with the provisions already in force, are brought to the attention of all the persons concerned by all appropriate means.

Article 6
Non-regression
Implementation of this Directive shall under no circumstances be sufficient grounds for a reduction in the general level of protection of workers in the areas to which it applies, without prejudice to the Member States' right to respond to changes in the situation by introducing laws, regulations and administrative provisions which differ from those in force on the notification of this Directive, provided that the minimum requirements of this Directive are complied with.

Article 7
Implementation
The Member States shall bring into force the laws, regulations and administrative provisions necessary for them to comply with this Directive by 1 January 2001. They shall immediately inform the Commission thereof.
When the Member States adopt those measures they shall contain a reference to this Directive or shall be accompanied by such a reference on the occasion of their official publication. The methods of making such references shall be laid down by the Member States.
The Member States shall communicate to the Commission, within two years of the entry into force of this Directive, all the information necessary for the Commission to draw up a report to the European Parliament and the Council on the application of this Directive.

Annex 8.21.

Decision No 50/2002/EC of the European Parliament and of the Council of 7 December 2001 establishing a programme of Community action to encourage cooperation between Member States to **combat social exclusion**
Official Journal L 010 , 12/01/2002 P. 0001 - 0007.I

MAIN PROVISIONS

Article 1
Establishment of the programme
A programme of Community action to encourage cooperation between Member States in order to combat social exclusion, hereinafter referred to as "the programme", shall be adopted for the period 1 January 2002 to 31 December 2006.

Article 2
Principles
1. The programme shall be part of an open method of coordination between Member States to give a decisive impetus to the elimination of social exclusion and poverty by setting appropriate objectives at Community level and by the implementation of national action plans.
2. The programme and the national action plans shall contribute to a better understanding of social exclusion, the mainstreaming of the combating of exclusion in Member States' and Community policies and measures, and the development of priority actions chosen by Member States in accordance with their particular situation.
3. In designing, implementing and following up the activities under the programme, account shall be taken of the experience of Member States at all levels involved and of people exposed to social exclusion and poverty, as well as social partners, non-governmental and voluntary organisations, bodies providing social services and other actors involved in the fight against social exclusion and poverty.

Article 3
Objectives
In the context of the open method of coordination referred to in Article 2(1), the programme shall support cooperation which enables the Community and the Member States to enhance the effectiveness and efficiency of policies to combat social exclusion by:
(a) improving the understanding of social exclusion and poverty with the help in particular of comparable indicators;
(b) organising exchanges on policies which are implemented and promoting mutual learning inter alia in the context of national action plans, with the help in particular of comparable indicators;
(c) developing the capacity of actors to address social exclusion and poverty effectively, and to promote innovative approaches, in particular through networking at European level, and by promoting dialogue with all those involved including at national and regional level.

Article 4
Community actions
1. With a view to achieving the objectives set out in Article 3, the following Community actions may be implemented within a transnational framework:
(a) analysis of characteristics, causes, processes and trends in social exclusion, including the collection of statistics on the various forms of social exclusion in order to compare these data, the study of quantitative and qualitative indicators, the development of common methodologies and thematic studies;
(b) exchange of information and best practices encouraging the development of quantitative and qualitative indicators, based on these objectives as agreed by the European Parliament and the Council, assessment criteria and benchmarks and monitoring, evaluation and peer review;
(c) promotion of dialogue involving the various actors and support for relevant networking at European level between organisations active in the fight against poverty and social exclusion, in particular non-governmental organisations.
2. Arrangements for the implementation of the Community actions described in paragraph 1 are set out in the Annex.

Article 5
Implementation and cooperation with the Member States

1. The Commission shall:
(a) ensure the implementation of the Community actions covered by the programme;
(b) have a regular exchange of views with representatives of non-governmental organisations and the social partners at European level on the design and implementation of and follow-up to the programme and on related policy orientations. To this end, the Commission shall make useful information available to non-governmental organisations and social partners. The Commission shall inform the Committee established under Article 8 of these views;
(c) promote active partnership and dialogue between all the partners involved in the programme to encourage an integrated and coordinated approach to the fight against social exclusion and poverty.
2. The Commission shall, in cooperation with the Member States, take the necessary steps to:
(a) promote the involvement in the programme of all the parties concerned;
(b) ensure the dissemination of the results of the Community actions undertaken within the framework of the programme;
(c) provide appropriate information, publicity and follow-up with regard to Community actions supported by the programme.

Article 6
Financing
1. The financial framework for the implementation of the programme for the period referred to in Article 1 is hereby set at EUR 75 million, including technical and administrative expenditure.
2. The annual appropriations, including those relating to human resources, shall be authorised by the budgetary authority within the limits of the financial perspective.

Article 7
Implementing measures
1. The measures necessary for the implementation of this Decision relating to the matters referred to below shall be adopted in accordance with the management procedure referred to in Article 8(2):
(a) the annual implementation of the programme's Community actions and the annual plan of work;
(b) the breakdown of the funds between the different strands of the programme;
(c) the arrangements for selecting activities and organisations for Community support;
(d) the criteria for evaluating the programme, including those relating to cost-effectiveness, and the arrangements for disseminating and transferring the results.
2. The measures necessary for the implementation of this Decision relating to all other matters shall be adopted in accordance with the advisory procedure referred to in Article 8(3).

Article 8
Committee
1. The Commission shall be assisted by a Committee.
2. Where reference is made to this paragraph, Articles 4 and 7 of Decision 1999/468/EC shall apply, having regard to the provisions of Article 8 thereof.
The period laid down in Article 4(3) of Decision 1999/468/EC shall be set at two months.
3. Where reference is made to this paragraph, Articles 3 and 7 of Decision 1999/468/EC shall apply, having regard to the provisions of Article 8 thereof.
4. The Committee shall adopt its rules of procedure.

Article 9
Cooperation with other committees and links with the Social Protection Committee
1. To ensure the consistency and complementarity of this programme with other measures referred to in Article 10, the Commission shall keep the Committee regularly informed about other Community action contributing to combating social exclusion. Where appropriate, the Commission shall establish regular and structured cooperation between this Committee and the monitoring committees established for other relevant policies, instruments and actions.
2. The Commission shall establish the necessary links with the Social Protection Committee within the framework of the Community actions referred to in this Decision.

Article 10
Consistency and complementarity
1. The Commission shall, in cooperation with the Member States, ensure overall consistency with other relevant Community policies, instruments and actions, in particular by establishing appropriate mechanisms to coordinate the activities of this programme with relevant activities relating to research, employment, economic,

industrial and enterprise policies, non-discrimination, immigration, equality between women and men, social protection, education, training and youth policy, health and in the field of enlargement and the Community's external relations.
2. The Member States shall make every possible effort to ensure consistency and complementarity between activities under this programme and those carried out at national, regional and local levels.
3. The Commission and the Member States shall ensure consistency and complementarity between action undertaken under this programme and action undertaken in the field of employment and also with Community action under the structural funds, in particular the Community initiative EQUAL.

Article 11
Participation of the EFTA/EEA countries, the associated countries of Central and Eastern Europe, Cyprus, Malta and Turkey
This programme shall be open to the participation of:
- the EFTA/EEA countries in accordance with the conditions established in the EEA Agreement;
- the associated central and eastern European countries in accordance with the conditions established in the Europe Agreements, in their additional protocols and in the decisions of the respective Association Councils;
- Cyprus, Malta and Turkey, funded by additional appropriations in accordance with procedures to be agreed with each country.

Article 12
Monitoring and evaluation
1. The Commission shall regularly monitor this programme in cooperation with the Member States in accordance with the procedure referred to in Article 8(2).
2. The Commission shall report on the overall consistency of policies with social cohesion including progress achieved under this programme in its annual summary report to the Spring European Council, on which the European Parliament shall express its views in due course.
3. The programme shall be evaluated by the Commission by the end of the third year and at the end of the programme with the assistance of independent experts. This evaluation will assess the relevance, effectiveness and cost-effectiveness of activities implemented with regard to the objectives referred to in Article 3. It will also examine the impact of the programme as a whole. The evaluation will also examine the complementarity between action under the programme and that pursued under other relevant Community policies, instruments and actions.
4. The Commission shall submit to the European Parliament, the Council, the Economic and Social Committee and the Committee of the Regions a final report on the implementation of the programme by 31 December 2006.

Annexes - Chapter 8: Living and Working Conditions

Chapter 9

PROTECTION OF SAFETY AND HEALTH

The activities of the European Community for the protection of the physical safety and health of its citizens are relatively new, since they are implemented since the decade of the 1980s. The Member States still have the main responsibility in those fields. The Community gives general guidelines of common policies in three directions: the safety and health at work (not to be confused with public safety); the health protection of citizens in general; and the protection of health and safety of consumers.

9.1. Safety and health at work

The **European Agency for Health and Safety at Work**, based in Bilbao has as main tasks: the collection and dissemination of technical, scientific and economic information on health and safety at work; the promotion of and support for exchanges of information and experience between Member States; the provision of information necessary for the Commission in the preparation and evaluation of legislation; and the operation of a network linking Member States' national networks[1].

The Community has for a long time been involved in the area of workers' safety. The ECSC and Euratom Treaties assigned more tasks to these Communities in this field than the EEC Treaty to the European Economic Community [see section 1.1.]. Article 46 of the **ECSC Treaty** called upon the High Authority (Commission) to "obtain the information it requires to assess the possibilities for improving working conditions and living standards for workers in the industries within its province and the threats to those standards". Article 55 called upon it to "promote technical and economic research relating" *inter alia* "to occupational safety" in those industries. ECSC "social research" has developed from multiannual programmes decided upon by the Commission in the fields of hygiene and safety in mines, the effort to combat pollution at the workplace and ergonomics[2]. A safety and Health Commission for the Mining and Other Extractive Industries prepares opinions and makes proposals to the Governments in those fields[3].

By virtue of the powers conferred on it by the **Euratom Treaty**, the Community has been able to implement an efficient policy for the protection of workers and the general public against the **risks linked with radioactivity**. The Council Directive of 1 June 1976 laying down the revised basic standards for the health protection of the general public and workers against the dangers of ionising radiation strengthened and improved the practical organisation of radiation pro-

[1] Regulation 2062/94, OJ L 216, 20.08.1994 and Regulation 1643/95, OJ L 156, 07.07.1995.
[2] Resolution OJ C 257, 14.10.1986.
[3] OJ 28, 31.08.1957.

tection in the Community[1]. That was highly appropriate at a time when public opinion was beginning to worry about the consequences of radioactivity for the environment and human health. In the health field, the Directive lays down basic measures for the radiation protection of persons undergoing medical examination or treatment.

Despite the limited competences that assigned the EEC Treaty to the European Community, Directives were adopted concerning the protection of workers, notably from the major accident hazards of certain industrial activities[2] and exposure to asbestos[3]. After the 1987 Single Act [see section 1.1.] had increased the Community's authority as regards the health and safety of the work force, the Commission set up a mutual information system for legislative and administrative acts of the Member States concerning health and security of workers at the place of work[4]. At the instigation of the Commission, the Council adopted, in 1989, a **Framework Directive** on the introduction of measures to encourage improvements in the safety and health of workers at the workplace[5] [see annex 9.1.]. This Directive lays down three main principles: the employer's general obligation to guarantee the workers' health and safety in all work-related aspects, in particular by preventing professional risks, by keeping the work force informed and by training; the obligation of every worker to contribute to his own health and safety and that of others by using the work facilities correctly and respecting the safety instructions; the absence or limited liability for employers for things caused by abnormal unforeseen circumstances or exceptional events. By laying down the main principles concerning health and safety at work in the Community, the framework Directive is the foundation on which all other directives aiming at the improvement of the working environment to protect workers' health and safety (Art. 137 TEC) are superimposed.

This is particularly the case as regards the specific Directives laying down **minimum requirements on**:

- workplaces[6] [see annex 9.2.];
- work equipment and machinery[7] [see annex 9.3.];
- personal protective equipment[8] [see annex 9.4.];
- the manual handling of loads involving some kind of risk - notably of dorsal/lumbar damage for workers[9] [see annex 9.5.];
- work using display screens[10] [see annex 9.6.];
- exposure at work to carcinogenic agents[11] [see annex 9.7.];
- exposure at work to biological agents[12]
- minimum health and safety requirements on temporary and mobile sites[13];
- safety and/or health signs in the workplace[14] [see annex 9.8.];
- the protection of workers in the mineral-extracting industries by drilling[15];
- the protection of workers in surface and underground mineral-extracting industries[16];
- the protection of workers from the risks related to hazardous chemical agents at the workplace[17] [see annex 9.9.];
- the protection of workers potentially at risk from explosive atmospheres (e.g. flammable and/or combustible gases, vapours, mists or dusts)[1];

---

1 Directive 96/29/Euratom, OJ L 159, 29.06.1996.
2 Directive 82/501, OJ L 230, 05.08.1982.
3 Directive 83/477, OJ L 263, 24.09.1983 and Directive 2003/18, OJ L 97, 15.04.2003.
4 Decision 88/383, OJ L 183, 14.07.1988.
5 Directive 89/391, OJ L 183, 29.06.1989.
6 Directive 89/654, OJ L 393, 30.12.1989.
7 Directive 89/655, OJ L 393, 30.12.1989 and Directive 95/63, OJ L 335, 30.12.1995.
8 Directive 89/656, OJ L 393, 30.12.1989.
9 Directive 90/269, OJ L 156, 21.06.1990.
10 Directive 90/270, OJ L 156, 21.06.1990.
11 Directive 90/394, OJ L 196, 26.07.1990 and OJ L 138, 01.06.1999.
12 Directive 2000/54, OJ L 262, 17.10.2000.
13 Directive 92/57, OJ L 245, 26.08.1992.
14 Directive 92/58, OJ L 245, 26.08.1992.
15 Directive 92/91, OJ L 348, 28.11.1992.
16 Directive 92/104, OJ L 404, 31.12.1992.
17 Directive 98/24, OJ L 131, 05.05.1998.

- exposure of workers to the risks arising from physical agents (mechanical vibrations)[2]; and
- exposure to the risks arising from physical agents (noise)[3] [see annex 9.10.].

These Directives guarantee the right to safety at work for the workers in all Member States, including those which previously had not high safety standards. Workers having an interim or specific duration work relation must enjoy the same health and safety conditions as the other workers of an undertaking[4]. As seen above, a directive aims at improving the health and safety of pregnant workers and workers who have recently given birth or are breastfeeding[5] [see section 8.5. and annex 8.19.]. The Council recommends that the Member States recognise, in the context of their policy on preventing occupational hazards and accidents, the right of self-employed workers to health and safety protection, and their duties in this area[6].

The **new Community strategy on health and safety at work** aims at a global approach to well-being at work, taking account of changes in the world of work and the emergence of new risks, especially of a psycho-social nature. According to the Commission, the strategy should be based on: consolidating a culture of risk prevention, including psychological and social risks such as stress, harassment, depression and alcoholism; combining a variety of political instruments, such as social dialogue and corporate social responsibility; and building partnerships between all players in the field of health and safety[7].

9.2. Public health protection

Public health was brought fully into the action scope of the European Union by a special title of the Maastricht Treaty, which, as amended at Amsterdam to heed the "mad cow" and dioxin lessons[8], states that a **high level of human health protection** shall be ensured in the definition and implementation of all Community policies and activities. Article 152 (TEC) invites the Community to contribute towards ensuring a high level of human health protection by encouraging cooperation between the Member States and by fostering cooperation with third countries and the competent international organisations.

The **programme of Community action** in the field of public health (2003-2008) complements national policies aiming to protect human health and improve public health[9] [see annex 9.11.]. The general objectives of the programme are: (a) to improve information and knowledge for the development of public health; (b) to enhance the capability of responding rapidly and in a coordinated fashion to threats to health; (c) to promote health and prevent disease through addressing health determinants across all policies and activities. The programme should thereby contribute to: ensuring a high level of human health protection in the definition and implementation of all Community policies and activities; tackling inequalities in health; and encouraging cooperation between Member States.

The measures under the programme underpin the **health strategy of the Community** and should yield Community added value by responding to needs arising out of conditions and structures established through Community action in other fields, by addressing new developments, new threats and new problems for which the Community would be in a better position to act to protect its people, by bringing together activities undertaken in relative isolation and with limited impact at national level and by complementing them in order to achieve positive results for the people of the Community. The programme can provide a significant added value to health promo-

---

1. Directive 1999/92, OJ L 23, 28.01.2000.
2. Directive 2002/44, OJ L 177, 06.07.2002.
3. Directive 2003/10, OJ L 42, 15.02.2003.
4. Directive 91/383, OJ L 206, 29.07.1991.
5. Directive 92/85, OJ L 348, 28.11.1992.
6. Recommendation 2003/134, OJ L 53, 28.02.2003.
7. Commission communication, COM (2002) 118, 11 March 2002.
8. Moussis (2004), sections 5.1.4. and 11.2.
9. Decision 1786/2002, OJ L 271, 09.10.2002.

tion by facilitating the exchange of experience and best practices and by providing a basis for a common analysis of the factors affecting public health. Also, the programme may have added value in the event of threats to public health of a cross-border nature, such as infectious diseases, environmental pollution or food contamination.

A Community **health-monitoring system** aims to facilitate the planning, monitoring and evaluation of Community programmes, provide the Member States with appropriate health information to make comparisons and to support their national health policies. It entails action aimed at establishing Community health indicators, developing a Community-wide network for sharing health data and facilitating analyses and reporting in the health sphere. Actually, the Community leads actions against AIDS, cancer, particularly by combating smoking, and drug dependence.

As regards the acquired immune deficiency syndrome (**AIDS**), the Member States decided, first, to introduce a procedure for the periodical and rapid exchange of epidemiological data at Community level and machinery for the exchange of information on national measures taken[1]. The Community **network for the epidemiological surveillance** and control of communicable diseases ensures continuous surveillance and provides an early warning and response system to deal with the appearance or recurrence of these diseases in the Member States[2]. The Community participates in a research and development programme aimed at developing new clinical interventions to combat HIV/AIDS, malaria and tuberculosis through a long-term partnership between Europe and developing countries, undertaken by several Member States[3].

In the framework of the **action plans to combat cancer**, the Community has adopted several measures against smoking, notably a Directive concerning the labelling of tobacco products[4] and a Directive concerning the maximum tar content of cigarettes[5]. A Resolution on banning smoking in places open to the public, which provided guidelines to the Member States for the protection of non-smokers from environmental tobacco smoke[6], was reinforced by a recommendation on the prevention of smoking and on initiatives to improve tobacco control[7]. A milestone Directive prohibits all forms of advertising and sponsorship of tobacco products in the media other than television, i.e. in the press and other printed publications, in radio broadcasting and in information society services[8] [see annex 9.12.]. Another Directive prohibits all forms of television advertising for cigarettes and other tobacco products and provides that television programmes may not be sponsored by undertakings whose principal activity is the manufacture or sale of cigarettes and other tobacco products[9].

For the **prevention of drug dependence,** the Community has set up a customs cooperation and has taken a number of measures in the framework of its justice and home affairs policy[10]. The European Monitoring Centre for Drugs and Drug Addiction (EMCDDA), established in Lisbon, has at its disposal, as a key instrument in its fight against drugs, a European Information Network on Drugs and Drug Addiction[11] [see annex 9.13.]. In connection with the European Union Drugs Strategy (2000-04), the Council made a number of recommendations concerning information and counselling, emergency services, networking between agencies, appropriate integration of health and social services, and training and qualification for professionals, in order to reduce substantially the incidence of drug-related health damage and the number of deaths[12].

---

1 OJ C 197, 27.07.1988, p. 8 and OJ C 329, 31.12.1990, p. 21-22.
2 OJ L 268, 03.10.1998.
3 Decision 1209/2003, OJ L 169, 08.07.2003.
4 Directive 89/622, OJ L 359, 08.12.1989 and Directive 92/41, OJ L 158, 11.06.1992.
5 Directive 90/239, OJ L 137, 30.05.1990.
6 OJ C 189, 26.07.1989, p. 1-2.
7 Recommendation 2003/54, OJ L 22, 25.01.2003.
8 Directive 2003/33, OJ L 152, 20.06.2003.
9 Directive 89/552, OJ L 298, 17.10.1989 and Directive 97/36, OJ L 202, 30.07.1997.
10 Moussis (2004), sections 5.1.5. and 8.1.2.
11 Regulation 302/93, OJ L 36, 12.02.1993 and Regulation 2220/2000, OJ L 253, 07.10.2000.
12 Recommendation 2003/488, OJ L 165, 03.07.2003.

The Council recommends that the Member States adopt a common strategy aiming to promote research into all the different aspects of problems associated with alcohol consumption by young people, to increase prevention, to combat the sale of alcohol to under age consumers and to take measures to combat dependency[1].

The activities carried out inside the thematic priority area "life sciences, genomics and biotechnology for health" of the **common research policy**[2] may have numerous applications in various health-related sectors, and notably in the development of new diagnostic tools and new treatments capable of helping to combat diseases that are not at present under control[3] [see annex 9.14.].

9.3. Protection of consumers' health and physical safety

The Community turned its attention to the physical safety of consumers in the 1970s. But for many years, efforts in this field were **overshadowed by other common policies**, notably the agricultural one and that of removing technical barriers to trade. This was particularly true of the Directive on the alignment of legislation on cosmetics[4] and that on the classification, packaging and labelling of dangerous preparations[5]. These directives, however, adapted over the years to technical progress, have gradually become more protective of human health. Other directives aim directly at this objective, notably the Directive concerning food additives authorised for use in foodstuffs intended for human consumption[6] and the Directive on measures to monitor certain substances and residues thereof in live animals and animal products[7].

The accident at the Chernobyl nuclear power plant in April 1986 gave the Community an opportunity to complete its legislation on **radioactive contamination**. In addition to ad hoc measures adopted in order to coordinate national measures covering agricultural produce[8] and definition of conditions under which agricultural produce originating in third countries could be imported[9], the Council adopted in December 1987 a Regulation setting maximum permitted levels of radioactive contamination of foodstuffs and of feeding stuffs following a nuclear accident or any other case of radiological emergency[10].

The effort to complete the internal market proved the effective trigger of a genuine policy to protect the health and physical safety of consumers. In the 1980s the Community placed the well-being of its citizens high on its list of priorities by adopting **general legislation guaranteeing the safety of individuals** in their capacity as users of products, regardless of the origin of the latter. This is the aim of a Directive on the approximation of the laws of the Member States concerning products which, appearing to be other than they are, endanger the health or safety of consumers[11] [see annex 9.15.]. This Directive prohibits the marketing, import and either manufacture or export of **dangerous imitations of foodstuffs**. Such products can be withdrawn from the market by a Member State and the Commission and the other Member States are informed of their existence.

A major Directive in the context of the single market was adopted in 1988 dealing with **toy safety**[12]. It sets the basic safety requirements that must be met by all toys manufactured in the Community or imported from third countries. The European standardisation committees then adopt harmonised standards and manufacturers respecting these are covered by a presumption

---

1 Recommendation 2001/458, OJ L 161, 16.06.2001.
2 Moussis (2004), section 18.4.1.
3 Decision 2002/834, OJ L 294, 29.10.2002.
4 Directive 76/68, OJ L 262, 27.09.1976 and Directive 98/62, OJ L 253, 15.09.1998.
5 Directive 1999/45, OJ L 200, 30.07.1999.
6 Directive 89/107, OJ L 40, 11.02.1989.
7 Directive 96/23, OJ L 125, 23.05.1996.
8 Recommendation 86/156, OJ L 118, 07.05.1986.
9 Regulation 3955/87, OJ L 371, 30.12.1987.
10 Regulation 3954/87, OJ L 371, 30.12.1987 and Regulation 2218/89, OJ L 211, 22.07.1989.
11 Directive 87/357, OJ L 192, 11.07.1987.
12 Directive 88/378, OJ L 187, 16.07.1988 and Directive 93/68, OJ L 220, 30.08.1993.

that their toys meet the basic safety requirements defined in the Directive. This Directive consequently promotes the free movement of goods while encouraging the manufacture of high-quality danger-free toys for the Union's children.

Since it is difficult to adopt Community legislation for every product, it is necessary to establish at Community level a general safety requirement. This general legal instrument is provided by a Directive on **general product safety**[1] [see annex 9.16.]. The purpose of this Directive is to ensure that products placed on the market, which are intended for consumers or likely, under reasonably foreseeable conditions, to be used by consumers even if not intended for them, are safe. Producers are obliged to place only safe products on the market, conforming to the specific rules of national law of the Member State in whose territory the product is marketed drawn up in conformity with the Treaty and in accordance with Directive 98/34 laying down a procedure for the provision of information in the field of technical standards and regulations[2]. Distributors are required to act with due care to help to ensure compliance with the applicable safety requirements, in particular by not supplying products which they know or should have presumed, on the basis of the information in their possession and as professionals, do not comply with those requirements. Where producers and distributors know or ought to know that a product that they have placed on the market poses risks to the consumer they must immediately inform the competent authorities of the Member States thereof. Member States must ensure that producers and distributors comply with their obligations, establish or nominate authorities competent to monitor the compliance of products with the general safety requirements and lay down the rules on penalties applicable to infringements of the national provisions adopted. The Commission must promote and take part in the operation in a European network of the authorities of the Member States competent for product safety. This network must be coordinated with other Community procedures, in particular the **Community Rapid Information System (RAPEX)**, which is described in Annex II of the directive and is essentially aimed at a rapid exchange of information in the event of a serious risk.

Thanks to **RAPEX**, the Member States and the Commission can take the necessary urgent steps when it becomes known that a particular consumer product is a source of immediate and serious danger to consumer health and physical safety. Managed by the Commission, the system has permitted the withdrawal from the market of several dangerous products, particularly foodstuffs. Early-warning systems cannot work properly, however, if the Member States do not apply the appropriate measures fully and in good time when a risk arises, as was the case of Belgium which infringed Community procedures by not informing the Commission and the other Member States immediately that dioxin had been found in foodstuffs and in animal feed in June 1999[3].

Another information network, the Community system of information and monitoring of **accidents in the home and during leisure (EHLASS)**, included in the programme of Community action on injury prevention (1999 to 2003), is geared to the collection of data from the casualty departments of 65 hospitals in the fifteen Member States and from household surveys covering the nature and origin of home and leisure accidents[4]. Analysis of the data enables Member States to take appropriate measures to reduce the number of accidents and victims by means of information campaigns, negotiation with industry and introduction of standards of regulations.

A Commission White Paper aims at a **common food safety strategy**, providing a high level of consumer protection through stringent Community rules and appropriate checks at all stages of the production chain, "from farm to table"[5]. Besides the establishment of a European Food Authority, made up of independent experts, the Commission envisages a programme of legislative measures consolidating the principles of food safety such as the responsibility of feed manufacturers, the traceability of products, risk analysis and application of the **precautionary principle**.

[1] Directive 2001/95, OJ L 11, 15.01.2002, repealing Directive 92/59, OJ L 228, 11.08.1992 from 15 January 2004.
[2] Moussis (2004), section 6.2.2.
[3] Moussis (2004), section 5.1.4.
[4] Decision 372/1999, OJ L 46, 20.02.1999
[5] COM (1999) 719, 12 January 2000.

This principle is an integral part of a structured approach to risk analysis based on assessment, management and communication of risk. The precautionary principle may prove necessary when scientific data are insufficient, inconclusive or uncertain and when preliminary scientific findings provide reasonable grounds for concern that the potentially dangerous effects on the environment or on human, animal or plant health may be inconsistent with the level of protection sought by the European Union[1]. Indeed, according to the Court of Justice, when there is uncertainty regarding the risk to human health or safety, the Community institutions are empowered to take protective measures without having to wait until the reality and seriousness of those risks becomes fully apparent[2].

The Court of First Instance has confirmed the approach taken by the Commission[3]. The precautionary principle could be applied only where there was a risk, notably for human health, which had not yet been conclusively demonstrated, but it could not be based on unverified conjecture. Before any preventive measures were taken, the competent public authority had to conduct a **risk assessment** with two complementary components: a scientific component (as thorough a scientific risk assessment as possible taking account notably of the urgency of the situation) and a political component (risk management), with the public authority determining the desired level of protection and consequently deciding on an appropriate measure given the level of risk it had determined. "Risk" thus constituted a function of the probability that use of a product or a procedure would adversely affect human health. "Hazard" ("danger") was, in this context, commonly used in a broader sense and described any product or procedure capable of having an adverse effect on human health.

Taking account of the bovine spongiform encephalopathy (BSE) experience[4], **animal-health rules** govern the placing on the market and importation from third countries of products of animal origin, with a view to preventing the spread of animal diseases[5]. Other rules are applicable to the collection, transport, storing, handling, processing and use or disposal of **animal by-products** in order to prevent them from presenting a risk to animal or public health[6]. They prohibit the recycling of dead animals and condemned animal material into the feed chain. The only raw material allowed to be used for the production of animal feed is material derived from animals declared fit for human consumption.

A directive aims to approximate the laws of the Member States with a view to maintaining both a high level of public health protection and the free circulation of products marketed in the Community as **foods containing concentrated sources of nutrients** (vitamins and minerals) and presented for supplementing the intake of those nutrients from the normal diet[7]. It establishes specific rules on labelling and criteria for fixing the maximum quantities of vitamins and minerals in these products. Foods and food ingredients treated with ionising radiation are also subjected to Community checks[8].

After the BSE or **"mad-cow" crisis** of 1996, the Commission set up a **Scientific Steering Committee**, made up of distinguished scientific experts, to provide sound scientific advice and coordinate the work of the various sector-specific scientific committees in the field of consumer health[9]. Eight scientific sector-specific committees are required to draw the Commission's attention to any specific or emerging problem falling within their remit and to provide scientific advice on the basis of trends in existing scientific data[10]. The Community "Food and Veterinary Office", has responsibility for monitoring the observance of veterinary and plant-health legislation and

---

1 COM (2000) 1, 2 February 2000.
2 Judgments of 5 May 1998, Cases C-180/96 and C-157/96, ECR 1998 I-2265.
3 Judgments of 11 September 2002, Case T-13/99 (ECR 1999, p. II-1961) *Pfizer Animal Health SA* v *Council* and Case T-70/99 *Alpharma Inc.* v *Council*, ECR 2002, p. II-3495.
4 Moussis (2004), sections 5.1.4 and 21.4.2.
5 Directive 2002/99, OJ L 18, 23.01.2003.
6 Regulation 1774/2002, OJ L 273, 10.10.2002.
7 Directive 2002/46, OJ L 183, 12.07.2002.
8 Directive 1999/2, OJ L 66, 13.03.1999.
9 Decision 97/404, OJ L 169, 27.06.1997.
10 Decision 97/579, OJ L 237, 28.08.1997.

food hygiene rules both within the European Union and in countries which provide it with foodstuffs. However, recommendations issued by the scientific committees are not always taken into consideration by the Member States[1].

Physical safety and health of consumers is integrated in **other common policies**, particularly: the agricultural policy (definition of dairy products and imitation dairy products, regulation of organic products, veterinary problems, promotion of high quality products and, in general, food policy)[2]; research policy (food quality and safety)[3]; the process of completing the internal market (machinery, foodstuffs, construction materials)[4]; and public health policy (measures to combat smoking, etc.)[5].

1 COM (1998) 598, 18 November 1998.
2 Moussis (2004), sections 5.1.4. and 21.4.2.
3 Ibid, section 18.4.1.
4 Ibid, section 6.2.
5 Ibid, section 13.5.8.

Annex 9

PROTECTION OF SAFETY AND HEALTH

Annex 9.1.

Council Directive 89/391/EEC of 12 June 1989 on the introduction of measures to **encourage improvements in the safety and health of workers at work**
Official Journal L 183 , 29/06/1989 P. 0001 - 0008.

MAIN PROVISIONS

Article 1
Object
1. The object of this Directive is to introduce measures to encourage improvements in the safety and health of workers at work.
2. To that end it contains general principles concerning the prevention of occupational risks, the protection of safety and health, the elimination of risk and accident factors, the informing, consultation, balanced participation in accordance with national laws and/or practices and training of workers and their representatives, as well as general guidelines for the implementation of the said principles.
3. This Directive shall be without prejudice to existing or future national and Community provisions which are more favourable to protection of the safety and health of workers at work.

Article 2
Scope
1. This Directive shall apply to all sectors of activity, both public and private (industrial, agricultural, commercial, administrative, service, educational, cultural, leisure, etc.).
2. This Directive shall not be applicable where characteristics peculiar to certain specific public service activities, such as the armed forces or the police, or to certain specific activities in the civil protection services inevitably conflict with it.
In that event, the safety and health of workers must be ensured as far as possible in the light of the objectives of this Directive.

Article 3
Definitions
For the purposes of this Directive, the following terms shall have the following meanings:
(a) worker: any person employed by an employer, including trainees and apprentices but excluding domestic servants;
(b) employer: any natural or legal person who has an employment relationship with the worker and has responsibility for the undertaking and/or establishment;
(c) workers' representative with specific responsibility for the safety and health of workers: any person elected, chosen or designated in accordance with national laws and/or practices to represent workers where problems arise relating to the safety and health protection of workers at work;
(d) prevention: all the steps or measures taken or planned at all stages of work in the undertaking to prevent or reduce occupational risks.

Article 4
1. Member States shall take the necessary steps to ensure that employers, workers and workers' representatives are subject to the legal provisions necessary for the implementation of this Directive.
2. In particular, Member States shall ensure adequate controls and supervision.

SECTION II
EMPLOYERS' OBLIGATIONS

Article 5
General provision
1. The employer shall have a duty to ensure the safety and health of workers in every aspect related to the work.
2. Where, pursuant to Article 7 (3), an employer enlists competent external services or persons, this shall not discharge him from his responsibilities in this area.
3. The workers' obligations in the field of safety and health at work shall not affect the principle of the responsibility of the employer.
4. This Directive shall not restrict the option of Member States to provide for the exclusion or the limitation of employers' responsibility where occurrences are due to unusual and unforeseeable circumstances, beyond the employers' control, or to exceptional events, the consequences of which could not have been avoided despite the exercise of all due care.
Member States need not exercise the option referred to in the first subparagraph.

Article 6
General obligations on employers
1. Within the context of his responsibilities, the employer shall take the measures necessary for the safety and health protection of workers, including prevention of occupational risks and provision of information and training, as well as provision of the necessary organization and means.
The employer shall be alert to the need to adjust these measures to take account of changing circumstances and aim to improve existing situations.
2. The employer shall implement the measures referred to in the first subparagraph of paragraph 1 on the basis of the following general principles of prevention:
(a)avoiding risks;
(b)evaluating the risks which cannot be avoided:
(c)combating the risks at source;
(d)adapting the work to the individual, especially as regards the design of work places, the choice of work equipment and the choice of working and production methods, with a view, in particular, to alleviating monotonous work and work at a predetermined work-rate and to reducing their effect on health.
(e)adapting to technical progress;
(f)replacing the dangerous by the non-dangerous or the less dangerous;
(g)developing a coherent overall prevention policy which covers technology, organization of work, working conditions, social relationships and the influence of factors related to the working environment;
(h)giving collective protective measures priority over individual protective measures;
(i)giving appropriate instructions to the workers.
3. Without prejudice to the other provisions of this Directive, the employer shall, taking into account the nature of the activities of the enterprise and/or establishment:
(a) evaluate the risks to the safety and health of workers, inter alia in the choice of work equipment, the chemical substances or preparations used, and the fitting-out of work places.
Subsequent to this evaluation and as necessary, the preventive measures and the working and production methods implemented by the employer must:
- assure an improvement in the level of protection afforded to workers with regard to safety and health,
- be integrated into all the activities of the undertaking and/or establishment and at all hierarchical levels;
(b) where he entrusts tasks to a worker, take into consideration the worker's capabilities as regards health and safety;
(c) ensure that the planning and introduction of new technologies are the subject of consultation with the workers and/or their representatives, as regards the consequences of the choice of equipment, the working conditions and the working environment for the safety and health of workers;
(d) take appropriate steps to ensure that only workers who have received adequate instructions may have access to areas where there is serious and specific danger.
4. Without prejudice to the other provisions of this Directive, where several undertakings share a work place, the employers shall cooperate in implementing the safety, health and occupational hygiene provisions and, taking into account the nature of the activities, shall coordinate their actions in matters of the protection and prevention of occupational risks, and shall inform one another and their respective workers and/or workers' representatives of these risks.
5. Measures related to safety, hygiene and health at work may in no circumstances involve the workers in financial cost.

Article 7
Protective and preventive services
1. Without prejudice to the obligations referred to in Articles 5 and 6, the employer shall designate one or more workers to carry out activities related to the protection and prevention of occupational risks for the undertaking and/or establishment.
2. Designated workers may not be placed at any disadvantage because of their activities related to the protection and prevention of occupational risks.
Designated workers shall be allowed adequate time to enable them to fulfil their obligations arising from this Directive.
3. If such protective and preventive measures cannot be organized for lack of competent personnel in the undertaking
and/or establishment, the employer shall enlist competent external services or persons.
4. Where the employer enlists such services or persons, he shall inform them of the factors known to affect, or suspected of affecting, the safety and health of the workers and they must have access to the information referred to in Article 10 (2).
5. In all cases:
- the workers designated must have the necessary capabilities and the necessary means,
- the external services or persons consulted must have the necessary aptitudes and the necessary personal and professional means, and
- the workers designated and the external services or persons consulted must be sufficient in number
to deal with the organization of protective and preventive measures, taking into account the size of the undertaking and/or establishment and/or the hazards to which the workers are exposed and their distribution throughout the entire undertaking and/or establishment.
6. The protection from, and prevention of, the health and safety risks which form the subject of this Article shall be the responsibility of one or more workers, of one service or of separate services whether from inside or outside the undertaking and/or establishment.
The worker(s) and/or agency(ies) must work together whenever necessary.
7. Member States may define, in the light of the nature of the activities and size of the undertakings, the categories of undertakings in which the employer, provided he is competent, may himself take responsibility for the measures referred to in paragraph 1.
8. Member States shall define the necessary capabilities and aptitudes referred to in paragraph 5.
They may determine the sufficient number referred to in paragraph 5.

Article 8
First aid, fire-fighting and evacuation of workers, serious and imminent danger
1. The employer shall:
- take the necessary measures for first aid, fire-fighting and evacuation of workers, adapted to the nature of the activities and the size of the undertaking and/or establishment and taking into account other persons present,
- arrange any necessary contacts with external services, particularly as regards first aid, emergency medical care, rescue work and fire-fighting.
2. Pursuant to paragraph 1, the employer shall, inter alia, for first aid, fire-fighting and the evacuation of workers, designate the workers required to implement such measures.
The number of such workers, their training and the equipment available to them shall be adequate, taking account of the size and/or specific hazards of the undertaking and/or establishment.
3. The employer shall:
(a) as soon as possible, inform all workers who are, or may be, exposed to serious and imminent danger of the risk involved and of the steps taken or to be taken as regards protection;
(b) take action and give instructions to enable workers in the event of serious, imminent and unavoidable danger to stop work and/or immediately to leave the work place and proceed to a place of safety;
(c) save in exceptional cases for reasons duly substantiated, refrain from asking workers to resume work in a working situation where there is still a serious and imminent danger.
4. Workers who, in the event of serious, imminent and unavoidable danger, leave their workstation and/or a dangerous area may not be placed at any disadvantage because of their action and must be protected against any harmful and unjustified consequences, in accordance with national laws and/or practices.
5. The employer shall ensure that all workers are able, in the event of serious and imminent danger to their own safety and/or that of other persons, and where the immediate superior responsible cannot be contacted, to take the appropriate steps in the light of their knowledge and the technical means at their disposal, to avoid the consequences of such danger.
Their actions shall not place them at any disadvantage, unless they acted carelessly or there was negligence on their part.

Article 9
Various obligations on employers
1. The employer shall:
(a) be in possession of an assessment of the risks to safety and health at work, including those facing groups of workers exposed to particular risks;
(b) decide on the protective measures to be taken and, if necessary, the protective equipment to be used;
(c) keep a list of occupational accidents resulting in a worker being unfit for work for more than three working days;
(d) draw up, for the responsible authorities and in accordance with national laws and/or practices, reports on occupational accidents suffered by his workers.
2. Member States shall define, in the light of the nature of the activities and size of the undertakings, the obligations to be met by the different categories of undertakings in respect of the drawing-up of the documents provided for in paragraph 1 (a) and (b) and when preparing the documents provided for in paragraph 1 (c) and (d).

Article 10
Worker information
1. The employer shall take appropriate measures so that workers and/or their representatives in the undertaking and/or establishment receive, in accordance with national laws and/or practices which may take account, inter alia, of the size of the undertaking and/or establishment, all the necessary information concerning:
(a) the safety and health risks and protective and preventive measures and activities in respect of both the undertaking and/or establishment in general and each type of workstation and/or job;
(b) the measures taken pursuant to Article 8 (2).
2. The employer shall take appropriate measures so that employers of workers from any outside undertakings and/or establishments engaged in work in his undertaking and/or establishment receive, in accordance with national laws and/or practices, adequate information concerning the points referred to in paragraph 1 (a) and (b) which is to be provided to the workers in question.
3. The employer shall take appropriate measures so that workers with specific functions in protecting the safety and health of workers, or workers' representatives with specific responsibility for the safety and health of workers shall have access, to carry out their functions and in accordance with national laws and/or practices, to:
(a) the risk assessment and protective measures referred to in Article 9 (1) (a) and (b);
(b) the list and reports referred to in Article 9 (1) (c) and (d);
(c) the information yielded by protective and preventive measures, inspection agencies and bodies responsible for safety and health.

Article 11
Consultation and participation of workers
1. Employers shall consult workers and/or their representatives and allow them to take part in discussions on all questions relating to safety and health at work.
This presupposes:
- the consultation of workers,
- the right of workers and/or their representatives to make proposals,
- balanced participation in accordance with national laws and/or practices.
2. Workers or workers' representatives with specific responsibility for the safety and health of workers shall take part in a balanced way, in accordance with national laws and/or practices, or shall be consulted in advance and in good time by the employer with regard to:
(a) any measure which may substantially affect safety and health;
(b) the designation of workers referred to in Articles 7 (1) and 8 (2) and the activities referred to in Article 7 (1);
(c) the information referred to in Articles 9 (1) and 10;
(d) the enlistment, where appropriate, of the competent services or persons outside the undertaking and/or establishment, as referred to in Article 7 (3);
(e) the planning and organization of the training referred to in Article 12.
3. Workers' representatives with specific responsibility for the safety and health of workers shall have the right to ask the employer to take appropriate measures and to submit proposals to him to that end to mitigate hazards for workers and/or to remove sources of danger.
4. The workers referred to in paragraph 2 and the workers' representatives referred to in paragraphs 2 and 3 may not be placed at a disadvantage because of their respective activities referred to in paragraphs 2 and 3.
5. Employers must allow workers' representatives with specific responsibility for the safety and health of workers adequate time off work, without loss of pay, and provide them with the necessary means to enable such representatives to exercise their rights and functions deriving from this Directive.

6. Workers and/or their representatives are entitled to appeal, in accordance with national law and/or practice, to the authority responsible for safety and health protection at work if they consider that the measures taken and the means employed by the employer are inadequate for the purposes of ensuring safety and health at work. Workers' representatives must be given the opportunity to submit their observations during inspection visits by the competent authority.

Article 12
Training of workers
1. The employer shall ensure that each worker receives adequate safety and health training, in particular in the form of information and instructions specific to his workstation or job:
- on recruitment,
- in the event of a transfer or a change of job,
- in the event of the introduction of new work equipment or a change in equipment,
- in the event of the introduction of any new technology.

The training shall be:
- adapted to take account of new or changed risks, and
- repeated periodically if necessary.

2. The employer shall ensure that workers from outside undertakings and/or establishments engaged in work in his undertaking and/or establishment have in fact received appropriate instructions regarding health and safety risks during their activities in his undertaking and/or establishment.
3. Workers' representatives with a specific role in protecting the safety and health of workers shall be entitled to appropriate training.
4. The training referred to in paragraphs 1 and 3 may not be at the workers' expense or at that of the workers' representatives.
The training referred to in paragraph 1 must take place during working hours.
The training referred to in paragraph 3 must take place during working hours or in accordance with national practice either within or outside the undertaking and/or the establishment.

SECTION III
WORKERS' OBLIGATIONS

Article 13
1. It shall be the responsibility of each worker to take care as far as possible of his own safety and health and that of other persons affected by his acts or Commissions at work in accordance with his training and the instructions given by his employer.
2. To this end, workers must in particular, in accordance with their training and the instructions given by their employer:
(a)make correct use of machinery, apparatus, tools, dangerous substances, transport equipment and other means of production;
(b)make correct use of the personal protective equipment supplied to them and, after use, return it to its proper place;
(c)refrain from disconnecting, changing or removing arbitrarily safety devices fitted, e.g. to machinery, apparatus, tools, plant and buildings, and use such safety devices correctly;
(d)immediately inform the employer and/or the workers with specific responsibility for the safety and health of workers of any work situation they have reasonable grounds for considering represents a serious and immediate danger to safety and health and of any shortcomings in the protection arrangements;
(e)cooperate, in accordance with national practice, with the employer and/or workers with specific responsibility for the safety and health of workers, for as long as may be necessary to enable any tasks or requirements imposed by the competent authority to protect the safety and health of workers at work to be carried out;
(f) cooperate, in accordance with national practice, with the employer and/or workers with specific responsibility for the safety and health of workers, for as long as may be necessary to enable the employer to ensure that the working environment and working conditions are safe and pose no risk to safety and health within their field of activity.

SECTION IV
MISCELLANEOUS PROVISIONS

Article 14
Health surveillance
1. To ensure that workers receive health surveillance appropriate to the health and safety risks they incur at work, measures shall be introduced in accordance with national law and/or practices.
2. The measures referred to in paragraph 1 shall be such that each worker, if he so wishes, may receive health surveillance at regular intervals.
3. Health surveillance may be provided as part of a national health system.

Article 15
Risk groups
Particularly sensitive risk groups must be protected against the dangers which specifically affect them.

Article 16
Individual Directives - Amendments
General scope of this Directive
1. The Council, acting on a proposal from the Commission based on Article 118a of the Treaty, shall adopt individual Directives, inter alia, in the areas listed in the Annex.
2. This Directive and, without prejudice to the procedure referred to in Article 17 concerning technical adjustments, the individual Directives may be amended in accordance with the procedure provided for in Article 118a of the Treaty.
3. The provisions of this Directive shall apply in full to all the areas covered by the individual Directives, without prejudice to more stringent and/or specific provisions contained in these individual Directives.

Article 17
Committee
1. For the purely technical adjustments to the individual Directives provided for in Article 16 (1) to take account of:
- the adoption of Directives in the field of technical harmonization and standardization, and/or
- technical progress, changes in international regulations or specifications, and new findings,
the Commission shall be assisted by a committee composed of the representatives of the Member States and chaired by the representative of the Commission.
2. The representative of the Commission shall submit to the committee a draft of the measures to be taken.
The committee shall deliver its opinion on the draft within a time limit which the chairman may lay down according to the urgency of the matter.
The opinion shall be delivered by the majority laid down in Article 148 (2) of the Treaty in the case of decisions which the Council is required to adopt on a proposal from the Commission.
The votes of the representatives of the Member States within the committee shall be weighted in the manner set out in that Article. The chairman shall not vote.
3. The Commission shall adopt the measures envisaged if they are in accordance with the opinion of the committee.
If the measures envisaged are not in accordance with the opinion of the committee, or if no opinion is delivered, the Commission shall, without delay, submit to the Council a proposal relating to the measures to be taken. The Council shall act by a qualified majority.
If, on the expiry of three months from the date of the referral to the Council, the Council has not acted, the proposed measures shall be adopted by the Commission.

Annex 9.2.

Council Directive 89/654/EEC of 30 November 1989 concerning the **minimum safety and health requirements for the workplace** (first individual directive within the meaning of Article 16 (1) of Directive 89/391/EEC)
Official Journal L 393 , 30/12/1989 P. 0001 - 0012.

MAIN PROVISIONS

Article 1
Subject
1. This Directive, which is the first individual directive within the meaning of Article 16 (1) of Directive 89/391/EEC, lays down minimum requirements for safety and health at the workplace, as defined in Article 2.
2. This Directive shall not apply to:
(a) means of transport used outside the undertaking and/or the establishment, or workplaces inside means of transport;
(b) temporary or mobile work sites;
(c) extractive industries;
(d) fishing boats;
(e) fields, woods and other land forming part of an agricultural or forestry undertaking but situated away from the undertaking's buildings.
3. The provisions of Directive 89/391/EEC are fully applicable to the whole scope referred to in paragraph 1, without prejudice to more restrictive and/or specific provisions contained in this Directive.

Article 2
Definition
For the purposes of this Directive, 'workplace' means the place intended to house workstations on the premises of the undertaking and/or establishment and any other place within the area of the undertaking and/or establishment to which the worker has access in the course of his employment.

SECTION II
EMPLOYERS' OBLIGATIONS

Article 3
Workplaces used for the first time
Workplaces used for the first time after 31 December 1992 must satisfy the minimum safety and health requirements laid down in Annex I.

Article 4
Workplaces already in use
Workplaces already in use before 1 January 1993 must satisfy the minimum safety and health requirements laid down in Annex II at the latest three years after that date.
However, as regards the Portuguese Republic, workplaces used before 1 January 1993 must satisfy, at the latest four years after that date, the minimum safety and health requirements appearing in Annex II.

Article 5
Modifications to workplaces
When workplaces undergo modifications, extensions and/or conversions after 31 December 1992, the employer shall take the measures necessary to ensure that those modifications, extensions and/or conversions are in compliance with the corresponding minimum requirements laid down in Annex I.

Article 6
General requirements
To safeguard the safety and health of workers, the employer shall see to it that:
- traffic routes to emergency exits and the exits themselves are kept clear at all times,
- technical maintenance of the workplace and of the equipment and devices, and in particular those referred to in Annexes I and II, is carried out and any faults found which are liable to affect the safety and health of workers are rectified as quickly as possible,
- the workplace and the equipment and devices, and in particular those referred to in Annex I, point 6, and

Annex II, point 6, are regularly cleaned to an adequate level of hygiene,
- safety equipment and devices intended to prevent or eliminate hazards, and in particular those referred to in Annexes I and II, are regularly maintained and checked.

Article 7
Information of workers
Without prejudice to Article 10 of Directive 89/391/EEC, workers and/or their representatives shall be informed of all measures to be taken concerning safety and health at the workplace.

Article 8
Consultation of workers and workers' participation
Consultation and participation of workers and/or of their representatives shall take place in accordance with Article 11 of Directive 89/391/EEC on the matters covered by this Directive, including the Annexes thereto.

SECTION III
MISCELLANEOUS PROVISIONS

Article 9
Amendments to the Annexes
Strictly technical amendments to the Annexes as a result of:
- the adoption of Directives on technical harmonization and standardization of the design, manufacture or construction of parts of workplaces, and/or
- technical progress, changes in international regulations or specifications and knowledge with regard to workplaces,
shall be adopted in accordance with the procedure laid down in Article 17 of Directive 89/391/EEC.

Article 10
Final provisions
1. Member States shall bring into force the laws, regulations and administrative provisions necessary to comply with this Directive by 31 December 1992. They shall forthwith inform the Commission thereof. However, the date applicable for the Hellenic Republic shall be 31 December 1994.
2. Member States shall communicate to the Commission the texts of the provisions of national law which they have already adopted or adopt in the field governed by this Directive.
3. Member States shall report to the Commission every five years on the practical implementation of the provisions of this Directive, indicating the points of view of employers and workers.
The Commission shall inform the European Parliament, the Council, the Economic and Social Committee and the Advisory Council on Safety, Hygiene and Health Protection at Work.
4. The Commission shall submit periodically to the European Parliament, the Council and the Economic and Social Committee a report on the implementation of this Directive, taking into account paragraphs 1 to 3.

Article 11
This Directive is addressed to the Member States.

Done at Brussels, 30 November 1989.
For the Council
The President
J. P. SOISSON
(1) OJ No C 141, 30. 5. 1988, p. 6,
OJ No C 115, 8. 5. 1989, p. 34 and
OJ No C 284, 10. 11. 1989, p. 8
(2) OJ No C 326, 19. 12. 1988, p. 123 and
OJ No C 256, 9. 10. 1988, p. 51.
(3) OJ No C 175, 4. 7. 1988, p. 28.
(4) OJ No C 28, 3. 2. 1988, p. 3.
(5) OJ No C 28, 3. 2. 1988, p. 1.
(6) OJ No L 183, 29. 6. 1989, p. 1.
(7) OJ No L 185, 9. 7. 1974, p. 15. (8) OJ No L 229, 7. 9. 1977, p. 12.

ANNEX I
MINIMUM SAFETY AND HEALTH REQUIREMENTS FOR WORKPLACES USED FOR THE FIRST TIME, AS REFERRED TO IN ARTICLE 3 OF THE DIRECTIVE

1. Preliminary note
The obligations laid down in this Annex apply whenever required by the features of the workplace, the activity, the circumstances or a hazard.
2. Stability and solidity
Buildings which house workplaces must have a structure and solidity appropriate to the nature of their use.
3. Electrical installations
Electrical installations must be designed and constructed so as not to present a fire or explosion hazard; persons must be adequately protected against the risk of accidents caused by direct or indirect contact.
The design, construction and choice of material and protection devices must be appropriate to the voltage, external conditions and the competence of persons with access to parts of the installation.
4. Emergency routes and exits
4.1. Emergency routes and exits must remain clear and lead as directly as possible to the open air or to a safe area.
4.2. In the event of danger, it must be possible for workers to evacuate all workstations quickly and as safely as possible.
4.3. The number, distribution and dimensions of the emergency routes and exits depend on the use, equipment and dimensions of the workplaces and the maximum number of persons that may be present.
4.4. Emergency doors must open outwards.
Sliding or revolving doors are not permitted if they are specifically intended as emergency exits.
Emergency doors should not be so locked or fastened that they cannot be easily and immediately opened by any person who may require to use them in an emergency.
4.5. Specific emergency routes and exits must be indicated by signs in accordance with the national regulations transposing Directive 77/576/EEC (8) into law.
Such signs must be placed at appropriate points and be made to last.
4.6. Emergency doors must not be locked.
The emergency routes and exits, and the traffic routes and doors giving access to them, must be free from obstruction so that they can be used at any time without hindrance.
4.7. Emergency routes and exits requiring illumination must be provided with emergency lighting of adequate intensity in case the lighting fails.
5. Fire detection and fire fighting
5.1. Depending on the dimensions and use of the buildings, the equipment they contain, the physical and chemical properties of the substances present and the maximum potential number of people present, workplaces must be equipped with appropriate fire-fighting equipment and, as necessary, with fire detectors and alarm systems.
5.2. Non-automatic fire-fighting equipment must be easily accessible and simple to use.
The equipment must be indicated by signs in accordance with the national regulations transposing Directive 77/576/EEC into law.
Such signs must be placed at appropriate points and be made to last.
6. Ventilation of enclosed workplaces
6.1. Steps shall be taken to see to it that there is sufficient fresh air in enclosed workplaces, having regard to the working methods used and the physical demands placed on the workers.
If a forced ventilation system is used, it shall be maintained in working order.
Any breakdown must be indicated by a control system where this is necessary for workers' health.
6.2. If air-conditioning or mechanical ventilation installations are used, they must operate in such a way that workers are not exposed to draughts which cause discomfort.
Any deposit or dirt likely to create an immediate danger to the health of workers by polluting the atmosphere must be removed without delay.
7. Room temperature
7.1. During working hours, the temperature in rooms containing workplaces must be adequate for human beings, having regard to the working methods being used and the physical demands placed on the workers.
7.2. The temperature in rest areas, rooms for duty staff, sanitary facilities, canteens and first aid rooms must be appropriate to the particular purpose of such areas.
7.3..Windows, skylights and glass partitions should allow excessive effects of sunlight in workplaces to be avoided, having regard to the nature of the work and of the workplace.
8. Natural and artificial room lighting
8.1. Workplaces must as far as possible receive sufficient natural light and be equipped with artificial lighting

adequate for the protection of workers' safety and health.
8.2. Lighting installations in rooms containing workplaces and in passageways must be placed in such a way that there is no risk of accident to workers as a result of the type of lighting fitted.
8.3. Workplaces in which workers are especially exposed to risks in the event of failure of artificial lighting must be provided with emergency lighting of adequate intensity.
9. Floors, walls, ceilings and roofs of rooms
9.1. The floors of workplaces must have no dangerous bumps, holes or slopes and must be fixed, stable and not slippery.
Workplaces containing workstations must be adequately insulated, bearing in mind the type of undertaking involved and the physical activity of the workers.
9.2. The surfaces of floors, walls and ceilings in rooms must be such that they can be cleaned or refurbished to an appropriate standard of hygiene.
9.3. Transparent or translucent walls, in particular all-glass partitions, in rooms or in the vicinity of workplaces and traffic routes must be clearly indicated and made of safety material or be shielded from such places or traffic routes to prevent workers from coming into contact with walls or being injured should the walls shatter.
9.4. Access to roofs made of materials of insufficient strength must not be permitted unless equipment is provided to ensure that the work can be carried out in a safe manner.
10. Windows and skylights
10.1. It must be possible for workers to open, close, adjust or secure windows, skylights and ventilators in a safe manner. When open, they must not be positioned so as to constitute a hazard to workers.
10.2. Windows and skylights must be designed in conjunction with equipment or otherwise fitted with devices allowing them to be cleaned without risk to the workers carrying out this work or to workers present in and around the building.
11. Doors and gates
11.1. The position, number and dimensions of doors and gates, and the materials used in their construction, are determined by the nature and use of the rooms or areas.
11.2.Transparent doors must be appropriately marked at a conspicuous level.
11.3. Swing doors and gates must be transparent or have see-through panels.
11.4. If transparent or translucent surfaces in doors and gates are not made of safety material and if there is a danger that workers may be injured if a door or gate should shatter, the surfaces must be protected against breakage.
11.5. Sliding doors must be fitted with a safety device to prevent them from being derailed and falling over.
11.6. Doors and gates opening upwards must be fitted with a mechanism to secure them against falling back.
11.7. Doors along escape routes must be appropriately marked.
It must be possible to open them from the inside at any time without special assistance.
It must be possible to open the doors when the workplaces are occupied.
11.8. Doors for pedestrians must be provided in the immediate vicinity of any gates intended essentially for vehicle traffic, unless it is safe for pedestrians to pass through; such doors must be clearly marked and left permanently unobstructed.
11.9. Mechanical doors and gates must function in such a way that there is no risk of accident to workers.
They must be fitted with easily identifiable and accessible emergency shut-down devices and, unless they open automatically in the event of a power failure, it must also be possible to open them manually.
12. Traffic routes - danger areas
12.1. Traffic routes, including stairs, fixed ladders and loading bays and ramps, must be located and dimensioned to ensure easy, safe and appropriate access for pedestrians or vehicles in such a way as not to endanger workers employed in the vicinity of these traffic routes.
12.2. Routes used for pedestrian traffic and/or goods traffic must be dimensioned in accordance with the number of potential users and the type of undertaking.
If means of transport are used on traffic routes, a sufficient safety clearance must be provided for pedestrians.
12.3. Sufficient clearance must be allowed between vehicle traffic routes and doors, gates, passages for pedestrians, corridors and staircases.
12.4. Where the use and equipment of rooms so requires for the protection of workers, traffic routes must be clearly identified.
12.5. If the workplaces contain danger areas in which, owing to the nature of the work, there is a risk of the worker or objects falling, the places must be equipped, as far as possible, with devices preventing unauthorized workers from entering those areas.
Appropriate measures must be taken to protect workers authorized to enter danger areas.
Danger areas must be clearly indicated.
13. Specific measures for escalators and travelators
Escalators and travelators must function safely.

They must be equipped with any necessary safety devices.
They must be fitted with easily identifiable and accessible emergency shut-down devices.
14. Loading bays and ramps
14.1. Loading bays and ramps must be suitable for the dimensions of the loads to be transported.
14.2. Loading bays must have at least one exit point.
Where technically feasible, bays over a certain length must have an exit point at each end.
14.3. Loading ramps must as far as possible be safe enough to prevent workers from falling off.
15. Room dimensions and air space in rooms - freedom of movement at the workstation
15.1. Workrooms must have sufficient surface area, height and air space to allow workers to perform their work without risk to their safety, health or well-being.
15.2. The dimensions of the free unoccupied area at the workstation must be calculated to allow workers sufficient freedom of movement to perform their work.
If this is not possible for reasons specific to the workplace, the worker must be provided with sufficient freedom of movement near his workstation.
16. Rest rooms
16.1. Where the safety or health of workers, in particular because of the type of activity carried out or the presence of more than a certain number of employees, so require, workers must be provided with an easily accessible rest room.
This provision does not apply if the workers are employed in offices or similar workrooms providing equivalent relaxation during breaks.
16.2. Rest rooms must be large enough and equipped with an adequate number of tables and seats with backs for the number of workers.
16.3. In rest rooms appropriate measures must be introduced for the protection of non-smokers against discomfort caused by tobacco smoke.
16.4.If working hours are regularly and frequently interrupted and there is no rest room, other rooms must be provided in which workers can stay during such interruptions, wherever this is required for the safety or health of workers.
Appropriate measures should be taken for the protection of non-smokers against discomfort caused by tobacco smoke.
17. Pregnant women and nursing mothers
Pregnant women and nursing mothers must be able to lie down to rest in appropriate conditions.
18. Sanitary equipment
18.1. Changing rooms and lockers
18.1.1. Appropriate changing rooms must be provided for workers if they have to wear special work clothes and where, for reasons of health or propriety, they cannot be expected to change in another room.
Changing rooms must be easily accessible, be of sufficient capacity and be provided with seating.
18.1.2. Changing rooms must be sufficiently large and have facilities to enable each worker to lock away his clothes during working hours.
If circumstances so require (e.g. dangerous substances, humidity, dirt), lockers for work clothes must be separate from those for ordinary clothes.
18.1.3. Provision must be made for separate changing rooms or separate use of changing rooms for men and women.
18.1.4. If changing rooms are not required under 18.1.1, each worker must be provided with a place to store his clothes.
18.2. Showers and washbasins
18.2.1.Adequate and suitable showers must be provided for workers if required by the nature of the work or for health reasons.
Provision must be made for separate shower rooms or separate use of shower rooms for men and women.
18.2.2. The shower rooms must be sufficiently large to permit each worker to wash without hindrance in conditions of an appropriate standard of hygiene.
The showers must be equipped with hot and cold running water.
18.2.3. Where showers are not required under the first subparagraph of 18.2.1, adequate and suitable washbasins with running water (hot water if necessary) must be provided in the vicinity of the workstations and the changing rooms.
Such washbasins must be separate for, or used separately by, men and women when so required for reasons of propriety.
18.2.4. Where the rooms housing the showers or washbasins are separate from the changing rooms, there must be easy communication between the two.
18.3. Lavatories and washbasins
Separate facilities must be provided in the vicinity of workstations, rest rooms, changing rooms and rooms

housing showers or washbasins, with an adequate number of lavatories and washbasins.
Provision must be made for separate lavatories or separate use of lavatories for men and women.
19. First aid rooms
19.1. One or more first aid rooms must be provided where the size of the premises, type of activity being carried out and frequency of accidents so dictate.
19.2. First aid rooms must be fitted with essential first aid installations and equipment and be easily accessible to stretchers.
They must be signposted in accordance with the national regulations transposing Directive 77/576/EEC into law.
19.3. In addition, first aid equipment must be available in all places where working conditions require it.
This equipment must be suitably marked and easily accessible.
20. Handicapped workers
Workplaces must be organized to take account of handicapped workers, if necessary.
This provision applies in particular to the doors, passageways, staircases, showers, washbasins, lavatories and workstations used or occupied directly by handicapped persons.
21. Outdoor workplaces (special provisions)
21.1. Workstations, traffic routes and other areas or installations outdoors which are used or occupied by the workers in the course of their activity must be organized in such a way that pedestrians and vehicles can circulate safely.
Sections 12, 13 and 14 also apply to main traffic routes on the site of the undertaking (traffic routes leading to fixed workstations), to traffic routes used for the regular maintenance and supervision of the undertaking's installations and to loading bays.
Section 12 is also applicable to outdoor workplaces.
21.2. Workplaces outdoors must be adequately lit by artificial lighting if daylight is not adequate.
21.3. When workers are employed at workstations outdoors, such workstations must as far as possible be arranged so that workers:
(a) are protected against inclement weather conditions and if necessary against falling objects;
(b) are not exposed to harmful noise levels nor to harmful external influences such as gases, vapours or dust;
(c) are able to leave their workstations swiftly in the event of danger or are able to be rapidly assisted;
(d) cannot slip or fall.

ANNEX II
MINIMUM HEALTH AND SAFETY REQUIREMENTS FOR WORKPLACES ALREADY IN USE, AS REFERRED TO IN ARTICLE 4 OF THE DIRECTIVE

1.Preliminary note
The obligations laid down in this Annex apply wherever required by the features of the workplace, the activity, the circumstances or a hazard.
2. Stability and solidity
Buildings which have workplaces must have a structure and solidity appropriate to the nature of their use.
3. Electrical installations
Electrical installations must be designed and constructed so as not to present a fire or explosion hazard; persons must be adequately protected against the risk of accidents caused by direct or indirect contact.
Electrical installations and protection devices must be appropriate to the voltage, external conditions and the competence of persons with access to parts of the installation.
4. Emergency routes and exits
4.1. Emergency routes and exits must remain clear and lead as directly as possible to the open air or to a safe area.
4.2. In the event of danger, it must be possible for workers to evacuate all workstations quickly and as safely as possible.
4.3. There must be an adequate number of escape routes and emergency exits.
4.4. Emergency exit doors must open outwards.
Sliding or revolving doors are not permitted if they are specifically intended as emergency exits.
Emergency doors should not be so locked or fastened that they cannot be easily and immediately opened by any person who may require to use them in an emergency.
4.5. Specific emergency routes and exits must be indicated by signs in accordance with the national regulations transposing Directive 77/576/EEC into law.
Such signs must be placed at appropriate points and be made to last.
4.6. Emergency doors must not be locked.
The emergency routes and exits, and the traffic routes and doors giving access to them, must be free from

obstruction so that they can be used at any time without hindrance.
4.7. Emergency routes and exits requiring illumination must be provided with emergency lighting of adequate intensity in case the lighting fails.
5. Fire detection and fire fighting
5.1. Depending on the dimensions and use of the buildings, the equipment they contain, the physical and chemical characteristics of the substances present and the maximum potential number of people present, workplaces must be equipped with appropriate fire-fighting equipment, and, as necessary, fire detectors and an alarm system.
5.2. Non-automatic fire-fighting equipment must be easily accessible and simple to use.
It must be indicated by signs in accordance with the national regulations transposing Directive 77/576/EEC into law.
Such signs must be placed at appropriate points and be made to last.
6. Ventilation of enclosed workplaces
Steps shall be taken to see to it that there is sufficient fresh air in enclosed workplaces, having regard to the working methods used and the physical demands placed on the workers.
If a forced ventilation system is used, it shall be maintained in working order.
Any breakdown must be indicated by a control system where this is necessary for the workers' health.
7. Room temperature
7.1. During working hours, the temperature in rooms containing workplaces must be adequate for human beings, having regard to the working methods being used and the physical demands placed on the workers.
7.2. The temperature in rest areas, rooms for duty staff, sanitary facilities, canteens and first aid rooms must be appropriate to the particular purpose of such areas.
8. Natural and artificial room lighting
8.1. Workplaces must as far as possible receive sufficient natural light and be equipped with artificial lighting adequate for workers' safety and health.
8.2. Workplaces in which workers are especially exposed to risks in the event of failure of artificial lighting must be provided with emergency lighting of adequate intensity.
9. Doors and gates
9.1. Transparent doors must be appropriately marked at a conspicuous level.
9.2. Swing doors and gates must be transparent or have see-through panels.
10. Danger areas
If the workplaces contain danger areas in which, owing to the nature of the work, there is a risk of the worker or objects falling, the places must be equipped, as far as possible, with devices preventing unauthorized workers from entering those areas.
Appropriate measures must be taken to protect workers authorized to enter danger areas.
Danger areas must be clearly indicated.
11. Rest rooms and rest areas
11.1. Where the safety or health of workers, in particular because of the type of activity carried out or the presence of more than a certain number of employees, so require, workers must be provided with an easily accessible rest room or appropriate rest area.
This provision does not apply if the workers are employed in offices or similar workrooms providing equivalent relaxation during breaks.
11.2. Rest rooms and rest areas must be equipped with tables and seats with backs.
11.3. In rest rooms and rest areas appropriate measures must be introduced for the protection of non-smokers against discomfort caused by tobacco smoke.
12. Pregnant women and nursing mothers
Pregnant women and nursing mothers must be able to lie down to rest in appropriate conditions.
13. Sanitary equipment
13.1. Changing rooms and lockers
13.1.1. Appropriate changing rooms must be provided for workers if they have to wear special work clothes and where, for reasons of health or propriety, they cannot be expected to change in another room.
Changing rooms must be easily accessible and of sufficient capacity.
13.1.2. Changing rooms must have facilities to enable each worker to lock away his clothes during working hours. If circumstances so require (e.g. dangerous substances, humidity, dirt), lockers for work clothes must be separate from those for ordinary clothes.
13.1.3. Provision must be made for separate changing rooms or separate use of changing rooms for men and women.
13.2. Showers, lavatories and washbasins
13.2.1. Workplaces must be fitted out in such a way that workers have in the vicinity:
- showers, if required by the nature of their work,

- special facilities equipped with an adequate number of lavatories and washbasins.
13.2.2. The showers and washbasins must be equipped with running water (hot water if necessary).
13.2.3. Provision must be made for separate showers or separate use of showers for men and women.
Provision must be made for separate lavatories or separate use of lavatories for men and women.
14. First aid equipment
Workplaces must be fitted with first aid equipment.
The equipment must be suitably marked and easily accessible.
15. Handicapped workers
Workplaces must be organized to take account of handicapped workers, if necessary.
This provision applies in particular to the doors, passageways, staircases, showers, washbasins, lavatories and workstations used or occupied directly by handicapped persons.
16. Movement of pedestrians and vehicles
Outdoor and indoor workplaces must be organized in such a way that pedestrians and vehicles can circulate in a safe manner.
17. Outdoor workplaces (special provisions)
When workers are employed at workstations outdoors, such workstations must as far as possible be organized so that workers:
(a) are protected against inclement weather conditions and if necessay against falling objects;
(b) are not exposed to harmful noise levels nor to harmful external influences such as gases, vapours or dust;
(c) are able to leave their workstations swiftly in the event of danger or are able to be rapidly assisted;
(d) cannot slip or fall.

Annex 9.3.

Council Directive 89/655/EEC of 30 November 1989 concerning the minimum safety and health requirements for **the use of work equipment by workers at work** (second individual Directive within the meaning of Article 16 (1) of Directive 89/391/EEC)
Official Journal L 393 , 30/12/1989 P. 0013 - 0017

MAIN PROVISIONS

Article 1
Subject
1. This Directive, which is the second individual directive within the meaning of Article 16 (1) of Directive 89/391/EEC, lays down minimum safety and health requirements for the use of work equipment by workers at work, as defined in Article 2.
2. The provisions of Directive 89/391/EEC are fully applicable to the whole scope referred to in paragraph 1, without prejudice to more restrictive and/or specific provisions contained in this Directive.

Article 2
Definitions
For the purposes of this Directive, the following terms shall have the following meanings:
(a) 'work equipment': any machine, apparatus, tool or installation used at work;
(b) 'use of work equipment': any activity involving work equipment such as starting or stopping the equipment, its use, transport, repair, modification, maintenance and servicing, including, in particular, cleaning;
(c) 'danger zone': any zone within and/or around work equipment in which an exposed worker is subject to a risk to his health or safety;
(d) 'exposed worker': any worker wholly or partially in a danger zone;
(e) 'operator': the worker or workers given the task of using work equipment.

SECTION II
EMPLOYERS' OBLIGATIONS

Article 3
General obligations
1. The employer shall take the measures necessary to ensure that the work equipment made available to workers in the undertaking and/or establishment is suitable for the work to be carried out or properly adapted for that purpose and may be used by workers without impairment to their safety or health.
In selecting the work equipment which he proposes to use, the employer shall pay attention to the specific working conditions and characteristics and to the hazards which exist in the undertaking and/or establishment, in particular at the workplace, for the safety and health of the workers, and/or any additional hazards posed by the use of work equipment in question.
2. Where it is not possible fully so to ensure that work equipment can be used by workers without risk to their safety or health, the employer shall take appropriate measures to minimize the risks.

Article 4
Rules concerning work equipment
1. Without prejudice to Article 3, the employer must obtain and/or use:
(a) work equipment which, if provided to workers in the undertaking and/or establishment for the first time after 31 December 1992, complies with:
i(i) the provisions of any relevant Community directive which is applicable;
(ii) the minimum requirements laid down in the Annex, to the extent that no other Community directive is applicable or is so only partially;
(b)
work equipment which, if already provided to workers in the undertaking and/or establishment by 31 December 1992, complies with the minimum requirements laid down in the Annex no later than four years after that date.
2. The employer shall take the measures necessary to ensure that, throughout its working life, work equipment is kept, by means of adequate maintenance, at a level such that it complies with the provisions of paragraph 1 (a) or (b) as applicable.

Article 5
Work equipment involving specific risks
When the use of work equipment is likely to involve a specific risk to the safety or health of workers, the employer shall take the measures necessary to ensure that:
- the use of work equipment is restricted to those persons given the task of using it;
- in the case of repairs, modifications, maintenance or servicing, the workers concerned are specifically designated to carry out such work.

Article 6
Informing workers
1. Without prejudice to Article 10 of Directive 89/391/EEC, the employer shall take the measures necessary to ensure that workers have at their disposal adequate information and, where appropriate, written instructions on the work equipment used at work.
2. The information and the written instructions must contain at least adequate safety and health information concerning:
- the conditions of use of work equipment,
- foreseeable abnormal situations,
- the conclusions to be drawn from experience, where appropriate, in using work equipment.
3. The information and the written instructions must be comprehensible to the workers concerned.

Article 7
Training of workers
Without prejudice to Article 12 of Directive 89/391/EEC, the employer shall take the measures necessary to ensure that:
- workers given the task of using work equipment receive adequate training, including training on any risks which such use may entail,
- workers referred to in the second indent of Article 5 receive adequate specific training.

Article 8
Consultation of workers and workers' participation
Consultation and participation of workers and/or of their representatives shall take place in accordance with Article 11 of Directive 89/391/EEC on the matters covered by this Directive, including the Annexes thereto.

SECTION III
MISCELLANEOUS PROVISIONS

Article 9
Amendment to the Annex
1. Addition to the Annex of the supplementary minimum requirements applicable to specific work equipment referred to in point 3 thereof shall be adopted by the Council in accordance with the procedure laid down in Article 118a of the Treaty.
2. Strictly technical adaptations of the Annex as a result of:
- the adoption of directives on technical harmonization and standardization of work equipment, and/or
- technical progress, changes in international regulations or specifications or knowledge in the field of work equipment
shall be adopted, in accordance with the procedure laid down in Article 17 of Directive 89/391/EEC.

Article 10
Final provisions
1. Member States shall bring into force the laws, regulations and administrative provisions necessary to comply with this Directive by 31 December 1992. They shall forthwith inform the Commission thereof.
2. Member States shall communicate to the Commission the texts of the provisions of national law which they have already adopted or adopt in the field governed by this Directive.
3. Member States shall report to the Commission every five years on the practical implementation of the provisions of this Directive, indicating the points of view of employers and workers.
The Commission shall accordingly inform the European Parliament, the Council, the Economic and Social Committee, and the Advisory Committee on Safety, Hygiene and Health Protection at Work.
4. The Commission shall submit periodically to the European Parliament, the Council and the Economic and Social Committee a report on the implementation of this Directive, taking into account paragraphs 1 to 3.

Article 11
This Directive is addressed to the Member States.

Done at Brussels, 30 November 1989.
For the Council
The President
J. P. SOISSON
(1) OJ No C 114, 30. 4. 1988, p. 3, OJ No C 106, 26. 4. 1989, p. 13 and
OJ No C 287, 15. 11. 1989, p. 12.
(2) OJ No C 326, 19. 12. 1988, p. 132 and
OJ No C 256, 9. 10. 1989, p. 65.
(3) OJ No C 318, 12. 12. 1988, p. 26.
(4) OJ No C 28, 3. 2. 1988, p. 3.
(5) OJ No C 28, 3. 2. 1988, p. 1.
(6) OJ No L 183, 29. 6. 1989, p. 1.
(7) OJ No L 109, 26. 4. 1983, p. 8.
(8) OJ No L 185, 9. 7. 1974, p. 15.

ANNEX
MINIMUM REQUIREMENTS REFERRED TO IN ARTICLE 4 (1) (a) (ii) and (b)

1. General comment
The obligations laid down in this Annex apply having regard to the provisions of the Directive and where the corresponding risk exists for the work equipment in question.

2. General minimum requirements applicable to work equipment
2.1. Work equipment control devices which affect safety must be clearly visible and identifiable and appropriately marked where necessary.
Except where necessary for certain control devices, control devices must be located outside danger zones and in such a way that their operation cannot cause additional hazard. They must not give rise to any hazard as a result of any unintentional operation.
If necessary, from the main control position, the operator must be able to ensure that no person is present in the danger zones. If this is impossible, a safe system such as an audible and/or visible warning signal must be given automatically whenever the machinery is about to start. An exposed worker must have the time and/or the means quickly to avoid hazards caused by the starting and/or stopping of the work equipment.
Control systems must be safe. A breakdown in, or damage to, control systems must not result in a dangerous situation.
2.2. It must be possible to start work equipment only by deliberate action on a control provided for the purpose.
The same shall apply:
- to restart it after a stoppage for whatever reason,
- for the control of a significant change in the operating conditions (e.g. speed, pressure, etc.),
unless such a restart or change does not subject exposed workers to any hazard.
This requirement does not apply to restarting or a change in operating conditions as a result of the normal operating cycle of an automatic device.
2.3. All work equipment must be fitted with a control to stop it completely and safely.
Each work station must be fitted with a control to stop some or all of the work equipment, depending on the type of hazard, so that the equipment is in a safe state. The equipment's stop control must have priority over the start controls. When the work equipment or the dangerous parts of it have stopped, the energy supply of the actuators concerned must be switched off.
2.4. Where appropriate, and depending on the hazards the equipment presents and its normal stopping time, work equipment must be fitted with an emergency stop device.
2.5. Work equipment presenting risk due to falling objects or projections must be fitted with appropriate safety devices corresponding to the risk.
Work equipment presenting hazards due to emissions of gas, vapour, liquid or dust must be fitted with appropriate containment and/or extraction devices near the sources of the hazard.
2.6. Work equipment and parts of such equipment must, where necessary for the safety and health of workers, be stabilized by clamping or some other means.
2.7. Where there is a risk of rupture or disintegration of parts of the work equipment, likely to pose significant danger to the safety and health of workers, appropriate protection measures must be taken.
2.8. Where there is a risk of mechanical contact with moving parts of work equipment which could lead to

accidents, those parts must be provided with guards or devices to prevent access to danger zones or to halt movements of dangerous parts before the danger zones are reached.
The guards and protection devices must:
- be of robust construction,
- not give rise to any additional hazard,
- not be easily removed or rendered inoperative,
- be situated at sufficient distance from the danger zone,
- not restrict more than necessary the view of the operating cycle of the equipment,
- allow operations necessary to fit or replace parts and for maintenance work, restricting access only to the area where the work is to be carried out and, if possible, without removal of the guard or protection device.

2.9. Areas and points for working on, or maintenance of, work equipment must be suitably lit in line with the operation to be carried out.

2.10. Work equipment parts at high or very low temperature must, where appropriate, be protected to avoid the risk of workers coming into contact or coming too close.

2.11. Warning devices on work equipment must be unambiguous and easily perceived and understood.

2.12. Work equipment may be used only for operations and under conditions for which it is appropriate.

2.13. It must be possible to carry out maintenance operations when the equipment is shut down. If this is not possible, it must be possible to take appropriate protection measures for the carrying out of such operations or for such operations to be carried out outside the danger zones.
If any machine has a maintenance log, it must be kept up to date.

2.14. All work equipment must be fitted with clearly identifiable means to isolate it from all its energy sources. Reconnection must be presumed to pose no risk to the workers concerned.

2.15. Work equipment must bear the warnings and markings essential to ensure the safety of workers.

2.16. Workers must have safe means of access to, and be able to remain safely in, all the areas necessary for production, adjustment and maintenance operations.

2.17. All work equipment must be appropriate for protecting workers against the risk of the work equipment catching fire or overheating, or of discharges of gas, dust, liquid, vapour or other substances produced, used or stored in the work equipment.

2.18. All work equipment must be appropriate for preventing the risk of explosion of the work equipment or of substances produced, used or stored in the work equipment.

2.19. All work equipment must be appropriate for protecting exposed workers against the risk of direct or indirect contact with electricity.

3. Minimum additional requirements applicable to specific work equipment,
as referred to in Article 9 (1) of the Directive.

Annex 9.4.

Council Directive 89/656/EEC of 30 November 1989 on the minimum health and safety requirements for **the use by workers of personal protective equipment at the workplace** (third individual directive within the meaning of Article 16 (1) of Directive 89/391/EEC)
Official Journal L 393 , 30/12/1989 P. 0018 - 0028

MAIN PROVISIONS

SECTION I
GENERAL PROVISIONS

Article 1
Subject
1. This Directive, which is the third individual directive within the meaning of Article 16 (1) of Directive 89/391/EEC, lays down minimum requirements for personal protective equipment used by workers at work.
2. The provisions of Directive 89/391/EEC are fully applicable to the whole scope referred to in paragraph 1, without prejudice to more restrictive and/or specific provisions contained in this Directive.

Article 2
Definition
1. For the purposes of this Directive, personal protective equipment shall mean all equipment designed to be worn or held by the worker to protect him against one or more hazards likely to endanger his safety and health at work, and any addition or accessory designed to meet this objective.
2. The definition in paragraph 1 excludes:
(a) ordinary working clothes and uniforms not specifically designed to protect the safety and health of the worker;
(b) equipment used by emergency and rescue services;
(c) personal protective equipment worn or used by the military, the police and other public order agencies;
(d) personal protective equipment for means of road transport;
(e) sports equipment;
(f) self-defence or deterrent equipment;
(g) portable devices for detecting and signalling risks and nuisances
.
Article 3
General rule
Personal protective equipment shall be used when the risks cannot be avoided or sufficiently limited by technical means of collective protection or by measures, methods or procedures of work organization.

SECTION II
EMPLOYERS' OBLIGATIONS

Article 4
General provisions
1. Personal protective equipment must comply with the relevant Community provisions on design and manufacture with respect to safety and health.
All personal protective equipment must:
(a) be appropriate for the risks involved, without itself leading to any increased risk;
(b) correspond to existing conditions at the workplace;
(c) take account of ergonomic requirements and the worker's state of health;
(d) fit the wearer correctly after any necessary adjustment.
2. Where the presence of more than one risk makes it necessary for a worker to wear simultaneously more than one item of personal protective equipment, such equipment must be compatible and continue to be effective against the risk or risks in question.
3. The conditions of use of personal protective equipment, in particular the period for which it is worn, shall be determined on the basis of the seriousness of the risk, the frequency of exposure to the risk, the characteristics of the workstation of each worker and the performance of the personal protective equipment.
4. Personal protective equipment is, in principle, intended for personal use.

If the circumstances require personal protective equipment to be worn by more than one person, appropriate measures shall be taken to ensure that such use does not create any health or hygiene problem for the different users.
5. Adequate information on each item of personal protective equipment, required under paragraphs 1 and 2, shall be provided and made available within the undertaking and/or establishment.
6. Personal protective equipment shall be provided free of charge by the employer, who shall ensure its good working order and satisfactory hygienic condition by means of the necessary maintenance, repair and replacements.
However, Member States may provide, in accordance with their national practice, that the worker be asked to contribute towards the cost of certain personal protective equipment in circumstances where use of the equipment is not exclusive to the workplace.
7. The employer shall first inform the worker of the risks against which the wearing of the personal protective equipment protects him.
8. The employer shall arrange for training and shall, if appropriate, organize demonstrations in the wearing of personal protective equipment.
9. Personal protective equipment may be used only for the purposes specified, except in specific and exceptional circumstances.
It must be used in accordance with instructions.
Such instructions must be understandable to the workers.

Article 5
Assessment of personal protective equipment
1. Before choosing personal protective equipment, the employer is required to assess whether the personal protective equipment he intends to use satisfies the requirements of Article 4 (1) and (2).
This assessment shall involve:
(a) an analysis and assessment of risks which cannot be avoided by other means;
(b) the definition of the characteristics which personal protective equipment must have in order to be effective against the risks referred to in (a), taking into account any risks which this equipment itself may create;
(c) comparison of the characteristics of the personal protective equipment available with the characteristics referred to in (b).
2. The assessment provided for in paragraph 1 shall be reviewed if any changes are made to any of its elements.

Article 6
(8) Rules for use
1. Without prejudice to Articles 3, 4 and 5, Member States shall ensure that general rules are established for the use of personal protective equipment and/or rules covering cases and situations where the employer must provide the personal protective equipment, taking account of Community legislation on the free movement of such equipment.
These rules shall indicate in particular the circumstances or the risk situations in which, without prejudice to the priority to be given to collective means of protection, the use of personal protective equipment is necessary.
Annexes I, II and III, which constitute a guide, contain useful information for establishing such rules.
2. When Member States adapt the rules referred to in paragraph 1, they shall take account of any significant changes to the risk, collective means of protection and personal protective equipment brought about by technological developments.
3. Member States shall consult the employers' and workers' organization on the rules referred to in paragraphs 1 and 2.

Article 7
Information for workers
Without prejudice to Article 10 of Directive 89/391/EEC, workers and/or their representatives shall be informed of all measures to be taken with regard to the health and safety of workers when personal protective equipment is used by workers at work.

Article 8
Consultation of workers and workers' participation
Consultation and participation of workers and/or of their representatives shall take place in accordance with Article 11 of Directive 89/391/EEC on the matters covered by this Directive, including the Annexes thereto.

SECTION III
MISCELLANEOUS PROVISIONS

Article 9
Adjustment of the Annexes
Alterations of a strictly technical nature to Annexes I, II and III resulting from:
- the adoption of technical harmonization and standardization directives relating to personal protective equipment, and/or
- technical progress and changes in international regulations and specifications or knowledge in the field of personal protective equipment,
shall be adopted in accordance with the procedure provided for in Article 17 of Directive 89/391/EEC.

Article 10
Final provisions
1. Member States shall bring into force the laws, regulations and administrative provisions necessary to comply with this Directive not later than 31 December 1992. They shall immediately inform the Commission thereof.
2. Member States shall communicate to the Commission the text of the provisions of national law which they adopt, as well as those already adopted, in the field covered by this Directive.
3. Member States shall report to the Commission every five years on the practical implementation of the provisions of this Directive, indicating the points of view of employers and workers.
The Commission shall inform the European Parliament, the Council, the Economic and Social Committee, and the Advisory Committee on Safety, Hygiene and Health Protection at Work.
4. The Commission shall report periodically to the European Parliament, the Council and the Economic and Social Committee on the implementation of the Directive in the light of paragraphs 1, 2 and 3.

Article 11
This Directive is addressed to the Member States.

Done at Brussels, 30 November 1989.
For the Council
The President
J. P. SOISSON
(1) OJ No C 161, 20. 6. 1988, p. 1,
OJ No C 115, 8. 5. 1989, p. 27 and
OJ No C 287, 15. 11. 1989, p. 11.
(2) OJ No C 12, 16. 1. 1989, p. 92 and
OJ No C 256, 9. 10. 1989, p. 61.
(3) OJ No C 318, 12. 12. 1988, p. 30.
(4) OJ No C 28, 3. 2. 1988, p. 3.
(5) OJ No C 28, 3. 2. 1988, p. 1.
(6) OJ No L 183, 29. 6. 1989, p. 1.
(7) OJ No L 185, 9. 7. 1974, p. 15. (8) See the Commission communication (OJ No C 328, 30. 12. 1989, p. 3).

ANNEX I
SPECIMEN RISK SURVEY TABLE FOR THE USE OF PERSONAL PROTECTIVE EQUIPMENT
RISKS
PHYSICAL
CHEMICAL
BIOLOGICAL
MECHANICAL
THERMAL
RADIATION
AEROSOLS
LIQUIDS
Falls from a height
Blows, cuts, impact, crushing
Stabs, cuts, grazes
Vibration
Slipping, falling over
Heat, fire

Cold
ELECTRICAL
Non-ionizing
Ionizing
NOISE
Dust, fibres
Fumes
Vapours
Immersion
Splashes, spurts
GASES, VAPOURS
Harmful bacteria
Harmful viruses
Mycotic fungi
Non-microbe biological antigens
Cranium
Ears
Eyes
Respiratory tract
Face
Whole head
Hands
Arms (parts)
Foot
Legs (parts)
Skin
Trunk/abdomen
Parenteral passages
Whole body

PARTS OF THE BODY
VARIOUS
LOWER
LIMBS
UPPER
LIMBS
HEAD

ANNEX II
NON-EXHAUSTIVE GUIDE LIST OF ITEMS OF PERSONAL PROTECTIVE EQUIPMENT
HEAD PROTECTION

- Protective helmets for use in industry (mines, building sites, other industrial uses).
- Scalp protection (caps, bonnets, hairnets - with or without eye shade).
- Protective headgear (bonnets, caps, sou'westers, etc. in fabric, fabric with proofing, etc.)

HEARING PROTECTION
- Earplugs and similar devices.
- Full acoustic helmets.
- Earmuffs which can be fitted to industrial helmets.
- Ear defenders with receiver for LF induction loop.
- Ear protection with intercom equipment.

EYE AND FACE PROTECTION
- Spectacles.
- Goggles.
- X-ray goggles, laser-beam goggles, ultra-violet, infra-red, visible radiation goggles.
- Face shields.

- Arc-welding masks and helmets (hand masks, headband masks or masks which can be fitted to protective helmets).

RESPIRATORY PROTECTION
- Dust filters, gas filters and radioactive dust filters.
- Insulating appliances with an air supply.
- Respiratory devices including a removable welding mask.
- Diving equipment.
- Diving suits.

HAND AND ARM PROTECTION
- Gloves to provide protection:
- from machinery (piercing, cuts, vibrations, etc.),
- from chemicals,
- for electricians and from heat.
- Mittens.
- Finger stalls.
- Oversleeves.
- Wrist protection for heavy work.
- Fingerless gloves.
- Protective gloves.

FOOT AND LEG PROTECTION
- Low shoes, ankle boots, calf-length boots, safety boots.
- Shoes which can be unlaced or unhooked rapidly.
- Shoes with additional protective toe-cap.
- Shoes and overshoes with heat-resistant soles.
- Heat-resistant shoes, boots and overboots.
- Thermal shoes, boots and overboots.
- Vibration-resistant shoes, boots and overboots.
- Anti-static shoes, boots and overboots.
- Insulating shoes, boots and overboots.
- Protective boots for chain saw operators.
- Clogs.
- Kneepads.
- Removable instep protectors.
- Gaiters.
- Removable soles (heat-proof, pierce-proof or sweat-proof).
- Removable spikes for ice, snow or slippery flooring.

SKIN PROTECTION
- Barrier creams/ointments.

TRUNK AND ABDOMEN PROTECTION
- Protective waistcoats, jackets and aprons to provide protection from machinery (piercing, cutting, molten metal splashes, etc.).
- Protective waistcoats, jackets and aprons to provide protection from chemicals.
- Heated waistcoats.
- Life jackets.
- Protective X-ray aprons.
- Body belts.

WHOLE BODY PROTECTION
- Equipment designed to prevent falls
- Fall-prevention equipment (full equipment with all necessary accessories).
- Braking equipment to absorb kinetic energy (full equipment with all necessary accessories).
- Body-holding devices (safety harness).
- Protective clothing
- 'Safety' working clothing (two-piece and overalls).

- Clothing to provide protection from machinery (piercing, cutting, etc.).
- Clothing to provide protection from chemicals.
- Clothing to provide protection from molten metal splashes and infra-red radiation.
- Heat-resistant clothing.
- Thermal clothing.
- Clothing to provide protection from radioactive contamination.
- Dust-proof clothing.
- Gas-proof clothing.
- Fluorescent signalling, retro-reflecting clothing and accessories (armbands,gloves, etc.).
- Protective coverings.

ANNEX III
NON-EXHAUSTIVE GUIDE LIST OF ACTIVITIES AND SECTORS OF ACTIVITY WHICH MAY REQUIRE THE PROVISION OF PERSONAL PROTECTIVE EQUIPMENT

1. HEAD PROTECTION (SKULL PROTECTION)
Protective helmets
- Building work, particularly work on, underneath or in the vicinity of scaffolding and elevated workplaces, erection and stripping of formwork, assembly and installation work, work on scaffolding and demolition work.
- Work on steel bridges, steel building construction, masts, towers, steel hydraulic structures, blast furnaces, steel works and rolling mills, large containers, large pipelines, boiler plants and power stations.
- Work in pits, trenches, shafts and tunnels.
- Earth and rock works.
- Work in underground workings, quarries, open diggings, coal stock removal.
- Work with bolt-driving tools.
- Blasting work.
- Work in the vicinity of lifts, lifting gear, cranes and conveyors.
- Work with blast furnaces, direct reduction plants, steelworks, rolling mills, metalworks, forging, drop forging and casting.
- Work with industrial furnaces, containers, machinery, silos, bunkers and pipelines.
- Shipbuilding.
- Railway shunting work.
- Slaughterhouses.

2. FOOT PROTECTION
Safety shoes with puncture-proof soles
- Carcase work, foundation work and roadworks.
- Scaffolding work.
- The demolition of carcase work.
- Work with concrete and prefabricated parts involving formwork erection and stripping.
- Work in contractors' yards and warehouses.
- Roof work.

Safety shoes without pierce-proof soles
- Work on steel bridges, steel building construction, masts, towers, lifts, steel hydraulic structures, blast furnaces, steelworks and rolling mills, large containers, large pipelines, cranes, boiler plants and power stations.
- Furnace construction, heating and ventilation installation and metal assembly work.
- Conversion and maintenance work.
- Work with blast furnaces, direct reduction plants, steelworks, rolling mills, metalworks, forging, drop forging, hot pressing and drawing plants.
- Work in quarries and open diggings, coal stock removal.
- Working and processing of rock.
- Flat glass products and container glassware manufacture, working and processing.
- Work with moulds in the ceramics industry.
- Lining of kilns in the ceramics industry.
- Moulding work in the ceramic ware and building materials industry.
- Transport and storage.
- Work with frozen meat blocks and preserved foods packaging.
- Shipbuilding.
- Railway shunting work.

Safety shoes with heels or wedges and pierce-proof soles

- Roof work.

Protective shoes with insulated soles

- Work with and on very hot or very cold materials.

Safety shoes which can easily be removed

- Where there is a risk of penetration by molten substances.

3. EYE OR FACE PROTECTION

Protective goggles, face shields or screens

- Welding, grinding and separating work.
- Caulking and chiselling.
- Rock working and processing.
- Work with bolt-driving tools.
- Work on stock removing machines for small chippings.
- Drop forging.
- The removal and breaking up of fragments.
- Spraying of abrasive substances.
- Work with acids and caustic solutions, disinfectants and corrosive cleaning products.
- Work with liquid sprays.
- Work with and in the vicinity of molten substances.
- Work with radiant heat.
- Work with lasers.

4. RESPIRATORY PROTECTION

Respirators/breathing apparatus

- Work in containers, restricted areas and gas-fired industrial furnaces where there may be gas or insufficient oxygen.
- Work in the vicinity of the blast furnace charge.
- Work in the vicinity of gas converters and blast furnace gas pipes.
- Work in the vicinity of blast furnace taps where there may be heavy metal fumes.
- Work on the lining of furnaces and ladles where there may be dust.
- Spray painting where dedusting is inadequate.
- Work in shafts, sewers and other underground areas connected with sewage.
- Work in refrigeration plants where there is a danger that the refrigerant may escape.

5. HEARING PROTECTION

Ear protectors

- Work with metal presses.
- Work with pneumatic drills.
- The work of ground staff at airports.
- Pile-driving work.
- Wood and textile working.

6. BODY, ARM AND HAND PROTECTION

Protective clothing

- Work with acids and caustic solutions, disinfectants and corrosive cleaning substances.
- Work with or in the vicinity of hot materials and where the effects of heat are felt.
- Work on flat glass products.
- Shot blasting.
- Work in deep-freeze rooms.

Fire-resistant protective clothing

- Welding in restricted areas.

Pierce-proof aprons

- Boning and cutting work.
- Work with hand knives involving drawing the knife towards the body.

Leather aprons

- Welding.
- Forging.
- Casting.

Forearm protection

- Boning and cutting.

Gloves
- Welding.
- Handling of sharp-edged objects, other than machines where there is a danger of the glove's being caught.
- Unprotected work with acids and caustic solutions.

Metal mesh gloves
- Boning and cutting.
- Regular cutting using a hand knife for production and slaughtering.
- Changing the knives of cutting machines.

7. WEATHERPROOF CLOTHING
- Work in the open air in rain and cold weather.

8. REFLECTIVE CLOTHING
- Work where the workers must be clearly visible.

9. SAFETY HARNESSES
- Work on scaffolding.
- Assembly of prefabricated parts.
- Work on masts.

10. SAFETY ROPES
- Work in high crane cabs.
- Work in high cabs of warehouse stacking and retrieval equipment.
- Work in high sections of drilling towers.
- Work in shafts and sewers.

11. SKIN PROTECTION
- Processing of coating materials.
- Tanning.

Annex 9.5.

Council Directive 90/269/EEC of 29 May 1990 on the minimum **health and safety requirements for the manual handling of loads** where there is a risk particularly of back injury to workers (fourth individual Directive within the meaning of Article 16 (1) of Directive 89/391/EEC)

Official Journal L 156 , 21/06/1990 P. 0009 - 0013

MAIN PROVISIONS

SECTION I
GENERAL PROVISIONS

Article 1
Subject
1. This Directive, which is the fourth individual Directive within the meaning of Article 16 (1) of Directive 89/391/EEC, lays down minimum health and safety requirements for the manual handling of loads where there is a risk particularly of back injury to workers.
2. The provisions of Directive 89/391/EEC shall be fully applicable to the whole sphere referred to in paragraph 1, without prejudice to more restrictive and/or specific provisions contained in this Directive.

Article 2
Definition
For the purposes of this Directives, 'manual handling of loads' means any transporting or supporting of a load, by one or more workers, including lifting, putting down, pushing, pulling, carrying or moving of a load, which, by reason of its characteristics or of unfavourable ergonomic conditions, involves a risk particularly of back injury to workers.

SECTION II
EMPLOYERS' OBLIGATIONS

Article 3
General provision
1. The employer shall take appropriate organizational measures, or shall use the appropriate means, in particular mechanical equipment, in order to avoid the need for the manual handling of loads by workers.
2. Where the need for the manual handling of loads by workers cannot be avoided, the employer shall take the appropriate organizational measures, use the appropriate means or provide workers with such means in order to reduce the risk involved in the manual handling of such loads, having regard to Annex I.

Article 4
Organization of workstations
Wherever the need for manual handling of loads by workers cannot be avoided, the employer shall organize workstations in such a way as to make such handling as safe and healthy as possible and:
(a) assess, in advance if possible, the health and safety conditions of the type of work involved, and in particular examine the characteristics of loads, taking account of Annex I;
(b) take care to avoid or reduce the risk particularly of back injury to workers, by taking appropriate measures, considering in particular the characteristics of the working environment and the requirements of the activity, taking account of Annex I.

Article 5
Reference to Annex II
For the implementation of Article 6 (3) (b) and Articles 14 and 15 of Directive 89/391/EEC, account should be taken of Annex II.

Article 6
Information for, and training of, workers
1. Without prejudice to Article 10 of Directive 89/391/EEC, workers and/or their representatives shall be informed of all measures to be implemented, pursuant to this Directive, with regard to the protection of safety and of health.

Employers must ensure that workers and/or their representatives receive general indications and, where possible, precise information on:
- the weight of a load,
- the centre of gravity of the heaviest side when a package is eccentrically loaded.
2. Without prejudice to Article 12 of Directive 83/391/EEC, employers must ensure that workers receive in addition proper training and information on how to handle loads correctly and the risks they might be open to particularly if these tasks are not performed correctly, having regard to Annexes I and II.

Article 7
Consultation of workers and workers' participation
Consultation and participation of workers and/or of their representatives shall take place in accordance with Article 11 of Directive 89/391/EEC on matters covered by this Directive, including the Annexes thereto.

SECTION III
MISCELLANEOUS PROVISIONS

Article 8
Adjustment of the Annexes
Alterations of a strictly technical nature to Annexes I and II resulting from technical progress and changes in international regulations and specifications or knowledge in the field of the manual handling of loads shall be adopted in accordance with the procedure provided for in Article 17 of Directive 89/391/EEC.

Article 9
Final provisions
1. Member States shall bring into force the laws, regulations and administrative provisions needed to comply with this Directive not later than 31 December 1992.
They shall forthwith inform the Commission thereof.
2. Member States shall communicate to the Commission the text of the provisions of national law which they adopt, or have adopted, in the field covered by this Directive.
3. Member States shall report to the Commission every four years on the practical implementation of the provisions of this Directive, indicating the points of view of employers and workers.
The Commission shall inform the European Parliament, the Council, the Economic and Social Committee and the Advisory Committee on Safety, Hygiene and Health Protection at Work thereof.
4. The Commission shall report periodically to the European Parliament, the Council and the Economic and Social Committee on the implementation of the Directive in the light of paragraphs 1, 2 and 3.

Article 10
This Directive is addressed to the Member States.

Done at Brussels, 29 May 1990.
For the Council
The President
B. AHERN

(1) OJ No C 117, 4. 5. 1988, p. 8.
(2) OJ No C 326, 19. 12. 1988, p. 137 and OJ No C 96, 17. 4. 1990, p. 82.
(3) OJ No C 318, 12. 12. 1988, p. 37.
(4) OJ No C 28, 3. 2. 1988, p. 3.
(5) OJ No C 28, 3. 2. 1988, p. 1.(6) OJ No L 183, 29. 6. 1983, p. 1.
(7) OJ No L 185, 9. 7. 1974, p. 15.

ANNEX I
(*) REFERENCE FACTORS (Article 3 (2), Article 4 (a) and (b) and Article 6 (2))

1. Characteristics of the load
The manual handling of a load may present a risk particularly of back injury if it is:
- too heavy or too large,
- unwieldy or difficult to grasp,

- unstable or has contents likely to shift,
- positioned in a manner requiring it to be held or manipulated at a distance from the trunk, or with a bending or twisting of the trunk,
- likely, because of its contours and/or consistency, to result in injury to workers, particularly in the event of a collision.

2. Physical effort required
A physical effort may present a risk particularly of back injury if it is:
- too strenuous,
- only achieved by a twisting movement of the trunk,
- likely to result in a sudden movement of the load,
- made with the body in an unstable posture.

3. Characteristics of the working environment
The characteristics of the work environment may increase a risk particularly of back injury if:
- there is not enough room, in particular vertically, to carry out the activity,
- the floor is uneven, thus presenting tripping hazards, or is slippery in relation to the worker's footwear,
- the place of work or the working environment prevents the handling of loads at a safe height or with good posture by the worker,
- there are variations in the level of the floor or the working surface, requiring the load to be manipulated on different levels,
- the floor or foot rest is unstable,
- the temperature, humidity or ventilation is unsuitable.

4. Requirements of the activity
The activity may present a risk particularly of back injury if it entails one or more of the following requirements:
- over-frequent or over-prolonged physical effort involving in particular the spine,
- an insufficient bodily rest or recovery period,
- excessive lifting, lowering or carrying distances,
- a rate of work imposed by a process which cannot be altered by the worker.
(*) With a view to making a multi-factor analysis, reference may be made simultaneously to the various factors listed in Annexes I and II.

ANNEX II
(*) INDIVIDUAL RISK FACTORS (Articles 5 and 6 (2))

The worker may be at risk if he/she:
- is physically unsuited to carry out the task in question,
- is wearing unsuitable clothing, footwear or other personal effects,
- does not have adequate or appropriate knowledge or training.
(*) With a view to multi-factor analysis, reference may be made simultaneously to the various factors listed in Annexes I and II.

Annex 9.6.

Council Directive 90/270/EEC of 29 May 1990 on the minimum **safety and health requirements for work with display screen equipment** (fifth individual Directive within the meaning of Article 16 (1) of Directive 89/391/EEC)
Official Journal L 156 , 21/06/1990 P. 0014 - 0018

MAIN PROVISIONS

SECTION I
GENERAL PROVISIONS

Article 1
Subject
1. This Directive, which is the fifth individual Directive within the meaning of Article 16 (1) of Directive 89/391/EEC, lays down minimum safety and health requirements for work with display screen equipment as defined in Article 2.
2. The provisions of Directive 89/391/EEC are fully applicable to the whole field referred to in paragraph 1, without prejudice to more stringent and/or specific provisions contained in the present Directive.
3. This Directive shall not apply to:
(a) drivers' cabs or control cabs for vehicles or machinery;
(b)computer systems on board a means of transport;
(c)computer systems mainly intended for public use;
(d)'portable' systems not in prolonged use at a workstation;
(e)calculators, cash registers and any equipment having a small data or measurement display required for direct use of the equipment;
(f)typewriters of traditional design, of the type known as 'typewriter with window'.

Article 2
Definitions
For the purpose of this Directive, the following terms shall have the following meanings:
(a) display screen equipment: an alphanumeric or graphic display screen, regardless of the display process employed;
(b)workstation: an assembly comprising display screen equipment, which may be provided with a keyboard or input device and/or software determining the operator/machine interface, optional accessories, peripherals including the diskette drive, telephone, modem, printer, document holder, work chair and work desk or work surface, and the immediate work environment;
(c)worker: any worker as defined in Article 3 (a) of Directive 89/391/EEC who habitually uses display screen equipment as a significant part of his normal work.

SECTION II
EMPLOYERS' OBLIGATIONS

Article 3
Analysis of workstations
1. Employers shall be obliged to perform an analysis of workstations in order to evaluate the safety and health conditions to which they give rise for their workers, particularly as regards possible risks to eyesight, physical problems and problems of mental stress.
2. Emyployers shall take appropriate measures to remedy the risks found, on the basis of the evaluation referred to in paragraph 1, taking account of the additional and/or combined effects of the risks so found.

Article 4
Workstations put into service for the first time
Employers must take the appropriate steps to ensure that workstations first put into service after 31 December 1992 meet the minimum requirements laid down in the Annex.

Article 5
Workstations already put into service
Employers must take the appropriate steps to ensure that workstations already put into service on or before 31

December 1992 are adapted to comply with the minimum requirements laid down in the Annex not later than four years after that date.

Article 6
Information for, and training of, workers
1. Without prejudice to Article 10 of Directive 89/391/EEC, workers shall receive information on all aspects of safety and health relating to their workstation, in particular information on such measures applicable to workstations as are implemented under Articles 3, 7 and 9.
In all cases, workers or their representatives shall be informed of any health and safety measure taken in compliance with this Directive.
2. Without prejudice to Article 12 of Directive 89/391/EEC, every worker shall also receive training in use of the workstation before commencing this type of work and whenever the organization of the workstation is substantially modified.

Article 7
Daily work routine
The employer must plan the worker's activities in such a way that daily work on a display screen is periodically interrupted by breaks or changes of activity reducing the workload at the display screen.

Article 8
Worker consultation and participation
Consultation and participation of workers and/or their representatives shall take place in accordance with Article 11 of Directive 89/391/EEC on the matters covered by this Directive, including its Annex.

Article 9
Protection of workers' eyes and eyesight
1. Workers shall be entitled to an appropriate eye and eyesight test carried out by a person with the necessary capabilities:
- before commencing display screen work,
- at regular intervals thereafter, and
- if they experience visual difficulties which may be due to display screen work.
2. Workers shall be entitled to an ophthalmological examination if the results of the test referred to in paragraph 1 show that this is necessary.
3. If the results of the test referred to in paragraph 1 or of the examination referred to in paragraph 2 show that it is necessary and if normal corrective appliances cannot be used, workers must be provided with special corrective appliances appropriate for the work concerned.
4. Measures taken pursuant to this Article may in no circumstances involve workes in additional financial cost.
5. Protection of workers' eyes and eyesight may be provided as part of a national health system.

SECTION III
MISCELLANEOUS PROVISIONS

Article 10
Adaptations to the Annex
The strictly technical adaptations to the Annex to take account of technical progress, developments in international regulations and specifications and knowledge in the field of
display screen equipment shall be adopted in accordance with the procedure laid down in Article 17 of Directive 89/391/EEC.

Article 11
Final provisions
1. Member States shall bring into force the laws, regulations and administrative provisions necessary to comply with this Directive by 31 December 1992.
They shall forthwith inform the Commission thereof.
2. Member States shall communicate to the Commission the texts of the provisions of national law which they adopt, or have already adopted, in the field covered by this Directive.
3. Member States shall report to the Commission every four years on the practical implementation of the provisions of this Directive, indicating the points of view of employers and workers.
The Commission shall inform the European Parliament, the Council, the Economic and Social Committee and the Advisory Committee on Safety, Hygiene and Health Protection at Work.

4. The Commission shall submit a report on the implementation of this Directive at regular intervals to the European Parliament, the Council and the Economic and Social Committee, taking into account paragraphs 1, 2 and 3.

Article 12
This Directive is addressed to the Member States.

Done at Brussels, 29 May 1990.
For the Council
The President
B. AHERN

(1) OJ No C 113, 29. 4. 1988, p. 7 and OJ No C 130, 26. 5. 1989, p. 5.
(2) OJ No C 12, 16. 1. 1989, p. 92 and OJ No C 113, 7. 5. 1990.
(3) OJ No C 318, 12. 12. 1988, p. 32.
(4) OJ No C 28, 3. 2. 1988, p. 3.
(5) OJ No C 28, 3. 2. 1988, p. 1.
(6) OJ No L 183, 29. 6. 1989, p. 1.
(7) OJ No L 185, 9. 7. 1974, p. 15.

Annex MINIMUM REQUIREMENTS (Articles 4 and 5)
Preliminary remark

The obligations laid down in this Annex shall apply in order to achieve the objectives of this Directive and to the extent that, firstly, the components concerned are present at the workstation, and secondly, the inherent requirements or characteristics of the task do not preclude it.

1. EQUIPMENT

(a) General comment
The use as such of the equipment must not be a source of risk for workers.
(b) Display screen
The characters on the screen shall be well-defined and clearly formed, of adequate size and with adequate spacing between the characters and lines.
The image on the screen should be stable, with no flickering or other forms of instability.
The brightness and/or the contrast between the characters and the background shall be easily adjustable by the operator, and also be easily adjustable to ambient conditions.
The screen must swivel and tilt easily and freely to suit the needs of the operator.
It shall be possible to use a separate base for the screen or an adjustable table.
The screen shall be free of reflective glare and reflections liable to cause discomfort to the user.
(c)Keyboard
The keyboard shall be tiltable and separate from the screen so as to allow the worker to find a comfortable working position avoiding fatigue in the arms or hands.
The space in front of the keyboard shall be sufficient to provide support for the hands and arms of the operator.
The keyboard shall have a matt surface to avoid reflective glare.
The arrangement of the keyboard and the characteristics of the keys shall be such as to facilitate the use of the keyboard.
The symbols on the keys shall be adequately contrasted and legible from the design working position.
(d) Work desk or work surface
The work desk or work surface shall have a sufficiently large, low-reflectance surface and allow a flexible arrangement of the screen, keyboard, documents and related equipment.
The document holder shall be stable and adjustable and shall be positioned so as to minimize the need for uncomfortable head and eye movements.
There shall be adequate space for workers to find a comfortable position.
(e)Work chair
The work chair shall be stable and allow the operator easy freedom of movement and a comfortable position.
The seat shall be adjustable in height.
The seat back shall be adjustable in both height and tilt.
A footrest shall be made available to any one who wishes for one

2. ENVIRONMENT

(a) Space requirements
The workstation shall be dimensioned and designed so as to provide sufficient space for the user to change position and vary movements.
(b) Lighting
Room lighting and/or spot lighting (work lamps) shall ensure satisfactory lighting conditions and an appropriate contrast between the screen and the background environment, taking into account the type of work and the user's vision requirements.
Possible disturbing glare and reflections on the screen or other equipment shall be prevented by coordinating workplace and workstation layout with the positioning and technical characteristics of the artificial light sources.
(c) Reflections and glare
Workstations shall be so designed that sources of light, such as windows and other openings, transparent or translucid walls, and brightly coloured fixtures or walls cause no direct glare and, as far as possible, no reflections on the screen.
Windows shall be fitted with a suitable system of adjustable covering to attenuate the daylight that falls on the workstation.
(d) Noise
Noise emitted by equipment belonging to workstation(s) shall be taken into account when a workstation is being equipped, in particular so as not to distract attention or disturb speech.
(e) Heat
Equipment belonging to workstation(s) shall not produce excess heat which could cause discomfort to workers.
(f) Radiation
All radiation with the exception of the visible part of the electromagnetic spectrum shall be reduced to negligible levels from the point of view of the protection of workers' safety and health.
(g) Humidity
An adequate level of humidity shall be established and maintained.

3. OPERATOR/COMPUTER INTERFACE

In designing, selecting, commissioning and modifying software, and in designing tasks using display screen equipment, the employer shall take into account the following principles:
(a) software must be suitable for the task;
(b) software must be easy to use and, where appropriate, adaptable to the operator's level of knowledge or experience; no quantitative or qualitative checking facility may be used without the knowledge of the workers;
(c) systems must provide feedback to workers on their performance;
(d) systems must display information in a format and at a pace which are adapted to operators;
(e) the principles of software ergonomics must be applied, in particular to human data processing.

Annex 9.7.

Council Directive 90/394/EEC of 28 June 1990 on the protection of workers from the risks related to **exposure to carcinogens at work** (Sixth individual Directive within the meaning of Article 16 (1) of Directive 89/391/EEC)
Official Journal L 196 , 26/07/1990 P. 0001 - 0007.

MAIN PROVISIONS

Article 1
Objective
1. This Directive, which is the sixth individual Directive within the meaning of Article 16 (1) of Directive 89/391/EEC, has as its aim the protection of workers against risks to their health and safety, including the prevention of such risks, arising or likely to arise from exposure to carcinogens at work.
It lays down particular minimum requirements in this area, including limit values.
2. This Directive shall not apply to workers exposed only to radiation covered by the Treaty establishing the European Atomic Energy Community.
3. Directive 89/391/EEC shall apply fully to the whole area referred to in paragraph 1, without prejudice to more stringent and/or specific provisions contained in this Directive.

Article 2
Definition
For the purposes of this Directive, 'carcinogen' means:
(a) a substance to which, in Annex I to Directive 67/548/EEC, the risk-phrase R 45 'may cause cancer' is applied;
(b) a preparation which, under Article 3 (5) (j) of Directive 88/379/EEC, must be labelled as R 45 'may cause cancer';
(c) a substance, a preparation or a process referred to in Annex I as well as a substance or preparation released by a process referred to in Annex I.

Article 3
Scope - determination and assessment of risks
1. This Directive shall apply to activities in which workers are or are likely to be exposed to carcinogens as a result of their work.
2. In the case of any activity likely to involve a risk of exposure to carcinogens, the nature, degree and duration of workers' exposure must be determined in order to make it possible to assess any risk to the workers' health or safety and to lay down the measures to be taken.
The assessment must be renewed regularly and in any event when any change occurs in the conditions which may affect workers' exposure to carcinogens.
The employer must supply the authorities responsible at
their request with the information used for making the assessment.
3. Furthermore, when assessing the risk, account shall be taken of all other cases of major exposure, such as those with harmful effects on the skin.
4. When the assessment referred to in paragraph 2 is carried out, employers shall give particular attention to any effects concerning the health or safety of workers at
particular risk and shall, inter alia, take account of the desirability of not employing such workers in areas where they may come into contact with carcinogens.

SECTION II
EMPLOYERS' OBLIGATIONS

Article 4
Reduction and replacement
1. The employer shall reduce the use of a carcinogen at the place of work, in particular by replacing it, in so far as is technically possible, by a substance, preparation or process which, under its conditions of use, is not dangerous or is less dangerous to workers' health or safety, as the case may be.
2. The employer shall, upon request, submit the findings of his investigations to the relevant authorities.

Article 5
Prevention and reduction of exposure
1. Where the results of the assessment referred to in Article 3 (2) reveal a risk to workers' health or safety, workers' exposure must be prevented.
2. Where it is not technically possible to replace the carcinogen by a substance, preparation or process which, under its conditions of use, is not dangerous or is less dangerous to health or safety, the employer shall ensure that the carcinogen is, in so far as is technically possible, manufactured and used in a closed system.
3. Where a closed system is not technically possible, the employer shall ensure that the level of exposure of workers is reduced to as low a level as is technically possible.
4. Wherever a carcinogen is used, the employer shall apply all the following measures:
(a) limitation of the quantities of a carcinogen at the place of work;
(b) keeping as low as possible the number of workers exposed or likely to be exposed;
(c) design of work processes and engineering control measures so as to avoid or minimize the release of carcinogens into the place of work;
(d) evacuation of carcinogens at source, local extraction system or general ventilation, all such methods to be appropriate and compatible with the need to protect public health and the environment;
(e) use of existing appropriate procedures for the measurement of carcinogens, in particular for the early detection of abnormal exposures resulting from an unforeseeable event or an accident;
(f) application of suitable working procedures and methods;
(g) collective protection measures and/or, where exposure cannot be avoided by other means, individual protection measures;
(h) hygiene measures, in particular regular cleaning of floors, walls and other surfaces;
(i) information for workers;
(j) demarcation of risk areas and use of adequate warning and safety signs including 'no smoking' signs in areas where workers are exposed or likely to be exposed to carcinogens;
(k) drawing up plans to deal with emergencies likely to result in abnormally high exposure;
(l) means for safe storage, handling and transportation, in particular by using sealed and clearly and visibly labelled containers;
(m) means for safe collection, storage and disposal of waste by workers, including the use of sealed and clearly and visibly labelled containers.

Article 6
Information for the competent authority
Where the results of the assessment referred to in Article 3 (2) reveal a risk to workers' health or safety, employers shall, when requested, make available to the competent authority appropriate information on:
(a) the activities and/or industrial processes carried out, including the reasons for which carcinogens are used;
(b) the quantities of substances or preparations manufactured or used which contain carcinogens;
(c) the number of workers exposed;
(d) the preventive measures taken;
(e) the type of protective equipment used;
(f) the nature and degree of exposure;
(g) the cases of replacement.

Article 7
Unforeseen exposure
1. In the event of an unforeseeable event or an accident which is likely to result in an abnormal exposure of workers, the employer shall inform the workers thereof.
2. Until the situation has been restored to normal and the causes of the abnormal exposure have been eliminated:
(a) only those workers who are essential to the carrying out of repairs and other necessary work shall be permitted to work in the affected area;
(b) the workers concerned shall be provided with protective clothing and individual respiratory protection equipment which they must wear; the exposure may not be permanent and shall be kept to the strict minimum of time necessary for each worker;
(c) unprotected workers shall not be allowed to work in the affected area.

Article 8
Foreseeable exposure
1. For certain activities such as maintenance, in respect of which it is foreseeable that there is the potential for a significant increase in exposure of workers, and in respect of which all scope for further technical preventive measures for limiting workers' exposure has already been exhausted, the employer shall determine, after

consultation of the workers and/or their representatives in the undertaking or establishment, without prejudice to the employer's responsibility, the measures necessary to reduce the duration of workers' exposure to the minimum possible and to ensure protection of workers while they are engaged in such activities.
Pursuant to the first subparagraph, the workers concerned shall be provided with protective clothing and individual respiratory protection equipment which they must wear as long as the abnormal exposure persists; that exposure may not be permanent and shall be kept to the strict minimum of time necessary for each worker.
2. Appropriate measures shall be taken to ensure that the areas in which the activities referred to in the first subparagraph of paragraph 1 take place are clearly demarcated and indicated or that unauthorized persons are prevented by other means from having access to such areas.

Article 9
Access to risk areas
Appropriate measures shall be taken by employers to ensure that access to areas in which the activities in respect of which the results of the assessment referred to in Article 3 (2) reveal
a risk to workers' safety or health take place are accessible solely to workers who, by reason of their work or duties, are required to enter them.

Article 10
Hygiene and individual protection
1. Employers shall be obliged, in the case of all activities for which there is a risk of contamination by carcinogens, to take appropriate measures to ensure that:
(a) workers do not eat, drink or smoke in working areas where there is a risk of contamination by carcinogens;
(b) workers are provided with appropriate protective clothing or other appropriate special clothing;
separate storage places are provided for working or protective clothing and for street clothes;
(c) workers are provided with appropriate and adequate washing and toilet facilities;
(d) protective equipment is properly stored in a well-defined place;
it is checked and cleaned if possible before, and in any case after, each use;
defective equipment is repaired or replaced before further use.
2. Workers may not be charged for the cost of these measures.

Article 11
Information and training of workers
1. Appropriate measures shall be taken by the employer to ensure that workers and/or workers' representatives in the undertaking or establishment receive sufficient and appropriate training, on the basis of all available information, in particular in the form of information and instructions, concerning:
(a) potential risks to health, including the additional risks due to tobacco consumption;
(b) precautions to be taken to prevent exposure;
(c) hygiene requirements;
(d) wearing and use of protective equipment and clothing;
(e) steps to be taken by workers, including rescue workers, in the case of incidents and to prevent incidents.
The training shall be:
- adapted to take account of new or changed risk, and
- repeated periodically if necessary.
2. Employers shall inform workers of installations and related containers containing carcinogens, ensure that all containers, packages and installations containing carcinogens are labelled clearly and legibly, and display clearly visible warning and hazard signs.

Article 12
Information for workers
Appropriate measures shall be taken to ensure that:
(a) workers and/or any workers' representatives in the undertaking or establishment can check that this Directive is applied or can be involved in its application, in particular with regard to:
i(i) the consequences for workers' safety and health of the selection, wearing and use of protective clothing and equipment, without prejudice to the employer's responsibility for determining the effectiveness of protective clothing and equipment;
(ii) the measures determined by the employer which are referred to in the first subparagraph of Article 8 (1), without prejudice to the employer's responsibility for determining such measures;
(b) workers and/or any workers' representatives in the undertaking or establishment are informed as quickly as possible of abnormal exposures, including those referred to in Article 8, of the causes thereof and of the measures taken or to be taken to rectify the situation;

(c) the employer keeps an up-to-date list of the workers engaged in the activities in respect of which the results of the assessment referred to in Article 3 (2) reveal a risk to workers' health or safety, indicating, if the information is available, the exposure to which they have been subjected;
(d) the doctor and/or the competent authority as well as all other persons who have responsibility for health and safety at work have access to the list referred to in subparagraph (c);
(e) each worker has access to the information on the list which relates to him personally;
(f) workers and/or any workers' representatives in the undertaking or establishment have access to anonymous collective information.

Article 13
Consultation and participation of workers
Consultation and participation of workers and/or their representatives in connection with matters covered by this Directive, including the Annexes hereto, shall take place in accordance with Article 11 of Directive 89/391/EEC.

SECTION III
MISCELLANEOUS PROVISIONS

Article 14
Health surveillance
1. The Member States shall establish, in accordance with national laws and/or practice, arrangements for carrying out relevant health surveillance of workers for whom the results of the assessment referred to in Article 3 (2) reveal a risk to health or safety.
2. The arrangements referred to in paragraph 1 shall be such that each worker shall be able to undergo, if appropriate, relevant health surveillance:
- prior to exposure,
- at regular intervals thereafter.
Those arrangements shall be such that it is directly possible to implement individual and occupational hygiene measures.
3. If a worker is found to be suffering from an abnormality which is suspected to be the result of exposure to carcinogens, the doctor or authority responsible for the health surveillance of workers may require other workers who have been similarly exposed to undergo health surveillance.
In that event, a reassessment of the risk of exposure shall be carried out in accordance with Article 3 (2).
4. In cases where health surveillance is carried out, an individual medical record shall be kept and the doctor or authority responsible for health surveillance shall propose any protective or preventive measures to be taken in respect of any individual workers.
5. Information and advice must be given to workers regarding any health surveillance which they may undergo following the end of exposure.
6. In accordance with national laws and/or practice:
- workers shall have access to the results of the health surveillance which concern them, and
- the workers concerned or the employer may request a review of the results of the health surveillance.
7. Practical recommendations for the health surveillance of workers are given in Annex II.
8. All cases of cancer identified in accordance with national laws and/or practice as resulting from occupational exposure to a carcinogen shall be notified to the competent authority.

Article 15
Record-keeping
1. The list referred to in Article 12 (c) and the medical record referred to in Article 14 (4) shall be kept for at least 40 years following the end of exposure, in accordance with national laws and/or practice.
2. Those documents shall be made available to the responsible authority in cases where the undertaking ceases activity, in accordance with national laws and/or practice.

Article 16
Limit values
1. The Council shall, in accordance with the procedure laid down in Article 118a of the Treaty, set out limit values in Directives on the basis of the available information, including scientific and technical data, in respect of all those carcinogens for which this is possible, and, where necessary, other directly related provisions.
2. Limit values and other directly related provisions shall be set out in Annex III.

Article 17
Annexes
1. Annexes I and III may be amended in accordance only with the procedure laid down in Article 118a of the Treaty.
2. Purely technical adjustments to Annex II in the light of technical progress, changes in international regulations or
specifications and new findings in the field of carcinogens shall be adopted in accordance with the procedure laid down in Article 17 of Directive 89/391/EEC.

Article 18
Use of data
The Commission shall have access to the use made by the competent national authorities of the information referred to in Article 14 (8).

Article 19
Final provisions
1. Member States shall bring into force the laws, regulations and administrative provisions necessary to comply with this Directive not later than 31 December 1992.
Should Directives 67/548/EEC or 88/379/EEC be amended by amending Directives after notification of this Directive with respect to the substances and preparations referred to in Article 2 (a) and (b), Member States shall bring into force the laws, regulations and administrative provisions necessary to introduce the amendments in question into the provisions referred to in the first subparagraph by the deadlines laid down for implementation of such amending Directives.
Member States shall forthwith inform the Commission that the provisions referred to in this paragraph have been brought into force.
2. Member States shall communicate to the Commission the provisions of national law already adopted or which they adopt in the future in the field governed by this Directive.

Article 20
This Directive is addressed to the Member States.

Done at Luxembourg, 28 June 1990.
For the Council
The President
M. GEOGHEGAN-QUINN

(1) OJ No C 34, 8. 2. 1988, p. 9.
(2) OJ No C 158, 26. 6. 1989, p. 121 and OJ No C 149, 18. 6. 1990.
(3) OJ No C 208, 8. 8. 1988, p. 43.
(4) OJ No C 67, 8. 3. 1984, p. 2.(5) OJ No C 28, 3. 2. 1988, p. 1.
(6) OJ No L 183, 29. 6. 1989, p. 1.
(7) OJ No 196, 16. 8. 1967, p. 1.
(8) OJ No L 259, 19. 9. 1988, p. 1.(9) OJ No L 187, 16. 7. 1988, p. 14.
(10) OJ No L 64, 8. 3. 1989, p. 18.
(11) OJ No L 185, 9. 7. 1974, p. 15.

ANNEX I
List of substances, preparations and processes (Article 2 (c))
1. Manufacture of auramine.
2. Work involving exposure to aromatic polycyclic hydrocarbons present in coal soots, tar, pitch, fumes or dust.
3. Work involving exposure to dusts, fumes and sprays produced during the roasting and electro-refining of cupro-nickel mattes.
4. Strong acid process in the manufacture of isopropyl alcohol.

ANNEX II
Practical recommendations for the health surveillance of workers (Article 14 (7))
1. The doctor and/or authority responsible for the health monitoring of workers exposed to carcinogens must be familiar with the exposure conditions or circumstances of each worker.
2. Health monitoring of workers must be carried out in accordance with the principles and practices of occupational medicine; it must include at least the following measures:

- keeping records of a worker's medical and occupational history,
- a personal interview,
- where appropriate, biological monitoring, as well as detection of early and reversible effects.

Further tests may be decided upon for each worker when he is the subject of health monitoring, in the light of the most recent knowledge available to occupational medicine.

Annex 9.8.

Council Directive 92/58/EEC of 24 June 1992 on the minimum requirements for the provision of **safety and/or health signs at work** (ninth individual Directive within the meaning of Article 16 (1) of Directive 89/391/EEC)
Official Journal L 245 , 26/08/1992 P. 0023 - 0042.

MAIN PROVISIONS

Article 1
Object
1. This Directive, which is the ninth individual Directive within the meaning of Article 16 (1) of Directive 89/391/EEC, lays down minimum requirements for the provision of safety and/or health signs at work.
2. This Directive shall not apply to signs for the placing on the market of dangerous substances and preparations, products and/or equipment, unless other Community provisions make specific reference thereto.
3. This Directive shall not apply to signs used for regulating road, rail, inland waterway, sea or air transport.
4. The provisions of Directive 89/391/EEC shall apply in full to the whole area referred to in paragraph 1, without prejudice to more stringent and/or specific provisions in this Directive.

Article 2
Definitions
For the purposes of this Directive:
(a) safety and/or health signs means signs referring to a specific object, activity or situation and providing information or instructions about safety and/or health at work by means of a signboard, a colour, an illuminated sign or acoustic signal, a verbal communication or a hand signal, as the case may be;
(b) prohibition sign means a sign prohibiting behaviour likely to incur or cause danger;
(c) warning sign means a sign giving warning of a hazard or danger;
(d) mandatory sign means a sign prescribing specific behaviour;
(e) emergency escape or first-aid sign means a sign giving information on emergency exits or first-aid or rescue facilities;
(f) information sign means a sign providing information other than that referred to in (b) to (e);
(g) signboard means a sign which provides specific information by a combination of a geometric shape, colours and a symbol or pictogram and which is rendered visible by lighting of sufficient intensity;
(h) supplementary signboard means a signboard used together with one of the signs described under (g), which provides supplementary information;
(i) safety colour means a colour to which a specific meaning is assigned;
(j) Symbol or pictogram means a figure which describes a situation or prescribes specific behaviour and which is used on a signboard or illuminated surface;
(k) illuminated sign means a sign produced by a device made of transparent or translucent materials which are illuminated from the inside or the rear in such a way as to give the appearance of a luminous surface;
(l) acoustic signal means a coded sound signal which is released and transmitted by a device designed for that purpose, without the use of a human or artificial voice;
(m) verbal communication means a predetermined spoken message communicated by a human or artificial voice;
(n) hand signal a movement and/or position of the arms and/or hands, in coded form, for guiding persons who are carrying out manoeuvres which constitute a hazard or danger for workers.

SECTION II EMPLOYERS' OBLIGATIONS
Article 3
General rules
1. Employers shall provide safety and/or health signs as laid down in this Directive where hazards cannot be avoided or adequately reduced by techniques for collective protection or measures, methods or procedures used in the organization of work, or ensure that such signs are in place.
Employers shall take into account any risk evaluation made in accordance with Article 6 (3) (a) of Directive 89/391/EEC.
2. Without prejudice to the provisions of Annex V, the signs used for road, rail, inland waterway, sea and air transport shall be installed, wherever appropriate for such forms of transport, inside undertakings and/or firms.

Article 4
Safety and/or health signs used for the first time
Without prejudice to Article 6, a safety and/or health sign used at work for the first time on or after the date referred to in Article 11 (1) first subparagraph must fulfil the minimum requirements set out in Annexes I to IX.

Article 5
Safety and/or health signs already in use
Without prejudice to Article 6, a safety and/or health sign which was already in use at work before the date referred to in Article 11 (1) first subparagraph must fulfil the minimum requirements set out in Annexes I to IX by no later than eighteen months after that date.

Article 6
Exemptions
1. Taking account of the types of activity and/or size of the undertakings concerned, Member States may specify categories of undertakings allowed to replace totally, partially or temporarily the illuminated signs, and/or acoustic signals provided for in this Directive by alternative measures which afford the same level of protection.
2. Member States may derogate, after consulting both sides of industry, from the application of Annex VIII, section 2 and/or Annex IX, section 3, whilst laying down alternative measures guaranteeing the same level of protection.
3. Member States shall consult, in accordance with national laws and/or practice, employers' and workers' organizations when implementing paragraph 1.

Article 7
Information and instruction for workers
1. Without prejudice to Article 10 of Directive 89/391/EEC, workers and/or their representatives shall be informed of all the measures to be taken concerning the safety and/or health signs used at work.
2. Without prejudice to Article 12 of Directive 89/391/EEC, workers must be given suitable instruction, in particular in the form of specific directions concerning the safety and/or health signs used at work.
In particular, the instruction referred to in the first subparagraph shall cover the meaning of the signs, especially signs incorporating words, and the general and specific behaviour to be adopted.

Article 8
Consultation of workers and workers' participation
Consultation and participation of workers and/or their representatives shall take place in accordance with Article 11 of Directive 89/391/EEC on the matters covered by this Directive, including Annexes I to IX.

SECTION III MISCELLANEOUS PROVISIONS

Article 9
Adaptation of the Annexes
Adaptations of a technical nature to Annexes I to IX shall be adopted, in accordance with the procedure provided for in Article 17 of Directive 89/391/EEC, in the light of:
- the adoption of directives on technical harmonization and standardisation concerning the design and manufacture of safety and/or health signs or devices at work,
- technical progress, changes in international rules or specifications and advances in knowledge in the field of safety and/or health signs at work.

Article 10
1. Directive 77/576/EEC shall be repealed on the date referred to in Article 11 (1), first subparagraph. However, in the cases referred to in Article 5, that Directive shall continue to apply for a maximum period of eighteen months following that date.
2. Any reference to the repealed Directive shall be taken to refer to the corresponding provisions of this Directive.

Article 11
Final provisions
1. Member States shall bring into force the laws, regulations and administrative provisions required to comply with this Directive no later than 24 June 1994.
They shall immediately inform the Commission thereof.
2. When Member States adopt these measures they shall contain a reference to this Directive or shall be

accompanied by such reference on the occasion of their official publication. The methods of making such a reference shall be laid down by the Member States.
3. Member States shall communicate to the Commission the text of the provisions of domestic law which they have already adopted or adopt in the field covered by this Directive.
4. Member States shall report to the Commission every five years on the practical implementation of the provisions of this Directive, indicating the views of employers and workers.
The Commission shall inform the European Parliament, the Council, the Economic and Social Committee and the Advisory Committee on Safety, Hygiene and Health at Work thereof.
5. The Commission shall forward periodically to the European Parliament, the Council and the Economic and Social Committee a report on the implementation of this Directive, taking into account paragraphs 1 to 4.

Article 12
This Directive is addressed to the Member States.
Done at Luxembourg, 24 June 1992.
For the Council
The President
José da SILVA PENEDA

(1) OJ No C 53, 28. 2. 1991, p. 46 and OJ No C 279, 26. 10. 1991, p. 13.
(2) OJ No C 240, 16. 9. 1991, p. 102 and OJ No C 150, 15. 6. 1992.
(3) OJ No C 159, 17. 6. 1991, p. 9.
(4) OJ No C 28, 3. 2. 1988, p. 3.
(5) OJ No L 229, 7. 9. 1977, p. 12. Last amended by Commission Directive 79/640/EEC. (OJ No L 183, 19. 7. 1979, p. 11.)
(6) OJ No C 28, 3. 2. 1989, p. 1.
(7) OJ No L 183, 29. 6. 1989, p. 1.
(8) OJ No L 185, 9. 7. 1974, p. 15.

ANNEX I
GENERAL MINIMUM REQUIREMENTS CONCERNING SAFETY AND/OR HEALTH SIGNS AT WORK

1. Preliminary remarks
1.1. Where health and/or safety signs are required by the general rule in Article 3 of the Directive, they must conform to the specific requirements in Annexes II to IX.
1.2. This Annex introduces those requirements, describes the different uses of safety and/or health signs, and gives general rules on the interchanging and combining of signs.
1.3. Health and/or safety signs must be used only to convey the message or information specified in the Directive.

2. Types of signs
2.1. Permanent signs
2.1.1. Permanent signboards must be used for signs relating to prohibitions, warnings and mandatory requirements and the location and identification of emergency escape routes and first-aid facilities.
Signboards and/or a safety colour must be used to mark permanently the location and identification of fire-fighting equipment.
2.1.2. Signboards on containers and pipes must be placed as laid down in Annex III.
2.1.3. Places where there is a risk of colliding with obstacles or of falling must be permanently marked with a safety colour and/or with signboards.
2.1.4. Traffic routes must be permanently marked with a safety colour.
2.2. Occasional signs
2.2.1. Illuminated signs, acoustic signals and/or verbal communication must be used where the occasion requires, taking into account the possibilities for interchanging and combining signs set out in Section 3, to signal danger, to call persons to take a specific course of action and for the emergency evacuation of persons.
2.2.2. Hand signals and/or verbal communication must be used where the occasion requires, to guide persons carrying out hazardous or dangerous manoeuvres.

3. Interchanging and combining signs
3.1. Any one of the following may be used if equally effective:
- a safety colour or a signboard to mark places where there is an obstacle or a drop,
- illuminated signs, acoustic signals or verbal communication,

- hand signals or verbal communication.
3.2. Some types of signs may be used together:
- illuminated signs and acoustic signals,
- illuminated signs and verbal communication,
- hand signals and verbal communication.

4. The instructions in the table below apply to all signs incorporating a safety colour:
Colour
Meaning or purpose
Instructions and information
Red
Prohibition sign
Dangerous behaviour
Danger alarm
Stop, shutdown, emergency cutout devices
Evacuate
Fire-fighting equipment
Identification and location
Yellow
or
Amber
Warning sign
Be careful, take precautions
Examine
Blue
Mandatory sign
Specific behaviour or action
Wear personal protective equipment
Green
Emergency escape, first aid sign
Doors, exits, routes, equipment, facilities
No danger
Return to normal

5. The effectiveness of a sign must not be adversely affected by:
5.1. the presence of another emission source of the same type which interferes with visibility or audibility; therefore, in particular,
5.1.1. the placing of too many signs too close together should be avoided;
5.1.2. two illuminated signs which are likely to be confused are not to be used at the same time;
5.1.3. an illuminated sign is not to be used in the proximity of another similar illuminated source;
5.1.4. two acoustic signals are not to be used at the same time;
5.1.5. an acoustic signal is not be used if there is too much ambient noise;
5.2. poor design, insufficient number, incorrect positioning, poor state of repair or incorrect functioning of the signs or signalling devices.

6. Depending on requirements, signs and signalling devices must be cleaned, maintained, checked, repaired, and if necessary replaced on a regular basis to ensure that they retain their intrinsic and/or functional qualities.
7. The number and positioning of signs or signalling devices to be installed will depend on the extent of the hazards or dangers or on the zone to be covered.
8. Signs requiring some form of power must be provided with a guaranteed emergency supply in the event of a power cut, unless the hazard has thereby been eliminated.
9. The triggering of an illuminated sign and/or acoustic signal indicates when the required action should start, the sign or signal must be activated for as long as the action requires.
Illuminated signs and acoustic signals must be reactivated immediately after use.
10. Illuminated signs and acoustic signals must be checked to ensure that they function correctly and that they are effective before they are put into service and subsequently at sufficiently frequent intervals.
11. If the hearing or the sight of the workers concerned is impaired, including impairment caused by the wearing of personal protective equipment, measures must be taken to supplement or replace the signs concerned.
12. Areas, rooms or enclosures used for the storage of significant quantities of dangerous substances or preparations must be indicated by a suitable warning sign taken from section 3.2. of Annex II, or marked as

provided in section 1 of Annex III, unless the labelling of the individual packages or containers is adequate for this purpose.

ANNEX II
MINIMUM GENERAL REQUIREMENTS CONCERNING SIGNBOARDS

1. Intrinsic features
1.1. The shape and colours of signboards are set out in section 3, in accordance with their specific object (signboards indicating a prohibition, a warning, a mandatory action, an escape route, an emergency or fire-fighting equipment).
1.2. Pictograms must be as simple as possible and should contain only essential details.
1.3. The pictograms used may be slightly different from or more detailed than those shown in section 3, provided that they convey the same meaning and that no difference or adaptation obscures the meaning.
1.4. Signboards are to be made of shock and weather-resistant material suitable for the surrounding environment.
1.5. The dimensions and colorimetric and photometric features of signboards must be such that they can be easily seen and understood.

2. Conditions of use
2.1. Signboards are in principle to be installed at a suitable height and in a position appropriate to the line of sight, taking account of any obstacles, either at the access point to an area in the case of a general hazard, or in the immediate vicinity of a specific hazard or object and in a well-lit and easily accessible and visible location. Without prejudice to the provisions of Directive 89/654/EEC, phosphorescent colours, reflective materials or artificial lighting should be used where the level of natural light is poor.
2.2. The signboard must be removed when the situation to which it refers ceases to exist.

ANNEX III
MINIMUM REQUIREMENTS GOVERNING SIGNS ON CONTAINERS AND PIPES

1. Containers used at work for dangerous substances or preparations defined in Directives 67/548/EEC (1) and 88/379/EEC (2) and containers used for the storage of such dangerous substances or preparations, together with the visible pipes containing or transporting dangerous substances and preparations, must be labelled (pictogram or symbol against a coloured background) in accordance with those Directives.
Paragraph 1 does not apply to containers used at work for brief periods nor to containers whose contents change frequently, provided that alternative adequate measures are taken, in particular for information and/or training, which guarantee the same level of protection.
The labels referred to in paragraph 1 may be:
- replaced by warning signs as provided for in Annex II, using the same pictograms or symbols,
- supplemented by additional information, such as the name and/or formula of the dangerous substance or preparation and details of the hazard,
- for the transporting of containers at the place of work, supplemented or replaced by signs applicable throughout the Community for the transport of dangerous substances or preparations.
2. Signs must be mounted as follows:
- on the visible side(s),
- in unpliable, self-adhesive or painted form.
3. Where appropriate, the signs referred to in section 1 of this Annex must have the intrinsic features defined in section 1.4. of Annex II and must fulfil the conditions of use for signboards laid down in section 2 of Annex II.
4. Without prejudice to sections 1, 2 and 3, the labels used on pipes must be positioned visibly in the vicinity of the most dangerous points, such as valves and joint, and at reasonable intervals.
5. Areas, rooms or enclosures used for the storage of significant quantities of dangerous substances or preparations must be indicated by a suitable warning sign taken from section 3.2 of Annex II, or marked as provided in section 1 of Annex III, unless the labelling of the individual packages or containers is adequate for this purpose, taking into account Annex II, point 1.5 with regard to dimensions.
Stores of a number of dangerous substances or preparations may be indicated by the warning sign for general danger.
The signs or labels referred to above must be positioned, as appropriate, near the storage area or on the door leading into the storage room.
(1) OJ No L 196, 16. 8. 1967, p. 1.
(2) OJ No L 187, 16. 7. 1988, p. 14.

ANNEX IV
MINIMUM REQUIREMENTS FOR THE IDENTIFICATION AND LOCATION OF FIRE-FIGHTING EQUIPMENT

1. Preliminary remark
This Annex applies to equipment used exclusively for fire-fighting purposes.
2. Fire-fighting equipment must be identified by using a specific colour for the equipment and placing a location signboard, and/or by using a specific colour for the places where such equipment is kept, or their access points.
3. The colour for identifying this equipment is red.
The red area must be sufficiently large to allow the equipment to be identified easily.
4. The signboards provided for in section 3.5 of Annex Ii must be used to mark the locations of this equipment.

ANNEX V
MINIMUM REQUIREMENTS GOVERNING SIGNS USED FOR OBSTACLES AND DANGEROUS LOCATIONS, AND FOR MARKING TRAFFIC ROUTES

1. Signs for obstacles and dangerous locations
1.1. Places where there is a risk of colliding with obstacles, of falling or of objects falling should be marked with alternating yellow and black, or red and white stripes in built-up zones in the undertaking to which workers have access during their work.
1.2. The dimensions of the markings must be commensurate with the scale of the obstacle or dangerous location in question.
1.3. The yellow and black or red and white stripes must be at an angle of approximately 45o and of more or less equal size.
1.4. Example:
2. Marking of traffic routes
2.1. Where the use and equipment of rooms so requires for the protection of workers, traffic routes for vehicles must be clearly identified by continuous stripes in a clearly visible colour, preferably white or yellow, taking into account the colour of the ground.
2.2. The stripes must be located so as to indicate the necessary safe distance between the vehicles and any object which may be near by, and between pedestrians and vehicles.
2.3. Permanent traffic routes in built-up areas outdoors should, as far as is practicable, be similarly marked, unless they are provided with suitable barriers or pavements.

ANNEX VI
MINIMUM REQUIREMENTS FOR ILLUMINATED SIGNS

1. Intrinsic features
1.1. The light emitted by a sign must produce a luminous contrast which is appropriate to its environment, in accordance with the intended conditions of use of the sign, but without producing glare for an excessive amount of light or poor visibility as a result of insufficient light.
1.2. The luminous area emitting a sign may be of a single colour or contain a pictogram on a specified background.
1.3. The single colour must correspond to the table of colours and their meanings set out in section 4 of Annex I.
1.4. Likewise, when the sign contains a pictogram, the latter must comply with all the relevant rules set out in Annex II.

2. Specific rules governing use
2.1. If a device can emit both continuous and intermittent signs, the intermittent sign should be used to indicate a higher level of danger or a more urgent need for the requested/imposed intervention or action than is indicated by the continuous sign.
The duration of each flash and the frequency of the flashers of an intermittent illuminated sign must be such as to
- ensure the proper perception of the message, and
- avoid any confusion either between different illuminated signs or with a continuous illuminated sign.
2.2. If a flashing sign is used instead of - or together with - an acoustic signal, identical codes must be used.
2.3. Devices for emitting flashing signs in the event of grave danger must be under special surveillance or be fitted with an auxiliary lamp.

ANNEX VII
MINIMUM REQUIREMENTS FOR ACOUSTIC SIGNS

1. Intrinsic features
1.1. Acoustic signals must:
(a) have a sound level which is considerably higher than the level of ambient noise, so that it is audible without being excessive or painful;
(b) be easily recognizable, particularly in terms of pulse length and the interval between pulses or groups of pulses, and be clearly distinct from any other acoustic signal and ambient noises.
1.2. If a device can emit an acoustic signal at variable and constant frequencies, the variable frequency should be used to indicate a higher level of danger or a more urgent need for the requested/imposed intervention or action in relation to the stable frequency.
2. Code
The signal for evacuation must be continuous.

ANNEX VIII
MINIMUM REQUIREMENTS FOR VERBAL COMMUNICATION

1. Intrinsic features
1.1. Verbal communication between a speaker or emitter and one or more hearers is to take the form of (sometimes coded) short texts, phrases, groups of words and/or individual words.
1.2. Spoken messages are to be as short, simple and clear as possible; the verbal skills of the speaker and the hearing abilities of the hearer(s) must be such as to ensure reliable verbal communication.
1.3. Verbal communication is direct (by means of the human voice) or indirect (by means of a human or artificial voice which is broadcast by whatever means is appropriate).
2. Specific rules governing use
2.1. The persons involved must have a good knowledge of the language used so that they are able to pronounce and understand the spoken message correctly and consequently behave in a way which is appropriate to health and/or safety.
2.2. If verbal communication is used instead of - or together with - gestures, code words should be used such as:
- start
to indicate the start of a command
- stop
to interrupt or end a movement
- end
to stop the operation
raise
to have a load raised
lower
to have a load lowered
- forwards
- backwards
- right
- left

aa
to be coordinated with the corresponding hand signals

- danger
for an emergency stop

- quickly
to speed up a movement for safety reasons.

ANNEX IX
MINIMUM REQUIREMENTS FOR HAND SIGNALS

1. Features
Hand signals must be precise, simple, expansive, easy to make and to understand, and clearly distinct from other such signals.

Where both arms are used at the same time, they must be moved symmetrically and for giving one sign only.
Provided that they fulfil the conditions given above, the signals used may vary slightly from or be more detailed than those shown in section 3; they must, however, be equally meaningful and comprehensible.
2. Specific rules governing use
2.1. The person giving the signs, hereinafter referred to as the 'signalman', will use arm/hand movements to give manoeuvring instructions to the person receiving the signs, hereinafter referred to as the (operator).
2.2. The signalman must be able to monitor all manoeuvres visually without being endangered thereby.
2.3. The signalman's duties must consist exclusively of directing manoeuvres and ensuring the safety of workers in the vicinity.
2.4. If the conditions described in point 2.2 are not fulfilled, one or more extra singnalmen should be deployed.
2.5. The operator must interrupt the ongoing manoeuvre in order to request new instructions when he is unable to carry out the orders he has received with the necessary safety guarantees.
2.6. Accessories:
The operator must be able to recognize the signalman without difficulty.
The signalman is to wear one or more appropriate distinctive items, e.g. a jacket, helmet, sleeves or armbandds, or carry bats.
The distinctive items are to be brightly coloured, preferably all of the same colour and for the exclusive use of signalmen.
3. Coded signals to be used
Preliminary remark:
The following set of coded signals are without prejudice to other codes applicable at Community level, used for the same manoeuvres in certain sectors:

Meaning
Description
Illustration

3. Meaning
Description
Illustration

A. General signals

START
Attention
Start of
command
both arms are extended horizontally with the palms facing forward
STOP
Interruption
End of movement
the right arm points upwards with the palm facing forwards
END
of the operation
both hands are clasped at chest height

B. Vertical movements

RAISE
the right arm points upwards with the palm facing forward and slowly makes a circle
LOWER
the right arm points downwards with the palm facing inwards and slowly makes a circle
VERTICAL DISTANCE
the hands indicate the relevant distance
3. Meaning
Description
Illustration

C. Horizontal Movements
MOVE FORWARDS

both arms are bent with the palms facing upwards, and the forearms make slow movements towards the body
MOVE BACKWARDS
both arms are bent with the palms facing downwards, and the forearms make slow movements away from the body
RIGHT
to the
signalman's
the right arm is extended more or less horizontally with the palm facing downwards and slowly makes small movements to the right
LEFT
to the
signalman's
the left arm is extended more or less horizontally with the palm facing downwards and slowly makes small movements to the left
HORIZONTAL DISTANCE
the hands indicate the relevant distance

3. Meaning
Description
Illustration
D. Danger
DANGER
Emergency stop
both arms point upwards with the palms facing forwards
QUICK
all movements faster
SLOW
all movements slower

Annex 9.9.

Council Directive 98/24/EC of 7 April 1998 on the protection of the health and safety of workers from the **risks related to chemical agents at work** (fourteenth individual Directive within the meaning of Article 16(1) of Directive 89/391/EEC)
Official Journal L 131 , 05/05/1998 P. 0011 - 0023.

MAIN PROVISIONS

Article 1

Objective and scope
1. This Directive, which is the fourteenth individual Directive within the meaning of Article 16(1) of Directive 89/391/EEC, lays down minimum requirements for the protection of workers from risks to their safety and health arising, or likely to arise, from the effects of chemical agents that are present at the workplace or as a result of any work activity involving chemical agents.
2. The requirements of this Directive apply where hazardous chemical agents are present or may be present at the workplace, without prejudice to the provisions for chemical agents to which measures for radiation protection apply pursuant to Directives adopted under the Treaty establishing the European Atomic Energy Community.
3. For carcinogens at work the provisions of this Directive shall apply without prejudice to more stringent and/or specific provisions contained in Council Directive 90/394/EEC of 28 June 1990 on the protection of workers from the risks related to exposure to carcinogens (sixth individual Directive within the meaning of Article 16(1) of Directive 89/391/EEC) (15).
4. The provisions of Directive 89/391/EEC shall apply fully to the whole field referred to in this Article, without prejudice to more stringent and/or specific provisions contained in this Directive.
5. As far as the transport of hazardous chemical agents is concerned, the provisions of this Directive shall apply without prejudice to more stringent and/or specific provisions contained in Directive 94/55/EC (16), in Directive 96/49/EC (17), in the provisions of the IMDG Code, IBC Code and IGC Code as defined in Article 2 of Directive 93/75/EEC (18), in the provisions of the European Agreement concerning the International Carriage of Dangerous Goods by Inland Waterway and of the Regulation for the Carriage of Dangerous Substances on the Rhine as incorporated in Community law and in the technical instructions for the safe transport of dangerous goods issued, at the date of entry into force of this Directive, by the International Civil Aviation Organisation.

Article 2

Definitions
For the purpose of this Directive, the terms used shall have the following meanings:
(a) 'Chemical agent` means any chemical element or compound, on its own or admixed, as it occurs in the natural state or as produced, used or released, including release as waste, by any work activity, whether or not produced intentionally and whether or not placed on the market;
(b) 'Hazardous chemical agent` means:
(i) any chemical agent which meets the criteria for classification as a dangerous substance according to the criteria in Annex VI to Directive 67/548/EEC, whether or not that substance is classified under that Directive, other than those substances which only meet the criteria for classification as dangerous for the environment;
(ii) any chemical agent which meets the criteria for classification as a dangerous preparation within the meaning of Directive 88/379/EEC, whether or not that preparation is classified under that Directive, other than those preparations which only meet the criteria for classification as dangerous for the environment;
(iii) any chemical agent which, whilst not meeting the criteria for classification as dangerous in accordance with (i) and (ii), may, because of its physico-chemical, chemical or toxicological properties and the way it is used or is present in the workplace, present a risk to the safety and health of workers, including any chemical agent assigned an occupational exposure limit value under Article 3.
(c) 'Activity involving chemical agents` means any work in which chemical agents are used, or are intended to be used, in any process, including production, handling, storage, transport or disposal and treatment, or which result from such work;
(d) 'Occupational exposure limit value` means, unless otherwise specified, the limit of the time-weighted average of the concentration of a chemical agent in the air within the breathing zone of a worker in relation to a specified reference period;
(e) 'Biological limit value` means the limit of the concentration in the appropriate biological medium of the

relevant agent, its metabolite, or an indicator of effect;
(f) 'Health surveillance` means the assessment of an individual worker to determine the state of health of that individual, as related to exposure to specific chemical agents at work;
(g) 'Hazard` means the intrinsic property of a chemical agent with the potential to cause harm;
(h) 'Risk` means the likelihood that the potential for harm will be attained under the conditions of use and/or exposure.

Article 3

Occupational exposure limit values and biological limit values
1. The Commission shall evaluate the relationship between the health effects of hazardous chemical agents and the level of occupational exposure by means of an independent scientific assessment of the latest available scientific data.
2. On the basis of the evaluation described in paragraph 1, the Commission, after first consulting the Advisory Committee on Safety, Hygiene and Health protection at Work, shall propose European objectives in the form of indicative occupational exposure limit values for the protection of workers from chemical risks, to be set at Community level.
These limit values shall be established or revised, taking into account the availability of measurement techniques, in accordance with the procedure laid down in Article 17 of Directive 89/391/EEC. Member States shall keep workers' and employers' organisations informed of indicative occupational exposure limit values set at Community level.
3. For any chemical agent for which an indicative occupational exposure limit value is established at Community level, Member States shall establish a national occupational exposure limit value, taking into account the Community limit value, determining its nature in accordance with national legislation and practice.
4. Binding occupational exposure limit values may be drawn up at Community level and, in addition to the factors considered when establishing indicative occupational exposure limit values, shall reflect feasibility factors while maintaining the aim of ensuring the health of workers at work. Such limit values shall be established in accordance with Article 118a of the Treaty and laid down in Annex I to this Directive.
5. For any chemical agent for which a binding occupational exposure limit value is established. Member States shall establish a corresponding national binding occupational exposure limit value based on, but not exceeding, the Community limit value.
6. Binding biological limit values may be drawn up at Community level on the basis of the evaluation described in paragraph 1 and of the availability of measurement techniques, and shall reflect feasibility factors while maintaining the aim of ensuring the health of workers at work. Such limit values shall be established in accordance with the procedure laid down in Article 118a of the Treaty and laid down in Annex II to this Directive, together with other relevant health surveillance information.
7. For any chemical agent for which a binding biological limit value is established, Member States shall establish a corresponding national binding biological limit value based on, but not exceeding, the Community limit value.
8. Where a Member State introduces or revises a national occupational exposure limit value or a national biological limit value for a chemical agent, it shall inform the Commission and other Member States thereof together with the relevant scientific and technical data. The Commission shall undertake the appropriate action.
9. On the basis of the reports provided by the Member States under Article 15, the Commission shall carry out an assessment of the way in which Member States have taken account of Community indicative limit values when establishing the corresponding national occupational exposure limit values.
10. Standardised methods for the measurement and evaluation of workplace air concentrations in relation to occupational exposure limit values shall be developed in accordance with Article 12(2).

SECTION II

EMPLOYERS' OBLIGATIONS

Article 4

Determination and assessment of risk of hazardous chemical agents
1. In carrying out the obligations laid down in Articles 6(3) and 9(1) of Directive 89/391/EEC, the employer shall first determine whether any hazardous chemical agents are present at the workplace. If so, he shall then assess any risk to the safety and health of workers arising from the presence of those chemical agents, taking into consideration the following:
- their hazardous properties,

- information on safety and health that shall be provided by the supplier, (e.g. the relevant safety data sheet in accordance with the provisions of Directive 67/548/EEC or Directive 88/379/EEC),
- the level, type and duration of exposure,
- the circumstances of work involving such agents, including their amount,
- any occupational exposure limit values or biological limit values established on the territory of the Member State in question,
- the effect of preventive measures taken or to be taken,
- where available, the conclusions to be drawn from any health surveillance already undertaken.

The employer shall obtain additional information which is needed for the risk assessment from the supplier or from other readily available sources. Where appropriate, this information shall comprise the specific assessment concerning the risk to users established on the basis of Community legislation on chemical agents.

2. The employer must be in possession of an assessment of the risk in accordance with Article 9 of Directive 89/391/EEC, and shall identify which measures have been taken in accordance with Articles 5 and 6 of this Directive. The risk assessment shall be documented in a suitable form according to national law and practice, and may include a justification by the employer that the nature and extent of the risks related to chemical agents make a further detailed risk assessment unnecessary. The risk assessment shall be kept up-to-date, particularly if there have been significant changes which could render it out-of-date, or when the results of health surveillance show it to be necessary.

3. Certain activities within the undertaking or establishment, such as maintenance, in respect of which it is foreseeable that there is a potential for significant exposure, or which may result in deleterious effects to safety and health for other reasons, even after all technical measures have been taken, shall be included in the risk assessment.

4. In the case of activities involving exposure to several hazardous chemical agents, the risk shall be assessed on the basis of the risk presented by all such chemical agents in combination.

5. In the case of a new activity involving hazardous chemical agents, work shall only commence after an assessment of the risk of that activity has been made and any preventive measures identified have been implemented.

6. Practical guidelines for the determination and assessment of risk, and for their review and, if necessary, adjustment, shall be developed in accordance with Article 12(2).

Article 5

General principles for prevention of risks associated with hazardous chemical agents and application of this Directive in relation to assessment of risks

1. In carrying out his obligation to ensure the health and safety of workers in any activity involving hazardous chemical agents the employer shall take the necessary preventive measures set out in Article 6(1) and (2) of Directive 89/391/EEC and include the measures set out in this Directive.

2. Risks to the health and safety of workers at work involving hazardous chemical agents shall be eliminated or reduced to a minimum by:
- the design and organisation of systems of work at the workplace,
- the provision of suitable equipment for work with chemical agents and maintenance procedures which ensure the health and safety of workers at work,
- reducing to a minimum the number of workers exposed or likely to be exposed,
- reducing to a minimum the duration and intensity of exposure,
- appropriate hygiene measures,
- reducing the quantity of chemical agents present at the workplace to the minimum required for the type of work concerned,
- suitable working procedures including arrangements for the safe handling, storage and transport within the workplace of hazardous chemical agents and waste containing such chemical agents.

Practical guidelines for preventive measures to control risk shall be developed in accordance with Article 12(2).

3. Where the results of the assessment referred to in Article 4(1) reveal a risk to the safety and health of workers, the specific protection, prevention and monitoring measures laid down in Articles 6, 7 and 10 shall be applied.

4. Where the results of the risk assessment referred to in Article 4(1) show that, because of the quantities of a hazardous chemical agent present in the workplace, there is only a slight risk to the safety and health of workers, and the measures taken in accordance with paragraphs 1 and 2 of this Article are sufficient to reduce that risk, the provisions of Articles 6, 7 and 10 shall not apply.

Article 6

Specific protection and prevention measures
1. The employer shall ensure that the risk from a hazardous chemical agent to the safety and health of workers at work is eliminated or reduced to a minimum.
2. In applying paragraph 1, substitution shall by preference be undertaken, whereby the employer shall avoid the use of a hazardous chemical agent by replacing it with a chemical agent or process which, under its condition of use, is not hazardous or less hazardous to workers' safety and health, as the case may be.
Where the nature of the activity does not permit risk to be eliminated by substitution, having regard to the activity and risk assessment referred to in Article 4, the employer shall ensure that the risk is reduced to a minimum by application of protection and prevention measures, consistent with the assessment of the risk made pursuant to Article 4. These will include, in order of priority:
(a) design of appropriate work processes and engineering controls and use of adequate equipment and materials, so as to avoid or minimise the release of hazardous chemical agents which may present a risk to workers' safety and health at the place of work;
(b) application of collective protection measures at the source of the risk, such as adequate ventilation and appropriate organizational measures;
(c) where exposure cannot be prevented by other means, application of individual protection measures including personal protective equipment.
Practical guidelines for protection and prevention measures to control risk shall be developed in accordance with Article 12(2).
3. The measures referred to in paragraph 2 of this Article shall be accompanied by health surveillance in accordance with Article 10 if it is appropriate to the nature of the risk.
4. Unless the employer clearly demonstrates by other means of evaluation that, in accordance with paragraph 2, adequate prevention and protection have been achieved, the employer shall carry out on a regular basis, and when any change occurs in the conditions which may affect workers' exposure to chemical agents, such measurements of chemical agents which may present a risk to worker's health at the workplace as are necessary, in particular in relation to the occupational exposure limit values.
5. The employer shall take into account the results of the procedures referred to in paragraph 4 of this Article in carrying out the obligations laid down in or resulting as a consequence of Article 4.
In any event, where an occupational exposure limit value effectively established on the territory of a Member State has been exceeded, the employer shall immediately take steps, taking into account the nature of that limit, to remedy the situation by carrying out preventive and protective measures.
6. On the basis of the overall assessment of and general principles for the prevention of risks in Articles 4 and 5, the employer shall take technical and/or organisational measures appropriate to the nature of the operation, including storage, handling and segregation of incompatible chemical agents, providing protection of workers against hazards arising from the physico-chemical properties of chemical agents. In particular he shall take measures, in order of priority, to:
(a) prevent the presence at the workplace of hazardous concentrations of inflammable substances or hazardous quantities of chemically unstable substances or, where the nature of the work does not allow that,
(b) avoid the presence of ignition sources which could give rise to fires and explosions, or adverse conditions which could cause chemically unstable substances or mixtures of substances to give rise to harmful physical effects, and
(c) mitigate the detrimental effects to the health and safety of workers in the event of fire or explosion due to the ignition of inflammable substances, or harmful physical effects arising from chemically unstable substances or mixtures of substances.
Work equipment and protective systems provided by the employer for the protection of workers shall comply with the relevant Community provisions on design, manufacture and supply with respect to health and safety. Technical and/or organisational measures taken by the employer shall take account of and be consistent with the equipment group categorisation in Annex I to Directive 94/9/EC of the European Parliament and of the Council of 23 March 1994 on the approximation of the laws of the Member States concerning equipment and protective systems intended for use in potentially explosive atmospheres (19).
The employer shall take measures to provide sufficient control of plant, equipment and machinery or provision of explosion suppression equipment or explosion pressure relief arrangements.

Article 7

Arrangements to deal with accidents, incidents and emergencies
1. Without prejudice to the obligations laid down in Article 8 of Directive 89/391/EEC, the employer shall, in order to protect the safety and health of workers from an accident, incident or emergency related to the presence

of hazardous chemical agents at the workplace, establish procedures (action plans) which can be put into effect when any such event occurs, so that appropriate action is taken. These arrangements shall include any relevant safety drills which are to be performed at regular intervals, and the provision of appropriate first aid facilities.
2. In the case of the occurrence of an event such as is mentioned in paragraph 1, the employer shall immediately take steps to mitigate the effects of the event and to inform the workers concerned thereof.
In order to restore the situation to normal:
- the employer shall implement appropriate measures to remedy the situation as soon as possible,
- only those workers who are essential to the carrying out of repairs and other necessary work shall be permitted to work in the affected area.
3. The workers who are permitted to work in the affected area shall be provided with appropriate protective clothing, personal protective equipment, specialised safety equipment and plant which they must use as long as the situation persists; that situation shall not be permanent.
Unprotected persons shall not be permitted to remain in the affected area.
4. Without prejudice to Article 8 of Directive 89/391/EEC the employer shall take the measures necessary to provide the warning and other communication systems required to signal an increased risk to safety and health, to enable an appropriate response and to launch remedial actions, assistance, escape and rescue operations immediately if the need arises.
5. The employer shall ensure that information on emergency arrangements involving hazardous chemical agents is available. The relevant internal and external accident and emergency services shall have access to this information. It shall include the following:
- advance notice of relevant work hazards, hazard identification arrangements, precautions and procedures, so that the emergency services can prepare their own response procedures and precautionary measures; and
- any available information concerning specific hazards arising, or likely to rise, at the time of an accident or emergency, including information on procedures prepared pursuant to this Article.

Article 8

Information and training for workers
1. Without prejudice to Articles 10 and 12 of Directive 89/391/EEC the employer shall ensure that workers and/or their representatives are provided with:
- the data obtained pursuant to Article 4 of this Directive, and further informed whenever a major alteration at the workplace leads to a change in these data,
- information on the hazardous chemical agents occurring in the workplace, such as the identity of those agents, the risks to safety and health, relevant occupational exposure limit values and other legislative provisions,
- training and information on appropriate precautions and actions to be taken in order to safeguard themselves and other workers at the workplace,
- access to any safety data sheet provided by the supplier in accordance with Article 10 of Directive 88/379/EEC and Article 27 of Directive 92/32/EEC (20);
and that the information is:
- provided in a manner appropriate to the outcome of the risk assessment pursuant to Article 4 of this Directive. This may vary from oral communication to individual instruction and training supported by information in writing, depending on the nature and degree of the risk revealed by the assessment required by the said Article,
- updated to take account of changing circumstances.
2. Where containers and pipes for hazardous chemical agents used at work are not marked in accordance with the relevant Community legislation on the labelling of chemical agents and on safety signs at the workplace, the employer shall, without prejudice to the derogations provided for in the abovementioned legislation, ensure that the contents of the containers and pipes, together with the nature of those contents and any associated hazards, are clearly identifiable.
3. Member States may take measures necessary to ensure that employers may, preferably from the producer or supplier, obtain on request all information on hazardous chemical agents needed to apply Article 4(1) of this Directive, insofar as Directives 67/548/EEC and 88/379/EEC do not include any obligation to provide information.

SECTION III

MISCELLANEOUS PROVISIONS

Article 9

Prohibitions

1. To prevent the exposure of workers to health risks from certain chemical agents and/or certain activities involving chemical agents, the production, manufacture or use at work of the chemical agents and the activities set out in Annex III shall be prohibited to the extent specified therein.
2. Member States may permit derogations from requirements of paragraph 1 in the following circumstances:
- for the sole purpose of scientific research and testing, including analysis,
- for activities intended to eliminate chemical agents that are present in the form of by-products or waste products,
- for the production of the chemical agents referred to in paragraph 1 for use as intermediates, and for such use.
The exposure of workers to chemical agents referred to in paragraph 1 must be prevented, in particular by providing that the production and earliest possible use of such chemical agents as intermediates must take place in a single closed system, from which the aforesaid chemical agents may be removed only to the extent necessary to monitor the process or service the system.
Member States may provide for systems of individual authorisations.
3. When derogations are permitted pursuant to paragraph 2, the competent authority shall request the employer to submit the following information:
- the reason for requesting the derogation,
- the quantity of the chemical agent to be used annually,
- the activities and/or reactions or processes involved,
- the number of workers liable to be involved,
- the precautions envisaged to protect the safety and health of workers concerned,
- the technical and organisational measures taken to prevent the exposure of workers.
4. The Council, in accordance with the procedure laid down in Article 118a of the Treaty, may amend the list of prohibitions under paragraph 1 of this Article, to include further chemical agents or activities.

Article 10

Health surveillance
1. Without prejudice to Article 14 of Directive 89/391/EEC, Member States shall introduce arrangements for carrying out appropriate health surveillance of workers for whom the results of the assessment referred to in Article 4 of this Directive reveal a risk to health. These arrangements, including the requirements specified for health and exposure records and their availability, shall be introduced in accordance with national laws and/or practice.
Health surveillance, the results of which shall be taken into account in applying preventive measures in the specific workplace, shall be appropriate where:
- the exposure of the worker to a hazardous chemical agent is such that an identifiable disease or adverse health effect may be related to the exposure, and
- there is a likelihood that the disease or effect may occur under the particular conditions of the worker's work, and
- the technique of investigation is of low risk to workers.
Furthermore, there shall be valid techniques for detecting indications of the disease or effect.
Where a binding biological limit value has been set as indicated in Annex II, health surveillance shall be a compulsory requirement for work with the hazardous chemical agent in question, in accordance with the procedures in that Annex. Workers shall be informed of this requirement before being assigned to the task involving risk of exposure to the hazardous chemical agent indicated.
2. Member States shall establish arrangements to ensure that for each worker who undergoes health surveillance in accordance with the requirements of paragraph 1, individual health and exposure records are made and kept up-to-date.
3. Health and exposure records shall contain a summary of the results of health surveillance carried out and of any monitoring data representative of the exposure of the individual. Biological monitoring and related requirements may form part of health surveillance.
Health and exposure records shall be kept in a suitable form so as to permit consultation at a later date, taking into account any confidentiality.
Copies of the appropriate records shall be supplied to the competent authority on request. The individual worker shall, at his request, have access to the health and exposure records relating to him personally.
Where an undertaking ceases to trade, the health and exposure records shall be made available to the competent authority.
4. Where, as a result of health surveillance:
- a worker is found to have an identifiable disease or adverse health effect which is considered by a doctor or occupational health-care professional to be the result of exposure at work to a hazardous chemical agent, or
- a binding biological limit value is found to have been exceeded,

the worker shall be informed by the doctor or other suitably qualified person of the result which relates to him personally, including information and advice regarding any health surveillance which he should undergo following the end of the exposure, and
the employer shall:
- review the risk assessment made pursuant to Article 4(1),
- review the measures provided to eliminate or reduce risks pursuant to Articles 5 and 6,
- take into account the advice of the occupational health-care professional or other suitably qualified person or the competent authority in implementing any measures required to eliminate or reduce risk in accordance with Article 6, including the possibility of assigning the worker to alternative work where there is no risk of further exposure, and
- arrange continued health surveillance and provide for a review of the health status of any other worker who has been similarly exposed. In such cases the competent doctor or occupational health-care professional or the competent authority may propose that exposed persons undergo a medical examination.

Article 11

Consultation and participation of workers
Consultation and participation of workers and/or their representatives shall take place in accordance with Article 11 of Directive 89/391/EEC on the matters covered by this Directive, including the Annexes hereto.

Article 12

Adaptation of the Annexes, preparation and adoption of technical guidance
1. Adjustments of a strictly technical nature to the Annexes in line with:
- the adoption of Directives in the field of technical harmonisation and standardisation concerning chemical agents, and/or
- technical progress, changes in international standards or specifications and new findings concerning chemical agents,
shall be adopted in accordance with the procedure laid down in Article 17 of Directive 89/391/EEC.
2. The Commission shall draw up practical guidelines of a non-binding nature. These guidelines shall address the topics referred to in Articles 3, 4, 5 and 6, and Annex II, section 1.
The Commission shall first consult the Advisory Committee on Safety, Hygiene and Health Protection at Work in accordance with Decision 74/325/EEC.
In the context of the application of this Directive, Member States shall take account as far as possible of these guidelines in drawing up their national policies for the protection of the health and safety of workers.

Article 13

Repeal and amendment of earlier Directives
1. Directives 80/1107/EEC, 82/605/EEC and 88/364/EEC shall be repealed on the date referred to in Article 14(1).
2. Council Directive 83/477/EEC of 19 September 1983 on the protection of workers from the risks related to exposure to asbestos at work (second individual Directive within the meaning of Article 8 of Directive 80/1107/EEC) (21), is amended as follows:
(a) in the first sentence of Article 1(1), the following words shall be deleted:
"which is the second individual Directive within the meaning of Article 8 of Directive 80/1107/EEC";
(b) Article 9(2) shall be replaced by the following:
"2. The amendments necessary to adapt the Annexes to this Directive to technical progress shall be adopted in accordance with the procedure laid down in Article 17 of Council Directive 89/391/EEC of 12 June 1989 on the introduction of measures to encourage improvements in the safety and health of workers at the workplace (*).
(*) OJ L 183, 29. 6. 1989, p. 1.";
(c) in the second subparagraph of Article 15(1) the words "in accordance with the procedure set out in Article 10 of Directive 80/1107/EEC` shall be replaced by "in accordance with the procedure laid down in Article 17 of Directive 89/391/EEC".
3. Council Directive 86/188/EEC of 12 May 1986 on the protection of workers from the risks related to exposure to noise at work (22) is amended as follows:
(a) in Article 1(1), the following words shall be deleted:
"which is the third individual Directive within the meaning of Directive 80/1107/EEC";
(b) in Article 12(2), the second subparagraph shall be replaced by the following:
"Annexes I and II shall be adapted to technical progress in accordance with the procedure laid down in Article

17 of Council Directive 89/391/EEC of 12 June 1989 on the introduction of measures to encourage improvements in the safety and health of workers at the workplace (*).
(*) OJ L 183, 29. 6. 1989, p. 1."
4. Any other reference in Directive 83/477/EEC and Directive 86/188/EEC to Directive 80/1107/EEC shall be obsolete from the date of repeal of the said Directive.
5. Directives 91/322/EEC and 96/94/EC remain in force.

SECTION IV

Final provisions

Article 14
1. Member States shall bring into force the laws, regulations and administrative provisions necessary to comply with this Directive not later than 5 May 2001. They shall forthwith inform the Commission thereof.
When Member States adopt these measures, they shall contain a reference to this Directive or shall be accompanied by such reference on the occasion of their official publication. The methods for making such reference shall be laid down by Member States.
2. Member States shall communicate to the Commission the texts of the provisions of national law which they have already adopted or which they adopt in the field governed by this Directive.

Article 15
Member States shall report to the Commission every five years on the practical implementation of this Directive, indicating the views of employers and workers.
The Commission shall inform the European Parliament, the Council and the Economic and Social Committee thereof.

Article 16
This Directive shall enter into force on the twentieth day following that of its publication in the Official Journal of the European Communities.

Article 17
This Directive is addressed to the Member States.

Done at Luxembourg, 7 April 1998.
For the Council
The President
D. BLUNKETT

(1) OJ C 165, 16. 6. 1993, p. 4.
(2) OJ C 34, 2. 2. 1994, p. 42.
(3) Opinion of the European Parliament of 20 April 1994 (OJ C 128, 9. 5. 1994, p. 167), Council common position of 7 October 1997 (OJ C 375, 10. 12. 1997, p. 2) and Decision of the European Parliament on 17 February 1998 (not yet published in the Official Journal).
(4) OJ L 327, 3. 12. 1980, p. 8. Directive as last amended by Directive 88/642/EEC (OJ L 356, 24. 12. 1988, p. 74).
(5) OJ L 247, 23. 8. 1982, p. 12.
(6) OJ L 179, 9. 7. 1988, p. 44.
(7) OJ L 183, 29. 6. 1989, p. 1.
(8) OJ 196, 16. 8. 1967, p. 1. Directive as last amended by Directive 96/56/EC (OJ L 236, 18. 9. 1996, p. 35).
(9) OJ L 187, 16. 7. 1988, p. 14. Directive as last amended by Commission Directive 96/65/EC (OJ L 265, 18. 10. 1996, p. 15).
(10) OJ L 275, 5. 10. 1990, p. 35.
(11) OJ L 245, 26. 8. 1992, p. 23.
(12) OJ L 177, 5. 7. 1991, p. 22.
(13) OJ L 338, 28. 12. 1996, p. 86.
(14) OJ L 185, 9. 7. 1974, p. 15. Decision as last amended by the 1994 Act of Accession.
(15) OJ L 196, 26. 7. 1990, p. 1.
(16) Council Directive 94/55/EC of 21 November 1994 on the approximation of the laws of the Member States with regard to the transport of dangerous goods by road (OJ L 319, 12. 12. 1994, p. 7). Directive as amended by Commission Directive 96/86/EC (OJ L 335, 24. 12. 1996, p. 43).

(17) Council Directive 96/49/EC of 23 July 1996 on the approximation of the laws of the Member States with regard to the transport of dangerous goods by rail (OJ L 235, 17. 9. 1996, p. 25). Directive as amended by Commission Directive 96/87/EC (OJ L 335, 24. 12. 1996, p. 45).
(18) Council Directive 93/75/EEC of 13 September 1993 concerning minimum requirements for vessels bound for or leaving Community ports and carrying dangerous or polluting goods (OJ L 247, 5. 10. 1993, p. 19). Directive as last amended by Commission Directive 97/34/EC (OJ L 158, 17. 6. 1997, p. 40).
(19) OJ L 100, 19. 4. 1994, p. 1.
(20) OJ L 154, 5. 6. 1992, p. 1.
(21) OJ L 263, 24. 9. 1983, p. 25. Directive as amended by Directive 91/382/EEC (OJ L 206, 29. 7. 1991, p. 16).
(22) OJ L 137, 24. 5. 1986, p. 28.

Annex 9.10.

Directive 2003/10/EC of the European Parliament and of the Council of 6 February 2003 on the minimum health and safety requirements regarding the **exposure of workers to the risks arising from physical agents (noise)** (Seventeenth individual Directive within the meaning of Article 16(1) of Directive 89/391/EEC)
Official Journal L 042 , 15/02/2003 P. 0038 - 0044

MAIN PROVISIONS

SECTION I
GENERAL PROVISIONS

Article 1
Aim and scope
1. This Directive, which is the 17th individual Directive within the meaning of Article 16(1) of Directive 89/391/EEC, lays down minimum requirements for the protection of workers from risks to their health and safety arising or likely to arise from exposure to noise and in particular the risk to hearing.
2. The requirements of this Directive shall apply to activities in which workers are or are likely to be exposed to risks from noise as a result of their work.
3. Directive 89/391/EEC shall apply fully to the whole area referred to in paragraph 1, without prejudice to more stringent and/or specific provisions contained in this Directive.

Article 2
Definitions
For the purposes of this Directive, the physical parameters used as risk predictors are defined as follows:
(a) peak sound pressure (ppeak): maximum value of the "C"-frequency weighted instantaneous noise pressure;
(b) daily noise exposure level (LEX,8h) (dB(A) re. 20 >ISO_7>μ>ISO_1>Pa): time-weighted average of the noise exposure levels for a nominal eight-hour working day as defined by international standard ISO 1999: 1990, point 3.6. It covers all noises present at work, including impulsive noise;
(c) weekly noise exposure level (LEX,8h): time-weighted average of the daily noise exposure levels for a nominal week of five eight-hour working days as defined by international standard ISO 1999:1990, point 3.6 (note 2).

Article 3
Exposure limit values and exposure action values
1. For the purposes of this Directive the exposure limit values and exposure action values in respect of the daily noise exposure levels and peak sound pressure are fixed at:
(a) exposure limit values: LEX,8h = 87 dB(A) and ppeak = 200 Pa(11) respectively;
(b) upper exposure action values: LEX,8h 85 dB(A) and ppeak = 140 Pa(12) respectively;
(c) lower exposure action values: LEX,8h = 80 dB(A) and ppeak = 112 Pa(13) respectively.
2. When applying the exposure limit values, the determination of the worker's effective exposure shall take account of the attenuation provided by the individual hearing protectors worn by the worker. The exposure action values shall not take account of the effect of any such protectors.
3. In duly justified circumstances, for activities where daily noise exposure varies markedly from one working day to the next, Member States may, for the purposes of applying the exposure limit values and the exposure action values, use the weekly noise exposure level in place of the daily noise exposure level to assess the levels of noise to which workers are exposed, on condition that:
(a) the weekly noise exposure level as shown by adequate monitoring does not exceed the exposure limit value of 87 dB(A); and
(b) appropriate measures are taken in order to reduce the risk associated with these activities to a minimum.

SECTION II
OBLIGATIONS OF EMPLOYERS

Article 4
Determination and assessment of risks
1. In carrying out the obligations laid down in Articles 6(3) and 9(1) of Directive 89/391/EEC, the employer shall assess and, if necessary, measure the levels of noise to which workers are exposed.

2. The methods and apparatus used shall be adapted to the prevailing conditions particularly in the light of the characteristics of the noise to be measured, the length of exposure, ambient factors and the characteristics of the measuring apparatus.
These methods and this apparatus shall make it possible to determine the parameters defined in Article 2 and to decide whether, in a given case, the values fixed in Article 3 have been exceeded.
3. The methods used may include sampling, which shall be representative of the personal exposure of a worker.
4. The assessment and measurement referred to in paragraph 1 shall be planned and carried out by competent services at suitable intervals, taking particular account of the provisions of Article 7 of Directive 89/391/EEC concerning the necessary competent services or persons. The data obtained from the assessment and/or measurement of the level of exposure to noise shall be preserved in a suitable form so as to permit consultation at a later stage.
5. When applying this Article, the assessment of the measurement results shall take into account the measurement inaccuracies determined in accordance with metrological practice.
6. Pursuant to Article 6(3) of Directive 89/391/EEC, the employer shall give particular attention, when carrying out the risk assessment, to the following:
(a) the level, type and duration of exposure, including any exposure to impulsive noise;
(b) the exposure limit values and the exposure action values laid down in Article 3 of this Directive;
(c) any effects concerning the health and safety of workers belonging to particularly sensitive risk groups;
(d) as far as technically achievable, any effects on workers' health and safety resulting from interactions between noise and work-related ototoxic substances, and between noise and vibrations;
(e) any indirect effects on workers' health and safety resulting from interactions between noise and warning signals or other sounds that need to be observed in order to reduce the risk of accidents;
(f) information on noise emission provided by manufacturers of work equipment in accordance with the relevant Community directives;
(g) the existence of alternative work equipment designed to reduce the noise emission;
(h) the extension of exposure to noise beyond normal working hours under the employer's responsibility;
(i) appropriate information obtained following health surveillance, including published information, as far as possible;
(j) the availability of hearing protectors with adequate attenuation characteristics.
7. The employer shall be in possession of an assessment of the risk in accordance with Article 9(1)(a) of Directive 89/391/EEC, and shall identify which measures must be taken in accordance with Articles 5, 6, 7 and 8 of this Directive. The risk assessment shall be recorded on a suitable medium, according to national law and practice. The risk assessment shall be kept up to date on a regular basis, particularly if there have been significant changes which could render it out of date, or when the results of health surveillance show it to be necessary.

Article 5
Provisions aimed at avoiding or reducing exposure
1. Taking account of technical progress and of the availability of measures to control the risk at source, the risks arising from exposure to noise shall be eliminated at their source or reduced to a minimum.
The reduction of such risks shall be based on the general principles of prevention set out in Article 6(2) of Directive 89/391/EEC, and take into account in particular:
(a) other working methods that require less exposure to noise;
(b) the choice of appropriate work equipment, taking account of the work to be done, emitting the least possible noise, including the possibility of making available to workers work equipment subject to Community provisions with the aim or effect of limiting exposure to noise;
(c) the design and layout of workplaces and work stations;
(d) adequate information and training to instruct workers to use work equipment correctly in order to reduce their exposure to noise to a minimum;
(e) noise reduction by technical means:
(i) reducing airborne noise, e.g. by shields, enclosures, sound-absorbent coverings;
(ii) reducing structure-borne noise, e.g. by damping or isolation;
(f) appropriate maintenance programmes for work equipment, the workplace and workplace systems;
(g) organisation of work to reduce noise:
(i) limitation of the duration and intensity of the exposure;
(ii) appropriate work schedules with adequate rest periods.
2. On the basis of the risk assessment referred to in Article 4, if the upper exposure action values are exceeded, the employer shall establish and implement a programme of technical and/or organisational measures intended to reduce the exposure to noise, taking into account in particular the measures referred to in paragraph 1.
3. On the basis of the risk assessment referred to in Article 4, workplaces where workers are likely to be

exposed to noise exceeding the upper exposure action values shall be marked with appropriate signs. The areas in question shall also be delimited and access to them restricted where this is technically feasible and the risk of exposure so justifies.
4. Where, owing to the nature of the activity, a worker benefits from the use of rest facilities under the responsibility of the employer, noise in these facilities shall be reduced to a level compatible with their purpose and the conditions of use.
5. Pursuant to Article 15 of Directive 89/391/EEC, the employer shall adapt the measures referred to in this Article to the requirements of workers belonging to particularly sensitive risk groups.

Article 6
Personal protection
1. If the risks arising from exposure to noise cannot be prevented by other means, appropriate, properly fitting individual hearing protectors shall be made available to workers and used by them in accordance with the provisions of Council Directive 89/656/EEC of 30 November 1989 on the minimum health and safety requirements for the use by workers of personal protective equipment at the workplace (third individual Directive within the meaning of Article 16(1) of Directive 89/391/EEC)(14) and Article 13(2) of Directive 89/391/EEC and under the conditions set out below:
(a) where noise exposure exceeds the lower exposure action values, the employer shall make individual hearing protectors available to workers;
(b) where noise exposure matches or exceeds the upper exposure action values, individual hearing protectors shall be used;
(c) the individual hearing protectors shall be so selected as to eliminate the risk to hearing or to reduce the risk to a minimum.
2. The employer shall make every effort to ensure the wearing of hearing protectors and shall be responsible for checking the effectiveness of the measures taken in compliance with this Article.

Article 7
Limitation of exposure
1. Under no circumstances shall the exposure of the worker as determined in accordance with Article 3(2) exceed the exposure limit values.
2. If, despite the measures taken to implement this Directive, exposures above the exposure limit values are detected, the employer shall:
(a) take immediate action to reduce the exposure to below the exposure limit values;
(b) identify the reasons why overexposure has occurred; and
(c) amend the protection and prevention measures in order to avoid any recurrence.

Article 8
Worker information and training
Without prejudice to Articles 10 and 12 of Directive 89/391/EEC the employer shall ensure that workers who are exposed to noise at work at or above the lower exposure action values, and/or their representatives, receive information and training relating to risks resulting from exposure to noise concerning, in particular:
(a) the nature of such risks;
(b) the measures taken to implement this Directive in order to eliminate or reduce to a minimum the risks from noise, including the circumstances in which the measures apply;
(c) the exposure limit values and the exposure action values laid down in Article 3 of this Directive;
(d) the results of the assessment and measurement of the noise carried out in accordance with Article 4 of this Directive together with an explanation of their significance and potential risks;
(e) the correct use of hearing protectors;
(f) why and how to detect and report signs of hearing damage;
(g) the circumstances in which workers are entitled to health surveillance and the purpose of health surveillance, in accordance with Article 10 of this Directive;
(h) safe working practices to minimise exposure to noise.

Article 9
Consultation and participation of workers
Consultation and participation of workers and/or of their representatives shall take place in accordance with Article 11 of Directive 89/391/EEC on the matters covered by this Directive, in particular:
- the assessment of risks and identification of measures to be taken, referred to in Article 4,
- the actions aimed at eliminating or reducing risks arising from exposure to noise, referred to in Article 5,
- the choice of individual hearing protectors referred to in Article 6(1)(c).

SECTION III
MISCELLANEOUS PROVISIONS

Article 10
Health surveillance
1. Without prejudice to Article 14 of Directive 89/391/EEC, Member States shall adopt provisions to ensure the appropriate health surveillance of workers where the results of the assessment and measurement provided for in Article 4(1) of this Directive indicate a risk to their health. Those provisions, including the requirements specified for health records and their availability, shall be introduced in accordance with national law and/or practice.
2. A worker whose exposure exceeds the upper exposure action values shall have the right to have his/her hearing checked by a doctor or by another suitably qualified person under the responsibility of a doctor, in accordance with national law and/or practice. Preventive audiometric testing shall also be available for workers whose exposure exceeds the lower exposure action values, where the assessment and measurement provided for in Article 4(1) indicate a risk to health.
The objectives of these checks are to provide early diagnosis of any loss of hearing due to noise, and to preserve the hearing function.
3. Member States shall establish arrangements to ensure that, for each worker who undergoes surveillance in accordance with paragraphs 1 and 2, individual health records are made and kept up to date. Health records shall contain a summary of the results of the health surveillance carried out. They shall be kept in a suitable form so as to permit any consultation at a later date, taking into account any confidentiality.
Copies of the appropriate records shall be supplied to the competent authority on request. The individual worker shall, at his or her request, have access to the health records relating to him or her personally.
4. Where, as a result of surveillance of the hearing function, a worker is found to have identifiable hearing damage, a doctor, or a specialist if the doctor considers it necessary, shall assess whether the damage is likely to be the result of exposure to noise at work. If this is the case:
(a) the worker shall be informed by the doctor or other suitably qualified person of the result which relates to him or her personally;
(b) the employer shall:
(i) review the risk assessment carried out pursuant to Article 4;
(ii) review the measures provided for to eliminate or reduce risks pursuant to Articles 5 and 6;
(iii) take into account the advice of the occupational healthcare professional or other suitably qualified person or the competent authority in implementing any measures required to eliminate or reduce risk in accordance with Articles 5 and 6, including the possibility of assigning the worker to alternative work where there is no risk of further exposure; and
(iv) arrange systematic health surveillance and provide for a review of the health status of any other worker who has been similarly exposed.

Article 11
Derogations
1. In exceptional situations where, because of the nature of the work, the full and proper use of individual hearing protectors would be likely to cause greater risk to health or safety than not using such protectors, Member States may grant derogations from the provisions of Articles 6(1)(a) and (b) and 7.
2. The derogations referred to in paragraph 1 shall be granted by Member States following consultation with both sides of industry and, where appropriate, with the medical authorities responsible, in accordance with national laws and/or practice. Such derogations must be accompanied by conditions which guarantee, taking into account the special circumstances, that the resulting risks are reduced to a minimum and that the workers concerned are subject to increased health surveillance. Such derogations shall be reviewed every four years and withdrawn as soon as the justifying circumstances no longer obtain.
3. Every four years Member States shall forward to the Commission a list of derogations referred to in paragraph 1, indicating the exact reasons and circumstances which made them decide to grant the derogations.

Article 12
Technical amendments
Amendments of a strictly technical nature shall be adopted in accordance with the regulatory procedure laid down in Article 13(2) and in line with:
(a) the adoption of directives in the field of technical harmonisation and standardisation with regard to the design, building, manufacture or construction of work equipment and/or workplaces; and
(b) technical progress, changes in the most appropriate harmonised European standards or specifications and new findings concerning noise.

Article 13
Committee
1. The Commission shall be assisted by the Committee referred to in Article 17 of Directive 89/391/EEC.
2. Where reference is made to this paragraph, Articles 5 and 7 of Council Decision 1999/468/EC shall apply, having regard to the provisions of Article 8 thereof.
The period laid down in Article 5(6) of Decision 1999/468/EC shall be set at three months.
3. The Committee shall adopt its Rules of Procedure.

Article 14
Code of conduct
In the context of the application of this directive Member States shall draw up in consultation with the social partners, in accordance with national law and practice, a code of conduct providing for practical guidelines to help workers and employers in the music and entertainment sectors to meet their legal obligations as laid down in this Directive.

Article 15
Repeal
Directive 86/188/EEC is hereby repealed with effect from the date set out in the first subparagraph of Article 17(1).

SECTION IV
FINAL PROVISIONS

Article 16
Reports
Every five years Member States shall provide a report to the Commission on the practical implementation of this Directive, indicating the points of view of both sides of industry. It shall contain a description of best practice for preventing noise with a harmful effect on health and of other forms of work organisation, together with the action taken by the Member States to impart knowledge of such best practice.
On the basis of those reports, the Commission shall carry out an overall assessment of the implementation of this Directive, including implementation in the light of research and scientific information, and, inter alia, taking into account the implications of this Directive for the music and entertainment sectors. The Commission shall inform the European Parliament, the Council, the European Economic and Social Committee and the Advisory Committee on Safety, Hygiene and Health Protection at Work thereof and, if necessary, propose amendments.

Article 17
Transposition
1. The Member States shall bring into force the laws, regulations and administrative provisions necessary to comply with this Directive before 15 February 2006. They shall forthwith inform the Commission thereof.
When Member States adopt these measures, they shall contain a reference to this Directive or shall be accompanied by such reference on the occasion of their official publication. The methods of making such reference shall be laid down by the Member States.
2. In order to take account of particular conditions, Member States may, if necessary, have an additional period of five years from 15 February 2006, that is to say a total of eight years, to implement the provisions of Article 7 with regard to the personnel on board seagoing vessels.
In order to allow for the drawing up of a code of conduct providing for practical guidelines for the implementation of the provisions of this Directive, Member States shall be entitled to make use of a maximum transitional period of two years from 15 February 2006, that is to say a total of five years from the entry into force of this Directive, to comply with this Directive, with regard to the music and entertainment sectors on the condition that during this period the levels of protection already achieved in individual Member States, with regard to the personnel in these sectors, are maintained.
3. The Member States shall communicate to the Commission the text of the provisions of national law which they adopt or have already adopted in the field covered by this Directive.

Annex 9.11.

Decision No 1786/2002/EC of the European Parliament and of the Council of 23 September 2002 adopting a **programme of Community action in the field of public health** (2003-2008) - Commission Statements
Official Journal L 271 , 09/10/2002 P. 0001 - 0012

MAIN PROVISIONS

Article 1
Establishment of the programme
1. This Decision establishes a programme of Community action in the field of public health, hereinafter referred to as "the programme".
2. The programme shall be implemented in the period starting on 1 January 2003 and ending on 31 December 2008.

Article 2
Overall aim and general objectives
1. The programme, which shall complement national policies, shall aim to protect human health and improve public health.
2. The general objectives of the programme shall be:
(a) to improve information and knowledge for the development of public health;
(b) to enhance the capability of responding rapidly and in a coordinated fashion to threats to health;
(c) to promote health and prevent disease through addressing health determinants across all policies and activities.
3. The programme shall thereby contribute to:
(a) ensuring a high level of human health protection in the definition and implementation of all Community policies and activities, through the promotion of an integrated and intersectoral health strategy;
(b) tackling inequalities in health;
(c) encouraging cooperation between Member States in the areas covered by Article 152 of the Treaty.

Article 3
Community actions and activities
1. The general objectives of the programme as set out in Article 2 shall be pursued by means of the actions listed in the Annex.
2. These actions shall be implemented in close cooperation with Member States through support to activities of a transversal nature, which may be used to implement all or part of the actions and which may, where appropriate, be combined. These activities are the following:
(a) Activities related to the monitoring and rapid reaction systems
(i) network activities operated through structures designated by Member States and other activities of Community interest for the purposes of public health monitoring and providing national information, as well as data at Community level, in furtherance of the objectives of the programme;
(ii) activities to counter health threats, including major diseases, and react to unforeseen events, enable investigations and coordinate response;
(iii) preparation, establishment and operation of appropriate structural arrangements coordinating and integrating networks for health monitoring and for rapid reaction to health threats;
(iv) development of appropriate links between the actions concerning the monitoring and rapid reaction systems.
(b) Activities on health determinants
development and implementation of health promotion and disease prevention activities across all Community policies and involving, as appropriate, non-governmental organisations, innovative or pilot projects and networks between national institutions and activities.
(c) Activities related to legislation
(i) preparatory work for Community legislative instruments in the field of public health;
(ii) health impact assessment of Community legislation;
(iii) coordination of the position of the Community and its Member States in fora in which health-related matters are discussed.
(d) Activities related to consultation, knowledge and information
(i) development and dissemination to competent authorities in Member States, to health and other professionals and, where appropriate, to other stakeholders and the general public of health information, knowledge, including

statistics, reports, reviews, analysis, and advice on issues of common interest to the Community and to Member States;
(ii) information and consultation on health and health-related matters at the Community level, involving all stakeholders such as patients' organisations, health professionals, health care providers, trade unions, social partners and NGOs in the field of public health;
(iii) sharing of experience and exchange of information on health-related matters between the Community and authorities and competent organisations of Member States;
(iv) encouraging education and vocational training in the field of public health relevant to the objectives of the programme;
(v) developing and maintaining networks for the exchange of information on best practice in public health and the effectiveness of health policies;
(vi) obtaining scientific information and advice from high-level scientists and experts;
(vii) supporting and promoting activities by the Community and the Member States with regard to good practice and to sound guidelines for public health based on scientific data.
(e) Promotion of coordination at the European level of non-governmental organisations which are developing activities defined as priorities under the programme. They may be operating either singly or in the form of several coordinated associations.

Article 4
Joint strategies and actions
To ensure a high level of human health protection in the definition and implementation of all Community policies and activities, the objectives of the programme may be implemented as joint strategies and joint actions by creating links with relevant Community programmes and actions, notably in the areas of consumer protection, social protection, health and safety at work, employment, research and technological development, internal market, information society and information technology, statistics, agriculture, education, transport, industry and environment, and with actions undertaken by the Joint Research Centre and relevant Community bodies with which cooperation shall be fostered.

Article 5
Implementation of the programme
1. The Commission shall ensure the implementation, in close cooperation with the Member States, of the actions set out in the programme, in accordance with the provisions of Article 9 and ensuring its harmonious and balanced development.
2. In order to assist implementation, the Commission shall ensure, through appropriate structural arrangements closely associating the Member States, the coordination and integration of networks for health monitoring and rapid reaction to health threats.
3. The Commission and Member States shall take appropriate action, within their respective areas of competence, to ensure the efficient running of the programme and to develop mechanisms at Community and Member State level to achieve the objectives of the programme. They shall ensure that appropriate information is provided about actions supported by the programme and that the widest possible participation is obtained in actions requiring implementation through local and regional authorities and non-governmental organisations.
4. The Commission shall, in close cooperation with the Member States, pursue the comparability of data and information and, where possible, the compatibility and interoperability of the systems and networks for exchange of data and information on health.
5. In implementing the programme the Commission, together with the Member States, shall ensure compliance with all relevant legal provisions regarding personal data protection and, where appropriate, the introduction of mechanisms to ensure the confidentiality and safety of such data.
6. The Commission, in close cooperation with the Member States, shall ensure the transition between those actions developed within the public health programmes adopted by the Decisions referred to in Article 13 which contribute to the priorities set out in this programme, and those to be implemented under this programme.

Article 6
Consistency and complementarity
The Commission shall ensure that there is consistency and complementarity between the actions to be implemented under the programme and those implemented under other Community policies and activities, including the policies mentioned in Article 4. In particular, the Commission shall identify those proposals of particular relevance to the objectives and actions of the programme, and inform the Committee referred to in Article 9 of how health considerations are taken into account in these proposals and of their expected health impact.

Article 7
Funding
1. The financial framework for the implementation of the programme for the period specified in Article 1 is hereby set at EUR 312 million.
Expenditure on technical and administrative assistance related to the structural arrangements referred to under Article 3(2)(a)(iii), and activities arising therefrom, shall be met from the overall budget of the programme.
2. The annual appropriations shall be authorised by the budgetary authority within the limits of the financial perspective.

Article 8
Implementation measures
1. The measures necessary for the implementation of this Decision relating to the matters referred to below shall be adopted in accordance with the management procedure referred to in Article 9(2):
(a) the annual plan of work for the implementation of the programme, setting out priorities and actions to be undertaken, including allocation of resources;
(b) the arrangements, criteria and procedures for selecting and financing the actions of the programme;
(c) the arrangements for implementing the joint strategies and actions referred to in Article 4;
(d) the arrangements for evaluating the programme referred to in Article 12;
(e) the arrangements for the preparation of any structural arrangements for the coordination of health monitoring and rapid reaction to health threats;
(f) the arrangements for transmitting, exchanging and disseminating information and for rapid reaction on health threats under the programme, without prejudice to the implementation measures carried out under Decision 2119/98/EC.
2. The measures necessary for the implementation of this Decision relating to all other matters shall be adopted in accordance with the advisory procedure referred to in Article 9(3).

Article 9
Committee
1. The Commission shall be assisted by a Committee.
2. Where reference is made to this paragraph, Articles 4 and 7 of Decision 1999/468/EC shall apply, having regard to the provisions of Article 8 thereof.
The period laid down in Article 4(3) of Decision 1999/468/EC shall be set at two months.
3. Where reference is made to this paragraph, Articles 3 and 7 of Decision 1999/468/EC shall apply, having regard to the provisions of Article 8 thereof.
4. The Committee shall adopt its rules of procedure.

Article 10
Participation of the EFTA/EEA countries, the associated central and eastern European countries, Cyprus, Malta and Turkey
The programme shall be open to the participation of:
(a) the EFTA/EEA countries in accordance with the conditions established in the EEA Agreement;
(b) the associated countries of central and eastern Europe, in accordance with the conditions laid down in the Europe Agreements, in their Additional Protocols and in the Decisions of the respective Association Councils;
(c) Cyprus, funded by additional appropriations in accordance with the procedures to be agreed with that country;
(d) Malta and Turkey, funded by additional appropriations in accordance with the provisions of the Treaty.

Article 11
International cooperation
In the course of implementing the programme, cooperation with third countries and with international organisations competent in the sphere of public health, in particular the World Health Organisation, the Council of Europe and the Organisation for Economic Cooperation and Development, or able to have an impact on public health such as the World Trade Organisation and the United Nations Food and Agriculture Organisation shall be encouraged in accordance with the procedure laid down in Article 9(3). In particular, the health information system and the capacity to respond to health threats should be, where appropriate and possible, coordinated with the activities of the World Health Organisation.

Article 12
Monitoring, evaluation and dissemination of results
1. The Commission, in close cooperation with the Member States, shall regularly monitor, where appropriate

with the help of experts, the implementation of the actions of the programme in the light of the objectives. It shall report annually to the Committee. The Commission shall transmit a copy of its main findings to the European Parliament and to the Council.
2. At the request of the Commission, Member States shall submit information on the implementation and the impact of this programme.
3. By the end of the fourth year of the programme, the Commission shall have an external assessment conducted by independent qualified experts of the implementation and achievements during the three first years of the programme. It shall also assess the impact achieved on health and the efficiency of the use of resources, as well as the consistency and complementarity with other relevant programmes, actions and initiatives implemented under other Community policies and activities. The Commission shall communicate the conclusions thereof, accompanied by its comments, to the European Parliament, the Council, the Economic and Social Committee and the Committee of the Regions. The Commission shall also submit to those institutions and bodies a final report on the implementation of the programme by the end of the year which follows the end of the programme.
4. The Commission shall make the results of actions undertaken and the evaluation reports publicly available.

Article 13
Repeal
The following Decisions are hereby repealed on 31 December 2002:
Decision No 645/96/EC, Decision No 646/96/EC, Decision No 647/96/EC, Decision No 102/97/EC, Decision No 1400/97/EC, Decision No 372/1999/EC, Decision No 1295/1999/EC, Decision No 1296/1999/EC.

Article 14
Entry into force
This Decision shall enter into force on the date of its publication in the Official Journal of the European Communities.

Done at Brussels, 23 September 2002.

For the European Parliament
The President
P. Cox

For the Council
The President
M. Fischer Boel

(1) OJ C 337 E, 28.11.2000, p. 122 and C 240 E, 28.8.2001, p. 168.
(2) OJ C 116, 20.4.2001, p. 75.
(3) OJ C 144, 16.5.2001, p. 43.
(4) Opinion of the European Parliament of 4 April 2001 (OJ C 21, 24.1.2002, p. 161), Council Common Position of 31 July 2001 (OJ C 307, 31.10.2001, p. 27) and Decision of the European Parliament of 12 December 2001 (not yet published in the Official Journal). Decision of the European Parliament of 3 July 2002 and Decision of the Council of 26 June 2002.
(5) OJ L 95, 16.4.1996, p. 1. Decision as last amended by Decision No 521/2001/EC (OJ L 79, 17.3.2001, p. 1).
(6) OJ L 95, 16.4.1996, p. 9. Decision as last amended by Decision No 521/2001/EC.
(7) OJ L 95, 16.4.1996, p. 16. Decision as last amended by Decision No 521/2001/EC.
(8) OJ L 19, 22.1.1997, p. 25. Decision as amended by Decision No 521/2001/EC.
(9) OJ L 193, 22.7.1997, p. 1. Decision as amended by Decision No 521/2001/EC.
(10) OJ L 46, 20.2.1999, p. 1.
(11) OJ L 155, 22.6.1999, p. 1.
(12) OJ L 155, 22.6.1999, p. 7. Decision as amended by Decision No 521/2001/EC.
(13) OJ L 268, 3.10.1998, p. 1.
(14) OJ L 21, 26.1.2000, p. 32.
(15) OJ L 203, 21.7.1998, p. 14.
(16) OJ L 199, 30.7.1999, p. 59.
(17) OJ C 390, 15.12.1998, p. 1.
(18) OJ C 200, 15.7.1999, p. 1.
(19) OJ C 407, 28.12.1998, p. 21.
(20) OJ C 51, 22.2.1999, p. 53.
(21) OJ C 175, 21.6.1999, p. 135.

(22) OJ C 172, 18.6.1999, p. 3.
(23) OJ L 184, 17.7.1999, p. 23.

ANNEX

ACTIONS AND SUPPORT MEASURES

1. To improve health information and knowledge for the development of public health by:
1.1. developing and operating a sustainable health monitoring system to establish comparable quantitative and qualitative indicators at Community level on the basis of existing work and of accomplished results, and to collect, analyse and disseminate comparable and compatible age- and gender-specific information on human health at Community level concerning health status, health policies and health determinants, including demography, geography and socioeconomic situations, personal and biological factors, health behaviours such as substance abuse, nutrition, physical activity, sexual behaviour, and living, working and environmental conditions, paying special attention to inequalities in health;
1.2. developing an information system for the early warning, detection and surveillance of health threats, both on communicable diseases, including with regard to the danger of cross-border spread of diseases (including resistant pathogens), and on non-communicable diseases;
1.3. improving the system for the transfer and sharing of information and health data including public access;
1.4. developing and using mechanisms for analysis, advice, reporting, information and consultation with Member States and stakeholders on health issues relevant at Community level;
1.5. improving analysis and knowledge of the impact of health policy developments and of other Community policies and activities, such as the internal market as it affects health systems, in contributing to a high level of human health protection, including developing criteria and methodologies for assessing policies for their impact on health and developing other links between public health and other policies;
1.6. reviewing, analysing, and supporting the exchange of experiences on, health technologies, including new information technologies;
1.7. supporting the exchange of information and experiences on good practice;
1.8. developing and operating a joint action with the plans drawn up under e-Europe to improve availability to the general public on the Internet of information on health matters, and considering the possibilities for establishing a system of recognisable Community seals of approval for Internet sites.
The existing data and the information provided by the system is to be easily accessible to the Community, relevant users in Member States and, as appropriate, international organisations.
The statistical element of the system will be developed, in collaboration with Member States, using as necessary the Community Statistical Programme to promote synergy and avoid duplication.

2. To enhance the capability of responding rapidly and in a coordinated fashion to threats to health by:
2.1. enhancing the capacity to tackle communicable diseases by supporting the further implementation of Decision No 2119/98/EC on the Community network on the epidemiological surveillance and control of communicable diseases;
2.2. supporting the network's operation, in the Member States and the countries participating on the basis of Article 10 of this decision, in particular in relation to common investigations, training, continuous assessment, quality assurance and, where appropriate, in relation to its contribution to the actions described in the Annex, points 1.2 and 1.3;
2.3. developing strategies and mechanisms for preventing, exchanging information on and responding to non-communicable disease threats, including gender-specific health threats and rare diseases;
2.4. exchanging information concerning strategies in order to counter health threats from physical, chemical or biological sources in emergency situations, including those relating to terrorist acts, and developing or using, when appropriate, Community approaches and mechanisms;
2.5. exchanging information on vaccination and immunisation strategies;
2.6. enhancing the safety and quality of organs and substances of human origin, including blood, blood components and blood precursors by developing high standards of quality and safety for the collection, processing, storage and distribution and use of these substances;
2.7. implementing vigilance networks for human products, such as blood, blood components and blood precursors;
2.8. promoting strategies and measures concerning the protection of human health from possible adverse effects from environmental agents such as ionising and non-ionising radiation and noise;
2.9. developing strategies for reducing antibiotic resistance.

3. To promote health and prevent disease through action on health determinants across all Community policies and activities by:
3.1. preparing and implementing strategies and measures, including those related to public awareness, on life-style related health determinants, such as nutrition, physical activity, tobacco, alcohol, drugs and other substances and on mental health, including measures to take in all Community policies and age- and gender-specific strategies;
3.2. analysing the situation and developing strategies on social and economic health determinants, in order to identify and combat inequalities in health and to assess the impact of social and economic factors on health;
3.3. analysing the situation and developing strategies on health determinants related to the environment and contributing to the identification and assessment of the health consequences of environmental factors;
3.4. analysing the situation and exchange information on genetic determinants and the use of genetic screening;
3.5. developing methods to evaluate quality and efficiency of health promotion strategies and measures;
3.6. encouraging relevant training activities related to the above measures.

4. Support measures
4.1. Community assistance may be provided to support the actions and activities referred to in Article 3.
4.2. In carrying out the programme, the Commission may require additional resources, including recourse to experts, for instance for the monitoring system, the evaluation of the programme or the preparation of new legislation. It may also require experts to work for the Community structural arrangements for the coordination and integration of networks for health monitoring and for rapid reaction to health threats. The report referred to in Article 12(1) shall be accompanied, if need be, by any proposal regarding adjustment of the requirements.
4.3. The Commission may also undertake information, publication and dissemination of actions. It may also undertake evaluation studies and organise seminars, colloquia or other meetings of experts.

Annex 9.12.

Directive 2003/33/EC of the European Parliament and of the Council of 26 May 2003 on the approximation of the laws, regulations and administrative provisions of the Member States relating to **the advertising and sponsorship of tobacco products** (Text with EEA relevance)
Official Journal L 152 , 20/06/2003 P. 0016 - 0019

MAIN PROVISIONS

Article 1
Subject-matter and scope
1. The objective of this Directive is to approximate the laws, regulations and administrative provisions of the Member States relating to the advertising of tobacco products and their promotion:
(a) in the press and other printed publications;
(b) in radio broadcasting;
(c) in information society services; and
(d) through tobacco related sponsorship, including the free distribution of tobacco products.
2. This Directive is intended to ensure the free movement of the media concerned and of related services and to eliminate obstacles to the operation of the Internal Market.

Article 2
Definitions
For the purposes of this Directive, the following definitions shall apply:
(a) "tobacco products" means all products intended to be smoked, sniffed, sucked or chewed inasmuch as they are made, even partly, of tobacco;
(b) "advertising" means any form of commercial communications with the aim or direct or indirect effect of promoting a tobacco product;
(c) "sponsorship" means any form of public or private contribution to any event, activity or individual with the aim or direct or indirect effect of promoting a tobacco product;
(d) "information society services" means services within the meaning of Article 1(2) of Directive 98/34/EC of the European Parliament and of the Council of 22 June 1998 laying down a procedure for the provision of information in the field of technical standards and regulations and of rules on information society services(11).

Article 3
Advertising in printed media and information society services
1. Advertising in the press and other printed publications shall be limited to publications intended exclusively for professionals in the tobacco trade and to publications which are printed and published in third countries, where those publications are not principally intended for the Community market.
Other advertising in the press and other printed publications shall be prohibited.
2. Advertising that is not permitted in the press and other printed publications shall not be permitted in information society services.

Article 4
Radio advertising and sponsorship
1. All forms of radio advertising for tobacco products shall be prohibited.
2. Radio programmes shall not be sponsored by undertakings whose principal activity is the manufacture or sale of tobacco products.

Article 5
Sponsorship of events
1. Sponsorship of events or activities involving or taking place in several Member States or otherwise having cross-border effects shall be prohibited.
2. Any free distribution of tobacco products in the context of the sponsorship of the events referred to in paragraph 1 having the purpose or the direct or indirect effect of promoting such products shall be prohibited.

Article 6
Report
No later than 20 June 2008, the Commission shall submit a report to the European Parliament, the Council and

the European Economic and Social Committee on the implementation of this Directive. That report shall be accompanied by any proposals for amendments to this Directive which the Commission deems necessary.

Article 7

Penalties and enforcement

Member States shall lay down the rules on penalties applicable to infringements of the national provisions adopted pursuant to this Directive and shall take all measures necessary to ensure that they are implemented. The penalties provided for must be effective, proportionate and dissuasive. The Member States shall notify those rules to the Commission by the date specified in Article 10 at the latest and shall notify it without delay of any subsequent amendment affecting them.

Those rules shall include provisions ensuring that persons or organisations which, under national legislation, can justify a legitimate interest in the suppression of advertising, sponsorship or other matters incompatible with this Directive, may take legal action against such advertising or sponsorship or bring such advertising or sponsorship to the attention of an administrative body competent either to pronounce on complaints or to institute the appropriate legal proceedings.

Article 8

Free movement of products and services

Member States shall not prohibit or restrict the free movement of products or services which comply with this Directive.

Article 9

References to Directive 98/43/EC

References to the annulled Directive 98/43/EC shall be construed as references to this Directive.

Article 10

Implementation

1. Member States shall bring into force the laws, regulations and administrative provisions necessary to comply with this Directive by 31 July 2005 at the latest. They shall forthwith inform the Commission thereof.

When Member States adopt those measures, they shall contain a reference to this Directive or be accompanied by such a reference on the occasion of their official publication. The methods of making such reference shall be laid down by the Member States.

2. Member States shall communicate to the Commission the text of the main provisions of national law which they adopt in the field covered by this Directive.

Annex 9.13.

Council Regulation (EEC) No 302/93 of 8 February 1993 on the establishment of a
European Monitoring Centre for Drugs and Drug Addiction
Official Journal L 036 , 12/02/1993 P. 0001 - 0008

MAIN PROVISIONS

Article 1

Objective
1. This Regulation establishes the European Monitoring Centre for Drugs and Drug Addiction (EDMC), hereinafter referred to as 'the Centre`.
2. The Centre's objective is to provide, in the areas referred to in Article 4, the Community and its Member States with objective, reliable and comparable information at European level concerning drugs and drug addiction and their consequences.
3. The statistical, documentary and technical information processed or produced is intended to help provide the Community and the Member States with an overall view of the drug and drug addiction situation when, in their respective areas of competence, they take measures or decide on action.
4. The Centre may not take any measure which in any way goes beyond the sphere of information and the processing thereof.
5. The Centre shall not collect any data making it possible to identify individuals or small groups of individuals. It shall refrain from any transmission of information relating to specific named cases.

Article 2

Tasks
In order to achieve the objective set out in Article 1, the Centre shall perform the following tasks within its areas of activity:
A. Collection and analysis of existing data
It shall:
1. collect, register and analyse information, including data resulting from research, communicated by Member States as well as that emanating from Community, non-governmental national sources and competent international organizations;
2. carry out surveys, preparatory studies and feasibility studies, together with any pilot projects necessary to accomplish its tasks; organize meetings of experts and whenever necesssary set up ad hoc working parties for the purpose; it shall set up and make available open scientific documentation resources and assist in the promotion of information activities;
3. provide an organizational and technical system capable of supplying information on similar or complementary programmes or action pursued by the Member States;
4. establish and coordinate, in consultation and in cooperation with the competent authorities and organizations in the Member States, the network referred to in Article 5;
5. facilitate exchanges of information between decision-makers, researchers, specialists and those involved in combating drugs in governmental and non-governmental organizations;

B. Improvement of data-comparison methods
6. ensure improved comparability, objectivity and reliability of data at European level by establishing indicators and common criteria of a non-binding nature, compliance with which may be recommended by the Centre, with a view to greater uniformity of the measurement methods used by the Member States and the Community;
7. facilitate and structure exchange of information, in terms of both quality and quantity (databases);

C. Dissemination of data
8. make the information produced by it available to the Community, the Member States and competent organizations;
9. ensure wide dissemination of work done in each Member State and by the Community itself, and, where appropriate, by non-Community countries or international organizations;
10. ensure wide dissemination of reliable non-confidential data, on the basis of data which it gathers it shall publish a yearly report on the state of the drugs problem;

D. Cooperation with European and international bodies and organizations and with non-Community countries
11. contribute to improving coordination between national and Community action in its areas of activity;
12. without prejudice to Member States' obligations with regard to transmission of information under the provisions of the United Nations Conventions on drugs, promote the incorporation of data on drugs and drug addiction gathered in the Member States or emanating from the Community into international monitoring and drug-control programmes, particularly those established by the United Nations Organization and its specialized agencies;
13. cooperate actively with the bodies referred to in Article 12.

Article 3

Work method
1. The Centre shall progressively carry out its tasks in the light of the objectives adopted in the three-year and annual work programmes and with due regard to the available resources.
2. In pursuing its activities, the Centre shall, in order to avoid duplication, take account of those already carried out by other existing or future institutions and agencies, notably the European Police Office (Europol), and shall ensure that it adds to their value.

Article 4

Priority areas of activity
The objectives and tasks of the Centre, as defined in Articles 1 and 2, shall be implemented following the order of priorities indicated in the Annex.

Article 5

European Information Network on Drugs and Drug Addiction (Reitox)
1. The Centre shall have at its disposal the European Information Network on Drugs and Drug Addiction (Reitox), a computer network forming the infrastructure for collecting and exchanging information and documentation; the network shall make use of, inter alia, an autonomous computer system linking the national drug information networks, the specialized centres in Member States and the information systems of the international or European organizations or bodies cooperating with the Centre.
2. In order to enable the network to be established as rapidly and efficiently as possible, the Member States shall, with in six months of the entry into force of this Regulation, notify the Centre of the main elements of their national information networks, including where appropriate the national monitoring centres, in the areas of activity mentioned in Article 4 and name any specialized Centres which in their judgment could make a useful contribution to the Centre's work.
3. The specialized centres shall be designated with the consent of the Member State in whose territory they are located, by a unanimous decision of the members of the management board, as referred to in the second subparagraph of Article 8 (2), for a period not exceeding the duration of each multiannual work programme as referred to in Article 8 (3). This designation shall be renewable.
4. The Centre may, with the consent of the Member State in whose territory the centres are located, enter into contractual relations, in particular subcontracting arrangements, with governmental or non-governmental specialized centres as referred to in paragraph 3, in order to fulfil any tasks which it may wish to entrust to them. With the consent of the respective Member States, it may also enter into contracts, on an ad hoc basis and for specific tasks, with bodies which are not part of Reitox.
5. The allocation of specific tasks to the specialized centres shall appear in the Centre's multiannual programme mentioned in Article 8 (3).

Article 6

Protection and confidentiality of data
1. Where on the basis of this Regulation personal data which do not enable natural persons to be identified are also forwarded to the Centre in accordance with national law, such data may be used only for the stated purpose and under the conditions prescribed by the forwarding authority. This shall apply mutatis mutandis where personal data are communicated by the Centre to the competent authorities of the Member States or to international organizations and other European institutions.
2. Data on drugs and drug addiction provided to or by the Centre may be published subject to compliance with Community and national rules on the dissemination and confidentiality of information. Personal data may not be published or made accessible to the public.

3. Member States and the specialized centres shall be under no obligation to provide information classified as confidential under their national legislation.

Article 7

Legal status
The Centre shall have legal personality. It shall enjoy, in each Member State, the most extensive legal status granted to legal persons under their laws; in particular, it may purchase or dispose of movable and immovable property and may institute legal proceedings.

Article 8

Management Board
1. The Centre shall have a management board consisting of one representative from each Member State, two representatives from the Commission and two scientists particularly qualified in the field of drugs, designated by the European Parliament on the basis of their particular qualification in that field.
Each member of the management board may be assisted or represented by an alternative member. In the absence of the full member, the alternative member may exercise his right to vote. The management board may call in as non-voting observers representatives of international organizations with which the Centre cooperates in accordance with Article 12.
2. The chairman of the management board shall be elected by its members for a three-year period: his term of office shall be renewable once. The chairman shall take part in the voting. Each member of the management board shall have one vote.
The decisions of the management board shall be taken by a two-thirds majority of its members, except in the cases referred to in Article 5 (3), for which a unanimous decision by the members is required, and in paragraph 3 of this Article. The management board shall draw up its own rules of procedure. The management board shall meet at least once a year.
3. The management board shall adopt a three-year work programme on the basis of a draft submitted by the Centre's Director, after consulting the Scientific Committee and seeking the opinions of the Commission and of the Council. The first three-year programme shall be adopted unanimously, within nine months of the entry into force of this Regulation. The management board, acting by a majority of three-quarters of its members, shall decide whether subsequent three-year programmes are to be adopted by the majority laid down in the second subparagraph of paragraph 2 of this Article or by unanimity.
4. Under the three-year work programme, the management board shall each year adopt the Centre's annual work programme on the basis of a draft submitted by the Director, after consulting the Scientific Committee and seeking the Commission's opinion. The programme may be adjusted in the course of the year in accordance with the same procedure.
5. By 31 January each year at the latest, the management board shall adopt an annual general report on the activities of the Centre. The Director shall forward this report to the European Parliament, the Council, the Commission and the Member States.

Article 9

Director
1. The Centre shall be headed by a Director appointed by the management board on a proposal from the Commission for a five-year period, which shall be renewable. The Director shall be responsible for:
- preparing and implementing the decisions and programmes adopted by the Centre's management board,
- day-to-day administration,
- preparing the Centre's work programmes,
- the preparation of a statement of revenue and expenditure and on the implementation of the budget,
- the preparation and publication of the reports provided for in this Regulation,
- all staff matters,
- performance of the tasks referred to in Article 1 and 2.
2. The Director shall be accountable for his activities to the management board and shall attend its meetings.
3. The Director shall be the Centre's legal representative.

Article 10

Scientific Committee
1. The management board and the Director shall be assisted by a Scientific Committee which shall deliver an

opinion where provided for in this Regulation on any scientific matter concerning the Centre's activities which the management board or the Director may submit to it.
The opinions of the Scientific Committee shall be published.
2. The Scientific Committee shall consist of one representative from each Member State. The management board may appoint up to six other members having regard to their particular qualifications.
3. Members shall serve on the Scientific Committee for a three-year period, which shall be renewable.
4. The Scientific Committee shall elect its chairman for a three-year period.
5. The Scientific Committee shall be convened by its chairman at least once a year.

Article 11

Budget
1. Estimates shall be drawn up of all the Centre's revenue and expenditure for each financial year, which shall correspond to the calendar year, and shall be entered in the Centre's budget.
2. By 15 February each year at the latest, the Director shall draw up a preliminary draft budget covering the operational expenditure and the programme of work anticipated for the following financial year, and shall forward this preliminary draft to the management board together with an establishment plan.
3. Revenue and expenditure shall be in balance.
4. The Centre's revenue shall, without prejudice to other resources, consist of a subsidy from the Community entered under a specific heading of the general budget of the European Communities (Commission Section), payments for services rendered and any financial contributions from the organizations and bodies and non-Community countries mentioned in Articles 12 and 13 respectively.
5. The Centre's expenditure shall include, inter alia:
- staff remuneration, administrative and infrastructure expenses, and operating costs,
- expenditure in support of the national information networks which form part of the Reitox network and expenditure relating to contracts with the specialized centres.
6. The management board shall adopt the draft budget and forward it to the Commission, which on that basis shall establish the relevant estimates in the preliminary draft general budget of the European Communities, which it shall put before the Council pursuant to Article 203 of the Treaty.
7. The management board shall adopt the Centre's final budget before the beginning of the financial year, adjusting it where necessary to the Community subsidy and the Centre's other resources.
8. The Director shall implement the budget.
9. Monitoring of the commitment and payment of all the Centre's expenditure and of the establishment and recovery of all the Centre's revenue shall be carried out by the Commission's financial controller.
10. By 31 March each year at the latest, the Director shall forward to the Commission, the management board and the Court of Auditors the accounts for all the Centre's revenue and expenditure in respect of the preceding financial year.
The Court of Auditors shall examine them in accordance with Article 206a of the Treaty.
11. The management board shall give a discharge to the Director in respect of the implementation of the budget.
12. The Financial Regulation applicable to the general budget of the European Communities shall apply to the Centre. The Council, acting by a qualified majority on a proposal from the Commission and after consulting the European Parliament and the management board, may grant derogations from the Financial Regulation when then specific requirements of the functioning of the Centre so dictate.

Article 12

Cooperation with other organizations and bodies
Without prejudice to relations which the Commission may maintain pursuant to Article 229 of the Treaty, the Centre shall actively seek the cooperation of international organizations and other, particularly European, governmental and non-governmental agencies competent in the sector of drugs.

Article 13

Non-Community countries
1. The Centre shall be open to the participation of those non-Community countries which share the Community's interests and those of its Member States in the Centre's objectives and work, on the basis of agreements entered into between them and the Community on the basis of Article 235 of the Treaty.
2. The management board may take a decision on the involvement of experts proposed by non-Community countries in the ad hoc working parties provided for in Article 2 (2), subject to an undertaking from the interested parties to observe the rules referred to in Article 6.

Article 14

Privileges and immunities
The Protocol on the Privileges and immunities of the European Communities shall apply to the Centre.

Article 15

Staff Regulations
The staff of the Centre shall be subject to the regulations and rules applicable to the officials and other servants of the European Communities.
The Centre shall exercise in respect of its staff the powers devolved to the appointing authority.
The management board shall, in agreement with the Commission, adopt the appropriate implementing rules.

Article 16

Liability
1. The contractual liability of the Centre shall be governed by the law applicable to the contract in question. The Court of Justice shall have jurisdiction pursuant to an arbitration clause contained in a contract concluded by the Centre.
2. In the case of non-contractual liability, the Centre shall, in accordance with the general principles common to the laws of the Member States, make good any damage caused by the Centre or its servants in the performance of their duties. The Court of Justice shall have jurisdiction in disputes relating to compensating for any such damage.
3. The personal liability of servants towards the Centre shall be governed by the provisions applying to the staff of the Centre.

Article 17

Jurisdiction of the Court of Justice
The Court of Justice shall have jurisdiction in actions brought against the Centre under the conditions provided for in Article 173 of the Treaty.

Article 18

Report
During the third year following the entry into force of this Regulation, the Commission shall forward to the European Parliament and to the Community a progress report on the Centre's activities, together with proposals, if appropriate, to modify or extend its tasks, taking into account, in particular, the evolution of Community powers.

Article 19

Entry into force
This Regulation shall enter into force on the day following the decision of the competent authorities on the seat of the Centre.

This Regulation shall be binding in its entirety and directly applicable in all Member States.
Done at Brussels, 8 February 1993.
For the Council
The President
J. TRØJBORG

(1) OJ No C 43, 18. 2. 1992, p. 2.
(2) OJ No C 150, 15. 6. 1992, p. 54.
(3) OJ No C 223, 31. 8. 1992, p. 26.
(4) OJ No L 326, 24. 11. 1990, p. 56.
(5) OJ No L 326, 24. 11. 1990, p. 57.
(6) OJ No L 357, 20. 12. 1990, p. 1. Regulation, as amended by Regulation (EEC) No 900/92 (OJ No L 96, 10. 4. 1992, p. 1).

(7) OJ No L 166, 28. 6. 1991, p. 77.
(8) OJ No C 185, 22. 7. 1989, p. 1.
ANNEX

A. The work of the Centre shall be carried out with due regard to the respective powers of the Community and its Member States in the area of drugs, as those powers are defined by the Treaty.
The information gathered by the Centre shall relate to the following priority areas:
1. demand and reduction of the demand for drugs;
2. national and Community strategies and policies (with special emphasis on international, bilateral and Community policies, action plans, legislation, activities and agreements);
3. international cooperation and geopolitics of supply (with special emphasis on cooperation programmes and information on producer and transit countries);
4. control of trade in narcotic drugs, psychotropic substances and precursors, as provided for in the relevant present or future international conventions and Community acts (1);
5. Implications of the drugs phenomenon for producer, consumer and transit countries, within areas covered by the Treaty, including money laundering, as laid down by the relevant present or future Community acts (2).

B. The Commission shall make available to the Centre, for dissemination, the information and statistical data which it possesses pursuant to its powers.

C. During the first three-year period special attention will be given to demand and demand reduction.
(1) - The relevant international conventions currently in force include, in particular, the United Nations Conventions, in so far as the Community is or could become party to them. - The relevant Community acts currently in force include in particular Council Regulation (EEC) No 3677/90 of 13 December 1990 laying down measures to be taken to discourage the diversion of certain subtances to the illicit manufacture of narcotic drugs and psychotropic substances. - This involves only information which the Member States are obliged to supply to the Commission on the basis of existing and future Community legislation.
(2) - Of the relevant Community acts currently in force the one concerning money laundering is the Council Directive of 10 June 1991 on prevention of the use of the financial system for the purpose of money laundering. - This involves only information which the Member States are obliged to supply to the Commission on the basis of existing and future Community legislation.

Annex 9.14.

2002/834/EC: Council Decision of 30 September 2002 adopting a **specific programme for research, technological development and demonstration**: "Integrating and strengthening the European Research Area" (2002-2006)
Official Journal L 294 , 29/10/2002 P. 0001 - 0043

MAIN PROVISIONS

Article 1
1. In accordance with the framework programme, a specific programme on integrating and strengthening the European Research Area (hereinafter referred to as "the specific programme") is hereby adopted for the period from 30 September 2002 to 31 December 2006.
2. The objectives and scientific and technological priorities for the specific programme are set out in Annex I.

Article 2
In accordance with Annex II of the framework programme, the amount deemed necessary for the execution of the specific programme is EUR 12905 million, including a maximum of 6,0 % for the Commission's administrative expenditure. An indicative breakdown of this amount is given in Annex II.

Article 3
All research activities carried out under the specific programme must be carried out in compliance with fundamental ethical principles.

Article 4
1. The detailed rules for financial participation by the Community in the specific programme shall be those referred to in Article 2(2) of the framework programme.
2. The specific programme shall be implemented by means of the instruments defined in Annex III to the framework programme and described in Annex III.
3. The rules for participation and dissemination shall apply to the specific programme.

Article 5
1. The Commission shall draw up a work programme for the implementation of the specific programme, setting out in greater detail the objectives and scientific and technological priorities set out in Annex I, and the timetable for implementation.
2. The work programme shall take account of relevant research activities carried out by the Member States, Associated States and European and international organisations. It shall be updated where appropriate.

Article 6
1. The Commission shall be responsible for the implementation of the specific programme.
2. The procedure laid down in Article 7(2) shall apply for the adoption of the following measures:
(a) the drawing up and updating of the work programme referred to in Article 5(1), including the instruments to be used on a priority basis, any subsequent adjustment to their use, the content of the calls for proposals as well as the evaluation and selection criteria to be applied;
(b) the approval of funding of:
(i) RTD actions involving networks of excellence and integrated projects,
(ii) RTD actions under the following priority thematic areas:
"Life sciences, genomics and biotechnology for health",
"Information society technologies",
"Nanotechnologies and nanosciences, knowledge-based multifunctional materials and new production processes and devices",
"Aeronautics and space",
"Food quality and safety",
"Sustainable development, global change and ecosystems",
where the estimated amount of the Community contribution under this programme is equal to or more than EUR 1,5 million,
(iii) RTD actions, other than those referred to in points (i) and (ii), where the estimated amount of the Community contribution under this programme is equal to or more than EUR 0,6 million;
(c) the drawing-up of the terms of reference for the external assessment provided for in Article 6(2) of the

framework programme;
(d) any adjustment to the indicative breakdown of the amount as set out in Annex II.
3. The procedure laid down in Article 7(3) shall apply for the adoption of the following measures:
- detailed implementing provisions concerning research activities involving human embryos and human embryonic stem cells,
- RTD actions involving the use of human embryos and human embryonic stem cells.

ANNEX I

SCIENTIFIC AND TECHNOLOGICAL OBJECTIVES AND BROAD LINES OF THE ACTIVITIES

INTRODUCTION

This programme will promote world class research in key priority areas of exceptional interest and added value to Europe and the competitiveness of its industry, which have been identified in the framework programme 2002-2006, as well as on topics that are identified as being of high importance during the course of implementation of the framework programme in view of the EU's policy needs and the opportunities arising in novel, leading edge research areas.
The programme will strive towards greater integration of research in Europe by means of:
- focused action in priority thematic research areas, using powerful financing instruments (integrated projects and networks of excellence) which bring together the research actors in appropriate configurations for the new challenges that these priority research areas represent, and with critical mass,
- systematic and coordinated planning and execution of research to support Community policies, and to explore new and emerging scientific and technological areas, taking account of needs expressed by the relevant actors throughout the European Union,
- promoting the networking and joint action of national and European frameworks for research and innovation, and the opening up of national programmes, in these priority areas, including where appropriate by the use of actions under Article 169 of the Treaty, as well as in other areas where such action would be of benefit to the performance of Europe's research base.
The programme is complementary to the programme "structuring the European Research Area" and the specific programme for the JRC, and its implementation will be coordinated with them.
International cooperation represents an important dimension of the Framework Programme. In this specific programme, international activities are carried out in the two forms of:
- participation of researchers, teams and institutions from third countries in projects within the different thematic priority fields, related to issues arising at world level and being subjects of international efforts,
- specific international cooperation activities with some groups of countries, as a support to Community external relations and development aid policies.
The objectives and forms of the international cooperation activities in the Framework Programme are described under the heading "Specific activities covering a wider field of research".
Participation of the candidate countries in this programme will be encouraged.
Participation of small and medium sized enterprises (SMEs) will be encouraged and gender equity will, overall, be assured in the implementation of the activities.
The activities carried out within the programme will be implemented in an integrated fashion to assure coherence and synergy between their various elements and, as appropriate, with other parts of the framework programme(1).

1. FOCUSING AND INTEGRATING COMMUNITY RESEARCH

1.1. PRIORITY THEMATIC AREAS OF RESEARCH

The priority thematic areas represent the bulk of expenditure under the sixth framework programme. Through a highly focused Community research effort, the intention is to generate a substantial leveraging effect which, together with actions in other parts of the framework programme and through open coordination with other - regional, national, European and international - frameworks, will result in a coherent and highly effective common endeavour towards their overall objectives.
The actions are therefore described in terms of:
- the overall objectives and expected achievements which are sought in each priority area,
- the research priorities to be pursued by means of Community action.
The priority thematic areas of research are described in terms of their overall objectives and the main research focus. The associated work programme will elaborate further on the detailed research content.
Within the thematic priority areas, the importance of the new instruments (integrated projects and networks of

excellence) is recognised as being an overall priority means to attain the objectives of critical mass, management simplification and European added value contributed by Community research in relation to what is already undertaken at national level, and of the integration of the research capacities. The size of projects is not a criterion for exclusion, and access to new instruments is ensured for SMEs and other small entities.
Networks of excellence and integrated projects will be used from the start of the programme in each thematic priority area and, where deemed appropriate, as a priority means, while maintaining the use of specific targeted projects and coordination actions. In addition to research and technological development, they may incorporate the following types of activity, where they are of specific relevance to the objectives sought: demonstration, dissemination and exploitation; cooperation with researchers and research teams from third countries; human resource development, including the promotion of training of researchers; development of research facilities and infrastructure of specific relevance to the research being undertaken; and promotion of better links between science and society, including women in science.
Specific targeted research projects and coordination actions, as well as specific support actions, may also be used in the spirit of the "stairway of excellence" in the implementation of the thematic priorities.
Innovation is an important dimension which must be taken into account in the design and implementation of RTD activities. In particular, networks of excellence and integrated projects will include activities relating to dissemination and exploitation of knowledge and, where relevant, to ensure transfer of technology and facilitate exploitation of results. Where appropriate, special attention will be given to technology transfer to SMEs and to the creation of research-based enterprises as a means of exploiting research results.
The priority research areas include, in certain cases, research at the borders of traditional disciplines where advances will require interdisciplinary and multidisciplinary effort. They will also each carry out, as appropriate, exploratory research at the leading edge of knowledge on subjects closely related to one or more topics within them. Measurement and testing aspects will also receive necessary emphasis. A particular attention will be given during the implementation of the programme to the coordination between the different priority areas, and between these areas and actions under the heading "policy support and anticipating scientific and technological needs".
The principle of sustainable development, and gender equality, will be duly taken into account. Furthermore, consideration of the ethical, social, legal and wider cultural aspects of the research to be undertaken and its potential applications, as well as socio-economic impacts of scientific and technological development and foresight, will where relevant form a part of the activities under this heading. Research on ethics related to scientific and technological developments will be carried out in the programme "Structuring the European Research Area".
During the implementation of this programme and in the research activities arising from it, fundamental ethical principles are to be respected. These include the principles reflected in the Charter of fundamental rights of the EU, including the following: protection of human dignity and human life, protection of personal data and privacy, as well as animals and the environment in accordance with Community law and relevant international conventions and codes of conduct, e.g. the Helsinki Declaration in its latest version, the Convention of the Council of Europe on Human Rights and Biomedicine signed in Oviedo on 4 April 1997, and the Additional Protocol on the Prohibition of Cloning Human Beings signed in Paris on 12 January 1998, the UN Convention on the Rights of the Child, the Universal Declaration on the human genome and human rights adopted by UNESCO, and the relevant World Health Organisation (WHO) resolutions.
Account will also be taken to the opinions of the European Group of Advisers on the Ethical Implications of Biotechnology (1991-1997) and the opinions of the European Group on Ethics in Science and New technologies (as from 1998).
In compliance with the principle of subsidiarity and the diversity of approaches existing in Europe, participants in research projects must conform to current legislation, regulations and ethical rules in the countries where the research will be carried out. In any case, national provisions apply and no research forbidden in any given Member State will be supported by Community funding in that Member State.
Where appropriate, participants in research projects must seek the approval of the relevant national or local ethics committees prior to the start of the RTD activities. An ethical review will be implemented systematically by the Commission for proposals dealing with ethically sensitive issues, in particular proposals involving the use of human embryos and human embryonic stem cells.
Any research project involving the use of human embryos and human embryonic stem cells, following the ethical review mentioned above, will be submitted to a Regulatory Committee.
In specific cases, an ethical review may take place during the implementation of a project.
The following fields of research shall not be financed under this programme:
- research activity aiming at human cloning for reproductive purposes,
- research activity intended to modify the genetic heritage of human beings which could make such changes heritable(2),
- research activities intended to create human embryos solely for the purpose of research or for the purpose of

stem cell procurement, including by means of somatic cell nuclear transfer.
In addition, funding of research activities that are prohibited in all the Member States is in all circumstances excluded.
In accordance with the Amsterdam protocol on animal protection and welfare, animal experiments must be replaced with alternatives wherever possible. Suffering by animals must be avoided or kept to a minimum. This particularly applies (pursuant to Directive 86/609/EEC) to animal experiments involving species which are closest to human beings. Altering the genetic heritage of animals and cloning of animals may be considered only if the aims are ethically justified and the conditions are such that the animals' welfare is guaranteed and the principles of biodiversity are respected.
These guidelines will apply in the implementation of this programme. Furthermore, scientific advances and national provisions will be regularly monitored by the Commission so as to take account of any relevant developments. This monitoring could lead as necessary to a revision of these guidelines.

1.1.1. Life sciences, genomics and biotechnology for health
The sequencing of the human genome and many other genomes heralds a new age in human biology, offering unprecedented opportunities to improve human health and to stimulate industrial and economic activity. In making its contribution to realising these benefits, this theme will focus on integrating post-genomic research, including research on related molecular mechanisms, into the more established biomedical and biotechnological approaches, and will facilitate the integration of research capacities (both public and private) across Europe to increase coherence and achieve critical mass. Integrated multidisciplinary research, which enables a strong interaction between technology and biology, is vital in this theme for translating genome data into practical applications. In addition, an essential element will be to involve key stakeholders, for example, as appropriate industry, healthcare providers and physicians, policy makers, regulatory authorities, patient associations, and experts on ethical matters, etc. in implementing the theme. Furthermore, attention will be paid to childhood diseases and related treatments, whenever appropriate, and gender equity in the research will be ensured(3).
This thematic priority area will stimulate and sustain multidisciplinary basic research to exploit the full potential of genome information to underpin applications to human health. In the field of applications, the emphasis will be put on research aimed at bringing basic knowledge through to the application stage ("translational" approach), to enable real and consistent and coordinated progress at European level in medicine and improve the quality of life. This research may also have implications for research on areas such as agriculture and environment, which are addressed under other thematic priorities; such implications should be duly taken into account in the course of the implementation of the thematic priorities concerned.
It will be an integral component of the European Community effort to enhance the European biotechnology industry in line with the conclusions of the Stockholm European Council. It will endeavour to create strong links with all activities that improve the framework conditions for innovation in the health sector of the biotechnology industry, especially in SMEs, including stimulating entrepreneurship and opportunities for investment through venture capital and the involvement of the European Investment Bank. Attention will also be paid to the identification of regulatory bottlenecks in the development of new applications for genomics, to the anticipation at the earliest possible stage of the ethical implications and to the broader implications of developments in genomics research for society and citizens.
This thematic priority area will also foster the implementation and development of the health strategy of the European Community.
Throughout the thematic priority, international collaboration will be encouraged. Where appropriate, due account will be given to the European Community's commitment to poverty reduction in developing countries and the importance that improved health will bring to the process - in line with Article 177 of the Treaty and with the European Community's accelerated actions to combat HIV/AIDS, malaria and tuberculosis.

Research priorities
(i) Advanced genomics and its applications for health
Fundamental knowledge and basic tools for functional genomics in all organisms
The strategic objective of this line is to foster the basic understanding of genomic information, by developing the knowledge base, tools and resources needed to decipher the function of genes and gene products relevant to human health and to explore their interactions with each other and with their environment. Research actions will encompass the following:
- Gene expression and proteomics: The objectives are to enable researchers to better decipher the functions of genes and gene products as well as to define the complex regulatory networks (biocomplexity) that control fundamental biological processes.
Research will focus on: developing high throughput tools and approaches for monitoring gene expression and protein profiles and for determining protein function and interactions of biological molecules within the living cell.

- Structural genomics: The objectives are to enable researchers to determine, more effectively and at a higher rate than is currently feasible, the 3-D structure of proteins and other macromolecules, which is important for elucidating protein function and essential for drug design.
Research will focus on: developing high throughput approaches for determining high-resolution 3-D structures of macromolecules.
- Comparative genomics and population genetics: The objectives are to enable researchers to use well-characterised model organisms for predicting and testing gene function and to take full advantage of specific population cohorts available in Europe to determine the relationship between gene function and health or disease.
Research will focus on: developing model organisms and transgenic tools; developing genetic epidemiology tools and standardised genotyping protocols.
- Bioinformatics: The objectives are to enable researchers to access efficient tools for managing and interpreting the ever-increasing quantities of genome data and for making it available to the research community in an accessible and usable form.
Research will focus on: developing bioinformatic tools and resources for data storage, mining and processing; developing computational biology approaches for in silico prediction of gene function and for the simulation of complex regulatory networks.
- Multidisciplinary functional genomics approaches to basic biological processes: The objectives are to enable researchers to study fundamental biological processes by integrating the above innovative approaches.
Research will focus on: elucidation of the mechanisms underlying fundamental cellular processes, to identify the genes involved and to decipher their biological functions in living organisms.
Applications of knowledge and technologies in the field of genomics and biotechnology for health
The strategic objective of this line is to foster the competitiveness of Europe's biotechnology industry by exploiting the wealth of biological data produced by genomics and advances in biotechnology. Research actions will encompass the following:
- Technological platforms for the developments in the fields of new diagnostic, prevention and therapeutic tools: In the context of preventing and treating diseases, the objectives are to foster academic and industrial collaboration through technological platforms where multidisciplinary approaches using cutting edge technologies arising from genomic research may contribute to health care progress and cost reduction through more precise diagnosis, individualised treatment and more efficient development pathways for new drugs and therapies (such as the selection of new drug candidates), and other novel products of the new technologies.
Research will focus on: rational and accelerated development of new, safer, more effective drugs including pharmacogenomics approaches; development of new diagnostics; development of new in vitro tests to replace animal experimentation; development and testing of new preventive and therapeutic tools, such as somatic gene and cell therapies (in particular stem cell therapies, for example those on neurological and neuromuscular disorders) and immunotherapies; innovative research in post-genomics, which has high potential for application.
With a view to ensuring socially responsible choices, public acceptance and an efficient development pathway for these new technologies, an active and early involvement in the above activities of regulators, experts on ethics, patients and society at large will be necessary.

(ii) Combating major diseases
Application-oriented genomic approaches to medical knowledge and technologies
The strategic objective of this line is to develop improved strategies for the prevention and management - using also advanced technologies for health - of human disease and for living and ageing healthily. It will concentrate exclusively on integrating genomic approaches through all relevant organisms into more established medical approaches for investigating disease and health determinants. The emphasis will be put on translational research aimed at bringing basic knowledge through to clinical application. Research actions will focus on the following:
- Combating cardiovascular diseases, diabetes, and rare diseases: The objectives are to improve the prevention and management of important causes of mortality and ill health in Europe and to pool Europe's research resources for tackling rare diseases.
Research will focus on: integrating clinical expertise and resources with relevant model systems and advanced tools in functional genomics to generate breakthroughs in the prevention and management of these diseases.
- Combating resistance to antibiotics and other drugs: The objectives are to confront the major threat to public health caused by drug resistant pathogens.
Research will focus on: exploitation of the knowledge of microbial genomes and on host-pathogen interactions for the development of vaccines and alternative therapeutic strategies to circumvent the problem of antimicrobial and other drug resistance; development of strategies for optimal usage of antimicrobials; support to the European Community network for epidemiological surveillance and control of communicable diseases.
- Studying the brain and combating diseases of the nervous system: The objectives are to use genome information to understand better the functioning and dysfunctioning of the brain, in order to gain new insight

into mental processes, to combat neurological disorders and diseases, and to improve brain repair.
Research will focus on: understanding the molecular and cellular bases of brain function, damage, plasticity and repair, learning, memory and cognition; developing strategies for prevention and management of neurological and mental disorders and diseases (such as Alzheimer's disease, Parkinson's disease and new variant Creutzfeldt-Jakob's disease), including those relating to drug dependence.
- Studying human development and the ageing process: The objective is to better understand human development, with special emphasis on the ageing process, in order to develop the evidence base for improving public health strategies to promote healthy living and healthy ageing.
Research will focus on: understanding human development from conception to adolescence; exploring the molecular and cellular determinants of healthy ageing including their interactions with environmental, behavioural and gender factors.

Combating cancer
The objective is to combat cancer by developing improved patient-oriented strategies, from prevention to more effective and earlier diagnosis and better treatment with minimal side effects. The research will therefore concentrate on translating the knowledge being created by genomics and other fields of basic research into applications that improve clinical practice and public health.
The patient-oriented approach will include four interlinked components. Research will focus on:
- Establishing facilities and developing initiatives for the exploitation of research on cancer in Europe; encouraging the development of evidence-based guidelines for good clinical practice and improved public health strategies by accelerating the translation of existing research results into applications.
- Supporting clinical research, particularly clinical trials, aimed at validating new and improved interventions.
- Supporting translational research aimed at bringing basic knowledge through to applications in clinical practice and public health.
- Other issues related to cancer, such as ageing and cancer, regional differences, psycho-social aspects, palliative care and guidance to support groups

Confronting the major communicable diseases linked to poverty
The strategic objective of this line is to confront the global emergency caused by the three major communicable diseases - HIV/AIDS, malaria and tuberculosis - through the development of effective disease interventions, particularly for use in developing countries. It is envisaged that developing countries will be significant partners in the implementation of this line and, as appropriate, participate directly in specific activities within it, in particular through the clinical trials programme.
Research will focus on: developing promising candidate interventions (vaccines, therapies and HIV microbicides) against the target diseases by sponsoring research over the full spectrum from basic molecular research, taking advantage of microbial genomics, through to pre-clinical testing and proof-of-principle; establishing a clinical trials programme to unite and support Europe's clinical trial activities specifically targeted at interventions for use in developing countries; establishing an AIDS Therapy Trials Network in Europe to improve the coherence and complementarity of clinical trials of AIDS therapies for European use.
The research activities carried out within this thematic priority area will include exploratory research at the leading edge of knowledge on subjects closely related to one or more topics within it. Two complementary approaches will be utilised: one receptive and open - the other proactive.

Annex 9.15.

Council Directive 87/357/EEC of 25 June 1987 on the approximation of the laws of the Member States **concerning products which, appearing to be other than they are, endanger the health or safety of consumers**

Official Journal L 192 , 11/07/1987 P. 0049 - 0050

MAIN PROVISIONS

Article 1

1. This Directive applies to the products, defined in paragraph 2 below, which, appearing to be other than they are, endanger the health or safety of consumers.

2. The products referred to in paragraph 1 above are those which, although not foodstuffs, possess a form, odour, colour, appearance, packaging, labelling, volume or size, such that it is likely that consumers, especially children, will confuse them with foodstuffs and in consequence place them in their mouths, or suck or ingest them, which might be dangerous and cause, for example, suffocation, poisoning, or the perforation or obstruction of the digestive tract.

Article 2

Member States shall take all the measures necessary to prohibit the marketing, import and either manufacture or export of the products referred to in this Directive.

Article 3

Member States shall in particular ensure that checks are carried out on products on the market to ascertain that no product falling within the scope of this Directive is being marketed and shall take all necessary measures to ensure that their competent authorities withdraw or cause to be withdrawn from their markets any product covered by this Directive.

Article 4

1. If a Member State takes a specific measure persuant to Articles 2 and 3, it shall inform the Commission thereof. It shall give a description of the product and the grounds for its decision.

Where details of the product are already required under Decision 84/133/EEC, no further notification is required under this Directive.

The Commission shall forward the details to the other Member States at the earliest opportunity.

2. The Committee set up by Decision 84/133/EEC may be requested by the Commission or a Member State to enter into an exchange of views on questions relating to the application of this Directive.

Article 5

Two years after the date referred to in Article 6, on the basis of a Commission report on experience gained, accompanied by appropriate proposals, the Council shall take a decision on a possible adjustment to this Directive, in particular with a view to extending its scope to cover dangerous imitations other than imitations of foodstuffs and any review of the procedures laid down in Article 4.

Article 6

1. Member States shall take the measures necessary to comply with this Directive not later than 26 June 1989. They shall forthwith inform the Commission thereof.

2. Member States shall communicate to the Commission the texts of provisions of national law which they adopt in the field governed by this Directive.

Annex 9.16.

Directive 2001/95/EC of the European Parliament and of the Council of 3 December 2001 on **general product safety** (Text with EEA relevance)
Official Journal L 011 , 15/01/2002 P. 0004 - 0017

MAIN PROVISIONS

CHAPTER I
Objective - Scope - Definitions

Article 1
1. The purpose of this Directive is to ensure that products placed on the market are safe.
2. This Directive shall apply to all the products defined in Article 2(a). Each of its provisions shall apply in so far as there are no specific provisions with the same objective in rules of Community law governing the safety of the products concerned.
Where products are subject to specific safety requirements imposed by Community legislation, this Directive shall apply only to the aspects and risks or categories of risks not covered by those requirements. This means that:
(a) Articles 2(b) and (c), 3 and 4 shall not apply to those products insofar as concerns the risks or categories of risks covered by the specific legislation;
(b) Articles 5 to 18 shall apply except where there are specific provisions governing the aspects covered by the said Articles with the same objective.

Article 2
For the purposes of this Directive:
(a) "product" shall mean any product - including in the context of providing a service - which is intended for consumers or likely, under reasonably foreseeable conditions, to be used by consumers even if not intended for them, and is supplied or made available, whether for consideration or not, in the course of a commercial activity, and whether new, used or reconditioned.
This definition shall not apply to second-hand products supplied as antiques or as products to be repaired or reconditioned prior to being used, provided that the supplier clearly informs the person to whom he supplies the product to that effect;
(b) "safe product" shall mean any product which, under normal or reasonably foreseeable conditions of use including duration and, where applicable, putting into service, installation and maintenance requirements, does not present any risk or only the minimum risks compatible with the product's use, considered to be acceptable and consistent with a high level of protection for the safety and health of persons, taking into account the following points in particular:
(i) the characteristics of the product, including its composition, packaging, instructions for assembly and, where applicable, for installation and maintenance;
(ii) the effect on other products, where it is reasonably foreseeable that it will be used with other products;
(iii) the presentation of the product, the labelling, any warnings and instructions for its use and disposal and any other indication or information regarding the product;
(iv) the categories of consumers at risk when using the product, in particular children and the elderly.
The feasibility of obtaining higher levels of safety or the availability of other products presenting a lesser degree of risk shall not constitute grounds for considering a product to be "dangerous";
(c) "dangerous product" shall mean any product which does not meet the definition of "safe product" in (b);
(d) "serious risk" shall mean any serious risk, including those the effects of which are not immediate, requiring rapid intervention by the public authorities;
(e) "producer" shall mean:
(i) the manufacturer of the product, when he is established in the Community, and any other person presenting himself as the manufacturer by affixing to the product his name, trade mark or other distinctive mark, or the person who reconditions the product;
(ii) the manufacturer's representative, when the manufacturer is not established in the Community or, if there is no representative established in the Community, the importer of the product;
(iii) other professionals in the supply chain, insofar as their activities may affect the safety properties of a product;
(f) "distributor" shall mean any professional in the supply chain whose activity does not affect the safety properties of a product;

(g) "recall" shall mean any measure aimed at achieving the return of a dangerous product that has already been supplied or made available to consumers by the producer or distributor;
(h) "withdrawal" shall mean any measure aimed at preventing the distribution, display and offer of a product dangerous to the consumer.

CHAPTER II
General safety requirement, conformity assessment criteria and European standards

Article 3
1. Producers shall be obliged to place only safe products on the market.
2. A product shall be deemed safe, as far as the aspects covered by the relevant national legislation are concerned, when, in the absence of specific Community provisions governing the safety of the product in question, it conforms to the specific rules of national law of the Member State in whose territory the product is marketed, such rules being drawn up in conformity with the Treaty, and in particular Articles 28 and 30 thereof, and laying down the health and safety requirements which the product must satisfy in order to be marketed.
A product shall be presumed safe as far as the risks and risk categories covered by relevant national standards are concerned when it conforms to voluntary national standards transposing European standards, the references of which have been published by the Commission in the Official Journal of the European Communities in accordance with Article 4. The Member States shall publish the references of such national standards.
3. In circumstances other than those referred to in paragraph 2, the conformity of a product to the general safety requirement shall be assessed by taking into account the following elements in particular, where they exist:
(a) voluntary national standards transposing relevant European standards other than those referred to in paragraph 2;
(b) the standards drawn up in the Member State in which the product is marketed;
(c) Commission recommendations setting guidelines on product safety assessment;
(d) product safety codes of good practice in force in the sector concerned;
(e) the state of the art and technology;
(f) reasonable consumer expectations concerning safety.
4. Conformity of a product with the criteria designed to ensure the general safety requirement, in particular the provisions mentioned in paragraphs 2 or 3, shall not bar the competent authorities of the Member States from taking appropriate measures to impose restrictions on its being placed on the market or to require its withdrawal from the market or recall where there is evidence that, despite such conformity, it is dangerous.

Article 4
1. For the purposes of this Directive, the European standards referred to in the second subparagraph of Article 3(2) shall be drawn up as follows:
(a) the requirements intended to ensure that products which conform to these standards satisfy the general safety requirement shall be determined in accordance with the procedure laid down in Article 15(2);
(b) on the basis of those requirements, the Commission shall, in accordance with Directive 98/34/EC of the European Parliament and of the Council of 22 June 1998 laying down a procedure for the provision of information in the field of technical standards and regulations and of rules on information society services(7) call on the European standardisation bodies to draw up standards which satisfy these requirements;
(c) on the basis of those mandates, the European standardisation bodies shall adopt the standards in accordance with the principles contained in the general guidelines for cooperation between the Commission and those bodies;
(d) the Commission shall report every three years to the European Parliament and the Council, within the framework of the report referred to in Article 19(2), on its programmes for setting the requirements and the mandates for standardisation provided for in subparagraphs (a) and (b) above. This report will, in particular, include an analysis of the decisions taken regarding requirements and mandates for standardisation referred to in subparagraphs (a) and (b) and regarding the standards referred to in subparagraph (c). It will also include information on the products for which the Commission intends to set the requirements and the mandates in question, the product risks to be considered and the results of any preparatory work launched in this area.
2. The Commission shall publish in the Official Journal of the European Communities the references of the European standards adopted in this way and drawn up in accordance with the requirements referred to in paragraph 1.
If a standard adopted by the European standardisation bodies before the entry into force of this Directive ensures compliance with the general safety requirement, the Commission shall decide to publish its references in the Official Journal of the European Communities.
If a standard does not ensure compliance with the general safety requirement, the Commission shall withdraw reference to the standard from publication in whole or in part.

In the cases referred to in the second and third subparagraphs, the Commission shall, on its own initiative or at the request of a Member State, decide in accordance with the procedure laid down in Article 15(2) whether the standard in question meets the general safety requirement. The Commission shall decide to publish or withdraw after consulting the Committee established by Article 5 of Directive 98/34/EC. The Commission shall notify the Member States of its decision.

CHAPTER III
Other obligations of producers and obligations of distributors

Article 5
1. Within the limits of their respective activities, producers shall provide consumers with the relevant information to enable them to assess the risks inherent in a product throughout the normal or reasonably foreseeable period of its use, where such risks are not immediately obvious without adequate warnings, and to take precautions against those risks.
The presence of warnings does not exempt any person from compliance with the other requirements laid down in this Directive.
Within the limits of their respective activities, producers shall adopt measures commensurate with the characteristics of the products which they supply, enabling them to:
(a) be informed of risks which these products might pose;
(b) choose to take appropriate action including, if necessary to avoid these risks, withdrawal from the market, adequately and effectively warning consumers or recall from consumers.
The measures referred to in the third subparagraph shall include, for example:
(a) an indication, by means of the product or its packaging, of the identity and details of the producer and the product reference or, where applicable, the batch of products to which it belongs, except where not to give such indication is justified and
(b) in all cases where appropriate, the carrying out of sample testing of marketed products, investigating and, if necessary, keeping a register of complaints and keeping distributors informed of such monitoring.
Action such as that referred to in (b) of the third subparagraph shall be undertaken on a voluntary basis or at the request of the competent authorities in accordance with Article 8(1)(f). Recall shall take place as a last resort, where other measures would not suffice to prevent the risks involved, in instances where the producers consider it necessary or where they are obliged to do so further to a measure taken by the competent authority. It may be effected within the framework of codes of good practice on the matter in the Member State concerned, where such codes exist.
2. Distributors shall be required to act with due care to help to ensure compliance with the applicable safety requirements, in particular by not supplying products which they know or should have presumed, on the basis of the information in their possession and as professionals, do not comply with those requirements. Moreover, within the limits of their respective activities, they shall participate in monitoring the safety of products placed on the market, especially by passing on information on product risks, keeping and providing the documentation necessary for tracing the origin of products, and cooperating in the action taken by producers and competent authorities to avoid the risks. Within the limits of their respective activities they shall take measures enabling them to cooperate efficiently.
3. Where producers and distributors know or ought to know, on the basis of the information in their possession and as professionals, that a product that they have placed on the market poses risks to the consumer that are incompatible with the general safety requirement, they shall immediately inform the competent authorities of the Member States thereof under the conditions laid down in Annex I, giving details, in particular, of action taken to prevent risk to the consumer.
The Commission shall, in accordance with the procedure referred to in Article 15(3), adapt the specific requirements relating to the obligation to provide information laid down in Annex I.
4. Producers and distributors shall, within the limits of their respective activities, cooperate with the competent authorities, at the request of the latter, on action taken to avoid the risks posed by products which they supply or have supplied. The procedures for such cooperation, including procedures for dialogue with the producers and distributors concerned on issues related to product safety, shall be established by the competent authorities.

CHAPTER IV
Specific obligations and powers of the Member States

Article 6
1. Member States shall ensure that producers and distributors comply with their obligations under this Directive in such a way that products placed on the market are safe.
2. Member States shall establish or nominate authorities competent to monitor the compliance of products with

the general safety requirements and arrange for such authorities to have and use the necessary powers to take the appropriate measures incumbent upon them under this Directive.
3. Member States shall define the tasks, powers, organisation and cooperation arrangements of the competent authorities. They shall keep the Commission informed, and the Commission shall pass on such information to the other Member States.

Article 7
Member States shall lay down the rules on penalties applicable to infringements of the national provisions adopted pursuant to this Directive and shall take all measures necessary to ensure that they are implemented. The penalties provided for shall be effective, proportionate and dissuasive. Member States shall notify those provisions to the Commission by 15 January 2004 and shall also notify it, without delay, of any amendment affecting them.

Article 8
1. For the purposes of this Directive, and in particular of Article 6 thereof, the competent authorities of the Member States shall be entitled to take, inter alia, the measures in (a) and in (b) to (f) below, where appropriate:
(a) for any product:
(i) to organise, even after its being placed on the market as being safe, appropriate checks on its safety properties, on an adequate scale, up to the final stage of use or consumption;
(ii) to require all necessary information from the parties concerned;
(iii) to take samples of products and subject them to safety checks;
(b) for any product that could pose risks in certain conditions:
(i) to require that it be marked with suitable, clearly worded and easily comprehensible warnings, in the official languages of the Member State in which the product is marketed, on the risks it may present;
(ii) to make its marketing subject to prior conditions so as to make it safe;
(c) for any product that could pose risks for certain persons:
to order that they be given warning of the risk in good time and in an appropriate form, including the publication of special warnings;
(d) for any product that could be dangerous:
for the period needed for the various safety evaluations, checks and controls, temporarily to ban its supply, the offer to supply it or its display;
(e) for any dangerous product:
to ban its marketing and introduce the accompanying measures required to ensure the ban is complied with;
(f) for any dangerous product already on the market:
(i) to order or organise its actual and immediate withdrawal, and alert consumers to the risks it presents;
(ii) to order or coordinate or, if appropriate, to organise together with producers and distributors its recall from consumers and its destruction in suitable conditions.
2. When the competent authorities of the Member States take measures such as those provided for in paragraph 1, in particular those referred to in (d) to (f), they shall act in accordance with the Treaty, and in particular Articles 28 and 30 thereof, in such a way as to implement the measures in a manner proportional to the seriousness of the risk, and taking due account of the precautionary principle.
In this context, they shall encourage and promote voluntary action by producers and distributors, in accordance with the obligations incumbent on them under this Directive, and in particular Chapter III thereof, including where applicable by the development of codes of good practice.
If necessary, they shall organise or order the measures provided for in paragraph 1(f) if the action undertaken by the producers and distributors in fulfilment of their obligations is unsatisfactory or insufficient. Recall shall take place as a last resort. It may be effected within the framework of codes of good practice on the matter in the Member State concerned, where such codes exist.
3. In particular, the competent authorities shall have the power to take the necessary action to apply with due dispatch appropriate measures such as those mentioned in paragraph 1, (b) to (f), in the case of products posing a serious risk. These circumstances shall be determined by the Member States, assessing each individual case on its merits, taking into account the guidelines referred to in point 8 of Annex II.
4. The measures to be taken by the competent authorities under this Article shall be addressed, as appropriate, to:
(a) the producer;
(b) within the limits of their respective activities, distributors and in particular the party responsible for the first stage of distribution on the national market;
(c) any other person, where necessary, with a view to cooperation in action taken to avoid risks arising from a product.

Article 9

1. In order to ensure effective market surveillance, aimed at guaranteeing a high level of consumer health and safety protection, which entails cooperation between their competent authorities, Member States shall ensure that approaches employing appropriate means and procedures are put in place, which may include in particular:
(a) establishment, periodical updating and implementation of sectoral surveillance programmes by categories of products or risks and the monitoring of surveillance activities, findings and results;
(b) follow-up and updating of scientific and technical knowledge concerning the safety of products;
(c) periodical review and assessment of the functioning of the control activities and their effectiveness and, if necessary, revision of the surveillance approach and organisation put in place.
2. Member States shall ensure that consumers and other interested parties are given an opportunity to submit complaints to the competent authorities on product safety and on surveillance and control activities and that these complaints are followed up as appropriate. Member States shall actively inform consumers and other interested parties of the procedures established to that end.

Article 10
1. The Commission shall promote and take part in the operation in a European network of the authorities of the Member States competent for product safety, in particular in the form of administrative cooperation.
2. This network operation shall develop in a coordinated manner with the other existing Community procedures particularly RAPEX. Its objective shall be, in particular, to facilitate:
(a) the exchange of information on risk assessment, dangerous products, test methods and results, recent scientific developments as well as other aspects relevant for control activities;
(b) the establishment and execution of joint surveillance and testing projects;
(c) the exchange of expertise and best practices and cooperation in training activities;
(d) improved cooperation at Community level with regard to the tracing, withdrawal and recall of dangerous products.

CHAPTER V
Exchanges of information and rapid intervention situations

Article 11
1. Where a Member State takes measures which restrict the placing on the market of products - or require their withdrawal or recall - such as those provided for in Article 8(1)(b) to (f), the Member State shall, to the extent that such notification is not required under Article 12 or any specific Community legislation, inform the Commission of the measures, specifying its reasons for adopting them. It shall also inform the Commission of any modification or lifting of such measures.
If the notifying Member State considers that the effects of the risk do not or cannot go beyond its territory, it shall notify the measures concerned insofar as they involve information likely to be of interest to Member State from the product safety standpoint, and in particular if they are in response to a new risk which has not yet beer reported in other notifications.
In accordance with the procedure laid down in Article 15(3) of this Directive, the Commission shall, while ensuring the effectiveness and proper functioning of the system, adopt the guidelines referred to in point 8 of Annex II. These shall propose the content and standard form for the notifications provided for in this Article, and, in particular, shall provide precise criteria for determining the conditions for which notification is relevant for the purposes of the second subparagraph.
2. The Commission shall forward the notification to the other Member States, unless it concludes, after examination on the basis of the information contained in the notification, that the measure does not comply wit Community law. In such a case, it shall immediately inform the Member State which initiated the action.

Article 12
1. Where a Member State adopts or decides to adopt, recommend or agree with producers and distributors, whether on a compulsory or voluntary basis, measures or actions to prevent, restrict or impose specific conditions on the possible marketing or use, within its own territory, of products by reason of a serious risk, it shall immediately notify the Commission thereof through RAPEX. It shall also inform the Commission withou delay of modification or withdrawal of any such measure or action.
If the notifying Member State considers that the effects of the risk do not or cannot go beyond its territory, it shall follow the procedure laid down in Article 11, taking into account the relevant criteria proposed in the guidelines referred to in point 8 of Annex II.
Without prejudice to the first subparagraph, before deciding to adopt such measures or to take such action, Member States may pass on to the Commission any information in their possession regarding the existence of a

serious risk.
In the case of a serious risk, they shall notify the Commission of the voluntary measures laid down in Article 5 of this Directive taken by producers and distributors.
2. On receiving such notifications, the Commission shall check whether they comply with this Article and with the requirements applicable to the functioning of RAPEX, and shall forward them to the other Member States, which, in turn, shall immediately inform the Commission of any measures adopted.
3. Detailed procedures for RAPEX are set out in Annex II. They shall be adapted by the Commission in accordance with the procedure referred to in Article 15(3).
4. Access to RAPEX shall be open to applicant countries, third countries or international organisations, within the framework of agreements between the Community and those countries or international organisations, according to arrangements defined in these agreements. Any such agreements shall be based on reciprocity and include provisions on confidentiality corresponding to those applicable in the Community.

Article 13
1. If the Commission becomes aware of a serious risk from certain products to the health and safety of consumers in various Member States, it may, after consulting the Member States, and, if scientific questions arise which fall within the competence of a Community Scientific Committee, the Scientific Committee competent to deal with the risk concerned, adopt a decision in the light of the result of those consultations, in accordance with the procedure laid down in Article 15(2), requiring Member States to take measures from among those listed in Article 8(1)(b) to (f) if, at one and the same time:
(a) it emerges from prior consultations with the Member States that they differ significantly on the approach adopted or to be adopted to deal with the risk; and
(b) the risk cannot be dealt with, in view of the nature of the safety issue posed by the product, in a manner compatible with the degree of urgency of the case, under other procedures laid down by the specific Community legislation applicable to the products concerned; and
(c) the risk can be eliminated effectively only by adopting appropriate measures applicable at Community level, in order to ensure a consistent and high level of protection of the health and safety of consumers and the proper functioning of the internal market.
2. The decisions referred to in paragraph 1 shall be valid for a period not exceeding one year and may be confirmed, under the same procedure, for additional periods none of which shall exceed one year.
However, decisions concerning specific, individually identified products or batches of products shall be valid without a time limit.
3. Export from the Community of dangerous products which have been the subject of a decision referred to in paragraph 1 shall be prohibited unless the decision provides otherwise.
4. Member States shall take all necessary measures to implement the decisions referred to in paragraph 1 within less than 20 days, unless a different period is specified in those decisions.
5. The competent authorities responsible for carrying out the measures referred to in paragraph 1 shall, within one month, give the parties concerned an opportunity to submit their views and shall inform the Commission accordingly.

CHAPTER VI
Committee procedures

Article 14
1. The measures necessary for the implementation of this Directive relating to the matters referred to below shall be adopted in accordance with the regulatory procedure provided for in Article 15(2):
(a) the measures referred to in Article 4 concerning standards adopted by the European standardisation bodies;
(b) the decisions referred to in Article 13 requiring Member States to take measures as listed in Article 8(1)(b) to (f).
2. The measures necessary for the implementation of this Directive in respect of all other matters shall be adopted in accordance with the advisory procedure provided for in Article 15(3).

Article 15
1. The Commission shall be assisted by a Committee.
2. Where reference is made to this paragraph, Articles 5 and 7 of Decision 1999/468/EC shall apply, having regard to the provisions of Article 8 thereof.
The period laid down in Article 5(6) of Decision 1999/468/EC shall be set at 15 days.
3. Where reference is made to this paragraph, Articles 3 and 7 of Decision 1999/468/EC shall apply, having regard to the provisions of Article 8 thereof.
4. The Committee shall adopt its rules of procedure.

CHAPTER VII
Final provisions

Article 16
1. Information available to the authorities of the Member States or the Commission relating to risks to consumer health and safety posed by products shall in general be available to the public, in accordance with the requirements of transparency and without prejudice to the restrictions required for monitoring and investigation activities. In particular the public shall have access to information on product identification, the nature of the risk and the measures taken.
However, Member States and the Commission shall take the steps necessary to ensure that their officials and agents are required not to disclose information obtained for the purposes of this Directive which, by its nature, is covered by professional secrecy in duly justified cases, except for information relating to the safety properties of products which must be made public if circumstances so require, in order to protect the health and safety of consumers.
2. Protection of professional secrecy shall not prevent the dissemination to the competent authorities of information relevant for ensuring the effectiveness of market monitoring and surveillance activities. The authorities receiving information covered by professional secrecy shall ensure its protection.

Article 17
This Directive shall be without prejudice to the application of Directive 85/374/EEC.

Article 18
1. Any measure adopted under this Directive and involving restrictions on the placing of a product on the market or requiring its withdrawal or recall must state the appropriate reasons on which it is based. It shall be notified as soon as possible to the party concerned and shall indicate the remedies available under the provisions in force in the Member State in question and the time limits applying to such remedies.
The parties concerned shall, whenever feasible, be given an opportunity to submit their views before the adoption of the measure. If this has not been done in advance because of the urgency of the measures to be taken, they shall be given such opportunity in due course after the measure has been implemented.
Measures requiring the withdrawal of a product or its recall shall take into consideration the need to encourage distributors, users and consumers to contribute to the implementation of such measures.
2. Member States shall ensure that any measure taken by the competent authorities involving restrictions on the placing of a product on the market or requiring its withdrawal or recall can be challenged before the competent courts.
3. Any decision taken by virtue of this Directive and involving restrictions on the placing of a product on the market or requiring its withdrawal or its recall shall be without prejudice to assessment of the liability of the party concerned, in the light of the national criminal law applying in the case in question.

Article 19
1. The Commission may bring before the Committee referred to in Article 15 any matter concerning the application of this Directive and particularly those relating to market monitoring and surveillance activities.
2. Every three years, following 15 January 2004, the Commission shall submit a report on the implementation of this Directive to the European Parliament and the Council.
The report shall in particular include information on the safety of consumer products, in particular on improved traceability of products, the functioning of market surveillance, standardisation work, the functioning of RAPEX and Community measures taken on the basis of Article 13. To this end the Commission shall conduct assessments of the relevant issues, in particular the approaches, systems and practices put in place in the Member States, in the light of the requirements of this Directive and the other Community legislation relating to product safety. The Member States shall provide the Commission with all the necessary assistance and information for carrying out the assessments and preparing the reports.

Article 20
The Commission shall identify the needs, possibilities and priorities for Community action on the safety of services and submit to the European Parliament and the Council, before 1 January 2003, a report, accompanied by proposals on the subject as appropriate.

Article 21
1. Member States shall bring into force the laws, regulations and administrative provisions necessary in order to comply with this Directive with effect from 15 January 2004. They shall forthwith inform the Commission thereof.

When Member States adopt those measures, they shall contain a reference to this Directive or be accompanied by such reference on the occasion of their official publication. The methods of making such reference shall be laid down by Member States.
2. Member States shall communicate to the Commission the provisions of national law which they adopt in the field covered by this Directive.

Article 22
Directive 92/59/EEC is hereby repealed from 15 January 2004, without prejudice to the obligations of Member States concerning the deadlines for transposition and application of the said Directive as indicated in Annex III. References to Directive 92/59/EEC shall be construed as references to this Directive and shall be read in accordance with the correlation table in Annex IV.

Article 23
This Directive shall enter into force on the day of its publication in the Official Journal of the European Communities.

Article 24
This Directive is addressed to the Member States.

Done at Brussels, 3 December 2001.

For the European Parliament
The President
N. Fontaine

For the Council
The President
F. Vandenbroucke

(1) OJ C 337 E, 28.11.2000, p. 109 and
OJ C 154 E, 29.5.2000, p. 265.
(2) OJ C 367, 20.12.2000, p. 34.
(3) Opinion of the European Parliament of 15.11.2000 (OJ C 223, 8.8.2001, p. 154), Council Common Position of 12.2.2001 (OJ C 93, 23.3.2001, p. 24) and Decision of the European Parliament of 16.5.2001 (not yet published in the Official Journal). Decision of the European Parliament of 4.10.2001 and Council Decision of 27.9.2001.
(4) OJ L 228, 11.8.1992, p. 24.
(5) OJ L 184, 17.7.1999, p. 23.
(6) OJ L 210, 7.8.1985, p. 29. Directive as amended by Directive 1999/34/EC of the European Parliament and of the Council (OJ L 141, 4.6.1999, p. 20).
(7) OJ L 204, 21.7.1998, p. 37. Directive amended by Directive 98/48/EC (OJ L 217, 5.8.1998, p. 18).

ANNEX I

REQUIREMENTS CONCERNING INFORMATION ON PRODUCTS THAT DO NOT COMPLY WITH THE GENERAL SAFETY REQUIREMENT TO BE PROVIDED TO THE COMPETENT AUTHORITIES BY PRODUCERS AND DISTRIBUTORS

1. The information specified in Article 5(3), or where applicable by specific requirements of Community rules on the product concerned, shall be passed to the competent authorities appointed for the purpose in the Member States where the products in question are or have been marketed or otherwise supplied to consumers.
2. The Commission, assisted by the Committee referred to in Article 15, shall define the content and draw up the standard form of the notifications provided for in this Annex, while ensuring the effectiveness and proper functioning of the system. In particular, it shall put forward, possibly in the form of a guide, simple and clear criteria for determining the special conditions, particularly those concerning isolated circumstances or products, for which notification is not relevant in relation to this Annex.
3. In the event of serious risks, this information shall include at least the following:
(a) information enabling a precise identification of the product or batch of products in question;
(b) a full description of the risk that the products in question present;
(c) all available information relevant for tracing the product;

(d) a description of the action undertaken to prevent risks to consumers.

ANNEX II

PROCEDURES FOR THE APPLICATION OF RAPEX AND GUIDELINES FOR NOTIFICATIONS

1. RAPEX covers products as defined in Article 2(a) that pose a serious risk to the health and safety of consumers.
Pharmaceuticals, which come under Directives 75/319/EEC(1) and 81/851/EEC(2), are excluded from the scope of RAPEX.
2. RAPEX is essentially aimed at a rapid exchange of information in the event of a serious risk. The guidelines referred to in point 8 define specific criteria for identifying serious risks.
3. Member States notifying under Article 12 shall provide all available details. In particular, the notification shall contain the information stipulated in the guidelines referred to in point 8 and at least:
(a) information enabling the product to be identified;
(b) a description of the risk involved, including a summary of the results of any tests/analyses and of their conclusions which are relevant to assessing the level of risk;
(c) the nature and the duration of the measures or action taken or decided on, if applicable;
(d) information on supply chains and distribution of the product, in particular on destination countries.
Such information must be transmitted using the special standard notification form and by the means stipulated in the guidelines referred to in point 8.
When the measure notified pursuant to Article 11 or Article 12 seeks to limit the marketing or use of a chemical substance or preparation, the Member States shall provide as soon as possible either a summary or the references of the relevant data relating to the substance or preparation considered and to known and available substitutes, where such information is available. They will also communicate the anticipated effects of the measure on consumer health and safety together with the assessment of the risk carried out in accordance with the general principles for the risk evaluation of chemical substances as referred to in Article 10(4) of Regulation (EEC) No 793/93(3) in the case of an existing substance or in Article 3(2) of Directive 67/548/EEC(4) in the case of a new substance. The guidelines referred to in point 8 shall define the details and procedures for the information requested in that respect.
4. When a Member State has informed the Commission, in accordance with Article 12(1), third subparagraph, of a serious risk before deciding to adopt measures, it must inform the Commission within 45 days whether it confirms or modifies this information.
5. The Commission shall, in the shortest time possible, verify the conformity with the provisions of the Directive of the information received under RAPEX and, may, when it considers it to be necessary and in order to assess product safety, carry out an investigation on its own initiative. In the case of such an investigation, Member States shall supply the Commission with the requested information to the best of their ability.
6. Upon receipt of a notification referred to in Article 12, the Member States are requested to inform the Commission, at the latest within the set period of time stipulated in the guidelines referred to in point 8, of the following:
(a) whether the product has been marketed in their territory;
(b) what measures concerning the product in question they may be adopting in the light of their own circumstances, stating the reasons, including any differing assessment of risk or any other special circumstance justifying their decision, in particular lack of action or of follow-up;
(c) any relevant supplementary information they have obtained on the risk involved, including the results of any tests or analyses carried out.
The guidelines referred to in point 8 shall provide precise criteria for notifying measures limited to national territory and shall specify how to deal with notifications concerning risks which are considered by the Member State not to go beyond its territory.
7. Member States shall immediately inform the Commission of any modification or lifting of the measure(s) or action(s) in question.
8. The Commission shall prepare and regularly update, in accordance with the procedure laid down in Article 15(3), guidelines concerning the management of RAPEX by the Commission and the Member States.
9. The Commission may inform the national contact points regarding products posing serious risks, imported into or exported from the Community and the European Economic Area.
10. Responsibility for the information provided lies with the notifying Member State.
11. The Commission shall ensure the proper functioning of the system, in particular classifying and indexing notifications according to the degree of urgency. Detailed procedures shall be laid down by the guidelines referred to in point 8.

Conclusions

APPRAISAL AND PERSPECTIVES OF THE COMMON SOCIAL POLICY

Economic and social cohesion is linked to the objective of economic and monetary union. Such a union, implying abandonment of the use of exchange rate adjustment as a means of balance of national economies, would be to the detriment of the poorer Member States without an efficient common structural policy revolving around sufficient capital transfers from the richer to the poorer regions of the EU [see section 3.1.]. Likewise, inside an economic and monetary union, where governments gradually lose the ability to confront separately the social problems of their peoples, since monetary and increasingly economic decisions are taken in common, the process of social integration is pursued through common employment, vocational training and social protection policies. The common social policy has already built a "European social model" which guarantees, not only fundamental human rights and the democratic and pluralistic principles, but also the fundamental rights of workers: training adapted to the technical progress, fair pay allowing decent living conditions and social protection covering the hazards of life, illness, unemployment and old age. This model is the social bedrock of the European integration process and places the European Union in the vanguard of social progress in the world.

The common social policy represents an **important contribution to European integration** as an essential building block. It is interesting to note in the following paragraphs that each of the four wings of this policy makes a different contribution to the integration process. They, nevertheless, reinforce each other and interact with other common policies, notably the economic and monetary, industrial, research and development ones, in fostering the social cohesion necessary in an economic and monetary union.

The **freedom of movement of workers** was essential for the completion of the common market. By virtue of the Community regulations adopted in their favour, migrant workers and self-employed persons from any Member State enjoy fair conditions compared with nationals of the host country with regard to access to employment, social security, the education and vocational training of their children, living and working conditions and the right to exercise union rights [see section 5.1.]. The common labour market is handicapped, however, by the existence of different languages, customs and working methods and, although the EU is taking measures to overcome these hurdles to the free movement of workers, it will certainly need much time before it encompasses a really homogeneous labour market.

The **common employment policy** is striving to ensure that the national employment policies and the common policies of the EU, notably in the economic and monetary field, work together in a consistent manner so as to boost economic reforms and employment while maintaining price stability. The coordinated employment strategy aims to harness structural reforms and modernisation to improve the efficiency of the labour market, while maintaining a non-inflationary growth dynamic [see section 6.2.]. The employment guidelines, agreed each year by the Council, help the Member States to devise their own employment strategies, while pursuing common goals, such as: improving employability, with the emphasis on suitable training; developing entrepreneurship;

encouraging the adaptability of the work force; and strengthening equal opportunities policies for women and men. The Lisbon agenda has shifted the focus of the European employment strategy from the fight against unemployment towards the wider priority of more and better jobs in an inclusive society and has helped employment creation in the EU. However, performance varies considerably among the Member States and reforms are not pursued in a sufficiently comprehensive way by all of them, whether in terms of creating and maintaining employment or improving vocational skills and the quality of jobs.

The joint Council and Commission reports on employment, drawn up in accordance with Article 128 of the EC Treaty, note the progress made in the employment field throughout the Union (increase in labour productivity, job creation, reduction in unemployment, etc.) in line with the objectives set at the Lisbon European Council. Significant persistent weaknesses nevertheless indicate the need for continuing structural reform, particularly in the face of a less favourable economic outlook. Key issues for the future include: measures to boost employment rates, improve the quality of work and promote equal opportunities and active ageing, investment in human resources, a more effective strategy geared to social inclusion and greater emphasis on regional disparities. The challenge of the European employment strategy consists in raising the employment rate by promoting employability and by removing obstacles and disincentives to take up or remain in a job, while preserving high protection standards of the European social model.

The common **education and training policies** complement the common employment policy by encouraging the adaptation of the work force to the new conditions of the industrial and service sectors in Europe and in the rest of the world. The cooperation and exchange of experiences through the Community programmes help the Member States develop the European dimension in education, the teaching of languages, the vocational training and retraining needed in the information society and in the global economy [see section 7.2.]. At the same time, these programmes build networks of teachers, instructors and young people who participate actively in the European integration process.

The common policy for the **improvement of living and working conditions** is aimed at the convergence of social protection systems and through it at the social cohesion of the Union. Community directives fixing common minimum standards guarantee the rights, the physical safety and health of workers, particularly the women and the young, in all Member States. The establishment of a framework of basic minimum standards provides a bulwark against using low social standards as an instrument of unfair economic competition [see sections 8.3, 8.4 and 8.5.]. The social bedrock, which is thus being built, is indispensable for the good functioning of economic and monetary union where the competition between the various regions of the Union is enhanced. However, economic and social developments in European countries make it necessary to modernise social protection systems in order to attain four main objectives: creating more incentives to work and provide a secure income; safeguarding pensions with sustainable pension schemes; promoting social inclusion; and ensuring the high quality and sustainability of health protection.

At present, the Community has to address major industrial change both of a quantitative and qualitative nature: the globalisation of production and markets, the acceleration of technological change and the changes to production systems. These factors as a whole are having a profound effect on the Community's industrial scene, and a significant impact on employment and the dynamics of human resources in the Community. EU labour markets must become more inclusive, with employment opportunities extended to all, at the same time as they become more adaptable to economic conditions. The Community's social policy must anticipate future changes in employment and in qualifications requirements. Workers' qualifications must be adapted to meet future changes and to minimise the economic and social cost of changes already occurring.

While wealth creation is essential for social progress, this progress cannot be founded simply on the basis of the competitiveness of economies, but also on the efficiency of European society as a whole. This efficiency can itself be founded on a well-educated, highly motivated and adaptable working population. **Economic and social progress must, therefore, go hand in hand** to preserve the shared values, which form the basis of the European social model. These include the market economy, democracy and pluralism, respect of individual rights, free collective bargaining equality of opportunity for all, social welfare and solidarity. The European social model needs to be constantly adapted to secure its long-term sustainability in the face of an ageing population, to ensure that work is financially worthwhile, to promote social inclusion and gender equality, and to provide quality health services. The Structural Funds have a major role to play in improving both the infrastructure necessary for the full use of the information society and the "intangible" elements, i.e. overcoming obstacles relating to economics, management, public administration and education of the less developed regions of the Union.

The big question is how **the Structural Funds of the Union** would cope with the accession of Central and Eastern European countries, when the disadvantaged regions of the Union would become far more numerous [see section 3.3.2.]. It is evident that a greater concentration of assistance would be necessary, in terms of fields covered and geographical eligibility, particularly in the most prosperous Member States. Actually, the pre-accession strategy includes the establishment of an Instrument for Structural Policies for Pre-accession (ISPA), which is directed towards aligning applicant countries on Community infrastructure standards and provide a financial contribution for environmental measures, and transport infrastructure measures. After accession, in May 2004, the common structural policy should be braced on helping the new Member States meet successively the requirements of the single market and of the single currency. A complete overhaul of the implementation of the Structural Funds and of the Cohesion Fund should be started to enable simplified procedures to be followed that were geared more to the structural problems of the new Member States.

The European Union should also promote the principles of the European social model in the rest of the world, which suffers from poverty, inequalities and exploitation. It is important that the respect of the fundamental human rights, in particular the right to association and collective bargaining as well as the protection against compulsory work and work of children, be enforced at international level in the framework of the United Nations Organisation. The EU could and should contribute to the **globalisation of solidarity and respect of human rights** in the world. This is not only in the interest of the poorest populations of the world, but also in its own interest, since it would limit the social dumping engendered by the globalisation of economies, which is endangering the European social model.

BIBLIOGRAPHY ON THE COMMON SOCIAL POLICY

- ADDIS Elisabetta. Gender Symmetry in the Reform of European Welfare States. Florence: European University Institute, 2002.
- BALDASSARRI Mario (ed.). The new welfare: unemployment and social security in Europe. Basingstoke: Palgrave Macmillan, 2003.
- BARNES Matt (et al.). Poverty and social exclusion in Europe. Cheltenham: Edward Elgar, 2002.
- BEGG Iain, BERGHMAN Jos (ed.). "Social Exclusion and Reforming the European Social Model", Journal of European Social Policy, v. 12, n. 3, August 2002, p. 179-239.
- BEST Edward, BOSSAERT Danielle (eds.). From Luxembourg to Lisbon and beyond: Making the Employment Strategy Work. Maastricht: European Institute of Public Administration, 2002.
- BIAGI Marco (ed.). Quality of Work and Employee Involvement in Europe. The Hague: Kluwer Law International, 2002.
- BLANPAIN Roger. Involvement of Employees in the European Union: European Works Councils, the European Company Statute, Information and Consultation Rights. The Hague: Kluwer Law International, 2002.
- BOUGRAB Jeannette. "L'égalité entre les femmes et les hommes dans les jurisprudences des cours suprêmes européennes et nationales", L'Actualité juridique. Droit administratif, année 59, n. 31, 22 septembre 2003, p. 1640-1647.
- BRÖDNER Peter, LATNIAK Erich. Sources of Innovation and Competitiveness: National Programmes Supporting the Development of Work Organisation. Brussels: European Commission, 2002.
- BUSSE Reinhard, WISMAR Matthias, BERMAN Philip, The European Union and Health Services: the Impact of the Single European Market on Member States, Amsterdam: IOS Press, 2002.
- DITCH John, ROBERTS Ellen. Integrated Approaches to Active Welfare and Employment Policies. Luxembourg: EUR-OP*, 2002.
- ENNALS Richard. The Existing Policy Framework to Promote Modernisation of Work: Its Weaknesses. Brussels: European Commission, 2002.
- ELLIS Evelyn. "Social advantages: a new lease of life?", Common Market Law Review, v. 40, n. 3, June 2003, p. 639-659.
- ERTL Hubert, PHILLIPS David. Implementing European Union education and training policy: a comparative study of issues in four Member States. Dordrecht - Boston: Kluwer Academic, 2003.
- EUROPEAN COMMISSION. Education and Training in Europe: Diverse Systems, Shared Goals for 2010: the Work Programme on the Future Objectives Education and Training Systems, Luxembourg: EUR-OP*, 2002.
  - A new Impetus for European Youth: European Commission White Paper. Luxembourg: EUR-OP*, 2002.
  - EU Cooperation in Higher Education, Luxembourg: EUR-OP*, 2003.
  - Training in Europe. Luxembourg: EUR-OP*, 2003.

- Leonardo da Vinci: Social and occupational integration of disadvantaged people. Luxembourg: EUR-OP*, 2003.
- The sectoral social dialogue in Europe. Luxembourg: EUR-OP*, 2003.

- EUZÉBY Alain, MARQUES Rosa Maria. "Mondialisation de l'économie et concurrence fiscale: des menaces pour le modèle social européen", Revue du Marché commun et de l'Union européenne, n. 468, mai 2003, p. 310-316.
- FODEN David, MAGNUSSON Lars. Five years' experience of the Luxembourg employment strategy. Brussels: European Trade Union Confederation, 2003.
- GALLIE Duncan, PAUGAM Serge. Social precarity and social integration. Luxembourg: EUR-OP*, 2003.
- GOUDSWAARD Anneke. The Use of Occupational Safety and Health Management Systems in the Member States of the European Union: Experiences at Company Level. Luxembourg: EUR-OP*, 2002.
- HUTSEBAUT Martin. "Social protection in Europe: a European trade union perspective", International Social Security Review, v. 56, n. 1, January-March 2003, p. 53-74.
- INOZEMTSEV Vladislav. "Le retour de l'Europe. Partie II.: à l'avant-garde du progrès, la politique sociale dans l'Union européenne", Revue du Marché commun et de l'Union européenne, n. 466, mars 2003, p. 167-178.
- JANSSENS Jos. Innovations in Lifelong Learning: Capitalising on ADAPT. Luxembourg: EUR-OP*, 2002.
- JOUSTEN Alain. "Départ à la retraite: une perspective internationale", Revue française d'économie, v. 18, n. 1, juillet 2003, p. 83-97.
- KESSLER Francis, LHERNOULD Jean-Philippe. Droit social et politiques sociales communautaires. Rueil-Malmaison: Éd. Liaisons, 2003.
- KUCHLER Birgit, GOEBEL Jan. "Incidence and intensity of smoothed income poverty in European countries", Journal of European Social Policy, v. 13, n. 4, November 2003, p. 357-369.
- LEGOUPIL Nathalie, ROUSSEL Régis. "Formation des personnes handicapées: droit français et européen", Actualité de la formation permanente, n. 185, juillet-août 2003, p. 33-41.
- LEÓN Margarita (et al.). (En)gendering the Convention: women and the future of the European Union. Florence: European University Institute, 2003.
- MAJOCCHI Alberto. "Globalisation, sustainable development and the European social model", The European Union Review, v. 8, n. 1-2, March-July 2003, p. 7-28.
- MOSHER James, TRUBEK David. "Alternative approaches to governance in the EU: EU social policy and the European Employment Strategy", Journal of Common Market Studies, v. 41, n. 1, March 2003, p. 63-88.
- MUFFELS Ruud, TSAKLOGLOU Panos, MAYES David. Social Exclusion in European Welfare States. Cheltenham: Edward Elgar, 2002.
- MURRAY Alasdair. Corporate social responsibility in the EU. London: Centre for European Reform, 2003.
- MOUSSIS Nicholas. *Access to European Union: Law, Economics, Policies*. 13th revised edition. Brussels: Euroconfidentiel, 2004.
  - *Guide to European Policies*. 9th revised edition. Brussels: European Study Service, 2003.
  - *Accès à l'Union européenne: droit économie, politiques*. 11ème edition révisée. Bruxelles: Bruylant; Paris: LGDJ; Athènes: Papazissis, 2004.
  - *Guide des politiques de l'Europe*. Bierges: Éditions Mols, 2002.
- NEAL Alan. European Labour Law and Policy: Cases and Materials. The Hague: Kluwer Law International, 2002.
- O'HAGAN Emer. Employee Relations in the Periphery of Europe: the Unfolding Story of the European Social Model. Basingstoke: Palgrave, 2002.
- STEWART Kitty. "Monitoring social inclusion in Europe's regions", Journal of European

Social Policy, v. 13, n. 4, November 2003, p. 335-356.
- THRELFALL Monica. "European social integration: harmonization, convergence and single social areas", Journal of European Social Policy, v. 13, n. 2, May 2003, p. 121-139.
- TRUBEK David, ZEITLIN Jonathan. Governing work and welfare in a new economy: European and American experiments. Oxford: Oxford University Press, 2003.
- VAUGHAN-WHITEHEAD Daniel. EU enlargement versus social Europe?: the uncertain future of the European social model. Cheltenham: Edward Elgar, 2003.
- WILLETTS David. Old Europe?: demographic change and pension reform. London: Centre for European Reform, 2003.

The publications of the Office for Official Publications of the European Communities (EUR-OP) exist generally in all official languages of the EU.